25 Years 2025-2001

ISC

CHAPTERWISE - TOPICWISE QUESTION BANK

Chemistry

Chemistry

Class 12

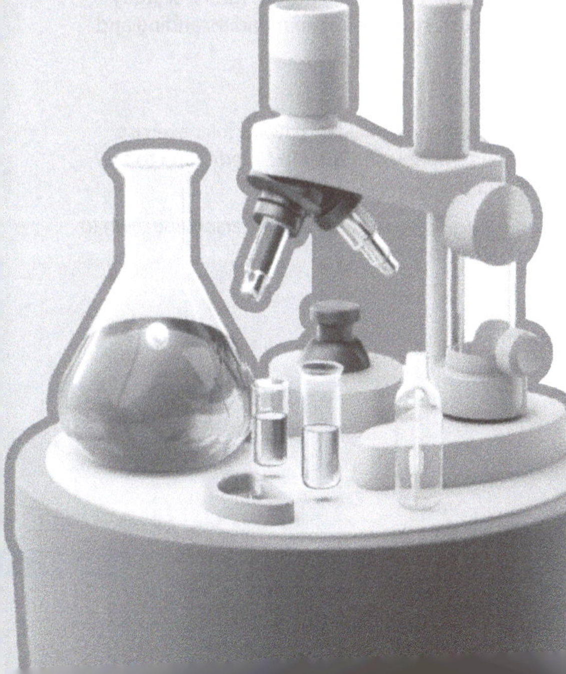

Author
Abhishika Kaushik

arihant
SUCCESS AND NOTHING LESS

arihant
SUCCESS AND NOTHING LESS

ARIHANT PRAKASHAN
(School Division Series)

ADMINISTRATIVE & PRODUCTION OFFICES

Regd. Office
'Ramchhaya' 4577/15, Agarwal Road, Darya Ganj, New Delhi -110002
Tele: 011- 47630600, 43518550

Head Office
Kalindi, TP Nagar, Meerut (UP) - 250002, Tel: 0121-7156203, 7156204

SALES & SUPPORT OFFICES

Agra, Ahmedabad, Bengaluru, Bareilly, Chennai, Delhi, Guwahati, Hyderabad, Jaipur, Jhansi, Kolkata, Lucknow, Nagpur & Pune.

PO No : TXT-XX-XXXXXXX-X-XX

Published By Arihant Publications (India) Ltd.

For further information about the books published by Arihant, log on to www.arihantbooks.com or e-mail at info@arihantbooks.com

PRICE ₹280.00

Follow us on

Achieving 99+ Marks in Board Exams

Achieving 99+ marks in board exams is definitely an ambitious goal, but with the right approach and these 7 tips from toppers, you can definitely increase your chances of success!

Here are the 7 Topper Tips to ace your board exams:

1. Master the art of consistency

Consistency builds understanding and confidence, both crucial for excelling in exams.

2. Build a winning study strategy

Create a personalised timetable that prioritises subjects based on your strengths and weaknesses.

3. Befriend the syllabus

Focus on high-weightage topics and prioritise mastering core concepts before moving on to advanced ones.

4. Embrace active learning

Explain concepts to yourself or in study groups to solidify understanding.

5. Conquer the past

Solve Past years' papers and Sample Papers under timed conditions to practice time management and understand paper pattern.

6. Seek help, when needed!

Don't hesitate to clarify doubts with teachers, tutors, or study groups. Asking questions strengthens your understanding and prevents confusion.

7. Prioritise well-being

Eat nutritious meals, get enough sleep, have regular exercise practice stress management techniques like meditation to stay calm and focused during exams.

These tips are just a starting point, and you can personalise them to fit your learning style and preferences.

Contents

ISC Chapterwise Question Bank 2025-2001

Latest Syllabus

There will be two papers in the subject.

Paper I	Theory : 3 hours	70 Marks
Paper II	Practical : 3 hours	15 Marks
	Project Work	10 Marks
	Practical File	5 Marks

PAPER I THEORY

70 Marks

S. No.	UNIT	TOTAL WEIGHTAGE	
1.	Solutions	Physical Chemistry	25 Marks
2.	Electrochemistry		
3.	Chemical Kinetics		
4.	*d*-and *f*-Block Elements	Inorganic Chemistry	14 Marks
5.	Coordination Compounds		
6.	Haloalkanes and Haloarenes	Organic Chemistry	31 Marks
7.	Alcohols, Phenols and Ethers		
8.	Aldehydes, Ketones and Carboxylic Acids		
9.	Organic Compounds Containing Nitrogen		
10.	Biomolecules		
	TOTAL		**70 Marks**

1. SOLUTIONS

Study of concentration of solutions of solids in liquids, liquid in liquid, solubility of gases in liquids, solid solutions, Colligative properties - Raoult's law of relative lowering of vapour pressure (1st and 2nd), elevation of boiling point, depression of freezing point, osmotic pressure. Use of colligative properties in determining molecular masses of solutes, abnormal molecular mass association and dissociation, van't Hoff factor.

Normality, molality, molarity, mole fraction, ppm, as measures of concentration. Definition of the above with examples. Simple problems based on the above.

(i) *Solubility of gases in liquids – Henry's law, simple numericals based on the above.*

(ii) *Raoult's law for volatile solutes and non-volatile solutes, ideal solution, non-ideal solution. Azeotropic mixtures – definition, types, graphical representation, fractional distillation with examples.*

(iii) *Colligative properties – definition and examples, and its use in determination of molecular mass.*

(a) *Relative lowering of vapour pressure: Definition and mathematical expression of Raoult's law. Determination of relative molecular mass by measurement of lowering of vapour pressure.*

(b) *Depression in freezing point: molal depression constant (cryoscopic constant) – definition and mathematical expression (derivation included).*

(c) *Elevation in boiling point method: molal elevation constant (ebullioscopic constant) definition and mathematical expression (derivation included).*

(d) *Osmotic pressure: definition and explanation. Natural and chemical semipermeable membranes, reverse osmosis, isotonic, hypotonic and hypertonic solutions. Comparison between diffusion and osmosis. Application of osmotic pressure in the determination of relative molecular mass. van't Hoff- Boyle's law, van't Hoff – Charles' law, van't Hoff - Avogadro's law.*

(e) *Abnormal molecular mass: Dissociation and Association with suitable examples.*

(f) van't Hoff factor for the electrolytes which dissociate and the molecules which associate in solution. Modification of the formula of colligative properties based on van't Hoff factor. Simple problems. Calculation of degree of dissociation and association. Experimental details not required.

Numerical problems based on all the above methods. Experimental details not required.

2. ELECTROCHEMISTRY

Electrolytic and electrochemical cells. Redox reactions in electrochemical cells. Electromotive Force (emf) of a cell, standard electrode potential, Nernst equation and its application to chemical cells. Relation between Gibb's energy change and emf of a cell.

Conductance in electrolytic solutions, specific, equivalent and molar conductivity, variations of conductivity with concentration, graphs; Kohlrausch's law of electrolysis and Faraday's laws of electrolysis. Dry cell and lead accumulator, fuel cells, corrosion.

(i) Electrochemical cells: introduction, redox reactions (principle of oxidation and reduction in a cell).

(ii) Galvanic cells - introduction; representation, principle – oxidation reduction. Mechanism of production of electric current in a galvanic cell.

(iii) Measurement of potential. Single electrode potentials. Standard hydrogen electrode (E°) - definition, preparation, application and limitations.

Standard electrode potential - Measurement of standard electrode potential of Zn^{2+} / Zn , Cu^{2+} / Cu, half-cell (using standard hydrogen electrode).

Cell notation – representation.

Factors affecting electrode potential with explanation - main emphasis on the temperature, concentration and nature of the electrode.

(iv) Electrochemical series. Its explanation on the basis of standard reduction potential. Prediction of the feasibility of a reaction.

(v) Nernst equation and correlation with the free energy of the reaction with suitable examples.

Prediction of spontaneity of a reaction based on the cell emf.

Numericals on standard electrode potential of half-cells, cell emf, relationship between free energy and equilibrium constant, standard electrode potential and free energy.

(vi) Comparison of metallic conductance and electrolytic conductance. Relationship between conductance and resistance. Specific resistance and specific conductance.

Cell constant: Calculation of cell constant. Meaning of equivalent conductance. Meaning of molar conductance. General relationship between specific conductance, molar conductance and equivalent conductance (units and graphs). Units, numericals. Molar conductance of a weak electrolyte at a given concentration and at infinite dilution. Kohlrausch's law – definition, applications and numericals.

(vii) Faraday's laws of electrolysis.

Faraday's first law of electrolysis. Statement, mathematical form. Simple problems.

Faraday's second law of electrolysis: Statement, mathematical form. Simple problems. Relation between Faraday, Avogadro's number and charge on an electron. $F = N_A e$ should be given (no details of Millikan's experiment are required).

(viii) Batteries: Primary and secondary cells: Leclanche cell, mercury cell, Lead storage battery and fuel cell – structure, reactions and uses.

(ix) Corrosion: Concept, mechanism of electrochemical reaction, factors affecting it and its prevention.

3. CHEMICAL KINETICS

Meaning of chemical kinetics – slow and fast reactions. Rate of a reaction - average and instantaneous rate (graphical representation). Factors affecting rate of reaction: surface area, nature of reactants, concentration, temperature, catalyst and radiation. Order and molecularity of a reaction, rate law and specific rate constant. Integrated rate equations and half-life (only for zero and first order reactions), concept of collision theory (elementary idea, no mathematical treatment). Concept of threshold and activation energy, Arrhenius equation.

(i) Meaning of chemical kinetics, scope and importance of kinetics of the reaction, slow and fast reactions – explanation in terms of bonds.

(ii) Rate of Reaction: definition, representation of rate of reaction in terms of reactants and products, determination of rate of reactions graphically, instantaneous and average rate of reaction. Factors affecting rate of reaction.

(iii) Law of mass action: statement and meaning of active mass. Explanation with an example – general reactions.

(iv) Effect of concentration of reactants on the rate of a reaction: Qualitative treatment, based on the law of mass action, statement of rate law, General rate equation – Rate = k(concentration of the reactant)$_n$, where k is rate constant and n is the order of the reaction, relationship between the rate of the reaction with rate constant with respect to various reactants.

(v) Order of a reaction: meaning, relation between order and stoichiometric coefficients in balanced equations, order as an experimental quantity, rate equation for zero order reaction and its unit, mathematical derivation of rate equation for first order reaction, characteristics of first order reaction – rate constant is independent of the initial concentration, units to be derived, definition of half-life period, derivation of expression of half-life period from first order rate equation.

Problems based on first order rate equation and half-life period.

(vi) Molecularity of the reaction: Meaning – physical picture, relation between order, molecularity and the rate of a reaction, Differences between order and molecularity of a reaction.

(vii) *The concept of energy: Exothermic and endothermic reactions, concept of energy barrier, threshold and activation energy, formation of activated complex, effect of catalyst on activation energy and reaction rate.*

(viii) *Collision theory: Condition for a chemical change – close contact, particles should collide. Collisions to be effective – optimum energy and proper orientation during collision. Energy barrier built-up when the collision is about to take place, Activated complex formation, difference in energy of the reactant and the product – exothermic and endothermic reactions with proper graphs and labelling.*

(ix) *Mechanism of the reaction: Meaning of elementary reaction, meaning of complex and overall reaction, explanation of the mechanism of the reaction, slowest step of the reaction. Relationship between the rate expression, order of reactants and products at the rate-determining step, units of rate constant – explanation with suitable examples.*

(x) *Effect of temperature on the rate constant of a reaction: Arrhenius equation :* $k = Ae^{-E_a/RT}$, *meaning of the symbols of Arrhenius equation, related graph, evaluation of* E_a *and A from the graph, meaning of slope of the graph, conversion from exponential to log form of the equation, relationship between the increase in temperature and the number of collisions. Numerical based on Arrhenius equation.*

4. *d*- and *f*-BLOCK ELEMENTS

Position in the periodic table, occurrence, electronic configuration and characteristics of transition metals, general trends in properties of the 3*d*-series of transition metals - metallic character, ionisation enthalpy, oxidation states, ionic radii, colour of ions, catalytic property, magnetic properties, interstitial compounds, alloy formation, preparation and properties of $K_2Cr_2O_7$ and $KMnO_4$.

Lanthanoids and actinoids

(i) *d-Block:* 3*d*, 4*d* and 5*d*- *series :*
Study in terms of metallic character, atomic and ionic radii, ionisation enthalpy, oxidisation states, variable valency, formation of coloured compounds, formation of complexes, alloy formation.

(ii) *f-Block: 4f and 5f- series: Electronic configuration, atomic and ionic radii, oxidisation states, formation of coloured compounds, formation of complexes, alloy formation. Lanthanoid contraction and its consequences. Chemical reactivity – with oxygen, hydrogen, halogen, sulphur, nitrogen, carbon and water. Actinoids - oxidation states and comparison with lanthanoids.*

(iii) *Potassium permanganate: structure, shape, equation of extraction from pyrolusite ore, its oxidising nature in acidic, basic and neutral medium, use in redox titration. Oxidising nature in acidic* [$FeSO_4$, $(COOH)_2.2H_2O$, KI], *basic* (KI) *and neutral* (H_2S) *mediums to be done.*

(iv) *Potassium dichromate: structure, shape, equation of extraction from chromite ore and its use in titration. Oxidising nature in acidic, basic and neutral medium, use in redox titration. Interconversion of chromate and dichromate ion (effect of* pH*).*

5. COORDINATION COMPOUNDS

Concept of complexes, definition of ligands, coordination number, oxidation number. IUPAC nomenclature of mononuclear coordination compounds. Isomerism (structural and stereo). Bonding, Werner's theory, VBT and CFT. Colour, magnetic properties and shapes. Importance of coordination compounds (in qualitative analysis, extraction of metals and biological system).

(i) *Definition of coordination compounds / complex compounds, differences with a double salt, study of ligands – mono-, bi-, tri-, tetra-, penta-, hexa- and polydentate, chelating ligands, definition of coordination number, its calculation for a complex coordination sphere, study of oxidation state of an element in a complex, its calculation, IUPAC rules of nomenclature of coordination compounds.*

(ii) *Isomerism – structural, stereo types and examples.*

(iii) *Valence bond theory of coordination compounds – examples of formation of inner orbital and outer orbital complexes (high and low spin, octahedral, tetrahedral and square planar), prediction of magnetic character.*

(iv) *Crystal field theory – crystal field splitting in tetra and octahedral systems. Explanation of colour and magnetic character.*

(v) *Stability of coordination compounds (explain stability on the basis of magnitude of K) as mentioned above.*

(vi) *Importance and uses.*

6. HALOALKANES AND HALOARENES

Haloalkanes: General formula, nomenclature and classification. Nature of C—*X* bond, physical and chemical properties, mechanism of substitution reactions, optical rotation.

Haloarenes: Basic idea, nature of C—*X* bond, substitution reactions (directive influence of halogen in monosubstituted compounds only).

Uses and environmental effects of — dichloromethane, trichloromethane, tetrachloromethane, iodoform, freons and DDT.

Nature of C — X bond

Naming the halogen derivatives of alkanes by using common system and IUPAC system for mono, di and tri-halo derivatives.
Preparation of haloalkanes from:
Alkane and halogen.

- *Alkene and hydrogen halide.*
- *Alcohols with* PX_3, PCl_5 *and* $SOCl_2$.
- *Halide exchange method (Finkelstein and Swarts)*
- *Silver salt of fatty acids (Hunsdiecker).*

Physical properties : *state, melting point, boiling point and solubility.*

Chemical properties : *nucleophilic substitution reactions* (S_N1, S_N2 *mechanism in terms of primary, secondary and tertiary halides). Reaction with: sodium hydroxide, water, sodium iodide, ammonia, primary amine, secondary amine, potassium cyanide, silver cyanide, potassium nitrite, silver nitrite, silver salt of fatty acid and lithium-aluminium hydride.*

Elimination reaction (Saytzeff's rule) / β-elimination. Reaction with metals: sodium and magnesium (Wurtz's reaction, Grignard's reagent preparation). Chloroform and iodoform: preparation and properties. Structure of freons. Preparation of haloarenes by Sandmeyer's and Gattermann's reaction, by electrophilic substitution.

Physical properties: *State, melting point, boiling point and solubility.*

Chemical properties : *Electrophilic substitution (chlorination nitration and sulphonation) with mechanism, Nucleophilic substitution (replacement of chlorine with —OH, —NH_2) with mechanism, Reduction to benzene, Wurtz-Fittig reaction, Fittig reaction, Addition reaction with magnesium (formation of Grignard reagent), Structure of DDT.*

7. ALCOHOLS, PHENOLS AND ETHERS

Alcohols: Classification, general formula, structure and nomenclature. Methods of preparation, physical and chemical properties (of primary alcohols only), identification of primary, secondary and tertiary alcohols, mechanism of dehydration, uses with special reference to methanol and ethanol.

(i) *Classification into monohydric, dihydric and polyhydric alcohols, general formulae, structure and nomenclature of alcohols. Difference between primary, secondary and tertiary alcohols in terms of structure, physical properties and chemical properties.*

(ii) *Methods of preparation:*

Hydration of Alkenes – direct hydration, indirect hydration, hydroboration oxidation, From Grignard's reagent, Hydrolysis of alkyl halides, Reduction of carbonyl compounds, From primary amines.

Manufacture of methanol by Bosch process and ethanol by fermentation of carbohydrates, chemical equations required (only outline of the method of manufacture, detail not required).

Properties:

Acidic nature of alcohols:, Reaction with sodium, Esterification with mechanism, Reaction with hydrogen halides. Reaction with PCl_3, PCl_5 and $SOCl_2$, Reaction with acid chlorides and acid anhydrides, Oxidation, Dehydration with mechanism.

Uses of alcohols.

(iii) *Conversion of one alcohol into another.*

(iv) *Distinction between primary, secondary and tertiary alcohols by Lucas test.*

Phenols: Classification and nomenclature. Methods of preparation, physical and chemical properties, acidic nature of phenol, electrophilic substitution reactions, uses of phenols.

Preparation of phenol from diazonium salt, chlorobenzene (Dow's process) and from benzene sulphonic acid. Manufacture from cumene.

Physical properties : *state and solubility*

Chemical properties : *Acidic character of phenol, Reaction with sodium hydroxide, Reaction with sodium, Reaction with zinc, Reaction with acetyl chloride and acetic anhydride, Reaction with phosphorus pentachloride, Bromination, nitration and sulphonation (Electrophilic substitution reactions), Kolbe's reaction (formation of salicylic acid), Reimer – Tiemann reaction, Test for phenol – $FeCl_3$ test, azo dye test.*

Aliphatic Ethers: General formula, structure and nomenclature. Methods of preparation, physical and chemical properties, uses.

Ethers: structure of ethereal group. Preparation from alcohol (Williamson's synthesis).

Physical properties: *state, miscibility.*

Chemical properties: *Reaction with chlorine, Oxidation (peroxide formation), Reaction with HI, Reaction with PCl_5.*

Aryl Ethers

Physical properties : *state and solubility.*

Chemical properties : *preparation of anisole (Williamson's synthesis), electrophilic substitution (halogenation, nitration and Friedel-Crafts reaction.) Uses of ether.*

8. ALDEHYDES, KETONES AND CARBOXYLIC ACIDS

Aldehydes and Ketones : Nomenclature, structure of methods of preparation of aldehydes and ketones, physical and chemical properties, mechanism of nucleophilic addition, reactivity of alpha hydrogen in aldehydes and uses.

Preparation: *From alcohol, From alkenes (ozonolysis), From alkynes (hydration), From acid chlorides (Rosenmund's reduction, reaction with dialkyl cadmium), From calcium salt of carboxylic acids, From nitriles (Stephen reaction, Grignard's reagent), From esters.*

Physical properties : *state and boiling point.*

Chemical properties : *Nucleophilic addition reactions with mechanism (ammonia and its derivatives, HCN, $NaHSO_3$ and Grignard's reagent), Oxidation reactions, iodoform reaction, Reduction: reduction to alcohol and alkanes (Clemmensen's reduction, Wolff-Kishner reduction, Red phosphorus and HI), Base catalysed reactions (with mechanism): Aldol condensation, Cross-Aldol condensation, Cannizzaro's reaction.*

Tests: difference between formaldehyde and acetaldehyde; aldehydes and ketones.

Uses of aldehydes and ketones.

Aromatic aldehyde (Benzaldehyde)

Lab preparation from toluene by oxidation with chromyl chloride.

Physical properties: *state and stability.*

Chemical properties: *Oxidation and reduction, Nucleophilic addition reaction (hydrogen cyanide and sodium bisulphite), Reactions with ammonia and its derivatives (hydroxyl amine, hydrazine and phenyl hydrazine), Reaction with phosphorus pentachloride, Cannizzaro reaction, Benzoin condensation, Perkin's reaction, Electrophilic substitution - halogenation, nitration and sulphonation.*

Test: distinction between aromatic and aliphatic aldehydes.

Uses of benzaldehyde.

Carboxylic Acids: Classification, general formula and structure of carboxylic group. Nomenclature, acidic nature, methods of preparation, physical and chemical properties and uses.

Classification of mono and di carboxylic acids with examples.

Preparation of aliphatic and aromatic carboxylic acid:

From alcohols, aldehydes, From nitriles, From Grignard's reagent.

Physical Properties: State boiling point and solubility.

Chemical properties: *Acidic character: (aliphatic, aromatic carboxylic acids with the effect of substituents on the acidic character–to be dealt with in detail).*

Reaction with active metals, alkalies, carbonates and bicarbonates, Formation of acid derivatives.

Decarboxylation (chemical and Kolbe's electrolytic reaction), HVZ *reactions, Substitution of benzene ring (meta directive effect of carboxylic acid group) nitration and sulphonation.*

Tests for acids: formic acid, acetic acid and benzoic acid.

Uses of formic acid, acetic acid and benzoic acid.

9. ORGANIC COMPOUNDS CONTAINING NITROGEN

Aliphatic Amines: General formula and, classification of amines. Structure of the amino group, nomenclature. Methods of preparation, physical and chemical properties, uses, identification of primary, secondary and tertiary amines.

Amines

Nomenclature, classification with examples, structure, general formula.

Methods of preparation: *From alcohol, From alkyl halide, From cyanide, From amide (Hofmann's degradation), From nitro compounds, Gabriel phthalimide synthesis.*

Physical properties : *comparison between primary, secondary and tertiary amines in terms of – state, solubility, boiling point (hydrogen bonding), comparison with alcohols.*

Chemical properties : *Basic character of amines – comparison between primary, secondary and tertiary alkyl amines/ ammonia/ aniline. Effect of substituents on the basic strength of aniline, Alkylation and acylation with mechanism, Reaction with nitrous acid, Carbylamine reaction.*

Distinction between primary, secondary and tertiary amines (Hinsberg's test)

Aniline

Preparation reduction of nitrobenzene.

Physical properties – state, solubility and boiling point.

Chemical properties:

Reaction with HCl *and* H_2SO_4, *Acetylation, alkylation, Benzoylation, Carbylamine reaction, Diazotisation, Electrophilic substitution (bromination, nitration and sulphonation)*

Tests for aniline.

Uses of aniline.

Cyanides and Isocyanides

Methods of preparation:

Cyanides : *From alkyl halide, From amide, Isocyanides, From alkyl halide, From primary amines*

Diazonium salts: Preparation, chemical reactions and importance in synthetic organic chemistry.

Preparation from aniline;

Properties: Sandmeyer's reaction, Gattermann reaction and Balz – Scheimann reaction, replacement of diazo group by — H, — OH, — NO_2, *coupling reaction with phenol and aniline.*

10. BIOMOLECULES

Carbohydrates – Definition, classification (aldoses and ketoses), monosaccharides (glucose and fructose), D-L configuration oligosaccharides (sucrose, lactose, maltose), polysaccharides (starch, cellulose, glycogen); Importance of carbohydrates.

Carbohydrates: definition, classification - mono (aldose, ketose), oligo (di, tri, tetra saccharides) and polysaccharides with examples: reducing sugars and non reducing sugars – examples and uses.

Establishment of structures for glucose and fructose (open and cyclic).heating with HI, *reaction with hydroxylamine, bromine water, acetic anhydride, nitric acid and phenyl hydrazine.*

Test for glucose and fructose (bromine water test with equation).

Disaccharides – structures of sucrose, maltose and lactose (glycosidic linkage).

Polysaccharides – starch, cellulose, glycogen.

Proteins – Structural units of proteins. Basic idea of - amino acids, peptide bond, polypeptides, proteins, structure of proteins - primary, secondary, tertiary structure and quaternary structures (qualitative idea only), denaturation of proteins. Enzymes, hormones - elementary idea only.

Proteins: Amino acids – general structure, classification and Zwitter ion formation. Isoelectric point. Classification of proteins on the basis of molecular shape; primary, secondary, tertiary and quaternary, structures of proteins, denaturation of proteins. (Definitions only. Details and diagrams are not required).

Vitamins - Classification and functions.

Vitamins A, B, C, D, E and K: classification (fat soluble and water soluble), deficiency diseases. (Chemical names and structures are not required).

Nucleic Acids - DNA and RNA.

Nucleic acids: basic unit – purine and pyrimidine, DNA *– structure (double helical),* RNA *(No chemical structure required). Differences between* DNA *and* RNA.

01

Solutions

TREND ANALYSIS 4 YEARS

		Average No. of Questions Across all Sets				
		Types of Questions	2024	2023	2020	2019
TOPIC 01	Relative Molecular Mass, Mole Concept, Expressing Concentration of Solutions	1 Mark	—	—	—	—
		2 Marks	—	—	—	—
		3 Marks	—	—	—	—
		5 Marks	—	—	—	—
TOPIC 02	Raoult's Law and Solubility of Gases in Liquids	1 Mark	—	—	—	—
		2 Marks	—	—	—	—
		3 Marks	—	—	—	—
		5 Marks	—	—	—	—
TOPIC 03	Colligative Properties and Relative Molecular Mass of Non-volatile Substances	1 Mark	1	—	—	1
		2 Marks	1	2	—	1
		3 Marks	2	1	—	2
		5 Marks	—	—	2	—

TOPIC 1

Relative Molecular Mass, Mole Concept, Expressing Concentration of Solutions

Relative Molecular Mass

The relative molecular mass of an element or a compound is the mass of one molecule of the element or compound compared with $\frac{1}{12}$th of the mass of an atom of ${}_6C^{12}$ isotope of carbon which is assigned as 12 units.

$$\text{Relative molecular mass} = \frac{\text{Actual mass of an element or a compound}}{\frac{1}{2} \times \text{Mass of an atom of } {}_6C^{12}}$$

Mole Concept

The number 6.02×10^{23} entities of a substance is called **Avogadro's number** (N_A), which stands for 1 mole of a substance.

$$\text{Number of moles of solute } (n) = \frac{\text{Mass of solute in gram } (w)}{\text{Gram molar mass of solute } (M)}$$

(Gram molar mass = Mass of 1 mole of solute in gram).

The volume occupied by one mole of a gas is called **molar volume**. At STP, one mole of a gaseous substance occupies 22.4 L.

Expressing Concentrations of Solutions

Solutions are homogeneous mixtures of two or more than two components. In solution, a **solute** is a substance which is dissolved in another substance, known as **solvent**. Solvent is present in a larger quantity in comparison to the solute.

The solutions containing two components are called **binary solutions**, e.g. salt solution.

Expressing of concentration terms and their relation with temperature

Terms	Formula	Definition	Effect of temperature
Mass percentage	$\frac{\text{Mass of solute}}{\text{Total mass of solution}}\times 100$	Amount of solute in grams present in 100 g of solution.	No effect
Mass by volume percentage	$\frac{\text{Mass of solute}}{\text{Total volume of solution in mL}}\times 100$	Amount of solute in grams dissolved in 100 mL of the solution.	Changes with change in temperature.
Volume percentage	$\frac{\text{Volume of solute}}{\text{Total volume of solution}}\times 100$	Volume of solute in mL dissolved in 100 mL of the solution.	Changes with change in temperature.
Strength	$\frac{\text{Mass of solute in grams}}{\text{Volume of solution in L / dm}^3}$	Amount of solute in grams present in one litre (or dm^3) of solution.	Changes with change in temperature.
Parts per million	$\frac{\text{No. of parts of solute}}{\text{Total no. of parts of all components of solution}}\times 10^6$	Number of parts of solute present in million (10^6) parts of solution.	No effect
Mole fraction	$\chi_A = \frac{n_A}{n_A + n_B}$	Ratio of number of moles of one component to the total number of moles of all the components.	No effect
Molarity	$\frac{\text{Moles of solute}}{\text{Volume of solution in L / dm}^3}$	Number of moles of solute dissolved one litre (or one dm^3) of solution.	Changes with change in temperature.
Molality	$\frac{\text{Moles of solute}}{\text{Mass of solvent in kg}}$	Number of moles of solute per 1 kg of the solvent.	No effect
Normality	$\frac{\text{No. of gram equivalent of solute}}{\text{Volume of solution in litres}}$	Number of gram equivalent of solute dissolved in one litre of solution at a certain temperature.	Changes with change in temperature.

PYQs Previous Years' Questions

1 Mark Questions

1. A solution of urea (molecular mass = 60) contains 8.6 g per litre. It is isotonic with a 5% solution of a non-volatile and non-electrolytic solute. What will be the molecular mass of the solute? **ISC 2021-22 (Sem-I)**
   (a) 34.9 g mol^{-1}
   (b) 349 g mol^{-1}
   (c) 861 g mol^{-1}
   (d) 3490 g mol^{-1}

2. If 5.85 g of NaCl are dissolved in 90 g of water, the mole fraction of solute is **ISC Specimen 2021-22 (Sem-I)**
   (a) 0.2632 (b) 0.0102
   (c) 0.0196 (d) 0.1045

3. Complete the following statement by selecting the correct alternative from the given choices of the following terms used for denoting concentration of a solution, the one which does not get affected by temperature is **ISC 2014**
   (a) molarity (b) molality
   (c) normality (d) formality

4. Correct the following statement.
   "Molarity of a solution is independent of temperature". **ISC 2005**

2 Marks Questions

5. A binary solution contains 92 g ethyl alcohol and 72 g water (Atomic weight of C = 12, H = 1, O = 16). **ISC Specimen 2021-22, (Sem-I)**
   (i) Mole fraction of ethyl alcohol is
   (a) 0.40 (b) 0.80 (c) 0.66 (d) 0.33
   (ii) Mole fraction of water is
   (a) 0.33 (b) 0.66 (c) 0.20 (d) 0.80

6. 46 g of ethyl alcohol is dissolved in 18 g of water. Calculate the mole fraction of ethyl alcohol. (Atomic weight of C = 12, O = 16 and H = 1) **ISC 2011**

7. If the molality of an aqueous solution of cane sugar is 0.4445, what is the mole fraction of cane sugar? **ISC 2008**

> **KEY IDEA**
> Using molality, we can calculate the moles of cane sugar present in 1000 g of water. Then, calculate the mole fraction of cane sugar using the formula, $\chi = \frac{n_{solute}}{n_{solute} + n_{solvent}}$

8. Calculate the mole fraction of water in a sodium hydroxide solution which has 80 g of NaOH and 54 g of H_2O. (Relative atomic masses of Na = 23, O = 16 and H = 1) **ISC 2005**

Explanations

1. (b) No. of moles of urea $= \frac{8.6}{60}$

   5% of unknown solution $= \frac{5}{100 \text{ mL}} = \frac{50}{1000 \text{ L}} = 5 \text{g/L}$

   No. of moles of unknown solute $= \frac{50}{m} \Rightarrow \frac{8.6}{60} = \frac{50}{m}$

   $\Rightarrow \quad m = 348.9 \sim 349 \text{ g/mol}$

2. (c) $w = 5.85$ g
   Weight of water = 90 g

   $$\text{Mole fraction of NaCl} = \frac{\text{No. of moles of NaCl}}{\text{Moles of water + Moles of NaCl}}$$

   $$= \frac{\frac{\text{Mass of NaCl}}{\text{Molar mass of NaCl}}}{\frac{\text{Mass of water}}{\text{Molar mass of water}} + \frac{\text{Mass of NaCl}}{\text{Molar mass of NaCl}}}$$

   $$\Rightarrow \frac{\frac{5.85}{58.5}}{\frac{90}{18} + \frac{5.85}{58.5}} \Rightarrow \frac{0.1}{5 + 0.1} = \frac{0.1}{5.1} = 0.0196$$

3. (b) Molality does not get affected by temperature because molality does not depend on the volume while other three terms depend on the volume and volume varies with temperature.

4. The correct statement is
   "Molarity of a solution depends on temperature".

> **Concept Enhancer** Only molality has weight term which do not depend on temperature, while molarity depends on volume which is affected by temperature.

5. (i) (d) No. of moles $= \dfrac{\text{Given mass}}{\text{Molar mass}}$

Moles of ethyl alcohol $= \dfrac{92}{46} = 2$ mol

Moles of water $= \dfrac{72}{18} = 4$ mol

Mole fraction of ethyl alcohol $= \dfrac{2}{2+4} = \dfrac{1}{3} \simeq 0.33$ **(1)**

(ii) (b) Mole fraction of water $= \dfrac{4}{2+4} = 0.66$ **(1)**

6. Given, mass of ethyl alcohol $(w) = 46$ g,

Mass of water $(W) = 18$ g

We know that,

Molecular weight of ethyl alcohol (C_2H_5OH)

$= 2 \times 12 + 5 \times 1 + 16 + 1 = 46$

Number of moles of ethyl alcohol in 46 g

$= \dfrac{\text{Mass of ethyl alcohol}}{\text{Molar mass of ethyl alcohol}} = \dfrac{46}{46} = 1$ mol

Molecular weight of water (H_2O) $= 2 \times 1 + 16 = 18$

Number of moles of water in 18 g $= \dfrac{18}{18} = 1$ mol

$\therefore$ Mole fraction of ethyl alcohol

$$= \frac{n_{C_2H_5OH}}{n_{C_2H_5OH} + n_{H_2O}} = \frac{1}{1+1} = \frac{1}{2} = 0.5$$

7. Given, molality of cane sugar solution

$= 0.4445$ mol/kg

That means, number of moles (n) of cane sugar present in 1 kg of water $= 0.4445$

We know that, number of moles of water,

$$(N) = \frac{1000}{18} = 55.5555$$

($\because$ Density of water $= 1000\ \text{kg}/\text{m}^3 = 1\ \text{g}/\text{cm}^3$, molecular weight of $H_2O = 18\ \text{g mol}^{-1}$)

Thus, molarity $= \dfrac{\text{Number of moles of water}}{\text{Volume (L)}}$

$= \dfrac{1000/18}{1} = 55.5555$M

Mole fraction of cane sugar

$$= \frac{n_{\text{solute}}}{n_{\text{solute}} + N_{\text{solvent}}} = \frac{n}{n+N}$$

$$= \frac{0.4445}{0.4445 + 55.5555} = \frac{0.4445}{56} = 0.0079$$

8. Molecular mass of NaOH

$= 23 + 16 + 1 = 40\ \text{g mol}^{-1}$

Number of moles of NaOH in 80 g

$$(n) = \frac{\text{Mass of NaOH}}{\text{Molecular mass of NaOH}}$$

$= \dfrac{80}{40} = 2$ mol

Molecular mass of water $= 2 + 16 = 18\ \text{g mol}^{-1}$

Number of moles of water in 54 g,

$(N) = \dfrac{54}{18} = 3$ mol

Total number of moles in solution $= n + N$

$= 2 + 3 = 5$ mol

Mole fraction of water in solution

$$= \frac{\text{Number of moles of water}}{\text{Total number of moles present in solution}}$$

$$= \frac{N}{n+N} = \frac{3}{5} = 0.6$$

TOPIC 2

Raoult's Law and Solubility of Gases in Liquids

Vapour Pressure of Solution

The maximum pressure exerted by the vapour of a liquid at a particular temperature in a state of dynamic equilibrium is known as **vapour pressure** of the liquid at that temperature.

The vapour pressure of a liquid depends on the following factors

(i) **Nature of liquid** Liquids having strong intermolecular forces possess lower vapour pressure at a given temperature.

(ii) **Temperature** Vapour pressure increases with increase in temperature.

(iii) **Presence of impurities** The presence of non-volatile impurities lowers the vapour pressure while that of volatile impurities raises the vapour pressure of a liquid.

Solubility of Gases in Liquids (Henry's Law)

According to Henry's law, 'at constant temperature, the solubility of a gas in a liquid is directly proportional to the pressure of the gas.' 'The partial pressure of the gas in vapour phase (p) is proportional to the mole fraction of the gas (χ) in the solution'.

$$p \propto \chi \quad \text{or} \quad \boxed{p = K_H \cdot \chi}$$

(where, K_H is Henry's law constant.)

Higher the value of K_H at a given pressure, the lower is the solubility of the gas in the liquid.

The solubility of a gas in liquid (or solvent) depends on the following factors :

(i) **Nature of the gas** Different gases possess different values of K_H. The solubility of gas is inversely proportional to the value of K_H. At a given pressure, higher the value of K_H, lower is the solubility of the gas.

(ii) **Temperature** In general, solubility of gases decreases as the temperature increases.

(iii) **Pressure** Solubility increases with increase of pressure.

Applications of Henry's Law

- To increase the solubility of CO_2 in soft drinks and soda water, the bottle is sealed under high pressure.
- To avoid bends (blocking of capillaries) and the toxic effects of high concentrations of N_2 in the blood, the tanks used by scuba divers are filled with air diluted with He. (11.7% of He + 56.2% N_2 + 32.1% O_2)

Limitations of Henry's Law

- It is applicable to ideal gases only. However, it can be applied to real gases at low pressure.
- It is not applicable to those gases which dissociate into ions in solution and those gases which undergoes a chemical change in solution.

Note In the solution of a liquid in a liquid, if one of the components is so volatile that it can exists as a gas, then we can say that Raoult's law becomes a special case of Henry's law in which K_H becomes equal to $p°$.

Raoult's Law

It states that for a solution of volatile solute, the partial vapour pressure of each component in the solution is directly proportional to its mole fraction present in solution, i.e. $p_1 = p_1^\circ \chi_1$ and $p_2 = p_2^\circ \chi_2$ w here, p_1° and p_2° are vapour pressures of pure components 1 and 2 respectively at the same temperature.

According to **Dalton's law of partial pressure,**

$$p_{total} = p_1 + p_2 = \chi_1 p_1^\circ + \chi_2 p_2^\circ = (1 - \chi_2) p_1^\circ + \chi_2 p_2^\circ$$
$$= p_1^\circ + (p_2^\circ - p_1^\circ)\chi_2.$$

If y_1 and y_2 are the mole fractions of the components 1 and 2 respectively in vapour phase, then $p_1 = y_1 \times p_{total}$ and $p_2 = y_2 \times p_{total}$.

Ideal and Non-ideal Solutions

On the basis of Raoult's liquid-liquid solutions can be divided into ideal and non ideal solutions.

Ideal Solutions

They obey Raoult's law over entire range of concentrations and temperatures. For these solutions, $\Delta H_{mix} = 0$ and $\Delta V_{mix} = 0$.

Solution of n-hexane and n-heptane, bromoethane and chloroethane, benzene and toluene, etc. are nearly ideal in behaviour.

Non-ideal Solutions

They do not obey Raoult's law over entire range of concentrations and temperatures.

For such solutions, $\Delta H_{mix} \neq 0$ and $\Delta V_{mix} \neq 0$

There are following two types of non-ideal solutions are

Solutions having positive deviation from ideal behaviour	Solutions having negative deviation from ideal behaviour
The intermolecular interactions, i.e. $A — B$ interactions are weaker than in pure components, i.e. between $A—A$ or $B—B$.	The intermolecular interactions, i.e. $A — B$ interactions are stronger than in pure components, i.e. between $A — A$ or $B — B$.
$p_1 > p_1^\circ\chi_1$ and $p_2 > p_2^\circ\chi_2$	$p_1 < p_1^\circ\chi_1$ and $p_2 < p_2^\circ\chi_2$
$\Delta_{mix}H$ = positive (endothermic)	$\Delta_{mix}H$ = negative (exothermic)
$\Delta_{mix}V$ = positive	$\Delta_{mix}V$ = negative
Heating increases solubility.	Heating decreases solubility.

Azeotropic Mixtures

The solutions of completely miscible liquids, which boils at constant temperature and can distilled over without any change in composition are called azeotropes or azeotropic mixtures.

The solutions which show large negative deviation from Raoult's law, form **maximum boiling azeotropes**. $H_2O + HCl$ and the solutions which shows large positive deviation from Raoult's law, form **minimum boiling azeotropes**. e.g. $C_2H_5OH + H_2O$.

For the separation of two liquids which have nearly equal boiling points, the process of simple distillation cannot be used. In such case fractional distillation is used.

PYQs Previous Years' Questions

1 Mark Questions

1. According to which law the solubility of a gas at equilibrium and constant temperature varies directly with the pressure of the gas, provided the gas does not undergo any chemical change during the dissolution? **ISC 2021-22 (Sem-I)**
   (a) Raoult's law (b) Nernst distribution law
   (c) Henry's law (d) Van't Hoff law

Or The solubility of a gas varies directly with pressure of the gas is based upon **ISC 2008**
   (a) Raoult's law (b) Henry's law
   (c) Nernst distribution law (d) None of these

2. A solution containing components A and B follows Raoult's law.
   With reference to the statement which of the following options is correct? **ISC 2021-22 (Sem-I)**
   (a) $A—B$ attraction force is greater than $A—A$ and $B—B$.
   (b) $A—B$ attraction force is less than $A—A$ and $B—B$.
   (c) $A—B$ attraction force remains the same as $A—A$ and $B—B$.
   (d) Total volume of solution is different from sum of volumes of both components A and B.

3. Solutions which distil without any change in composition and temperature are called **ISC Specimen 2021-22 (Sem-I)**
   (a) ideal (b) supersaturated
   (c) azeotropic (d) isotonic

4. Solutions which strictly obey ...... law are called .... solutions. **ISC 2012**

5. The .... pressure of an aqueous solution of 0.1 M cane sugar is .... than that of pure water. **ISC 2010**

2 Marks Questions

6. 5 moles of sucrose (molecular mass = 342 g mol^{-1}) dissolved in 1000 g of water (molecular mass = 18 g mol^{-1}). Vapour pressure of pure water at 298 K = 4.57 mm Hg. **ISC 2021-22 (Sem-I)**
   (i) What will be the vapour pressure of sucrose solution at the same temperature?
   (a) 0.419 mm Hg (b) 6.570 mm Hg
   (c) 4.190 mm Hg (d) 0.657 mm Hg
   (ii) What will be the mole fraction of sucrose in water?
   (a) 0.8261 (b) 0.0826 (c) 0.4376 (d) 0.0435

7. A solution is prepared by dissolving 2.0 g of sucrose and 2.0 g of urea in 100 g of water at 298 K. Calculate the vapour pressure of the solution, if the vapour pressure of pure water at 298 K is 23.56 torr. (Molecular weight of urea = 60 and sucrose = 342) **ISC 2006**

KEY IDEA
Calculate vapour pressure of a solution using formula for relative lowering of vapour pressure

$$\frac{p_A^\circ - p_S}{p_A^\circ} = \frac{n_B}{n_A} = \frac{W_B \times M_A}{M_B \times W_A}.$$

3 Marks Questions

8. What is the mass of a non-volatile solute (molar mass 60) that needs to be dissolved in 100 g of water in order to decrease the vapour pressure of water by 25%? What will be the molality of the solution? **ISC 2010**

Explanations

1. (c) Henry's law

Or

(b) It is based upon Henry's law.

2. (c) The solution which obey Raoult's law is always ideal solution. In ideal solution, attraction force remains same in $A—A$ and $B—B$.

3. (c) Azeotropic mixture is a constant boiling mixture in which the compositon remains same throughout the boiling.

4. Solutions which strictly obey **Raoult's** law are called **ideal** solutions.

5. The **vapour** pressure of an aqueous solution of 0.1 M cane sugar is **less** than that of pure water (as it is non-volatile solute).

6. (i) (c) According to Raoult's law,

$$p_{\text{solution}} = p^{\circ}_{\text{solvent}} \times \chi_{\text{solvent}} = 4.57 \times \frac{\frac{1000}{18}}{\frac{1000}{18}+5}$$

$$= 4.57 \times \frac{55.55}{55.55+5} = 4.192 \text{ mm of Hg}$$ **(1)**

(ii) (b) Mole fraction of sucrose

$$= \frac{\text{No. of moles of sucrose}}{\text{Moles of sucrose + Moles of water}}$$

$$= \frac{5}{5+\frac{1000}{18}} = 0.0826$$ **(1)**

7. The expression for Raoult's law for the solution containing non-volatile solute is

$$\frac{\Delta p}{p^{\circ}} = \frac{p^{\circ}-p}{p^{\circ}} = \frac{n}{n+N}$$

$$= \frac{w/m}{w/m+W/M}$$

Given that, $p^{\circ} = 23.56$ torr

Number of moles of solute,

n = Number of moles of sucrose + Number of moles of urea

$$= \frac{w_s}{m_s} + \frac{w_u}{m_u}$$

$$n = \frac{2}{342} + \frac{2}{60}$$

Number of moles of solvent (water),

$$N = \frac{100}{18}$$

$$\therefore \frac{23.56-p}{23.56} = \frac{\frac{2}{342}+\frac{2}{60}}{\frac{2}{342}+\frac{2}{60}+\frac{100}{18}} = 0.007$$

$$23.56 - p = 0.007 \times 23.56 = 0.165$$

$$p = 23.56 - 0.165$$

$$= 23.395 \text{ torr}$$

Hence, the vapour pressure of the solution is 23.395 torr.

8. According to Raoult's law,

$$\frac{\Delta p}{p^{\circ}} = \frac{p^{\circ}-p}{p^{\circ}} = \frac{n}{n+N}$$

$$= \frac{w/m}{w/m+W/M}$$

Given, $\Delta p = 25\%$ (atm), i.e. $p^{\circ} = 100$ (atm), $m = 60$, $W = 100$ g, $M = 18$ (for water), $w = ?$

$$\frac{25}{100} = \frac{w/60}{w/60+100/18}$$

$$\Rightarrow \quad \frac{1}{4} = \frac{w/60}{\frac{18w+60\times 100}{18\times 60}}$$

$$\Rightarrow \quad w = 111.11 \text{ g}$$

Mass of solute required is 111.11 g.

Now, Molality (m)

$$= \frac{\text{Number of moles of solute}}{\text{Mass of solvent in kg}}$$

$$= \frac{111.11/60}{100/1000}$$

$$= 18.518$$

Hence, molality of the solution is 18.518 mol kg^{-1}.

TOPIC 3

Colligative Properties and Relative Molecular Mass of Non-volatile Substances

Colligative Properties

The properties of the solutions which depends only on the number of solute particles, but not on the nature of the solute particles are known as colligative properties.

$$\text{Colligative properties} \propto \text{Number of solute particles in the solution} \propto \frac{1}{\text{Molar mass of solute}}$$

Colligative properties of solutions are

- relative lowering of vapour pressure.
- depression in freezing point.
- elevation in boiling point.
- osmotic pressure.

Relative Lowering of Vapour Pressure

Relative lowering of vapour pressure of an ideal solution containing the non-volatile solute is equal to the mole fraction of the solute at a given temperature.

Relative lowering of vapour pressure (Raoult's law for non-volatile solutes) is given by

$$\frac{p^\circ - p}{p^\circ} = \chi_{\text{solute}}$$

(where, p° is the vapour pressure of pure solvent, p is vapour pressure of solution, χ_{solute} is mole fraction of solute).

$$\Rightarrow \quad \frac{p^\circ - p}{p^\circ} = \frac{n}{n+N} \qquad \left(\text{Since, } \chi_{\text{solute}} = \frac{n}{n+N}\right)$$

or $$\frac{p^\circ - p}{p^\circ} = \frac{n}{N} \text{ for dilute solutions, } (n << N)$$

$$= \frac{w_2 \times M_1}{M_2 \times W_1} \qquad \left(n = \frac{w_2}{M_2} \text{ and } N = \frac{W_1}{M_1}\right)$$

where, n = moles of solute and N is moles of solvent.

w_2 and W_1 = mass of solute and solvent respectively.

M_1 and M_2 = molecular weight of solvent and solute respectively.

Depression in Freezing Point

When a non-volatile solute is added to a solvent, the freezing point of the solution is always lower than that of pure solvent as the vapour pressure of the solvent decreases in the presence of non-volatile solute. This difference in freezing point is known as depression in freezing point.

Note Depression in freezing point is colligative property but the freezing point is not.

Depression in freezing point, $\Delta T_f \propto$ Lowering in vapour pressure, $\Delta T_f = T_f^\circ - T_f$.

where, T_f = freezing point of solution

T_f° = freezing point of pure solvent.

For dilute solutions, $\Delta T_f \propto m$, $\Delta T_f = K_f \cdot m$ or

$$\Delta T_f = \frac{K_f \times w \times 1000}{M' \times W(\text{g})}$$

$\frac{w}{M' W}$ represents the molality (m) of the solution,

$$\boxed{M' = \frac{K_f \times w \times 1000}{\Delta T_f \times W\,(\text{g})}}$$

The **cryoscopic constant**, i.e. K_f the **depression in freezing point** produced on dissolving one mole of a substance in 1000 g of the solvent. Its unit is K molal^{-1}, °C molal^{-1} or K kg mol^{-1}.

Elevation in Boiling Point

When a non-volatile solute is added to a solvent, the boiling point of the solution is always higher than that of pure solvent as the vapour pressure of the solvent decreases in the presence of non-volatile solute and to make it boil we have to increase the vapour pressure to atmospheric pressure by raising the temperature.

This difference in boiling point is known as elevation in boiling point, i.e. $\Delta T_b = T_b - T_b^\circ$.

where, T_b = boiling point of solution

T_b° = boiling point of pure solvent.

Note Elevation in boiling point is colligative property but the boiling point is not.

In terms of molality (m), $\Delta T_b = K_b \times m$.

For dilute solutions, $\Delta T_b \propto m$ or $\Delta T_b = K_b \times m$

$$= K_b\left(\frac{w_B \times 1000}{M_B \times w_A}\right)$$

or $$M_B = \left(\frac{1000 \times w_B \times K_b}{\Delta T_b \times W_A}\right)$$

The **ebullioscopic constant** is the elevation of boiling point produced on dissolving 1 mole of a substance in 1000 g of the solvent. Its unit is K $molal^{-1}$, °C $molal^{-1}$ or K kg mol^{-1}.

Molal depression constant (K_f) and molal elevation constant (K_b) for a particular solvent can be calculated as

$$K_f = \frac{R \times M \times T_f^2}{1000 \times \Delta_{fus}H} \quad \text{and} \quad K_b = \frac{R \times M \times T_b^2}{1000 \times \Delta_{vap}H}$$

where, R and M are gas constant and molar mass of the solvent, respectively. T_f and T_b are freezing point and boiling point of the pure solvent, respectively (in K). $\Delta_{fus}H$ and $\Delta_{vap}H$ are enthalpies for the fusion and vaporisation of the solvent, respectively.

Osmosis and Osmotic Pressure

The process of flow of solvent molecules through semipermeable membrane from the solution of lower concentration to solution of higher concentration is known as **osmosis.**

Osmotic pressure of the solution is the pressure which just prevents the flow of solvent molecules. In the other words, the pressure that must be applied to the solution in order to prevent the passage of solvent molecules into the solution through a semipermeable membrane separating the two is called **osmotic pressure**.

Osmotic pressure, $\pi = R\frac{nT}{V}$ or CRT $\left(\text{where, } C = \frac{n}{V}\right)$

or $\pi V = nRT = \frac{w}{M'}RT$ or $\boxed{M' = \frac{wRT}{\pi V}}$

where, n = moles of solute

V = volume of solution (in L)

W = weight of solute

M = molecular weight of solute.

The value of R is taken to be 0.0821 L atm $K^{-1}mol^{-1}$ when π is expressed in atmosphere, V in litres and T in Kelvin.

Types of Solution on the Basis of Osmotic Pressure

(i) **Isotonic solutions** Two solutions having same osmotic pressure at a given temperature are called isotonic solutions.

(ii) **Hypotonic and hypertonic solutions** A solution having lower osmotic pressure than the other is called hypotonic while the one with higher osmotic pressure is called hypertonic.

Note People taking salty food experience water retention in tissue cells and intercellular spaces due to osmosis. The resulting puffiness is called **edema.**

Abnormal Molecular Mass

For the substances undergoing association, dissociation, etc., in the solution, experimentally observed molecular mass determined from colligative properties is different from the normal value as expected from its chemical formula.

This observed molecular mass is known as abnormal molecular mass.

The reason is that, Molecular mass of solute

$$(M') \propto \frac{1}{\text{Number of particles of solute in solution}}$$

The molecular association of a solute in solution leads to a observed molar mass higher than normal molar mass of solute while molecular dissociation of an observed solute leads to a molar mass which is less than the normal value of the molar mass of the solute.

Note Larger the value of molecular mass of the solute, smaller the observed value of colligative properties, i.e. relative lowering of vapour pressure, elevation in boiling point (ΔT_b), depression of freezing point (ΔT_f) and osmotic pressure (π).

van't Hoff Factor

It is the ratio of the experimental (observed) value of the colligative property to the calculated (normal) value of the same colligative property. It is used to find out the extent of dissociation or association.

$$\text{van't Hoff factor, } i = \frac{\text{Normal molar mass}}{\text{Abnormal molar mass}}$$

$$= \frac{\text{Total number of moles of particles after association or dissociation}}{\text{Number of moles of particles before association or dissociation}}$$

$$= \frac{\text{Observed colligative property}}{\text{Calculated colligative property}}$$

If $i > 1$, solute undergoes dissociation, and if $i < 1$, solute undergoes association.

Calculation of Degree of Association or Dissociation

- For association, when molecules of solute form dimer, $n = 2$.

$$\text{Degree of association, } \alpha = \frac{i - 1}{(1/n - 1)}$$

where, n = number of solute molecules associating to make bigger molecular species.

- For dissociation, of the solute AB type, $m=2$ and of the solute AB_2 or A_2B type ($CaCl_2, Na_2SO_4$), $m=3$.

  Degree of dissociation, $\alpha = \frac{i-1}{m-1}$.

  where, m = number of particles formed per molecule of the electrolyte.

Inclusion of van't Hoff factor modifies the equations for colligative properties,

- Relative lowering in vapour pressure of solvent, $\frac{p^\circ - p}{p^\circ} = i\frac{n}{N}$.
- Elevation in boiling point, $\Delta T_b = iK_b m$.
- Depression in freezing point, $\Delta T_f = iK_f m$.
- Osmotic pressure of solution, $\pi = i\frac{n}{V}RT$.

PYQs Previous Years' Questions

1 Mark Questions

1. An equimolar solution of non-volatile solutes A and B, shows a depression in freezing point in the ratio of 2:1. If A remains in its normal state in the solution, the state of B in the solution will be **ISC 2024**

   (a) normal (b) hydrolysed
   (c) associated (d) dissociated

2. Which of the following aqueous solution has lowest vapour pressure? **ISC Specimen 2024**

   (a) 1 M NaCl (b) 1 M K_2SO_4
   (c) 1 M Glucose (d) 1 M Sucrose

3. The value of molal depression constant or cryoscopic constant (K_f) depends on which of the following ? **ISC 2021-22 (Sem-I)**

   (a) Nature of solvent
   (b) Heat of the solution of the solute in the solvent
   (c) Nature of solute
   (d) Vapour pressure of the solution

4. If molality of the dilute solution of a non-volatile, non-dissociating and non-associating electrolyte is doubled, the value of molal elevation constant or Ebullioscopic constant (K_b) will be **ISC Specimen 2021-22 (Sem-I)**

   (a) doubled (b) halved
   (c) tripled (d) unchanged

5. Colligative properties depend on **ISC Specimen 2021-22 (Sem-I)**

   (a) the nature of solute particles in solution
   (b) the number of solute particles in solution
   (c) the nature of solute and solvent particles
   (d) the physical properties of solute particles in solution

6. The elevation of boiling point of 0.5 M K_2SO_4 solution is .... that of 0.5 M urea solution. The elevation of boiling point of 0.5 M KCl solution is ...... that of 0.5 M K_2SO_4 solution. (more than, less than) **ISC 2019**

7. An aqueous solution of urea freezes at $-0.186°C$, K_f for water = 1.86 K kg mol^{-1}, K_b for water = 0.522 K kg mol^{-1}. The boiling point of urea solution will be **ISC 2018**

   (a) 375.065 K (b) 373.186 K
   (c) 375.512 K (d) 373.0512 K

8. The molal freezing point constant of water is 1.86 K kg mol^{-1}. Therefore, the freezing point of 0.1m NaCl solution in water is expected to be **ISC Specimen 2018**

   (a) $-1.86°C$ (b) $-0.372°C$
   (c) $-0.186°C$ (d) $+0.372°C$

9. Why the freezing point depression (ΔT_f) of 0.4 M NaCl solution is nearly twice than that of 0.4 M glucose solution? **ISC 2017**

10. The molal freezing point constant of water is 1.86 K kg mol^{-1}. Therefore, the freezing point of 0.1 M NaCl solution in water is expected to be

    (a) $-1.86°$ C (b) $-0.372°$ C
    (c) $-0.186°$ C (d) $+0.372°$ C **ISC 2015**

11. The van't Hoff factor of acetic acid solution is .... than one and the value of normal colligative property is .... than the observed colligative property of this solution. **ISC 2014**

12. Define Raoult's law for the elevation in boiling point of a solution. **ISC 2014**

13. What is the unit of molal depression constant? **ISC 2014**

14. Define cryoscopic constant. **ISC 2013**

15. Which is colligative property among the following? Polysaccharide, osmotic pressure, aldol condensation, polarimeter? **ISC 2013**

16. A solution X is prepared by dissolving 3 moles of glucose in one litre of water and a solution Y is prepared by dissolving 1.5 moles of sodium chloride in one litre of water. Will the osmotic pressure of X be higher, lower or equal to that of Y ?
Give a reason for your answer. **ISC 2012**

17. 0.1 M urea solution shows less depression in freezing point than 0.1 M $MgCl_2$ solution. Explain. **ISC 2011**

18. Out of the following solutions, the one having the highest boiling point will be **ISC 2011**
(a) 0.1 M NaCl (b) 0.1 M $BaCl_2$
(c) 0.1 M KNO_3 (d) 0.1 M $K_4[Fe(CN)_6]$

19. For a dissociated solute in solution, the value of van't Hoff factor is **ISC 2010**
(a) zero (b) one
(c) greater than one (d) less than one

20. An example of intensive property is **ISC 2010**
(a) number of moles
(b) mass
(c) volume
(d) density

21. The elevation in boiling point produced by dilute equimolar solution of three substances are in the order $A >$ glucose $> B$. Suggest a reason for this observation. **ISC 2010**

22. The osmotic pressure of 0.25 M urea solution is 2.67 atm. What will be the osmotic pressure of a 0.25 M solution of potassium sulphate? **ISC 2010**

23. The .... of the boiling point of solvent by the addition of a solute is .... proportional to the molality of the solutions. **ISC 2009**

24. The molecular weight of sodium chloride determined by measuring the osmotic pressure of its aqueous solution is **ISC 2009**
(a) double the theoretical value
(b) same as the theoretical value
(c) half the theoretical value
(d) three times the theoretical value

25. Correct the following statement by changing the underlined part of the sentence.
Water boils <u>below 100°C</u> by the addition of NaCl.
ISC 2008

26. The lowest freezing point of 0.1 M aqueous solution of **ISC 2006**
(a) K_2SO_4 (b) NaCl
(c) urea (d) glucose

27. Correct the given statement :
"Osmotic pressure and boiling point are colligative properties." **ISC 2004**

28. Correct the given statement.
"Addition of sodium chloride lowers the boiling point and freezing point of water." **ISC 2003**

29. Correct the given statement.
"Freezing point of a solution is directly proportional to its molality." **ISC 2001**

2 Marks Questions

30. If 200 cm^3 of an aqueous solution of protein contains 1.26 g of protein, the osmotic pressure of the solution at 300 K is found to be 2.57×10^{-3} atm.
Calculate the molar mass of protein.
($R = 0.0821$ L atm K^{-1} mol^{-1}) **ISC 2024**

31. John was making noodles in boiling water. When he added common salt (NaCl) to boiling water, the water stopped boiling for a short while. If John had added 15.0 g of NaCl to 250.0 g of water, calculate the boiling point of solution assuming that NaCl dissociates completely in water. (K_b for water $= 0.512$ K kg mol^{-1}, molecular mass of NaCl $= 58.44$ g mol^{-1}). **ISC Specimen 2024**

32. The osmotic pressure of blood at 37°C is 8.21 atm. How much glucose in grams should be used per litre of aqueous solution for an intravenous injection so that it is isotonic with blood? (Molecular wt. of glucose = 180 g/mol) **ISC 2023**

33. Calculate the mass of ascorbic acid (molecular mass = 176 g/mol) that should be dissolved in 155 g of acetic acid to cause a depression of freeing point by 1.15 K. Assume that ascorbic acid does not dissociate or associate in the solution.
[K_f for acetic acid = 3.9 K kg/mol] **ISC 2023**

34. The osmotic pressure of 20 g haemoglobin in 500 mL of solution is 0.016 atm at 25°C. Calculate the molecular mass of haemoglobin. **ISC Specimen 2023**

35. A solution of urea in water has boiling point 100.128°C. Calculate the freezing point of the same solution. Molal constants for water are $K_b = 0.512$ K kg mol^{-1} and $K_f = 1.86$ K kg mol^{-1} respectively.
ISC Specimen 2023

36. A solution contains 54 g of glucose (molecular mass = 180 g mol^{-1}) in 250 g of water (K_f for water = 1.86 K kg mol^{-1}). **ISC 2021-22 (Sem-I)**

(i) What will be the freezing point of this glucose solution?
(a) 276.402 K (b) 270.768 K
(c) 370.402 K (d) 272.563 K

(ii) What will be the molality of this glucose solution?
(a) 1.20 m (b) 0.12 m (c) 2.40 m (d) 0.24 m

37. 0.76 g of glucose (molecular mass = 180 g mol^{-1}) is dissolved in 20 mL of aqueous solution at 298 K. (R = 0.0821 L-atm $K^{-1} mol^{-1}$) **ISC 2021-22 (Sem-I)**

(i) What is the osmotic pressure of solution at 298 K?
(a) 8.41 atm (b) 0.48 atm
(c) 4.89 atm (d) 5.16 atm

(ii) What is the molarity of the glucose solution?
(a) 0.42 M (b) 0.21 M (c) 4.01 M (d) 2.02 M

38. A solution of sucrose (molecular weight 342 g mol^{-1}) has been prepared by dissolving 68.4 g of sucrose in 1000 g of water. **ISC Specimen 2021-22 (Sem-I)**

(K_f for water = 1.86 K kg mol^{-1})

(i) The freezing point of the solution obtained will be
(a) – 0.52°C (b) + 0.52°C
(c) – 0.372°C (d) + 0.372°C

(ii) The molality of sucrose solution will be
(a) 0.1 (b) 0.2 (c) 0.3 (d) 0.4

39. An aqueous solution containing one gram of urea (molecular weight = 60) boils at 100.25°C. The same solution freezes at – 0.894°C.

The aqueous solution containing 3 g of glucose (molecular weight = 180) in the same volume of solution **ISC Specimen 2021-22 (Sem-I)**

(i) What is the boiling point of glucose?
(a) 100.75°C (b) 100.50°C
(c) 100.25°C (d) 100.08°C

(ii) What is the freezing point of glucose?
(a) + 0.894°C (b) – 0.894°C
(c) + 0.447°C (d) – 0.447°C

40. Calculate the boiling point of urea solution when 6 g of urea is dissolved in 200 g of water.
(K_b for water = 0.52 K kg mol^{-1}, boiling point of pure water = 373 K, mol. wt. of urea = 60) **ISC 2019**

41. Calculate the osmotic pressure of a solution prepared by dissolving 0.025 g of K_2SO_4 in 2.0 litres of water at 25°C.

Assuming that K_2SO_4 is completely dissociated (molecular weight of K_2SO_4 = 174 g mol^{-1}). **ISC 2018**

42. Calculate the mass of compound (molar mass = 256 g mol^{-1}) to be dissolved in 75 g of benzene to lower its freezing point by 0.48 K.
(K_f = 5.12 K kg mol^{-1}). **ISC Specimen 2018**

43. A 2 molal solution of sodium chloride in water causes an elevation in the boiling point of water by 1.88 K. What is the value of van't Hoff factor? What does it signify?
(K_b = 0.52 K kg mol^{-1}) **ISC 2014**

44. The freezing point of a solution containing 0.3 g of acetic acid in 30 g of benzene is lowered by 0.45 K. Calculate the van't Hoff factor. (Atomic weight of C = 12, H = 1, O = 16, K_f for benzene = 5.12 K kg mol^{-1}) **ISC 2013**

45. A solution of urea in water has a boiling point of 100.18°C. Calculate the freezing point of the solution.
(K_f for water is 1.86 K kg mol^{-1} and K_b for water is 0.512 K kg mol^{-1}) **ISC 2012**

KEY IDEA
(i) First, calculate the molality (m) of the solution, by using the formula, $\Delta T_b = K_b \times m$.
(ii) Then, find out the depression of freezing point using molality of solution, using the formula, $\Delta T_f = K_f \times m$ and then the freezing point of solution by
$\Delta T_f = T'_f - T_f^{\circ}$.

46. The boiling point of pure water is 373 K. Calculate the boiling point of an aqueous solution containing 18 g of glucose (W=180) in 100 g of water. Molal elevation constant of water is 0.52 K kg mol^{-1}. **ISC 2009**

47. Equal weights of two substances X and Y are dissolved in equal volumes of water. The osmotic pressure of the solution containing Y is five times the osmotic pressure of the solution containing X. What is the molecular weight of X if that of Y is 60? **ISC 2009**

48. Which of the following solutions will have a lower vapour pressure and why?
(i) A 5% solution of cane sugar ($C_{12}H_{22}O_{11}$).
(ii) A 5% solution of urea (NH_2CONH_2).
(Relative atomic masses of H = 1, C = 12, O = 16, N = 14) **ISC 2009**

49. The molecular weights of sodium chloride and glucose are determined by the depression of freezing point method. Compared to their theoretical molecular weight, what will be their observed molecular weights when determined by the above method? Justify your answer. **ISC 2007**

50. An aqueous solution containing 1.70 g of cane sugar in 100 mL water begins to freeze at – 0.093° C. The cryoscopic constant (molal depression constant) of water is 1.86 kg mol^{-1}. Calculate the molecular weight of cane sugar. **ISC 2007**

51. A decinormal solution of sodium chloride exerts an osmotic pressure of 4.82 atm at 27°C. Calculate the degree of dissociation of sodium chloride. **ISC 2007**

52. The depression in the freezing point of a sugar was found to be 0.402°C. Calculate pressure of the sugar solution at 27°C. (K_f = 1.86 K kg mol^{-1}) **ISC 2007**

53. Why does soda water fizz when the bottle is opened? Name the law that explains this phenomenon. **ISC 2004**

54. An aqueous solution containing 0.2 g of compound *A* in 21.7 g of water freezes at 272.914 K. If the value of K_f for water is 1.86 K kg mol^{-1}, calculate molecular weight of compound *A*. **ISC 2004**

55. What is a colligative property? Give two examples. **ISC 2003**

3 Marks Questions

56. Read the passage given below and answer the questions that follow. **ISC 2024**

When two solutions are separated by a semipermeable membrane, the solvent molecules move from a solution of lower molar concentration to a solution of higher molar concentration through osmosis.

(i) Samar removed the outer hard shell of two different eggs while cooking at home. He then placed one egg in pure water and the other egg in saturated solution of sucrose. What change is he likely to observe in the eggs after few hours?

(ii) Which solution, hypertonic or hypotonic, has a higher amount of solute in same quantity of solution?

(iii) A 5% aqueous solution of glucose (molar mass = 180 g mol^{-1}) is isotonic with 1.66% aqueous solution of urea. Calculate the molar mass of urea.

57. An aqueous solution containing 12.50 g of barium chloride in 1000 g of water boils at 373.0834 K. Calculate the degree of dissociation of barium chloride.

[Given K_b for H_2O = 0.52 K kg mol^{-1}; molecular mass of $BaCl_2$ = 208.34 g mol^{-1}] **ISC 2024**

58. Read the passage given below carefully and answer the questions that follow. **ISC Specimen 2024**

During the winter season in a particular year, Kashmir experienced heavy snowfall. It was an unexpected snowfall. Thousands of visitors were stranded because it was dangerous to travel on snowy roads and vehicles could not move as water froze in the car radiators. In such conditions officials decided to sprinkle rock salt or $CaCl_2$ on roads.

(i) Why was it decided to sprinkle rock salt or $CaCl_2$ on the roads?

(ii) A mixture of ethylene glycol and water is used as coolant in car radiators. Why?

(iii) How many grams of ethylene glycol (Mol. wt. = 62 g mol^{-1}) should be added to 10 kg of water so that the solution freezes at –10°C? (K_f for water = 1.86 K kg mol^{-1})

59. Water vapours and liquid water are in equilibrium in a container. At room temperature, the vapour pressure of water is 25 mm of Hg. The volume of water is *V* mL. **ISC Specimen 2024**

(i) What will be the vapour pressure of water if the volume of water is reduced to *V*/4 mL without any change in temperature? Give a reason.

(ii) Will there be a change in vapour pressure if more water (at room temperature) is added to the container? Give a reason.

60. When 2g of benzoic acid is dissolved in 25g of benzene, it shows a depression in freezing point equal to 1.62K. Molal depression constant (K_f) of benzene is 4.9 K kg mol^{-1} and molecular weight of benzoic acid = 122 g/mol. What will be the percentage association of the benzoic acid? **ISC 2023**
(Benzoic acid forms dimer when dissolved benzene.)

61. An aqueous solution containing 12.48 g of barium chloride in 1000 g of water boils at 373.0832K. Calculate the degree of dissociation (α) of barium chloride. **ISC Specimen 2023**
K_b for H_2O = 0.52 K kg mol^{-1}, molecular mass of $BaCl_2$ = 208.34 g mol^{-1}.

62. When 0.4 g of oxalic acid is dissolved in 40g of benzene, the freezing point of the solution is lowered by 0.45 K. Calculate the degree of association of acetic acid. Acetic acid forms dimer when dissolved in benzene. (K_f for benzene = 5.12 K kg mol^{-1}, at. wt. C = 12, H = 1, O = 16) **ISC 2019**

63. A solution is prepared by dissolving 9.25 g of non-volatile solute in 450 mL of water. It has an osmotic pressure of 350 mm of Hg at 27°C. Assuming the solute is non-electrolyte, determine its molecular mass.
($R = 0.0821\,L\,atm\,K^{-1}mol^{-1}$) *ISC 2019*

> **KEY IDEA**
>
> (i) Find the value of osmotic pressure by using the formula
>
> $$\pi = CRT \text{ where, } C = \frac{n}{V} = \frac{w_B}{M_B \times V}$$
>
> (ii) Then, calculate the value of M_B by using formula
>
> $$M_B = \frac{w_B \times 1000 \times R \times T}{V \times \pi}$$

64. The freezing point of a solution containing 5.85 g of NaCl in 100 g of water is – 3.348°C. Calculate van't Hoff factor 'i' for this solution. What will be the experimental molecular weight of NaCl?
(K_f for water = 1.86 K kg mol^{-1}, atomic weight of Na = 23, Cl = 35.5) *ISC 2018*

65. An aqueous solution containing 12.48 g of barium chloride ($BaCl_2$) in 1000 g of water, boils at 100.0832°C. Calculate the degree of dissociation of barium chloride. (K_b for water = 0.52 kg mol^{-1}, atomic weight Ba = 137, Cl=35.5) *ISC 2018*

66. Calculate the amount of $CaCl_2$ (molar mass = 111 g mol^{-1}) which must be added to 500 g of water to lower its freezing point by 2 K, assuming $CaCl_2$ is completely dissociated. (K_f for water = 1.86 K kg mol^{-1}). *ISC Specimen 2018*

67. A solution containing 0.5 g of KCl dissolves in 100 g of water and freezes at – 0.24°C. Calculate the degree of dissociation of the salt.
(K_f for water = 1.86°C). *ISC Specimen 2018*

68. What will be the vapour pressure of a solution containing 5 moles of sucrose ($C_{12}H_{22}O_{11}$) in 1 kg of water, if the vapour pressure of pure water is 4.57 mm of Hg? (C = 12, H = 1, O = 16) *ISC 2014*

69. Ethylene glycol is used as an antifreeze agent. Calculate the amount of ethylene glycol to be added to 4 kg of water to prevent it from freezing at –6° C.(K_f for H_2O = 1.85 K mol^{-1}kg) *ISC 2013*

70. A solution of lactose containing 8.45 g of lactose in 100 g of water has a vapour pressure of 4.559 mm of Hg at 0°C. If the vapour pressure of pure water is 4.579 mm of Hg, calculate the molecular weight of lactose. *ISC 2012*

71. The osmotic pressure of 0.01 molar solution of an electrolyte is found to be 0.65 atm at 27°C. Calculate the van't Hoff factor. What conclusion can you draw about the molecular state of the solute in the solution? *ISC 2011*

> **KEY IDEA**
>
> (i) First find out the value of osmotic pressure by using the formula $\pi_{cal} = CRT$.
>
> (ii) Then find the value of i, by using formula, $i = \frac{\pi_{obs}}{\pi_{cal}}$.

72. Albumins are the most abundant proteins in blood. At 25°C, 3.5g of albumin in 100 mL of water produces an osmotic pressure of 0.014 atm. What is the molecular weight of albumin? *ISC 2008*

73. The osmotic pressure of blood is 7.65 atm at 27°C. How much glucose should be used per litre to prepare an intravenous injection that has the same osmotic pressure as blood? *ISC 2003, 2001*

74. 0.5 g of a non-volatile solute is dissolved in 100 g of ethyl acetate at 20°C. The vapour pressure of the solution and pure ethyl acetate are 72.0 torr and 72.8 torr, respectively at – 28°C. Calculate molecular weight of the solute. *ISC 2001*

4 Marks Questions

75. (i) The freezing point of nitrobenzene is 278.8 K. A 0.25 molal solution of a substance (molecular weight = 120) in nitrobenzene has a freezing point of 276.8 K. Calculate the molal depression constant of nitrobenzene.

(ii) Calculate osmotic pressure of a solution containing 3.42 g of sucrose in 1 L of water at 400 K. *ISC 2002*

76. (i) The cryoscopic constant of water is 1.86 Kmol^{-1}kg^{-1}. An aqueous solution of cane sugar freezes at – 0.372°C. Calculate molality of the solution.

(ii) The molecular weights of potassium chloride and glucose are determined by the depression in freezing point method. As compared to their theoretical molecular weights, what do you expect are their molecular weights determined by this experiment? Why? *ISC 2000*

5 Marks Questions

77. (i) The elevation in boiling point when 0.30 g of acetic acid is dissolved in 100 g of benzene is 0.0633°C. Calculate the molecular weight of acetic acid from this data. What conclusion can you draw about the molecular state of the solute in the solution? (Given K_b for benzene $= 2.53$ K kg mol^{-1}, at. wt. of C = 12, H = 1, O = 16).

(ii) Determine the osmotic pressure of a solution prepared by dissolving 0.025 g of K_2SO_4 in 2 litres of water at 25°C, assuming that K_2SO_4 is completely dissociated. ($R = 0.0821$ L atm K^{-1}mol^{-1}, mol. wt. of $K_2SO_4 = 174$ g mol^{-1}). **ISC 2020**

KEY IDEA

- First calculate the value of M_B by using formula

$$M_B = \frac{K_b \times M_b \times 1000}{W_A \times \Delta T_b}$$

- Then calculate the value of i by using formula

$$i = \frac{\text{Normal molar mass}}{\text{Abnormal molar mass}}$$

For $i > 1 \Rightarrow$ Dissociation and for $i < 1 \Rightarrow$ Association.

78. (i) An aqueous solution of a non-volatile solute freezes at 272.4 K, while pure water freezes at 273.0 K.

Determine the following : (Given, $K_f = 1.86$ K kg mol^{-1}, $K_b = 0.512$ K kg mol^{-1} and vapour pressure of water at 298 K = 23.756 mm of Hg)

(a) The molality of solution.

(b) Boiling point of solution.

(c) The lowering of vapour pressure of water at 298 K.

(ii) A solution containing 1.23 g of calcium nitrate in 10 g of water, boils at 100.975°C at 760 mm of Hg. Calculate the van't Hoff factor for the salt at this concentration. (K_b for water = 0.52 K kg mol^{-1}, molecular weight of calcium nitrate = 164 g mol^{-1}) **ISC 2020**

79. (i) Determine the freezing point of a solution containing 0.625 g of glucose ($C_6H_{12}O_6$) dissolved in 102.8 g of water. (Freezing point of water = 273 K, K_f for water = 1.87 K kg mol^{-1}, at. wt. of C = 12, H = 1 and O = 16)

(ii) A 0.15 M aqueous solution of KCl exerts an osmotic pressure of 6.8 atm at 310 K. Calculate the degree of dissociation of KCl. ($R = 0.0821$ L atm K^{-1}mol^{-1}).

(iii) A solution containing 8.44 g of sucrose in 100 g of water has a vapour pressure 4.56 mm of Hg at 273K. If the vapour pressure of pure water is 4.58 mm of Hg at the same temperature, calculate the molecular weight of sucrose. **ISC 2017**

80. (i) A 10% aqueous solution of cane sugar (mol.wt. = 342) is isotonic with 1.754% aqueous solution of urea. Find the molecular mass of urea.

(ii) The molecular weight of an organic compound is 58 g mol^{-1}. What will be the boiling point of a solution containing 48 g of the solute in 1200 g of water?

[K_b for water = 0.513°C kg mol^{-1}; boiling point of water = 100°C]

(iii) What will be the value of van't Hoff factor (i) of benzoic acid, if it dimerises in aqueous solution? How will the experimental molecular weight vary as compared to the normal molecular weight? **ISC 2016**

81. (i) A solution containing 0.5 g of KCl dissolves in 100 g of water and freezes at – 0.24°C. Calculate the degree of dissociation of the salt. (K_f for water = 1.86°C). (Atomic weights of K = 39, Cl = 35.5)

(ii) If 1.71 g of sugar (molar mass = 342 g/mol) are dissolved in 500 mL of an aqueous solution at 300 K, what will be its osmotic pressure?

(iii) 0.70 g of an organic compound when dissolved in 32 g of acetone produces an elevation of 0.25°C in the boiling point. Calculate the molecular mass of organic compound.

(K_b for acetone = 1.72 K kg mol^{-1}) **ISC 2015**

82. Define osmotic pressure. Arrange the following in increasing order of osmotic pressure and give reasons in support of your answer.

(i) 34.2 g per litre of sucrose (Molecular weight = 342).

(ii) 90.0 g per litre of glucose (Molecular weight = 180).

(iii) 5.85 g per litre of sodium chloride (Molecular weight = 58.5). **ISC 2004**

Explanations

1. (d) Dissociated
2. (b) 1 M K_2SO_4 has maximum number of ions, hence have lowest vapour pressure.
3. (a) Nature of solvent
4. (d) K_b is a characteristic property of solvent. It has nothing to do with solute concentration.
5. (b) Colligative properties depend on the total number of solute particles in the solution. It does not depend on the chemical nature of its components.
6. more than, less than
7. (d) Given,

Freezing point of the solution,

$$T_f = -0.186°C$$

Converting in Kelvin, $T_f = -0.186 + 273$

$$= 272.814 K$$

As $T_f = T_f^\circ - \Delta T_f$

$$272.814 = 273 - \Delta T_f$$

$$\Delta T_f = 0.186 K$$

Now, calculate molality of solution by using the formula

$$\Delta T_f = K_f m$$

$$0.186 K = 1.86 K \text{ kg mol}^{-1} \times m$$

$$m = 0.1 \text{ mol kg}^{-1}$$

To calculate elevation in boiling point, we use

$$\Delta T_b = K_b m$$

Given, $K_b = 0.512$ K kg mol^{-1}

$m = 0.1$ mol kg^{-1}

$$\Delta T_b = 0.512 \text{ K kg mol}^{-1} \times 0.1 \text{ mol kg}^{-1},$$

$$\Delta T_b = 0.0512 K$$

Boiling point of a solution $(T_b) = T_b^\circ + \Delta T_b$

$= (373 + 0.0512)$ K

$= 373.0512$ K

8. (c) Given, $K_f = 1.86$ K kg mol^{-1}

Molality of NaCl $= 0.1$ m

Depression in freezing point,

$$\Delta T_f = K_f \times m = 1.86 \times 0.1$$

$$\Delta T_f = 0.186$$

$$\Delta T_f = 0 - T_f = 0 - 0.186$$

$$T_f = -0.186°C$$

Concept Enhancer The value of change in temperature (ΔT) will be same in units of Kelvin as well as °C.

9. Depression in freezing point is a colligative property which depends on the number of particles. Glucose is a molecular compound, it remains as a single molecule in solution.

NaCl ionises in solution to give two particles (ions)

$$NaCl \longrightarrow Na^+ + Cl^-$$

Thus, depression in freezing point (ΔT_f) of 0.4 M NaCl is greater than 0.4 M glucose solution.

10. (c) The molal freezing point constant of water is 1.86 K kg mol^{-1}.

Assume that molality = molarity

Then $m = 0.1$ M

From equation, $\Delta T_f = K_f \times$ molality

$= 1.86$ K kg mol^{-1} $\times 0.1$

$= 0.186$ K $= 0.186$ °C

Depression in freezing point is -0.186 °C.

11. The van't Hoff factor of acetic acid solution is less than one because two molecules of acetic acid associate together to form a dimer, as shown below :

$$2\,CH_3COOH \rightleftharpoons (CH_3COOH)_2$$

For association, $i < 1$.

and the value of normal colligative property is more than the observed colligative property of this solution.

It is because,

$$i = \frac{\text{Observed value of a colligative property}}{\text{Normal calculated colligative property}}$$

For association, $i < 1$.

12. Raoult's law states that relative lowering of vapour pressure is directly proportional to the mole fraction of the solute particles. The elevation in boiling point (ΔT_b) is directly proportional to the lowering in vapour pressure (Δp).

$\therefore \quad \Delta T_b \propto \Delta p$

and $\quad \dfrac{\Delta p}{p^\circ} = \dfrac{w}{M'}\dfrac{M}{W}$ (Raoult's law)

or $\quad \Delta p \propto \dfrac{w}{M'W}$

and $\quad \Delta T_b \propto \dfrac{w}{M'W}$

13. The unit of molal depression constant is K kg mol^{-1}.

14. It is the depression in freezing point produced on dissolving one mole of a substance in 1000 g or 1 kg of the solvent.

15. Osmotic pressure is a colligative property.

16. Osmotic pressure is a colligative property which depends on the number of particles present in solution. Since, glucose is non-electrolyte.

$\therefore$ Value of van't Hoff factor i for sodium chloride.

$$= 1 \text{ and } n = 3 \text{ mol}$$

Value of van't Hoff factor i for sodium chloride

$$= 2 \text{ and } n = 1.5 \text{ mol}$$

Now for glucose, osmotic pressure, $\pi = \frac{inRT}{V}$

[Here, volume (V) of water = 1000 mL]

$$= 1 \times 3RT / 1000 = 3RT / 1000$$

For NaCl, osmotic pressure, $\pi = \frac{inRT}{V}$

$$= 2 \times 1.5 RT / 1000 = 3RT / 1000$$

So, π is same for both the solutions.

17. Depression in freezing point is a colligative property which depends on the number of particles. Urea is a molecular compound, it remains as a single molecule. In solution magnesium chloride is an ionic compound, it ionises as follows to give three particles.

$$MgCl_2 \longrightarrow Mg^{2+} + 2Cl^-$$

Thus, 0.1 M urea solution shows less depression in freezing point than 0.1 M $MgCl_2$ solution.

18. (d) 0.1 M $K_4[Fe(CN)_6]$ has highest boiling point. It is because, $K_4[Fe(CN)_6]$ dissociates to give maximum number of particles as follows

$$K_4[Fe(CN)_6] \longrightarrow 4K^+ + [Fe(CN)_6]^{4-}$$

Therefore, its solution has highest boiling point. Hence, option (d) is correct.

19. (c) For a dissociated solute in solution the value of van't Hoff factor is greater than one, i.e. $i > 1$.

20. (d) Density is the intensive property as it depends on the nature of the substance and is independent of its amount present in the system. Hence, option (d) is correct.

21. Elevation in boiling point is a colligative property which depends upon number of particles of non-volatile solute present in the solution. Larger the molecular mass of the solute, smaller is the value of elevation in boiling point.

On dissociation, molecular mass of the solute decreases while elevation in boiling point rises and *vice-versa*. Thus, the reason for the given observation in substance A dissociates while substance B associates in the solution.

22. Osmotic pressure, $\pi = iCRT$ where, i is van't Hoff factor.

Value of i for urea is 1 (one) while i for potassium sulphate is 3 (strong electrolyte). Also, molarity, M for the two solutions is same (0.25 M).

$$\pi_{(K_2SO_4 \text{ solution})} = i \times \pi_{\text{urea}} = 3 \times 2.67 = 8.01 \text{ atm}$$

(as $\pi_{\text{urea}} = 2.67$ atm)

23. The **elevation** of the boiling point of a solvent by the addition of a solute is **directly** proportional to the molality of the solution.

i.e. $\Delta T_b \propto m$

24. (c) Molecular weight of NaCl determined by measuring the osmotic pressure of its aqueous solution is half the theoretical value, because it is a strong electrolyte and dissociates into 2 ions.

$$NaCl \longrightarrow Na^+ + Cl^-$$

According to van't Hoff factor, observed molecular mass

$$= \frac{\text{Normal molecular mass}}{\text{Number of particles per molecule}}$$

$$= \frac{\text{Normal molecular mass}}{2}$$

Hence, option (c) is correct.

25. The correct statement is as follows

Water boils **above 100°C** by the addition of NaCl. It is because, NaCl is a strong electrolyte and it dissociates into 2 ions, therefore its van't Hoff value, i is 2 and the elevation of boiling point ΔT_b, is proportional to i.

26. (a) K_2SO_4 has the lowest freezing point as it dissociates to give more number of particles.

$$K_2SO_4 \rightleftharpoons 2K^+ + SO_4^{2-}$$

Hence, option (a) is correct.

27. Osmotic pressure and elevation in boiling point are colligative properties.

28. Addition of sodium chloride increases the boiling point and decreases the freezing point of water.

29. Depression in freezing point of a solvent is directly proportional to its molality.

i.e. $\Delta T_f \propto m$

30. Given, Volume of aqueous solution of a protein $= 200\ cm^3$

Amount of protein $= 1.26$ g

Osmotic pressure, $\pi = 2.57 \times 10^{-3}$ atm

$R = 0.0821$ L atm K^{-1} mol^{-1} or $T = 300$ K

as $\pi = CRT$

$$\therefore 2.57 \times 10^{-3} = \frac{1.26 \times 1000 \times 0.0821 \times 300}{M \times 200}$$

$$M = \frac{1.26 \times 1000 \times 0.0821 \times 300}{2.57 \times 10^{-3} \times 200}$$

$$= 0.06 \times 10^6 \text{ g/mol}^{-1}$$

31. Mass of NaCl = 15 g

Weight of the solvent = 250 g

Boiling point of water $= T_0 = 373$ K

Boiling point of solution $= T$

$K_b = 0.512$ K kg/mol

$\Delta T = K_b \times$ molality

$$= 0.512 \times \frac{\text{mass of NaCl}}{\text{molar mass of NaCl} \times \text{weight of the solvent 1 kg}}$$

$$\Delta T = 0.512 \times \frac{15\text{ g} \times 1000}{58.5\text{ g/mol} \times 250} = 0.53\text{ K}$$

$\Delta T = 0.523$ K

$= T - T_0 = T - 373$ K

$\Rightarrow T = 373.53$ K

32. Given, $\pi_{blood} = 8.21$ atm, $V = 1$ L, $T = 37 + 273 = 310$ K

Blood and glucose are isotonic,

So, both will have same osmotic pressure,

We know, $\pi = CRT$

$$\pi = \frac{n}{V} RT$$

$$\pi V = nRT$$

$$n = \frac{\pi V}{RT}$$

$$n = \frac{8.21 \times 1.0}{0.0821 \times 310} = \frac{10}{31}$$

Weight of glucose $= n \times$ molecular weight

$$= \frac{10}{31} \times 180 = 58.064\text{ g}$$

Concept Enhancer Two isotonic solutions have same osmotic pressure at given same temperature.

33. W_1, Mass of acetic acid = 155 g

M_2, Molecular mass of $(C_6H_8O_6) = 176$ g/mol

Depression of freezing point = 1.15 K

We know,

$$\Delta T_f = \frac{K_f \times 1000 \times w_2}{M_2 \times W_1}$$

$$1.15 = \frac{3.9 \times 1000 \times w_2}{176 \times 155}$$

$$w_2 = \frac{176 \times 155 \times 1.15}{3.9 \times 1000} = 8.04\text{ g}$$

34. Osmotic pressure (π) is given by

$$\pi = CRT = \frac{nRT}{V} \qquad \left(\because n = \frac{W}{M}\right)$$

$$= \frac{WRT}{MV}$$

Given, $\pi = 0.016$ atm, $V = 500$ mL, $T = 25°C = 298$ K

$$0.016 = \frac{20 \times 0.0821 \times 298 \times 1000}{M \times 500}$$

$M = 61164.5$ g/mol

35. Boiling point of solution = 100.128°C

$K_b = 0.512$ K kg mol^{-1}

$K_f = 1.86$ K kg mol^{-1}

$\Delta T_b = 100.128°C - 100°C = 0.128°C$

$\Delta T_b = K_b \times$ molality

$$\text{Molality} = \frac{0.128}{0.512} = 0.25$$

Now, $\Delta T_{freezing} = K_f \times$ molality

$= 1.86 \times 0.25 = 0.465$

Freezing point of solution $= 0 - 0.46 = -0.46°C$

36. (i) (b) Given, $K_f = 1.86$ K kg mol^{-1}; $m = 1.2$ mol kg^{-1}

$\Delta T_f = K_f \times m$

$= 1.86\text{K kg mol}^{-1} \times 1.20\text{ mol kg}^{-1}$

$= 2.232$ K

$T_f = T_f' - \Delta T_f = 273\text{ K} - 2.232\text{ K}$

$= 270.768$ K **(1)**

(ii) (a) Weight of glucose (w) = 54 g

Molecular mass of glucose (M') = 180 g/mol

Mass of water (W) = 250 g

$$\text{Molality } (m) = \frac{w \times 1000}{M' \times W(\text{g})} = \frac{54 \times 1000}{180 \times 250} = 1.20\text{ m}$$ **(1)**

37. $\pi = CRT$

where, π = osmotic pressure

R = gas constant = 0.082 $dm^3 atm\ mol^{-1} K^{-1}$

T = temperature = 298 K

$$C = \text{molarity} = \frac{n}{V} = \frac{w}{M \times V}$$

where, n = no. of moles

w = weight of solute glucose = 0.76 g

M = molecular weight of solute glucose = 180 g

V = volume of solution = 2011 mL = 0.02 L

(i) (c) $\pi = 0.2 \times 0.0821 \times 298 = 4.89$ atm

i.e. option (c) is correct. **(1)**

(ii) (b) $C = \frac{0.76}{180 \times 0.02} = 0.211\,M$

i.e. option (b) is correct. **(1)**

38. (i) (c) Given, molecular weight = 342 g mol^{-1}.

Amount of sucrose = 68.4 g

Amount of water = 1000 g

K_f for water = 1.86 K kg mol^{-1}.

$$\Delta T_f = K_f \times m \text{ also } \left(\text{also } m = \frac{w_B \times 1000}{M_B \cdot W_A}\right)$$

$$= \frac{1.86 \times 68.4 \times 1000}{342 \times 1000}$$

$$\Delta T_f = 1.86 \times 0.2 = 0.372 \text{ K}$$

$$T_f' - T_f = 0.372$$

$$273 - T_f = 0.372 \text{ K}$$

$$T_f = 273 - 0.372 = 272.628 \text{ K}$$

$$T_b = 273 - 272.628 = -0.372°C$$ **(1)**

(ii) (b) Molality $(m) = \frac{w \times 1000}{M' \times W(g)} = \frac{68.4 \times 1000}{342 \times 1000} = 0.2$ m **(1)**

39. Moles of urea $= \frac{1}{60}$ mol

Moles of glucose $= \frac{3}{180} = \frac{1}{60}$ mol

When moles are same, then molality is also similar and K_b and K_f will remain unchanged.

Thus, temperature will also remain unchanged.

(i) (c) Boiling point of glucose is 100.25°C. **(1)**

(ii) (b) And freezing point of glucose is – 0.894°C. **(1)**

40. Given,

Mass of solute (urea), i.e. $w_B = 6$ g

Mass of water (solvent), i.e. $W_A = 200$ g

Molar mass of urea, $M_B = 60$ g mol^{-1}

K_f for water = 0.52 K kg mol^{-1}

Boiling point (b.p) of pure water = 373 K

$\because \Delta T_b$ (elevation in b.p)

$$= K_f \times \frac{w_B}{M_B} \times \frac{1000}{W_A} = \frac{0.52 \text{K kg mol}^{-1} \times 6 \text{ g} \times 1000}{60 \text{ g mol}^{-1} \times 200 \text{ g}}$$

$$\Delta T_b = 0.26° \text{ K}$$

Thus, boiling point of solution,

$$T = T° + \Delta T_b = 373 + 0.26 = 373.26 \text{ K.}$$

41. By using formula $\pi = CRT$, we can calculate the value of osmotic pressure (π).

Given, mass of K_2SO_4 = 0.025 g,

Molar mass of K_2SO_4 = 174 g mol^{-1}

Number of moles of solute dissolved(n)

$$= \frac{0.025 \text{g}}{174 \text{g mol}^{-1}} = \frac{0.025}{174} \text{ mol}, V = 2\text{L}$$

$$T = 25°C = 25 + 273 = 298\text{K}$$

$$R = 8.314 \text{ kPa L K}^{-1}\text{mol}^{-1} = 8.314 \times 10^3 \text{ Pa LK}^{-1}\text{mol}^{-1}$$

Substituting these values, in formula

$\pi = \frac{n}{V} RT$, we get,

$$\pi = \frac{0.025}{174} \text{mol} \times \frac{1}{2\text{L}} \times 8.314 \times 10^3 \text{Pa LK}^{-1}\text{mol}^{-1} \times 298\text{K},$$

$$\pi = 177.98 \text{ Pa}$$

Common Mistake In such type of questions one can make mistake by taking the value of R as 8.314 k Pa $LK^{-1}mol^{-1}$ instead of 8.314×10^3 Pa $LK^{-1}mol^{-1}$.

42. Given that, K_f = 5.12 K kg mol^{-1}

Mass of benzene, $W_1 = 75$ g

Depression in freezing point, $\Delta T_f = 0.48$ K,

Molar mass of compound, $M_2 = 256$ g mol^{-1}

If w_2 is the mass of compound,

Then, $$\Delta T_f = \frac{K_f \times w_2 \times 1000}{W_1 \times M_2}$$

$$0.48 = \frac{5.12 \times w_2 \times 1000}{75 \times 256}$$

$$w_2 = \frac{0.48 \times 75 \times 256}{5.12 \times 1000} = 1.8 \text{ g}$$

43. Given : Molality, $m = 2$,

Elevation in boiling point, $\Delta T_b = 1.88$ K,

van't Hoff factor, $i = ?$,

$$K_b = 0.52 \text{ K kg mol}^{-1}$$

We know that, $\Delta T_b = i K_b \, m$

van't Hoff factor, $i = \Delta T_b / K_b \times m$

$$= \frac{1.88}{0.52 \times 2}$$

$$= 1.807$$

Since, value of van't Hoff factor is greater than one, it signifies that solute undergoes dissociation.

44. Given, amount of acetic acid $(w) = 0.3$ g,

amount of benzene $(W) = 30$ g,

depression in freezing point,

$$\Delta T_f = 0.45 \text{ K},$$

$$K_f = 5.12 \text{ K kg mol}^{-1}$$

We know that, $\Delta T_f = i K_f \, m$

(where, m is molality and i represents van't Hoff factor)

$$\text{Molality, } m = \frac{w \times 1000}{M' \times W} = \frac{0.3 \times 1000}{60 \times 30}$$

$$= 0.166 \approx 0.17$$

[as molar mass of acetic acid (CH_3COOH)

$M' = 2 \times 12 + 4 \times 1 + 2 \times 16 = 60 \text{ g mol}^{-1}$]

$$\text{Now, } i = \frac{\Delta T_f}{K_f \times m} = \frac{0.45}{5.12 \times 0.17} = 0.517$$

45. Calculation of molality (m) of the solution

Given, boiling point of solution

$$= 100.18 + 273$$

$$= 373.18 \text{ K}$$

Boiling point of water $= 100 + 273 = 373$ K

$\therefore$ Elevation in boiling point,

$$\Delta T_b = 373.18°\text{K} - 373°\text{K} = 0.18 \text{ K}$$

We know that, $\Delta T_b = K_b \times m$

$$\therefore \text{Molality, } m = \frac{\Delta T_b}{K_b} = \frac{0.18}{0.512} = 0.351 \text{ mol kg}^{-1}$$

(as $K_b = 0.512 \text{ K kg mol}^{-1}$)

Calculation of freezing point

We know that,

$$\Delta T_f = K_f \times m = 1.86 \times 0.351 = 0.652 \text{K}$$

(as $K_f = 1.86 \text{ K kg mol}^{-1}$)

$$T_f = T_f' - \Delta T_f$$

$$= 273 \text{ K} - 0.652 \text{ K}$$

$$= 272.34 \text{ K}$$

(as freezing point of water $= 0°\text{C} = 273$ K)

$$T_f = -0.652 \, °\text{C}$$

46. Given, boiling point of pure water $= 373$ K

Weight of solute, $w = 18$ g,

Weight of solvent, $W = 100$ g,

Molecular weight of solute, $m = 180 \text{ g mol}^{-1}$

K_b for water $= 0.52 \text{ K kg mol}^{-1}$

For glucose as solute $i = 1$

$$\therefore \quad \Delta T_b = \frac{1000 \times K_b \times w}{m \times W}$$

$$= \frac{1000 \times 0.52 \times 18}{180 \times 100} = 0.52 \text{ K}$$

$\therefore$ Boiling point of solution $= T_b + \Delta T_b$

(where, T_b is boiling point of water $= 100°\text{C} = 373$ K)

$$= 373 + 0.52 = 373.52 \text{ K}$$

47. Suppose weight of X and Y are w g and volume of water for each solution $= V$

If π is osmotic pressure of solution containing X, then osmotic pressure of Y is 5 times the solution containing X i.e. 5π.

Now, for solution containing X,

$$\pi = \frac{wRT}{mV} \quad \text{...(i)}$$

for solution containing Y,

$$5\pi = \frac{wRT}{60V} \quad (\text{As, } m \text{ for } Y = 60) \quad \text{...(ii)}$$

On dividing Eq. (i) by Eq. (ii), we get

$$\frac{\pi}{5\pi} = \frac{wRT \times 60V}{mV \times wRT}$$

$$\Rightarrow \quad \frac{1}{5} = \frac{60}{m}$$

$$\Rightarrow \quad m = 300$$

Therefore, molecular weight of $X = 300 \text{g mol}^{-1}$

48. Vapour pressure of solution $\propto$ Mole fraction of solvent. Let, 5 g of cane sugar be dissolved in 100 g of water

Mole fraction of water in (i)

$$= \frac{N}{N + n} = \frac{W/M}{\frac{w}{M'} + \frac{W}{M}}$$

$$= \frac{100/18}{100/18 + 5/342} = \frac{5.55}{5.55 + 0.0146} = 0.9973$$

$$\left(\text{where, } N = \frac{W}{M} = \frac{100}{18} \text{ and } n = \frac{w}{M'} = \frac{5}{342}\right)$$

Mole fraction of water in (ii),

$$\frac{N}{N + n'} = \frac{\frac{100}{18}}{\frac{100}{18} + \frac{5}{60}} = 0.98526 \qquad \left(\text{where, } n' = \frac{5}{60}\right)$$

Vapour pressure of 5% solution of urea will be lower because mole fraction of water is lower than that of 5% solution of cane sugar.

49. Observed molecular mass of sodium chloride will be half of its theoretical mass.

This is because depression in freezing point method is a colligative property which depends upon the number of solute particles present in solution.

One molecule of sodium chloride furnishes two particles, Na^+ and Cl^- in aqueous solution as it is a strong electrolyte.

$$NaCl \longrightarrow Na^+ + Cl^-$$

According to van't Hoff factor, observed molecular mass

$$= \frac{\text{Normal molecular mass}}{\text{Number of particles formed per molecule}}$$

Observed molecular mass of glucose as determined by the depression of freezing point method will be same as its theoretical molecular mass. It is because glucose neither shows association nor dissociation in aqueous solution as it is a weak electrolyte.

50. We know that, molecular mass $= \dfrac{i \times 1000 \times K_f \times w}{\Delta T \times W(\text{g})}$

For cane sugar $i = 1$, w (cane sugar) $= 1.70$ g,

$W = 100$ g water

$$\Delta T = 0 - (-0.093) = 0.093$$

$$K_f = 1.86 \text{ K kg mol}^{-1}$$

$$\therefore \text{ Molecular mass} = \frac{1 \times 1000 \times 1.86 \times 1.7}{0.093 \times 100}$$

$$= 340 \text{ g mol}^{-1}$$

51. Equivalent weight of NaCl = Molecular weight of NaCl.

$\therefore$ 0.1 N NaCl = 0.1M NaCl

If NaCl does not dissociate in aqueous solution then for a given solution, it is given that,

$C = 0.1\text{M}$, $T = 300$ K $(27 + 273)$

$$\pi = CRT$$

$$= 0.1 \text{ M} \times 0.082 \text{ L atm K}^{-1}\text{mol}^{-1} \times 300\text{K}$$

$$= 2.46 \text{ atm}$$

But observed $\pi = 4.82$ atm

van't Hoff factor,

$$i = \frac{\text{Observed magnitude of } \pi}{\text{Normal magnitude of } \pi} = \frac{4082}{2046} = 1.95 \approx 2$$

If degree of dissociation is α, then

For NaCl, $m = 2$ as the number of solute particles formed in its aqueous solution is almost double the number of NaCl molecules.

$$\therefore \quad \alpha = \frac{i-1}{m-1} = \frac{2-1}{2-1} = 1 \text{ or } 100\%$$

52. Sugar is a non-electrolyte. Therefore, for sugar solution, depression in freezing point takes place.

Given that, $\Delta T_f = 0.402$ °C,

$$K_f = 1.86 \text{ K kg mol}^{-1}$$

$$T = 27 + 273 = 300 \text{ K}$$

$$\Delta T_f = m \times K_f$$

or $$m = \frac{\Delta T_f}{K_f} = \frac{0.402}{1.86} = 0.216 \text{ mol kg}^{-1}$$

Now, for same solution.

Osmotic pressure, $\pi = CRT = m \times R \times T$

$$= 0.216 \times 0.0821 \times 300$$

$$= 5.32 \text{ atm}$$

53. Soda water is prepared by dissolving CO_2 in water under a pressure of 5 to 10 atm. The bottle is tightly capped to prevent the escape of CO_2.

When the bottle is opened, the pressure reduced and most of the dissolved CO_2 gas escapes from the solution in the form of fizz or effervescence. This phenomenon is based upon Henry's law of solubility of gases. This law states that, 'at constant temperature, the solubility of gas in a liquid is directly proportional to the pressure of the gas.'

54. Given, $w = 0.2$ g, $W = 21.7$ g

$$T_{f'} = 272.914 \text{ K}$$

$$K_f = 1.86 \text{ K kg mol}^{-1}$$

$$\Delta T_f = T_f - T_{f'} = 273 - 272.914$$

$$(\because T_f \text{ of water} = 0°\text{C} = 273 \text{ K})$$

$$= 0.086 \text{ K}$$

If the compound A is non-electrolyte, then $i = 1$.

Now, $\Delta T_f = i \times K_f \times \frac{w \times 1000}{W \times M'}$

$$M' = i \times K_f \times \frac{w \times 1000}{W \times \Delta T_f}$$

$$= 1 \times 1.86 \times \frac{0.2 \times 1000}{21.7 \times 0.086} = 199.33 \text{ g mol}^{-1}$$

55. The properties of dilute solutions which depend only on the number of solute particles but not upon their nature are called colligative properties.

Two colligative properties of solutions are

(i) Relative lowering of vapour pressure

(ii) Elevation in boiling point

56. (i) The egg placed in water will get swollen. It is due to the osmosis of pure water into the egg. While, when the egg is placed in the saturated solution of sucrose, it will shrink because osmosis always occurs from higher concentration of solvent to lower concentration of solvent.

(ii) Hypertonic solution has a higher amount of solute in same quality of solution.

(iii) Given, molar mass = 180 g mol^{-1}

Aqueous solution of glucose = 5%

The above solution is isotonic with 1.66% aqueous solution of urea.

As solution is isotonic.

$\therefore \quad \pi_{sugar} = \pi_{urea}$

$$C_1RT = C_2RT$$

or $\quad C_1 = C_2$

$$\frac{5}{180} = \frac{1.66}{M}$$

$$M = \frac{1.66}{5} \times 180$$

$$= 59.76 \text{ g}$$

57. Given, boiling point of water = 373.0834 K

Actual boiling point of water = 373 K

$\therefore \quad \Delta T = 373.0834 - 373$

$$= 0.0834 \text{ K}$$

Amount of $BaCl_2$ = 12.5 g

Amount of water = 1000 g

K_b for H_2O = 0.52 K kg mol^{-1}

Molecular mass of $BaCl_2$ = 208.34 g mol^{-1}.

Moles of $BaCl_2 = \frac{12.5}{208.34} = 0.0599 \approx 0.06$

$$\text{Molality} = \frac{0.06 \times 1000}{1000} = 0.06 \text{ mol/kg}$$

Now, $\Delta T_b = K_b \cdot m \cdot i$

$$0.0834 = 0.52 \times 0.06 \times i$$

$$i = \frac{0.0834}{0.52 \times 0.06}$$

$$= 2.67 \simeq 2.7$$

As, $\underset{1-x}{BaCl_2} \rightleftharpoons \underset{x}{Ba^{2+}} + \underset{2x}{2Cl^-}$

$$i = 1 - x + x + 2x$$

$$2.7 = 1 + 2x$$

$$\Rightarrow \quad x = \frac{1.7}{2} = 0.85$$

Therefore, degree of dissociation is 85%.

58. (i) When rock salt is spread over snow covered roads, snow starts melting from the surface because of the depression in freezing point of water and it helps in clearing the roads.

(ii) Ethylene glycol lowers the freezing point of water. Due to this, the coolant in radiators will not freeze. Otherwise, the radiator will burst due to the freezing of coolant.

(iii) $\Delta T_f = K_f \times \text{molality}$

$$0 - (-10) = 1.86 \times \frac{\frac{w}{62}}{10}$$

$$10 = \frac{1.86 \times w}{62 \times 10}$$

$$w = \frac{62 \times 100}{1.86} = 3333.3 \text{ g} = 3.33 \text{ kg}$$

59. (i) Vapour pressure of water remains same if the volume of water is reduced to $V/4$ mL without any change in temperature because it doesn't depend on the volume, it depends only on the temperature.

(ii) The vapour pressure of a liquid is independent of the volume of the liquid in the container, whether one litre or thirty litres, both samples will have the same vapour pressure at the same temperature.

60. Given, $w_{\text{Benzoic acid}} = 2 \text{ g}, K_f = 4.9 \text{ K kg mol}^{-1}$

$$W_{\text{Benzene}} = 25 \text{ g}, \Delta T_f = 1.62 \text{ K}.$$

Now, $\quad \Delta T_f = K_f \times \frac{w_{\text{Benzoic acid}} \times 1000}{M_{\text{Benzoic acid}} \times W_{\text{Benzene}}}$

$$1.62 = \frac{4.9 \times 2\text{g} \times 1000}{M_{\text{Benzoic}} \times 25\text{g}}$$

$$M_{Benzoic acid} = \frac{4.9 \times 2 \times 1000}{1.62 \times 25} = 241.98 \text{ g /mol}$$

Degree of association of benzoic acid is

$$2C_6H_5COOH \rightleftharpoons (C_6H_5COOH)_2$$

At $t = 0$	1	0
At $t = t_{eq}$	$1-x$	$x/2$

So, total no. of moles of particles at equilibrium

$$= 1 - x + \frac{x}{2} = 1 - \frac{x}{2} = i.$$

$$i = \frac{\text{Normal molecular mass}}{\text{Abnormal molecular mass}}$$

$$1 - \frac{x}{2} = \frac{122}{241.98}$$

$$\frac{x}{2} = 1 - \frac{122}{241.98} \Rightarrow x = 0.992 \Rightarrow 99.2\%$$

61. Given, boiling point of water = 373.0832 K

Actual boiling point of water = 373 K

$$\Delta T = 373.0832 - 373$$
$$= 0.0832$$

$$\text{Moles of } BaCl_2 = \frac{\text{Given mass}}{\text{Molar mass}} = \frac{12.48}{208.34} = 0.06$$

$$\Delta T_b = K_b \times m \times i \text{ } (i = \text{van't Hoff factor})$$
$$0.0832 = 0.52 \times 0.06 \times i$$
$$i = \frac{0.0832}{0.52 \times 0.06} = 2.67$$

$\Rightarrow$ $1 + (n-1) \times \alpha = 2.67$ (degree of dissociation)

$\Rightarrow$ $1 + 2\alpha = 2.67$

$\Rightarrow$ $2\alpha = 1.67$

$\Rightarrow$ $\alpha = 0.835$

62. Given,

Mass of oxalic acid = 0.4 g (w_B)

Mass of benzene = 40 g (W_A)

K_f for benzene = 5.12 K kg mol^{-1}

Molar mass of oxalic acid [$C_2O_4H_2$] = 90 g mol^{-1} ($2 \times 12 + 4 \times 16 + 2 \times 1$), i.e. ($M_B$)

ΔT_f (lowering in freezing point) = 0.45 K

$$\text{Now, } \Delta T_f = i \times K_f \times \frac{w_B}{M_B} \times \frac{1000}{W_A}$$

$$i = \frac{\Delta T_f \times M_B \times W_A}{K_f \times w_B \times 1000}$$

$$i = \frac{0.45 \text{ K} \times 90 \text{ g mol}^{-1} \times 40 \text{ g}}{5.12 \text{ K kg mol}^{-1} \times 0.4 \text{ g} \times 1000} = 0.79$$

Also, $i = 1 - \alpha + \frac{\alpha}{2}$ (For association)

where, i = vant' Hoff factor and

α = degree of association.

$$0.79 = 1 - \alpha + \frac{\alpha}{2} = 1 - \alpha\left[1 - \frac{1}{2}\right]$$

$$0.79 = 1 - \frac{\alpha}{2}$$

$$\frac{\alpha}{2} = 1 - 0.79 = 0.21$$

$\therefore$ $\alpha = 0.42$ or 42%

63. Given : Mass of non-volatile solute (w_B) = 9.25 g

Volume of water (V_A) = 450 mL

Osmotic pressure (π) = $\frac{350}{760}$ = 0.46 atm

Temperature (T) = 27 + 273 = 300 K

Gas constant (R) = 0.0821 L atm K^{-1}mol^{-1}

Now,

$$\because \quad \pi = CRT = \frac{w_B \times 1000 \times RT}{M_B \times V}$$

$\therefore M_B$ [molecular mass of non-volatile solute]

$$= \frac{w_B \times 1000 \times R \times T}{V \times \pi}$$

$$\text{or,} \quad M_B = \frac{w_B \times 1000 \times R \times T}{V \times \pi}$$

$$\text{or,} = \frac{9.25 \text{ g} \times 1000 \times 0.0821 \text{ L atm K}^{-1} \text{ mol}^{-1} \times 300 \text{ K}}{450 \text{ mL} \times 0.46 \text{ atm}}$$

$$M_B = \frac{2278275}{20.7} = 1100.6 \text{ g mol}^{-1}$$

Hence, molecular mass of non-volatile solute

$= 1100.6$ g mol^{-1}

64. Given, $w_2 = 5.85$ g, $W_1 = 100$ g,

$m_1 = 18$ g mol^{-1} for H_2O

Depression in freezing point

$$(\Delta T_f) = T_f^\circ - T_f$$

$$\Delta T_f = 0°C - (-3.348)°C = 3.348°C = 3.348K$$

$$\therefore \quad M_2 = \frac{1000 \times K_f \times w_2}{\Delta T_f \times W_1}$$

$$\therefore \quad M_2 = \frac{1000 \times 1.86 \text{K kg mol}^{-1} \times 5.85 \text{ g}}{3.348 \text{ K} \times 100 \text{g}}$$

$= 32.5$ g mol^{-1}

Calculated molecular mass of NaCl

$= 23+35.5 = 58.5 \text{ g mol}^{-1}$

Now, $i = \dfrac{\text{Calculated molecular mass}}{\text{Observed molecular mass}}$

$i = \dfrac{58.5}{32.5} = 1.8$

$\therefore$ van't Hoff factor $(i) = 1.8$

65. Given, $W_2 = 12.48\text{g}, W_1 = 1000\text{g}$,

$T_{b\,(\text{solution})} = (100.0832 + 273)\text{ K} = 373.0832\text{K}$

K_b for $H_2O = 0.52 \text{ kg mol}^{-1}$

and $M_{2(BaCl_2)} = 208 \text{ g mol}^{-1}$

$\Delta T_b = T_b - T_b^{\circ} = 373.0832\text{K} - 373\text{K} = 0.0832 \text{ K}$

$$M_{2(\text{Observed})} = \frac{K_b \times w_2 \times 1000}{\Delta T_b \times W_1}$$

$$= \frac{0.52 \text{ kg mol}^{-1} \times 12.48\text{g} \times 1000}{0.0832 \text{ K} \times 1000\text{g}}$$

$$M_{2(\text{Observed})} = 78 \text{ g mol}^{-1}$$

$$i = \frac{M_{2(\text{Calculated})}}{M_{2(\text{Observed})}} = \frac{208\text{g mol}^{-1}}{78\text{g mol}^{-1}} = 2.67$$

For $BaCl_2$, $m = 3$ as it gives 3 ions on dissociation

$$\alpha = \frac{i-1}{m-1}$$

$$= \frac{2.67-1}{3-1} = \frac{1.67}{2} = 0.835, \ \alpha = 83.5\%$$

66. Given, $K_f = 1.86 \text{ K kg mol}^{-1}$, $\Delta T_f = 2 \text{ K}$,

Amount of water taken $(W_1) = 500$ g

Amount of $CaCl_2\,(w_2) = ?$,

Molar mass of $CaCl_2\,(M_2) = 111 \text{ g mol}^{-1}$

It is given that $CaCl_2$ is completely dissociated,

$$CaCl_2 \longrightarrow Ca^{2+} + 2Cl^-$$

$\therefore$ Number of particles after dissociation $= 3$

van't Hoff factor, $i = 3$

$$\Delta T_f = \frac{i \times K_f \times w_2 \times 1000}{W_1 \times M_2}$$

$$w_2 = \frac{\Delta T_f \times W_1 \times M_2}{i \times K_f \times 1000} = \frac{2 \times 500 \times 111}{3 \times 1.86 \times 1000} = 19.89 \text{ g}$$

67. Given, K_f for water $= 1.86°\text{C}$

Amount of KCl taken $(w_2) = 0.5$ g

Amount of water taken $(W_1) = 100$ g

$$\Delta T_f = 0 - (-0.24) = 0.24°\text{C}$$

Observed molecular mass of

$$KCl\,(M_2) = \frac{1000 \times K_f \times w_2}{\Delta T_f \times W_1}$$

$$= \frac{1000 \times 1.86 \times 0.5}{0.24 \times 100} = 38.75 \text{ g mol}^{-1}$$

Normal molecular mass of $KCl = 39 + 35.5$

$= 74.5 \text{ g mol}^{-1}$

van't Hoff factor $= \dfrac{\text{Normal molecular mass}}{\text{Observed molecular mass}}$

$$i = \frac{74.5}{38.75} = 1.92$$

	$KCl \rightleftharpoons$	K^+	+ Cl^-
Initial moles	1 mol	0	0
Moles after dissociation	$1-\alpha$	α	α

Total number of moles after dissociation

$$= 1 - \alpha + \alpha + \alpha = 1 + \alpha$$

$$i = 1 + \alpha$$

$$1.92 = 1 + \alpha$$

So, degree of dissociation, $\alpha = 1.92 - 1 = 0.92$, i.e. 92% dissociated.

68. Given, number of moles of sucrose $(n) = 5$ mol

Mass of solvent (water) $= 1$ kg

Vapour pressure of pure water $(p°) = 4.57$ mm of Hg

Vapour pressure of solution $(p) = ?$

According to Raoult's law,

$$\frac{p° - p}{p°} = \frac{n}{n+N}$$

(where, N is number of moles of water)

$$\frac{4.57 - p}{4.57} = \frac{5}{5 + 55.5} \quad \left(\text{as } N = \frac{1000}{18} = 55.5 \text{ mol}\right)$$

$$4.57 - p = \frac{4.57 \times 5}{60.5} = 0.377$$

$\therefore \qquad p = 4.57 - 0.377 = 4.193$ mm of Hg

69. Given, mass of water $(W) = 4$ kg,

$K_f = 1.85 \text{ K kg mol}^{-1}$

$\Delta T_f = 0 - (-6) = 6°\text{C}$

(as, freezing point of pure water is 0°C.)

Mass of ethylene glycol $(w) = ?$

Molar mass of ethylene glycol

$[CH_2OH \cdot CH_2OH]$, $M' = 62 \text{ g mol}^{-1}$

We know that,

$$\Delta T_f = \frac{K_f \times w}{M' \times W\,(\text{kg})}$$

$$\therefore \quad w = \frac{\Delta T_f \times M' \times W(\text{kg})}{K_f}$$

$$= \frac{6 \times 62 \times 4}{1.85} = 804.32\text{ g}$$

70. Given, vapour pressure of pure water

$$(p^\circ) = 4.579 \text{ mm of Hg}$$

Vapour pressure of solution

$$(p) = 4.559 \text{ mm of Hg}$$

Mass of lactose $(w) = 8.45$ g

Mass of water $(W) = 100$ g

Molecular mass of H_2O $(M) = 18$ g

Molecular mass of lactose $(m) = ?$

According to Raoult's law,

$$\frac{p^\circ - p}{p^\circ} = \frac{wM}{W \cdot m}$$

$$\frac{4.579 - 4.559}{4.579} = \frac{8.45 \times 18}{100 \times m}$$

$$\therefore \quad m = \frac{8.45 \times 18 \times 4.579}{100 \times 0.02} = 348.232 \text{ g mol}^{-1}$$

71. Given, osmotic pressure $(\pi_{obs}) = 0.65$ atm

Temperature, $T = 27°C = (27 + 273)K = 300K$

Concentration, $C = 0.01$ M

van't Hoff factor, $i = ?$

We know that, $\pi_{cal.} = CRT$

$$= 0.01 \text{ M} \times 0.0821 \text{ L atm K}^{-1} \times 300 \text{ K}$$

$$= 0.2463 \text{ atm}$$

But, $\pi_{calc} = 0.65$ atm

van't Hoff factor, $i = \frac{\pi_{obs.}}{\pi_{cal.}} = \frac{0.2463}{0.65} = 0.3789$

i.e. $\quad i < 1$

When $i < 1$, the solute undergoes association. Thus, it gets associated in solution.

72. We know that, osmotic pressure $\pi = CRT = \frac{wRT}{M \times V}$

or $\quad M = \frac{wRT}{\pi \times V}$

Given, $w = 3.5$ g, $R = 0.0821 \text{ dm}^3 \text{ atm K}^{-1}$,

$T = 273 + 25 = 298$ K, $\pi = 0.014$ atm,

$V = 100$ mL

$\therefore$ Molecular weight of albumin,

$$M = \frac{3.5 \times 0.082 \times 298 \times 1000}{0.014 \times 100} = 61090 \text{ g mol}^{-1}$$

Molecular weight of albumin is 61090 g mol^{-1}.

73. Let, the weight of glucose is wg.

If glucose solution has same osmotic pressure as blood.

Thus, $\pi_{glucose} = \pi_{blood} = 7.65$ atm

$$\therefore \quad \pi = \frac{w \times R \times T}{M \times V}$$

Given : Volume of solution, $V = 1$ L

Gas constant, $R = 0.0821 \text{ L atm mol}^{-1} \text{ K}^{-1}$

Temperature, $T = 27°C = (27 + 273)$ K $= 300$ K

Molecular weight of glucose, $M = 180 \text{ g mol}^{-1}$

Thus, $\quad \pi = \frac{w \times 0.0821 \times 300}{180 \times 1}$

$$\Rightarrow \quad w = \frac{7.65 \times 180}{0.0821 \times 300} = 55.9 \text{ g mol}^{-1}$$

74. Given that, weight of solvent, $w = 100$ g

Vapour pressure of solution, $\quad p = 72.0$ torr

Vapour pressure of solvent (ethyl acetate),

$$p^\circ = 72.8 \text{ torr}$$

Molecular weight of solvent = 88 g mol^{-1}

According to Raoult's law, $\frac{p^\circ - p}{p^\circ} = \frac{n}{N + n}$

But for dilute solutions, $n <<< N$

Thus, $\quad \frac{p^\circ - p}{p^\circ} = \frac{n}{N}$

$$\Rightarrow \quad \frac{72.8 - 72}{72.8} = \frac{0.5/m}{100/88}$$

$$\Rightarrow \quad m = \frac{0.5}{0.8} \times \frac{88}{100} \times 72.8 = 40.04$$

Hence, molecular weight of non-volatile solute is 40.04 g mol^{-1}.

75. (i) Given that, $T_f^\circ = 278.8$ K

Molality of a solution, $m = 0.25$ m

Molecular weight of solute,

$$w = 120 \text{ g mol}^{-1}$$

Freezing point of solution,

$$T_{f'} = 276.8 \text{ K}$$

It is known that,

$$\Delta T_f = i \times K_f \times m$$

$$\Rightarrow \quad K_f = \frac{\Delta T_f}{i \times m}$$

Here, van't Hoff factor, i for solute is considered as 1.
Depression in freezing point,

$$\Delta T_f = T_f^\circ - T_f' = 278.8 - 276.8 \text{ K} = 2 \text{ K}$$

$$\therefore \; K_f = \frac{2}{1 \times 0.25} = 8 \text{ K molal}^{-1}$$ **(1½)**

(ii) Given that, weight of sucrose = 3.42 g
Volume of solution = 1 L

$T = 400\text{K}$

Molecular weight of sucrose = 342 g mol^{-1}

Gas constant, $R = 0.0821 \text{ atm K}^{-1}\text{mol}^{-1}$

Osmotic pressure (π) of a solution is given by

$$\pi = \frac{w \times R \times T}{mV} = \frac{3.42 \times 0.0821 \times 400}{342 \times 1} = 0.328 \text{ atm}$$

≈ 0.33 atm **(1½)**

76. (i) Given : Cryoscopic constant, $K_f = 1.86 \text{ K mol}^{-1} \text{ kg}^{-1}$

Freezing point of solution,

$T_{f'} = -0.327°\text{C}$

$= [273 + (-0.327)]\text{K} = 272.673 \text{ K}$

Freezing point of pure water,

$T_f^\circ = 0°\text{C} = 273 \text{ K}$

Depression in freezing point,

$$\Delta T_f = T_f^\circ - T_{f'} = 273 - 272.673 \text{ K} = 0.327 \text{ K}$$

We know that, $\Delta T_f = i \times K_f \times m$

Since, cane sugar is a non-electrolyte, thus i (van't Hoff factor) is equal to 1.

$\therefore \; 0.327 = 1 \times 1.86 \times m$

$$m = \frac{0.327}{1.86} = 0.17 \text{ molal} \approx 0.2 \text{ molal}$$ **(1½)**

Hence, molality of solution is 0.2 molal.

(ii) The molecular weight of solutes can be determined by using the depression of freezing point as,

$$m = \frac{i \times 1000 \times K_f \times w}{\Delta T_f \times W}.$$

The molecular weight calculated by above equation is usually found to be slightly different from the theoretical value because the solute which is added to the solution acts as an electrolyte. It undergoes either association or dissociation which results in either increase or decrease in their molecular weights.

KCl being an electrolyte undergoes dissociation and releases two ions [K^+ and Cl^-] for which value of i comes out to be greater than, 1 i.e. 2.

Hence, in case of KCl, experimental molecular weight comes out to be larger than observed value.

While for glucose, its experimental value comes out to be same as observed value as it is non-electrolyte for which value of i is 1. **(1½)**

77. (i) Given, weight of solute $(w_B) = 0.30$ g
weight of solvent $(W_A) = 100$ g.

$\Delta T_b = 0.0633°\text{C} \Rightarrow 0.0633$ K.

$K_b = 2.53 \text{ K kg mol}^{-1}$.

$$M_B = \frac{K_b \times w_B \times 1000}{W_A \times \Delta T_b} = \frac{2.53 \times 1000 \times 0.30}{100 \times 0.0633}$$

$= 119.9$ g/mol

$$i = \frac{\text{Normal molar mass}}{\text{Abnormal molar mass}} \Rightarrow \frac{60}{119.90} = 0.5$$

$\therefore \; i < 1$

As i is less than 1, thus association will take place. **(2)**

(ii) Given, mass of $K_2SO_4 (W) = 25 \text{ mg} = 0.025 \text{ g}$; volume$(V) = 2\text{L}$, $T = 298$ K.

The reaction of dissociation of K_2SO_4.

$$\Rightarrow \quad K_2SO_4 \longrightarrow 2K^+ + SO_4^{2-}$$

Number of ions produced $i = 2 + 1 = 3$

as $\quad \pi = i\dfrac{n}{V}RT = i\dfrac{W}{MV}RT$

where, $R = 0.082 \text{ L atm K}^{-1} \text{ mol}^{-1}$, molar mass of $K_2SO_4 = 174$ g/mol

By substituting the value we get

$$T_1 = \frac{3 \times 0.025}{174 \times 2} \times 0.0821 \times 298 = 5.27 \times 10^{-3} \text{ atm}$$ **(3)**

78. (i) (a) Given : $T_f = 272.4 \text{ K}, T_f^\circ = 273.0 \text{ K}$

$K_f = 1.86 \text{ K kg mol}^{-1}$

$K_b = 0.512 \text{ K kg mol}^{-1}$

Vapour pressure of water at 298 K
$= 23.756$ mm Hg

$m = ?$

As we know, $\Delta T_f = K_f \times m$

$$\therefore \quad 0.6 = 1.86 \times m \text{ or } m = \frac{0.6}{1.86}$$

Thus, molality of solution = 0.323 m **(1)**

(b) T_b (Boiling point of solution) = ?

We know , $\dfrac{\Delta T_f}{\Delta T_b} = \dfrac{K_f}{K_b}$

$$\therefore \quad \frac{0.6}{\Delta T_b} = \frac{1.86}{0.512}$$

or $$\Delta T_b = \frac{0.6 \times 0.512}{1.86} = 0.17 \text{ K}$$

Also, $\Delta T_b = T_b - T_b^\circ$

$\Rightarrow \quad 0.17 = T_b - 273$

$\therefore \quad 0.17 + 273 = T_b$

$273.17\text{ K} = T_b$

$\therefore$ Boiling point of solution is 273.17 K.

(c) Lowering of vapour pressure at 298 K = ?

we know, $\dfrac{p^\circ - p}{p^\circ} = \dfrac{(760 - 23.756)\text{ mm Hg}}{760\text{ mm Hg}}$

$\therefore \quad \dfrac{p^\circ - p}{p^\circ} = 0.969$ **(2)**

(ii) Given, mass of calcium nitrate = 1.23 g

Mass of water = 10 g

T_b for solution = 100.975° C

K_b for water = 0.52 K kg mol^{-1}

Molecular weight of calcium nitrate = 164 g mol^{-1}

As we know,

$$\Delta T_b = i \times K_b \times m$$

$$\Rightarrow \quad \Delta T_b = i \times K_b \times \frac{w_B}{M_B} \times \frac{1000}{W_A}$$

$$100.975 - 100℃ = i \times 0.52 \times \frac{1.23}{164} \times \frac{1000}{10}$$

or $\quad 0.975 = i \times 0.52 \times 0.75$

$\therefore \quad i = 2.5$ **(3)**

79. (i) Given : Freezing point of water = 273 K

Weight of solute (glucose) $w = 0.625$ g

Weight of solvent, $W = 102.8$ g

Molecular weight of solute, $m = (C_6H_{12}O_6)$

$= 12 \times 6 + 1 \times 12 + 16 \times 6 = 180\text{ g mol}^{-1}$

K_f for water = 1.87 K kg mol^{-1}

For glucose as solute, $i = 1$

$$\Delta T_f = \frac{1000 \times K_f \times w}{m \times W}$$

$$= \frac{1000 \times 1.87 \times 0.625}{180 \times 102.8}$$

$= 0.063$ K

$\therefore$ Freezing point of solution $= T_f + \Delta T_f$

(where, T_f is freezing point of water = 0°C = 273 K)

$= 273 + 0.063 = 273.063$ K **(2)**

(ii) Osmotic pressure $(\pi) = CRT$

Given, $C = 0.15$ M, $R = 0.0821$ L atm K^{-1} mol^{-1}

$T = 310$ K

$\therefore \quad \pi = CRT$

$= 0.15\text{ M} \times 0.0821\text{ L atm K}^{-1}\text{ mol}^{-1} \times 310\text{ K}$

$= 3.82$ atm

Observed $\pi = 6.8$ atm

$\therefore$ van't Hoff Factor,

$$i = \frac{\text{Observed magnitude of } \pi}{\text{Normal magnitude of } \pi} = \frac{6.8}{3.82} = 1.78$$

If degree of dissociation is α, then for KCl, $n = 2$ as the number of solute particles in its aqueous solution is almost double the number of NaCl molecules.

$$\therefore \quad \alpha = \frac{i-1}{n-1} = \frac{1.78 - 1}{2-1} = 0.78 = 78\%$$ **(2)**

(iii) Similar to question 70. **(1)**

80. (i) Isotonic solutions have same osmotic pressure at same temperature.

Here, W_1 = weight of cane sugar solution = 10g,

M_1 = molecular weight of cane sugar = 342 g,

w_2 = weight of urea solution = 1.754g

$$\pi = CRT = \frac{w}{m}\frac{RT}{V}$$

For cane sugar and urea solution, π, R, T and V are same.

For cane sugar solution, $\pi = \dfrac{10RT}{342V}$

For urea solution, $\pi = \dfrac{1.754RT}{MV}$

$$\because \quad \frac{10RT}{342V} = \frac{1.754RT}{MV}$$

$$\therefore \quad M = \frac{1.754 \times 342}{10} = 59.98\text{ g}$$ **(2)**

(ii) Given,

W_a = Weight of H_2O (solvent) = 1200 g

w_b = Weight of organic compound = 48 g

$T_b{}^\circ = 100°C$, $K_b = 0.513°C$ kg mol^{-1}

M_b = molecular mass of solute = 58 g mol^{-1}

$$\Delta T_b = \frac{K_b \times 1000 \times w_b}{M_b \times W_a}$$

$$= \frac{(0.513\text{ °C kg mol}^{-1}) \times 100 \times 48\text{ g}}{(58\text{ g mol}^{-1}) \times 1200\text{ g}}$$

$= 0.0353$ °C

As we know that, $\Delta T_b = T_b - T_b^\circ$

$0.0353 = T_b - 100$

$T_b = 100 + 0.0353$

$= 100.0353$ °C $= 373.1853$ K **(2)**

(iii) van't Hoff factor (i)

$$= \frac{\text{Total number of moles of particles after association / dissociation}}{\text{Number of moles of particles before association / dissociation}}$$

Two molecules of benzoic acid dimerises to give one bigger molecule.

$\therefore \quad i = \frac{1}{2}$

So, in case of association

$$i = \frac{\text{Normal molecular weight}}{\text{Experimental molecular weight}}$$

$\because \quad i = \frac{1}{2}$

$\therefore$ Experimental molecular weight

$= 2 \times$ normal molecular weight

Hence, experimental molecular weight will become twice of normal molecular weight. **(1)**

81. (i) Given : Weight of KCl (solute) $= 0.5$ g

Weight of solvent (water) $= 100$ g

Freezing point (T_f) $= -0.24°C$

$K_f = 1.86°C$

Molecular mass of KCl $= 39 + 35.5 = 74.5$

From depression in freezing point

$$T_f = i \times K_f \times m$$

$$0.24°C = i \times 1.86°C \times \frac{0.5}{74.5} \times \frac{1000}{100} \Rightarrow i = 1.92$$

For KCl, $\quad i = 1 + \alpha$

(where α is the degree of dissociation)

$\alpha = 1.92 - 1 \Rightarrow \alpha = .92$ or 92% **(2)**

(ii) Given: Weight of sugar $= 1.71$ g

Molar mass of sugar $= 342$ g/mol

Volume of solvent $= 500$ mL

Temperature $= 300$ K

Osmotic pressure, $\pi = CRT$

$$C = \frac{1.71}{342} \times \frac{1000}{500}$$

$$\pi = 0.01 \times 0.0821 \text{ L atm/K/mol} \times 300 \text{ K}$$

$C = 0.01$ mol/L, $\pi = 0.2463$ atm **(2)**

(iii) Given $\Delta T_b = 0.25°$, or 0.25 K, $K_b = 1.72$ kg mol^{-1}

$$\Rightarrow \quad \Delta T_b = K_b \times m$$

$$0.25 = 1.72 \times \frac{0.70}{\text{molecular weight}} \times \frac{1000}{32 \text{ g}}$$

Molecular weight $= 150.5$ g **(1)**

82. The pressure which must be applied to the solution in order to prevent the passage of solvent molecules into the solution through a semipermeable membrane separating the two is called **osmotic pressure.**

Osmotic pressure is a colligative property which depends upon the number of solute particles.

(i) Moles of sucrose $= \frac{w_{\text{sucrose}}}{M} = \frac{34.2}{342} = 0.1$ mol

Since, 1 mole of sucrose $= 6.022 \times 10^{23}$ particles

$\therefore \quad 0.1$ mole of sucrose $= 6.022 \times 10^{23} \times 0.1$

$= 6.022 \times 10^{22}$ particles

Hence, 34.2 g per litre of sucrose contains 6.022×10^{22} particles. **(1)**

(ii) Moles of glucose $= \frac{90.0}{180} = 0.5$ mol

Since, 1 mole of glucose $= 6.022 \times 10^{23}$ particles

$\therefore$ 0.5 mole of glucose $= 6.022 \times 10^{23} \times 0.5$

$= 30.11 \times 10^{22}$ particles

$= 3.011 \times 10^{23}$ particles

Hence, 90.0 g per litre of glucose contains 3.011×10^{23} particles. **(2)**

(iii) Moles of NaCl $= \frac{5.85}{58.5} = 0.1$ mol

Since, 1 mole of NaCl $= 2 \times 6.023 \times 10^{23}$ particles

($\because NaCl \rightleftharpoons Na^+ + Cl^-$)

$\therefore$0.1 mol of NaCl $= 2 \times 6.023 \times 10^{23} \times 0.1$

$= 12.046 \times 10^{22}$ particles

Hence, 5.85 g per litre of NaCl contains 12.046×10^{22} particles.

Among all the above, 90.0 g per litre of glucose contains maximum number of particles followed by NaCl and sucrose.

Thus, glucose would possess maximum osmotic pressure.

Hence, the increasing order of their osmotic pressure is sucrose < NaCl < glucose. **(2)**

Concept Enhancer Osmotic pressure $(\pi) = iCRT, C = \frac{n}{V} = \frac{w_B}{M_B \times V}$.

Here, C is the molar concentration of solution. On increasing the molar concentration, osmotic pressure increases. If the weight of all solutes and its solution volumes are equal, osmotic pressure will only be depend on molar mass of solute.

CHAPTER TEST

01 Mark Questions

1. Fill in the blanks by choosing the appropriate word(s) from those given in the brackets.

[molarity, molality, volume, weight, zero, positive, Raoult's law, Henry's law, concentration, mole fraction]

(i) .... does not get affected by temperature because it does not depend on the ....

(ii) The solutions which show .... deviation from .... are non-ideal solutions.

(iii) Ideal solutions obey .... over entire range of ....

(iv) .... states that the partial vapour pressure is proportional to the ...... of the gas in the solution.

2. Select and write the correct alternatives from the choices given below.

(i) The density of a 3.6 M H_2SO_4 solution having 29% H_2SO_4 is

(a) 1.84 g mL^{-1} (b) 1.85 g mL^{-1}
(c) 1.44 g mL^{-1} (d) 1.22 g mL^{-1}

(ii) A solution which has higher osmotic pressure than its standard solution. The term given to that type of solution is

(a) isotonic (b) hypertonic
(c) dilute (d) hypotonic

(iii) The unit of ebullioscopic constant is

(a) K kg mol^{-1} (b) mol^{-1} kg K^{-1}
(c) kg mol^{-1} K^{-1} (d) K mol^{-1} kg^{-1}

(iv) For which solution, Raoult's law is not applicable?

(a) 0.1 M NaCl (b) 0.1 M Urea
(c) 0.1 M Glucose (d) 0.1 M Sucrose

3. (i) **Assertion** (A) High blood pressure patients are advised to take the minimum quantity of salt.

Reason (R) From common salt Na^+ and Cl^- ion concentration increases in the body fluid, which may rupture the blood cells.

(a) Both (A) and (R) are correct and (R) is the correct explanation of (A).
(b) Both (A) and (R) are correct but (R) is not the correct explanation of (A).
(c) (A) is correct and (R) is incorrect.
(d) (A) is incorrect and (R) is correct.

(ii) **Assertion** (A) Cryoscopy constant can not be used for the determination of molecular weight of macromolecules.

Reason (R) High molecular weight solute leads to very low value of ΔT_f.

(a) Both (A) and (R) are correct and (R) is the correct explanation of (A).
(b) Both (A) and (R) are correct but (R) is not the correct explanation of (A).
(c) (A) is correct and (R) is incorrect.
(d) (A) is incorrect and (R) is correct.

02 Marks Questions

4. Define the term colligative properties. Why is elevation of boiling point a colligative property?

5. Give reason for the following.

(i) Solution containing non-volatile solute have higher boiling point than the pure solvent.

(ii) Elevation of boiling point of 1M KCl solution is nearly double than that of same concentration sugar solution.

6. Give reason for the following.

(i) Aquatic species are more comfortable in cold water than warm water.

(ii) At higher altitudes people suffer from anoxia resulting in inability to think.

7. Define van't Hoff factor? What possible values can it have if the solute molecules undergo association?

8. Calculate the mass of compound (molar mass $= 250\ g\ mol^{-1}$) to be dissolved in 76.8 g of benzene to lower its freezing point by 0.48 K.
($K_f = 5.12$ K kg mol^{-1})

9. Find the boiling point of a solution containing 1.04 g glucose ($C_6H_{12}O_6$) dissolved in 80.2 g of water.
($K_b = 0.52$ Km^{-1})

10. The vapour pressure of water is 12.4 kPa at 300 K. Calculate the vapour pressure of a molal solution of a non-volatile, non-ionic solute in water.

03 Marks Questions

11. Calculate the molality of a solution of 222.6 g of ethylene glycol ($C_2H_4(OH)_2$) and 500 g of water. If the density of this solution is 1.072, then what will be the molarity of the solution?

12. The freezing point of benzene decreases by 0.45°C when 0.2 g of acetic acid is added to 20 g of benzene. If acetic acid associates to give a dimer of benzene, the % association of acetic acid in benzene will be (K_f for benzene) = 5.12 K kg mol^{-1}.

13. Account for the following.
(i) The use of pressure cooker reduces cooking time.
(ii) Why we cannot separate the azeotropic mixture by distillation?
(iii) An example of a solid solution in which the solute is a gas.

14. Give any three differences between ideal and non-ideal solution.

15. State Raoult's law. Why does a solution of chloroform and acetone show negative deviation from Raoult's law?

05 Marks Questions

16. (i) The air is a mixture of a number of gases. The major components are oxygen and nitrogen with approximate proportion of 20% is to 79% by volume at 298 K, respectively. The water is in equilibrium with air at a pressure of 10 atm. At 298 K, if the Henry's law constant for oxygen and nitrogen are 3.30×10^7 mm and 6.51×10^7 mm respectively.
Calculate the composition of these gases in water.
(ii) Which of the following solutions will have the highest and lowest osmotic pressure and why?
(a) Sugar in water.
(b) Salt in water.

17. (i) An aqueous solution containing 12.48 g of $BaCl_2$ in 1 kg of water boils at 373.083 K. Calculate the degree of dissociation of $BaCl_2$.
(K_b for H_2O = 0.52 Km^{-1})
(ii) Calculate the lowering of vapour pressure for 0.1 m aqueous solution of non-electrolyte at 75°C.
($\Delta H = 9.720$ kcal mol^{-1}, $p_2 = 742.96$ torr)

18. (i) At what partial pressure, oxygen will have a solubility of 0.05 g L^{-1} in water at 19.85°C. K_H for O_2 in water at 19.85°C = 34.86 K bar. (Assume that density is same for solvent and solution).
(ii) A solution of 10.50 g of $MgBr_2$ in 200 g of water is prepared. Calculate its freezing point.
(Molar mass of $MgBr_2$ = 184 g,
K_f (water) = 1.86 K kg mol^{-1})

Answers

1. (i) molality, volume (ii) positive, Raoult's law (iii) Raoult's law, concentration (iv) Henry's law, mole fraction.
2. (i) (d) (ii) (b) (iii) (a) (iv) (a) **3.** (i) (a) (ii) (a)
8. 1.8g **9.** 373.04 K **10.** 12.08 kPa
11. Molality = 7.18 mol kg^{-1}, Molarity = 5.33 M **12.** 94.6%
16. (i) $\chi_{O_2} = 4.6 \times 10^{-5}$, $\chi_{N_2} = 9.22 \times 10^{-5}$
17. (i) 8.333% (ii) 0.533 **18.** (i) 1.834 bar (ii) 273 K

02

Electrochemistry

TREND ANALYSIS 4 YEARS

Average No. of Questions Across all Sets

Topic	Types of Questions	2024	2023	2020	2019
TOPIC 01 Metallic and Electrolytic Conduction, Electrolysis and Faraday's Laws of Electrolysis	1 Mark	—	—	—	—
	2 Marks	—	—	—	1
	3 Marks	—	—	—	—
	5 Marks	—	—	—	—
TOPIC 02 Electrochemical Cells, Galvanic Cell, Standard Hydrogen Electrode, Nernst Equation	1 Mark	—	2	—	1
	2 Marks	1	1	—	—
	3 Marks	—	—	1	—
	5 Marks	1	—	—	—
TOPIC 03 Conductance in Electrolytic Solutions, Corrosion and Batteries	1 Mark	2	—	1	—
	2 Marks	—	—	1	—
	3 Marks	—	—	1	—
	5 Marks	1	—	—	1

TOPIC 1

Metallic and Electrolytic Conduction, Electrolysis and Faraday's Laws of Electrolysis

Electrochemistry is the branch of chemistry which deals with the study of conversion of chemical energy into electrical energy or *vice-versa* and their mutual relationship.

The substances which allow the passage of current through them are called **electrical conductors**.

The substances which do not allow the passage of electric current through them are called **electrical insulators**.

Classification of Electrical Conductors

These are classified into two categories

(i) **Metallic conduction** The phenomenon of conduction of current by metals is called metallic conduction. It decreases with increase in temperature.

(ii) **Electrolytic conduction** The phenomenon of the flow of current due to the movement of ions is called electrolytic conduction. It increases with increase in temperature.

Electrolytes and Electrolysis

Electrolytes

The substances which conduct electric current either in aqueous state or fused state on account of the movement of ions and undergo a chemical change (decomposition) during the passage of electric current through them are called electrolytes.

Those substances which are completely ionised in aqueous solution and conduct large quantity of electricity are called **strong electrolytes**, e.g. NaCl, KCl, etc.

Those substances which are feebly ionised and conduct small quantity of electricity are called **weak electrolytes**. e.g. CH_3COOH, NH_4OH, etc.

Electrolysis

It is the process by which an electrolyte in molten state or in aqueous solution conducts an electric current and gets decomposed into its constituent ions that move towards the oppositely charged electrodes.

Faraday's Laws of Electrolysis

Michael Faraday studied the phenomenon of electrolysis and formulated two important quantitative laws governing electrolysis. These are as follows

1. Faraday's First Law of Electrolysis

It states that the amount of substance deposited at a particular electrode as a result of electrolysis is directly proportional to the quantity of electricity passed.

$$w = Z \times Q$$

where, Q is the quantity of electricity (charge) passed, Z is the electrochemical equivalent of the substance, w is the amount of substance deposited at the electrode.

or $$\boxed{w = Z \times it} \quad [\because Q = i \times t]$$

where, i = amount of current (in A)

t = time for which current is passed

Relation between electrochemical constant and chemical equivalent

Equivalent weight $(E) = Z \times 96500$ (and 1F = 96500 C).

2. Faraday's Second Law of Electrolysis

When the same quantity of electricity is passed through the solutions of different electrolytes connected in series, the masses of the substances produced at the electrodes are directly proportional to their equivalent weights.

$$\frac{\text{Weight of } A}{\text{Weight of } B} = \frac{\text{Equivalent weight of } A}{\text{Equivalent weight of } B}$$

where, A and B are the elements discharged at electrodes.

PYQs Previous Years' Questions

1 Mark Questions

1. Electrochemical equivalent is the amount of substance which gets deposited from its solution on passing electrical charge equal to **ISC 2021-22 (Sem-I), 2016**

   (a) 96500 C (b) 1 C (c) 60 C (d) 965 C

2. Name the law or principle to which the following observations confirm:
   When 96500 coulombs of electricity is passed through a solution of copper sulphate, 3.175 g of copper is deposited on the cathode (At. wt. of Cu = 63.5). **ISC 2017, 2013**

3. Calculate the number of coulombs required to deposit 5.4 g of Al, when the electrode reaction is

   $$Al^{3+} + 3e^- \longrightarrow Al$$

   [Atomic weight of Al = 27g/mol] **ISC 2016**

4. How many hours does it take to reduce 3 moles of Fe^{3+} to Fe^{2+} with 2.0 A current intensity? **ISC 2016**

5. A current liberates 0.50 g of hydrogen in 2 h. The weight of copper (atomic weight = 63.5) deposited at the same time by the same current through copper sulphate solution is **ISC 2014**

   (a) 63.5 g (b) 31.8 g (c) 15.9 g (d) 15.5 g

6. The quantity of electricity required to deposit 1.15 g of sodium from molten NaCl (Na = 23, Cl = 35.5) is **ISC 2012**

   (a) 1F (b) 0.5 F (c) 0.05 F (d) 1.5 F

7. The number of Faraday's required to reduce one mole of Cu^{2+} to metallic copper is **ISC 2009**

   (a) one (b) two (c) three (d) four

8. Electrolysis follows ... . *ISC 2009*

9. The number of Faraday's which will be required to reduce 4 g equivalents of Cu^{2+} to Cu metal is *ISC 2005*

(a) 1 (b) 2

(c) 3 (d) 4

10. According to Faraday's law, one gram equivalent of ion is liberated by ... . *ISC 2002*

2 Marks Questions

11. When two Faradays of electricity is passed through an aqueous solution of $CuSO_4$ and an aqueous solution of $AgNO_3$.
(Atomic weight of $Cu = 63.5 \text{ g mol}^{-1}$, $Ag = 108 \text{ g mol}^{-1}$) *ISC Specimen 2021-22 (Sem-I)*

(i) The mass of copper deposited at the cathode is
(a) 127.02 g
(b) 63.50 g
(c) 31.75 g
(d) 15.87 g

(ii) The mass of silver deposited at the cathode is
(a) 54 g (b) 108 g
(c) 216 g (d) 270 g

12. Calculate the mass of silver deposited at cathode when a current of 2 amperes is passed through a solution of $AgNO_3$ for 15 min. *ISC 2019*
(At. wt. of Ag= 108, 1 F= 96500 C)

KEY IDEA

(i) First, find the amount of charge by using formula
$$q = i \times t$$
(ii) Then, find the mass of silver deposited using the formula,
$$m = Z \times Q = \frac{\text{Eq. weight}}{96500} \times Q$$

13. (i) State Faraday's first law of electrolysis.
(ii) How many electrons will flow when a current of 5 A is passed through a solution for 200 s? *ISC 2011*

14. A current of 10 A is passed for 80 min and 27 s through a cell containing dilute sulphuric acid.
(i) How many moles of oxygen gas will be liberated at the anode?
(ii) Calculate the amount of zinc deposited at the cathode when another cell containing $ZnSO_4$ solution is connected in series $(Zn = 65)$. *ISC 2007*

3 Marks Questions

15. 0.3605 g of a metal is deposited on the electrode by passing 1.2 A of current for 15 min through a salt solution. The atomic weight of the metal is 96. What is the valency of metal? *ISC 2014*

16. A current of 4 A is passed through a molten solution for 45 min 2.977 g of metal is deposited. Calculate the charge carried by the metal cation if its atomic mass is 106.4 g/mol. *ISC 2002*

Explanations

1. (a) 96500 C

2. Faraday's first law of electrolysis is confirmed from the given statement which states that 'the amount of substance deposited at a particular electrode as a result of electrolysis is directly proportional to the quantity of electricity passed'.

3. $Al^{3+} + 3e^- \longrightarrow Al$

For 27g (1 mol) of Al required $= 3 \times 96500$ C

$\therefore$ 1 g of Al required $= \frac{3 \times 96500}{27}$ C

$\therefore$ 5.4 g of Al required $= \frac{3 \times 96500}{27} \times 5.4 = 57900$ C

Thus, the number of coulombs required to deposit 5.4 g of Al is 57900 C.

4. Given, current = 2 A

Number of moles of iron = 3 mol

From number of moles, weight of iron $= 3 \times 55.8 = 168$ g

From Faraday's equation, $w = ZIt$

$$t = \frac{168 \times 96500}{56 \times 2 \times 3600} \Rightarrow t = 40.2 \text{ h}$$

5. (b) Given, weight of hydrogen deposited in 2 h = 0.50 g

Atomic weight of Cu = 63.5 g

Weight of Cu deposited in 2 h = ?

From Faraday's second law, 'the amount of substance obtained by the same quantity of electricity is directly proportional to their equivalent weights'.

Hence, $\frac{\text{Weight of hydrogen}}{\text{Weight of copper}}$

$= \frac{\text{Equivalent weight of hydrogen}}{\text{Equivalent weight of copper}}$

Let, w is the weight of Cu, then $\frac{0.5}{w} = \frac{1}{63.5}$

($\because$ equivalent weight of H = 1, equivalent weight of Cu = 63.5)

$$w = 63.5 \times 0.5 = 31.75 \approx 31.8 \text{ g}$$

Hence, option (b) is correct.

6. (c) Given, weight of Na = 1.15 g

In molten state, NaCl ionises as

$$\underset{\text{Molten}}{NaCl} \longrightarrow Na^+ + Cl^-$$

and $Na^+ + e^- \longrightarrow Na$

1 Faraday will deposit 1 mole of Na, i.e. 23 g.

$\because$ The quantity of electricity required to deposit 23 g of Na from NaCl = 1F

$\therefore$ 1.15 g of Na will be deposited by

$$\frac{1 \times 1.15}{23} \text{ F} = 0.05 \text{ F}$$

Hence, option (c) is correct.

7. (b) Number of electrons give the number of Faraday's required for the number of moles of that substance in the balanced equation.

$$Cu^{2+} + 2e^- \longrightarrow Cu$$

To reduce 1 mole of $Cu^{2+} \longrightarrow Cu$, we need 2 moles of e^-. Hence, 2F required. Thus, the option (b) is correct.

Concept Enhancer The product of electrolysis depend on the nature of material being electrolysed, type of electrodes being used, different oxidising and reducing species present in the electrolytic cell and overvoltage (kinetic barrier).

8. Electrolysis follows **Faraday's laws of electrolysis.**

9. (d) Given, $\underset{\text{4 g equivalents}}{Cu^{2+}} + 2e^- \longrightarrow Cu$

According to Faraday's first law of electrolysis, 1F is the electrical charge required to deposit one gram equivalent of substance.

$$\underset{\substack{\text{1 mol} \\ \text{4 g equivalents}}}{Cu^{2+}} + \underset{\substack{\text{2 mol of } e^- \\ \text{4 g equivalents}}}{2\ e^-} \longrightarrow \underset{\substack{\text{1 mol} \\ \text{4 g equivalents}}}{Cu}$$

(According to mole concept)

(According to law of equivalent)

Therefore, the number of Faraday's required to reduce 4 g equivalents of Cu^{2+} to Cu metal is 4.

Hence, option (d) is correct.

10. According to Faraday's first law of electrolysis, one Faraday is the quantity of electricity required to deposit one gram equivalent of any substance.

Thus, one gram equivalent of ion is liberated by 96500 C.

11. (i) (b) The reaction is $Cu^{2+} + 2e^- \longrightarrow Cu$.

2 moles of electrons react with 1 mole of Cu^{2+} to deposit 1 mole of Cu = 63.5 g of copper.

We know,

$\because$ 2 Faradays of electricity corresponds to 2 moles of electrons. Hence, they will deposit 63.5 g of Cu at cathode. **(1)**

(ii) (c) Reaction at cathode is $Ag^+ + e^- \longrightarrow Ag$

1 mole of election react with 1 mole of Ag^+ to deposit 1 mole of Ag = 108 g mol^{-1}.

We know,

$\because$ 2 Faradays of electricity corresponds to 2 moles of electrons.

So, 2 Faradays of electricity

$= 2 \times 1$ mole of Ag^+

$= 2 \times 1$ mole of Ag deposited at cathode

$= 2 \times 108$ g mol^{-1}

$= 216$ g mol^{-1} **(1)**

12. Given, current $(i) = 2$ amperes.

time $(t) = 15 \text{ min} = 15 \times 60 = 900$ s

$\therefore \quad Q = i \times t = 2 \times 900 = 1800$ C

and atomic mass of Ag = 108

$\because$ 96500 C deposit silver (Ag) = 108 g

$\therefore$ 1800 C deposit silver (Ag) $= \frac{108 \times 1800}{96500} = 2.01$ g

Hence, silver deposited = 2.01 g

Common Mistake One can mistake by taking the value of time in minutes without converting it into seconds.

13. (i) **Faraday's first law of electrolysis** The amount of chemical deposition at the respective electrodes (anode and cathode) from an electrolytic solution is directly proportional to the charge passed through the electrolytic solution.

$$w \propto Q$$

or $$w \propto it$$

or $$w = Zit$$

where, Z is a constant known as electrochemical equivalent of the given substance, i is current, t is time, w is the amount of substance and Q is charge. **(1)**

(ii) Given, current, $i = 5\text{A}$ and time, $t = 200\text{ s}$

Amount of charge,

$Q = it$ (from Faraday's first law)

$= 5 \times 200 = 1000\text{ C}$

$\because$ 96500 C of electric charge is carried by 6.0×10^{23} electrons.

$\therefore$ 1000 C of electric charge is carried by

$$= \frac{6.0 \times 10^{23}}{96500} \times 1000 \Rightarrow \frac{6000 \times 10^{23}}{96500}$$

$= 6.217 \times 10^{21}$ electrons **(1)**

14. (i) Given, current, $i = 10\text{ A}$

$t = 80\text{ min } 27\text{ s} = 80 \times 60 + 27\text{ s} = 4827\text{ s}$

Equivalent weight, E for oxygen $= 8$

$$\text{Weight of } O_2 \text{ liberated} = \frac{8 \times 10 \times 4827}{96500} = 4\text{ g}$$

$$\text{Moles of oxygen} = \frac{\text{Weight}}{\text{Molecular weight}}$$

(Molecular weight of $O_2 = 16 \times 2 = 32$)

$$= \frac{4}{32} = 0.125 \text{ moles of } O_2$$ **(1)**

(ii) **According to Faraday's second law of electrolysis**

When the same quantity of electricity is passed through the solutions of different electrolytes connected in series, the masses of the substances liberated (or deposited) at the electrodes are directly proportional to their equivalent masses.

$$\frac{\text{Mass of } O_2}{\text{Mass of Zn}} = \frac{\text{Equivalent weight of } O_2}{\text{Equivalent weight of Zn}}$$

Let x be the amount of Zn deposited

$\therefore \quad \dfrac{4}{x} = \dfrac{8}{65/2}$ (equivalent weight of Zn = 65 / 2)

$$x = 4 \times \frac{65}{2 \times 8} = 16.25\text{ g}$$ **(1)**

15. Given, amount of metal, $w = 0.3605\text{ g}$,

Current, $i = 1.2\text{ A}$, time, $t = 15\text{ min} = 15 \times 60\text{ s}$

$$0.3605 = \frac{E}{96500} \times 1.2 \times 15 \times 60$$

(where, E is equivalent weight of metal.)

$$E = \frac{0.3605 \times 96500}{1.2 \times 15 \times 60} = 32.211$$ **(1½)**

$E = 32.21$

$$\text{Equivalent weight} = \frac{\text{Atomic weight}}{\text{Valency}}$$

$$\text{Valency} = \frac{96}{32.21} = 2.98 \cong 3$$

(As atomic weight of metal is 96)

Hence, valency of metal $= 3$ **(1½)**

16. Given, current, $i = 4\text{ A}$,

time, $t = 45\text{ min} = 45 \times 60\text{ s}$,

weight of metal, $w = 2.977\text{ g}$

$$2.977 = \frac{E \times 4 \times 45 \times 60}{96500}$$

(where, E is equivalent weight of metal.)

$$E = \frac{96500 \times 2.977}{4 \times 45 \times 60}$$

$= 26.6$ g of metal **(1½)**

Equivalent weight of the metal = 26.60 g

$$\text{Equivalent weight} = \frac{\text{Atomic weight}}{\text{Valency}}$$

$$\text{Valency} = \frac{106.4}{26.6} = 4$$

Hence, valency of the element = 4.

The metal cation can be M^{4+}.

The charge of an electron is 1.6×10^{-19} C.

$$M^{4+} + 4e^- \longrightarrow M$$

Charge of 4 electrons $= 1.6 \times 10^{-19} \times 4$

(As $Q = ne^-$ where, n is the number of electrons) $= 6.4 \times 10^{-19}$ C **(1½)**

TOPIC 2

Electrochemical Cells, Galvanic Cell, Standard Hydrogen Electrode, Nernst Equation

Electrochemical Cells

An electrochemical cell is a device in which chemical energy of the redox reaction is converted into electrical energy while electrolytic cell do the reverse.

$$\text{Chemical energy} \underset{\text{Electrolytic cell}}{\overset{\text{Electrochemical cell}}{\rightleftharpoons}} \text{Electrical energy}$$

Note A chemical reaction in which electrons are lost by one substance and gained by another is called redox reaction. In redox reaction, transfer of electrons take place which generate electric current.

Galvanic Cell

The most common electrochemical cell is a galvanic cell or a voltaic cell, e.g. Daniell cell, an improvement of galvanic cell.

Representation of Galvanic Cell

While representing a galvanic cell, the oxidation electrode (anode) is always written at the left and the reduction electrode (cathode) always at the right. Direct contact of the two solutions (i.e. through a porous diaphragm) is shown by a single vertical line (|) while the contact of the two solutions through a salt-bridge is shown by two parallel vertical lines (||).

$$\underset{\text{Anode}}{Zn(s) \mid Zn^{2+}(aq,\ C_1)} \,||\, \underset{\text{Cathode}}{Cu^{2+}(aq,\ C_2) \mid Cu(s)}$$

$$\underset{\substack{\text{Oxidation electrode}\\ \text{Oxidation half-cell}}}{\text{Negative electrode }(-)} \xrightarrow{\text{Flow of electrons}} \underset{\substack{\text{Reduction electrode}\\ \text{Reduction half-cell}}}{\text{Positive electrode }(+)}$$

- Oxidation half-cell reaction,

$$Zn(s) \longrightarrow Zn^{2+}(aq) + 2e^-$$

- Reduction half-cell reaction,

$$Cu^{2+}(aq) + 2e^- \longrightarrow Cu(s)$$

Electrode Potential

The potential difference developed between a metal and a solution containing its own ions (in equilibrium) is called **electrode potential of that metal** or **electrode**. It is the tendency of an electrode to lose or gain electrons, when it is in contact with its own ions in a solution.

Factors Affecting the Magnitude of Electrode Potential

- Nature of metal or electrode.
- Concentration of metal ions in solution.
- Temperature

Measurement of Electrode Potential

In order to compute the emf of a cell, we have to apply the relationship

$$E_{cell} = E_{right} - E_{left}$$

However, individual cell emf cannot be measured. It is the potential difference between the two electrodes that is measurable in a circuit by a voltmeter.

Therefore, in order to measure the half-cell potential, the other half-cell in this set up has to be assigned an arbitrary value. This is done by assigning a potential of zero called a **Standard Hydrogen Electrode** (SHE).

The SHE is written as: $Pt(s) \mid H_2(g) \mid H^+(aq)$

in which the reaction occurs as

$$H^+(aq) + e^- \longrightarrow \frac{1}{2}H_2(g)$$

and is assigned a zero potential at all temperatures.

Limitation The hydrogen electrode is not a convenient reference electrode to use in measurements because maintaining a stream of hydrogen at 1 atm takes careful management. It is usual to employ a secondary standard such as the saturated calomel electrode.

Standard Electrode Potential (E°)

The potential difference between the standard hydrogen half-cell and the half-cell placed in contact with SHE is called standard electrode potential, provided all dissolved species at unit molarity; all gases at one atmospheric pressure, all solids in their most stable form and temperature is maintained at 25°C.

Note The oxidation potential and reduction potential of a given electrode is related by

Oxidation electrode potential (E_{ox}) = − Reduction electrode potential (E_{red})

EMF of an Electrochemical Cell

The difference between the electrode potentials of two half-cells is known as cell potential or cell voltage.

If no current is drawn from the cell, it is called electromotive force (emf) of the cell.

$$E^\circ_{cell} = E^\circ_{cathode} - E^\circ_{anode} = (E^\circ_{red})_{cathode} - (E^\circ_{red})_{anode}$$

Electrochemical Series

The arrangement of various electrode systems in the increasing order of their standard reduction potential values is called electrochemical series.

The standard electrode potentials at 298 K
(Electrochemical series)

(Increasing strength of oxidising agent ↑; Increasing strength of reducing agent ↓)

Reaction (oxidised form + ne^-	$\longrightarrow$ reduced form)	$E^\ominus$ / V
$F_2(g) + 2e^-$	$\longrightarrow 2F^-$	2.87
$Co^{3+} + e^-$	$\longrightarrow Co^{2+}$	1.81
$H_2O_2 + 2H^+ + 2e^-$	$\longrightarrow 2H_2O$	1.78
$MnO_4^- + 8H^+ + 5e^-$	$\longrightarrow Mn^{2+} + 4H_2O$	1.51
$Au^{3+} + 3e^-$	$\longrightarrow Au(s)$	1.40
$Cl_2(g) + 2e^-$	$\longrightarrow 2Cl^-$	1.36
$Cr_2O_7^{2-} + 14H^+ + 6e^-$	$\longrightarrow 2Cr^{3+} + 7H_2O$	1.33
$O_2(g) + 4H^+ + 4e^-$	$\longrightarrow 2H_2O$	1.23
$MnO_2(s) + 4H^+ + 2e^-$	$\longrightarrow Mn^{2+} + 2H_2O$	1.23
$Br_2 + 2e^-$	$\longrightarrow 2Br^-$	1.09
$NO_3^- + 4H^+ + 3e^-$	$\longrightarrow NO(g) + 2H_2O$	0.97
$2Hg^{2+} + 2e^-$	$\longrightarrow Hg_2^{2+}$	0.92
$Ag^+ + e^-$	$\longrightarrow Ag(s)$	0.80
$Fe^{3+} + e^-$	$\longrightarrow Fe^{2+}$	0.77
$O_2(g) + 2H^+ + 2e^-$	$\longrightarrow H_2O_2$	0.68
$I_2 + 2e^-$	$\longrightarrow 2I^-$	0.54
$Cu^+ + e^-$	$\longrightarrow Cu(s)$	0.52
$Cu^{2+} + 2e^-$	$\longrightarrow Cu(s)$	0.34
$AgCl(s) + e^-$	$\longrightarrow Ag(s) + Cl^-$	0.22
$AgBr(s) + e^-$	$\longrightarrow Ag(s) + Br^-$	0.10
$2H^+ + 2e^-$	$\longrightarrow H_2(g)$	0.00
$Pb^{2+} + 2e^-$	$\longrightarrow Pb(s)$	−0.13
$Sn^{2+} + 2e^-$	$\longrightarrow Sn(s)$	−0.14
$Ni^{2+} + 2e^-$	$\longrightarrow Ni(s)$	−0.25
$Fe^{2+} + 2e^-$	$\longrightarrow Fe(s)$	−0.44
$Cr^{3+} + 3e^-$	$\longrightarrow Cr(s)$	−0.74
$Zn^{2+} + 2e^-$	$\longrightarrow Zn(s)$	−0.76
$2H_2O + 2e^-$	$\longrightarrow H_2(g) + 2OH^-(aq)$	−0.83
$Al^{3+} + 3e^-$	$\longrightarrow Al(s)$	−1.66
$Mg^{2+} + 2e^-$	$\longrightarrow Mg(s)$	−2.36
$Na^+ + e^-$	$\longrightarrow Na(s)$	−2.71
$Ca^{2+} + 2e^-$	$\longrightarrow Ca(s)$	−2.87
$K^+ + e^-$	$\longrightarrow K(s)$	−2.93
$Li^+ + e^-$	$\longrightarrow Li(s)$	−3.05

Note
- Negative E° means, the redox couple is stronger reducing agent than H^+ / H_2, e.g. Zn (−0.76).
- Positive E° means, the redox couple is a weaker reducing agent than H^+ / H_2, e.g. Ag (+ 0.80).

Important Features of Electrochemical Series

- The electrode having negative value of standard reduction potential acts as anode while that having positive value acts as cathode, when connected to a SHE.
- On moving from top to bottom in the series, tendency to gain electrons (reduction) increases and *vice-versa* occur from bottom to top.

Applications of Electrochemical Series

(i) **Feasibility of a redox reaction** A redox reaction is feasible when the substance having higher reduction potential gets reduced and the one having lower reduction potential gets oxidised. If E°_{cell} value is positive, then the reaction is feasible. In case, the value of E°_{cell} is negative, the reaction is not feasible. When E°_{cell} is zero, the reaction is in equilibrium.

(ii) **Reactivity of metals** In electrochemical series, the tendency of the substances to get oxidised decreases from top to bottom, thus the reactivity of the metals decreases in going down the series.

(iii) **Displacement of metals from salt solution** A metal can displace the other metal placed below it in the series from the salt solution of the latter.

(iv) **Displacement of hydrogen by metals from dilute acids** Any metal placed above hydrogen in the electrochemical series can displace H_2 from a dilute acid.

Nernst Equation

This equation gives the relation between electrode potential, temperature and concentration of metal ions. For an electrode involving the process of reduction, Nernst equation can be written as follows

$$M^{n+}(aq) + ne^- \longrightarrow M(s)$$

$$E_{M^{n+}/M} = E^\circ_{M^{n+}/M} - \frac{2.303\,RT}{nF}\log\frac{[M(s)]}{[M^{n+}(aq)]}$$

or

$$E_{cell} = E^\circ_{cell} - \frac{2.303RT}{nF}\log\frac{[M(s)]}{[M^{n+}(aq)]}$$

For emf of cell under standard conditions,

$$E_{cell} = E^{\circ}_{cell} - \frac{0.05912}{n} \log \frac{1}{(\text{Concentration of reactant } [M^{n+}])} [M(s) = 1]$$

Electrochemical Cell and Gibbs Energy of the Reaction

Let nF is the amount of charge passed, E is the emf of the cell and $\Delta_r G$ is the Gibbs energy of the reaction

$$\Delta_r G = -nFE_{cell}$$

Under standard conditions,

$$\Delta_r G^{\circ} = -nFE^{\circ}_{cell}$$

or $$\Delta_r G^{\circ} = -RT \ln K_C = -2.303RT \log K_C.$$

Additional Notes

At the stage of chemical equilibrium in the cell,

$$E_{cell} = 0$$

$$\Delta_r G = -nFE_{cell} = -nF \times 0 = 0$$

The reaction is feasible only, when E_{cell} = positive

or $\Delta_r G$ = negative.

PYQs Previous Years' Questions

1 Mark Questions

1. A potassium iodide (KI) solution containing starch turns blue on the addition of chlorine. Which one of the following statements explain this? ***ISC Specimen 2024***
   (P) The reduction potential of Cl_2 is more than that of I_2.
   (Q) The oxidation potential of Cl_2 is more than that of I_2.
   (R) The product formed when Cl_2 combines with starch is blue.
   (S) The product formed when I_2 combines with starch is blue.
   (a) Only P and R (b) Only Q and R
   (c) Only Q and S (d) Only P and S

2. Which one of the following statements is true for the Galvanic cell? ***ISC 2023***
   (a) Electrons flow from copper electrode to zinc electrode.
   (b) Current flows from zinc electrode to copper electrode.
   (c) Cations move towards copper electrode.
   (d) Cations move towards zinc electrode.

   Or

   Which of the following statement is true for electrochemical cell? ***ISC 2021-22 (Sem-I)***
   (a) Cations move towards zinc electrode
   (b) Cations move towards copper electrode
   (c) Current flows from zinc electrode to copper electrode
   (d) Electrons flow from copper electrode to zinc electrode

3. **Assertion** (A) If a solution contains both H^+ and Na^+ ions, the H^+ ions are reduced first at cathode.
   Reason (R) Cations with higher E° value are reduced first at cathode. ***ISC 2023***
   (a) Both (A) and (R) are correct and (R) is the correct explanation for (A).
   (b) Both (A) and (R) are correct but (R) is not the correct explanation for (A).
   (c) (A) is correct but (R) is incorrect.
   (d) (A) is incorrect but (R) is correct.

4. For a spontaneous reaction E°_{cell} and ΔG° will be respectively ***ISC Specimen 2023, Specimen 2021-22 (Sem-I), 2017***
   (a) – ve and – ve (b) – ve and + ve
   (c) + ve and – ve (d) + ve and + ve

5. The standard reduction electrode potential of Cu^{2+}/Cu is +0.34 V and that of Cr^{3+}/Cr is – 0.74 V. These two electrodes are connected in their standard state to make an electrochemical cell. What will be the standard electrode potential (E°) of this cell ? ***ISC 2021-22 (Sem-I)***
   (a) 1.19 V (b) 1.08 V (c) 0.69 V (d) 1.83 V

6. The standard reduction potential values of three metallic cations X, Y and Z are 0.52 V, – 3.03 V and – 1.18 V respectively.
   The order of reducing power of the corresponding metals is ***ISC Specimen 2021-22 (Sem-I)***
   (a) $Y > Z > X$ (b) $X > Y > Z$
   (c) $Z > Y > X$ (d) $Z > X > Y$

7. When zinc granule is dipped into copper sulphate solution, copper is precipitated because **ISC Specimen 2021-22 (Sem-I), 2011**
   (a) both copper and zinc have a positive reduction potential.
   (b) both copper and zinc have a negative reduction potential.
   (c) reduction potential of zinc is higher than that of copper.
   (d) reduction potential of copper is higher than that of zinc.

8. The cell reaction is spontaneous or feasible when emf of the cell is **ISC 2019**
   (a) negative
   (b) positive
   (c) zero
   (d) either positive or negative

9. A galvanic cell converts ...... energy into ...... energy. (electrical/chemical) **ISC 2018**

10. What happens when a nickel rod is dipped into a copper sulphate solution? Justify your answer.
   ($E^\circ_{Ni^{2+}/Ni} = -0.25V$ and $E^\circ_{Cu^{2+}/Cu} = +0.34V$). **ISC 2014**

   Or

   Will nickel displace copper from a 1 M solution of copper sulphate? Justify your answer.
   ($E^\circ_{Ni^{2+}/Ni} = -0.25$ V, $E^\circ_{Cu^{2+}/Cu} = +0.34$ V) **ISC 2010**

11. What is standard hydrogen electrode? **ISC 2014**

12. Two metallic elements A and B have the following standard potentials:
   $A = 0.40V$, $B = 0.80V$, what would you expect if element A was added to an aqueous salt solution of element B? Give a reason for your answer. **ISC 2013**

13. Arrange Ag, Cr and Hg metals in the increasing order of reducing power.
   Given: $E^\circ_{Ag^+/Ag} = +0.80$ V, $E^\circ_{Cr^{3+}/Cr} = -0.74$ V
   $E^\circ_{Hg^{2+}/Hg} = +0.79$ V **ISC 2013**

14. In galvanic cell, electrons flow from ...... to ...... through the connecting wires. **ISC 2013**

15. Nernst equation is used for ...... cell. **ISC 2012**

16. The reduction potential of a metal X is -0.76 V while that of Y is -2.38 V. Which of the two metals is a stronger reducing agent? Give a reason for your answer. **ISC 2010**

17. The standard electrode potentials of four elements A, B, C and D are -3.05, 1.66, -0.40 and 0.80 V, respectively. The highest chemical activity will be shown by **ISC 2006**
   (a) A (b) B (c) C (d) D

18. Copper displaces ...... from its solution because it has a ...... reduction potential. **ISC 2002**

19. Correct the following statement. Copper displaces both zinc and silver from their solutions. **ISC 2000**

2 Marks Questions

20. Calculate the maximum possible electrical work that can be obtained from a galvanic cell under standard conditions at 298 K **ISC 2024**

$$\underset{}{Zn}\,|\underset{(aq)}{Zn^{2+}}||\underset{(aq)}{Ag^{+}}|\,Ag$$

   Given $E^\circ_{(Zn^{2+}/Zn)} = -0.76$ V; $E^\circ_{Ag^+/Ag} = +0.80$ V

21. (i) A rusted piece of iron undergoes electrochemical reactions. Write the chemical reaction taking place at: **ISC Specimen 2024**
   (a) the electrode that behaves as an anode.
   (b) the electrode that behaves as a cathode.
   (ii) Given that the standard reduction potential for $Al^{3+}/Al = -1.66$ V and $\frac{1}{2}I_2/I^- = 0.54$ V, what will be the standard potential of the cell made by using Al^{3+} and I^-?

22. Calculate the emf of the following cell at 298 K. **ISC 2023**

$$Cu|Cu^{2+}(0.025\text{ M})||Ag^+(0.005\text{ M})|Ag$$

   Given : $E^\circ_{Cu^{2+}/Cu} = 0.34$ V, $E^\circ_{Ag^+/Ag} = 0.80$ V.
   1 Faraday = 96500 C mol^{-1}

23. Calculate the standard free energy change (ΔG°) for the following chemical reaction. **ISC Specimen 2023**

$$Cd(s) + 2Ag^+ \longrightarrow Cd^{2+} + 2Ag(s)$$

$$E^\circ_{Cd^{2+}/Cd} = -0.40\text{ V}, E^\circ_{Ag^+/Ag} = +0.80\text{ V}$$

24. The standard reduction electrode potential for Sn^{4+}/Sn^{2+} couple is $+0.15$ V and that for the Cr^{3+}/Cr couple is -0.74 V. These two couples in their standard state are connected to make a cell (1 Faraday = 96500 C mol^{-1}). **ISC 2021-22 (Sem-I)**
   (i) What will be the value of E°_{cell}?
   (a) + 1.19 V (b) + 0.89 V
   (c) + 0.18 V (d) + 1.83 V

(ii) What will be the value of standard Gibbs energy ($\Delta G°$)?

(a) – 650.3 kJ (b) – 515.3 kJ
(c) – 226.4 kJ (d) – 406.8 kJ

25. The standard electrode potential for the reaction is **ISC Specimen 2021-22 (Sem-I)**

I. $Ag^+ + e^- \longrightarrow Ag(s)$; $E°_{Ag^+/Ag} = +0.80$ V

II. $Sn^{2+} + 2e^- \longrightarrow Sn(s)$; $E°_{Sn^{2+}/Sn} = -0.14$ V

(i) The $E°_{cell}$ will be

(a) 0.66 V (b) 0.88 V
(c) 0.94 V (d) 1.08 V

(ii) The value of standard Gibbs energy ($\Delta G°$) will be ($F = 96{,}000$ C mol^{-1})

(a) –181.42 kJ (b) –90.71 kJ
(c) –45.36 kJ (d) –22.68 kJ

26. What is an electrochemical series? How is it useful in predicting whether a metal can liberate hydrogen from acid or not? **ISC 2018**

27. Calculate the emf of the following cell reaction at 298 K:

$Mg(g) + Cu^{2+}(0.0001\,M) \longrightarrow Mg^{2+}(0.001\,M) + Cu(s)$

The standard potential ($E°$) of the cell is 2.71 V. **ISC 2015**

28. Mention any two factors affecting the electrode potential of a metal. **ISC 2009**

29. Calculate E_{cell} at 25°C for the reaction,

$Zn + Cu^{2+}(0.20\,M) \longrightarrow Zn^{2+}(0.50\,M) + Cu$

Given : $E°_{(Zn^{2+}/Zn)} = -0.76$ V; $E°_{(Cu^{2+}/Cu)} = 0.34$ V **ISC 2007**

3 Marks Questions

30. Calculate the emf and ΔG for the given cell at 25°C.

$Cr(s)|Cr^{3+}(0.1\,M)||Fe^{2+}(0.01M)|Fe(s)$ **ISC 2020**

Given, $E°_{Cr^{3+}/Cr} = -0.74$ V, $E°_{Fe^{2+}/Fe} = -0.44$ V

($1\,F = 96500$ C, $R = 8.314$ JK^{-1} mol^{-1})

31. Calculate the emf and ΔG for the cell reaction at 298 K. **ISC 2019**

$Mg(s)\,|\,Mg^{2+}(0.1M)\,||\,Cu^{2+}(0.01M)|\,Cu(s)$

Given, $E°_{cell} = 2.71$ V, $1F = 96500$ C

KEY IDEA

First, find the number of electrons (n) taking part in the reaction then calculate the $\Delta G°$ and E_{cell} by using formula, $\Delta G° = -nFE°_{cell}$ and Nernst equation respectively.

32. Calculate the emf and $\Delta G°$ for the cell reaction at 25°C. **ISC 2018**

$Zn(s)|\underset{(0.1\,M)}{Zn^{2+}(aq)^{2+}}||\underset{(0.01\,M)}{Cd^{2+}(aq)}|Cd(s)$

Given, $E°_{Zn^{2+}/Zn} = -0.763$ and $E°_{Cd^{2+}/Cd} = -0.403$V

33. For the cell, $Zn\,|\,Zn^{2+}(\alpha = 1)\,||\,Cu^{2+}(\alpha = 1)\,|Cu$

Given that, $E°_{Zn^{2+}/Zn} = -0.76$ V, $E°_{Cu^{2+}/Cu} = +0.339$ V

(i) Write the cell reaction.

(ii) Calculate the emf and free energy change at 298 K involved in the cell.

(Faraday's constant equivalent^{-1}) **ISC 2017, 2005**

34. Calculate the value of E_{cell} at 298 K for the following cell : $Al\,|\,Al^{3+}(0.01\,M)||\,Sn^{2+}(0.015\,M)\,|\,Sn$

Given: $E°_{Al^{3+}/Al} = -1.66$ V and $E°_{Sn^{2+}/Sn} = -0.14$ V **ISC 2013**

KEY IDEA

Write half-cell equations to calculate

$$E°_{cell} = E°_{cathode} - E°_{anode}$$

Then, calculate the number of electrons taking part in reaction to calculate E_{cell} by using Nernst equation.

i.e. $$E_{cell} = E°_{cell} - \frac{0.059}{n}\log_{10}\frac{[\text{Product}]}{[\text{Reactant}]}$$

35. Calculate the maximum work that can be obtained from the given electrochemical cell constructed with two metals M and N.

($E°_{M^{2+}/M} = -0.76$ V, $E°_{N^{2+}/N} = +0.34$ V)

The cell reaction is $M + N^{2+} \longrightarrow M^{2+} + N$ **ISC 2012**

36. For the following cell, calculate the emf.

$Al\,|\,Al^{3+}(0.01\,M)\,||\,Fe^{2+}(0.02M)\,|\,Fe$

Given: $E°_{Al^{3+}/Al} = -1.66$ V, $E°_{Fe^{2+}/Fe} = -0.44$ V **ISC 2009**

37. A cell is constructed by dipping a zinc rod in 0.1 M zinc nitrate solution and a lead rod in a 0.2 M lead nitrate solution.

$E°_{Pb^{2+}/Pb} = -0.13$ V and $E°_{Zn^{2+}/Zn} = -0.76$ V

(i) Write the spontaneous cell reaction.

(ii) Calculate standard emf and emf of the cell. **ISC 2004**

4 Marks Questions

38. Consider the reaction, $2Ag^+ + Cd \longrightarrow 2Ag + Cd^{2+}$

The standard reduction of Ag^+/Ag and Cd^{2+}/Cd are + 0.80 V and – 0.40 V respectively.

(i) Give the cell representation.
(ii) What is the standard cell emf, E°?
(iii) What will be the emf of the cell if concentration of Cd^{2+} is 0.1 M and Ag^+ is 0.2 M?
(iv) Will the cell work spontaneously for the condition shown in (iii) above? **ISC 2016, 2011**

39. For the cell, $Cu|Cu^{2+}(0.13\text{ M})||Ag^+(0.01\text{ M})|Ag$

(i) Calculate the reduction potential of each electrode if the standard reduction potential for copper and silver electrodes are 0.34 V and 0.80 V respectively.
(ii) Calculate the emf of the cell.
(iii) Write the cell reaction.
(iv) Is this cell reaction spontaneous? Why? **ISC 2001**

5 Marks Questions

40. (i) Study the diagram given below that represents Cu-Ag electrochemical cell and answer the questions that follow. **ISC 2024**

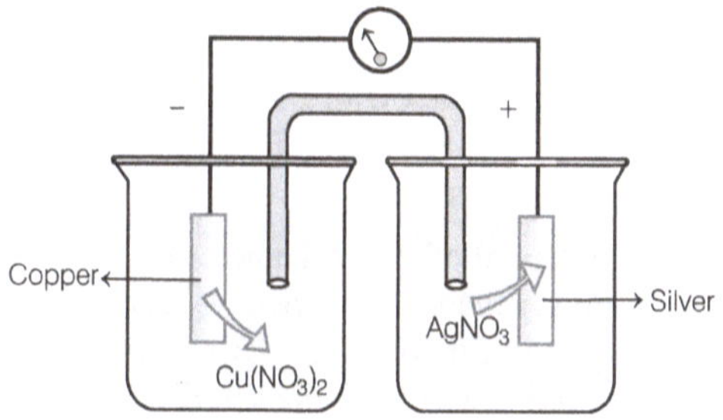

Given, $E^\circ_{(Cu^{2+}/Cu)} = 0.337\text{ V}$; $E^\circ_{(Ag^+/Ag)} = 0.799\text{ V}$

(a) Write the cell reaction for the above cell.
(b) Calculate the standard emf of the cell.
(c) It the concentration of $[Cu^{2+}]$ is 0.1 M and E_{cell} is 0.422 V, at 25°C, calculate the concentration of $[Ag^+]$.
(d) Calculate ΔG for the cell.

(ii) Calculate Λ°_m for $BaCl_2$ and $Al_2(SO_4)_3$ from the following data.

For $\Lambda^\circ_m\ Ba^{2+} = 127.2\text{ S cm}^2\text{ mol}^{-1}$,
$\Lambda^\circ_m Al^{3+} = 189\text{ S cm}^2\text{ mol}^{-1}$
$\Lambda^\circ_m Cl^- = 76.3\text{ S cm}^2\text{ mol}^{-1}$,
$\Lambda^\circ_m\ SO_4^{2-} = 160\text{ S cm}^2\text{ mol}^{-1}$

41. (i) Calculate the value of E° cell and ΔG° that can be obtained from the following cell under the standard conditions at 25°C **ISC Specimen 2024**

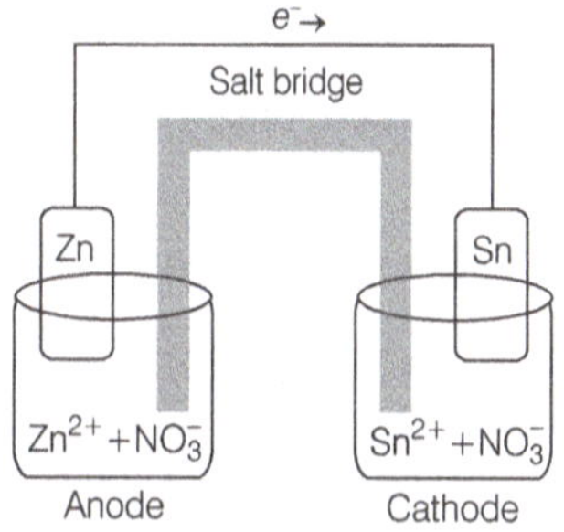

Given $E^\circ_{Zn^{2+}/Zn} = -0.76\text{ V}$;
$E^\circ_{Sn^{2+}/Sn} = -0.14\text{ V}$

1 Faraday = 96500 C mol^{-1}

(ii) How much electricity in Faraday is required for the complete reduction of MnO_4^- ions present in 500 mL of 0.5 M solution to Mn^{2+}?

42. (i) Calculate emf of the following cell at 298 K.

$Mg(s)|Mg^{2+}(0.1\text{ M})||Cu^{2+}(0.01\text{ M})|Cu(s)$

[Given : $E^\circ_{cell} = +2.71\text{ V}$, 1 Faraday $= 96500\text{ C mol}^{-1}$] **ISC Specimen 2018**

(ii) State Faraday's first law of electrolysis. Calculate the charge required in terms of Faraday for the reduction of 1 mole of Cu^{2+} to Cu.

Explanations

1. (c) Chlorine is placed below iodine in electrochemical series, so Cl_2 undergoes reduction and I^- undergoes oxidation.

$$2I^- \longrightarrow I_2 + 2e^-$$
$$Cl_2 + 2e^- \longrightarrow 2Cl^-$$
$$Cl_2 + 2I^- \longrightarrow I_2 + 2Cl^-$$

So, iodine absorbed in reaction which changes the starch colour changes to blue.

2. (c) In Galvanic cell, cations move towards Cu electrode (cathode) and accumulated as Cu metal.

Or

(b) Refer to sol. 2.

3. (a) Both (A) and (R) are correct and (R) is the correct explanation for (A).

When a solution contain both H^+ and Na^+ ions H^+ ions are reduced first because $E°$ for hydrogen is 0V which is higher than $E^\circ_{(Na^+)} = -2.71$ V.

4. (c) For a spontaneous reaction, E°_{cell} and ΔG° will be positive and negative respectively.

5. (b) At cathode,

$$Cu^{2+} + 2e^- \longrightarrow Cu, \quad E^\circ_{cell} = 0.34 \text{ V}$$

At anode, $$Cr \longrightarrow Cr^{3+} + 3e^-, \; E^\circ_{cell} = -0.74 \text{ V}$$

$$E^\circ_{cell} = E^\circ_{cathode} - E^\circ_{anode}$$
$$= 0.34 - (-0.74)$$
$$= 1.08 \text{ V}$$

6. (a) $Y > Z > X$.
More negative is the reduction potential more is its reducing power.

7. (d) $Zn + CuSO_4 \longrightarrow ZnSO_4 + \underset{ppt.}{Cu\downarrow}$

Zn reducing the Cu due to its high reduction potential than Cu.

8. (b) Free energy, i.e. $\Delta G°$ must be negative for a cell reaction to be spontaneous or feasible and

$$\Delta G° = -nFE^\circ_{cell} = (-) \text{ ve}$$

where, n = number of electrons
F = charge in Faraday
$E°$ = emf of the cell

Therefore, E°_{cell}, i.e. emf of the cell must be positive and (b) is the correct option.

9. chemical, electrical

10. Since, the standard electrode potential of Ni is less than that of Cu and possesses greater reducing power. So, nickel can displace copper from copper sulphate solution.

$$Cu^{2+}(aq) + Ni(s) \longrightarrow Ni^{2+}(aq) + Cu(s)$$

Or

Since, $E^\circ_{Ni^{2+}/Ni}$ (−0.25 V) < $E^\circ_{Cu^{2+}/Cu}$ (+0.34 V) therefore, Ni possesses a greater reducing power. Hence, Ni displaces Cu from $CuSO_4$ solution.

11. Standard Hydrogen Electrode (SHE) is an electrode in which H_2 gas at one atmospheric pressure is passed through a solution of H^+ ions of 1 M concentration at 25°C placed in contact with Pt foil. This electrode is also called Normal Hydrogen Electrode (NHE). Its potential is taken as zero.

12. Standard potential of $A < B$. Hence, A has more reducing power than B. So, when A is added to an aqueous salt solution of B, then B will form precipitate and A will form the salt displacing B from its solution.

13. Since, the standard potential values are in the order of

$$E^\circ_{Cr^{3+}/Cr}(-0.74 \text{ V}) < E^\circ_{Hg^{2+}/Hg}(0.79 \text{ V}) < E^\circ_{Ag^+/Ag}(0.80 \text{ V})$$

i.e. arranged in the increasing order to gain electrons. To lose electron or to act as reducing agent, the order will be reverse,

i.e. $$E^\circ_{Ag^+/Ag} < E^\circ_{Hg^{2+}/Hg} < E^\circ_{Cr^{3+}/Cr}$$

Concept Enhancer More the negative value of reducing potential, more is the tendency to get oxidised.

14. In galvanic cell, electrons flow from anode to cathode through the connecting wires.

15. Nernst equation is used for electrochemical cell.

16. Reduction potential of $X(-0.76 \text{ V}) > Y(-2.38 \text{ V})$. Strong reducing agents have a large negative value. Hence, metal Y is a stronger reducing agent than metal X.

17. (a) Element with large negative electrode potential acts as strong reducing agent and thus, possesses large chemical reactivity.

Hence, (*A*) shows highest chemical activity among the given options.

18. Copper displaces silver from its solution because it has a lower reduction potential.

19. Zinc displaces both **copper** and **silver** from their solutions.

Or **Copper** displaces **only** silver from the solution not zinc.

The reduction potential of three elements is in the order Zn< Cu< Ag. Hence, zinc is more reactive.

20. Given, $E^\circ_{(Zn^{2+}/Zn)} = -0.76$ V

$$E^\circ_{(Ag^+/Ag)} = 0.80 \text{ V}$$

$$E^\circ_{cell} = 0.8 - (-0.76) = 1.56 \text{ V}$$

$$W_{electrical} = -nFE^\circ_{cell}$$

$$= -2 \times 96500 \times [1.56]$$

$$= -301,080 \text{ J} = -301.1 \text{ kJ}$$

21. (i) In corrosion of iron, the reactions that take place at the cathode and anode are

(a) At anode,

$$2Fe(s) \longrightarrow 2Fe^{2+} + 4e^-$$

(b) At cathode,

$$O_2 + 4H^+ + 4e^- \longrightarrow 2H_2O(l)$$

(ii) At anode,

$$Al \longrightarrow Al^{3+} + 3e^- ; E^\circ_{Al^{3+}/Al} = -1.66 \text{ V}$$

At cathode,

$$I_2(s) + 2e^- \longrightarrow 2I^- ; E^\circ_{I_2/I^-} = 0.54 \text{ V}$$

$$E^\circ_{cell} = E^\circ_{cathode} - E^\circ_{anode} = 0.54 + 1.66$$

$$E^\circ_{cell} = -2.2 \text{ V}$$

22. At cathode,

$$[Ag^+ + e^- \longrightarrow Ag] \times 2; E^\circ_{Ag^+/Ag} = 0.80 \text{ V} \quad \ldots \text{(i)}$$

At anode,

$$Cu \longrightarrow Cu^{2+} + 2e; E^\circ_{Cu/Cu^{2+}} = -0.34 \text{ V} \ldots \text{(ii)}$$

Overall equation,

$$2Ag^+ + Cu \longrightarrow Cu^{2+} + 2Ag$$

$$E^\circ_{cell} = E^\circ_{cathode} - E^\circ_{anode}$$

$$= 0.80 - 0.34 = 0.46 \text{ V}$$

Applying Nernst equation,

$$E = E^\circ - \frac{0.0591}{n} \log \frac{[Cu^{2+}][Ag]^2}{[Ag^+]^2[Cu]}$$

$$= E^\circ - \frac{0.0591}{n} \log \frac{[Cu^{2+}]}{[Ag^+]^2}$$

$$= 0.46 - \frac{0.0591}{2} \log \frac{0.025}{[0.005]^2}$$

$$= 0.46 - 0.0885 = 0.3715 \text{ V} \quad \textbf{(2)}$$

Concept Enhancer The value of E°_{cell} of a half-cell reaction does not depend on stoichiometric coefficient of reactant or product.

23. The standard Gibbs energy is given by formula

$$\Delta G = -nFE^\circ_{cell}$$

where, n = no. of electrons lost of gained

F = Faraday's constant = 96500 C

$E°$ = EMF of cell

At cathode, $2Ag^+ + 2e^- \longrightarrow 2Ag$

At anode, $Cd \longrightarrow Cd^{2+} + 2e^-$

$$E^\circ_{cell} = E^\circ_{cathode} - E^\circ_{anode}$$

$$= 0.80 - (-0.40) = 1.20$$

According to reaction given the change in oxidation state (n) = 2

$$\Delta G = -2 \times 96500 (1.20)$$

$$= -231600 \text{ J} = -231.6 \text{ kJ} \quad \textbf{(2)}$$

24. At cathode, $(Sn^{4+} + 2e^- \longrightarrow Sn^{2+}) \times 3$

At anode, $(Cr \longrightarrow Cr^{3+} + 3e^-) \times 2$

Hence, $n = 6$

(i) (b) $E^\circ_{cell} = E^\circ_{cathode} - E^\circ_{anode}$

$$= 0.15 - (-0.74) = 0.89 \text{ V} \quad \textbf{(1)}$$

(ii) (b) $\Delta G° = -nFE^\circ_{cell}$

$$= -6 \times 96500 \times 0.89 = -515.3 \text{ kJ}$$

Hence, option (b) is correct. **(1)**

Concept Enhancer If two half reactions having potential E°_1 and E°_2 are combined to give a third-half reaction having a potential E°_3, then $\Delta G^\circ_3 = \Delta G^\circ_1 + \Delta G^\circ_2$

or $$E^\circ_3 = \frac{n_1E^\circ_1 + n_2E^\circ_2}{n_3}$$

25. (i) At anode, $Sn \longrightarrow Sn^{2+} + 2e^-$

At cathode, $\dfrac{[Ag^+ + e^- \longrightarrow Ag] \times 2}{Sn + 2Ag^+ \longrightarrow Sn^{2+} + 2Ag}$

So, $n = 2$

$$E^\circ_{cell} = E^\circ_{cathode} - E^\circ_{anode}$$
$$= -0.80 - (-0.14)$$
$$E^\circ_{cell} = 0.94 V \quad \textbf{(1)}$$

(ii) $\Delta G^\circ = -nFE^\circ_{cell}$
$$= -2 \times 96500 \times 0.94$$
$$= 181420 \text{ J}$$
$$= -181.42 \text{ kJ} \quad \textbf{(1)}$$

26. The arrangement of various standard half-cells in the order of their decreasing values of standard reduction potentials is called **electrochemical series**. **(1)**

In the electrochemical series, metals that are placed above hydrogen are reactive metals and these reacts with acids like HCl (dil.), H_2SO_4 (dil.) to produce salt and hydrogen gas and have, placed below hydrogen.

Metal + Dil. acid $\longrightarrow$ Salt + Hydrogen

e.g. $\underset{\text{Zinc}}{Zn(s)} + \underset{\text{(Dil.)}}{2HCl(aq)} \longrightarrow \underset{\text{Zinc chloride}}{ZnCl_2(aq)} + \underset{\text{Hydrogen gas}}{H_2(g)\uparrow}$ **(1)**

27. $Mg(g) + Cu^{2+}(0.0001M) \longrightarrow Mg^{2+}(0.001M) + Cu(s)$

Standard electrode potential = 2.71 V

$$E = E^\circ_{cell} - \frac{0.0591}{n} \log \frac{[Mg^{2+}]}{[Cu^{2+}]}$$
$$E = 2.71 - \frac{0.0591}{2} \log \frac{0.001}{0.0001}$$
$$= 2.71 - \frac{0.0591}{2} \log 10$$
$$E = 2.71 - 0.02955 = 2.68 \text{ V} \quad \textbf{(2)}$$

28. Two factors affecting electrode potential of a metal are as follows

(i) **Position of the metal in electrochemical series** More reactive the metal, greater is the tendency to lose electrons and hence, lower is the value of reduction potential of the metal. Thus, act as a strong reducing agent. **(1)**

(ii) **Concentration of metal ions in the solution** Dependence of the electrode potential of a metal on concentration of the electrolyte is given by Nernst equation.

For the electrode reaction,

$$M^{n+}(aq) + ne^- \longrightarrow M(s)$$
$$E_{M^{n+}/M} = E^\circ_{M^{n+}/M} + \frac{RT}{nF} \log_e \frac{[M^{n+}(aq)]}{[M(s)]} \quad \textbf{(1)}$$

29. Given, $Zn + \underset{(0.20M)}{Cu^{2+}} \longrightarrow \underset{(0.50M)}{Zn^{2+}} + Cu$

$$Zn \longrightarrow Zn^{2+} + 2e^-; \ (E^\circ_{Zn^{2+}/Zn}) = -0.76 \text{ V}$$
$$Cu^{2+} + 2e^- \longrightarrow Cu; \ (E^\circ_{Cu^{2+}/Cu}) = 0.34 \text{ V}$$

Hence, $n = 2$

$$E^\circ_{cell} = E^\circ_{cathode} - E^\circ_{anode}$$
$$= 0.34 - (-0.76) = 1.10 \text{ V}$$
$$E_{cell} = E^\circ_{cell} - \frac{0.059}{n} \log_{10} \frac{[Zn^{2+}]}{[Cu^{2+}]}$$

Putting values in Nernst equation,

$$E_{cell} = 1.10 - \frac{0.059}{2} \log \frac{(0.50)}{(0.20)} = 1.088 \text{ V}$$

30. Given, $E^\circ_{Cr^{3+}/Cr} = -0.74$ V, $E^\circ_{Fe^{2+}/Fe} = -0.44$ V

For the cell,

At cathode, $(Fe^{2+} + 2e^- \longrightarrow Fe) \times 3$

At anode, $(Cr \longrightarrow Cr^{3+} + 3e^-) \times 2$

Hence, $n = 6$

According to Nernst equation,

$$E_{cell} = E^\circ_{cell} - \frac{0.0591}{n} \log_{10} \frac{[\text{Product}]}{[\text{Reactant}]}$$
$$= E^\circ_{cell} - \frac{0.0591}{6} \log \frac{[Cr^{3+}]^2}{[Fe^{2+}]^3}$$
$$E^\circ_{cell} = E_{cathode} - E_{anode}$$
$$= -0.44 - (-0.74) = 030 \text{ V}$$

Given, $[Cr^{3+}] = 0.1$ M and $[Fe^{2+}] = 0.01$ M

$$E_{cell} = 0.30 - \frac{0.0591}{6} \log \frac{[0.1]^2}{[0.1]^3} = 0.2902 \text{ V}$$

Also, we know, $\Delta G = -nFE_{cell}$
$$= -6 \times 96500 \times 02902$$
$$= -1680258 \text{ J} = -16803 \text{ kJ}$$

31. $\Delta G^\circ = -nFE^\circ_{cell}$

where, n = no. of electrons participate = 2

Given, $E^\circ_{cell} = 2.71$ V = emf of cell

$F = 96500$ C

$\therefore\ \Delta G = -2 \times 96500 \times 2.71$

$= -523030 \text{ J mol}^{-1}$

$\Delta G = -523.030 \text{ kJ/mol}$

Now, $E_{cell} = E^\circ_{cell} - \dfrac{0.0591}{n} \log \dfrac{[Mg^{2+}]}{[Cu^{2+}]}$

$= 2.71 - \dfrac{0.0591}{2} \log \dfrac{[0.1]}{[0.01]}$

$= 2.71 - 0.02955$

$= 2.68045$

$\therefore$ EMF of cell $= 2.68045$

32. The cell reaction is

$$Zn(s) + Cd^{2+}(aq) \longrightarrow Cd(s) + Zn^{2+}(aq)$$

E°_{cell} of the cell is given by

$E^\circ_{cell} = E^\circ_{right} - E^\circ_{left}$

$= -0.403 - (-0.763) = 0.36 \text{ V}$

Applying Nernst equation to the cell reaction

$$E_{cell} = E^\circ_{cell} - \frac{0.059}{n} \log \frac{[Zn^{2+}(aq)]}{[Cd^{2+}(aq)]}$$

$E_{cell} = 0.36 - \dfrac{0.059}{2} \log \dfrac{0.1}{0.01}$ $\quad (\because n = 2)$

$E_{cell} = 0.36 - 0.0295 \log 10$

$= 0.36 - 0.0295 \times 1 = 0.3305 \text{ V}$

Now, $\Delta_r G^\circ = -nFE^\circ_{cell}$

$= -2 \times 96500 \times 0.33$

$= -63690 \text{ J mol}^{-1}$

$= -63.69 \text{ kJ mol}^{-1}$

33. According to thermodynamics, free energy change (ΔG°) is equal to maximum work.

Hence, $-W_{max} = \Delta G^\circ = -nFE^\circ_{cell}$

At cathode,

$Cu^{2+} + 2e^- \longrightarrow Cu;\ E^\circ = 0.339 \text{ V}$

At anode,

$Zn \longrightarrow Zn^{2+} + 2e^-;\ E^\circ = 0.761 \text{ V}$

(i) Cell reaction,

$Zn(s) + Cu^{2+}(aq) \longrightarrow Cu(s) + Zn^{2+}(aq)$

(ii) $E^\circ_{cell} = E^\circ_{cathode} - E^\circ_{anode}$

Given: $E^\circ_{Zn^{2+}/Zn} = -0.761 \text{ V}$

$E_{Cu^{2+},Cu} = +0.339 \text{ V}$

or $\quad E^\circ_{Zn/Zn^{2+}} = 0.761 \text{ V}$

Hence, $E^\circ_{cell} = E^\circ_{Cu^{2+}/Cu} - E^\circ_{Zn^{2+}/Zn}$

$= 0.339 - (-0.761) = 1.1 \text{ V}$

Putting the value of E°_{cell} in $\Delta G^\circ = -nFE^\circ_{cell}$

where, $n = 2, F = 96500 \text{ C}$

$\Delta G^\circ = -2 \times 96500 \times 1.1$

$= -212300 \text{ J}$

$= -212.3 \text{ kJ}$ **(3)**

Concept Enhancer According to thermodynamics, free energy change (ΔG°) is equal to maximum work, i.e. $W_{max} = \Delta G = -nFE^\circ_{cell}$

34. Given, $\quad E^\circ_{Al^{3+}/Al} = -1.66 \text{ V}$

and $\quad E^\circ_{Sn^{2+}/Sn} = -0.14 \text{ V}$

At anode, $\quad Al \longrightarrow Al^{3+} + 3e^-\ \} \times 2$

At cathode, $\quad Sn^{2+} + 2e^- \longrightarrow Sn\ \} \times 3$

Hence, $n = 6$

$E^\circ_{cell} = E^\circ_{cathode} - E^\circ_{anode}$

$= -0.14 - (-1.66) = -0.14 + 1.66 = 1.52 \text{ V}$

$E_{cell} = E^\circ_{cell} - \dfrac{0.059}{n} \log \dfrac{[Al^{3+}]^2}{[Sn^{2+}]^3}$

$= 1.52 - \dfrac{0.059}{6} \log \dfrac{(0.01)^2}{(0.015)^3}$

$= 1.52 - \dfrac{0.059}{6} \times 1.47$

$= 1.52 - 0.0144$

$= 1.5055 \text{ V}$ **(3)**

35. Given: $E^\circ_{M^{2+}/M} = -0.76 \text{ V}, E^\circ_{N^{2+}/N} = +0.34 \text{ V}$

So, $n = 2$

For the cell

At cathode, $\quad N^{2+} + 2e^- \longrightarrow N$

At anode, $\quad M \longrightarrow M^{2+} + 2e^-$

$E^\circ_{cell} = E^\circ_{cathode} - E^\circ_{anode}$

$= 0.34 - (-0.76) = 1.1 \text{ V}$

$W_{max} = -nFE^\circ_{cell}$

$= -2 \times 96500 \times 1.1$ $\quad (\because 1 \text{ F} = 96500 \text{ C})$

$= -212300 \text{ J}$

$= -212.3 \text{ kJ}$

36. Given: $E^\circ_{Al^{3+}/Al} = -1.66$ V, $E^\circ_{Fe^{2+}/Fe} = -0.44$ V

For the cell,

At cathode, $(Fe^{2+} + 2e^- \longrightarrow Fe) \times 3;$

$E^\circ = -0.44$ V

At anode, $(Al \longrightarrow Al^{3+} + 3e^-) \times 2;\ E^\circ = -1.66$ V

Hence, $n = 6$

According to Nernst equation,

$$E_{cell} = E^\circ_{cell} - \frac{0.0591}{n}\log_{10}\frac{[\text{Product}]}{[\text{Reactant}]}$$

$$= E^\circ_{cell} - \frac{0.0591}{6}\log\frac{[Al^{3+}]^2}{[Fe^{2+}]^3}$$

$$E^\circ_{cell} = E^\circ_{cathode} - E^\circ_{anode} = -0.44 - (-1.66)$$

$$= -0.44 + 1.66 = 1.22$$

Given, $[Al^{3+}] = 0.01$ M, $[Fe^{2+}] = 0.02$M

$$E_{cell} = 1.22 - \frac{0.0591}{6}\log\frac{(0.01)^2}{(0.02)^3}$$

$$= 1.22 - 9.85 \times 10^{-3}\log(12.5)$$

$$= 1.22 - 9.85 \times 10^{-3} \times 1.097$$

$$= 1.22 - 0.012 = 1.208 \text{ V}$$ **(3)**

37. (i) Since, $E^\circ_{Pb^{2+}/Pb} > E^\circ_{Zn^{2+}/Zn}$

Hence, Pb will reduce and zinc will oxidise, i.e. Pb^{2+} will move towards cathode and Zn towards anode.

At anode, $Zn \longrightarrow Zn^{2+} + 2e^-;\ E^\circ = -0.76$ V

At cathode, $Pb^{2+} + 2e^- \longrightarrow Pb;\ E^\circ = -0.13$ V

Cell reaction, $Zn + Pb^{2+} \longrightarrow Pb + Zn^{2+}$

Cell representation is

$$Zn \mid Zn^{2+}(0.1\text{ M}) \mid\mid Pb^{2+}(0.2\text{M}) \mid Pb$$

(ii) $E^\circ_{cell} = E^\circ_{cathode} - E^\circ_{anode}$

$$= E^\circ_{Pb^{2+}/Pb} - E^\circ_{Zn^{2+}/Zn}$$

$$= -0.13 - (-0.76) = -0.13 + 0.76$$

$$E^\circ_{cell} = +0.63 \text{ V}$$

$$E_{cell} = E^\circ_{cell} - \frac{0.059}{n}\log\frac{[\text{Product}]}{[\text{Reactant}]} \quad (\text{Here, } n = 2)$$

$$= 0.63 - \frac{0.059}{2}\log\frac{(0.1)}{(0.2)}$$

$$= 0.63 - 0.0295\log(0.5)$$

$$= 0.63 - 0.0295(-0.30) = 0.63 + 8.85 \times 10^{-3}$$

$$E_{cell} = 0.6388 \text{ V}$$ **(3)**

38. (i) Given reaction is

$$2\,Ag^+ + Cd \longrightarrow 2\,Ag + Cd^{2+}$$

Reduction potential of $\underset{(0.80)}{Ag^+/Ag} > \underset{(-0.40)}{Cd^{2+}/Cd}$

Hence, Ag^+ will move towards cathode and Cd towards anode.

At cathode, $(Ag^+ + e^- \longrightarrow Ag) \times 2$, $E^\circ = 0.80$ V

At anode, $Cd \longrightarrow Cd^{2+} + 2e^-$, $E^\circ = +0.40$ V

Hence, cell representation is

$$Cd \mid Cd^{2+} \mid\mid Ag^+ / Ag$$ **(1)**

(ii) Given: $E^\circ_{Ag^+/Ag} = +0.80$ V

and $E^\circ_{Cd^{2+}/Cd} = -0.40$ V

Standard cell emf,

$$E^\circ_{cell} = E^\circ_{cathode} - E^\circ_{anode}$$

$$= 0.80 - (-0.40)$$

$$= 0.80 + 0.40$$

$$= 1.20 \text{ V}$$ **(1)**

(iii) Given, $[Cd^{2+}] = 0.1$ M and $[Ag^+] = 0.2$ M

According to Nernst equation,

$$E_{cell} = E^\circ_{cell} - \frac{0.0591}{n}\log\frac{[\text{Product}]}{[\text{Reactant}]}$$

$$= E^\circ_{cell} - \frac{0.0591}{n}\log\frac{[Cd^{2+}]}{[Ag^+]^2}$$

Here, $n = 2$

Hence, $E_{cell} = 1.20 - \frac{0.059}{2}\log\frac{(0.1)}{(0.2)^2}$

$$= 1.20 - \frac{0.059}{2}[\log 10 - 2\log 2]$$

$$= 1.20 - \frac{0.059}{2} \times 0.398$$

$$= 1.20 - 0.01 = 1.19 \text{ V}$$ **(1)**

(iv) For a reaction to be spontaneous, ΔG should be negative, i.e.

$$\Delta G = -nFE^\circ_{cell}$$

As $E^\circ_{cell} = 1.19$ V, which is positive, hence, ΔG is negative. Thus, the reaction would be spontaneous. **(1)**

39. (i) Reduction potential of $Ag^+ > Cu^{2+}$. Hence, Ag^+ will get reduced and Cu will get oxidised. Hence, Ag^+ will move towards cathode and Cu towards anode.

At anode, $Cu \longrightarrow Cu^{2+} + 2e^-, \; E° = 0.39\,V$

At cathode, $(Ag^+ + e^- \longrightarrow Ag) \times 2, \; E° = 0.80\,V$

Given : $[Ag^+] = 0.01M, \; E^\circ_{Ag^+/Ag} = 0.8\,V$

Reduction potential at cathode

$$E_{Ag^+/Ag} = E^\circ_{Ag^+/Ag} + \frac{0.0591}{1} \log [Ag^+]$$
$$= 0.8 + \frac{0.0591}{1} \log (0.01)$$
$$= 0.8 - 0.0591 \times 2$$
$$= 0.8 - 0.1182$$
$$= 0.6818\,V$$

Reduction potential at anode

$$E_{Cu^{2+}/Cu} = E^\circ_{Cu^{2+}/Cu} + \frac{0.0591}{2} \log [Cu^{2+}]$$
$$([Cu^{2+}] = 0.13M)$$
$$= 0.39 + \frac{0.0591}{2} \log (0.13V)$$
$$= 0.3638\,V (E^\circ_{Cu^{2+}/Cu} = 0.39\,V)$$ **(1)**

(ii) $E^\circ_{cell} = E^\circ_{cathode} - E^\circ_{anode}$
$$= 0.6818 - 0.3638$$
$$E^\circ_{cell} = 0.3180\,V$$ **(1)**

(iii) Cell reaction

At cathode, $2Ag^+ + 2e^- \longrightarrow 2Ag$

At anode, $Cu \longrightarrow Cu^{2+} + 2e^-$

$Cu + 2Ag^+ \longrightarrow Cu^{2+} + 2Ag$ **(1)**

(iv) For a reaction to be spontaneous, ΔG should be negative. For this cell, E_{cell} is positive and $\Delta G = -nFE^\circ$. Hence, this cell reaction is spontaneous.

Concept Enhancer More positive is the value of reduction potential, more is the tendency to get reduced.
(Reduction occurs at cathode and oxidation at anode)

40. (i) (a) The cell reaction for the given cell

$2Ag^+(aq) + 2e^- \longrightarrow 2Ag(s)$ [Reduction half- cell]

$Cu(s) \longrightarrow Cu^{2+}(aq) + 2e^-$ [Oxidation half- cell]

Overall reaction is given as

$2Ag^+(aq) + Cu(s) \longrightarrow 2Ag(s) + Cu^{2+}(aq)$

(b) Standard emf of the cell, i.e.

$$E^\circ_{Cell} = E_{Cathode} - E_{Anode}$$
$$= E^\circ_{Ag^+/Ag} - E_{Cu^{2+}/Cu}$$
$$= (0.799 - 0.337)\,V$$
$$E^\circ_{cell} = 0.462\,V$$

(c) Given, concentration of Cu^{2+}, i.e. $[Cu^{2+}] = 0.1\,M$

$E_{cell} = 0.422\,V$

$T = 25°C$

Concentration of Ag^+, i.e. $[Ag^+] = ?$

As, we know that,

$$E_{cell} = E^\circ_{cell} - \frac{0.059}{2} \log \frac{[Cu^{2+}]}{[Ag^+]^2}$$
$$0.422 = 0.462 - \frac{0.059}{2} \log \frac{[0.1]}{[Ag^+]^2}$$
$$= 0.462 - 0.0295\,[\log[0.1] - \log[Ag^+]^2]$$
$$= 0.462 - 0.0295 \log[0.1] + 0.0295 \times 2 \log[Ag^+]$$
$$= 0.462 + 0.0295 + 0.059 \log[Ag^+]$$
$$= 0.4915 + 0.0591 \log[Ag^+]$$
$$-0.0695 = 0.059 \log[Ag^+] - 1.178 = \log[Ag^+]$$
$$[Ag^+] = 0.066\,M$$

(d) $\Delta G° = -nFE^\circ_{cell}$
$$= -2 \times 96500 \times 0.462$$
$$= -89166\,J\,mol^{-1}$$
$$= -89.166\,kJ\,mol^{-1}$$

(ii) Given, $\Lambda^\circ_m Ba^{2+} = 127.2\,S\,cm^2\,mol^{-1}$

$\Lambda^\circ_m Al^{3+} = 189\,S\,cm^2\,mol^{-1}$

$\Lambda^\circ_m Cl = 76.3\,S\,cm^2\,mol^{-1}$

$\Lambda^\circ_m SO_4^{2-} = 160\,S\,cm^2\,mol^{-1}$

$$\Lambda^\circ_m BaCl_2 = \Lambda^\circ_m Ba^{2+} + 2\Lambda^\circ_m Cl^-$$
$$= 127.2 + 2 \times 76.3 = 127.2 + 152.6$$
$$= 279.8\,S\,cm^2 mol^{-1}$$
$$\Lambda^\circ_m Al_2(SO_4)_3 = 2\Lambda^\circ_m Al^{3+} + 3\Lambda^\circ_m SO_4^{2-}$$
$$= 2 \times 189 + 3 \times 160 = 858\,S\,cm^2\,mol^{-1}$$

41. (i) At anode,

$$Zn \longrightarrow Zn^{2+} + 2e^- ; E_{Zn^{2+}/Zn} = -0.76 \text{ V}$$

At cathode,

$$Sn^{2+} + 2e^- \longrightarrow Sn; E_{Sn^{2+}/Sn} = -0.14 \text{ V}$$

$$\therefore \quad E^\circ_{cell} = E^\circ_{cathode} - E^\circ_{anode}$$

$$= -0.14 + 0.76 = 0.62 \text{ V}$$

We know that,

$$\Delta G^\circ = -nFE^\circ_{cell}$$

$$= -2 \times 96500 \times 0.62 \qquad (\because n = 2)$$

$$= -119660 \text{ J}$$

$$= -119.66 \text{ kJ}$$

(ii) $\underset{+7}{MnO_4^-} \longrightarrow \underset{+2}{Mn^{2+}}$

So, one mole of it will require 5 moles of electrons.

$$\because \text{ Molarity} = \frac{\text{No. of moles}}{\text{Volume of solution}}$$

$$0.5 = \frac{\text{no. of moles}}{500 \times 10^{-3}}$$

$\therefore$ No. of moles = 0.25

Hence, 0.25 moles will require

$5 \times 0.25 = 1.25$ moles of electron.

42. (i) For the given cell, the half-cell reactions will be given as below.

At anode, $Mg \longrightarrow Mg^{2+} + 2e^-$

At cathode, $Cu^{2+} + 2e^- \longrightarrow Cu$

Therefore, the overall cell reaction will be

$$Mg + Cu^{2+} \longrightarrow Mg^{2+} + Cu$$

According to the Nernst equation,

$$E_{cell} = E^\circ_{cell} - \frac{0.0591}{n} \log\left[\frac{Mg^{2+}}{Cu^{2+}}\right]$$

In this case, $n = 2$

$$\therefore \quad E_{cell} = 2.71 - \frac{0.0591}{2} \log\left[\frac{0.1}{0.01}\right]$$

$$= 2.71 - 0.0295 \log 10 = 2.71 - 0.0295$$

$$E_{cell} = 2.68 \text{ V}$$ **(3)**

(ii) **Faraday's first law** It states that the amount of chemical reaction occurring at any electrode by passing current is directly proportional to the quantity of electricity passed through the electrolyte (in solution or in molten state).

Thus, w g of the substance gets deposited on passing Q coulomb of electricity

$$w \propto Q \text{ or } w = ZQ$$

$$w = Z \times it \qquad (\because Q = it)$$

where, Q = quantity of electricity, i = current (in A),
t = time (in s),
Z = constant of proportionality called electrochemical equivalent.

Charged required for the reduction of 1 mole of $Cu^{2+} = 2F = 2 \times 96500 \text{ C} = 193000 \text{ C}$ **(2)**

TOPIC 3

Conductance in Electrolytic Solutions, Corrosion and Batteries

Before introducing the concept of conductance of electricity through electrolytic solutions, we should study few terms related to conductance of electricity.

Conductance of Electrolytic Solutions

Ohm's Law

The strength of current, I flowing through a conductor is directly proportional to the potential difference, V across the conductor, i.e. $I \propto V$.

Hence, $I = \frac{V}{R}$ or $\frac{V}{I} = R$ (constant),

where R is proportionality constant and known as **resistance** of the conductor. Its unit is **ohm** (Ω).

Resistance (R)

It is defined as the hinderance provided by the conductor in the passage of current. Every substance offers resistance to the flow of electricity to a small or large extent.

Conductance (C)

The ease with which current flows through a conductor is known as its conductance.

It is the reciprocal of resistance (R), i.e. $C = \frac{1}{R}$.

Its unit is ohm^{-1} or mho or Siemen (S).

Specific Resistance or Resistivity (ρ)

It is defined as the resistance in ohm's of a specimen of 1 cm in length and 1 cm^2 in cross-section. If l is the length and A is the area of cross-section of a conductor, then resistance, $R \propto l/A$ or $R = \rho l/A$, where ρ (rho) is the specific resistance of the conductor. Its unit is Ω cm.

Specific Conductance or Conductivity (κ)

It is the conductance of a solution taken in a cell whose electrodes are at unit distance from each other and each has area equal to 1 cm^2. It is the reciprocal of resistivity. It is also called conductivity. Its unit is $ohm^{-1}cm^{-1}$ or Siemen cm^{-1} (S cm^{-1}).

$$\kappa = \frac{1}{\rho} = \frac{l}{RA}$$

Cell Constant (G)

The quantity l/A is called cell constant.

$$\text{Cell constant} = \text{Conductivity} \times \text{Resistance} = \frac{\text{Conductivity}}{\text{Conductance}}$$

Equivalent Conductance or Equivalent Conductivity (Λ_{eq})

It is defined as the conductance of a volume of solution containing 1g equivalent of dissolved substance when placed between two parallel electrodes of 1 cm apart and large enough to contain whole solution between them. Its unit is $ohm^{-1}cm^2equiv^{-1}$ or S cm^2equiv^{-1}.

Note Relation between κ and Λ_{eq}, $\Lambda_{eq} = \frac{1000}{C} \times \kappa = \kappa \times V$ (where, V is the volume in cm^3 of the solution containing 1 g equivalent of the electrolyte.).

Molar Conductance or Molar Conductivity (Λ_m)

The conductance of solution, whose volume contains one mole of solution placed between two parallel electrodes separated by 1 cm and have large cross-sectional area to kept whole solution.

$$\Lambda_m = \frac{1000}{C} \times \kappa$$

Note Relation between Λ_{eq} and Λ_m, $\Lambda_{eq} = \frac{\Lambda_m}{Z}$

(where, Z = number of individual charges that are being carried by the ions of the electrolyte)

Factors on which Conductance Depends

- Nature of electrode
- Concentration of solution
- Temperature

Variation of Conductivity and Molar Conductivity with Concentration

Conductivity always decreases with decrease in concentration (i.e. with dilution) of both the strong and weak electrolytes. This is due to the fact that the number of ions that carry current in a unit volume of solution always decreases with decrease in concentration.

Variation of Molar Conductivity with Concentration

Variation of molar conductivity for strong and weak electrolyte are as follows

1. For Strong Electrolytes

For these kind of electrolytes, Λ_m increases slowly with dilution. This can be represented by equation, **Debye-Huckel-Onsager equation.**

$$\Lambda_m = \Lambda_m^\circ - A\sqrt{C}$$

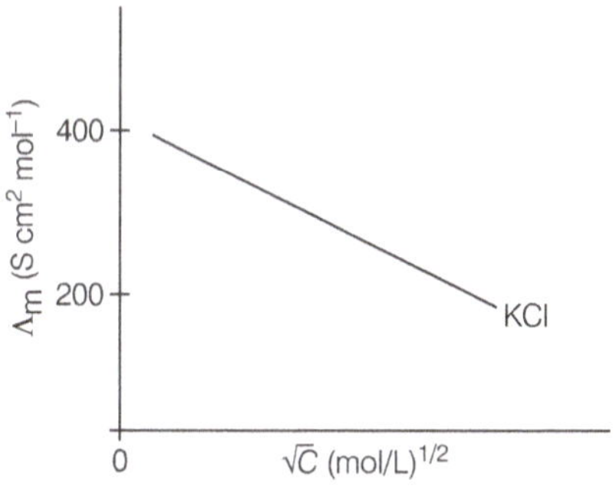

If we plot Λ_m against $\sqrt{C}$, we get a straight line with slope as $-A$ and intercept as Λ_m°.

The value of A depends on the type of electrolyte used.

Thus, NaCl, $CaCl_2$, $MgSO_4$ are known as strong electrolytes, respectively.

2. For Weak Electrolytes

A weak electrolyte (like acetic acid) is not completely dissociated at all concentrations. With dilution, the degree of dissociation increases, resulting in increase in the number of ions.

In this case the Λ_m° value increases steeply with dilution, especially in the low concentration region.

In this region, the graph of weak electrolytes in a plot of Λ_m against $\sqrt{C}$ becomes parallel to the Y-axis.

So, the limiting molar conductivity of a weak electrolyte cannot be determined by extrapolation of the plot. At infinite dilution ($C \rightarrow$ zero) electrolyte dissociates completely ($\alpha = 1$), but at such low concentration the conductivity of the solution is so low that it cannot be measured accurately.

It is rather determined by applying the Kohlrausch law of independent migration of ions. Through Kohlrausch law, we can determine λ°_{m} values of weak electrolyte.

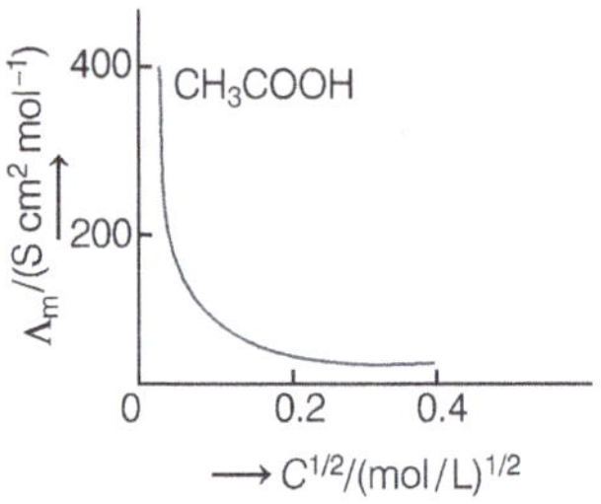

Kohlrausch's Law

Molar conductance of an electrolyte at infinite dilution is equal to the sum of the individual molar conductances of cations and anions with each conductance term multiplied by the number of respective ions present in the formula unit of the electrolyte.

$$\Lambda^{\circ}_{m} = \lambda^{\circ}_{+} + \lambda^{\circ}_{-} \text{ or } \nu_{+}\lambda^{\circ}_{+} + \nu_{-}\lambda^{\circ}_{-}$$

(where, λ°_{+} and λ°_{-} are the molar conductivities of cations and anions respectively and ν_{+} and ν_{-} are the number of cations and anions per formula unit of the electrolyte, respectively).

For weak electrolyte, $\alpha = \dfrac{\Lambda_m}{\Lambda^{\circ}_{m}}$

and $K_{\alpha} = \dfrac{C\alpha^2}{(1-\alpha)} = \dfrac{C\Lambda^2_m}{\Lambda^{\circ 2}_{m}\left(1 - \dfrac{\Lambda_m}{\Lambda^{\circ}_{m}}\right)} = \dfrac{C\Lambda^2_m}{\Lambda^{\circ}_{m}(\Lambda^{\circ}_{m} - \Lambda_m)}$

Battery

It is the arrangement of two or more galvanic cells connected together in series.

For a battery to be of practical use, it should be reasonably light, compact and its voltage should not vary appreciably during its use.

These are of two types

(i) **Primary cell** In this, redox reaction occurs once and hence it becomes dead after some time, e.g. dry cell, mercury cell both have zinc as anode and graphite as cathode.

(ii) **Secondary cell** It can be recharged again by passing a direct current in it. It is also called rechargeable cell, e.g. lead storage battery and nickel cadmium storage cell.

Some important secondary batteries

Cell	Reaction at anode	Reaction at cathode
Dry cell	$Zn(s) \longrightarrow Zn^{2+}(aq) + 2e^-$	$MnO_2(s) + NH_4^+(aq) + e^- \longrightarrow MnO(OH)(s) + NH_3(g)$
Mercury cell	$Zn(s) + 2OH^-(aq) \longrightarrow ZnO(s) + H_2O(l) + 2e^-$	$HgO_2(s) + H_2O(l) + 2e^- \longrightarrow Hg(l) + 2OH^-(aq)$
Lead storage call	$Pb(s) + SO_4^{2-}(aq) \longrightarrow PbSO_4(s) + 2e^-$	$PbO_2(s) + SO_4^{2-}(aq) + 4H^+(aq) + 2e^- \longrightarrow PbSO_4(s) + 2H_2O(l)$
Nickel-cadmium cell	$Cd(s) + 2OH^-(aq) \longrightarrow Cd(OH)_2(s) + 2e^-$	$NiO_2(s) + 2H_2O(l) + 2e^- \longrightarrow Ni(OH)_2(s) + 2OH^-(aq)$
Fuel cell	$2H_2(g) + 4OH^-(aq) \longrightarrow 4H_2O(l) + 4e^-$	$O_2(g) + 2H_2O(l) + e^- \longrightarrow 4OH^-(aq)$

Corrosion

The process of slow conversion of metals into their undesirable compounds by the action of moisture and other gases present in the atmosphere is called corrosion, e.g. rusting of iron.

It involves the following reaction,

$$4Fe(s) + \underset{\text{(From air)}}{3O_2(g)} + 2x \cdot H_2O \longrightarrow \underset{\text{Rust}}{2Fe_2O_3 \cdot x\, H_2O(s)}$$

Mechanism of Electrochemical Reaction of Corrosion

According to the electrochemical theory, corrosion is an electrochemical phenomenon.

Overall reaction that takes place in a miniature galvanic cell on the surface of iron is

At anode, $Fe(s) \longrightarrow Fe^{2+}(aq) + 2e^-] \times 2$

At cathode, $O_2(g) + 4H^+(aq) + 4e^- \longrightarrow 2H_2O(l)$

$$2Fe(s) + O_2(g) + 4H^+(aq) \longrightarrow 2Fe^{2+}(aq) + 2H_2O(l)$$

Atmospheric oxidation,

$$2Fe^{2+}(aq) + 2H_2O(l) + \frac{1}{2}O_2(g) \longrightarrow Fe_2O_3(s) + 4H^+(aq)$$

Factors Affecting Corrosion

Presence of air, moisture, carbon dioxide, electrolytes in water, etc.

Prevention of Corrosion

It can be prevented by barrier protection, sacrificial protection and cathodic protection.

PYQs Previous Years' Questions

1 Mark Questions

1. Which one of the following statements is correct regarding the dry cell?
   (P) Zinc container acts as an anode in dry cell.
   (Q) Zinc container touches the paste of MnO_2 and carbon.
   (R) Dry cell can be charged easily. *(ISC 2024)*
   (S) Graphite rod acts as a cathode in dry cell.
   (a) Only (P) and (R)
   (b) Only (Q) and (R)
   (c) Only (P) and (S)
   (d) Only (Q) and (S)

2. **Assertion** (A) Specific conductiity of all electrolytes decreases on dilution.

   Reason (R) On dilution, the number of ions per unit volume decreases. *ISC 2024*
   (a) Both Assertion and Reason are true and Reason is the correct explanation for Assertion.
   (b) Both Assertion and Reason are true but Reason is not the correct explanation for Assertion.
   (c) Assertion is true but Reason is false.
   (d) Assertion is false but Reason is true.

3. **Assertion** (A) Adding water to two beakers '*A*' and '*B*' containing NaOH and CH_3COOH solutions respectively will increase the molar conductance (Λ_m) of the solutions sharply in beaker '*A*' and slowly in beaker '*B*'.

   Reason (R) Molar conductance (Λ_m) increases with a decrease in concentration or upon dilution. *ISC Specimen 2024*
   (a) Both Assertion and Reason are true and Reason is the correct explanation of Assertion.
   (b) Both Assertion and Reason are true but Reason is not the correct explanation for Assertion.
   (c) Assertion is true but Reason is false.
   (d) Assertion is false but Reason is true.

4. **Assertion** (A) Specific conductance of all electrolytes decreases on dilution. *ISC Specimen 2023*

   Reason (R) On dilution, number of ions per unit volume decreases.
   (a) Both (A) and (R) are correct, and (R) is the correct explanation for (A).
   (b) Both (A) and (R) are correct, but (R) is not the correct explanation for (A).
   (c) (A) is correct but (R) is incorrect.
   (d) (A) is incorrect but (R) is correct.

5. The ionic conductance at infinite dilution for Ba^{2+} and Cl^- ions are 127 $ohm^{-1}cm^2mol^{-1}$ and 76 $ohm^{-1}cm^2mol^{-1}$ respectively. What will be the molar conductance of $BaCl_2$ at infinte dilution?
   (a) 139.5 $ohm^{-1}cm^2mol^{-1}$ *ISC 2021-22 (Sem-I)*
   (b) 279.0 $ohm^{-1}cm^2mol^{-1}$
   (c) 203.0 $ohm^{-1}cm^2mol^{-1}$
   (d) 101.5 $ohm^{-1}cm^2mol^{-1}$

6. On dilution, the specific conductance of a solution
   (a) remains unchanged *ISC Specimen 2021-22 (Sem-I)*
   (b) increases
   (c) decreases
   (d) first increases then decreases

7. Equivalent conductivity is the conducting power of all the ions furnished by one .... of an electrolyte present in a definite .... of the solution (volume, gram equivalent). *ISC 2020*

8. The molar conductance of a solution .... with dilution while its specific conductance .... with dilution. *ISC Specimen 2018*

9. Specific conductivity of 0.20 M solution of KCl at 298 K is 0.025 S cm^{-1}. Calculate its molar conductivity. *ISC 2017*

10. The unit of conductance is .... and that of specific conductance is .... *ISC 2016*

11. The molar conductance of a solution ... with dilution, while its specific conductance ... with dilution. *ISC 2014*

12. Kohlrausch's law is related to ... . *ISC 2014*

13. The unit of equivalent conductance is
    (a) ohm^{-1} cm^2 $equiv^{-1}$ (b) ohm^{-1} cm^2 g^{-1}
    (c) ohm cm^2 $equiv^{-1}$ (d) $ohm^{-1}mol^{-1}$ *ISC 2010*

14. Give a reason for the following.
    Specific conductance decreases with dilution whereas equivalent conductance increases with dilution. *ISC 2007*

15. The degree of dissociation of a weak electrolyte is ... proportional to the ... of its molar concentration. *ISC 2006*

16. As concentration of an electrolytic solution increases, its ... conductance increases but ... conductance decreases. *ISC 2003*

17. Correct the following statement.
For a strong electrolyte, the plot of equivalent conductance *versus* concentration of the solution is a straight line. *ISC 2002*

18. Correct the following statement.
On dilution of a solution, its equivalent and specific conductance increases. *ISC 2001*

2 Marks Questions

19. A conductivity cell is filled with 0.05 M NaOH solution offering a resistance of 31.6 ohm. If the cell constant of the cell is 0.367 cm^{-1}, calculate the following

(i) The value of specific conductance
(a) $1.29\times10^{-2}\Omega^{-1}cm^{-1}$ (b) $1.29\times10^{-3}\Omega^{-1}cm^{-1}$
(c) $1.16\times10^{-2}\Omega^{-1}cm^{-1}$ (d) $11.6\times10^{-2}\Omega^{-1}cm^{-1}$

(ii) The value of molar conductance
(a) $232.20\,\Omega^{-1}cm^2mol^{-1}$
(b) $23.22\,\Omega^{-1}cm^2mol^{-1}$
(c) $119.07\,\Omega^{-1}cm^2mol^{-1}$
(d) $165.36\,\Omega^{-1}cm^2mol^{-1}$ *ISC 2021-22 (Sem-I)*

20. A solution containing 2 g of anhydrous barium chloride in 400 cm^3 of water has a specific conductivity of 0.0058 S cm^{-1}.
(At. wt. of Ba = 137, Cl = 35.5)

(i) What is the molarity of the above solution?
(a) 0.204 M (b) 0.024 M
(c) 0.420 M (d) 4.021 M

(ii) What is the molar conductivity of the above solution?
(a) 241.67 S cm^2/mol (b) 261.47 S cm^2/mol
(c) 247.17 S cm^2/mol (d) 361.47 S cm^2/mol
ISC 2021-22 (Sem-I)

21. The limiting molar conductivities (Λ_m^∞) for NaCl, KBr and KCl are 126, 152 and 150 $ohm^{-1}cm^2mol^{-1}$ respectively. *ISC Specimen 2021-22 (Sem-I)*

(i) The molar conductivity at infinite dilution for NaBr is
(a) 128 $ohm^{-1}cm^2mol^{-1}$ (b) 176 $ohm^{-1}cm^2mol^{-1}$
(c) 278 $ohm^{-1}cm^2mol^{-1}$ (d) 302 $ohm^{-1}cm^2mol^{-1}$

(ii) The law applied to determine the molar conductivity of infinite dilution is known as
(a) Faraday's law (b) Avogadro's law
(c) Kohlrausch law (d) Ohm's law

22. The molar conductivity of NaCl, CH_3COONa and HCl at infinite dilution is 126.45, 91.0 and 426.16 ohm^{-1} cm^2 mol^{-1} respectively.
Calculate the molar conductivity (λ_m°) for CH_3COOH at infinite dilution. *ISC 2020*

23. Define the following terms.
(i) Equivalent conductivity
(ii) Corrosion of metals *ISC 2018*

24. Define molar conductance of a solution. State its unit. How is it related to the specific conductance of a solution? *ISC 2013*

25. The conductivity of 0.2 M KCl solution is $3\times10^{-2}ohm^{-1}cm^{-1}$. Calculate its molar conductance. *ISC 2012*

26. A solution of 0.1 N KCl offers a resistance of 245 Ω. Calculate the specific conductance and the equivalent conductance of the solution if the cell constant is 0.571 cm^{-1}. *ISC 2010*

27. A 0.05 M NaOH solution offered a resistance of 31.6 Ω in a conductivity cell. If the cell constant of the conductivity cell is 0.378 cm^{-1}, determine the molar conductance of NaOH solution at this temperature. *ISC 2008*

> **KEY IDEA**
> Find conductivity using the formula, $\kappa = \frac{1}{R}\times\frac{l}{A}$ where, $\frac{l}{A}$ cell constant.
> Then, find molar conductivity of solution by using the formula, $\lambda_m = \frac{\kappa\times1000}{C}$

28. Calculate the equivalent conductivity of 1 M H_2SO_4 whose specific conductivity is $26\times10^{-2}ohm^{-1}cm^{-1}$. *ISC 2006*

3 Marks Questions

29. Calculate the degree of dissociation (α) of acetic acid, if its molar conductivity (Λ_m) is 39.05 S cm^2 mol^{-1}.
(Given: $\lambda^\circ_{(H^+)}$ = 349.6 S cm^2mol^{-1} and
$\lambda^\circ_{(CH_3COO^-)}$ = 40.95 S cm^2 mol^{-1}) *ISC 2020*

30. The specific conductivity of a solution containing 5 g of anhydrous $BaCl_2$ (molecular weight = 208) in 1000 cm^3 of a solution is found to be 0.0058 $ohm^{-1}cm^{-1}$. Calculate the molar and equivalent conductivity of the solution. *ISC 2018*

31. A 0.05 M NH_4OH solution offers the resistance of 50 Ω to a conductivity cell at 298 K. If the cell constant is 0.50 cm^{-1} and molar conductance of NH_4OH at infinite dilution is 471.4 Ω^{-1} cm^2 mol^{-1}.
Calculate.
(i) Specific conductance
(ii) Molar conductance
(iii) Degree of dissociation **ISC 2016**

32. The specific conductance of a 0.01 M solution of acetic acid at 298 K is $1.65 \times 10^{-4} \Omega^{-1} cm^{-1}$.
The molar conductance at infinite dilution for H^+ ion and CH_3COO^- ion are 349.1 $\Omega^{-1}cm^2mol^{-1}$ and 40.9 $\Omega^{-1}cm^2mol^{-1}$ respectively, calculate
(i) molar conductance of the solution.
(ii) degree of dissociation of CH_3COOH.
(iii) dissociation constant for acetic acid.

33. 0.05 M NaOH solution offered a resistance of 31.6 Ω in a conductivity cell at 298 K. If the cell constant of the cell is 0.367cm^{-1}, calculate the molar conductivity of the NaOH solution. **ISC 2014**

KEY IDEA
Using molar conductivity $\Lambda_m = \frac{1000}{C} \times \kappa$
where, κ = specific conductivity
$$\kappa = \frac{l}{RA} = \frac{\text{cell constant } (G)}{R}$$

34. State Kohlrausch's law and give its mathematical expression mentioning the terms involved in it. **ISC 2010**

35. A conductivity cell has a cell constant of 0.5 cm^{-1}. This cell when filled with 0.01M sodium chloride solution has a resistance of 384 Ω at 25°C. Calculate the equivalent conductivity of 0.01 M sodium chloride at 25°C. **ISC 2000**

KEY IDEA
$\Lambda_{eq} = \frac{1000}{C} \times \kappa$, where, Λ_{eq} = equivalent conductance,
κ = specific conductance, C is concentration in gram equivalent per unit volume.
$$\kappa = \frac{\text{Cell constant } (G^*)}{\text{Resistance } (R)}$$

5 Marks Questions

36. (i) A 0.05 M NH_4OH solution offers the resistance of 30.8 ohms to a conductivity cell at 298 K. If the cell constant is 0.343 cm^{-1} and molar conductance of NH_4OH at infinite dilution is 471.4 S cm^2 mol^{-1}, calculate the following.
(a) Specific conductance
(b) Molar conductance
(c) Degree of dissociation

(ii) In the diagram of the electrolytic cell given below, *A*, *B* and *C* are connected in series having electrolytes of $ZnSO_4$, $AgNO_3$ and $CuSO_4$ respectively. A steady current of 1.5 A was passed until 1.45 g of Ag was deposited at the cathode of cell *B*.

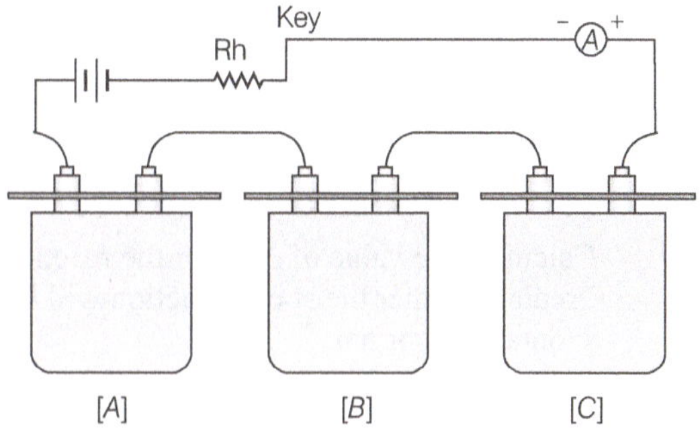

(Atomic mass of Ag = 108, Cu = 63.5, Zn = 65.3)
Answer the following questions.
(a) How long did the current flow?
(b) What weight of Cu and Zn was deposited at cathode? **ISC 2024**

37. (i) The molar conductivity *vs* $\sqrt{C}$ curve for Na_2SO_4, H_2SO_4 and NH_4OH are shown below in random order. **ISC Specimen 2024**

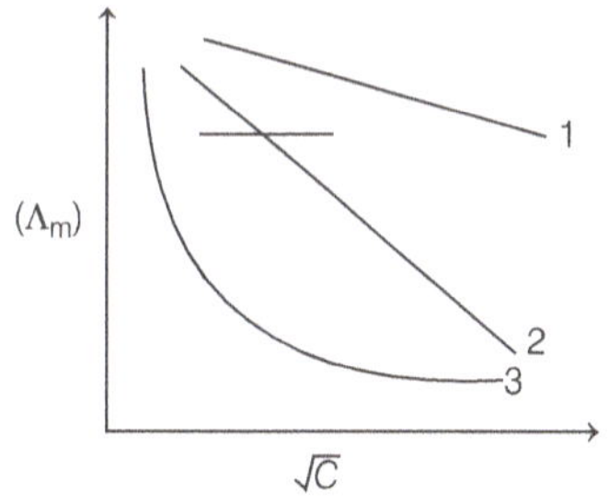

Identify the curve that corresponds to Na_2SO_4, H_2SO_4 and NH_4OH. Justify your answer.

(ii) The molar conductivity (Λ_m) of a dilute solution of methanoic acid is 34.1 S cm^2/mol. Calculate its degree of dissociation. (Given : $\lambda^\circ_{(H^+)}$ = 349.6 S cm^2/mol and $\lambda^\circ_{(HCOO^-)}$ = 54.6 S cm^2/mol)

38. (i) The resistance of a conductivity cell with 0.1 M KCl solution is 200 ohm. When the same cell is filled with 0.02 M NaCl solution, the resistance is 1100 ohm. If the conductivity of 0.1M KCl solution is 0.0129 ohm^{-1} cm^{-1}, calculate the cell constant and molar conductivity of 0.02 M NaCl solution.

> **KEY IDEA**
>
> First, we calculate cell constant using the formula,
>
> $$\kappa = \frac{G^*}{R} \text{ (} G^* \text{ is cell constant)}$$
>
> Then, find molar conductivity of solution by using the formula, $\lambda_m = \frac{\kappa \times 1000}{\text{Molarity}}$.

(ii) The emf (E°_{cell}) of the following reaction is 0.89 V

$$3Sn^{4+} + 2Cr \longrightarrow 3Sn^{2+} + 2Cr^{3+}$$

Calculate the value of ΔG° for the reaction. Predict whether the above reaction will be spontaneous or not.

39. (i) The specific conductance of 2.5×10^4 M formic acid is 5.25×10^{-5} $ohm^{-1} cm^{-1}$. Calculate its molar conductivity and degree of dissociation.

Given: $\lambda^\circ_{(H^+)} = 349.5$ $ohm^{-1} cm^2 mol^{-1}$ and $\lambda^\circ_{(HCOO^-)} = 50.5$ $ohm^{-1} cm^2 mol^{-1}$

(ii) Calculate the time taken to deposit 1.27 g of copper at cathode when a current of 2 amp, is passed through the solution of $CuSO_4$.
(Atomic weight of Cu = 63.5 g mol^{-1})

40. (i) A 0.06 molar CH_3COOH solution offers a resistance of 55 ohms to a conductivity cell at 25°C. If the cell constant is 0.45 cm^{-1} and the molar conductance of CH_3COOH at infinite dilution is 398.5 ohm^{-1} cm^2 mol^{-1}. Calculate. *ISC Specimen 2023*

(a) Specific conductance
(b) Molar conductance
(c) Degree of dissociation

(ii) Calculate the number of coulombs of charge required to deposit 24.35g of aluminium from a solution containing Al^{3+} ions.
(Atomic weight of Al = 27)

41. (i) Write the Nernst equation for the cell reaction given below and calculate the emf of the cell at 298K. *ISC Specimen 2023*

$$2Cr(s) + 3Fe^{2+}(0.1\,M) \longrightarrow 2Cr^{3+}(0.01\,M) + 3Fe(s)$$

Given: $E^\circ_{(Cr^{3+}/Cr)} = -0.74$ V, $E^\circ_{(Fe^{2+}/Fe)} = -0.44$ V

(ii) Calculate the molar conductance at infinite dilution (Λ°_m) for NH_4OH. Given that Λ°_m for $Ba(OH)_2$, $BaCl_2$ and NH_4Cl are 457 ohm^{-1} cm^2 mol^{-1}, 240 ohm^{-1} $cm^2 mol^{-1}$ and 129 ohm^{-1} $cm^2 mol^{-1}$ respectively.

42. (i) Define the following terms.
(a) Specific conductance (b) Kohlrausch law

(ii) The resistance of a conductivity cell containing 0.001 M KCl solution at 298 K is 1500 ohm. What is the cell constant and molar conductivity of 0.001 M KCl solution, if the conductivity of this solution is 0.146×10^{-3} $ohm^{-1} cm^{-1}$ at 298 K? *ISC 2019*

43. (i) Resistance of a conductivity cell filled with 0.1 mol L^{-1} KCl solution is 100 Ω. If the resistance of the same cell when filled with 0.02 mol L^{-1} KCl solution is 520 Ω, calculate the conductivity and molar conductivity of 0.02 mol L^{-1} KCl solution. The conductivity of 0.1 mol L^{-1} KCl solution is $1.29 \times 10^{-2} \Omega^{-1} cm^{-1}$. *ISC Specimen 2018*

(ii) Define the following terms.
(a) Limiting molar conductivity
(b) Fuel cell

Explanations

1. (c) Among the given statements (P) and (S) are correct while (Q) and (R) are incorrect.
   - Zinc container cannot touch is the paste of MnO_2 and carbon as the space between the electrode is filled with moist paste of ammonium chloride and zinc chloride.
   - Dry cell cannot be charged easily.
2. (a) Both Assertion and Reason are true and the Reason is the correct explanation of Assertion.
3. (a) When NaOH is added to acetic acid, there is firstly a gradual increase in the conductance and then there is a rapid increase in the conductance. This is because firstly the more hydrated protons are replaced by sodium ions and then after neutralisation of acetic acid.

   Sodium ions and hydroxide ions are added to the solution.
4. (a) Both (A) and (R) are correct and (R) is the correct explanation of Assertion.

   Specific conductance always decreases with the decrease in concentration both for weak and strong electrolytes.
5. (b) The equivalent weight of $BaCl_2 = \dfrac{\text{molecular weight}}{2}$

   $$\lambda^{\circ}_{m} \text{ for } BaCl_2 = \lambda^{\circ}_{m(Ba^{2+})} + 2\lambda^{\circ}_{m(Cl^-)}$$
   $$= 127 + 76 \times 2$$
   $$= 279 \text{ ohm}^{-1}\text{cm}^2\text{mol}^{-1}$$

   The correct answer is (b).
6. (c) decreases
7. gram equivalent, volume
8. increases, decreases.
9. Given, Specific conductivity $(\kappa) = 0.025 \text{ S cm}^{-1}$

   Concentration (C) = 0.20 M

   Now, molar conductivity $(\Lambda_m) = \dfrac{1000}{C} \times \kappa$

   $$= \frac{1000}{0.2} \times 0.025 = 125 \text{ S cm}^2\text{mol}^{-1}$$
10. Siemen or $\Omega^{-1}, \Omega^{-1}\text{ cm}^{-1}$.
11. The molar conductance of a solution **increases** with dilution, while its specific conductance **decreases** with dilution.

> **Concept Enhancer** Molar conductance depends on moles of ion present in the solution. On dilution, number of ions increases whereas, in case of specific conductance, with dilution, number of ions present per centimetre cube of solution becomes less.

12. Kohlrausch's law is related to **infinite dilution**.
13. (a) The unit of equivalent conductance is $\text{ohm}^{-1}\text{ cm}^2\text{ equiv}^{-1}$. Hence, the option (a) is correct.
14. Specific conductance depends on number of ions per unit volume. On dilution, number of ions will decrease per unit volume. Hence, specific conductance of the solution will decrease.

    Equivalent conductance is the product of specific conductivity and volume of the solution containing one gram equivalent of the electrolyte.

    As the decreasing value of specific conductivity is more than compensated by the increasing value of V, so the value of Λ_{eq} increases with dilution.
15. The degree of dissociation of a weak electrolyte is **inversely** proportional to the **square root** of its molar concentration.
16. As concentration of an electrolytic solution increases, its **specific** conductance increases but **equivalent** conductance decreases.
17. For a strong electrolyte, the plot of molar conductance *versus* square root of concentration of solution is a straight line.
18. On dilution of a solution, its equivalent conductance increases and specific conductance decreases.
19. Molarity of solution = 0.05 M

    Resistance of solution, $R = 31.6$ ohm

    Cell constant of the cell $= 0.367 \text{ cm}^{-1}$

    Conductance $= \dfrac{1}{R} = \dfrac{1}{31.6}\text{ ohm}^{-1}$

    (i) (c) Specific conductance = conductance × cell constant

    $$= \frac{1}{31.6}\text{ohm}^{-1} \times 0.367 \text{ cm}^{-1}$$
    $$= 0.0116 \text{ ohm}^{-1}\text{ cm}^{-1}$$
    $$= 1.16 \times 10^{-2}\Omega^{-1}\text{cm}^{-1},$$

    i.e. option (c) is correct. **(1)**

(ii) (a) Molar conductance,

$$\Lambda_m = \frac{\kappa \times 1000 \text{ cm}^3}{\text{Molarity}}$$

$$= \frac{0.0116 \text{ ohm}^{-1}\text{cm}^{-1} \times 1000 \text{ cm}^3}{0.05 \text{ mol}}$$

$$= 232 \text{ ohm}^{-1}\text{cm}^2\text{mol}^{-1}$$

Hence, option (a) is correct **(1)**

20. (i) (b) ***Step* I.** Analysing the given data

Mass of $BaCl_2 = 2$ g

Molar mass of $BaCl_2 = 207$ g

Number of moles of $BaCl_2$

$$= \frac{\text{Number or moles of } BaCl_2}{\text{Molar mass of } BaCl_2}$$

$$= \frac{2}{207} = 9.6 \times 10^{-3}$$

***Step* II.** Volume of solution = 400 cc = 0.4 L

Conductivity $(\kappa) = 0.0058 \text{ ohm}^{-1}\text{cm}^{-1}$

$$\text{Molarity } (M) = \frac{\text{Moles}}{\text{Volume (L)}} = \frac{0.009}{0.4}$$

Molarity $(M) = 0.024$ M, i.e. option (b) is correct. **(1)**

(ii) (a) Molar conductivity $= \dfrac{\kappa \times 1000}{M}$

$$\text{Molar conductivity} = \frac{0.0058 \Omega^{-1}\text{cm}^{-1} \times 1000 \text{ cm}^3}{0.024 \text{ mol}}$$

Molar conductivity $= 241.66 \text{ S cm}^2\text{mol}^{-1}$

Hence, option (a) is correct. **(1)**

21. (i) (a) $\Lambda^\circ_{NaBr} = \Lambda^\circ_{NaCl} + \Lambda^\circ_{KBr} - \Lambda^\circ_{KCl}$

$$\Lambda_{NaBr} = (126 + 152 - 150) \text{ S cm}^2 \text{ mol}^{-1}$$

$$= 128 \text{ S cm}^2 \text{ mol}^{-1}$$ **(1)**

(ii) (c) Kohlrausch law is used to find the molar conductivity of weak electrolyte using strong electrolytes at infinite dilution. **(1)**

22. Given, $\Lambda^\circ_{NaCl} = 126.45 \text{ ohm}^{-1}\text{cm}^2\text{mol}^{-1}$

$$\Lambda^\circ_{CH_3COONa} = 91.0 \text{ ohm}^{-1} \text{ cm}^2 \text{ mol}^{-1}$$

$$\Lambda^\circ_{HCl} = 426.16 \text{ ohm}^{-1} \text{ cm}^2 \text{ mol}^{-1}$$

$$\Lambda^\circ_{CH_3COOH} = \Lambda^\circ_{CH_3COONa} + \Lambda^\circ_{HCl} - \Lambda^\circ_{NaCl}$$

$$= (91.0 + 426.16) - 126.45$$

$$= 390.71 \text{ ohm}^{-1}\text{cm}^2\text{mol}^{-1}$$

23. (i) **Equivalent conductivity** of a solution is defined as the conductance of all the ions produced from one gram equivalent of the electrolyte dissolved in V cm^3 of the solution when the distance between the electrodes is one cm and the area of electrodes is so large that whole of the solution is contained between them. It is represented by Λ_{eq}. **(1)**

(ii) **Corrosion of metals** is basically an electrochemical phenomenon in which a metal oxide or other salt of the metal forms a coating on the metal surface, e.g. rusting of iron. **(1)**

24. The conductance of that volume of solution which contains one mole of the solute and is placed between two parallel electrodes of 1 cm distance apart and having sufficient area to hold the whole of the solution is called its **molar conductance**.

It is denoted by Λ_m. If the concentration of a solution is C mol/L, then volume of the solution containing 1 mole of the electrolyte will be $1/C$ L or $1000/C$ cc.

Hence, Λ_m and κ can be related as $\Lambda_m = \dfrac{1000}{C} \times \kappa$,

where, κ is specific conductance.

Its units are $\text{ohm}^{-1} \text{ cm}^2 \text{ mol}^{-1}$ in CGS and $\text{ohm}^{-1} \text{ m}^2 \text{ mol}^{-1}$ in SI system.

25. Given, C for KCl = 0.2 M, $\kappa = 3 \times 10^{-2} \Omega^{-1} \text{ cm}^{-1}$

$$\text{Putting value, } \Lambda_m = \frac{1000}{0.2} \times 3 \times 10^{-2}$$

$$= \frac{30}{0.2} = 1.5 \times 10^2 \Omega^{-1} \text{ cm}^2 \text{ mol}^{-1}$$

26. Given, $R = 245\Omega$, Cell constant = 0.571 cm^{-1}

Hence, specific conductance $= \dfrac{\text{Cell constant}}{\text{Resistance}}$

$$\kappa = \frac{0.571}{245} = 0.00233 \Omega^{-1} \text{ cm}^{-1}$$

$$= 2.33 \times 10^{-3} \Omega^{-1} \text{ cm}^{-1}$$

Equivalent conductance $\Lambda_{eq} = \dfrac{1000}{C} \times \kappa$

Concentration, $C = 0.1$ N

$$\Lambda_{eq} = \frac{1000}{0.1} \times 2.33 \times 10^{-3}$$

$$= 23.3 \Omega^{-1} \text{ cm}^2 \text{ equiv}^{-1}$$

27. Given, concentration, $C = 0.05$ M,

resistance $(R) = 31.6 \Omega$,

cell constant $(G^*) = 0.378 \text{ cm}^{-1}$.

$$\kappa = \frac{\text{Cell constant}}{\text{Resistance}} = \frac{0.378}{31.6} \Omega^{-1}\text{cm}^{-1}$$

Molar conductance,

$$\Lambda_m = \frac{1000}{0.05} \times \frac{0.378}{31.6} = 239.24\Omega^{-1}\ cm^2\ mol^{-1}$$

28. Given, concentration, $C = 1\,M, = 1 \times 2\,M = 2\,M$

Specific conductivity, $\kappa = 26 \times 10^{-2}\Omega^{-1}\ cm^{-1}$

Equivalent conductance,

$$\Lambda_{eq} = \frac{1000}{1 \times 2} \times 26 \times 10^{-2} = 130\ S\ cm^2\ equiv^{-1}$$

Common Mistake While calculating the equivalent conductivity, one can make mistake by taking the concentration in term of molarity instead of normality.

---

29. Given, $\Lambda_m = 39.05\ S\ cm^2 mol^{-1}$

We know that,

Degree of dissociation $(\alpha) = \frac{\Lambda_m}{\Lambda^\circ_m}$

$$\lambda^\circ_{CH_3COOH} = \lambda^\circ_{CH_3COO^-} + \lambda^\circ_{H^+}$$

$$\Lambda^\circ_{CH_3COOH} = 40.95 + 349.6 = 390.55\ S\ cm^2\ mol^{-1}$$

Now, $\alpha = \frac{39.05}{390.55} = 0.099$

30. Specific conductivity $(\kappa) = 0.0058\ ohm^{-1}\ cm^{-1}$

Molar mass of $BaCl_2 = 208\ g\ mol^{-1}$

As 5 g of $BaCl_2$ is present in $1000\ cm^3$ of the solution.

$\therefore$ Molar concentration (C)

$$= \frac{1}{208} \times \frac{5}{1000} \times 1000 = 0.0240\ mol\ L^{-1}$$

$\therefore$ Molar conductivity, $\Lambda_m = \frac{\kappa \times 1000}{M}$

$$= \frac{0.0058\ ohm^{-1}cm^{-1} \times 1000\ cm^3 L^{-1}}{0.0240\ mol\ L^{-1}}$$

$$= 241.67\ ohm^{-1} cm^2 mol^{-1}$$

In $BaCl_2$, equivalent weight

$$= \frac{\text{molecular weight}}{2} = \frac{208}{2} = 104$$

$\therefore$ Concentration of solution in gram equivalent per litre

$$= \frac{1}{104} \times \frac{1}{200} \times 1000 = 0.0480$$

$\therefore$ Equivalent conductivity, $\Lambda_{eq} = \frac{\kappa \times 1000}{N}$

$$= \frac{0.0058\ ohm^{-1}cm^{-1} \times 1000\ cm^3 L^{-1}}{0.0480\ g\ eqL^{-1}}$$

$$= 120.83\ ohm^{-1}cm^2 eq^{-1}$$ **(3)**

31. Given, $R = 50\Omega$, concentration $= 0.05\ M$

Cell constant, $G^* = 0.50\ cm^{-1}$,

Molar conductance at infinite dilution,

$$\Lambda^\circ = 471.4\Omega^{-1}\ cm^2\ mol^{-1}$$

(i) Specific conductance $= G^*/R$

$$\kappa = \frac{0.5}{50} = 0.01\Omega^{-1}\ cm^{-1}$$ **(1)**

(ii) Molar conductance, $\Lambda_m = \frac{1000 \times \kappa}{\text{molarity}}$

$$= \frac{1000 \times 0.01\Omega^{-1}\ cm^{-1}}{0.05\ mol\ cm^{-3}}$$

$$= 200\Omega^{-1}\ cm^2\ mol^{-1}$$ **(1)**

(iii) Degree of dissociation $(\alpha) = \frac{\Lambda_m}{\Lambda^\circ_m}$

$$= \frac{200\ W^{-1}\ cm^2 mol^{-1}}{471.4\ W^{-1}\ cm^2\ mol^{-1}} = 0.42$$ **(1)**

32. (i) Specific conductance $= 1.65 \times 10^{-4}\ \Omega^{-1}cm^{-1}$

Concentration $= 0.01\ M$

Limiting molar conductivity,

$$\Lambda^\circ_{CH_3COOH} = (349.1 + 40.9)\Omega^{-1}cm^2\ mol^{-1}$$

$$= 390\Omega^{-1}\ cm^2\ mol^{-1}$$

$$\Lambda_m = \frac{\kappa \times 1000}{C}$$

$$= \frac{1.65 \times 10^{-4}\ \Omega^{-1}cm^{-1} \times 1000}{0.01}$$

$$= 16.5\Omega^{-1}\ cm^2\ mol^{-1}$$ **(1)**

(ii) Degree of dissociation,

$$\alpha = \frac{\text{Molar conductance of substance}}{\text{Molar conductance at infinite dilution}}$$

$$\alpha = \frac{16.5}{390} = 0.042$$ **(1)**

(iii) Dissociation constant for acetic acid

$$K = \frac{C\alpha^2}{1-\alpha} = \frac{0.01 \times (0.042)^2}{1 - 0.042}$$

$$\Rightarrow \quad K = 1.8 \times 10^{-5}\ mol/L$$ **(1)**

33. Given, concentration, $C = 0.05$ M,

Resistance, $R = 31.6\Omega$

Cell constant $= 0.367\ cm^{-1}$

$$\kappa = \frac{0.367}{31.6}\Omega^{-1}cm^{-1}$$

$$\Lambda_m = \frac{1000}{C} \times \kappa = \frac{1000}{C} \times \frac{G^*}{R}$$

$$\Lambda_m = \frac{1000}{0.05} \times \frac{0.367}{31.6}$$

$$= 232.278\Omega^{-1}\ cm^2\ mol^{-1}$$

34. Kohlrausch's law states that the molar conductance of an electrolyte at infinite dilution is equal to the sum of the molar conductance of the two ions (cations and anions).'

$$\Lambda^\circ_m = \Lambda^\circ_+ + \Lambda^\circ_-$$

where, Λ°_+ and Λ°_- are the ionic conductivities of the cation and anion, respectively.

If an electrolyte furnishes more than one cation and anion then, according to Kohlrausch's law,

$$\Lambda^\circ_m (A_m B_n) = m\Lambda^\circ_A + n\Lambda^\circ_B$$

where, m and n are the number of cations and anions per formula unit of electrolyte. Λ°_A and Λ°_B are the ionic conductivities of the ions A and B.

35. Given, cell constant $= 0.5\ cm^{-1}$,

Concentration, $C = 0.01$ M, $R = 384\Omega$

Equivalent conductance,

$$\Lambda_{eq} = \frac{1000}{0.01} \times \kappa = \frac{1000}{0.01} \times \frac{G^*}{R} = \frac{1000}{0.01} \times \frac{0.5}{384}$$

(For NaCl, 0.01 M = 0.01 N)

$$= 130.2\Omega^{-1}\ cm^2\ equiv^{-1}$$

36. (i) Given, concentration of NH_4OH solution $= 0.05$ M

Resistance $= 30.8$ ohm

Temperature $= 298$ K

Cell constant $(G^*) = \frac{l}{A} = 0.343\ cm^{-1}$

Molar conductance Λ^∞_m of NH_4OH at infinite dilution

$$= 471.4\ S\ cm^2\ mol^{-1}$$

(a) **Specific conductance** $= \frac{1}{\rho} = \frac{1}{R} \times \frac{l}{A}$

$$= \frac{1}{30.8\ (ohm)} \times 0.343\ cm^{-1}$$

$$= 0.01113\ ohm^{-1}\ cm^{-1}$$

(b) **Molar conductance,** $\Lambda^c_m = \frac{\kappa \times 1000}{\text{Molarity}}$

$$= \frac{0.01113 \times 1000}{0.05} \approx 222\ S\ cm^2\ mol^{-1}$$

(c) **Degree of dissociation** $\alpha = \frac{\Lambda^c_m}{\Lambda^\infty_m} = \frac{222.6}{471.4} = 0.472$

(ii) (a) Given, Current $= 1.5$ A

Amount of Ag = 1.45 g

For Cell *B* Atomic mass of Ag = 108, Cu = 63.5, Zn = 65.3

As $Ag^+ + e^- \rightleftharpoons Ag$ (at cathode)

1 mole of Ag is deposited by 96500 C

1.45 g of Ag will be deposited by

$$= \frac{96500 \times 1.45}{108} = 1295.6\ C$$

Now, $Q = It$

$$1295.6 = 1.5 \times t$$

$$t = 864\ s$$

(b) **For Cell *A*** $Zn^{2+} + 2e^- \longrightarrow Zn$

$\therefore$ 2 moles of electrons (2×96500 C of current) produces 1 mole (65.3 g) of zinc.

$\therefore$ 1295.6 of electricity will deposit

$$= \frac{65.3}{2 \times 96500} \times 1295.6 = 0.438\ g\ of\ zinc$$

For Cell *C* $Cu^{2+} + 2e^- \longrightarrow Cu$

2 moles of electrons (2×96500 C of current) produces 1 mole (63.5 g) of Cu

1295.6 C of electricity will deposit

$$= \frac{63.5 \times 1295.6}{2 \times 96500} = 0.426\ g\ of\ Cu$$

37. (i) In any graph of molar conductivity *vs* $\sqrt{C}$, a weak electrolyte gives a curved decreasing graph.

Strong eletrolytes gives straight line decreasing graphs, in which the graph of stronger electrolyte will always be above the graph of the comparatively weaker electrolyte.

Graph 3 is curved which corresponds to NH_4OH that is a weak electrolyte.

Graph 2 and 1 respectively represent Na_2SO_4 and H_2SO_4.

($\because$ H_2SO_4 is a stronger electrolyte among the two.)

(ii) We are given,

$$\lambda^{\circ}_{(H^+)} = 349.6\ S\ cm^2/mol$$

$$\lambda^{\circ}_{(HCOO^-)} = 54.6\ S\ cm^2/mol$$

$$\lambda^{\circ}_{(HCOOH)} = \lambda^{\circ}_{(H^+)} + \lambda^{\circ}_{(HCOO^-)}$$

$$= 349.6 + 54.6$$

$$= 404.2\ S\ cm^2\ /\ mol$$

$$\text{Degree of dissociation } (\alpha) = \frac{\Lambda^c_m}{\Lambda^{\circ}_m} = \frac{34.1}{404.2} = 0.084$$

38. (i) For 0.1M KCl solution, $R = 200\,\Omega$

$$\kappa_{KCl} = 0.0129\,\Omega^{-1}cm^{-1}$$

$$\text{So, } \kappa_{KCl} = \frac{G^*}{R} \quad (G^* = \text{cell constant})$$

$$0.0129 = \frac{G^*}{200} \Rightarrow G^* = 200 \times 0.0129 = 2.58\ cm^{-1}$$

Given, cell is same, so $\kappa_{KCl} = \kappa_{NaCl}$

for 0.02 M NaCl solution,

$$\lambda_m = \frac{\kappa_{NaCl} \times 1000}{C}$$

$$= \frac{0.0129 \times 1000}{0.02} = 645\,\Omega^{-1}\ cm^2\ mol^{-1}$$

(3)

(ii) At cathode, $(Sn^{4+} + 2e^- \longrightarrow Sn^{2+}) \times 3$

At anode, $\underline{(Cr \longrightarrow Cr^{3+} + 3e^-) \times 2}$

$3\ Sn^{4+} + 2Cr + 6e^- \longrightarrow 3\ Sn^{2+} + 2Cr^{3+} + 6e^-$

So, $n = 6$

Given, $E^{\circ}_{cell} = 0.89\ V$

By the equation, $\Delta G^{\circ} = -nFE^{\circ}_{cell}$

$$= -6 \times 96500 \times 0.89$$

$$= -515.3\ kJ$$

ΔG° is –ve so the reaction will be spontaneous. **(2)**

39. (i) $\Lambda_m = \dfrac{\kappa \times 1000}{C} \qquad (\Omega^{-1}\ cm^{-1} = s)$

$$= \frac{5.25 \times 10^{-5}\Omega^{-1}cm^{-1} \times 1000}{2.5 \times 0^{-4}\ mol\ cm^{-3}}$$

$$= 210\ S\ cm^2 mol^{-1}$$

$$\Lambda^{\circ}_{(HCOOH)} = \Lambda^{\circ}_{(HCOO^-)} + \Lambda^{\circ}_{H^+}$$

$$= 50.5 + 349.5 = 400\ S\ cm^2 mol^{-1}$$

$$\alpha = \frac{\Lambda_m}{\Lambda^{\circ}_m} = \frac{210}{400} = 0.52 \text{ or } 52\%$$

(3)

(ii) Reaction taking place is

$$Cu^{2+} + 2e^- \longrightarrow Cu\ (n = 2)$$

By Faraday's first law,

$$W = ZQ \Rightarrow Zit$$

where, w = amount deposit, i = current and t = time

$$Z = \frac{\text{atomic weight}}{\text{no. of } e^- \times F}$$

$$\text{So, we get } 127 = \frac{63.5 \times 2 \times t}{2 \times 96500}$$

$$t = \frac{96500 \times 127}{63.5} = 1930\ s$$

(2)

40. (i) (a) Specific conductance is given by

$$R = \rho\frac{l}{a} \qquad \ldots(i)$$

where, R = resistance, ρ = specific resistivity

and $\dfrac{l}{a}$ = cell constant

By putting these value in Eq. (i) we get,

$$55 = \rho \times 0.45$$

$$\rho = \frac{55}{0.45} = 122.2\ \text{ohm cm}$$

$$\text{Specific conductance } (\kappa) = \frac{1}{\rho} = \frac{1}{122.2}$$

$$= 0.0082\ \text{ohm}^{-1}\ cm^{-1}.$$

(b) $\lambda_m = \kappa \times \dfrac{1000}{M}$

$$= \frac{0.0082 \times 1000}{0.06} = 136.66\ cm^2\ mol^{-1}$$

(c) Degree of dissociation $(\alpha) = \dfrac{\Lambda_m}{\Lambda^0}$

Λ_m = molar conductivity

Λ^0 = molar conductivity at infinite dilution

$$\therefore\ \alpha = \frac{1350}{398.5} = 3.38$$

(3)

(ii) $Al^{3+} + 3e^- \longrightarrow Al$

$3\text{ mol } e^- \longrightarrow 27\text{ g of Al}$

$$24.35\text{ g} \longrightarrow \frac{3}{27} \times 24.35 = 2.70\text{ mole of } e^-$$

$$\text{No. of } F = \frac{Q}{96500} = 2.70$$

$$Q = 2.70 \times 96500 = 26550\text{ C}$$ **(2)**

41. (i) The emf of cell is given by

$$E^\circ_{\text{cell}} = E^\circ_{\text{cathode}} - E^\circ_{\text{anode}}$$

$$= E^\circ_{Fe^{2+}/Fe} - E^\circ_{Cr^{3+}/Cr}$$

$$= -0.44 - (-0.74) = 0.30\text{ V}$$

The Nernst equation is formulated as

$$E_{\text{cell}} = E^\circ_{\text{cell}} - \frac{0.0591}{n} \log \frac{M^{n+}}{M}$$

$$= 0.30 - \frac{0.0591}{6} \log \frac{(0.01)^2}{(0.1)^3}$$

$$= 0.30 + \frac{0.0591}{6} = 0.30985\text{ V}$$ **(3)**

(ii) $\lambda^\circ_{m(NH_4OH)} = \lambda^\circ_{m(Ba(OH)_2)} + \lambda^\circ_{m(NH_4Cl)} - \lambda^\circ_{m(BaCl_2)}$

$$= 457 + 129 - 240$$

$$= 346\text{ ohm}^{-1}\text{cm}^2\text{mol}^{-1}$$ **(2)**

42. (i)(a) **Specific conductance** It is also known as conductivity and represented by symbol κ called 'kappa'. The specific conductance can be defined as the conductance of a solution of 1cm length with area of cross section equal to 1 cm^2.

or, $G = \kappa(\text{kappa}).\frac{A}{l}$

$\Rightarrow \kappa = G \cdot \frac{l}{A}$

where, l = 1cm and A = 1cm^2

$\frac{l}{A}$ is cell constant.

(b) Refer to Sol. 34. **(2)**

(ii) Given, concentration (C) of KCl solution = 0.001 M

Resistance (R) of 0.001 M KCl = 1500 Ω.

Conductivity (κ) at 298 K of KCl solution

$$= 0.146 \times 10^{-3}\,\Omega^{-1}\text{cm}^{-1}$$

Also, ∵ $\kappa(\text{Kappa}) = \frac{1}{R} \times \frac{l}{a}$

where, $\frac{l}{a}$ = cell constant

$\therefore \frac{l}{a} = \kappa(\text{Kappa}) \times R = 0.146 \times 10^{-3} \times 1500$

Cell constant = $219 \times 10^{-3}\text{cm}^{-1}$

and Λ_m (molar conductivity)

$$= \frac{\kappa \times 1000}{C} = \frac{0.146 \times 10^{-3} \times 1000}{0.001}$$

$$= 146\text{ S cm}^2\text{mol}^{-1}$$

Hence, cell constant = $219 \times 10^{-3}\text{cm}^{-1}$

Molar conductivity = 146 S cm^2 mol^{-1} **(3)**

43. (i) For electrolyte having 0.01 mol L^{-1} KCl solution,

Molarity = 0.1 mol L^{-1}

Resistance = 100Ω

Conductivity = $1.29 \times 10^{-2}\Omega^{-1}\text{ cm}^{-1}$

Cell constant (G^*)

= Resistance (R) × Conductivity (κ)

= $100\Omega \times 1.29 \times 10^{-2}\Omega^{-1}\text{cm}^{-1} = 1.29\text{cm}^{-1}$

For electrolyte having 0.01 mol L^{-1} KCl solution,

Molarity = 0.02 mol L^{-1}

Resistance = 520Ω, Conductivity = ?

Conductivity of 0.02 mol L^{-1} KCl solution,

$$\kappa = \frac{\text{Cell constant}}{\text{Resistance}} = \frac{1.29\ (\text{cm}^{-1})}{520\ \ (\Omega)}$$

$$= 2.481 \times 10^{-3}\text{cm}^{-1}\,\Omega^{-1}$$

Molar conductivity, $\Lambda_m = \frac{\kappa \times 1000}{\text{Molarity}}$

$$= \frac{2.481 \times 10^{-3} \times 1000}{0.02}$$

$$= 124\Omega^{-1}\text{cm}^2\text{mol}^{-1}$$ **(3)**

(ii)(a) **Limiting molar conductivity** When the concentration of electrolyte in solution approaches zero, the molar conductivity reaches a limiting value, known as limiting molar conductivity. It is denoted as Λ°_m.

(b) **Fuel cell** It is a type of galvanic cells, in which reactants are continuously feed to the electrodes, which react to produce electricity and product thus formed are continuously removed. They are designed to convert the energy of combustion of fuels like hydrogen, methane, methanol etc. directly into highly efficient electrical energy. The electrode reactions are given below.

At cathode,

$$O_2(g) + 2H_2O(l) + 4e^- \longrightarrow 4OH^-(aq)$$

At anode,

$$2H_2(g) + 4OH^-(aq) \longrightarrow 4H_2O(l) + 4e^-$$

Overall reaction, $2H_2(g) + O_2(g) \longrightarrow 2H_2O(l)$ **(2)**

CHAPTER TEST

01 Mark Questions

1. Fill in the blanks by choosing the appropriate word(s) from these given in the bracket.

[$PbSO_4$, Pb, PbO_2, chemical, electrical, zero, infinite increases, decreases]

(i) While charging the lead storage battery .... at anode is reduced to ....

(ii) Electrochemical cell is a device that converts the .... energy into .... energy.

(iii) Superconductors have .... resistivity or .... conductivity.

(iv) Conductivity .... but molar conductivity .... with increase in dilution.

2. Select and write the correct alternatives from the choices given below.

(i) Which among the options is the correct representation of the given cell reaction?

$$Zn + H_2SO_4 \longrightarrow ZnSO_4 + H_2$$

(a) $Zn|Zn^{2+}||H^+|H_2$

(b) $Zn|Zn^{2+}||H^+, H_2|Pt$

(c) $Zn|ZnSO_4||H_2|Zn$

(d) $Zn|H_2SO_4||ZnSO_4|H_2$

(ii) On changing the concentration of the ions to double in a cell reaction, the effect on E°_{cell} will be

(a) doubled (b) halved

(c) four times increases (d) unchanged

(iii) KCl solution is generally used to determine the cell constant because

(a) it is highly ionic in nature.

(b) its conductivity is known accurately at various concentration and different temperatures .

(c) size of cations and anions are comparable.

(d) All of the above

(iv) How many coulombs are required in order to reduce 12.3 g of nitrobenzene to aniline?

(a) 579 C (b) 5790 C

(c) 57900 C (d) 579000 C

3. (i) **Assertion** (A) Anhyd. HCl is a bad conductor of electricity, while *aq*. HCl is a good conductor.

Reason (R) Aqueous HCl is not fully ionised but anhyd. HCl is ionised to produce H^+ and Cl^- ions.

(a) Both (A) and (R) are correct and (R) is the correct explanation of (A).

(b) Both (A) and (R) are correct but (R) is not the correct explanation of (A).

(c) (A) is correct and (R) is incorrect.

(d) (A) is incorrect and (R) is correct.

(ii) **Assertion** (A) Solid NaCl does not conduct electricity.

Reason (R) Solid NaCl has no free ions.

(a) Both (A) and (R) are correct and (R) is the correct explanation of (A).

(b) Both (A) and (R) are correct but (R) is not the correct explanation of (A).

(c) (A) is correct and (R) is incorrect.

(d) (A) is incorrect and (R) is correct.

02 Marks Questions

4. Calculate the degree of dissociation (α) of acetic acid, if its molar conductivity (Λ_m) is $34.04 \text{ S cm}^2\text{mol}^{-1}$.

Given : $\lambda^\circ_{(H^+)} = 310.1 \text{ S cm}^2\text{mol}^{-1}$

$\lambda^\circ_{(CH_3COO^-)} = 30.3 \text{ S cm}^2\text{mol}^{-1}$

5. Give a relevant for the following.

(i) Dry cell become dead after a long time even if it has not been used.

(ii) Iron does not rust even if zinc coating is broken in a galvanised iron rod.

6. Calculate the electrode potential of the following cell at 298 K.

$$Ni \mid Ni^{2+}(0.50\text{ M}) \mid\mid Al^{3+}(0.001\text{ M}) \mid Al$$

Given : $E^\circ_{Ni^{2+}|Ni} = -0.25\text{ V}, E^\circ_{Al^{3+}|Al} = -1.66\text{ V}$

7. For the cell,

$$Zn(s) \mid Zn^{2+} \mid\mid Cu^{2+} \mid Cu(s)$$

(i) Write the half-cell reaction for each.

(ii) Calculate standard electrode potential.

8. Calculate the time taken to deposit 0.6 g of copper at cathode when a current of 1 ampere is passed through the solution of $CuSO_4$.

(Atomic weight of Cu $= 63.5 \text{ g mol}^{-1}$)

9. Predict the products of electrolysis in each case.

(i) An aqueous solution of $AgNO_3$ with platinum electrode.

(ii) An aqueous solution of H_2SO_4 with platinum electrode.

10. Calculate the emf of the given cell.

$$Cr\,|\,Cr^{3+}\,(0.1\,M)\,||\,Fe^{2+}\,(0.01\,M)\,|\,Fe$$

Given, $E^\circ_{Cr|Cr^{3+}} = -0.74$ V, $E^\circ_{(Fe^{2+}|Fe)} = -0.44$ V

03 Marks Questions

11. (i) Rusting of iron is quicker in saline water than in ordinary water.

(ii) Alkaline medium inhibits the rusting of iron.

(iii) An electrochemical cell stops working after sometime.

12. Consider the following cell reaction.

$$2Fe(s) + O_2(g) + 4H^+(aq) \longrightarrow 2Fe^{2+}(aq) + 2H_2O(l), \quad E^\circ = 1.67\text{ V}$$

at $[Fe^{2+}] = 10^{-6}$ M, $p_{(O_2)} = 0.1$ and pH = 6. What is the cell potential at 25°C?

13. Given the half-cell reactions in the following batteries.

(i) Leclanche cell (ii) Mercury cell

(iii) Nickel-cadmium cell

14. An aqueous solution of copper sulphate, $CuSO_4$ was electrolysed between platinum electrodes using a current of 0.145 A for 44 min. [Given, atomic mass of Cu = 63.5 g mol^{-1}]

(i) Write the cathodic reaction.

(ii) Calculate

(a) Electric charge passed during electrolysis.

(b) Mass of copper deposited at the cathode.

[Given, 1 F = 96500 C mol^{-1}]

15. The cell reaction is given below.

$$CrO_3(aq) + 6H^+ + 6e^- \longrightarrow Cr(s) + 3H_2O$$

Calculate how many grams of chromium will be electroplated by 22,000 coulombs. How long will it take to electroplate 0.5 g chromium using 11.0 A current? [Atomic mass of Cr = 52 g mol]

[1F = 96500 C mol^{-1}]

05 Marks Questions

16. (i) Define the following terms.

(a) Molar conductivity

(b) Limiting molar conductivity

(c) Fuel cell

(ii) Calculate λ°_m for acetic acid, If

$\lambda^\circ_{m(HCl)} = 420$ S $cm^2 mol^{-1}$

$\lambda^\circ_{m(NaCl)} = 120$ S $cm^2 mol^{-1}$ and

$\lambda^\circ_{m(CH_3COONa)} = 90$ S $cm^2 mol^{-1}$.

17. (i) The conductivity of 0.1 mol L^{-1} solution of acetic acid is 3.905×10^{-3} S cm^{-1}. Calculate its molar conductivity and degree of dissociation (α). Given, $\lambda^\circ_{(H^+)} = 349.6$ S $cm^2 mol^{-1}$ and $\lambda^\circ_{(CH_3COO^-)} = 40.9$ S $cm^2 mol^{-1}$.

(ii) Calculate the time to deposit 2.12 g of copper at cathode when a current of 3.5 A was passed through the solution of $CuSO_4$, (Molar mass of Cu = 63.5 g mol^{-1}, 1F = 96500 C mol^{-1})

18. (i) Write the cell reaction and calculate the emf of the following cell at 298 K.

$$Sn(s)\,|\,Sn^{2+}\,(0.004\,M)\,||\,H^+\,(0.020\,M)\,|\,H_2(g)\,(1\text{ bar})\,|\,Pt(s)$$

(Given : $E^\circ_{Sn^{2+}|Sn} = -0.14$ V)

(ii) Give reasons :

(a) On the basis of E° values, O_2 gas should be liberated at anode, but it is Cl_2 gas which is liberated in the electrolysis of aqueous NaCl.

(b) Conductivity of CH_3COOH decreases on dilution.

Answers

1. (i) $PbSO_4$, Pb (ii) electrical, chemical (iii) zero, infinite (iv) decreases, increases

2. (i) (b), (ii) (d), (iii) (b), (iv) (c) **3.** (i) (c), (ii) (a) **4.** $\alpha = 0.1$ **6.** $E_{cell} = 1.4602$ V

8. 911.8 sec **10.** 0.26 V **14.** (ii) charge passed = 382.8 C, mass deposited = 0.126 g

15. mass = 1.97 g, time = 8.4 min **16.** (ii) 390 $Scm^2 mol^{-1}$

17. (i) $\Lambda_m = 39.05$ Scm^2/mol, $\alpha = 0.1$ (ii) $t = 306$ min **18.** $E_{cell} = 0.111$ V

03

Chemical Kinetics

TREND ANALYSIS 4 YEARS

Topic	Types of Questions	2024	2023	2020	2019
TOPIC 01 Rate of Reaction and Factors Influencing the Reaction Rate	1 Marks	1	—	—	—
	2 Marks	—	—	—	1
	3 Marks	1	—	—	—
	5 Marks	—	—	—	—
TOPIC 02 Integrated Rate of Equation and Half-life of the Reaction	1 Mark	—	2	—	1
	2 Marks	—	—	—	2
	3 Marks	—	1	—	—
	5 Marks	—	—	—	—
TOPIC 03 Activation Energy, Collision Theory of Chemical Reactions	1 Mark	—	1	—	1
	2 Marks	—	—	—	—
	3 Marks	1	1	1	—
	5 Marks	—	—	—	—

Average No. of Questions Across all Sets

TOPIC 1

Rate of Reaction and Factors Influencing the Reaction Rate

The branch of chemistry which deals with the study of reaction rates and the mechanism by which the reactions occur is called **chemical kinetics**.

Comparison with Chemical Dynamics

In chemical dynamics, we study rate and mechanism of chemical reactions. It also involves the study of how energy is transferred among molecules alongwith their chemical kinetics.

Reaction Rate and its Measurement

The rate of a chemical reaction may be defined as the change in concentration of any of the reactants or products per unit time.

Units of rate of reaction is mol $L^{-1}s^{-1}$ or atm s^{-1} (when reactants and products are in gaseous state).

Average Rate of a Reaction

The change in concentration of any of the reactants or products per unit time over a specified interval of time is called the average rate of the given reaction.

Representation of rate of reaction in terms of reactants and products.

For a reaction like $A + 2B \longrightarrow 3C$

$$\text{Rate} = -\frac{\Delta[A]}{\Delta t} = -\frac{1}{2}\frac{\Delta[B]}{\Delta t} = \frac{1}{3}\frac{\Delta[C]}{\Delta t}$$

(Here, –ve sign indicates the rate of decrease of concentration of A and B otherwise rate of reaction is always positive.)

Instantaneous Rate of a Reaction

The rate of change of concentration of any of the reactants or products at a particular instant of time for a given temperature is called the instantaneous rate of a given reaction at that instant of time.

$$r_{\text{ins}} = \frac{-d[A]}{dt} = \frac{-1}{2}\frac{d[B]}{dt} = \frac{1}{3}\frac{d[C]}{dt}$$

Graphically Determination of Rate of Reaction

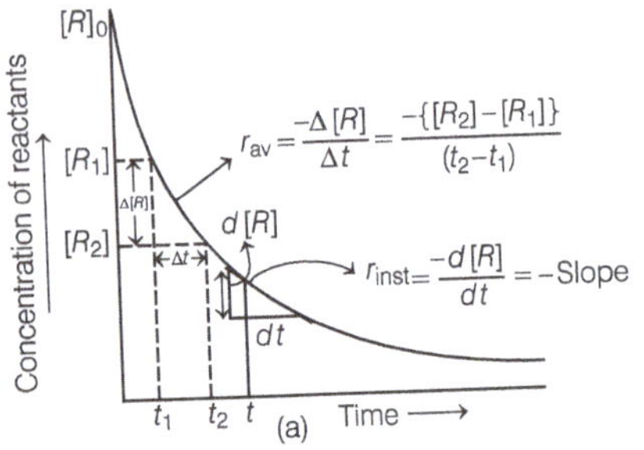

Determination of instantaneous and average rate of a reaction

Factors Affecting the Reaction Rate

Some of the factors that affect rate of reaction rate are as follows

(i) **Nature of reactants** The reactions involving polar and ionic substances are quite fast, whereas the reactions involving covalent compounds are much slower.

(ii) **Concentration of reactants** Rate of reaction increases on increasing the concentration of reactants due to increase in molecular collisions.

(iii) **Temperature** Usually, rate increases with increase in temperature. For most of the homogeneous reactions, the rate becomes doubled for each $10°$ rise in temperature.

(iv) **Presence of catalyst** If a catalyst increases the rate of a reaction, it is called positive catalyst and if it slows down the reaction, it is called negative catalyst.

(v) **Surface area** The rate of a reaction increases with an increase in surface area of the reactant.

(vi) **Radiation** Rate of reaction increased by the use of certain radiations. The photons of these radiations having frequencies (ν) possess sufficient energies ($E = h\nu$) to break certain bonds in reactants.

Dependence of Rate of a Reaction on the Concentration of Reactants

Law of Mass Action

At constant temperature, the rate of a chemical reaction is directly proportional to the product of active masses of reacting species, with each active mass term raised to the power equal to the stoichiometric coefficient of that species in the chemical reaction.

e.g. For a general reaction, $aA + bB \longrightarrow$ Products

Rate $\propto [A]^a\,[B]^b$, where $[A]$ and $[B]$ are active masses of reactants A and B respectively.

Active mass of a substance in the solution or gas phase is equal to its molar concentration.

Rate Law

It is the expression in which reaction rate is given in terms of molar concentration of reactants with each term raised to some power, which may or may not be same as the stoichiometric coefficient of reacting species in a balanced chemical equation. It is also called **rate equation** or **rate expression**.

For a general reaction, $aA + bB \longrightarrow cC + dD$

Rate $= k[A]^x[B]^y$, where x and y may or may not be equal to the stoichiometric coefficients (a and b) of the reactants.

$$\frac{-d[R]}{dt} = k[A]^x[B]^y$$

The above equation is known as **differential rate equation.** Rate law for any reaction cannot be predicted by merely looking at the balanced chemical equation, i.e. theoretically but must be determined experimentally.

e.g. For the decomposition of $N_2O_5(g)$,

$$2N_2O_5(g) \longrightarrow 4NO_2(g) + O_2(g);\ \text{Rate} = k[N_2O_5]$$

Rate Constant (Specific Reaction Rate)

The rate constant of a reaction is equal to the rate of reaction when the concentration of each of the reactants is unity.

For reaction, $aA + bB \longrightarrow$ Products, rate law is given by,

Rate $\propto [A]^a [B]^b$ and Rate $= k[A]^a [B]^b$, k = rate constant.

The general unit of rate constant is $mol^{1-n} L^{n-1} s^{-1}$, where, n represents the overall sum of the powers appearing in the rate law. For a gaseous reaction, unit of rate constant is $atm^{1-n} s^{-1}$.

Characteristics of Rate Constant

Some characteristics of rate constant are as follows.

- Higher the value of k, greater is the rate of the reaction.
- A particular reaction has a definite value of k at a particular temperature.
- The value of rate constant for a particular reaction increases with an increase in temperature.
- The rate constant does not depend upon the initial concentration of reactants.
- Its units depend upon the overall order of the reaction (the sum of the powers to which the concentration terms have been raised is the rate law).

Order of a Reaction

The sum of all the powers to which all the concentration terms in the rate law are raised to express the observed rate of reaction is called the overall order of reaction.

e.g. For the general reaction,

$$aA + bB + cC \longrightarrow \text{Products},$$

Rate $= k[A]^p [B]^q [C]^r$

where, p, q and r represent the order of reaction with respect to A, B and C respectively.

Therefore, overall order of reaction $= p + q + r$

- Order of a reaction is experimentally determined, which may be zero, whole number, fractional or negative.
- p, q and r may or may not be equal to stoichiometric coefficients.

Rate law and the units of rate constant for reactions of different order

Type of reaction	Rate law	Units of rate constant (k)		
		General units	Units when concentration is expressed (in mol L^{-1}) and time (in s)	For gaseous reactions when partial pressure is expressed (in atm)
Reaction of order, n	Rate $= k\,[\text{Reactants}]^n$	$\text{concentration}^{1-n}\text{time}^{-1}$	$mol^{1-n} L^{n-1} s^{-1}$	$atm^{1-n} s^{-1}$
Zero order reaction	Rate $= k$	concentraton time^{-1}	$mol\, L^{-1} s^{-1}$	$atm\, s^{-1}$
First order reaction	Rate $= k\,[\text{Reactants}]^1$	time^{-1}	s^{-1}	s^{-1}
Second order reaction	Rate $= k\,[\text{Reactants}]^2$	$\text{concentration}^{-1}\ \text{time}^{-1}$	$mol^{-1} L\, s^{-1}$	$atm^{-1} s^{-1}$
Third order reaction	Rate $= k\,[\text{Reactants}]^3$	$\text{concentration}^{-2}\ \text{time}^{-1}$	$mol^{-2} L^2 s^{-1}$	$atm^{-2} s^{-1}$

Molecularity

It is the number of reacting species taking part in an elementary reaction, which must collide simultaneously in order to bring about a chemical reaction. It is a theoretical concept and can never be zero or fractional.

Mechanism of a Reaction

A sequence of intermediate steps or all elementary processes proposed to account for the overall stoichiometry of a reaction is called the mechanism of the reaction. The simple chemical reactions which occur only in one step are called **elementary reactions**, whereas the reactions which occur in two or more steps are called **complex reactions**.

A complex reaction proceeds through a series of elementary reactions. Each elementary reaction has its own molecularity and its own rate. The overall rate of a complex reaction is governed by the rate of slowest elementary step, which is known as **rate determining step**.

Reaction Involving Slow Step

Those reactions which occur by a sequence of steps and among them the slowest step is considered as the rate determining step of that reaction.

e.g. $$NO_2 + CO \xrightarrow{500\,K} CO_2 + NO$$

Mechanism

***Step* I** $$NO_2 + NO_2 \xrightarrow{\text{Slow}} NO + NO_3$$

***Step* II** $$NO_3 + CO \xrightarrow{\text{Fast}} CO_2 + NO_2$$

Step I is the slowest step and also the rate determining step of the reaction, thus rate $= k[NO_2]^2$, i.e. the rate of reaction does not depend upon the concentration of CO but depends upon $[NO_2]^2$.

Note **Bottle neck principle** Generally in a complex reaction, the order of reaction is equal to the molecularity of the slowest step, yet the order of any reaction has always to be determined experimentally.

Differences between order and molecularity of a reaction

Order of a reaction	Molecularity of a reaction
It is the sum of the powers of concentration terms on which the rate of reaction actually depends or it is the sum of the exponents of the concentrations in the rate law equation.	It is the number of atoms, ions or molecules that must collide with one another simultaneously so as to result into a chemical reaction.
It can be fractional as well as zero.	It is always a whole number.
It can be determined experimentally only and cannot be calculated theoretically.	It can be calculated by adding the molecules of the slowest step. Therefore, it is a theoretical concept.
It tells us about slowest step in the mechanism and hence, gives some clue about mechanism of the reaction.	It does not tell us anything about the mechanism of the reaction.
Even the order of a simple reaction may not be equal to the number of molecules of the reactants as seen from the balanced equation.	For simple reactions, the molecularity can usually be obtained from the stoichiometry of the equation.

PYQs Previous Years' Questions

1 Mark Questions

1. For a particular reaction, the value of rate constant is $0.05\ s^{-1}$. The reaction is of .... order and will be .... of the initial concentration. **ISC 2024**

2. When the concentration of a reactant of first order reaction is tripled, the rate of reaction becomes .... times. The unit of rate constant (k) for the first order reaction is .... **ISC Specimen 2023**

3. When the concentration of a reactant of first order reaction is doubled, the rate of reaction becomes .... times.
   The unit of rate constant (k) for the first order reaction is .... **ISC Specimen 2021-22 (Sem-II)**

4. Identify the order of reaction from each of the following units of rate constant (k).
   (i) $mol\ L^{-1}s^{-1}$ (ii) $mol^{-1}L\ s^{-1}$ **ISC 2017**

5. Name the order of reaction which proceeds with a uniform rate throughout. **ISC 2017**

6. Unit of rate of reaction is .... . **ISC 2014**

7. For a first order reaction, the unit of rate of reaction is ... and that of rate constant is ... . **ISC 2011**

8. Correct the following statement by changing the underlined part of the sentence.
   (Do not change the whole sentence.)
   The rate constant of a first order reaction is directly proportional to the concentration of the reactant. **ISC 2008, 2004**

9. The reaction between X and Y is first order with respect to X and second order with respect to Y. If the concentration of X is halved and the concentration of Y is doubled, the rate of reaction will be **ISC 2008**
   (a) same as the initial value
   (b) three times the initial value
   (c) double the initial value
   (d) half the initial value

10. Define molecularity of a reaction. Give one difference between the order of a reaction and its molecularity. **ISC 2007**

2 Marks Questions

11. For the reaction $A + B \longrightarrow C + D$, the initial rate for different reactions and initial concentration of reactants are given below. **ISC 2019**

S.No.	Initial conc. $[A]\ mol\ L^{-1}$	Initial conc. $[B]\ mol\ L^{-1}$	Initial rate $(mol\ L^{-1}\ s^{-1})$
1.	1.0	1.0	2×10^{-3}
2.	2.0	1.0	4×10^{-3}
3.	4.0	1.0	8×10^{-3}
4.	1.0	2.0	2×10^{-3}
5.	1.0	4.0	2×10^{-3}

(i) What is the overall order of reaction?
(ii) Write the rate law equation.

12. (i) Write the rate law expression for the reaction $A + B + C \longrightarrow D + E$. If the order of reaction is first, second and zero with respect to A, B and C respectively.

(ii) How many times the rate of reaction will increase, if the concentration of A, B and C are doubled in the equation given in (i) above? **ISC 2018**

13. Identify the reaction order from each of the following rate constants. **ISC Specimen 2018**

(i) $k = 2.3 \times 10^{-5} \, L \, mol^{-1} \, s^{-1}$ (ii) $k = 3 \times 10^{-4} \, s^{-1}$

14. What is the difference between order of a reaction and the molecularity of a reaction? **ISC Specimen 2018, 2017, 2015**

15. For the reaction $2H_2 + 2NO \rightleftharpoons 2H_2O + N_2$, the following rate data was obtained:

S.No.	[NO] mol L^{-1}	$[H_2]$ mol L^{-1}	Rate : mol L^{-1} s^{-1}
1.	0.40	0.40	4.6×10^{-3}
2.	0.80	0.40	18.4×10^{-3}
3.	0.40	0.80	9.2×10^{-3}

Calculate the following.

(i) The overall order of reaction.

(ii) The rate law.

(iii) The value of rate constant (k). **ISC 2017**

16. A study of chemical kinetics of the reaction

$$A + B \longrightarrow \text{products},$$

gave the following data at 25°C.

Experiment	[A]	[B]	$\frac{d \text{ (Product)}}{dt}$
1.	1.0	0.15	4.20×10^{-6}
2.	2.0	0.15	8.40×10^{-6}
3.	1.0	0.20	5.60×10^{-6}

Find

(i) the order of reaction with respect to A.

(ii) the order of reaction with respect to B.

(iii) the rate law. **ISC 2012**

3 Marks Questions

17. For the reaction $A + B \rightleftharpoons$ Product, following data was obtained. **ISC 2024**

Experiment number	Initial concentration of [A] (mol L^{-1})	Initial concentration of [B] (mol L^{-1})	Initial rate (mol L^{-1} min^{-1})
1	0.15	0.15	9.6×10^{-2}
2	0.30	0.15	3.84×10^{-1}
3	0.15	0.30	1.92×10^{-1}
4	0.30	0.30	7.68×10^{-1}

Calculate the following.

(i) The overall order of the reaction.

(ii) The rate law equation.

(iii) The value of rate constant.

18. The data in the table given below was obtained in a series of experiments on the rate of the reaction between compounds [A] and [B] at a constant temperature: **ISC Specimen 2024**

Experiment	The initial concentration of [A] mol dm^{-3}	The initial concentration of [B] mol dm^{-3}	Initial rate mol dm^{-3} s^{-1}
1	0.15	0.30	1.10×10^{-4}
2	0.30	0.30	4.40×10^{-4}
3	0.60	0.15	8.80×10^{-4}

Show how this data can be used to deduce the rate expression for the reaction between [A] and [B].

19. The initial rate of a reaction, $A + B \longrightarrow$ products, is doubled when the initial concentration of A is doubled and increases eight fold when the initial concentration of both A and B were doubled. State the order of the reaction with respect to A and with respect to B. Write the rate equation. **ISC 2004**

20. List any two factors that influence the rate of chemical reaction. Indicate whether the rate constant of the reaction is dependent or independent on these factors. **ISC 2002**

5 Marks Question

21. Consider the reaction, $A + B \longrightarrow C + D$

The initial rates for different initial concentrations of the reactants are given below.

	Initial concentration (mol/L)		Initial rate (mol/L-s)
	[A]	[B]	
(a)	1.0	1.0	2.0×10^{-3}
(b)	2.0	1.0	4.0×10^{-3}
(c)	4.0	1.0	8.0×10^{-3}
(d)	1.0	2.0	2.0×10^{-3}
(e)	1.0	4.0	2.0×10^{-3}

(i) What are the order of reaction with respect to A and B?

(ii) What is the overall order?

(iii) Write the rate law equation.

(iv) Calculate the rate constant.

(v) Suggest a possible mechanism. **ISC 2005**

Explanations

1. First; independent
2. 3, s^{-1}
3. two, s^{-1}
4. (i) mol $L^{-1}s^{-1}$ $\rightarrow$ Zero order reaction.
   (ii) mol^{-1} L s^{-1} $\rightarrow$ Second order reaction.
5. Zero order reaction.
6. The unit of rate of reaction is mol $L^{-1}s^{-1}$.
   It is because rate of reaction
   $$= \frac{\text{Change in concentration of a reactant or product}}{\text{Time interval}}$$
   $$= \frac{\text{mol / L}}{\text{s}} = \text{mol L}^{-1}\text{s}^{-1}$$
7. For a first order reaction, the unit of rate of reaction is mol L^{-1} s^{-1} and that of rate constant is s^{-1}.
   For rate constant, general unit is mol^{1-n} L^{n-1} s^{-1}. where, n is the order of reaction.
   For first order reaction, $n = 1$.
   $\therefore$ Unit of rate constant for first order reaction
   $$= mol^{1-1}\ L^{1-1}\ s^{-1}$$
   $$= s^{-1}$$
8. **The rate of a first order reaction** is directly proportional to the concentration of the reactants.
   Rate of a reaction $\propto$ [Concentration of reactant]^n
   where, n = order of reaction.
   For first order,
   Rate of reaction $\propto$ [Concentration of reactant]^1
9. (c) Given, $X + Y \longrightarrow$ Product.
   As the reaction is first order with respect to X and second order with respect to Y.
   Hence, rate of reaction, $r_1 = k[X]^1[Y]^2$
   If concentration of X is halved, i.e. $\frac{[X]}{2}$ and concentration of Y is doubled, i.e. $[2Y]$.
   Then, new rate of reaction, $r_2 = k\left[\frac{X}{2}\right]^1[2Y]^2$
   $$= k \times 2[X][Y]^2$$
   Hence, $r_2 = 2r_1$.
   Hence, option (c) is correct.
10. **Molecularity** is the number of reacting species taking part in a chemical reaction to bring about the chemical change in a single step.

Difference between molecularity and order of a reaction Molecularity of a reaction is always a whole number, while order of a reaction may be zero or a fractional number.

11. Rate $= k[A]^a[B]^b$
    where, a = order of A and b = order of B
    By dividing rate (2) by rate (1), we get
    $$\frac{(\text{Rate})_2}{(\text{Rate})_1} = \frac{[A]_2^a[B]_2^b}{[A]_1^a[B]_1^b}$$
    $$\frac{4\times10^{-3}}{2\times10^{-3}} = \frac{(2)^a(1)^b}{(1)^a(1)^b}$$
    $$2 = (2)^a \Rightarrow a = 1$$
    $\therefore$ Order of $A = 1$ (½)
    Similarly, on dividing rate (1) and rate (4), we get
    $$\frac{(\text{Rate})_4}{(\text{Rate})_1} = \frac{[A]_4^a[B]_4^b}{[A]_1^a[B]_1^b}$$
    $$\frac{2\times10^{-3}}{2\times10^{-3}} = \frac{(1)^a(2)^b}{(1)^a(1)^b}$$
    $$(1) = (1)^a$$
    $\Rightarrow$ $a = 0$
    $\therefore$ Order of $B = 0$ (½)
    (i) Therefore, overall order of reaction
    $= 1 + 0 = 1$, (½)
    (ii) and rate law is $r = k[A]$. (½)
12. (i) The rate law expression for the reaction
    $A + B + C \longrightarrow D + E$ is $r = k[A][B]^2$.
    The order of reaction is first, second and zero with respect to A, B and C respectively. (1)
    (ii) If the concentration of A, B and C are doubled, then rate is given by
    $$r_1 = k[2A][2B]^2 \text{ and } r_1 = 8k[A][B]^2$$
    $\therefore$ New rate r_1 is 8 times of previous rate, r. Hence, rate of reaction increases by 8 times. (1)

Concept Enhancer A zero-order reaction is independent of the reactant concentration and the unit of rate is same as that of the rate constant.

13. (i) Rate constant 2.3×10^{-5} L mol^{-1} s^{-1} is for second order reaction. (1)
    (ii) Rate constant $3\times10^{-4}s^{-1}$ is for first order reaction. (1)

14. Refer to text on page 66.

15. Given, $2H_2 + 2NO \rightleftharpoons 2H_2O + N_2$

Let, the given reaction is of order q with respect to H_2 and p with respect to NO.

The rate of formation of H_2O and N_2 can also be written as,

$$4.6\times10^{-3} = k\,[A]^p\,[B]^q = k\,[0.4]^p\,[0.4]^q \quad ...(i)$$

$$18.4\times10^{-3} = k[0.8]^p\,[0.4]^q \quad ...(ii)$$

$$9.2\times10^{-3} = k[0.4]^p\,[0.8]^q \quad ...(iii)$$

From Eqs. (i) and (ii), we get

$$\frac{18.4\times10^{-3}}{4.6\times10^{-3}} = \frac{k(0.8)^p\,(0.4)^q}{k(0.4)^p\,(0.4)^q}$$

$$4 = (2)^p \Rightarrow (2)^2 = (2)^p$$

Hence, $p = 2$

From Eqs. (i) and (iii), we get

$$\frac{9.2\times10^{-3}}{4.6\times10^{-3}} = \frac{k(0.4)^p\,(0.8)^q}{k(0.4)^p\,(0.4)^q} \Rightarrow 2 = (2)^q \quad \textbf{(1)}$$

$\therefore \quad q = 1$

(i) Overall order of reaction is $(2+1) = 3$

(ii) Rate law equation, $r = k\,[NO]^2\,[H_2]$

(iii) $r = k\,[H_2]^2\,[NO]$

Rate constant, k

$$= \frac{r}{[H_2][NO]^2} = \frac{4.6\times10^{-3}}{[0.4][0.4]^2}$$

$$= 7.18\times10^{-2}\ \text{mol}^{-2}\text{L}^2\text{s}^{-1} \quad \textbf{(1)}$$

Common Mistake The order of reaction is an experimental value. It is not always necessary that the order of reaction is equal to the sum of stoichiometric coefficients in balanced reaction. So, use experimental data if it is given in question.

16. Given, $\quad A + B \longrightarrow \text{Products}$

Suppose the given reaction is of order p with respect to A and q with respect to B. The rate of formation of product can be written as

$$4.20\times10^{-6} = k\,[1.0]^p\,[0.15]^q \quad ...(i)$$

$$8.40\times10^{-6} = k\,[2.0]^p\,[0.15]^q \quad ...(ii)$$

$$5.60\times10^{-6} = k\,[1.0]^p\,[0.20]^q \quad ...(iii)$$

On dividing Eq. (ii) by Eq. (i), we get

$$\frac{8.40\times10^{-6}}{4.20\times10^{-6}} = \left[\frac{2.0}{1.0}\right]^p$$

$\Rightarrow \quad (2)^1 = 2^p$

$\therefore \quad p = 1$

On dividing Eq. (iii) by Eq. (i), we get

$$\frac{5.60\times10^{-6}}{4.20\times10^{-6}} = \left[\frac{0.20}{0.15}\right]^q \Rightarrow \left(\frac{4}{3}\right)^1 = \left(\frac{4}{3}\right)^q$$

$\therefore \quad q = 1$

Hence,

(i) The order of reaction with respect to A is 1. **(1)**

(ii) The order of reaction with respect to B is 1.

(iii) The rate law can be written as,

Rate $= k\,[A][B]$ **(1)**

17. Let, the order w.r.t A and B be α and β respectively.

Rate law expression may be written as

Rate $= k[A]^\alpha\,[B]^\beta$

$$\therefore \quad 9.6\times10^{-2} = k[0.15]^\alpha\,[0.15]^\beta \quad ...(i)$$

$$\text{or} \quad 3.84\times10^{-1} = k[0.3]^\alpha\,[0.15]^\beta \quad ...(ii)$$

$$\text{or} \quad 1.92\times10^{-1} = k[0.15]^\alpha\,[0.3]^\beta \quad ...(iii)$$

$$\text{or} \quad 7.68\times10^{-1} = k[0.3]^\alpha\,[0.3]^\beta \quad ...(iv)$$

Dividing Eqs. (i) by (ii), we get

$$\frac{9.6\times10^{-2}}{3.84\times10^{-1}} = \frac{k[0.15]^\alpha\,\cancel{[0.15]^\beta}}{k[0.3]^\alpha\,\cancel{[0.15]^\beta}}$$

$$\left[\frac{1}{4}\right] = \left[\frac{1}{2}\right]^\alpha \Rightarrow \left[\frac{1}{2}\right]^2 = \left[\frac{1}{2}\right]^\alpha$$

$\therefore \quad \alpha = 2$

Dividing Eqs. (i) by (iii), we get

$$\frac{9.6\times10^{-2}}{1.92\times10^{-1}} = \frac{\cancel{k[0.15]^\alpha}\,[0.15]^\beta}{\cancel{k[0.15]^\alpha}\,[0.3]^\beta}$$

$$\Rightarrow \quad \left[\frac{1}{2}\right]^1 = \left[\frac{1}{2}\right]^\beta \Rightarrow \beta = 1$$

(i) The overall order of the reaction is 3.

(ii) Rate law expression.

$$\text{Rate} = k[A]^2\,[B]^1$$

(iii) From expression (i) rate constant can be calculated as

$$9.6\times10^{-2} = k[0.15]^2\,[0.15]^1$$

$$k = \frac{9.6\times10^{-2}\ \text{mol L}^{-1}\ \text{min}^{-1}}{[0.15]^3\ (\text{mol L}^{-1})^3}$$

$$= 28.44\ \text{mol}^{-2}\ \text{L}^2\ \text{min}^{-1}$$

18. Let the rate be given by $r = k[A]^x[B]^y$

Where order of the reaction $= x + y$

Substituting given data

$$1.10\times10^{-4} = k[0.15]^x\,[0.30]^y \quad ...(i)$$

$$4.40\times10^{-4}=k[0.30]^x\,[0.30]^y \quad \ldots(ii)$$
$$8.80\times10^{-4}=k[0.60]^x\,[0.15]^y \quad \ldots(iii)$$

From Eqs. (i) and (ii)

$$\frac{1.1\times10^{-4}}{4.4\times10^{-4}}=\left[\frac{0.15}{0.30}\right]^x \Rightarrow \frac{1}{4}=\left(\frac{1}{2}\right)^x$$

$\Rightarrow \quad x=2$

From Eqs. (ii) and (iii)

$$\frac{4.40\times10^{-4}}{8.80\times10^{-4}}=\left[\frac{0.30}{0.60}\right]^x\left[\frac{0.30}{0.15}\right]^y$$

$$\Rightarrow \quad \frac{1}{2}=\left(\frac{1}{2}\right)^2[2]^y$$

$$\Rightarrow \quad \frac{2^2}{2}=2^y$$

$$\Rightarrow \quad y=1$$

From Eq. (ii),

$$4.40\times10^{-4}=k[0.30]^2\,[0.30]^1$$

$$\Rightarrow \quad k=\frac{4.40\times10^{-4}}{0.027}$$
$$=162.96\times10^{-4}=1.63\times10^{-2}$$

$$\therefore \quad R=1.63\times10^{-2}\,[A]^2[B]^1$$

19. Given, $A+B\longrightarrow$ Products

According to law of mass action,

Rate $\propto[A]^m\,[B]^n$ if the reaction is of order m with respect to $[A]$ and n with respect to $[B]$.

Hence, rate $=k\,[A]^m\,[B]^n$ ... (i)

(where, $k=$ Rate constant)

In case I, i.e. when concentration of A is doubled.

$$2\times \text{Rate}=k\,[2A]^m\,[B]^n \quad \ldots(ii)$$

In case II, i.e. when concentrations of A and B are doubled.

$$8\times \text{Rate}=k\,[2A]^m\,[2B]^n \quad \ldots(iii)$$

On dividing Eq. (iii) by Eq. (ii), we get

$$\frac{8\times \text{Rate}}{2\times \text{Rate}}=\frac{k\,[2A]^m\,[2B]^n}{k\,[2A]^m\,[B]^n}$$

$$\Rightarrow \quad (2)^2=[2]^n \Rightarrow n=2$$

Similarly, on dividing Eq. (ii) by Eq. (i), m comes out to be 1, thus $m=1$, $n=2$

Hence, reaction is of first order with respect to A and of second order with respect to B.

So, $\quad$ rate $=k\,[A][B]^2$

20. The two factors which influence the rate of reaction are

(i) **Concentration** Generally, rate of reaction increases with increase in the concentration of reactants. Rate constant does not depend upon initial concentration of reactants, i.e. it is independent on initial concentration of the reactants. **(1½)**

(ii) **Temperature** The rate of reaction usually increases on increasing the temperature.

The value of rate constant for a particular reaction increases with an increase in temperature. **(1½)**

21. Given reaction, $A+B\longrightarrow C+D$

Suppose the given reaction is of order p with respect to A and q with respect to B.

The rate of formation of C and D can also be written as

$$2.0\times10^{-3}=k\,[A]^p\,[B]^q=k(1)^p\,(1)^q \quad \ldots(i)$$
$$4.0\times10^{-3}=k\,(2)^p\,(1)^q \quad \ldots(ii)$$
$$2.0\times10^{-3}=k\,(1)^p\,(2)^q \quad \ldots(iii)$$

From Eqs. (i) and (ii), we get

$$\frac{4.0\times10^{-3}}{2.0\times10^{-3}}=\frac{k(2)^p\,(1)^q}{k\,(1)^p\,(1)^q} \Rightarrow (2)^1=2^p$$

Hence, $\quad p=1$

From Eqs. (i) and (iii), we get

$$\frac{2.0\times10^{-3}}{2.0\times10^{-3}}=\frac{k(1)^p\,(2)^q}{k\,(1)^p\,(1)^q}$$

$$\Rightarrow \quad 1=2^q \quad \Rightarrow 2^0=2^q$$

Hence, $\quad q=0$

(i) The order of reaction with respect to A is first order, i.e. $r\propto[A]$ and with respect to B is zero order, i.e. $r\propto[B]^0$.

(ii) Overall order is one $(1+0=1)$.

(iii) Rate law equation is, $r=k\,[A][B]^0$

where, k is rate constant.

(iv) Since, $r=k\,[A]$. Then rate constant,

$$k=\frac{r}{[A]}=\frac{2\times10^{-3}}{1.0}=2\times10^{-3}\,\text{s}^{-1}$$

(v) So first either A or B takes part in the reaction to generate reactive intermediate, which the attacks on other to give the product.

$$A\longrightarrow A^*$$
$$A^*+B\longrightarrow C+D$$

(1 × 5)

TOPIC 2

Integrated Rate of Equation and Half-life of the Reaction

Integrated Rate Equation

This equation can be obtained by integrating the differential rate equation to get a relation between directly measured experimental data.

The integrated rate equations are different for the reactions of different reaction orders.

Zero Order Reaction

It means that the rate of the reaction is directly proportional to zeroth power of the concentration of reactant A, i.e. rate does not depend upon the concentration of reactants.

$$\text{Rate} = k[A]^0$$

or

$$k = \frac{[A]_0 - [A]}{t}$$

where, $[A]_0$ is the initial concentration of reactant and $[A]$ is the concentration of reactant at time t.

- Unit of rate constant $= \text{mol}^{1-n}\text{L}^{n-1}\text{s}^{-1}$ $(n = 0)$
  $= \text{mol L}^{-1}\text{s}^{-1}$ or atm/s
- A plot of $[A]$ with time (t) is a straight line with slope $-k$, which is shown below.

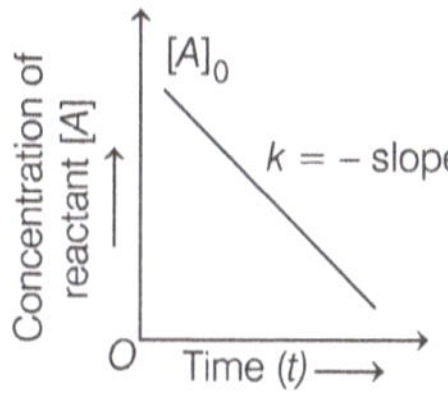

First Order Reaction

It means that rate of reaction is directly proportional to the first power of the concentration of the reactant A.

i.e. $\text{Rate} = k\ [A]$

$$k = \frac{2.303}{t}\log_{10}\frac{[A]_0}{[A]}$$

where, $[A]_0$ is the initial concentration and $[A]$ is the concentration of the reactant at time t,

Unit of rate constant $= \text{mol}^{1-n}\ \text{L}^{n-1}\ \text{s}^{-1}$

$(n = 1 \text{ for first order}) = \text{s}^{-1}$

Graphical Representation of a First Order Reaction

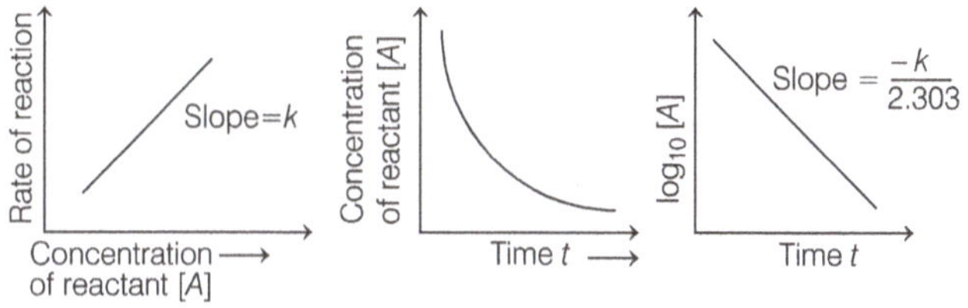

Pseudo First Order Reaction

The reactions which apparently seem to be of higher order but behave as first order reaction under certain conditions, are known as **pseudo first order reactions**, e.g. hydrolysis of ethyl acetate in the presence of acid and inversion of cane sugar.

Half-life of a Reaction ($t_{1/2}$)

The time taken for half of the reactant to react or the time taken for half of the reaction to get completed or the time in which the concentration of a reactant is reduced to half of its original value is called **half-life of the reaction**.

For a zero order reaction,

$$t_{1/2} = \frac{[A]_0}{2k}$$

For a first order reaction,

$$\therefore \quad t_{1/2} = \frac{2.303}{k}\log_{10}2 = \frac{0.693}{k}$$

where, k is rate constant.

Determination of Order of Reaction

(i) **Graphical method** This method is used when only one reactant is involved.

Rate $\propto [A]^n$, where $[A]$ is concentration of reactant A and n is the order of reaction.

So, for first order, plot of rate of reaction *vs* [concentration] for second order, plot of rate of reaction *vs* $[\text{concentration}]^2$ and for thier order, plot of rate of reaction *vs* $[\text{concentration}]^3$, is a straight line.

(ii) **Initial rate method** This method is used when the reaction involves more than one reactant.
Rate law of reaction is determined by determining orders of reaction with respect to all reactants one by one.

(iii) **Half-life method** Half-life of a reaction, $t_{1/2}$ and initial concentration of reactant $[A]_0$ are related to each other as follows : $t_{1/2} \propto 1/[A]_0^{n-1}$,
where, n is the order of reaction.

(iv) **Integrated rate law method** Data obtained from experiment is fed into rate equation of a particular order. After that, the values of rate constant k are calculated for different sets of observations. If the values of k are constant for all sets of data, the reaction is supposed to obey that particular rate law and follows the order suggested by that integrated rate law.
In case, the values of k are not constant, the data is used in the rate equation for other orders.

PYQs Previous Years' Questions

1 Mark Questions

1. For a first order reaction, the half-life period ($t_{1/2}$) is
   (a) proportional to the initial concentration **ISC 2023**
   (b) inversely proportional to the initial concentration
   (c) proportional to the square root of the initial concentration
   (d) independent of the initial concentration

2. For a first order reaction, when 100 g of the reactant is taken, 75 g of the reactant reacts in 8 minutes. If 200 g of the same reactant is taken, in how much time 150 g of the reactant will react? **ISC 2023**
   (a) 8 minutes (b) 16 minutes
   (c) 20 minutes (d) 24 minutes

3. Half-life period of a ... order reaction is .... on the concentration of the reactant. **ISC 2022 (Sem-II), 2013**

4. When the concentration of a reactant of first order reaction is doubled, the rate of reaction becomes .... times, but for a .... order reaction, the rate of reaction remains the same. **ISC 2019**

5. The half-life period of a first order reaction is 20 minutes. The time required for the concentration of the reactant to change from 0.16 M to 0.02 M is
   (a) 80 minutes (b) 60 minutes **ISC 2017**
   (c) 40 minutes (d) 20 minutes

6. What is the order of reaction whose rate constant has the same unit as the rate of reaction? **ISC 2016**

7. For a first order reaction the rate constant for the decomposition of N_2O_5 is $6 \times 10^{-4} s^{-1}$. The half-life period for the decomposition (in seconds) is **ISC 2015**
   (a) 11.55 (b) 115.5
   (c) 1155 (d) 1.155

8. If the half-life period of a first order reaction is 69.3 s. What is the value of its rate constant? **ISC 2013**

> **KEY IDEA**
> Using half-life period, $t_{½} = \frac{0.693}{k}$ for first order reaction we can calculate the value of k.

9. 75% of a first order reaction was completed in 32 min. When was 50% of the reaction completed? **ISC 2011**
   (a) 24 min (b) 16 min
   (c) 8 min (d) 4 min

2 Marks Questions

10. 25% of a first order reaction is completed in 30 minutes. Calculate the time taken in minutes for the reaction to go to 90% completion. **ISC 2019**

11. Show that for a first order reaction the time required to complete 75% of reaction is about 2 times more than that required to complete 50% of the reaction. **ISC 2019**

12. 40% of a first order reaction is completed in 50 minutes. How much time will it take for the completion of 80% of this reaction? **ISC 2018**

13. A substance decomposes by following first order kinetics. If 50% of the compound is decomposed in 120 minutes, how long will it take for 90% of the compound to decompose? **ISC Specimen 2018**

14. In a first order reaction, 10% of the reactant is consumed in 25 min. Calculate
    (i) the half-life period of the reaction.
    (ii) the time required for completing 87.5% of the reaction. **ISC 2016**

> **KEY IDEA**
> To calculate $t_{1/2}$ for a first order reaction k is required, so first calculate k by using formula $k = \frac{2.303}{t}\log\frac{a}{a-x}$
> and then calculate $t_{1/2} = \frac{0.693}{k}$.

15. A substance decomposes by the following first order kinetics. If 50% of the compound is decomposed in 120 min, how long will it take for 90% of the compound to decompose? **ISC 2015**

16. In a first order reaction, 10% of the reactant is consumed in 25 min. Calculate
(i) half-life of the reaction.
(ii) the time required for completing 17% of the reaction. **ISC 2013**

17. A first order reaction is 50% complete in 30 min at 27°C. Calculate
(i) the rate constant of the reaction at 27°C.
(ii) the time required for completing 10% of the reaction.

> **KEY IDEA**
> Using formula for first order reaction,
> $$t_{1/2} = \frac{0.693}{k} \text{ to calculate } k$$
> then calculate $t_{10\%}$ using the formula,
> $$t = \frac{2.303}{k}\log\frac{a}{a-x}$$

3 Marks Questions

18. 20% of a first order reaction is completed in five minutes. How much time will the 60% reaction take to complete? Calculate the half-life period ($t_{1/2}$) for the above reaction. **ISC 2023**

19. Suppose 50 bacterias are placed in a flask containing nutrients, so that they can multiply. A study at 35°C gave the following results: **ISC Specimen 2023**

Time (in minutes)	0	15	30	45	60
Number of bacteria	100	200	400	800	1600

Answer the following questions.
(i) This multiplication of bacteria follows
(a) zero order reaction (b) first order reaction
(c) second order reaction (d) third order reaction
(ii) The rate constant for the reaction is
(a) 0.0462 min^{-1} (b) 0.462 min^{-1}
(c) 4.62 min^{-1} (d) 46.2 min^{-1}
(iii) The half-life period ($t_{1/2}$) of the reaction is
(a) 1500 minutes (b) 150 minutes
(c) 15 minutes (d) 1.5 minutes

20. Answer the following questions.
(i) A first order reaction takes 100 minutes for completion of 60% of the reaction. Find the time required when 90% of the reaction will be completed.
(ii) In a reaction, $mA + nB \longrightarrow$ Products, when the concentration of A is doubled, the rate of reaction is also doubled. When the concentration of B is doubled, the rate of reaction becomes four times. Find the overall order of reaction **ISC 2021-22 (Sem-II)**

21. Answer the following questions.
(i) Mention any two factors that influence the rate of a chemical reaction.
(ii) In a first order reaction, 20% of a reactant is consumed in 30 minutes. Calculate
(a) the half-life period of the reaction.
(b) the time required for completing 93.75% of the reaction. **ISC 2021-22 (Sem-II)**

22. Answer the following. **ISC Specimen 2021-22 (Sem-II)**
(i) Define molecularity of a reaction. Give one difference between the order of reaction and its molecularity.
(ii) The rate constant (k) of a first order reaction is $4.5\times 10^{-2} s^{-1}$. What will be the time required for the initial concentration of 0.4 M of the reactant to be reduced to 0.2 M?

23. Answer the following. **ISC Specimen 2021-22, (Sem-II)**
(i) For a first order reaction, show that the time required for the completion of 99% reaction is twice the time required for the completion of 90% of the reaction.
(ii) For a reaction, rate $= k[A]^1[B]^{1.5}[C]^0$. What is the overall order of reaction?

> **KEY IDEA**
> Find t for 99% completion of reaction by using,
> $$t = \frac{2.303}{k}\log\frac{a}{a-x}.$$
> Similarly, find t for 90% completion.
> Then compare the above two values to find relation between $t_{99\%}$ and $t_{90\%}$.

24. Show that the time required for the completion of 75% of a reaction of first order is twice the time required for the completion of 50% of the reaction. **ISC 2010**

Explanations

1. (d) For first order reaction,

$$t_{1/2} = \frac{0.693}{k}$$

So, $t_{1/2}$ does not depend on initial concentration.

2. (a) For the first order reaction,

$$k = \frac{2.303}{t}\log\frac{[A_0]}{[A]} = \frac{2.303}{8}\log\frac{100}{25}$$

For 200 g,

$$\frac{2.303}{8}\log\frac{100}{25} = \frac{2.303}{t}\log\frac{200}{50}$$

$$t = \frac{8\times 2.303}{2.303} = 8 \text{ minutes}$$

3. Half-life period of a **first** order reaction is **independent** on the concentration of the reactant.

For first order, $t_{1/2} = \frac{0.693}{k}$ (where, k is disintegration constant or rate constant)

4. two, zero

5. (b) Given, $t_{1/2} = 20$ min

$[A]_0$ = initial concentration $= 0.16$ M

$[A]$ = concentration left after time 't' $= 0.02$ M

$$k = \frac{0.693}{t_{1/2}} = \frac{0.693}{20} = 0.03465 \text{ min}^{-1}$$

For first order reaction,

$$\text{Rate constant } (k) = \frac{2.303}{t}\log\frac{[A]_0}{[A]}$$

$$\therefore t = \frac{2.303}{0.03465}\log\frac{[0.16]}{[0.02]} = 60 \text{ minutes.}$$

6. Zero order of reaction whose unit of rate constant and rate of reaction has the same unit, i.e. mol L^{-1} s^{-1}.

7. (c) Given, rate constant for first order reaction of N_2O_5 decomposition $= 6\times 10^{-4} s^{-1}$

Half-life period = ?

From half-life equation of first order reaction.

$$t_{1/2} = \frac{0.693}{k} = \frac{0.693}{6\times 10^{-4}} \Rightarrow t_{1/2} = 1155$$

8. Given, half-life period, $t_{1/2} = 69.3$ s

Rate constant, k = ?

$$k = \frac{0.693}{69.3} = 0.01 \text{ s}^{-1}$$

9. Given, time $t_{75\%} = 32$ min, suppose the initial concentration is $[A]_0$. Since, the reaction is 75% complete in 32 min, the concentration left after 32 min will be given by

$$[A] = [A_0]\times\frac{(100-75)}{100} = [A_0]\times\frac{1}{4}$$

Then from the formula,

$$k = \frac{2.303}{t}\log\frac{[A]_0}{[A]}$$

We get,

$$k = \frac{2.303}{32}\log\frac{[A]_0}{[A]_0/4} = \frac{2.303}{32}\times\log 4$$

For 50% completion, $t_{1/2} = \frac{0.693}{k}$

$$t_{1/2} = \frac{0.693\times 32}{2.303\times\log 4}$$

where, $[\log 4 = 0.602]$

$$= \frac{0.693\times 32}{2.303\times 0.602} = 15.99 \approx 16 \text{ min}$$

Hence, option (b) is correct.

10. Given, time for 25% completion of reaction = 30 min

Let, [initial concentration] = 100

Then, $[a-x]$,

$$= 100 - 25 = 75\%$$

and $t = 30$ min

$$\text{Therefore, } k = \frac{2.303}{t}\log\frac{a}{a-x}$$

$$= \frac{2.303}{30}\log\frac{100}{75}$$

$$= 0.0767 \log 1.333$$

$$= 0.0767\times 0.1250 = 0.00958$$

$$k = 0.0096 \text{ min}^{-1}$$

$\therefore$ Time taken to complete 90% of reaction will be

$$t = \frac{2.303}{k}\log\frac{100}{10}$$

$$= \frac{2.303}{0.0096}\log 10$$

$$= \frac{2.303}{0.0096}\times 1 = 239.89 \approx 240 \text{ min}$$

11. Let, initial amount $(a) = 100$

Time required to complete 75% $= t_{75\%}$.

Amount at $t_{75\%}$, i.e. $(a-x)_1 = 100 - 75 = 25$.

Amount at $t_{50\%}$, i.e. $(a-x)_2 = 100 - 50 = 50$.

Where, time required to complete 50% $= t_{50\%}$.

Now, $$\frac{t_{75\%}}{t_{50\%}} = \frac{\log\left[\frac{a}{(a-x)_1}\right]}{\log\left[\frac{a}{(a-x)_2}\right]} = \frac{\log \frac{100}{25}}{\log \frac{100}{50}}$$

$$\frac{t_{75\%}}{t_{50\%}} = \frac{\log 4}{\log 2} = \frac{0.6020}{0.3010} = 2$$

Hence, $t_{75\%} = 2 \times t_{50\%}$, i.e. time required to complete 75% of a reaction is about 2 times more than that required to complete 50% of the reaction.

12. For the first order reaction,

$$k = \frac{2.303}{t} \log \frac{a}{a-x}$$

when, $x = \frac{40\,a}{100} = 0.4a$, $t = 50$ min.

$$\therefore \quad k = \frac{2.303}{50 \text{ min}} \log \frac{a}{a - 0.4a}$$

or $$k = \frac{2.303}{50 \text{ min}} \log \frac{a}{0.6\,a} = 0.010138 \text{min}^{-1}$$

Now, $t = ?$

when reaction is 80% complete, i.e. $x = 0.8a$

$$k = 0.010138 \text{ min}^{-1}$$

$$\therefore \quad t = \frac{2.303}{k} \log \frac{a}{a-x} = \frac{2.303}{0.010138 \text{min}^{-1}} \log \frac{a}{a - 0.8a}$$

$$= \frac{2.303}{0.010138 \text{ min}^{-1}} \log \frac{1}{0.2} = 158.78 \text{ min}$$

13. Given, first order reaction complete 50% in 120 minutes,

Let, $[x]_0 = 100$ M, $[x]_{120} = 100 - 50 = 50$ M and $t = 120$ min.

$$k = \frac{2.303}{t} \log \frac{[x_0]}{[x]} = \frac{2.303}{120} \log \frac{100}{50}$$

$$= 0.019 \log 2 = 5.78 \times 10^{-3} \text{ min}^{-1}$$

Time taken to complete 90% reaction = ?

$[x]_0 = 100$ M, $[x]_{90 \text{ min}} = 100 - 90 = 10$ M

$k = 5.78 \times 10^{-3} \text{ min}^{-1}$

$$t = \frac{2.303}{k} \log \frac{[x_0]}{[x]} = \frac{2.303}{5.78 \times 10^{-3}} \log \frac{100}{10}$$

$= 0.3984 \times 10^{+3} \times \log 10 = 398.4$ min $[\because \log 10 = 1]$

14. (i) Given, $t = 25$ min, suppose $[A_0] = 100$

$$[A] = 100 - \left(\frac{10 \times 100}{100}\right) = 100 - 10$$

Then, $$k = \frac{2.303}{25} \log_{10}\left(\frac{100}{100 - 10}\right)$$

[As, $\log 1.11 = 0.0457$]

$$= \frac{2.303}{25} \times 0.0457 = 0.004 \text{ min}^{-1}$$

Now, half-life

$$t_{1/2} = \frac{0.693}{k} = \frac{0.693}{0.004} = 173.25 \text{ min}$$ (1)

(ii) Given so, $[A] = 100 - 87.5$,

From the formula of rate constant,

$$k = \frac{2.303}{t} \log_{10} \frac{[A_0]}{[A]}$$

$$0.004 = \frac{2.303}{t} \log_{10} \frac{100}{100 - 87.5}$$

$$t = \frac{2.303}{0.004} \times 0.9030 \quad [\text{As}, \log 8 = 0.9030]$$

$$t = 519.90 \text{ min}$$ (1)

15. If $a = 100$, $a - x = 100 - 50 = 50$

For 50% completion of the reaction.

$$t_{50\%} = \frac{2.303}{k} \log \frac{100}{50}$$

$$\Rightarrow \quad 120 = \frac{2.303}{k} \times 0.3010 \quad [\text{As}, \log 2 = 0.3010]$$

$$k = \frac{2.303}{120} \times 0.3010$$

$$\Rightarrow \quad k = 0.0057$$

For 90% completion of the reaction.

If $a = 100$; $a - x = 100 - 90 = 10$

$$t_{90\%} = \frac{2.303}{k} \log \frac{100}{10}$$

$$\Rightarrow \quad t_{90\%} = \frac{2.303}{0.0057} \times 1 \quad [\text{As}, \log 10 = 1]$$

$$t_{90\%} = 404 \text{ min}$$

16. (i) Given, $t = 25$ min, suppose $[A]_0 = 100$

$$[A] = 100 - \left(\frac{10 \times 100}{100}\right) = 100 - 10$$

Then, $$k = \frac{2.303}{25} \log\left(\frac{100}{100 - 10}\right)$$

[As, $\log 1.11 = 0.0457$]

$$= \frac{2.303}{25} \times 0.0457 = 0.004 \text{ min}^{-1}$$

Now, half-life

$$t_{1/2} = \frac{0.693}{k} = \frac{0.693}{0.004} = 173.25 \text{ min}$$

(ii) From the formula of rate constant, when, $[A] = 100 - 17$, we get

$$k = \frac{2.303}{t} \log \frac{[A]_0}{[A]}$$

$$0.004 = \frac{2.303}{t} \log \frac{100}{100-17}$$

$$\Rightarrow \quad t = \frac{2.303}{0.004} \times 0.0809$$

[As, log 1.205 = 0.0809]

$$= 46.57 \text{ min}$$

17. (i) As the reaction is 50% completed in 30 min, thus, $t_{1/2} = 30$ min

$$k = \frac{0.693}{t_{1/2}} = \frac{0.693}{30} = 0.0231 \text{ min}^{-1}$$ **(1)**

(ii) For the formula of rate constant

$$k = \frac{2.303}{t} \log \frac{[A]_0}{[A]}$$

When $[A] = 100 - 10 = 90$

$$\Rightarrow \quad k = \frac{2.303}{t} \log \frac{[100]}{[90]}$$

$$t = \frac{2.303}{0.0231} \log \frac{[10]}{9}$$

$$t = 4.56 \text{ min}$$ **(1)**

18. Given, $t_{20\%} = 5$ min

Let, $[A]$ be initial concentration $= 100$

After 5 min, $[A] = 100 - 20 = 80$

For 1st order reaction,

$$k = \frac{2.303}{t} \log_{10} \frac{[A]_0}{[A]}$$

$$k = \frac{2.303}{5} \log_{10} \frac{100}{80}$$

$$= 0.0446 \text{ min}^{-1}$$

For 60% completion of reaction, the time will be

$$t = \frac{2.303}{k} \log \frac{[A]_0}{[A]}$$

Here, $[A]_0 = 100$ and $[A] = 100 - 60 = 40$

So, $$t = \frac{2.303}{0.0446} \times \log \frac{100}{40}$$

$$= \frac{2.303}{0.0446} \log 2.5$$

$$t = 20.5 \text{ min}$$

$t_{1/2}$ for this reaction is

$$t_{1/2} = \frac{0.693}{k} = \frac{0.693}{0.0446 \text{ min}^{-1}}$$

$$= 15.538 \text{ min}$$

19. (i) (b) In this data, as the time increases the growth of bacteria increases in the same order. So, it follows first order reaction. **(1)**

(ii) (a) The rate constant of first order is given by

$$k = -\frac{2.303}{t} \log \frac{[A]}{[A_0]}$$

$$k = \frac{-2.303}{15} \log \frac{100}{200}$$

$$k = \frac{-2.303}{15} \times (-0.301)$$

$$k = 0.0462 \text{ min}^{-1}$$

(iii) (c) Half-life of first order reaction is $t_{1/2} = \frac{0.693}{k}$

$$= \frac{0.693}{0.0462} = 15 \text{ min}$$ **(2)**

20. (i) For the reaction of first order

$$k = \frac{2.303}{t} \log \frac{a}{a-x}$$

$$k = \frac{2.303}{100} \log \frac{100}{40} = 0.00916$$

$$\Rightarrow 0.00916 = \frac{2.303}{t} \log \frac{100}{10}$$

$$\Rightarrow \quad t = \frac{2.303}{0.00916} \log 10 = 251.4 \text{ min}$$ **(1)**

(ii) The expression for the rate of the reaction is

$$r = k[A]^n[B]^m \quad \ldots\text{(i)}$$

When the concentration of A is doubled and the concentration of B remains same, the rate expression becomes $2r = k[2A]^n[B]^m$ ...(ii)

When the concentration of B is doubled, the rate expression becomes

$$4r = k[A]^n[2B]^m \quad \ldots\text{(iii)}$$

Divide Eq. (ii) with Eq. (i) to obtain $n = 1$

Divide Eq. (iii) with Eq. (i) to obtain $m = 2$

Hence, $n + m = 1 + 2 = 3$

The overall order of the reaction is 3. **(2)**

21. (i) Two factors that influence the rate of a chemical reaction are

(a) Temperature **(½)**

(b) Pressure or concentration of reactants **(½)**

(ii) $t = 30$ min

Let $a = 100, x = 20$ and $a - x = 80$

$$k = \frac{2.303}{t}\log\frac{a}{a-x}$$

$$= \frac{2.303}{30}\log\frac{100}{80} = 0.076 \times 0.097$$

$$= 0.0074\, s^{-1}$$ (1)

(a) $$t_{1/2} = \frac{0.693}{k}$$

$$= \frac{0.693}{0.0074} = 93.64 \text{ s}$$ (½)

(b) $$t = \frac{2.303}{0.0074}\log\frac{100}{6.25} = 374.74 \text{ s}$$ (½)

22. (i) The number of reacting species (atoms, ions or molecules) taking part in an elementary reaction, which must collide simultaneously in order to bring about a chemical reaction is called molecularity of the reaction. (½)

Difference between order and molecularity are as follows

Order	Molecularity
It is applicable to elementary as well as complex reactions.	It is applicable to elementary reactions. For complex reactions, it has no meaning.

(½)

(ii) Given, $k = 4.5 \times 10^{-2}\, s^{-1}$

$[A]_0 = 0.4$ M

$[A] = 0.2$ M

Time $(t) = ?$

For first order reaction,

$$t = \frac{2.303}{k}\log\frac{[A]_0}{[A]}$$

$$= \frac{2.303}{4.5 \times 10^{-2}} \times \log\left[\frac{0.4}{0.2}\right]$$

$$= 51.17 \times \log 2$$

$$= 51.17 \times 0.301 = 15.40 \text{ s}$$ (2)

23. (i) ***Case* I** If $a = 100$, $(a - x) = (100 - 99) = 1$

For 99% completion of the reaction,

$$t_{99\%} = \frac{2303}{k}\log\frac{100}{1}$$

$$= \frac{2303}{k}\log 10^2$$

$$= \frac{2303 \times 2}{k}$$

$$t_{99\%} = \frac{4.606}{k} \quad \text{...(i)}$$ (1)

***Case* II** If $a = 100$

$(a - x) = (100 - 90) = 10$

For 90% completion of the reaction

$$t_{90\%} = \frac{2303}{k}\log\frac{100}{10}$$

$$= \frac{2303}{k}\log 10 = \frac{2303}{k} \quad \text{...(ii)}$$

On dividing Eq. (i) by Eq. (ii), we get

$$\frac{t_{99\%}}{t_{90\%}} = \frac{4.606}{k} \times \frac{k}{2.303} = 2$$

It means that time required for 99% completion of the reaction is twice the time required to complete 90% of the reaction. (1)

(ii) The rate law expression is $= k[A]^1[B]^{1.5}[C]^0$

Order of reaction $= 1 + 1.5 + 0 = 25$ (1)

24. For 75% completion, suppose $[A]_0 = 100$,

then $[A] = 100 - 75 = 25$

$$k = \frac{2.303}{t}\log\frac{100}{25}$$

$$= \frac{1.386}{t} \quad [\text{As, } \log 4 = 2\log 2 = 2 \times 0.3010]$$

For 50% completion, $k = \dfrac{0.693}{t_{1/2}}$

But, for a given reaction, k is constant

$$\therefore \quad \frac{1.386}{t} = \frac{0.693}{t_{1/2}}$$

$$\Rightarrow \quad \frac{t}{t_{1/2}} = \frac{1.386}{0.693} = 2$$

or $t = 2\, t_{1/2}$

So, time (t) required for completion of 75% of a reaction is twice the time required for completion of 50% (half-life) of the reaction.

TOPIC 3

Activation Energy, Collision Theory of Chemical Reactions

Types of Reactions on the Basis of Concept of Energy

(i) **Endothermic reaction** A reaction in which energy is supplied to the reactants from the surroundings for the reaction is called endothermic reaction.

(ii) **Exothermic reaction** A reaction in which energy is evolved alongwith the products is called exothermic reaction.

Dependence of Reaction Rate on Temperature

Temperature Coefficient

It is defined as the ratio of the rate constants of the reaction at two different temperatures differing by 10°C.

Collision Theory

In order to explain the effect of temperature on reaction rates, a theory known as collision theory of reaction rate was proposed.

Conditions for a Chemical Change

- A reaction occurs only when the reactant molecules undergo collisions with one another.
- Only those collisions are effective which acquire a definite amount of energy. The minimum amount of energy required by the reacting molecules to produce effective collisions is called **threshold energy**.

  Only effective collisions lead to the formation of products.

  The number of effective collisions are governed by

  (a) Energy barrier

  (b) Orientation barrier

Concept for Increase in Reaction Rate with Temperature

As the temperature increases, the number of effective collisions increases. Hence, the rate of reaction increases appreciably even with small rise in temperature.

Activation Energy

It is the excess energy that the reactant molecules must acquire in order to cross the energy barrier and to change into the products.

Thus, activation energy = (Threshold energy) − (Average energy possessed by the reactant molecules)

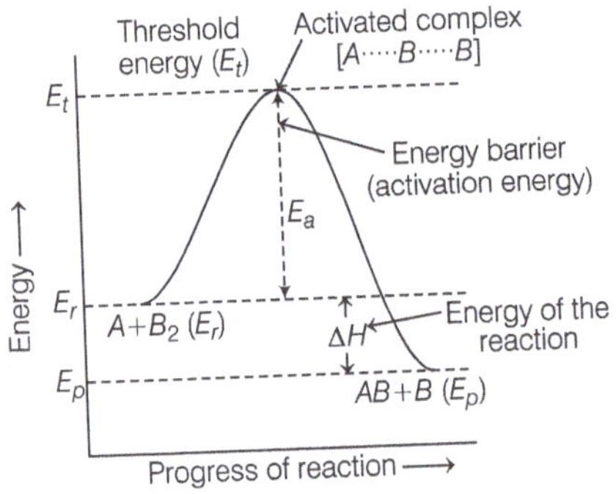

Thus, $$E_a = E_t - E_r$$

Activation Energy and Reversible Reaction

For a reversible reaction, overall energy change,

$$\Delta H = E_a(\text{forward}) - E_a(\text{backward})$$

[E_a = Activation energy of a reaction]

- For exothermic reaction ($\Delta H = -$ ve)
- For endothermic reaction ($\Delta H = +$ve)

Arrhenius Equation

It can be expressed as $k = Ae^{-E_a/RT}$

where, A is a constant (pre-exponential factor) known as frequency factor. It denotes the frequency of binary collisions of reactant molecules per second per litre. E_a is activation energy, R is gas constant, T represents temperature (in K) and k is the rate constant of the reaction.

On taking log on both sides, we get

$$\log_{10} k = \frac{-E_a}{2.303\,RT} + \log_{10} A$$

Calculation of Activation Energy

(i) **Graphical method** On comparing equation $\left(\log_{10} k = \frac{-E_a}{2.303\,RT} + \log_{10} A\right)$ with straight line equation, i.e. $y = mx + c$, and a graph is plotted between the values of $\log_{10} k$ against $\frac{1}{T}$, a straight line of slope $-\frac{E_a}{2.303\,R}$ is obtained.

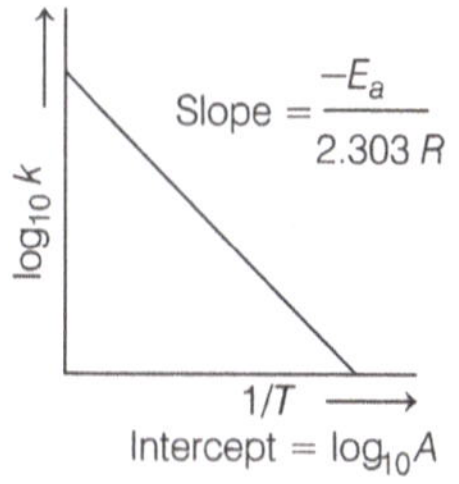

Knowing the value of slope and gas constant, E_a can be calculated as

$$E_a = -2.303\,R \times \text{slope}$$

(ii) **Rate constant method** If k_1 and k_2 are rate constants measured at two temperatures T_1 and T_2, respectively.

Then, $$\log_{10} \frac{k_2}{k_1} = \frac{E_a}{2.303\,R}\left(\frac{1}{T_1} - \frac{1}{T_2}\right)$$

From equation, it is clear that on increasing temperature, the value of k and rate of reaction increases due to increase in number of effective collisions.

Effect of Catalyst on Activation Energy

The formation of activated complex provides an alternative path of lower activation energy as compared to uncatalysed reaction.

This allows a large number of reactant molecules to cross over the energy barrier in order to transform into products.

PYQs Previous Years' Questions

1 Mark Questions

1. In the Haber's process, iron changes the .... of reaction while molybdenum increases the efficiency of the .... **ISC Specimen 2024**

2. The intermediate activated complex in a chemical reaction is highly .... due to .... energy. **ISC 2023**

3. A catalyst is a substance which **ISC 2019**
   (a) changes the equilibrium constant of the reaction
   (b) increases the equilibrium constant of the reaction
   (c) supplies energy to the reaction
   (d) shortens the time to reach equilibrium

4. Activation energy can be determined by .... **ISC 2013**

5. In a plot of $\log k$ *vs* $1/T$, the slope is **ISC 2012**
   (a) $-E_a / 2.303$
   (b) $E_a / 2.303\,R$
   (c) $E_a / 2.303$
   (d) $-E_a / 2.303\,R$

6. Write Arrhenius equation. **ISC 2005**

7. Correct the following statement.
   The rate constant of a reaction increases linearly with increase in temperature. **ISC 2003**

8. Arrhenius equation is related to .... **ISC 2002**

2 Marks Questions

9. A first order reaction is 50% complete in 30 minutes at 27°C and the same reaction is again 30% complete in 10 minutes at 47°C. Calculate the activation energy of the reaction ($R = 8.314\ \text{JK}^{-1}\text{mol}^{-1}$). **ISC 2021-22 (Sem-II)**

10. The rate of reaction becomes four times when the temperature changes from 293K to 313 K. Calculate the energy of activation (E_a) of the reaction assuming that it does not change with temperature.
    ($R = 8.314\ \text{JK}^{-1}\text{mol}^{-1}$)
    ISC Specimen 2021-22 (Sem-II), 2018

11. Draw a graph which is used to calculate the activation energy of a reaction. Give the appropriate expressions used to calculate the activation energy graphically. **ISC 2006**

3 Marks Questions

12. (i) The half-life period (t½) for decay of radioactive ^{14}C is 5730 years. An ancient piece of wood has only 80% of the ^{14}C found in a living tree. Calculate the age of the piece of wood.
    (ii) The rate of most of the reactions becomes double when the temperature is raised from 298 K to 308 K. Calculate the activation energy.
    ($R = 8.314\ \text{J K}^{-1}\ \text{mol}^{-1}$) **ISC Specimen 2024**

13. (i) The rate constant of a reaction at 500 K and 700 K are $0.02\ s^{-1}$ and $0.07\ s^{-1}$ respectively. Calculate the value of E_a (activation energy).

(ii) A radioactive substance which emits alpha particle follows first order reaction. The half-life period of this radioactive substance is 30 hours. Calculate the fraction in percent (%) of the radioactive substance which remains after 90 hours. *ISC 2024*

14. A first order reaction is 50% completed in 40 minutes at 300 K and in 20 minutes at 320 K.Calculate the activation energy of the reaction. *ISC 2023*

15. The rate constant for a first order reaction becomes six times when the temperature is increased from 350 K to 410 K. Calculate activation energy (E_a) for the reaction. *ISC Specimen 2023*

16. A first order reaction is 50% completed in 30 minutes at 300 K and in 10 minutes at 320 K. Calculate the activation energy of the reaction. ($R = 8.314\ JK^{-1}\ mol^{-1}$). *ISC 2020*

KEY IDEA

First, find the relation between k_1 [for 50% completion at 300 K) and k_2 (for 50% completion at 320 K) by using the formula $k = \frac{0.693}{t_{1/2}}$ Then, use the formula $\log\frac{k_2}{k_1} = \frac{E_a}{2.303R}\left[\frac{T_2 - T_1}{T_1T_2}\right]$ to calculate the value of E_a.

17. (i) Write the mathematical expression relating the variation of rate constant of a reaction with temperature.

(ii) How can you graphically find the activation energy of the reaction from the above expression?

(iii) The slope of the line in the graph of log k (k = rate constant) *versus* $\frac{1}{T}$ is −5841.

Calculate the activation energy of the reaction. *ISC 2014*

Explanations

1. Activation energy; catalyst
2. unstable, high.
3. (d) According to definition of a catalyst, the substance which alters the rate of chemical reaction without it self undergoing any chemical change is known as catalyst, i.e. a catalyst can shortens the time to reach equilibrium. The catalyst can do so by providing an alternative path of lower activation energy.

   Hence, (d) is the correct answer.
4. Activation energy can be determined by **Arrhenius equation.**
5. (d) In the plot of log k *vs* $1/T$ the slope is $-E_a/2303R$
6. Arrhenius equation can be expressed as

$$k = Ae^{-E_a/RT}$$

where, k = rate constant,
A = collision or frequency factor
E_a = activation energy
R = universal gas constant
T = temperature (in K)

7. According to Arrhenius equation,

$$k = Ae^{-E_a/RT}.$$

The rate constant of a reaction increases exponentially with increase in temperature.

8. Arrhenius equation is related to **rate constant.** Refer to solution 5.

Concept Enhancer Activation energy has term 'A' called frequency factor. It has same unit as the rate constant, i.e. s^{-1}.

9. Given, Time required to complete 50% of reaction $t_{1/2}$ at 27°C = 30 min

Time required to complete 30% of same reaction at 47°C = 10 min

$$T_1 = 27°C = 300\ K$$
$$T_2 = 47°C = 320\ K$$

We know that, $k_1 = \frac{0.693}{t_{1/2}} = \frac{0.693}{30}$

$$k_1 = 0.0231\ min^{-1}$$

$$k_2 = \frac{2.303}{t}\log\frac{a}{a-x}$$

$a = 100, a - x = 100 - 30 = 70, t = 10$ min

$$k = \frac{2.303}{10}\log\frac{100}{70}$$
$$= \frac{2.303}{10}\log\frac{10}{7} = \frac{2.303}{10} \times 0.155$$
$$= 0.036\ min$$

According to Arrhenius equation,

$$\log \frac{k_2}{k_1} = \frac{E_a}{2.303R} \times \frac{T_2 - T_1}{T_1 \times T_2}$$

By putting the values in equation we get

$$\log\left(\frac{0.036}{0.023}\right) = \frac{E_a}{2.303 \times 8.314}\left[\frac{320-300}{300 \times 320}\right]$$

$$\log(1.56) = \frac{E_a}{19.15}\left[\frac{20}{96000}\right]$$

$$E_a = \frac{0.1 \times 19.15 \times 96000}{20}$$

$$= 9192 \text{ J mol}^{-1}$$

$$= 9.192 \text{ kJ mol}^{-1}$$

Common Mistake One can make mistake by taking the temperature term in celsius scale instead of Kelvin scale.

10. Given , $T_1 = 293\text{K}$, $k_1 = k$ (Suppose)

when $T_2 = 313\text{K}$, $k_2 = 4k$

Substituting these values in the equation,

$$\log \frac{k_2}{k_1} = \frac{E_a}{2.303R}\left(\frac{T_2 - T_1}{T_1 T_2}\right)$$

$$\log \frac{4k}{k} = \frac{E_a}{2.303 \times 8.314 \text{ JK}^{-1}\text{mol}^{-1}} \times \left(\frac{313\text{ K} - 293\text{ K}}{313\text{ K} \times 293\text{ K}}\right)$$

$$\log 4 = \frac{E_a}{2.303 \times 8.314} \times \frac{20}{313 \times 293}$$

$$\therefore \quad E_a = \frac{0.6021 \times 2.303 \times 8.314 \times 313 \times 293}{20} \text{ J mol}^{-1}$$

$$E_a = 52.86 \text{ kJ mol}^{-1}$$

11. According to Arrhenius equation,

$$k = Ae^{-E_a/RT}$$

Taking log on both sides, we get

$$\log k = \log A - \frac{E_a}{2.303RT}$$

Comparing the above equation with straight line equation, i.e. $y = mx + c$

where, $y = \log k$, $x = \frac{1}{T}$

$$m(\text{slope}) = -\frac{E_a}{2.303\,R}$$

Intercept $c = \log A$

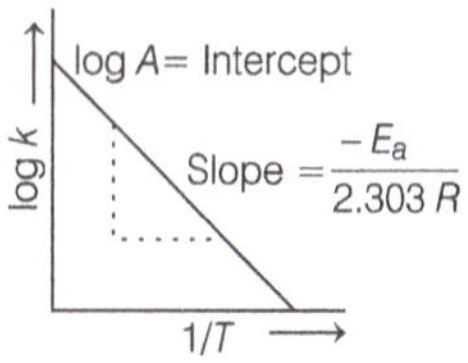

Graph between log k and $1/T$

After plotting, $\log k$ *vs* $\frac{1}{T}$ graph, slope of line will be $-\frac{E_a}{2.303\,R}$. Knowing the value of the slope and gas constant, the activation energy can be calculated with the help of equation, $E_a = -2.303R \times \text{slope}$.

12. (i) Decay constant

$$k = \frac{0.693}{t_{1/2}} = \frac{0.693}{5730 \text{ year}} = 1.209 \times 10^{-4}/\text{year}$$

The rate of counts is proportional to the number of C-14 atoms in the sample.

$$N_0 = 100,\ N = 80$$

The age of the sample $t = \frac{2.303}{k} \log\left(\frac{N_0}{N}\right)$

$$t = \frac{2.303}{1.209 \times 10^{-4}} \times \log\left(\frac{100}{80}\right) = 1846 \text{ years}$$

(ii) Using Arrhenius equation, $k = A_0 e^{-\frac{E_a}{RT}}$

$$\log \frac{k_2}{k_1} = \frac{E_a}{2.303}\left(\frac{1}{T_1} - \frac{1}{T_2}\right)$$

Given, rate of reaction doubles when temperature is raised from 208 to 308 K.

$$\frac{k_2}{k_1} = 2$$

$$E_a = \frac{2.303 \times 8.314 \times 298 \times 308 \times 0.3014}{1000}$$

$$= 52.89 \text{ kJ/mol}$$

13. (i) Given, $T_1 = 500$ K, $T_2 = 700$ K

$k_1 = 0.02 \text{ s}^{-1}$, $k_2 = 0.07 \text{ s}^{-1}$

We know that,

$$\log \frac{k_2}{k_1} = \frac{E_a}{2.303R}\left(\frac{1}{T_1} - \frac{1}{T_2}\right)$$

$$\log\left(\frac{0.07}{0.02}\right) = \frac{E_a}{2.303 \times 8.314}\left(\frac{1}{500} - \frac{1}{700}\right)$$

$$\log(3.5) = \frac{E_a}{19.15}\left[\frac{200}{350000}\right]$$

$$E_a = \frac{0.54 \times 19.15 \times 350000}{200}$$

$$= 18096.75 \text{ J mol}^{-1} = 18.096 \text{ kJ mol}^{-1}$$

(ii) Given, Half-life of radioactive substance = 30 hr = 1800 min

We know that, $t_{1/2} = \frac{0.693}{k}$

$$\Rightarrow \quad k = \frac{0.693}{t_{1/2}} = \frac{0.693}{1800}$$

$$= 0.000385 \text{ min}^{-1}$$

Also for first order reaction,

$$t = \frac{2.303}{k} \log \frac{[N_0]}{[N]}$$

$$90 \times 60 = \frac{2303}{0.000385} \log \frac{[N_0]}{[N]}$$

$$\log\left[\frac{N_0}{N}\right] = \frac{90 \times 60 \times 0.000385}{2303} = 0.9027$$

$$\frac{N_0}{N} = \text{Antilog } [0.9027]$$

$$= 7.9928$$

14. $t_{1/2}$ for first order reaction is given by, $t_{1/2} = \frac{0.693}{k}$

At 300 K, $k_1 = \frac{0.693}{40}$

At 320 K, $k_2 = \frac{0.693}{20}$

From Arrhenius equation,

$$\log\left(\frac{k_2}{k_1}\right) = \frac{E_a}{2303R}\left(\frac{1}{T_1} - \frac{1}{T_2}\right)$$

$$\log\left(\frac{40}{20}\right) = \frac{E_a}{2.303 \times 8.314 \text{ J mol}^{-1}\text{K}^{-1}}\left[\frac{1}{300} - \frac{1}{320}\right]$$

$$\log 2 = \frac{E_a}{19.147 \text{ J mol}^{-1}\text{K}^{-1}}\left[\frac{320 - 300}{300 \times 320}\right]$$

$$0.3010 = \frac{E_a}{19.147 \text{ J mol}^{-1}\text{K}^{-1}} \times 0.0002083 \text{ K}^{-1}$$

$$E_a = 27668 \text{ J/mol}$$

Common Mistake Generally, one can make mistake in finding the activation energy at two temperatures T_1 and T_2 by taking the formula as $\log \frac{k^2}{k^1} = \frac{E_a}{R}\left[\frac{1}{T_1} - \frac{1}{T_2}\right]$ instead of $\log \frac{k^2}{k^1} = \frac{E_a}{2.303R}\left[\frac{1}{T_1} - \frac{1}{T_2}\right]$

15. Let $k_1 = k$ and $k_2 = 6k$

Given, $T_1 = 350$ K, $T_2 = 410$ K

$$\log \frac{k_2}{k_1} = \frac{E_a}{2303\, R}\left[\frac{T_2 - T_1}{T_1 \cdot T_2}\right]$$

$$\log \frac{6k}{k} = \frac{E_a}{2303 \times 8314}\left[\frac{410 - 350}{410 \times 350}\right]$$

$$\frac{0.77 \times 2303 \times 8314 \times 410 \times 350}{60} = E_a$$

$$E_a = 352 \text{ kJ mol}^{-1} = 3563433 \text{ J mol}^{-1}$$

16. Given, time taken for 50% completion of reaction at 300 K = 300 min time taken for 50% of same reaction at 320 K = 10 min.

As $\quad k = \frac{0.693}{t_{1/2}}$

$$\therefore \quad k_{300} = \frac{0.693}{t_{1/2}} = \frac{0.693}{30} \quad \text{...(i)}$$

and $\quad k_{320} = \frac{0.693}{10} \quad$ ...(ii)

According to Arrhenius equation, we know, that

$$\log \frac{k_2}{k_1} = \frac{E_a}{2303 \times R}\left[\frac{1}{T_1} - \frac{1}{T_2}\right]$$

$$\Rightarrow \quad \log \frac{k_{320}}{k_{300}} = \frac{E_a}{2303 \times 8314}\left[\frac{1}{300} - \frac{1}{320}\right]$$

$$\Rightarrow \quad \log \frac{\frac{0.693}{10}}{\frac{0.693}{30}} = \frac{E_a}{2303 \times 8314}\left[\frac{320 - 300}{300 \times 320}\right]$$

$$\Rightarrow \quad \frac{(\log 3) \times 8314 \times 2303 \times 300 \times 320}{20} = E_a$$

$$\Rightarrow \quad E_a = 43.85 \text{ kJ/mol}$$

Thus, activation energy for the given reaction is 43.85 kJ/mol.

17. (i) Refer to page 79. **(1)**

(ii) Refer to page 79. **(1)**

(iii) Given, slope = − 5841

We know that, Slope $= -\frac{E_a}{2.303\, R}$

$$\therefore \quad E_a = -2.303\, R \times \text{slope}$$

$$= -2.303 \times 8.314 \times (-5841)$$

$$= 111838.4 \text{ J/mol}$$

$$E_a = 111.838 \text{ kJ/mol} \quad \textbf{(1)}$$

CHAPTER TEST

01 Mark Questions

1. Fill in the blanks by choosing the appropriate word(s) from those given in the bracket.
[increases, decreases, lower, higher, slow, s^{-1}, atm s^{-1}, mol L^{-1} s^{-1}, $atm^{-1}s^{-1}$, frequency factor, collision factor, activation energy, collision energy]
   (i) Rate of reaction .... with .... in concentration of reactants.
   (ii) A catalyst .... the rate of reaction by providing a path of .... activation energy.
   (iii) For first order reaction, the unit of rate constant in terms of gaseous and solution phase is/are .... and ..... respectively.
   (iv) In equation $k = Ae^{-E_a/RT}$, A is ...... and E_a is ......

2. Select and write the correct alternatives from the choices given below.
   (i) The correct statement about the $t_{1/2}$ for a first order reaction is
   (a) independent of concentration of reactant
   (b) proportional to concentration of reactants
   (c) inversely proportional to concentration of reactants
   (d) inversely proportional to the square of the concentration of reactant
   (ii) In order to produce effective collisions, the colloiding molecules must have
   (a) proper orientation
   (b) minimum amount of energy
   (c) both sufficient threshold energy and proper orientation
   (d) energy equal to or greater than threshold energy.
   (iii) The correct expression for the half-life of a zero-order reaction.
   (a) $t_{1/2} = \frac{[R]}{2k}$ (b) $t_{1/2} = \frac{[R]_0}{2k}$
   (c) $t_{1/2} = \frac{0.693}{k}$ (d) $t_{1/2} = \frac{0.069}{k}$
   (iv) In the presence of a catalyst the heat evolved or absorbed during the reaction
   (a) increases
   (b) remains unchanged
   (c) decreases
   (d) may increase or decrease

3. (i) **Assertion** (A) The rate law may not depend on the concentration of every reactant.
   Reason (R) With increase in temperature, the rate of reaction increases.
   (a) Both (A) and (R) are correct and (R) is the correct explanation of (A).
   (b) Both (A) and (R) are correct but (R) is not the correct explanation of (A).
   (c) (A) is correct and (R) is incorrect.
   (d) (A) is incorrect and (R) is correct.
   (ii) **Assertion** (A) E_a of the forward reaction is higher than that of the backward reaction in a reversible endothermic reaction.
   Reason (R) Threshold energy of the forward reaction is more than that of backward reaction.
   (a) Both (A) and (R) are correct and (R) is the correct explanation of (A).
   (b) Both (A) and (R) are correct but (R) is not the correct explanation of (A).
   (c) (A) is correct and (R) is incorrect.
   (d) (A) is incorrect and (R) is correct.

02 Marks Questions

4. The rate law for the reaction,
$CH_3COOCH_3 + H^+ \longrightarrow CH_3COOH + CH_3OH$ is given as $\frac{dx}{dt} = k[CH_3COOCH_3][H^+]^0$
What would be the effect on the rate if
   (i) concentration of the ester is halved?
   (ii) concentration of $[H^+]$ is doubled?

5. Explain the effect of adding a catalyst on each of the following.
   (i) Activation energy (ii) Gibbs energy of a reaction

6. For a reaction,
$$H_2 + Cl_2 \xrightarrow{h\nu} 2HCl; \qquad \text{Rate} = k$$
   (i) Write the order and molecularity of this reaction.
   (ii) Write the unit of rate constant.

7. A first order reaction takes 20 minutes for 20% decomposition. Calculate its $t_{1/2}$.

8. The rate constant for a first order reaction is 50 s^{-1}. How much time will it take to reduce the initial concentration of the reactant to its $\frac{1}{16}$th value?

9. The rate constant of a reaction at 50°C and 100°C is $1.5 \times 10^7 \text{ s}^{-1}$ and $4.5 \times 10^7 \text{ s}^{-1}$ respectively. Calculate the energy of activation (E_a).
(Using $R = 8.314 \text{ JK}^{-1} \text{ mol}^{-1}$)

10. For a reaction, the energy of activation is zero. What is the value of rate constant at 500 K, if $k = 2.0 \times 10^6 \text{ s}^{-1}$ at 280 K?

03 Marks Questions

11. The rate of a particular reaction becomes twice when temperature changes from 60°C to 100°C. Calculate the energy of activation of the reaction in kJ.

12. The rate constant for the first order decomposition of H_2O_2 is given by the following equation:

$$\log k = 5.4 - \frac{212}{T} + 5.7 \log T$$

Calculate E_a at 273°C.

13. For the reaction, $2NO(g) + Cl_2(g) \longrightarrow 2NOCl(g)$
The following data were collected. All the measurements were taken at 263 K.

Exp. No.	Initial [NO] (M)	Initial $[Cl_2]$ (M)	Initial rate of disappearance of Cl_2 (M/min)
1.	0.15	0.15	0.60
2.	0.15	0.30	1.20
3.	0.30	0.15	2.40
4.	0.25	0.25	?

(i) Write the expression for rate law.
(ii) Calculate the value of rate constant and specify its units.
(iii) What is the initial rate of disappearance of Cl_2 in experiment 4?

14. In the Arrhenius equation for a certain reaction, the value of A (frequency factor) and E_a (activation energy) are $4 \times 10^{13} \text{ s}^{-1}$ and 98.6 kJ mol^{-1}, respectively. If the reaction is of first order, then find that at what temperature will its half-life period be 10 min?

15. (i) Explain why H_2 and O_2 do not react at room temperature.
(ii) Write the rate equation for the reaction, $A_2 + 3B_2 \longrightarrow 2C$, if the overall order of the reaction is zero.
(iii) Catalysts have no effect on the equilibrium constant. Why?

05 Marks Questions

16. Consider the following reaction,

$$2NO(g) + Cl_2(g) \longrightarrow 2NOCl(g)$$

The rate of reaction becomes double when the concentration of Cl_2 is doubled. However, when the concentration of both the reactants are doubled, the rate becomes eight times. What is the order with respect to NO and with respect to reactant chlorine? What is the overall order of reaction?

17. (i) For a reaction $A + B \longrightarrow P$, the rate is given by Rate $= k[A][B]^2$
(a) How is the rate of the reaction affected if the concentration of B is tripled?
(b) What is the overall order of the reaction if A is present in excess?
(c) How is the rate of reaction affected if concentration of A is halved?
(ii) In a first order reaction, the concentration of the reactant is reduced from 0.9 mol L^{-1} to 0.3 mol L^{-1} in 3 minutes. Calculate the rate constant of the reaction.

18. (i) Define the following terms.
(a) Activation energy (b) Rate constant
(c) Order of reaction
(ii) The graph of conc. *vs* time is shown below.

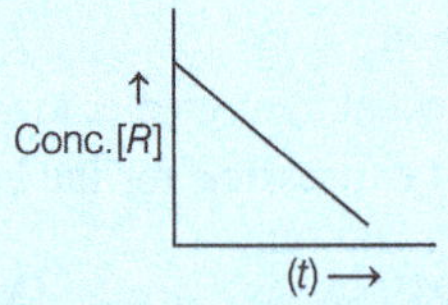

(a) Find the order of reaction.
(b) What does the slope of curve signifies?

Answers

1. (i) decreases, decreases (ii) increases, lower (iii) s^{-1}, s^{-1}
(iv) frequency factor, activation energy
2. (i) (a), (ii) (c), (iii) (b), (iv) (b) **3.** (i) (b), (ii) (c) **7.** $t_{1/2} = 61.87$ min **8.** $t = 5.52 \times 10^{-2}$ s
9. $E_a = 22.01 \text{ kJ mol}^{-1}$ **10.** $k_{500\,K} = 2.0 \times 10^6 \text{ s}^{-1}$ **11.** 17.88 kJ **12.** 4.059 kJ/mol
13. (ii) $k = 177.51 \text{ mol}^{-2} \text{ L}^2 \text{ mol}^{-1}$ **14.** $T \simeq 311.53$ K **16.** Order = 3 **17.** (ii) $k = 0.366 \text{ min}^{-1}$

04

d- and *f*-Block Elements

TREND ANALYSIS 4 YEARS

Topic	Types of Questions	2024	2023	2020	2019
		Average No. of Questions Across all Sets			
TOPIC 01 Chemistry of Transition and Inner-Transition Elements	1 Mark	—	1	—	3
	2 Marks	3	2	2	1
	3 Marks	—	—	—	—
	5 Marks	—	—	—	—
TOPIC 02 Compounds : Potassium Permanganate and Potassium Dichromate	1 Mark	1	—	1	—
	2 Marks	—	—	—	—
	3 Marks	—	—	—	1
	5 Marks	—	—	—	—

TOPIC 1

Chemistry of Transition and Inner-Transition Elements

d-Block Elements

The elements in which last electron enters into the *d*-subshell of penultimate shell are called *d*-block elements or **transition elements**. The general electronic configuration of transition elements is $(n-1)d^{1-10}ns^{1-2}$.

d-block consist of four transition series. i.e.

- 1st transition series or 3*d*-series - $_{21}Sc$ - $_{30}Zn$
- 2nd transition series or 4*d*-series - $_{39}Y$ - $_{48}Cd$
- 3rd transition series or 5*d*-series - $_{57}La$ - $_{30}Hf$
- 4th transition series or 6*d*-series - $_{89}Ac$, $_{104}Rf$ - $_{112}Cn$

Transition elements possess partially filled *d*-orbitals in their elementary form or in their ions existing in chemically significant oxidation states.

Hence, Zn, Cd and Hg are not regarded as transition elements due to the absence of partly filled *d*-orbitals in their commonly occurring ions. Copper is also regarded as a transition element only in +2 oxidation state.

Properties of Transition Elements

General properties of transition elements are discussed below

(i) Atomic Radii and Ionic Radii

Atomic radii of a particular series decreases with increase in atomic number. However, there is a slight increase in the atomic radii near the end of series. The atomic radii of corresponding elements of second and third transition series are nearly same due to **lanthanoid contraction**.

For the same oxidation state, ionic radii generally decreases with increase in nuclear charge in a given transition series.

(ii) Metallic Character

Almost all transition elements exhibit typical metallic properties like metallic lustre, malleability, ductility, high tensile strength, etc. (except Hg, which is a liquid at room temperature).

(iii) Ionisation Enthalpy

The ionisation energies of transition elements lies between those of *s*-block and *p*-block elements. The first ionisation energy increases with increase in atomic number across a given transition series, although the increase is not very regular.

The first ionisation energies of the elements of third transition series are higher than those of elements of first and second transition series due to poor shielding effect of 4*f*-orbitals.

(iv) Oxidation State

The most common oxidation state of elements of first transition series is +2 , (except Sc), due to loss of two 4*s*-electrons. For a transition metal, oxidation state with more negative value of standard reduction potential is more stable in aqueous medium.

The highest oxidation state shown by transition element is + 8. Hence, transition metal shows **variable valency**. The bonds formed in + 2 and + 3 oxidation state are generally ionic, whereas other are covalent.

(v) Formation of Coloured Compounds

Most of the compounds of transition metals are coloured both in solid state and in aqueous solution, due to *d-d* transition taking place between splitted *d*-orbitals of unpaired electron.

The transition metal ions having completely filled *d*-orbital (e.g. Zn^{2+}, Cu^{+}) and completely vacant *d*-orbitals are colourless (e.g. Sc^{3+}).

(vi) Magnetic Properties

Due to the presence of unpaired electrons in *d*-orbital, many compounds of transition elements are paramagnetic in nature. As the number of unpaired electron increases, paramagnetic character increases. Whereas, the presence of paired electrons causes diamagnetic character in elements and their compounds.

Ferromagnetism as in iron is due to maximum number of unpaired electrons. A paramagnetic substance is characterised by its magnetic moment which is calculated by 'spin only' formula, i.e. $\mu = \sqrt{n(n+2)}$ BM,

n = number of unpaired electrons.

(vii) Complex Compounds

The tendency to form complex ions/compounds is due to small size, high charge on the transition metal ions and availability of vacant *d*-orbitals of suitable energy to accommodate lone pair of electrons donated by the ligand atoms, e.g. $[Fe(CN)_6]^{3-}, [Fe(CN)_6]^{4-}$, etc.

(viii) Catalytic Property

Most of the transition metals and their compounds act as a catalyst because of the variable oxidation states and the presence of vacant *d*-orbitals due to which they can form a variety of unstable intermediates. Further, large surface area of transition metals also attributes to their catalytic property.

(ix) Alloy Formation

A large number of alloys are formed due to their similar atomic size.

f-Block Elements

The elements in which the differentiating electrons enter into $(n-2)f$-subshell, i.e. the *f*-orbitals of antipenultimate shell, are called **inner-transition elements** or *f*-block elements.

f-block elements consist of two series called **lanthanoid** series and **actinoid** series.

All *f*-block elements are metals and found rarely in earth's crust, thus, they are also called **rare earth metals**.

Lanthanoids or Lanthanoid Series

These elements follow lanthanum (La) in the periodic table and resemble it strongly in physical and chemical properties. There are 14 elements in this series, starting with cerium, Ce ($Z = 58$) to lutetium, Lu ($Z = 71$).

The general properties of lanthanoid series are as follows

(i) General Electronic Configuration

In general the electronic configuration of lanthanoid elements is $[Xe]4f^{1-14}5d^{0-1}6s^2$.

(ii) **Atomic and Ionic Radii**

On moving from La to Lu in lanthanoid series, the size of atoms and ions decreases regularly. This is because the 4*f*-orbitals containing electrons are too diffused to screen the nucleus as effectively as the more localised inner shell.

Hence, the attraction of the nucleus for the outermost electrons increases steadily with increase in the atomic number.

Thus, due to imperfect shielding of 4*f*-electrons, a contraction in the electron cloud of $4f$-subshell increases. This contraction is called **lanthanoid contraction**.

(iii) **Oxidation State**

The most common oxidation state of lanthanoids is $+3$. In aqueous solution and solid state, $+3$ oxidation state is more stable than other two oxidation states $+2$ and $+4$. This is due to the sum of ionisation and lattice energies of their tripositive ions is more negative as compared to that of $+2$ and $+4$ ions.

(iv) **Formation of Coloured Compounds**

Several trivalent (M^{3+}) lanthanide ions are coloured in solid state as well as in aqueous solution. Colour of compounds of members of this series arises due to f-f electronic transition, as f-subshells are partially filled.

(v) **Complex formation**

Lanthanide ions have very less tendency to form complexes. This is because of their low charge density, i.e. charge to size ratio. They form complexes with strong chelating agents like EDTA, β-diketones, oxime etc. No complex with π-bonding ligands are known.

(vi) **Formation of Interstitial Compounds**

Some *d*-block elements form interstitial compounds. They are generally non-stoichiometric and are neither typically ionic nor covalent. e.g. Mn_4N, TiC, Fe_3H, TiH etc.

The formulas quoted do not correspond to any normal oxidation state of the metal.

(vii) **Alloy formation and Catalytic Property**

An alloy of lanthanide metal is **misch metal.** It has lanthanide metal (95%) and iron about 5% with traces of S, C, Ca and Al. It is used in the production of bullets, shells and lighter flint.

Mixed oxides of lanthanides are used as catalysts in petroleum cracking.

(viii) **Chemical Reactivity**

Lanthanoid metal (M)

$$\xrightarrow{+O_2} M_2O_3$$
$$\xrightarrow{+N_2} MN$$
$$\xrightarrow{+S} M_2S_3$$
$$\xrightarrow{+C} MC_2$$
$$\xrightarrow{+X} MX_3$$
$$\xrightarrow{+H_2O} M(OH)_3$$
$$\xrightarrow{+H_2} MH_3$$

Actinoids or Actinoid Series

These elements follow actinium (Ac) up to lawrencium (Lr) and closely resemble it in physical and chemical properties.

The general properties of actinoid series are as follows

General Electronic Configuration

Actinoids follow general electronic configuration of $[Rn]5f^{1-14}6d^{0-1}7s^2$.

Oxidation States

Actinoids show a variety of oxidation states, i.e. +2, + 4, + 5, +6 and + 7 due to comparable energies of $5f$, $6d$ and $7s$ energy levels. The dominant oxidation state of actinoids is +3 which show increasing stability for the heavier elements.

Comparison of lanthanoids and actinoids

Lanthanoids	Actinoids
The maximum oxidation state shown by them is + 4, the other oxidation states being +2 and + 3.	The maximum oxidation state shown by them is +7, others being + 2, + 3, + 4, + 5 and + 6.
Their paramagnetic properties can be explained easily.	Their paramagnetic properties are difficult to be explained.
Except promethium, lanthanoids are non-radioactive.	Actinoids are radioactive.
Their compounds are less basic.	Their compounds are more basic.

Uses of Lanthanoids and Actinoids

- U and Pu are used as fuels in atomic reactors.
- In medicine, in the treatment of cancer, Th salts are used.
- Th and its compounds are used in nuclear chemistry.
- U salts are used in ceramic, glass and textile industry.
- Lanthanoids are useful in the form of their alloys and compounds, e.g. an alloy containing Mg and about 3% misch metal is used in jet engine parts.
- Mixed oxides of lanthanoids are used as catalysts in petroleum cracking.

PYQs Previous Years' Questions

1 Mark Questions

1. Which one of the following compounds is diamagnetic and colourless? **ISC 2023**

   (a) $K_2Cr_2O_7$ (b) $ZnSO_4$ (c) $KMnO_4$ (d) $Cr_2(SO_4)_3$

2. Which of the following pairs of transition elements have exceptional electronic configuration? **ISC Specimen 2023**

   (a) Sc and Cu (b) Fe and Ni
   (c) Cr and Cu (d) Mn and Zn

3. The transition metals show '*A*' character because of the presence of unpaired electrons while Cu^+ is '*B*' because its electronic configuration is $[Ar]3d^{10}$.

   Or **ISC Specimen 2021-22 (Sem-II), 2015**

   In the above sentence '*A*' and '*B*' are

   (a) paramagnetic, diamagnetic
   (b) noble, paramagnetic
   (c) noble, diamagnetic
   (d) diamagnetic, paramagnetic **ISC 2015**

4. Give reason Zn^{2+} salts are white but Cu^{2+} salts are blue in colour. **ISC 2019, 2014, 2013, 2010**

5. Explain, why Cu^+ is diamagnetic but Cu^{2+} paramagnetic $(Z = 29)$? **ISC 2019, 2013**

6. Which trivalent ion has maximum size in the lanthanoid series, i.e. lanthanum ion (La^{3+}) to lutetium ion (Lu^{3+})? (At. no. of lanthanum = 57 and lutetium = 71) **ISC 2019**

7. Why is zinc not regarded as a transition element? (Atomic number Zn = 30) **ISC 2018**

8. What is the electronic configuration of chromium atom $(Z = 24)$? Give a reason for your answer. **ISC 2012**

9. State the common oxidation state of

   (i) lanthanoids (ii) actinoids **ISC 2011**

10. The chemistry of actinoids is not so smooth as that of lanthanoids. Give reason.

11. La^{3+} $(Z = 57)$ and Lu^{3+} $(Z = 71)$ do not show any colour in solutions. Give reason.

2 Marks Questions

12. Give a reason for each of the following.

    (i) Zinc, cadmium and mercury are considered as *d*-block elements but not regarded as transition elements.

    (ii) Transition metals possess a great tendency to form complex compounds. **ISC 2024**

13. (i) Why is Mn^{+2} ion more stable the Fe^{+2} ion?
    (Atomic number of Mn = 25 and Fe = 26)

    (ii) Trivalent lanthanoid ions such as La^{3+} $(Z = 57)$ and Lu^{+3} $(Z = 71)$ do not show any colour in their solution. Give a reaction. **ISC 2024**

14. Account for each of the following. **ISC 2024**

    (i) Zirconium (Zr) and Hafnium (Hf) are difficult to separate.

    (ii) Salts of cupric (Cu^{2+}) ion are coloured whereas salts of cuprous (Cu^+) ion are colourless.

15. Give a reason for each of the following: **ISC Specimen 2024**

    (i) The size of the trivalent cations in lanthanoid series decreases steadily as the atomic number increases.

    (ii) The third ionisation energy of manganese $(Z = 25)$ is unexpectedly high.

16. Account for the following: **ISC Specimen 2024**

    (i) Salts of cuprous (Cu^+) ion are colourless whereas the salts of cupric (Cu^{2+}) ion are coloured.

    (ii) Zinc is not regarded as a transition element. (at. no. of Zn = 30)

17. (i) Give a reason to explain why transition metals can act as a good catalyst. **ISC Specimen 2024**

    (ii) Scandium $(Z = 21)$ does not exhibit variable oxidation states and yet it is regarded as transition element. Why?

18. Give a reason for the following. **ISC 2023**

    (i) Cu^{+2} salts are paramagnetic while Cu^+ salts are diamagnetic.

    (ii) Mn^{+2} compounds are more stable than Fe^{+2} compounds.

19. State a reason for each of the following. **ISC 2023**

    (i) $La(OH)_3$ is more basic than $Lu(OH)_3$.

    (ii) Transition elements and their compounds act as catalyst.

20. Why are Zn, Cd and Hg not regarded as transition elements? *ISC Specimen 2023*

21. Give reason for the following. *ISC Specimen 2023*
    (i) Transition metals form large number of complex compounds.
    (ii) Transition elements show variable oxidation states.

22. Why Zn^{2+} ions are colourless while Ni^{2+} ions are green and Cu^{2+} ions are blue in colour? *ISC 2020*

23. Explain the following.
    (i) Transition metals and their compounds generally exhibit a paramagnetic behaviour. *ISC 2020*
    (ii) There is an increase in density of elements from titanium ($Z = 22$) to copper ($Z = 29$) in the $3d$-series of transition elements. *ISC 2018*

24. Explain why,
    (i) transition elements form alloys?
    (ii) transition metals and their compounds act as catalyst? *ISC 2019*

25. Explain why? *ISC 2018*
    (i) Mn^{2+} is more stable than Fe^{2+} towards oxidation to + 3 state. (Atomic number of Mn = 25, Fe = 26)
    (ii) Zr and Hf exhibit similar properties. (Atomic number of Zr = 40, Hf = 72)

KEY IDEA
First find the electronic configuration of Mn^{2+} and Fe^{2+}. Then compare them to find the stability (in term) of half-filled or fully-filled electronic configuration.

26. Why do the transition elements have higher enthalpies of atomisation? In $3d$-series (Sc to Zn), which element has the lowest enthalpy of atomisation and why? *ISC Specimen 2018*

KEY IDEA
Enthalpy of atomisation is related to the stability of crystal lattice and strength of the metallic bond. Greater the number of unpaired electrons stronger is the resultant bonding.

27. Explain the following.
    (i) Why do transition metal ions possess a great tendency to form complexes?
    (ii) The paramagnetic character in $3d$-transition series elements increases upto Mn and then decreases. *ISC 2015*

28. Explain why transition metals form complex compounds? *ISC 2012*

29. In a given transition series, there is no significant changes in the atomic radii of elements with increase in atomic number. Explain why? *ISC 2011*

30. Iron is ferromagnetic in nature. Explain why? *ISC 2011*

3 Marks Questions

31. (i) The size of the trivalent cations in the lanthanoid series decreases steadily as the atomic number increases. What is this phenomenon called ? *ISC 2021-22 (Sem-II), 2018*
    (ii) Why are the compounds of transition elements coloured?

KEY IDEA
Transition element exhibit colour due to *d-d* transition which is possible only when *d*-orbital have unpaired electron.

32. (i) What is the basic difference between the electronic configuration of transition and inner transition elements? *ISC Specimen 2021-22 (Sem-II)*
    (ii) Why are Zn^{2+} ions colourless while Ni^{2+} ions are green in colour?

33. Account for the following. Explain why ? *ISC Specimen 2018*
    (i) Transition metals exhibit variable oxidation states.
    (ii) Zr ($Z = 40$) and Hf ($Z = 72$) have almost identical radii.
    (iii) Transition metals and their compounds act as a catalyst.

34. Compare the chemistry of the actinoids with that of lanthanoids with reference to the following :
    (i) Electronic configuration
    (ii) Oxidation states
    (iii) Chemical reactivity

Explanations

1. (b) In $ZnSO_4$, Zn^{2+} has $[Ar]3d^{10}4s^0$ configuration in which, there is no unpaired electrons is present. Thus, it is diamagnetic in nature and colourless.

2. (c) The elements having configuration against Aufbau rule are called to have abnormal configuration.

   Among the given option. $Cr = [Ar]3d^5 4s^1$ and $Cu = [Ar]3d^{10} 4s^1$ have abnormal configuration.

   This is due to the less energy gap between the 4*s* and 3*d* energy levels.

   So, electron easily moves from the 4*s*-orbital to the 3*d*-orbital resulting in a stable electronic configuration. **(1)**

3. paramagnetic, diagmagnetic.

   Or

   (a) paramagnetic, diamagnetic.

4. The transition metal ions having completely filled *d*-orbitals or completely empty *d*-orbitals are colourless or white.

   Since, Zn^{2+} possesses completely filled *d*-orbitals as electronic configuration of Zn^{2+} is $1s^2, 2s^2, 2p^6, 3s^2, 3p^6, 3d^{10}$.

   Thus, its salts are white or colourless. On the other hand, Cu^{2+} possesses an electronic configuration of $1s^2\ 2s^2\ 2p^6\ 3s^2\ 3p^6\ 3d^9$.

   This suggest that it has partly filled *d*-orbitals (an unpaired e^-) which undergoes *d*-*d* transition. Hence, Cu^{2+} salts are coloured.

5. The electronic configuration of

   $$Cu^+ = 1s^2, 2s^2, 2p^6, 3s^2, 3p^6, 4s^0, 3d^{10} \text{ and}$$
   $$Cu^{2+} = 1s^2, 2s^2, 2p^6, 3s^2, 3p^6, 4s^0, 3d^9$$

   In Cu^+ ion, all electrons are paired. Hence, Cu^+ is diamagnetic in nature. Whereas, Cu^{2+} has one unpaired electron thus, shows paramagnetic character.

6. Among trivalent ions in the lanthanoid series, there is a gradual decrease in ionic size due to lanthanoid contraction. Therefore, size of La^{3+} is more than that of Lu^{3+}, i.e. La^{3+} has ionic size 106 pm (approx.) and of Lu^{3+} has ionic size less than 86 pm.

7. Zinc with electronic configuration $[Ar]3d^{10}4s^2$ has completely filled shells of *d*-orbitals and therefore, it is not regarded as transition element. However, it is often studied with transition elements because of similarities in some of its properties to those of transition elements.

8. The electronic configuration of chromium atom ($Z = 24$) is

   $$1s^2, 2s^2, 2p^6, 3s^2, 3p^6, 4s^1, 3d^5.$$

   To maximise stability, electron from 4*s*-orbital jumps to 3*d*-orbital. So, that maximum number of half-filled orbitals can be obtained which is a stable arrangement of electrons. **(1)**

9. (i) In aqueous solution or in solid state, +3 state is more stable than other two oxidation states, i.e. +2 and +4 in lanthanoid. This is due to sum of ionisation and lattice energies of their tripositive ion which is more negative than other two oxidation states. **(1/2)**

   (ii) The most common state for actinoids is +3. It is due to more negative value of sum of ionisation and lattice energy of their tripositive ion than other oxidation states. **(1/2)**

10. Chemistry of the actinoids is more complex in the view of their ability to exist in different oxidation states.

    Further, many of the actinoid elements are radioactive which make the study of these elements rather difficult.

11. La^{3+} (lanthanum) have $4f^0$ and Lu^{3+} (lutetium) have $4f^{14}$ subshell. Because of the absence of partially filled *f*-subshell, these ions impart no colour to the solution.

12. (i) As zinc, cadmium and mercury of group 12 have completely filled *d*-orbitals in their common oxidation states, thus they are not regarded as transition metals, but they are studied along with the chemistry of the transition metals.

    (ii) The transition metals form a large number of complex compound due to the comparatively smaller size of the metal ions, their high charge density and vacant *d*-orbitals for bond formation.

13. (i) Mn^{2+} ion has half-filled configuration, i.e. $3d^5$, while Fe^{2+} ion does not (i.e. $3d^6$). Therefore, Mn^{2+} ion is more stable than Fe^{2+} ion.

    (ii) Ion which does not have unpaired electrons does not impart colour to the solution. La^{3+} has $5d^0 6s^0$ and Lu^{3+} has $4f^{14}5d^0 6s^0$ configuration. Thus, both do not have unpaired electron. Thus, they do not shown any colour in their solution.

14. (i) Due to lanthanoid contraction, there is a small difference in the size of Zr and Hf. So, there is difference in some properties of lanthanoids like solubility, degree of hydration and complex formation. These differences enable the separation of lanthanoids by ion exchange method.

(ii) Cu^{2+} ion has an electronic configuration $3d^9$ whereas Cu^+ ion has an $3d^{10}$. Hence, an unpaired electron is present in Cu^{2+} due to which $d-d$ electronic transition takes place. The energy of excitation corresponds to the frequency of light absorbed. The colour observed corresponds to the complementary colour of the light absorbed. In contrast, due to lack of unpaired electrons Cu^+ is colourless.

15. (i) The ionic radii of trivalent lanthanides decreases with the increasing atomic number due to poor shielding which results in higher effective nuclear charge Z_{eff}.

(ii) Atomic no. of Mn = 25 and electronic configuration is $[Ar]4s^2 3d^5$. Loss of two electrons gives the electronic configuration of Mn^{2+} as $[Ar]3d^5$ where d-orbital is half-filled and thus very stable. Therefore, the third ionisation energy is unexpectedly high for removing electron from the stable configuration of Mn^{2+}.

16. (i) Cuprous ion (Cu^+) has the electronic configuration of $[Ar]3d^{10} 4s^0$ which is fully-filled.

Cupric ion (Cu^{2+}) has electronic configuration $[Ar]3d^9 4s^0$ so it can undergoes d-d transition.

Hence, the cuprous ion is colourless and the cupric ion has a colour.

(ii) As, zinc atom has completely filled d-orbitals $(3d^{10})$ in its ground state as well as oxidised state, therefore it is not regarded as transition element.

17. (i) Transition elements can act as good catalyst because they are capable of exhibiting different oxidation states and hence they can act as both oxidising and reducing agents at the same time.

(ii) Scandium $(Z = 21)$ does not exhibit variable oxidation states and yet it is regarded as a transition element because it has partially filled d-orbitals, in the ground state $(3d^1 4s^2)$.

18. (i) Refer to sol. 5. **(1)**

(ii) Magnesium in +2 oxidation state form stable compounds than iron in +2 oxidation state.

$Mn^{2+} = 1s^2 2s^2 2p^6 3p^6 3d^5$ (half-filled d-orbital)

$Fe^{2+} = 1s^2 2s^2 2p^6 3s^2 3p^6 3d^6$

Mn^{2+} compounds are more stable due to half-filled d-orbitals. Fe^{2+} compounds are comparatively less stable as they have six electrons in their $3d$-orbitals. **(1)**

19. (i) $La(OH)_3$ is more basic than $Lu(OH)_3$ due to lanthanoid contraction. The size of lanthanoid ions decreases from La^{3+} to Lu^{3+}, the covalent character of the hydroxides increases and hence the basic strength decreases as we move from La^{3+} to Lu^{3+}. **(1)**

(ii) Most of the transition metals and their compounds act as a catalyst because of the variable oxidation states and the presence of vacant d-orbitals due to which they can form a variety of unstable intermediates.

Further, large surface area of transition metals also attributes to their catalytic property. **(1)**

20. Transition metals are defined as the elements having incompletely filled d-orbitals. Since, Zn, Cd and Hg have completely filled d-orbital, they are not regarded as transition elements.

21. (i) Transition elements form a large number of complex compounds due to the comparatively smaller sizes of the metal ions, their high charge density and the availability of vacant d-orbitals for bond formation. **(1)**

(ii) Transition elements show variable oxidation states in their compounds because there is a very small energy difference in between $(n-1)d$ and ns-orbitals.

As a result, electrons of $(n-1)d$-orbitals as well as ns-orbitals take part in bond formation. **(1)**

22. Refer to text on page 86 (Formation of coloured compounds) and Refer to Q. no. 32 (ii).

23. (i) Transition metals have one or more unpaired electron. So, they readily occur paramagnetic nature. **(1)**

(ii) While going from left to right in a period, the radii of transition elements remain similar but their atomic masses increases gradually. As a result, their density increases corresponding. **(1)**

Common Mistake Generally, students give the explanation about above trend in terms of increase in atomic number instead of increase in atomic mass.

24. (i) The atomic radii of the transition elements in any series are not much different from each other. As a result, they can very easily replace each other in the lattice and form solid solutions over an appreciable composition range. Such solid solution are called alloys. **(1)**

(ii) Many transition metals and their compounds are used as catalyst. This catalytic activity is due to their ability to adopt multiple oxidation states and to form complexes. Transition metals, because of their variable valencies sometimes form unstable intermediate compounds and provide a new path with lower activation energy for the reaction and thus, acts as a catalyst. **(1)**

25. (i) Electronic configuration of Mn^{2+} is $3d^5$ which is half-filled and hence stable. Therefore, third ionisation enthalpy is very high, i.e. third electron cannot be lost easily. In case of Fe^{2+}, electronic configuration is $3d^6$. Hence, it can lose electron easily to give stable configuration, i.e. $3d^5$. **(1)**

(ii) Due to lanthanoid contraction, Hf ($Z = 72$) has similar. size to that of Zr ($Z = 40$). Hence, their properties are similar **(1)**

Concept Enhancer The filling of 4*f*-orbital before 5*d*-orbital results irregular decrease in atomic radii called lanthanoid contraction. The factor responsible for this contraction is the imperfect shielding of one electron by another in the same set of orbitals.

26. The transition metals have high enthalpy of atomisation. It can be explained on the basis of strong inter-atomic interaction due to unpaired electrons. Greater the number of unpaired electrons, stronger is the resultant bonding.

In 3*d*-series Zn has the least enthalpy of atomisation because it has stable ground state configuration due to its completely filled *d*-orbital.

Thus, zinc has least tendency to form metallic bonds in the series.

27. (i) Due to small size of transition metal atoms or their cations and high effective nuclear charge, they have a high positive charge density on them. This high positive charged density makes the atoms or cation to attract the lone pair of electrons from the ligand and transition metal cation or atoms have vacant *d*-orbital in which they can accommodate the lone pair of electrons donated by ligands and thus, can form $L \rightarrow M$ coordinate bonds. **(1)**

(ii) Paramagnetic character increases with the increase in the number of unpaired electrons.

The larger is the number of unpaired electron in central atom or ion greater is the paramagnetic character hence on moving from Sc to Mn, number of unpaired electron increases and then from Fe to Zn decreases.

Thus, paramagnetic character also increases from Sc to Mn and then decreases from Fe to Zn. **(1)**

28. Transition metal form a large number of complex compounds due to the following reasons.

(i) Small size

(ii) High nuclear charge

(iii) Availability of vacant *d*-orbitals of suitable energy for accommodating the lone pair of electrons donated by the ligands. Also refer to sol. 27 (i).

29. Generally, atomic radii of transition elements belonging to a particular series decreases with increase in atomic number. As atomic number increases, the added electron enters in $(n-1)d$ subshell and thus, the shielding effect increases along with increase in nuclear charge.

However, the decrease in size with increase in nuclear charge due to increase in atomic number is counter balanced by the increased shielding effect of $(n-1)d$ electrons. Hence, in a given transition series, there is no significant changes in the atomic radii of elements with increase in atomic number.

30. Ferromagnetism is a special case of paramagnetism in which a substance acquires a permanent magnetic moment.

Paramagnetism is due to the presence of unpaired electrons in $(n-1)d$ orbital. As number of unpaired electrons increases, paramagnetism increases. Iron is much more paramagnetic than rest of the elements due to more number of unpaired electrons $[3d^6 4s^2]$ and hence, it is termed as ferromagnetic. It is used to prepare permanent magnets.

31. (i) This phenomenon is called lanthanoid contraction. **(1)**

(ii) Most of the complexes of transition elements are coloured. This is because of the absorption of radiation from visible light region to promote an electron from one of the *d*-orbitals to another.

The ions of transition elements absorb the radiation of a particular wavelength and the rest is reflected, imparting colour to the solution. **(2)**

32. (i) The general electronic configuration of transition elements is $(n-1)d^{1-10}ns^{1-2}$ and for the inner transition elements the general electronic configuration is $(n-2)f^{1-14}(n-1)d^{0-1}ns^{0-2}$.

In transition metals elements, last electron enters in $(n-1)d$-orbitals. While in inner-transition elements, it enters in $(n-2)f$-orbitals. **(1½)**

(ii) Zn^{+2} has completely filled d-orbitals ($Zn^{+2} = [Ar]\,3d^{10}4s^0$) while Ni^{2+} has incomplete filled d-orbitals. $Ni^{+2} = [Ar]3d^8 4s^0$.

Thus, d-d transition takes place in Ni^{2+} and shows colour. **(1½)**

33. (i) Transition metal exhibit variable oxidation states. This is because of the fact that the difference in the energy of $(n-1)$ d-electrons and ns-electrons is low which implies that electrons from both energy levels can take part in bonding. **(1)**

(ii) In lanthanoid due to poor shielding effect of $4f$-electrons the attraction between the electrons and the nucleus increases and hence atomic radius decreases. This is called lanthanoid contraction.

Because of this reason Zr and Hf have almost identical radii. **(1)**

(iii) Many transition metals and their compounds are used as catalyst. Their catalytic activity is due to their ability to adopt multiple oxidation states and to form complexes. **(1)**

34. (i) **Electronic configuration**

Lanthanoids = $[Xe]\,4f^{0\text{-}14}\,5d^{0\text{-}1}\,6s^2$

Actinoids = $[Rn]5f^{0\text{-}14}\,6d^{0\text{-}1}\,7s^2$ **(1)**

(ii) **Oxidation states** In lanthanoids, +3 oxidation state is most common alongwith + 2 and + 4. While in actinoids, there is a greater range of oxidation states because $5f$, $6d$ and $7s$ levels are of comparable energies.

They show + 2, + 3, + 4, + 5, + 6 and + 7 oxidation states. Common oxidation state in actinoids is + 3. **(1)**

(iii) **Chemical reactivity** Lanthanoids are less reactive than actinoids. Actually, earlier members of lanthanoids are quite reactive similar to calcium but with increasing atomic number, they behave more like aluminium.

Lanthanoids react with dilute acids to liberate H_2 gas while actinoids react with boiling water and gives a mixture of oxide and hydride. **(1)**

TOPIC 2

Compounds: Potassium Permanganate and Potassium Dichromate

Potassium Permanganate ($KMnO_4$)

Preparation

Various methods of preparation are as follows

From Pyrolusite, MnO_2

$$2MnO_2 + 4KOH + O_2 \xrightarrow[\text{KNO}_3\ \text{(Oxidising agent)}]{\text{Heat}} \underset{\text{Green}}{2K_2MnO_4} + 2H_2O$$

By Oxidation of K_2MnO_4

(i) **Chemical method**

$$3K_2MnO_4 + 2CO_2 \longrightarrow 2KMnO_4 + MnO_2 + 2K_2CO_3$$

(ii) **Electrolytic method** Iron electrodes as iron pipe (as cathode) with a rotating wire net (as anode).

$$\underset{\text{(Green)}}{MnO_4^{2-}} \longrightarrow \underset{\text{(Purple)}}{MnO_4^-} + e^- \qquad \text{(at anode)}$$

$$2H^+ + 2e^- \longrightarrow H_2 \qquad \text{(at cathode)}$$

The purple solution so obtained is evaporated under controlled conditions to obtain crystals of $KMnO_4$.

Structure of Manganate and Permanganate Ion

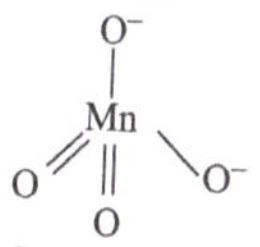

Tetrahedral manganate (green) ion

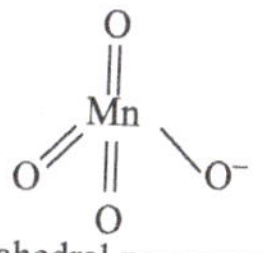

Tetrahedral permanganate (purple) ion

Properties-Redox Reaction

$KMnO_4$ shows oxidising nature in acidic medium, basic medium and neutral medium. These are as follows

(i) **Acidic medium**

(a) **Ferrous salts to ferric salts**

$$2KMnO_4 + 8H_2SO_4 + \underset{\text{Ferrous sulphate}}{10\,FeSO_4} \longrightarrow K_2SO_4 + 2MnSO_4 + \underset{\text{Ferric sulphate}}{5Fe_2(SO_4)_3} + 8\,H_2O$$

(b) **Potassium iodide to iodine**

$$2KMnO_4 + 8H_2SO_4 + 10KI \longrightarrow 6K_2SO_4 + 2MnSO_4 + 8H_2O + 5I_2$$

(c) **Oxalic acid to carbon dioxide**

$$2KMnO_4 + 3\,H_2SO_4 + 5\underset{\text{Oxalic acid}}{\begin{matrix}COOH\\ | \\ COOH\end{matrix}} \longrightarrow K_2SO_4 + 2MnSO_4 + 8H_2O + 10\,CO_2$$

(ii) **Basic medium** It oxidises potassium iodide to potassium iodate.

$$2KMnO_4 + KI + H_2O \longrightarrow 2MnO_2 + 2KOH + KIO_3$$

(iii) **Neutral medium** It oxidises hydrogen sulphide to sulphur.

$$2KMnO_4 + 3\,H_2S \longrightarrow 2KOH + 2MnO_2 + 2H_2O + 3S$$

Uses

- Widely used in laboratory and industry as an oxidising agent in redox reaction.
- Germicide, sterilising wells of drinking water, washing wounds.

Potassium Dichromate ($K_2Cr_2O_7$)

From Chromite Ore ($FeO \cdot Cr_2O_3$ or $FeCr_2O_4$)

Potassium dichromate is generally manufactured from chromite ore. The reactions involved in the preparation are as follows

$$\underset{\text{(Chromite ore)}}{4FeO \cdot Cr_2O_3} + 8Na_2CO_3 + 7O_2 \xrightarrow{\text{Roasted}} 8Na_2CrO_4 + 2Fe_2O_3 + 8CO_2$$

$$\underset{\text{(Sodium chromate)}}{2Na_2CrO_4} + H_2SO_4 \longrightarrow Na_2Cr_2O_7 + Na_2SO_4 + H_2O$$

$$\underset{\text{(Sodium dichromate)}}{Na_2Cr_2O_7} + 2KCl \longrightarrow \underset{\text{(Potassium dichromate)}}{\underset{\text{Orange}}{K_2Cr_2O_7}} + 2NaCl$$

Structure of Chromate and Dichromate Ions

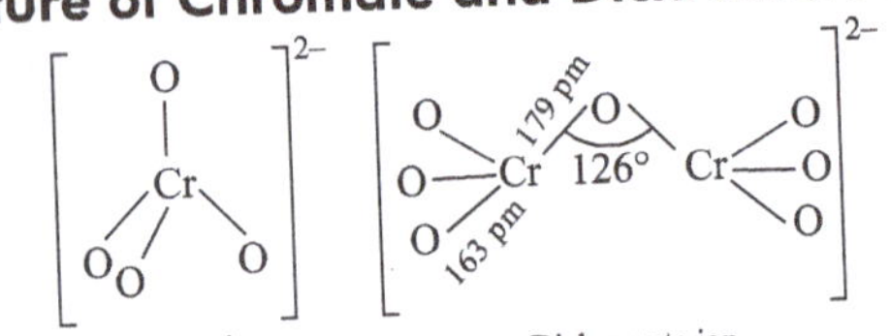

Chromate ion (Tetrahedral)

Dichromate ion

Chemical Properties

(i) Oxidising Properties in Acidic Medium

$K_2Cr_2O_7$ act as a good oxidising agent in acidic medium.

$$\underset{\text{(Orange)}}{K_2Cr_2O_7} + 4H_2SO_4 \longrightarrow K_2SO_4 + \underset{\text{Green}}{Cr_2(SO_4)_3} + 4H_2O + 3[O]$$

(ii) Oxidising Properties in Basic Medium

In alkaline solution (pH > 7), orange colour of $Cr_2O_7^{2-}$ (dichromate ion) changes to yellow colour due to the formation of CrO_4^{2-} (chromate ion).

$$\underset{\text{Orange red}}{K_2Cr_2O_7} + 2KOH \longrightarrow \underset{\text{Yellow}}{2K_2CrO_4} + H_2O$$

(iii) Interconversion of K_2CrO_4 and $K_2Cr_2O_7$

On acidifying the K_2CrO_4 solution, the colour changes to orange-red due to the reformation of dichromate.

$$2K_2CrO_4 + H_2SO_4 \longrightarrow K_2Cr_2O_7 + K_2SO_4 + H_2O$$

or $$2CrO_4^{2-} + 2H^+ \longrightarrow Cr_2O_7^{2-} + H_2O$$

Reason for inter conversion In dichromate solution, the orange-red $Cr_2O_7^{2-}$ ions are invariably in equilibrium with yellow CrO_4^{2-} ions.

$$\underset{\text{Orange-red}}{Cr_2O_7^{2-}} + H_2O \rightleftharpoons \underset{\text{Yellow}}{2CrO_4^{2-}} + 2H^+$$

(iv) Use in Redox Titration : Estimation

$K_2Cr_2O_7$ is determined volumetrically using Fe^{2+} or I^- (Iodometrically)

$$Cr_2O_7^{2-} + 6Fe^{2+} + 14H^+ \longrightarrow 2Cr^{3+} + 7H_2O \quad Cr_2O_7^{2-} \equiv 6Fe^{2+}$$

$$Cr_2O_7^{2-} + 6I^- + 14H^+ \longrightarrow 2Cr^{3+} + 3I_2 + 7H_2O$$

$$I_2 + 2S_2O_3^{2-} \longrightarrow S_4O_6^{2-} + 2I^-$$

Uses

- Oxidising agent in organic chemistry.
- In the estimation of Fe^{2+} and I^- ions in volumetric analysis.

PYQs Previous Years' Questions

1 Mark Questions

1. When $KMnO_4$ is heated with acidified oxalic acid, gas bubbles are evolved. These gas bubbles are evolved due to the formation of **ISC 2024**
   (a) SO_2 (b) CO_2
   (c) SO_3 (d) O_2

2. Acidified $K_2Cr_2O_7$ solution turns green when Na_2SO_3 is added to it. This is due to the formation of : **ISC Specimen 2024**
   (a) CrO_4^{2-} (b) $Cr_3(SO_3)_2$
   (c) Cr_2O_3 (d) $Cr_2(SO_4)_3$

3. $K_2Cr_2O_7$ acts as a powerful oxidising agent in acidic medium. Explain. **ISC 2020**

4. Give balanced equation for the following reaction. 'Potassium permanganate is heated with concentrated hydrochloric acid'. **ISC 2017**

5. Give balanced equation for the following reaction. Potassium dichromate is treated with acidified ferrous sulphate solution. **ISC 2016**

6. Give balanced equation when potassium iodide is treated with acidified potassium permanganate solution. **ISC 2013**

7. Give the balanced equation for acidified potassium permanganate and oxalic acid. **ISC 2012**

> **KEY IDEA**
>
> Acidified $KMnO_4$ acts as good oxidising agent, it oxidises oxalic acid to CO_2 and reduced itself to Mn^{2+} ion.

2 Marks Questions

8. Complete and balance the following chemical equations. **ISC Specimen 2023**
   (i) $KMnO_4 + H_2SO_4 + FeSO_4 \longrightarrow ...... + ... + ... + ...$
   (ii) $K_2Cr_2O_7 + KI + H_2SO_4 \longrightarrow ...... + ... + ... + ...$

9. Describe the oxidising action of potassium dichromate and write the ionic equations for its reactions with (i) iodide and (ii) H_2S.

10. Complete the following chemical reaction equations:
    (i) $MnO_4^-(aq) + C_2O_4^{2-}(aq) + H^+(aq) \longrightarrow$
    (ii) $Cr_2O_7^{2-}(aq) + Fe^{2+}(aq) + H^+(aq) \longrightarrow$

3 Marks Questions

11. Complete and balance the following chemical equations. **ISC 2019**
    (i) $KMnO_4 + H_2SO_4 + H_2C_2O_4 \longrightarrow ...... + ... + ... + ...$
    (ii) $K_2Cr_2O_7 + H_2SO_4 + KI \longrightarrow ...... + ... + ... + ...$
    (iii) $K_2Cr_2O_7 + H_2SO_4 + FeSO_4 \rightarrow ...... + ... + ... + ...$

12. Complete and balance the following chemical equations. **ISC 2018**
    (i) $KMnO_4 + KI + H_2SO_4 \longrightarrow .... + ... + ... + ...$
    (ii) $K_2Cr_2O_7 + H_2SO_4 + H_2S \longrightarrow .... + ... + ... + ...$
    (iii) $KMnO_4 + H_2SO_4 + FeSO_4 \longrightarrow .... + ... + ... + ...$

13. Complete the following chemical equations. **ISC Specimen 2018**
    (i) $K_2Cr_2O_7 + H_2SO_4 + FeSO_4 \longrightarrow$
    (ii) $K_2Cr_2O_7 + H_2SO_4 + H_2S \longrightarrow$
    (iii) $KMnO_4 + H_2SO_4 + H_2C_2O_4 \longrightarrow$

14. How does potassium dichromate prepared from a sample of chromite ore? Give the balanced equations for the chemical reactions involved. **ISC 2014**

Explanations

1. (*b*) These gas bubbles are evolved due to the formation of CO_2 gas.

$$2MnO_4^- + 5C_2O_4^{2-} + 16H^+ \longrightarrow 2Mn^{2+} + 10CO_2 + 8H_2O$$

2. (*d*) Acidified $K_2Cr_2O_7$ solution turns green when Na_2SO_3 is added to it. This is due to $Cr_2(SO_4)_3$.

3. In $K_2Cr_2O_7$, the oxidation number of Cr is +6 which is the highest oxidation number of Cr. Thus, $K_2Cr_2O_7$ can act as an oxidising agent and is reduced to Cr^{3+} ions. Equation involved is as follows

$$Cr_2O_7^{2-} + 14H^+ + 6e^- \longrightarrow 2Cr^{3+} + 7H_2O \ (E^\circ = 133 \text{ V})$$

4. $$\underset{\text{(Conc.)}}{16HCl} + 2KMnO_4 \xrightarrow{\Delta} 2KCl + 2MnCl_2 + 5Cl_2 + 8H_2O$$

5. $$\underset{\text{Ferrous sulphate}}{6FeSO_4} + \underset{\text{Potassium dichromate}}{K_2Cr_2O_7} + \underset{\text{Sulphuric acid}}{7H_2SO_4} \longrightarrow \underset{\text{Ferric sulphate}}{3Fe_2(SO_4)_3} + \underset{\text{Potassium sulphate}}{K_2SO_4} + \underset{\text{Chromium sulphate}}{Cr_2(SO_4)_3} + \underset{\text{Water}}{7H_2O}$$

6. An acidified $KMnO_4$ solution oxidised potassium iodide to iodine.

$$2KMnO_4 + 3H_2SO_4 \longrightarrow K_2SO_4 + 2MnSO_4 + 3H_2O + 5O$$
$$[2KI + H_2SO_4 \longrightarrow K_2SO_4 + 2HI] \times 5$$
$$[2HI + O \longrightarrow H_2O + I_2] \times 5$$
$$\overline{2KMnO_4 + 8H_2SO_4 + 10KI \longrightarrow 6K_2SO_4 + 2MnSO_4 + 8H_2O + 5I_2}$$

7. Thus, first write the balanced reduction and oxidation half reaction for $KMnO_4$ and oxalic acid respectively.

Then, write the overall balanced redox reaction. $KMnO_4$ oxidises oxalic acid (or oxalates) to carbon dioxide.

$$2KMnO_4 + 3H_2SO_4 \longrightarrow K_2SO_4 + 2MnSO_4 + 3H_2O + 5O$$
$$\left[\begin{matrix}COOH\\ |\\ COOH\end{matrix} + O \longrightarrow 2CO_2 + H_2O\right] \times 5$$
$$\overline{2KMnO_4 + 3H_2SO_4 + 5\underset{\text{Oxalic acid}}{\begin{matrix}COOH\\ |\\ COOH\end{matrix}} \longrightarrow K_2SO_4 + 2MnSO_4 + 8H_2O + 10CO_2}$$

8. (i) The given reaction takes place in acidic medium in which the ferrous salt is converted to ferric salt.

$$2KMnO_4 + 3H_2SO_4 \longrightarrow K_2SO_4 + 2MnSO_4 \ 3H_2O + 5O$$
$$[2FeSO_4 + H_2SO_4 + O \longrightarrow Fe_2(SO_4)_3 + H_2O] \times 5$$
$$\overline{2KMnO_4 + 8H_2SO_4 + 10FeSO_4 \longrightarrow K_2SO_4 + 2MnSO_4 + 5Fe_2(SO_4)_3 + 8H_2O}$$ (1)

(ii) In acidic medium $Cr_2O_7^{2-}$ is converted to Cr^{3+} and I^- is converted to I_2.

$$Cr_2O_7^{2-} + 14H^+ + 6e^- \longrightarrow 2Cr^{3+} + 7H_2O$$
$$6I^- \longrightarrow 3I_2 + 6e^-$$
$$\overline{Cr_2O_7^{2-} + 14H^+ + 6I^- \longrightarrow 2Cr^{3+} + 7H_2O + 3I_2}$$ (1)

9. Potassium dichromate is a strong oxidising agent. In acidic solution, its oxidising action is represented as

$$Cr_2O_7^{2-} + 14H^+ + 6e^- \longrightarrow 2Cr^{3+} + 7H_2O$$

(i) Reaction of $K_2Cr_2O_7$ with I^-

$$Cr_2O_7^{2-} + 14H^+ + 6I^- \longrightarrow 2Cr^{3+} + 3I_2 + 7H_2O$$ (1)

(ii) Reaction of $K_2Cr_2O_7$ with H_2S

$$Cr_2O_7^{2-} + 8H^+ + 3H_2S \longrightarrow 2Cr^{3+} + 3S + 7H_2O$$ (1)

10. (i) $2MnO_4^-(aq) + 5C_2O_4^{2-}(aq) + 16H^+(aq) \longrightarrow 2Mn^{2+} + 8H_2O(l) + 10CO_2(g)$ (1)

(ii) $Cr_2O_7^{2-}(aq) + 6Fe^{2+}(aq) + 14H^+(aq) \longrightarrow 2Cr^{3+}(aq) + 6Fe^{3+}(aq) + 7H_2O(l)$ (1)

11. (i) $2KMnO_4 + 5H_2C_2O_4 + 3H_2SO_4 \xrightarrow{60^\circ C} 2MnSO_4 + 10CO_2 + K_2SO_4 + 8H_2O$

(ii) $K_2Cr_2O_7 + 6KI + 7H_2SO_4 \longrightarrow 3I_2 + Cr_2(SO_4)_3 + 4K_2SO_4 + 7H_2O$

(iii) $K_2Cr_2O_7 + 7H_2SO_4 + 6FeSO_4 \longrightarrow 3Fe_2(SO_4)_3 + K_2SO_4 + Cr_2(SO_4)_3 + 7H_2O$ (1×3)

12. (i) $2KMnO_4 + 10KI + 3H_2SO_4 \longrightarrow K_2SO_4 + 2MnSO_4 + 8H_2O + 5I_2$

(ii) $K_2Cr_2O_7 + 4H_2SO_4 + 3H_2S \longrightarrow K_2SO_4 + Cr_2(SO_4)_3 + 7H_2O + 3S$

(iii) $2KMnO_4 + 8H_2SO_4 + 10FeSO_4 \longrightarrow K_2SO_4 + 2MnSO_4 + 5Fe_2(SO_4)_3 + 8H_2O$ (1×3)

13. (i) $K_2Cr_2O_7 + 7H_2SO_4 + 6FeSO_4 \longrightarrow$
$K_2SO_4 + Cr_2(SO_4)_3 + 3Fe_2(SO_4)_3 + 7H_2O$

(ii) $K_2Cr_2O_7 + 4H_2SO_4 + 3H_2S \longrightarrow$
$K_2SO_4 + Cr_2(SO_4)_3 + 7H_2O + 3S$

(iii) $2KMnO_4 + 3H_2SO_4 + 5C_2H_2O_4 \longrightarrow$
$K_2SO_4 + 2MnSO_4 + 8H_2O + 10CO_2$ **(1 × 3)**

14. Potassium dichromate is generally manufactured from chromite ore $FeO \cdot Cr_2O_3$ or $FeCr_2O_4$.
The steps involved are

(i) Finely powdered chromite ore is mixed with Na_2CO_3 and quicklime.
The mixture is roasted in a reverberatory furnace in the presence of excess of air. On account of roasting, a yellow mass containing sodium chromate is obtained.

$$4\,FeCr_2O_4 + O_2 \longrightarrow 2FeO_3 + 4Cr_2O_3$$
$$4Cr_2O_3 + 8Na_2CO_3 + 6O_2 \longrightarrow 8Na_2CrO_4 + 8CO_2$$
$$4FeCr_2O_4 + 8Na_2CO_3 + 7O_2 \longrightarrow 2Fe_2O_3 + 8Na_2CrO_4 + 8CO_2$$ **(1)**

(ii) Sodium chromate obtained is treated with concentrated sulphuric acid where it is converted into sodium dichromate.

$$2Na_2CrO_4 + H_2SO_4 \longrightarrow Na_2Cr_2O_7 + Na_2SO_4 + H_2O$$

The solution is concentrated when less soluble sodium sulphate $Na_2SO_4 \cdot 10H_2O$ crystallises out. This solution is filtered hot.
The solution is now cooled till sodium dichromate crystals $(Na_2Cr_2O_7 \cdot 2H_2O)$ separates out. **(1)**

(iii) Hot concentrated solution of sodium dichromate is treated with calculated amount of potassium chloride and the mixture is cooled till orange crystals of potassium dichromate are obtained.

$$\underset{\text{(Hot and Conc.)}}{Na_2Cr_2O_7} + 2KCl \longrightarrow \underset{\text{(Orange)}}{K_2Cr_2O_7} + 2NaCl$$ **(1)**

CHAPTER TEST

01 Mark Questions

1. Fill in the blanks by choosing the appropriate word(s) from those given in the bracket.

[colourless, coloured, paramagnetic, diamagnetic, Zr, Ce, lanthanoid, actinoid, purple, red *d-d* transition, charge transfer]

(i) Most of the lanthanoids are ..... and .... in nature.

(ii) The green manganate and purple permanganate are .... and .... respectively.

(iii) ..... and Hf have almost same radii due to ...... contraction.

(iv) Potassium permanganate is ...... coloured crystalline solid. The colour is due to ....

2. Select and write the correct alternatives from the choices given below.

(i) Which of the following will not form interstitial compounds?

(a) Fe (b) Ni (c) Co (d) Zn

(ii) The correct order of basic strength of lanthanoid hydroxides given below is

$$\underset{\text{I}}{La(OH)_3}, \underset{\text{II}}{Lu(OH)_3}, \underset{\text{III}}{Ce(OH)_3}$$

(a) I > II > II (b) I < III < II
(c) I > II > III (d) I < I < III

(iii) Which of the following factors is not responsible for the formation of the complex compounds by transition elements?

(a) Smaller size of metal ions
(b) High ionic charges on metal
(c) Availability of only *d*-orbitals
(d) Availability of both *d*-and *f*-orbitals

(iv) Which of the following has maximum number of unpaired *d*-electrons?

(a) Zn^{2+} (b) Ni^{2+} (c) Fe^{2+} (d) Co^{2+}

3. (i) **Assertion** (A) First ionisation enthalpy of Cr is lower than that of Zn.

Reason (R) IE of Cr is lower due to the stability of d^5.

(a) Both (A) and (R) are correct and (R) is the correct explanation of (A).
(b) Both (A) and (R) are correct but (R) is not the correct explanation of (A).
(c) (A) is correct and (R) is incorrect.
(d) (A) is incorrect and (R) is correct.

(ii) **Assertion** (A) Actinoids form relatively less stable complexes as compared to lanthanoids.

Reason (R) Actinoids can utilise their $5f$-orbitals alongwith 6*d*-orbitals in bonding but lanthanoids do not use their $4f$-orbitals for bonding.

(a) Both (A) and (R) are correct and (R) is the correct explanation of (A).
(b) Both (A) and (R) are correct but (R) is not the correct explanation of (A).
(c) (A) is correct and (R) is incorrect.
(d) (A) is incorrect and (R) is correct.

02 Marks Questions

4. What is lanthanoid contraction? Write any two consequences.

5. Complete the following chemical equation.

(i) $Cr_2O_7^{2-} + 2OH^- \longrightarrow$

(ii) $Cr_2O_7^{2-} + I^- + H^+ \longrightarrow$

6. Give a relevant reason for the following

(i) Transition metal exhibit paramagnetic behaviour.
(ii) Transition metals exhibit variable oxidation state.

7. Complete and balance the reactions.

(i) $Fe^{2+} + MnO_4^- + H^+ \longrightarrow$

(ii) $MnO_4^- + NO_2^- + H^+ \longrightarrow$

8. Give reason for the following.

(i) The transition metals (except Zn, Cd and Hg) are hard and have high melting and boiling points.
(ii) Metal-metal bonding is more frequent for the 4*d* and 5*d*-series transition metals than that for the 3*d*-series.

9. Write one difference and one similarity between the chemistry of lanthanoids and actinoids.

10. Write the electronic configuration of Eu^{2+} ion and calculate its magnetic moment. (Atomic number of Eu = 63)

03 Marks Questions

11. Give reason for the following.

(i) La^{3+} (Z=57) and Lu^{3+} (Z = 71) do not show any colour in solutions.

(ii) Mn shows the highest oxidation state of +7 with oxygen but with fluorine it shows + 4 as the highest oxidation state.

(iii) Yb^{2+} act as a strong reducing agent.

12. Complete the following reactions.

(i) $2MnO_4^- + 5S^{2-} + 16H^+ \longrightarrow$

(ii) $MnO_4^- + H_2O + I^- \longrightarrow$

(iii) $MnO_4^- + S_2O_3^{2-} + H_2O \longrightarrow$

13. Account for the following.

(i) Fe has higher enthalpy of atomisation than that of Cu.

(ii) Mn^{3+} undergoes disproportionation reaction easily.

(iii) Ti^{3+} is coloured in aqueous solution whereas Sc^{3+} is colourless.

14. Describe the preparation of sodium dichromate from chromite ore.

Write the ionic equation for the reaction that takes place between acidified $Na_2Cr_2O_7$ and iron (II) ions.

15. Give reason for the following.

(i) Cu^+ ion is not stable in aqueous solution.

(ii) $E^\circ_{M^{2+}/M}$ value of copper is positive.

(iii) Copper atom has completely filled d-orbitals in its ground state, yet it is regarded as a transition element.

05 Marks Questions

16. (i) Give reason for the following.

(a) Actinoids show irregularities in their electronic configuration.

(b) Lanthanoids show less oxidation state than actinoids.

(c) Eu^{2+} is a strong reducing agent.

(ii) How do you prepare

(a) K_2MnO_4 from MnO_2

(b) $Na_2Cr_2O_7$ from Na_2CrO_4

17. (i) Account for the following.

(a) Sc(21) is a transition metal but Ca(20) is not.

(b) Cu^+ is not known in aqueous solution.

(c) Many transition elements are known to form interstitial compounds.

(ii) Complete and balance the reaction.

(a) $Cr_2O_7^{2-} + OH^- \longrightarrow$

(b) $MnO_2 + KOH + O_2 \xrightarrow{\Delta}$

18. (i) A blackish brown coloured solid A which is an oxide of manganese, when fused with alkali metal hydroxide and an oxidising agent like KNO_3, produces a dark green coloured compound B which on disproportionation in neutral and acidic solution gives a purple coloured compound C.

Identify A, B and C and write the reaction involved when compound C is heated to 513 K.

(ii) (a) $E^\circ_{M^{3+}/M^{2+}}$ values for the first series of transition elements are given below.

E°(V)	Ti	V	Cr	Mn	Fe	Co
M^{3+}/M^{2+}	− 0.37	− 0.26	− 0.41	+ 1.57	+ 0.77	+ 197

Identify the two strongest oxidising agents in the aqueous solution from the above data.

(b) Copper (I) ion is not known in aqueous solution. Explain.

(c) In this series the highest oxidation state of a metal is exhibited in its oxide. Identify the metal.

Answers

1. (i) coloured, paramagnetic (ii) paramagnetic, diamagnetic (iii) Zr, lanthanoid (iv) purple, charge transfer

2. (i) (d) (ii) (b) (iii) (d) (iv) (c)

3. (i) (a) (ii) (d)

05

Coordination Compounds

TREND ANALYSIS 4 YEARS

Average No. of Questions Across all Sets

Topic	Types of Questions	2024	2023	2020	2019
TOPIC 01 Concept of Complexes, Ligands and IUPAC Nomenclature	1 Mark	1	1	—	—
	2 Marks	—	—	—	3
	3 Marks	—	—	1	—
	5 Marks	—	—	—	—
TOPIC 02 Isomerism, Magnetic Characteristics, Stability Constant of Coordination Compounds	1 Mark	1	—	1	—
	2 Marks	—	—	1	1
	3 Marks	—	—	—	—
	5 Marks	1	1	1	—

TOPIC 1

Concept of Complexes, Ligands and IUPAC Nomenclature

Addition Compounds

When two or more stable compounds combine together in stoichiometric ratio, then the compound formed is called addition compound. It is of following types

Coordination Compound

The compounds in which a central metal atom or ion is surrounded by a fixed number of oppositely charged ions or neutral molecules through coordinate bonds are called coordination compounds or **complex compounds**, e.g. $K_4[Fe(CN)_6]$. These type of compounds exhibit properties completely different from their constituents and retain identity even in solution state.

Double Salt

These are formed by mixing two saturated compounds. They lose their identity when dissolved in water as they dissociate completely into ions,
e.g. $[FeSO_4(NH_4)_2SO_4 \cdot 6H_2O]$ (Mohr's salt).

Werner's Theory of Coordination Compounds

Alfred Werner, a Swiss chemist was the first to formulate his idea about the structures of coordination compounds. He proposed the concept of primary valence and secondary valence.

According to Werner's theory,

- Metals possess two types of valencies, called **primary** or ionisable valency (oxidation number) and **secondary** or non-ionisable valency (coordination number).
- Every metal atom must satisfy both of its valencies.
- Primary valencies are satisfied by negative ions, whereas secondary valencies are satisfied by neutral molecules or negative ions.
- Primary valencies are non-directional. Secondary valencies are directed in space towards fixed position giving a definite shape to the complex.
- The ions/groups bound by the secondary linkages to the metal have characteristic spatial arrangements corresponding to coordination numbers. In modern formulations such spatial arrangements is called **coordination polyhedra.**

Some Important Terms Used in Coordination Chemistry

Some of the important terms are given below

Central Metal Atoms or Ions

In a coordination entity, the metal atoms or ions with which a definite number of ligands are attached in a definite geometry are called **central metal atoms or ions**.

e.g. $Fe^{2+}, Cu^{2+}, Ni^{2+}, Pt^{2+}$ are central metal ions which are also known as **Lewis acids**.

Ligand

It is a charged ion or neutral molecule which is capable of donating a pair of electrons to the **central atom or ion** for the formation of a coordinate bond. It is a **Lewis base**.

Ligands can be classified as

(i) **Monodentate ligands** These have only one donor atom which donates one lone pair of electrons, e.g. Cl^-, NH_3, CO, H_2O, etc.

(ii) **Bidentate ligands** These have two donor atoms which donates two lone pairs of electrons, e.g. 1, 2-ethanediamine (en).

(iii) **Polydentate ligands** These have more than two donor atoms in the molecule. e.g. Ethylenediamine tetraacetate (EDTA) is a hexadentate ligand.

(iv) **Chelating ligands** The ligands coordinating through two or more donor groups leading to formation of a ring with metal ion are called chelating ligands, e.g. $[Pt(en)_2]Cl_2$.

(v) **Ambidentate ligands** When a ligand containing two different donor atoms attach to the central metal atom through any of its donor atoms, is called ambidentate ligand, e.g. SCN^-, ONO^-, etc.

Coordination Sphere

The central atom/ion and the ligands present in the square brackets are collectively known as coordination sphere.

Ionisation Sphere

The part of the coordination compound which is present outside the square brackets [coordination sphere] is known as ionisation sphere.

Coordination Number

It is the maximum number of ligands which can be attached to the central metal atom or ion.

Oxidation Number

Oxidation number of the central metal atom is the electrical charge it would carry, if all the ligands are removed alongwith the lone pairs of electrons that are shared with the central atom.

e.g. Oxidation state of Fe in $[Fe(CN)_6]^{4-}$ can be calculated as

Let the oxidation state of Fe in $[Fe(CN)_6]^{4-}$ be x, then

$$x + 6 \times (-1) = -4$$

$$x - 6 = -4 \quad \Rightarrow \quad x = +2$$

Nomenclature of Coordination Compounds

The formula and names adopted for coordination entities are based on the recommendations of the IUPAC.

Formulae of Mononuclear Coordination Entities

Following rules are applied while writing the formulae

- The central atom is listed first.
- The ligands are then listed in alphabetical order. The placement of a ligand, in the list does not depend on its charge.
- Polydentate ligands are also listed alphabetically. In case of abbreviated ligand, the first letter of the abbreviation is used to determine the position of the ligand in the alphabetical order.
- The formula for the entire coordination entity, whether charged or not, is enclosed in square brackets. When ligands are polyatomic, their formulae are enclosed in parentheses. Ligand abbreviations are also enclosed in parentheses.

- There should be no space between the ligands and the metal within a coordination sphere.
- When the formula of a charged coordination entity is to be written without that of the counter ion, the charge is indicated outside the square brackets as a right superscript with the number before the sign.
  e.g. $[Co(CN)_6]^{3-}$, $[Cr(H_2O)_6]^{3+}$, etc.
- The charge of the cation(s) is balanced by the charge of the anion(s).

IUPAC Rules for Naming Complex Compounds

- If the counter ions are positively charged (cations), they are named first and if they are negatively charged (anions) they are named at the end.
- In **complex ions**, ligands are named first. The number of a particular type of ligand is written as di for 2, tri for 3, tetra for 4, penta for 5, hexa for 6 and so on. If the name of ligand involves numerical prefix such as di, tri, tetra, etc., the number of such ligands are : *bis* for 2, *tris* for 3, *tetrakis* for 4.
- If there are more than one type of ligands are present then, their names are written in alphabetical order. The negative and positive ligands are named by putting suffix *–o* and *–ium* respectively.
- The ligands are named in an alphabetical order before the name of the central atom/ion. (This procedure is reversed from writing formula).
- Names of the anionic ligands end in -'o', those of neutral and cationic ligands are the same except aqua for H_2O, ammine for NH_3, carbonyl for CO and nitrosyl for NO. These are placed within enclosing marks ( ).
- The oxidation state of central metal ion can be indicated by roman numerals I, II, III and IV etc., in bracket at the end of the name of the complex.
- If the complex ion is a cation, the metal is named same as the element, e.g. Co in a complex cation is called cobalt and Pt is called platinum.
- If the complex ion is an anion, the name of the metal ends with the suffix—'ate', e.g. Co in a complex anion, $[Co(SCN)_4]^{2-}$ is called cobaltate. For some metals, the Latin names are used in the complex anions, e.g. ferrate for Fe.
- When a ligand coordinates through more than one atom, the point of attachment of the ligand is indicated by putting the symbol of the atom through which coordination occurs after the name of ligand.
- In naming complexes containing two or more metal atoms joined by bridging ligands, the word μ added with hyphen before the name of ligand.

PYQs Previous Years' Questions

1 Mark Questions

1. The number of ions that will be produced when potassium ferrocyanide, $K_4[Fe(CN)_6]$, dissolves in water is .... This shows that .... is the ligand in the coordination compound. *ISC Specimen 2024*
2. The coordination number and oxidation state of the complex $K_4[Fe(CN)_6]$ are ..... and ..... respectively. *ISC 2023*
3. In coordination complexes, the central metal atom or ion behaves as .... and the ligands behave as .... *ISC Specimen 2023*
4. The coordination number and oxidation state of the element '*E*' in the complex $[E(NH_3)_4Cl_2]NO_3$ are respectively. *ISC 2021-22 (Sem-II)*
   (a) 6 and 3 (b) 6 and 2 (c) 4 and 2 (d) 4 and 3
5. Write the IUPAC name of $[Co(NH_3)_4Cl_2]Cl$. *ISC 2021-22 (Sem-II)*
6. Coordination compounds structure was first proposed by .... *ISC 2009*
7. Correct the following statement by changing the underlined part of sentence.
   In a coordination complex, donation of electron pair takes place from the <u>central metal atom to the ligands.</u> *ISC 2009*

2 Marks Questions

8. When a coordination compound $CoCl_3 \cdot 6NH_3$ is mixed with $AgNO_3$, three moles of AgCl are precipitated per mole of the compound. Write the structural formula and IUPAC name of the coordination compound. *ISC 2019*

9. (i) Write the IUPAC names of the following. *ISC 2019*

(a) $K_3[Fe(C_2O_4)_3]$

(b) $[Co(NH_3)_5Cl]SO_4$

(ii) $[Fe(CN)_6]^{4-}$ is a coordination complex ion. *ISC 2019*

(a) Calculate the oxidation number of iron in the complex.

(b) Write the IUPAC name of the complex ion.

10. Write the formula of the following compounds.

(i) Potassiumtrioxalatoaluminate (III)

(ii) Hexaaquairon (II) sulphate *ISC 2017*

11. Write the IUPAC names of the following coordination compounds.

(i) $[Cr(NH_3)_4(H_2O)_2]Cl_3$

(ii) $[PtCl_2(NH_3)_4][PtCl_4]$ *ISC 2015*

12. Write the formula of the following compounds.

(i) Triamminetriaquachromium (III) chloride

(ii) Potassiumhexacyanoferrate (III) *ISC 2014*

> **KEY IDEA**
>
> First, identify that complex is cationic or anionic. For cationic complex, general formula is [metal symbol + ligand (with their number as subscript)]. In this case, the counter ion satisfying the valency of metal or oxidation state of complex.
>
> For anionic complex, general formula is counter ion satisfying valency of metal [metal symbol + ligand (with their number as subscript)]

13. Give the IUPAC names of the following coordination compounds. *ISC 2013*

(i) $K_2[Zn(OH)_4]$ (ii) $[Co(NH_3)_5(CO_3)]Cl$

14. Write the formula of the following coordination compounds.

(i) Potassiumtetracyanonickelate (0)

(ii) Triamminetrinitrocobalt (III) *ISC 2012*

15. Give the IUPAC name for the following. *ISC 2011*

(i) $Na_3[AlF_6]$ (ii) $[Co(NH_3)_6]Cl_3$

16. Write the formula of the following coordination compound.

(i) Tetracarbonylnickel (0)

(ii) Potassiumdicyanoargentate (I) *ISC 2010*

3 Marks Questions

17. (i) Write the formula of each of the following compounds. *ISC Specimen 2021-22 (Sem-II)*

(a) Potassium trioxalatoaluminate (III)

(b) Triammine triaquachromium (III) chloride

(ii) For the complex ion $[Co(NH_3)_6]^{3+}$, state the oxidation state of central metal atom and the coordination number of the complex ion.

18. Write the IUPAC names of the following complexes.

(i) $[Cu(NH_3)_4]SO_4$ (ii) $[Co(en)_2Cl_2]$ *ISC 2020*

(iii) $K_3[Al(C_2O_4)_3]$

Explanations

1. Five, CN^-
2. 6, 2
3. Lewis acid, Lewis base
4. (a) 6 and 3
5. Tetraaminedichlorocobalt (IV) chloride.

> **Common Mistake** Generally, students make mistake in mentioning the oxidation state of central metal ion, while writing the IUPAC name of a coordination compound.

6. Coordination compounds structure was first proposed by **Alfred Werner**.
7. In a coordination complex, donation of electron pair takes place from the **ligands to the central metal atom**.
8. On mixing the coordination compound, $CoCl_3 \cdot 6NH_3$ with $AgNO_3$, three moles of AgCl are precipitated. It indicates the presence of three chlorine atoms outside the coordination sphere, i.e. 3 moles of chlorine are ionisable.

Therefore, structural formula of the given complex is $[Co(NH_3)_6]Cl_3$.

IUPAC name of the complex is hexaamminecobalt (III) chloride.

9. (i) (a) $K_3[Fe(C_2O_4)_3]$

Potassiumtrioxalato ferrate (III)

(b) $[Co(NH_3)_5Cl]SO_4$

Pentaamminechlorocobalt (III) sulphate (1)

(ii) $[Fe(CN)_6]^{4-}$ ion

(a) Let the oxidation number of iron in the complex, $[Fe(CN)_6]^{4-}$ be x.

$\therefore \quad x + 6(-1) = -4, \Rightarrow x - 6 = -4$

$x = 6 - 4 = 2$

(b) Hexacyanoferrate(II) **(1)**

10. (i) $K_3[Al(ox)_3]$ or $K_3[Al(C_2O_4)_3]$

(ii) $[Fe(H_2O)_6]\,SO_4$ **(1 × 2)**

11. IUPAC name

(i) $[Cr(NH_3)_4(H_2O)_2]\,Cl_3$

Tetraamminediaquachromium (III) chloride

(i) $[PtCl_2(NH_3)_4][PtCl_4]$

Tetraamminedichloroplatinum (IV) tetrachloroplatinate (II) **(1 × 2)**

12. (i) $[Cr(NH_3)_3(H_2O)_3]Cl_3$

(ii) $K_3[Fe(CN)_6]$ **(1 × 2)**

13. (i) Potassiumtetrahydroxyzincate (II)

(ii) Pentaamminecarbonatocobalt (III) chloride **(1 × 2)**

14. (i) $K_4[Ni(CN)_4]$

(ii) $[Co(NH_3)_3(NO_2)_3]$ **(1 × 2)**

15. (i) Sodiumhexafluoroaluminate (III)

(ii) Hexaamminecobalt (III) chloride **(1 × 2)**

16. (i) $[Ni(CO)_4]$ (ii) $K[Ag(CN)_2]$ **(1 × 2)**

17. (i) (a) $K_3[Al(C_2O_4)_3]$

(b) $[Cr(NH_3)_3(H_2O)_3]Cl_3$ **(1)**

(ii) Let, the oxidation state of Co in the complex $[Co(NH_3)_6]^{3+}$ be x.

$\therefore \quad x + 6 \times 0 = +3$

$x = +3$

As six ammonia molecule is attached to Co (central metal). Thus, coordination number is 6. **(2)**

18. (i) Tetraamine copper (II) sulphate

(ii) Dichloro*bis*-(ethane-1, 2-diammine) cobalt (II)

(iii) Potassium trioxalatoaluminate (III) **(1 × 3)**

TOPIC 2

Isomerism, Magnetic Characteristics, Stability Constant of Coordination Compounds

Isomerism in Coordination Compounds

Compounds having same molecular formula but different structures are called **isomers** and this phenomenon is called **isomerism**.

Coordination compounds show two major types of isomerism, i.e. structural isomerism and stereoisomerism.

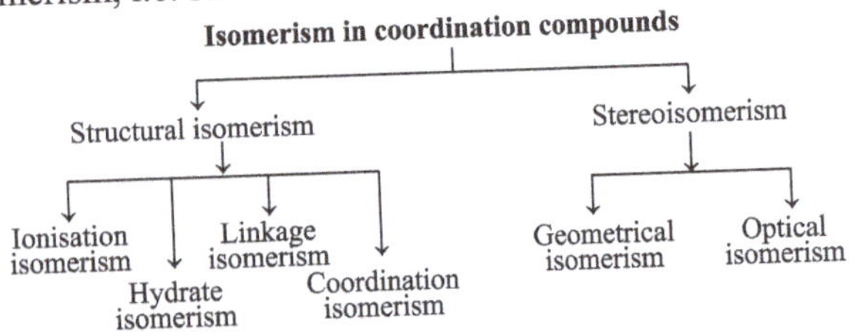

Structural Isomerism

The coordination compounds having same chemical formula and chemical bonds but are different due to different structural arrangement.

These are of following four types

(i) Ionisation Isomerism

It is shown by those compounds which have same composition but give different ions in solution, e.g. $[Co(NH_3)_5Br]\,SO_4$ and $[Co(NH_3)_5(SO_4)]\,Br$.

(ii) Hydrate Isomerism

It is shown by the compounds having difference in number of water molecules present as ligand (i.e. in the coordination sphere) and as free hydrate molecules (i.e. present outside the coordination sphere), e.g. $[Cr(H_2O)_5Cl]Cl_2 \cdot H_2O$ and $[Cr(H_2O)_6]Cl_3$.

(iii) Linkage Isomerism

It is shown by the compounds which have more than one atom in a monodentate ligand that functions as a donor, e.g. $[Co(NH_3)_5(NO_2)]Cl_2$ and $[Co(NH_3)_5ONO]Cl_2$.

(iv) Coordination Isomerism

It is shown by the compounds when both positive and negative ions of the compounds are complex ions and the two isomers differ in the distribution of ligands in the cation and the anion, e.g. $[Co(CN)_6]\,[Cr(NH_3)_6]$ and $[Cr(CN)_6]\,[Co(NH_3)_6]$.

Stereoisomerism

Coordination compounds having same molecular as well as the structural formula but show different arrangement in space around the central atom in the polyhedral are called stereoisomerism. It is of two types

(i) Geometrical or *cis-trans* Isomerism

When two identical ligands occupy adjacent position, we have *cis*-isomer and when they are arranged opposite to each other, we have *trans*-isomer. This phenomenon is called geometrical isomerism.

- **A square planar complex of the type** $[MX_2L_2]$ (X and L are unidentate) shows two geometrical isomers.

e.g.

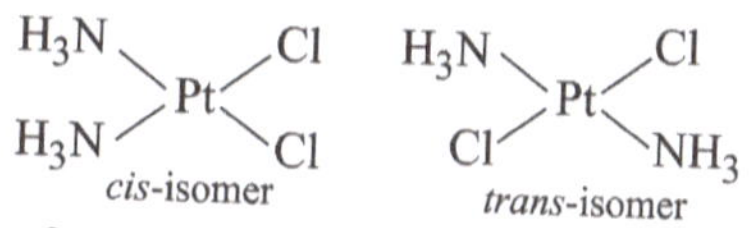

cis-isomer *trans*-isomer

Geometrical isomers of $[Pt(NH_3)_2Cl_2]$

- Other **square planar complex of the type** $[MABXL]$ ($ABXL$ are unidentate) shows three isomers-two *cis* and one *trans*.
- **Octahedral complexes of the type** $[MX_2L_4]$ in which two ligands X may be oriented *cis* or *trans* to each other.

e.g.

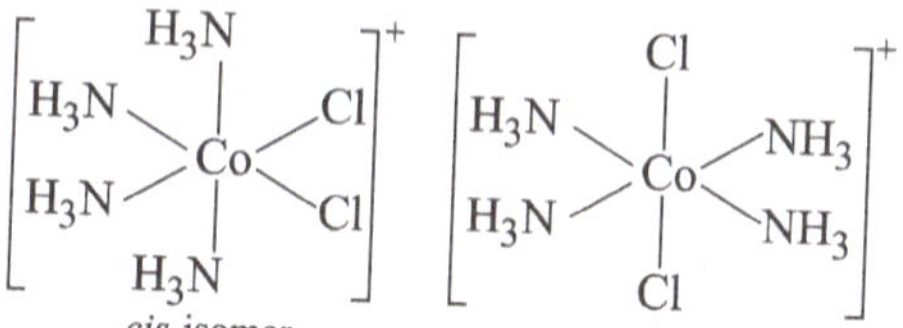

cis-isomer *trans*-isomer

Geometrical isomers of $[Co(NH_3)_4Cl_2]^+$

- **Octahedral coordination entities of the type** $[Ma_3b_3]$ shows geometrical isomerism. When three donor atoms of same ligands are occupying adjacent position in the polyhedra is known as **facial** (*fac*) **isomer**.

Whereas when three same ligands are occupying position around the meridian of the octahedral, it is known as **meridional** (*mer*) **isomer**.

e.g.

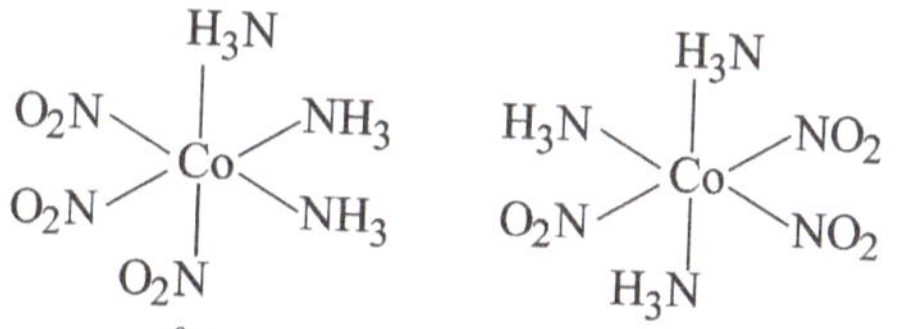

fac *mer*

Facial (*fac*) and meridional (*mer*) isomers of $[Co(NH_3)_3(NO_2)_3]$

Note **Tetrahedral complex** does not show geometrical isomerism because the relative positions of unidentate ligands attached to the central metal atom are the same with respect to each other.

- **Octahedral coordination complex of the type** $[M(AA)_2X_2]$

Mirror

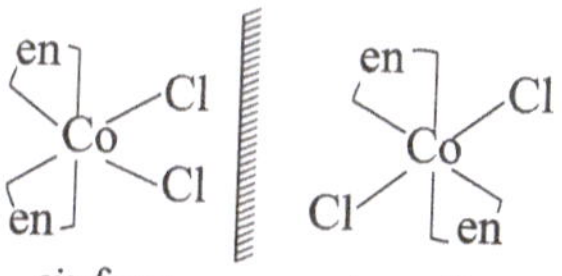

cis-form *trans*-form

(ii) Optical Isomerism

The compounds which do not have a plane of symmetry show optical isomerism. The optically active isomers which possesses non-superimposable mirror images are called **chiral**.

The isomer which rotates the plane of polarised light to the right is called ***dextro*** **(*d*) rotatory**, whereas the isomer which rotates the plane of polarised light to the left is called ***laevo*** **(*l*) rotatory**. The two forms of the molecule which are mirror images of each other are called **enantiomers.**

An equimolar mixture of *dextro* (*d*) and *laevo* (*l*) rotatory isomers is called **racemic mixture**. Optical isomerism is commonly shown by the octahedral complexes involving didentate ligands.

Some examples of octahedral complexes showing optical isomerism

Type	Example	Structure
$M(AA)_3$	$[Co(en)_3]^{3+}$, $[Cr(ox)_3]^{3-}$	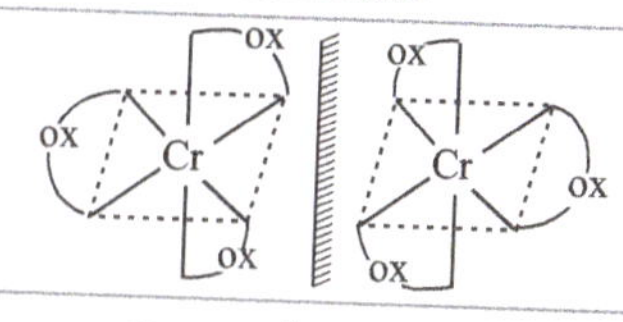
$[M(AA)_2X_2]^{n+}$ or $[M(AA)_2XY]^{n+}$	$[Co(en)_2Cl_2]^{3+}$	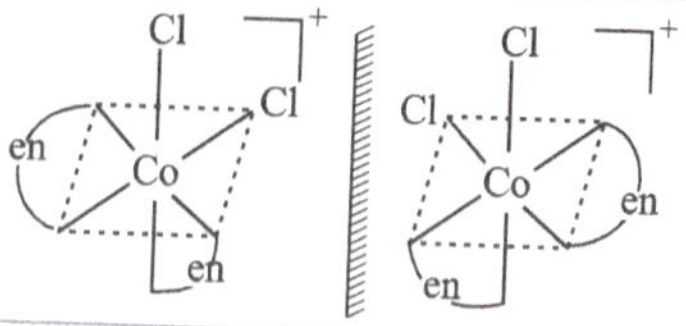
$[M(AA)_2X_2Y_2]$	$[Co(en)(NH_3)_2Cl_2]^+$	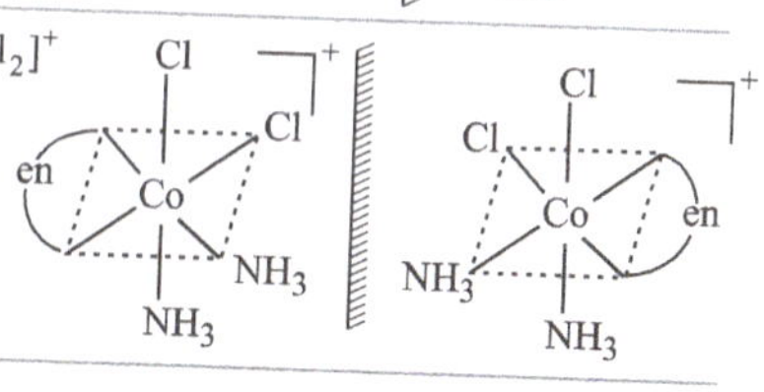

Bonding in Coordination Compounds

Many approaches have been put to explain the nature of bonding in coordination compounds, some of them are explained below.

Valence Bond Theory (VBT)

It was developed by **Linus Pauling**. In brief,

- Central atom/ion makes available required number of empty orbitals.

- These orbitals undergo hybridisation to give same number of hybrid orbitals of equal energy.
- These hybridised orbitals are allowed to overlap with ligand orbitals that can donate electron pairs for bonding, and form strong ligand-metal coordinate covalent bonds.

Hybridisation and geometry of complexes

Coordination number	Type of hybridisation	Geometry of the complex formed
2	sp	Linear
3	sp^2	Trigonal planar
4	sp^3	Tetrahedral
4	dsp^2	Square planar
5	dsp^3, sp^3d	Trigonal bipyramidal
6	sp^3d^2, d^2sp^3	Octahedral

- Ligands must have one sigma orbital containing lone pair of electrons.
- During complex formation, the Hund's rule of maximum multiplicity is followed while, in case of strong ligands, unpaired electrons get paired.
- A complex is **paramagnetic** if it contains unpaired electrons. If all the electrons are paired, the complex is **diamagnetic** in nature.
- The **outer orbital** (high spin) or **inner orbital** (low spin) **complexes** are formed depending whether outer d-orbitals or inner d-orbitals of metal ion are used, Using VBT, formation of $[Ni(CO)_4]$ can be represented as

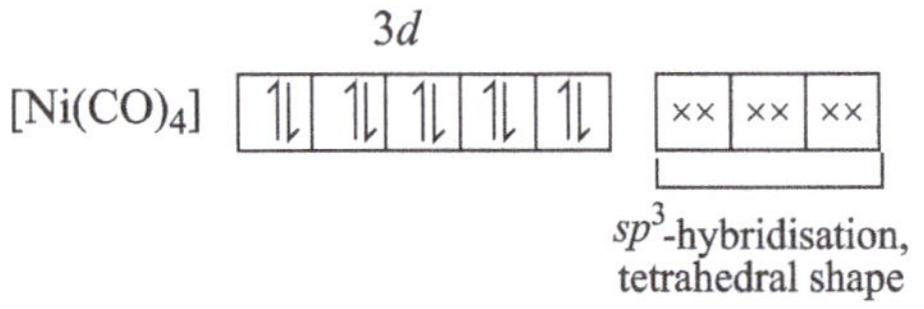

It is diamagnetic as all the electrons are paired.

Crystal Field Theory

This theory is an electrostatic model which considers the metal-ligand bond to be ionic arising purely from electrostatic interactions between the metal ion and the ligand.

The main characteristics of CFT are as follows

- The metal ion and ligand act as point charges and the interaction is purely electrostatic.
- When ligand approach free metal ion, all five degenerate (having similar energy) d-orbitals get split into two point groups t_{2g} (d_{xy}, d_{yz}, d_{zx}) and e_g $(d_{x^2-y^2}, d_{z^2})$. This type of splitting is called **crystal field splitting**.
- Due to different orientation, orbitals experience different interaction from ligand. Orbitals lying in the direction of ligand will have energy more than in symmetric field whereas orbitals lying in between the ligands will have lower energy.
- On the approach of ligands, two sets of d-orbitals having different energies are obtained. This difference in energies is called **crystal field splitting energy** (Δ_o or 10 Dq).
- Due to electrical field of ligand, the accommodation of electron in splitted d-orbitals is in accordance to Hund's rule.

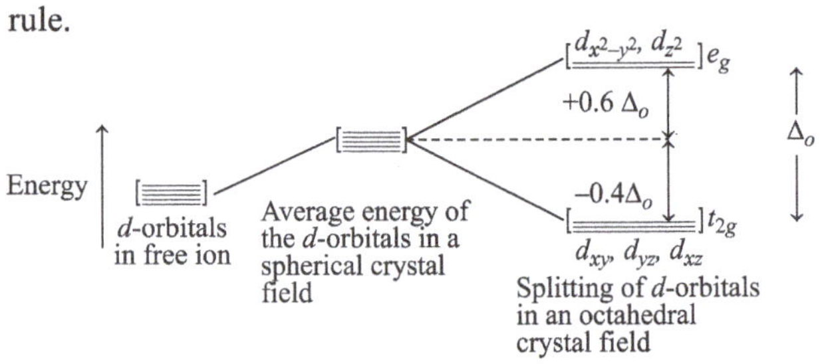

d-orbital splitting in an octahedral crystal field

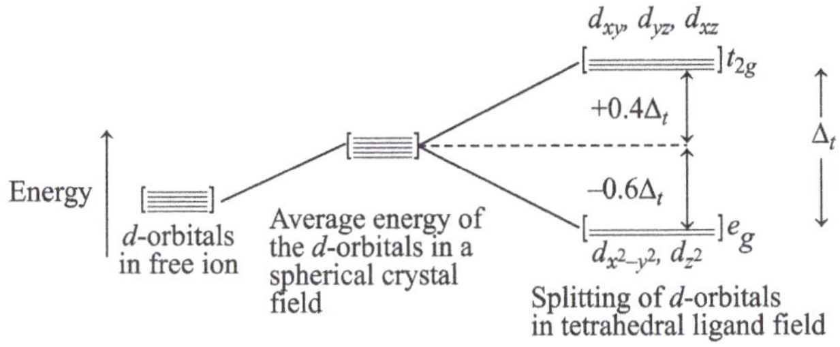

d-orbital splitting in a tetrahedral crystal

High Spin and Low Spin Complex

If $\Delta_o < P$ it will be high spin complex and if $\Delta_o > P$ it will be low spin complex.

where, Δ = crystal field splitting energy, P = energy required for electron pairing in an orbital. Weak field ligands form high spin complexes, while strong field ligands form low spin complexes.

Colour of Coordination Compounds

According to the crystal field theory, colour of complexes is due to d-d transitions of electrons. When light of certain frequency falls on the complex, it absorbs light from visible range for transition of electron from lower to higher level. This absorption depends upon the energy difference of the two levels. Colour of the compound is the complementary colour of the absorbed light. This electronic transition is known as d-d transition.

Complex having d^0 and d^{10} electronic configuration are colourless.

Magnetic Property of Coordination Compounds

Coordination compounds containing unpaired electrons are paramagnetic, while coordination compounds containing all electrons paired are diamagnetic in nature.

Stability of Coordination Compounds (Complex Ion)

It depends on the charge present on central atom, nature of metal ion, basic nature of ligand, presence of chelate ring and effect of multidentate cyclic ligand. If the interaction between metal ion and ligands is strong, the complex formed would be thermodynamically more stable.

For the reaction, $M^{a+} + nL^{x-} \rightleftharpoons [ML_n]^{b+}$, the equilibrium constant is termed as stability constant (K). It is

$$K = \frac{[ML_n]^{b+}}{[M^{a+}][L^{x-}]^n}$$

Higher the value of stability constant K, greater will be the stability of complex.

More the charge density on the ion, greater will be the stability of the complex. Also, greater the basic strength of the ligand, greater is the stability of the complex.

Importance and Uses of Coordination Compounds

(i) **Analytical chemistry** Qualitative detection and quantitative estimation of metal ions.

(ii) **Metallurgy** Extraction of metal.

(iii) **In biological system** Haemoglobin (complex of iron), chlorophyll (complex of magnesium).

(iv) **In industry** As catalyst, in electroplating.

(v) **In medicine** *cis*-platin (*cis*-$[PtCl_2(NH_3)_2]$) used in the treatment of cancer.

PYQs Previous Years' Questions

1 Mark Questions

1. EDTA is used in the treatment of .... while *cis*-platin is used in the treatment of .... *ISC 2024*

2. Crystal field splitting energy (CFSE) for high spin d^4-octahedral complex is: *ISC Specimen 2024*
   (a) $-1.6\,\Delta_o$ (b) $-1.2\,\Delta_o$
   (c) $-0.8\,\Delta_o$ (d) $-0.6\,\Delta_o$

3. Paramagnetic compounds are generally .... and contain .... electrons. *ISC 2021-22 (Sem-II)*

4. The type of hybridisation involved in octahedral complexes is *ISC Specimen 2021-22 (Sem-II)*
   (a) sp^3 (b) dsp^2
   (c) sp^3d (d) d^2sp^3

5. Outer orbital complexes involve .... hybridisation and are .... spin complexes. *ISC 2020*

6. In the complexes $[Fe(CN)_6]^{3-}$ and $[Pt(en)(H_2O)_2(NO_2)(Cl)]^{2+}$ the respective oxidation numbers of central metal atoms are *ISC 2018, 2015*
   (a) +3 and +4 (b) +6 and +4
   (c) +6 and +3 (d) +3 and +3

7. State the hybridisation and magnetic property of $[Fe(CN)_6]^{3-}$ ion according to the valence bond theory. *ISC 2018, 2015*

8. Name the types of isomerism shown by the following pairs of compounds: *ISC 2017*
   (i) $[Cu(NH_3)_4][PtCl_4]$ and $[Pt(NH_3)_4][CuCl_4]$
   (ii) $[Co(Pn)_2Cl_2]^+$ and $[Co(Tn)_2Cl_2]^+$

9. The complex ion $[Ni(CN)_4]^{2-}$ is *ISC 2017*
   (a) square planar and diamagnetic
   (b) tetrahedral and paramagnetic
   (c) square planar and paramagnetic
   (d) tetrahedral and diamagnetic

10. For the complex ion of $[Co(NH_3)_6]^{3+}$
    (i) state the hybridisation of the complex.
    (ii) state the magnetic nature of the complex. *ISC 2014*

11. Draw the structural isomer of $[Co(NH_3)_5NO_2]Cl_2$ and name the type of isomerism. *ISC 2012*

12. Among the following coordination compounds, the one giving a white precipitate with $BaCl_2$ solution is *ISC 2012*
    (a) $[Cr(H_2O)_5Br]SO_4$ (b) $[Cr(H_2O)_5SCN]$
    (c) $[Co(NH_3)_5SO_4]Br$ (d) $[Pt(NH_3)_6Cl_4]$

13. The hybridisation of the iron atom in $[Fe(CN)_6]^{3-}$ complex is **ISC 2010**
(a) sp^3 (b) d^2sp^3 (c) sp^3d^2 (d) dsp^2

14. Draw the geometrical isomers exhibited by the compound $[PtCl_2(NH_3)_2]$. **ISC 2010**

2 Marks Questions

15. $[Fe(CN)_6]^{4-}$ is a coordination complex ion. **ISC 2021-22 (Sem-II), 2019**
(i) Is the complex ion diamagnetic or paramagnetic ?
(ii) What is the hybridisation state of the central metal atom?

16. (i) What type of isomers are $[Co(NH_3)_5Br]SO_4$ and $[Co(NH_3)_5SO_4]Br$? Give a chemical test to distinguish between them. **ISC 2021-22 (Sem-II), 2015, 2013**
(ii) Write the structures of optical isomers of the complex ion $[Co(en)_2Cl_2]^+$.

17. Name the type of isomerism shown by each of the following pairs of compounds. **ISC Specimen 2021-22 (Sem-II)**
(i) $[CoCl_2(NH_3)_4]Cl \cdot H_2O$ and $[CoCl(H_2O)(NH_3)_4]Cl_2$
(ii) $[Cr(NH_3)_5Br]SO_4$ and $[Cr(NH_3)_5SO_4]Br$

18. With reference to the coordination complex ion $[Fe(H_2O)_6]^{2+}$ answer the following. (Atomic number of Fe = 26) **ISC 2020**
(i) Give the IUPAC name of the complex ion.
(ii) What is the oxidation number of the central metal atom?
(iii) How many unpaired electrons are there in the complex ion?
(iv) State the type of hybridisation of the complex ion.

19. What type of isomerism is shown by the following coordination compounds?
$[PtCl_2(NH_3)_4]Br_2$ and $[PtBr_2(NH_3)_4]Cl_2$
Write their IUPAC names. **ISC 2018**

20. Write the IUPAC name of the complex, $[Cr(NH_3)_4Cl_2]^+$. Which type of isomerism will be exhibited by it? **ISC Specimen 2018**

21. Write the IUPAC name of $[Co(en)_2Cl_2]^+$ ion and draw the structures of its geometrical isomers. **ISC 2018**

22. For the coordination complex ion $[Co(NH_3)_6]^{3+}$
(i) Give the IUPAC name of the complex ion.
(ii) What is the oxidation number of cobalt in the complex ion?
(iii) State the type of hybridisation of the complex ion.
(iv) State the magnetic behaviour of the complex ion. **ISC 2017**

23. Name the type of isomerism shown by the following pair of compounds. **ISC 2014**
(i) $[CoCl(H_2O)(NH_3)_4]Cl_2$ and $[CoCl_2(NH_3)_4]Cl \cdot H_2O$
(ii) $[Pt(NH_3)_4][PtCl_6]$ and $[Pt(NH_3)_4Cl_2][PtCl_4]$

24. $[CoF_6]^{3-}$ is a coordination complex ion.
(i) What is the oxidation number of cobalt in the complex?
(ii) How many unpaired electrons are there in the complex?
(iii) State the magnetic behaviour of the complex.
(iv) Give the IUPAC name of the complex. **ISC 2012**

25. Name the type of isomerism shown by the following pair of compounds, $[PtCl_2(NH_3)_4]Br_2$ and $[PtBr_2(NH_3)_4]Cl_2$. Give a chemical test to distinguish between the given pair of isomers. **ISC 2010**

26. Name the type of isomerism shown by the following pairs of coordination compounds.
(i) $[Co(NH_3)_5NO_2]Cl_2$ and $[Co(NH_3)_5ONO]Cl_2$
(ii) $[Cr(H_2O)_5Cl]Cl_2 \cdot H_2O$ and $[Cr(H_2O)_4Cl_2]Cl \cdot 2H_2O$ **ISC 2009**

3 Marks Questions

27. (i) What type of isomers are $[Co(NH_3)_5Br]SO_4$ and $[Co(NH_3)_5SO_4]Br$? Give a chemical test to distinguish between the two isomers.
(ii) Write the structures of optical isomers of the complex ion $[Co(en)_2Cl_2]^+$. **Specimen 2018**

28. For the complex ion of $[Fe(CN)_6]^{3-}$.
(i) Show hybridisation diagramatically.
(ii) Is it an inner orbital complex or an outer orbital complex?
(iii) State its magnetic property. **ISC 2011**

5 Marks Questions

29. (i) A coordination compound has a formula $CoCl_3 \cdot 4NH_3$. It precipitates silver ions as AgCl and its molar conductance corresponds to a total of two ions. **ISC Specimen 2024**
Based on this information, answer the following questions.
(a) Deduce structural formula of the complex compound.

(b) Write the IUPAC name of the complex compound.

(c) Draw the geometrical isomers of the complex compound.

(ii) Give a chemical test to show that $[Co(NH_3)_5Cl]SO_4$ and $[Co(NH_3)_5SO_4]Cl$ are ionisation isomers.

30. (i) When one mole of an isomer of the complex $[Cr(H_2O)_6]Cl_3$ is treated with $AgNO_3$, it produces 1 mole of a white precipitate of AgCl. Write the formula of this isomer of the complex and show how the metal-ligand bonding differs in the isomers. **ISC Specimen 2024**

(ii) A coordination compound shows d^2sp^3-hybridisation. Identify the nature of ligand as weak or strong. What will be the geometry of the compound?

31. (i) Name the type of isomerism exhibited by the following pairs of compounds. **2023**

(a) $[Co(NH_3)_5(ONO)]Cl_2$ and $[Co(NH_3)_5(NO)_2]Cl_2$

(b) $[Cr(H_2O)_5Cl]Cl_2 \cdot H_2O$ and $[Cr(H_2O)_4Cl_2]Cl \cdot 2H_2O$

(c) $[Pt(NH_3)_4Cl_2]Br_2$ and $[Pt(NH_3)_4Br_2]Cl_2$

(ii) Write the IUPAC names of the following complexes.

(a) $[Co(NH_3)_4(H_2O)_2]Cl_3$ (b) $K_2[Ni(CN)_4]$

32. (i) Name the type of isomerism shown by the following pairs of coordination compounds.

(a) $[Pt(H_2O)_4Cl_2]Cl_2 \cdot H_2O$ and $[Pt(H_2O)_3Cl_3]Cl \cdot 2H_2O$ **ISC Specimen 2023**

(b) $[Co(NH_3)_4Cl_2]Br_2$ and $[Co(NH_3)_4Br_2]Cl_2$

(c) $[Cr(H_2O)_5(SCN)]Cl_2$ and $[Cr(H_2O)_5(NCS)]Cl_2$

(ii) Consider the complex ion $[Co(CN)_6]^{3-}$ and answer the following questions.

(Atomic number of Co = 27)

(a) Type of hybridisation of central metal atom.

(b) Magnetic nature.

(c) Geometry of the complex ion.

(d) Low spin complex or high spin complex.

33. (i) Name of the type of isomerism exhibited by the following pairs of compounds. **ISC 2020**

(a) $[Co(ONO)(NH_3)_5]^{2+}$ and $[Co(NO_2)(NH_3)_5]^{2+}$

(b) $[Cr(H_2O)_4Cl_2]Cl \cdot 2H_2O$ and $[Cr(H_2O)_5Cl]Cl_2 \cdot H_2O$

(c) $[Co(NH_3)_6][Cr(CN)_6]$ and $[Cr(NH_3)_6][Co(CN)_6]$

(ii) Using the valence bond approach, predict the shape, hybridisation and magnetic behaviour of $[Ni(CO)_4]$. (Atomic number of Ni = 28)

34. (i) Write the IUPAC names of the following.

(a) $[Co(NH_3)_4SO_4]NO_3$

(b) $K[Pt(NH_3)Cl_3]$

(ii) What type of isomerism is exhibited by the following pairs of compounds?

(a) $[PtCl_2(NH_3)_4]Br_2$ and $[PtBr_2(NH_3)_4]Cl_2$

(b) $[Cr(SCN)(H_2O)_5]^{2+}$ and $[Cr(NCS)(H_2O)_5]^{2+}$

(iii) How does $K_2[PtCl_4]$ get ionised when dissolved in water? Will it form precipitate, when $AgNO_3$ solution is added to it? Give a reason for your answer.

ISC 2017

Explanations

1. Lead poisoning, cancer

2. (d) For high spin, $d^4 = t_{2g}^3 e_g^1$

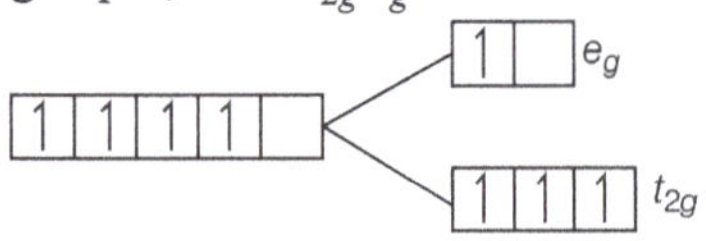

$\therefore$ $\quad$ $\text{CFSE} = (-0.4 \times 3 + 0.6 \times 1)\Delta_0$

$= (-1.2 + 0.6)\Delta_0 = -0.6\,\Delta_0$

3. coloured, unpaired $\quad$ 4. (d) d^2sp^3 $\quad$ 5. sp^3d^2, high

6. (a) $[Fe(CN)_6]^{3-}$

Let the oxidation number of Fe = x

$x + 6 \times (-1) = -3 \Rightarrow x = +3$

$[Pt(en)(H_2O)_2(NO_2)(Cl)]^{2+}$

Let the oxidation number of Pt = x,

$x + (0) + 2(0) + (-1) + (-1) = +2 \Rightarrow x = +4$

7. Oxidation number of Fe in the complex, $[Fe(CN)_6]^{3-}$ is

$$x + 6(-1) = -3 \Rightarrow x = +3$$

Electronic configuration of Fe is $[Ar]3d^6\,4s^2$.

Orbitals of Fe atom

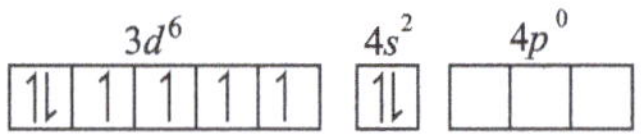

Orbitals of Fe^{3+} ion

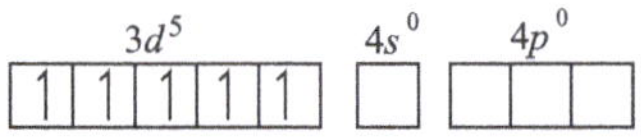

CN^- being strong field ligand, paired up the d-electrons of the metal.

Thus, $[Fe(CN)_6]^{3-}$ =

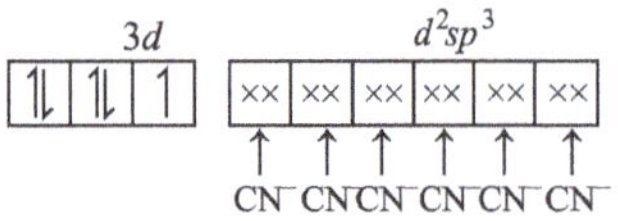

(i) Coordination number of the complex is 6. Hence, hybridisation is d^2sp^3, so geometry is octahedral.

(ii) Since, there is one unpaired electron, so it is paramagnetic.

8. (i) Coordination isomerism

(ii) Ligand isomerism

9. (a) Square planar and diamagnetic.

Concept Enhancer In case of strong field ligand, the complexes having C.N = 4 always form square planar geometry irrespective of metal.

10. **Oxidation number of Co in the complex $[Co(NH_3)_6]^{3+}$ is**

$$x + 6 \times (0) = +3, x = +3$$

Electronic configuration of Co is $[Ar]3d^7 4s^2$.

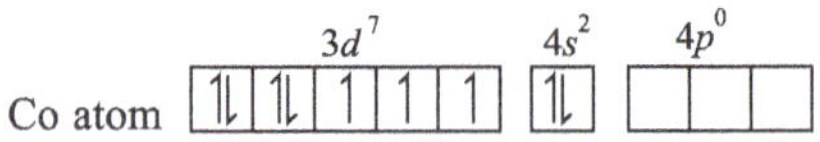

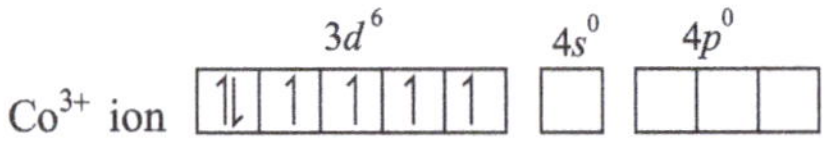

NH_3 is a strong field ligand, it causes pairing of $3d^6$ electrons.

Thus,

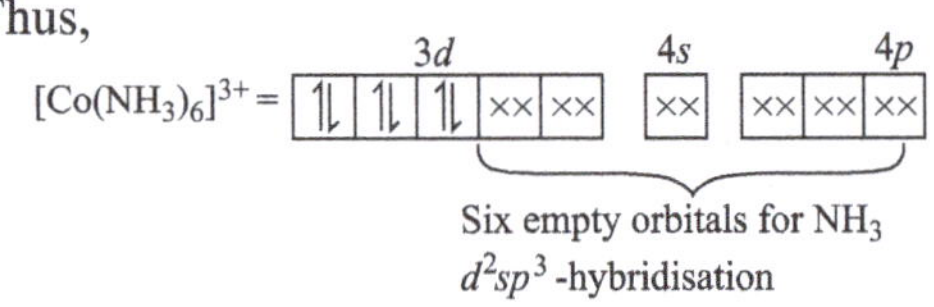

(i) Coordination number of the complex is 6. Hence, hybridisation is d^2sp^3.

(ii) All electrons are paired. So, it is diamagnetic.

11. The isomerism is linkage isomerism, i.e. more than one atom in a monodentate ligand may functions as donor. For this, in NO_2^- ion, either nitrogen or an oxygen atom may functions as donor.

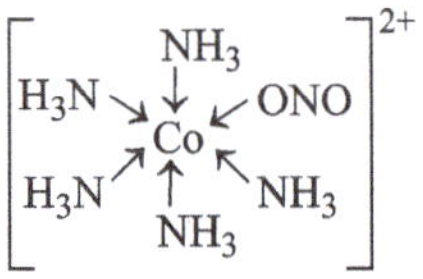

Pentaamminenitrito-O-cobalt (III) ion

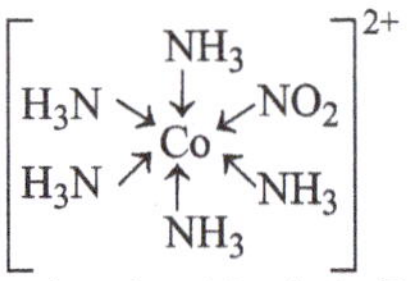

Pentaamminenitro-N-cobalt (III) ion

12. (a) $[Cr(H_2O)_5Br]SO_4$ gives a white precipitate of $BaSO_4$ when reacted with $BaCl_2$ solution, as it gives SO_4^{2-} ions in solution. Hence, option (a) is correct.

13. (b) Coordination number of complex is 6 and CN^- is a strong field ligand which paired up the d-electrons of the metal. So, hybridisation is d^2sp^3. Hence, option (b) is correct.

Concept Enhancer Strong field ligand form inner orbital complexes while weak field ligands form outer orbital complexes.

14. $[PtCl_2(NH_3)_2]$ exists in two geometrical isomers, i.e. *cis* and *trans*-forms.

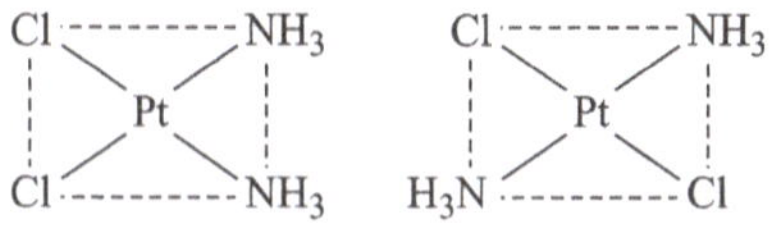

cis-isomer *trans*-isomer

15. (i) In the complex $[Fe(CN)_6]^{4-}$, iron exists in the + 2 oxidation state. Electronic configuration of Fe^{2+} is $4s^0 3d^6$. As CN^- is a strong field ligand, it causes the pairing of the unpaired 3*d* electrons. Hence, it is diamagnetic. **(1)**

(ii) In the given complex, hybridisation state of the central metal atom is d^2sp^3.

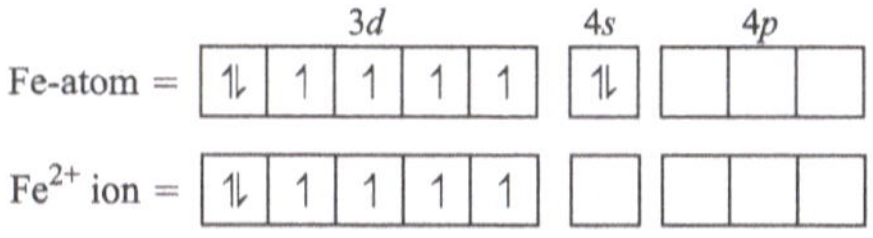

CN^- is a strong field ligand, thus it can pair the unpaired electrons of Fe^{2+}.

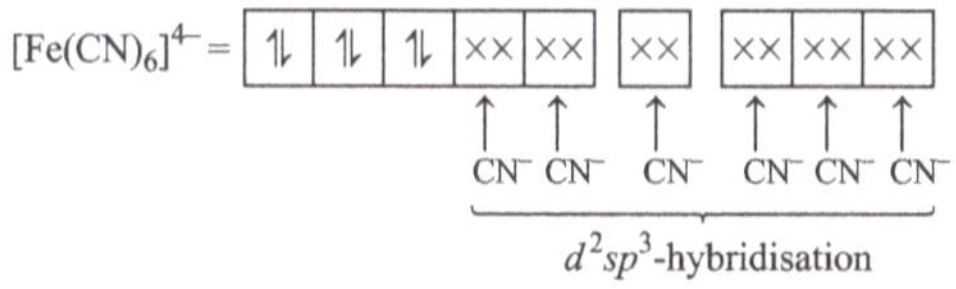

(1)

16. (i) The compounds will give different ions in solution, although they have same composition. Hence, they represent ionisation isomers. These compounds ionise in solution as given below

$[CoBr(NH_3)_5]\ SO_4 \longrightarrow [CoBr(NH_3)_5]^{2+} + SO_4^{2-}$

$[Co(SO_4)(NH_3)_5]Br \longrightarrow [Co(SO_4)(NH_3)_5]^+ + Br^-$

The complex $[CoBr(NH_3)_5]SO_4$ is red violet and its aqueous solution gives a white precipitate of $BaSO_4$ with $BaCl_2$.

Thus this reaction confirms the presence of SO_4^{2-} ions in the solution. Whereas the complex $[Co(SO_4)(NH_3)_5]Br$ is red in colour and its aqueous solution gives a light yellow precipitate of AgBr with $AgNO_3$ thus confirming the presence of Br^- ions in the solution.

$\underset{\text{Red violet}}{[CoBr(NH_3)_5]SO_4} + BaCl_2 \rightarrow$ White ppt. due to SO_4^{2-} ion

$\underset{\text{Red}}{[Co(NH_3)_5SO_4]Br} + BaCl_2 \longrightarrow$ No ppt. **(1)**

(ii) *cis*-form of $[Co(en)_2Cl_2]^+$ give optical isomers.

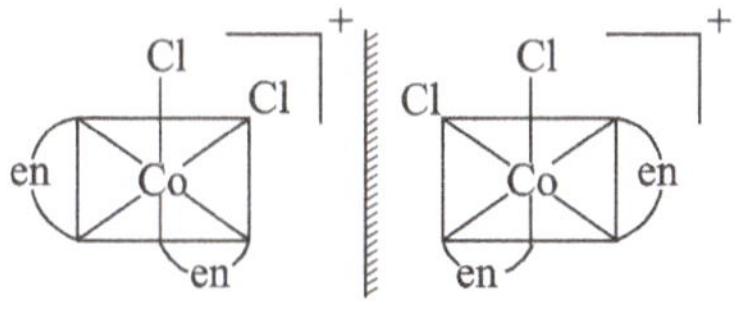

Non-superimposable mirror image structure **(1)**

17. (i) Given compounds show **hydrate isomerism.** These type of isomerism are shown by those isomers which have same composition but different number of water molecules attached to metal ion. **(1)**

(ii) Given compounds show **ionisation isomerism.** These type of isomerism are shown by those isomers which have same composition but yield different ions in solution. **(1)**

18. (i) Hexaaquairon (II) ion. **(1/2)**

(ii) Oxidation number is +2. **(1/2)**

(iii) In $[Fe(H_2O)_6]^{2+}$, four unpaired electrons are present as H_2O is a weak field ligand. **(1/2)**

$[Fe(H_2O)_6]^{2+}$, Fe is in +2 oxidation state

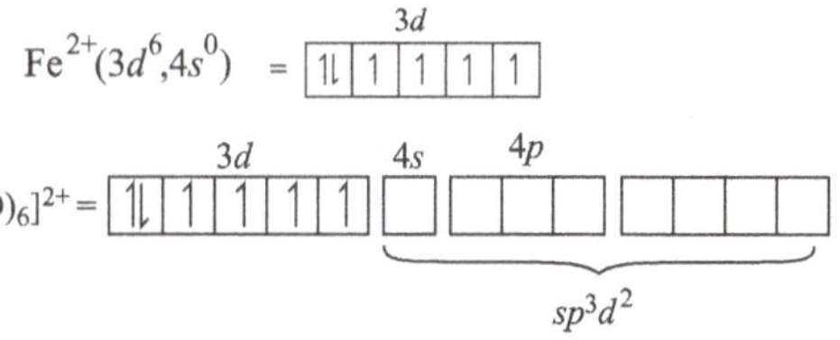

(iv) sp^3d^2-hybridisation **(1/2)**

19. $[Pt\ Cl_2(NH_3)_4]Br_2$ and $[PtBr_2(NH_3)_4]Cl_2$ shows ionisation isomerism as both of these compounds will give different type of ions in solution IUPAC names of the given compounds are

$[PtCl_2(NH_3)_4]Br_2$:

Tetraamminedichloroplatinum (IV) bromide

$[PtBr_2(NH_3)_4]Cl_2$:

Tetramminedibromoplatinum (IV) chloride

Common Mistake Some students write 'amine' instead of 'ammine' for NH_3 ligand.

20. IUPAC name of complex, $[Cr(NH_3)_4Cl_2]^+$ is tetraamminedichlorochromium (III) ion.

It shows geometrical isomerism as follows:

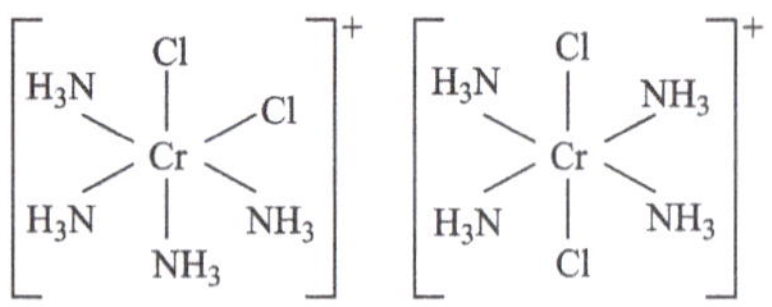

cis-isomer *trans*-isomer

21. $[Co(en)_2Cl_2]^+$

IUPAC name Dichloro *bis*-(ethane-1, 2-diamine) cobalt (III) ion.

Structure of its geometrical isomers (*cis* and *trans*) are given below.

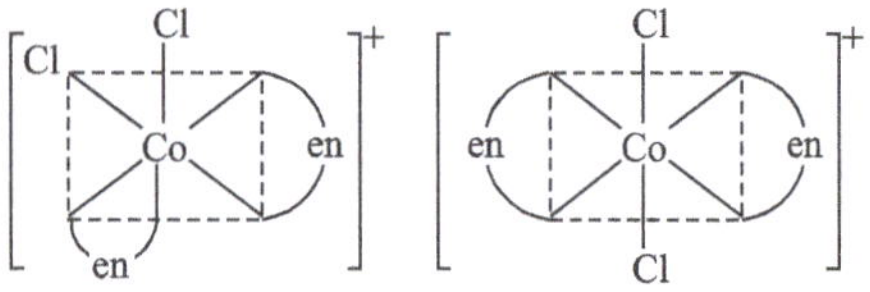

cis *trans*

22. (i) Hexaamminecobalt (III) ion. **(1/2)**

(ii) Let the oxidation number of Co in the complex $[Co(NH_3)_6]^{3+}$ be x.

$$x + 6 \times (0) = +3$$
$$x = +3$$ **(1/2)**

(iii) Electronic configuration of Co is $[Ar]3d^7 4s^2$.

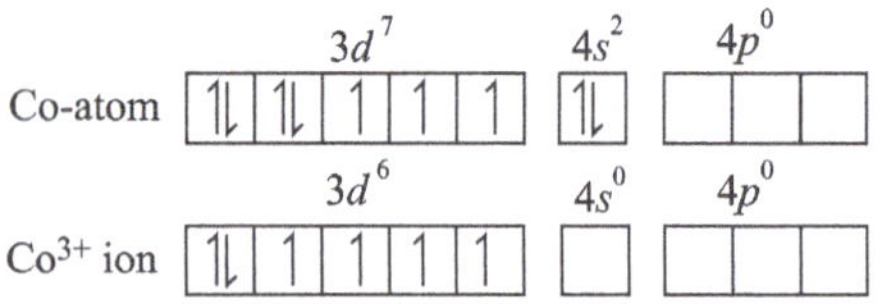

NH_3 is a strong field ligand, it causes pairing of $3d^6$ electrons.

Thus, $[Co(NH_3)_6]^{3+}$ =

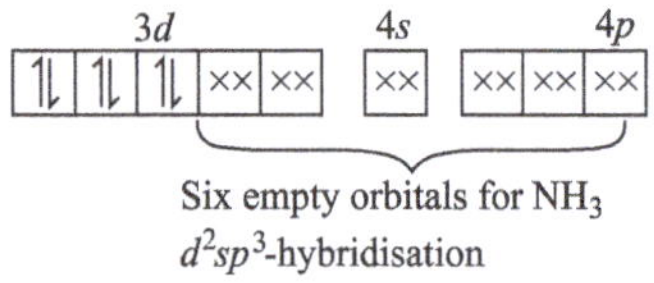

Thus, hybridisation of $[Co(NH_3)_6]^{3+}$ is d^2sp^3. **(1/2)**

(iv) As all electrons are paired so, it is diamagnetic. **(1/2)**

23. (i) In both compounds the difference is in the number of water molecule present as ligand (i.e. in coordination sphere) and as molecule of water of crystallisation (i.e. outside the coordination sphere). Hence, they are called hydrate isomers. **(1)**

(ii) In these compounds, both positive and negative ions of salt are complex ions and the two isomers differ in the distribution of ligands in cation and anion. Hence, they are coordination isomers. **(1)**

24. (i) Let the oxidation number of Co in the complex ion $[CoF_6]^{3-}$ is x, then

$$x + 6(-1) = -3$$
$$\Rightarrow \quad x = +3$$ **(1/2)**

(ii) Electronic configuration of

$$Co = [Ar]\ 3d^7, 4s^2$$

Co atom = 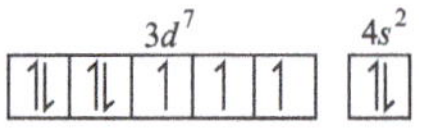

For Co^{3+} = $[Ar]\ 3d^6, 4s^0$

Co^{3+} ion = 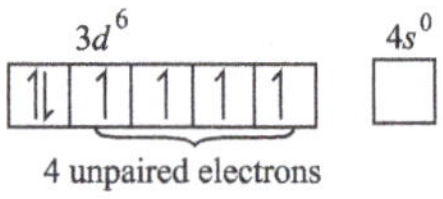

F^- is a weak field ligand, thus pairing of electron does not take place.

$\therefore [CoF_6]^{3-}$ =

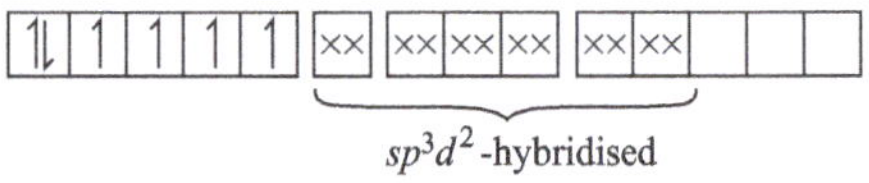

Therefore, there are 4 unpaired electrons. **(1/2)**

(iii) As it contains four unpaired electrons, so it is paramagnetic. **(1/2)**

(iv) Hexafluoridocobalt (III) ion. **(1/2)**

25. They show ionisation isomerism. It is because both compounds give different ions in solution and have same composition,

$$[PtCl_2(NH_3)_4]Br_2 \xrightleftharpoons{H_2O} [PtCl_2(NH_3)_4]^{2+} + 2Br^-$$

$$[PtBr_2(NH_3)_4]Cl_2 \xrightleftharpoons{H_2O} [Pt\,Br_2(NH_3)_4]^{2+} + 2Cl^-$$

Test When, above compounds are reacted with $AgNO_3$, they give different colour of ppt.

$$[Pt\,Cl_2(NH_3)_4]Br_2 + AgNO_3 \longrightarrow \underset{\text{Pale yellow ppt.}}{AgBr}$$

$$[Pt\,Br_2(NH_3)_4]Cl_2 + AgNO_3 \longrightarrow \underset{\text{White ppt.}}{AgCl}$$

26. (i) In both compounds, ambident ligand NO_2 is present. In $[Co(NH_3)_5NO_2]Cl_2$, NO_2 is coordinated through N and in $[Co(NH_3)_5ONO]Cl_2$, NO_2 is coordinated through O.

Hence, they show linkage isomerism. **(1)**

(ii) These isomers differ from each other in number of water molecules coordinated to central metal atom, i.e. (Cr). So, they show hydrate isomerism. **(1)**

27. (i) $[Co(NH_3)_5Br]SO_4$ and $[Co(NH_3)_5SO_4]Br$ shows ionisation isomerism.

Chemical test to distinguish between these two isomers are as follows

Dissolve both the compounds in water in different test tubes. To the both test tubes,

Test I Add $BaCl_2$ solution, one compound gives white precipitate indicating the presence of SO_4^{2-} ions.

The other compound does not give white precipitate, indicating the absence of SO_4^{2-} ions.

$$[Co(NH_3)_5Br]SO_4 + BaCl_2\,(aq) \longrightarrow [Co(NH_3)_5Br]Cl_2 + \underset{\text{White ppt.}}{BaSO_4(s)\downarrow}$$

$$[Co(NH_3)_5SO_4]Br + BaCl_2(aq) \longrightarrow \text{No reaction}$$

Test II Add $AgNO_3$ solution to both the compounds in separate test tubes.

Only $[Co(NH_3)_5SO_4]$ Br compound gives yellow precipitate, not $[Co(NH_3)_5Br]SO_4$, due to the absence of Br^- as counter ion.

$$[Co(NH_3)_5SO_4]Br + AgNO_3\,(aq) \longrightarrow [Co(NH_3)_5SO_4]NO_3 + \underset{\text{Yellow ppt.}}{AgBr(s)\downarrow}$$

$$[Co(NH_3)_5Cl]SO_4 + AgNO_3(aq) \longrightarrow \text{No reaction}$$

These two tests prove that the given two compounds are a pair of ionisation isomers. **(2)**

Note Write any of the above test in the answer.

(ii) The structure of optical isomers of the complex ion $[Co(en)_2Cl_2]^+$ are shown below.

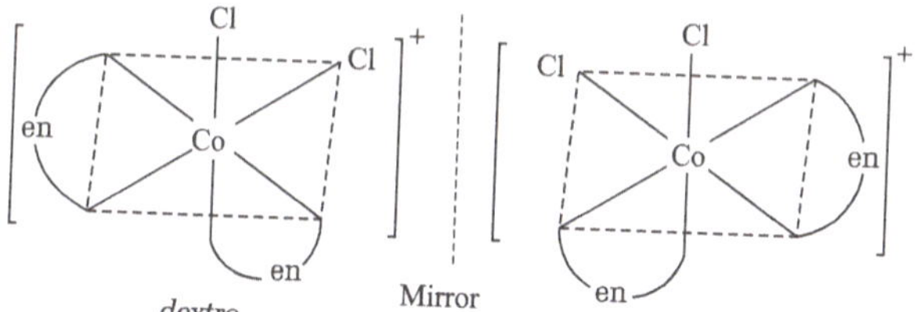

dextro Mirror *laevo* **(1)**

28. (i) Let the oxidation number of Fe in the complex ion $[Fe(CN)_6]^{3-}$ be x.

Then, $x + 6(-1) = -3$

$\Rightarrow$ $x = +3$

Electronic configuration

$\Rightarrow$ $Fe = [Ar]\,3d^6 4s^2$

For Fe^{3+}

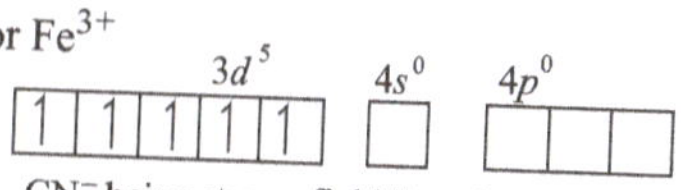

CN^- being strong field ligand, paired up the d-electrons of the metal

For $[Fe(CN)_6]^{3-}$ =

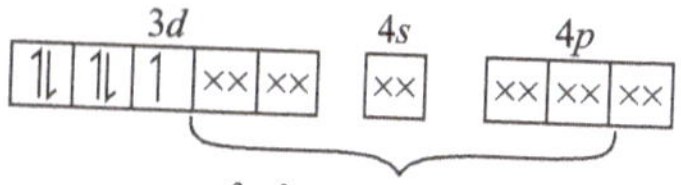

d^2sp^3-hybridisation
Six pairs of electrons from six CN^- ions **(1)**

(ii) It is an inner orbital complex as inner d-orbitals take part in hybridisation. **(1)**

(iii) It is paramagnetic due to the presence of unpaired electron. **(1)**

29. (i) It is given that $CoCl_3 \cdot 4NH_3$ precipitates silver ions as AgCl and its molar conductance corresponds to a total of two ions. Thus, the formula of the compound will be $[CoCl_2(NH_3)_4]Cl$ as it satisfies both the conditions.

(a) The structural formula of the complex compound is $[CoCl_2(NH_3)_4]Cl$.

(b) IUPAC name = Tetraamminedichloridocobalt-(III) chloride

(c) Geometrical isomers of $[CoCl_2(NH_3)_4]$ Cl are as follows

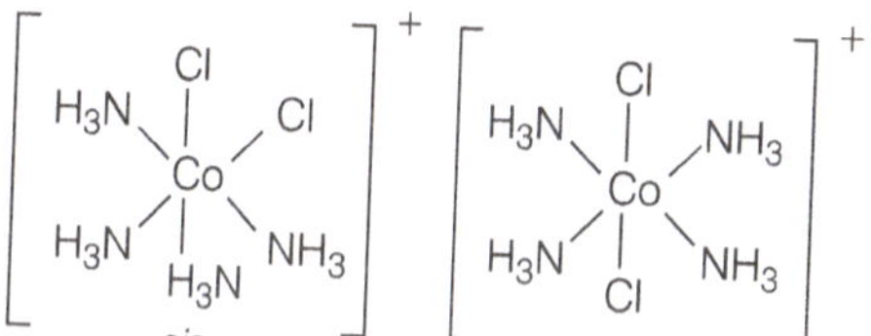

cis *trans*

(ii) The $[Co(NH_3)_5SO_4]Cl$ complex gives white precipitate with silver nitrate solution while $[Co(NH_3)_5Cl]$ SO_4 does not gives such precipitate. This shows that $[Co(NH_3)_5SO_4]Cl$ and $[Co(NH_3)_5Cl]SO_4$ are ionisation isomers.

30. (i) Isomer of the complex is $[Cr(H_2O)_5Cl]Cl_2 \cdot H_2O$ is grey-green in colour. IUPAC name is pentaquachloridochromium (III) chloride monohydrate. This isomer gives 1 mole of silver chloride upon reaction with silver nitrate and loses two moles of water when stored in a desiccator.

In $[Cr(H_2O)_6]Cl_3$ there are six water molecules attached to chromium metal but in $[Cr(H_2O)_5Cl]Cl_2 \cdot H_2O$ there are 5 water molecules and one chlorine ligand attached to chromium metal in coordination sphere.

(ii) Transition metal ion forming octahedral complexes undergo d^2sp^3-hybridisation.

In presence of strong field ligands, the unpaired electrons of the metal pair up which results in d^2sp^3-hybridisation.

31. (i) (a) In both compounds, ambidentate ligand NO_2 is present in $[Co(NH_3)_5(ONO)]Cl_2$ complex ONO is attached through O with Co while in $[Co(NH_3)_5(NO_2)]Cl_2$ complex NO_2 is attached through N with Co. Hence, they show linkage isomerism. **(1)**

(b) Given compounds with have different no. of water molecules in coordination sphere which are directly attached to metal ion. Hence, they show hydration isomerism. **(1)**

(c) Given compounds will give different number of ions in solution, although they have same composition.

Hence, they show ionisation isomerism. **(1)**

(ii) (a) Tetraaminediaquacobalt (III) chloride

(b) Potassium tetracyanonickelate (II) **(2)**

32. (i) (a) Hydrate isomerism

(b) Ionisation isomerism

(c) Linkage isomerism **(1 × 3)**

(ii) (a) Electronic configuration for

$_{27}Co \longrightarrow [Ar]3d^7 4s^2$

Oxidation state of Co in $[Co(CN)_6]^{3-} = +3$

E.C of Co = 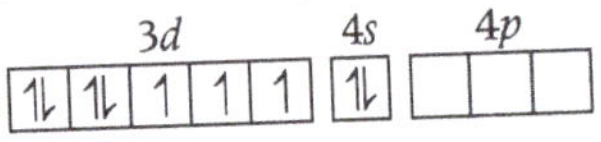

E.C of Co^{3+} = 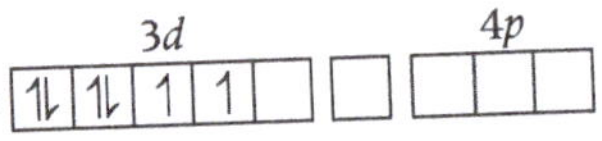

Since, CN^- is a strong ligand, it will pair up electron to form low spin complex.

$[Cu(CN)_6]^{3-}$ =

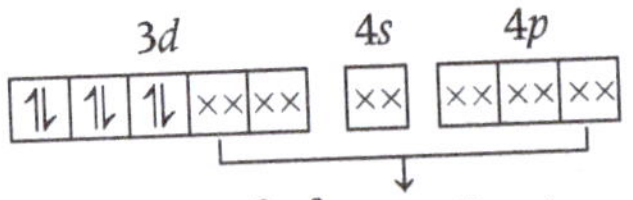

d^2sp^3-hybridisation

Hence, $[Cu(CN)_6]^{3-}$ is d^2sp^3 hybridised. **(1/2)**

(b) Since, all electrons are paired, so it is diamagnetic in nature. **(1/2)**

(c) The geometry of $[Co(CN)_6]^{3-}$ is octahedral **(1/2)**

(d) It form low spin complex as CN^- is a strong field ligand, so it will pair up the electrons. **(1/2)**

Common Mistake By considering CN^- as a weak field ligand, one can write the hybridsation 'sp^3d^2' instead of 'd^2sp^3'.

33. (i) (a) Linkage isomerism

(b) Hydrate isomerism

(c) Coordination isomerism **(1 ×3)**

(ii) Refer to text on pages 105 and 106 (VBT). **(2)**

34. (i)(a) Tetraaminesulphatecobalt (III) nitrate

(b) Potassiumaminetrichloroplatinate (II) **(1×2)**

(ii)(a) Given compounds will give different ions in solution, although they have same composition.

Hence, they exhibit ionisation isomerism. **(1)**

(b) In both compounds, ambidentate ligand SCN is present.

In $[Cr(SCN)(H_2O)_5]^{2+}$ complex SCN is attached through S with Cr while in $[Cr(NCS)(H_2O)_5]^{+2}$ complex SCN is attached through -N- . Hence, they show linkage isomerism. **(1)**

(iii) $K_2[PtCl_4]$ ionise in water as

$$K_2[PtCl_4] \longrightarrow 2K^+ + [PtCl_4]^{2-}$$

The compound does not ionise to give free chloride ions, therefore, it will not form precipitate when $AgNO_3$ solution is added to it. **(1)**

CHAPTER TEST

01 Mark Questions

1. Fill in the blanks by choosing the appropriate word(s) from the given brackets.

[+3, −3, metal, ligand, homoleptic, 6, 9, heteroleptic, one, two, d^2sp^3, sp^3d^2, diamagnetic, paramagnetic]

(i) The coordination number and oxidation state of the complex $[Cr(NH_3)_3(H_2O)_3]Cl_3$ are .... and .... respectively.

(ii) In coordination complex, donation of electrons pair take place from the ..... to ..... .

(iii) In $[Co(NH_3)_6]^{3+}$ complex, a metal is bound to ...... type of donar group are known as ....

(iv) $[Co(NH_3)_6]^{3+}$ has ...... hybridisation and ...... in nature.

2. Select and write the correct alternatives from the choices given below.

(i) The coordination number of platinum in $[Pt(NH_3)_4Cl_2]^{3+}$ ion is

(a) 2 (b) 4 (c) 3 (d) 6

(ii) The oxidation number of Co in $[CoF_6]^{3-}$ is

(a) +3 (b) +6 (c) −3 (d) 0

(iii) The IUPAC name of $[K_3Fe(CN)_6]$ is

(a) potassium ferrocyanoferrate (I)
(b) potassium hexacyanoferrate (III)
(c) potassium hexacyanoferrate (II)
(d) potassium hexaferricyanide

(iv) The geometry of $Ni(PPh_3)_2Cl_2$ is

(a) tetrahedral
(b) square planar
(c) octahedral
(d) None of the above

3. (i) **Assertion** (A) Usually a sulphate ion is a bidentate ligand but it can also act as monodentate in certain complexes.

Reason (R) Many times multidentate ligands do have flexidentate character.

(a) Both (A) and (R) are correct and (R) is the correct explanation of (A).
(b) Both (A) and (R) are correct but (R) is not the correct explanation of (A).
(c) (A) is correct and (R) is incorrect.
(d) (A) is incorrect and (R) is correct.

(ii) **Assertion** (A) $[Ni(CN)_4]^{2-}$ is square planar and diamagnetic.

Reason (R) It has no unpaired electrons due to the presence of strong field ligand.

(a) Both (A) and (R) are correct and (R) is the correct explanation of (A).
(b) Both (A) and (R) are correct but (R) is not the correct explanation of (A).
(c) (A) is correct and (R) is incorrect.
(d) (A) is incorrect and (R) is correct.

02 Marks Questions

4. Write the IUPAC name of the complex.

(i) $Pt(en)_2Cl_2$
(ii) $Pt(NH_2CH_3)(NH_3)_2Cl]Cl$

5. Write the formulae for the following.

(i) Pentaaninenitrito-O-cobalt (III) ion
(ii) Tetraaminechloronitrito-N-platinum (IV) sulphate

6. Write the IUPAC name of the complex $[Cr(en)_2Cl_2]^+$. Draw structures of geometrical isomers for this complex.

7. When $CrCl_3 \cdot 6H_2O$ is mixed with $AgNO_3$, 2 moles of AgCl are precipitated per mole of the compound. Write its

(i) structural formula of the complex and
(ii) IUPAC name.

8. Write the hybridisation and shape of the following complexes.

(i) $[Co(CN)_6]^{3-}$ (ii) $[NiF_4]^{2-}$

9. State reason for the following.

(i) CO is stronger ligand than Cl^-.
(ii) The molecular shape of $[CoF_6]^{3-}$ and $[Co(en)_3]^{3+}$ are different.

10. Write the type of isomerism shown by the complex $[Co(NH_3)_5(SCN)]^{2+}$. Also give its IUPAC name.

03 Marks Questions

11. (i) Write the formula of the following coordination compound.

Sodium dicyanidoaurate (I)

(ii) What type of isomerism is exhibited by the complex $[Co(NH_3)_5Cl]SO_4$?

(iii) Write the hybridisation and number of unpaired electrons in the complex $[Co(C_2O_4)_3]^{3-}$ (Atomic number of Co = 27)

12. (i) What is meant by CFSE?

(ii) On the basis of crystal field theory, written the electronic configuration for d^4 ion if (a) $\Delta_o > P$, (b) $\Delta_o < P$.

13. Using VBT, state the hybridisation, shape and magnetic behaviour of the following complexes.

(i) $[Co(NH_3)_6]^{3+}$ (ii) $[Cr(H_2O)_2(C_2O_4)_2]^{2-}$

(iii) $[Co(en)_3]Cl_3$

14. For the complex $[Fe(H_2O)_6]^{2+}$ write the

(i) hybridisation (ii) magnetic moment and

(iii) IUPAC name.

15. Name the following coordination complexes and give their structure.

(i) $[Fe(CN)_6]^{4-}$ (ii) $[Cr(NH_3)_4Cl_2]^{+}$

(iii) $[NiF_4]^{2-}$

(Atomic number of Fe = 26, Cr = 24, Ni = 28)

05 Marks Questions

16. Explain the following terms.

(i) Ambidentate ligands

(ii) Denticity of ligand

(iii) Crystal field splitting in an octahedral field

(iv) Spectrochemical series

(v) Chelate effect

17. (i) Write the IUPAC name and deduce the geometry and magnetic behaviour of the complex $K_4[Mn(CN)_6]$.

(ii) Draw the geometrical isomers of complex $[Pt(en)_2Cl_2]^{2+}$ and name them.

18. $PtCl_4$ and NH_3 may form five complexes, $A(PtCl_4 \cdot 6NH_3)$, $B(PtCl_4 \cdot 5NH_3)$, $C(PtCl_4 \cdot 4NH_3)$, $D(PtCl_4 \cdot 3NH_3)$ and $E(PtCl_4 \cdot 2NH_3)$. One mole of each A, B, C, D and E reacts with excess of $AgNO_3$ to yield 4, 3, 2 and 1 mole(s) of AgCl respectively, while E gives, no AgCl. The conductance of their solutions are in the order $A > B > C > D > E$. On the basis of Werner's theory, write their structure and give the total number of ions given by one complex.

Answers

1. (i) 6, +3 (ii) ligand, metal (iii) one, homoleptic (iv) d^2sp^3, diamagnetic

2. (i) (d), (ii) (a), (iii) (b), (iv) (a)

3. (i) (a), (ii) (a)

06

Haloalkanes and Haloarenes

TREND ANALYSIS 4 YEARS

Average No. of Questions Across all Sets

	Types of Questions	2024	2023	2020	2019
TOPIC 01 Nomenclature, Preparation and Properties of Haloalkanes and Haloarenes	1 Mark	—	—	—	—
	2 Marks	—	—	3	—
	3 Marks	—	—	—	1
	5 Marks	—	—	—	—
TOPIC 02 Properties of Haloalkanes and Haloarenes including Polyhalogens Compounds	1 Mark	1	1	—	1
	2 Marks	1	—	1	—
	3 Marks	—	—	—	—
	5 Marks	—	—	—	—

TOPIC 1

Nomenclature, Preparation and Properties of Haloalkanes and Haloarenes

Alkyl and aryl halides are obtained by the replacement of a hydrogen atom of an alkane and arene respectively by a halogen atom (i.e. F, Cl, Br, I).

Nomenclature

Nomenclature of haloalkanes and haloarenes are discussed below one by one.

(i) For Monosubstituted Haloalkanes

- In **common system,** monohalogen derivatives of alkanes (alkyl halides) are named by adding the word 'halide' to the name of the corresponding alkyl group.
- In **IUPAC system,** alkyl halides are named as halosubstituted hydrocarbons, i.e. haloalkanes.
- The names are written by prefixing the word 'halo' to the name of alkane corresponding to the longest continuous carbon chain having the halogen atom.

e.g. $CH_3CH_2CH_2Br$,

Common name *n*-propylbromide
IUPAC name 1- bromopropane

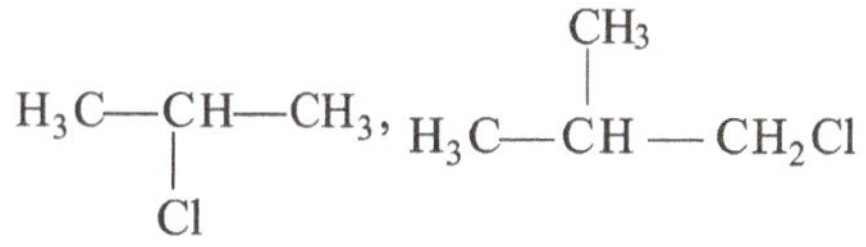

Common name *Iso*-propylchloride, *Iso*-butylchloride
IUPAC name 2-chloropropane, 1-chloro-2-methylpropane

(ii) For Disubstituted Haloalkane

The dihaloalkane having the same type of halogen atoms are named as alkylidene or alkylene dihalides.

The dihalo compounds having same type of halogen atoms are further classified as ***Geminal* halide** and ***Vicinal* halides**.

In **common name** system, *gem* halides are named as alkylidene halides, whereas *vic*-dihalides are named as alkylene dihalides. In **IUPAC** system, they are named as dihaloalkanes.

(iii) For Haloarenes

They are named by prefixing 'halo' before the name of the aromatic hydrocarbon.

Haloarenes are the common as well as IUPAC names of aryl halides. For dihalogen derivatives, the prefixes, *o*-, *m*-, *p*- are used in common system but in IUPAC system, the numerals 1, 2; 1, 3 and 1,4 are used.

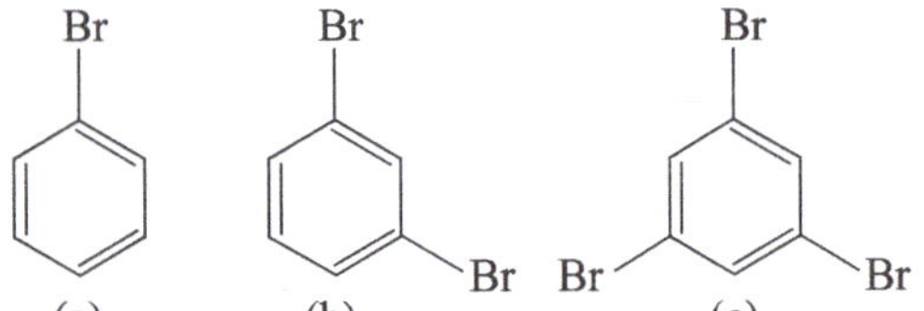

(a) (b) (c)

	(a)	(b)	(c)
Common name	Bromobenzene	*m*-dibromobenzene	*sym*-tribromobenzene
IUPAC name	Bromobenzene	1,3-dibromobenzene	1,3,5-tribomobenzene

Preparation

Important preparation of haloalkanes and haloarenes are

1. For Haloalkanes

Method of preparation of haloalkanes are as follows

From Alkane (By free radical halogenation)

Free radical chlorination or bromination of alkanes usually gives a complex mixture of isomeric mono and polyhaloalkanes.

e.g. $$CH_4 + Cl_2 \xrightarrow{\text{UV light, } \Delta} CH_3Cl + CH_2Cl_2 + CHCl_3 + CCl_4 + HCl$$

For the ease of substitution, various hydrogen follows the sequence as $3° > 2° > 1°$. Iodination is reversible as HI formed is strong reducing agent.

So, the reaction is carried out in the presence of an oxidising agent like HNO_3, HIO_3 or HIO_4. Fluorination is carried out through indirect methods as it is explosive.

From Alkene

Halogen acid when treated with alkene undergo addition reaction to yield haloalkane. Unsymmetrical alkene follow **Markownikoff's rule**.

e.g. $$\underset{\text{Propene}}{CH_3—CH{=}CH_2} + HBr \longrightarrow \underset{\text{2-bromopropane}}{CH_3—\overset{\overset{\displaystyle Br}{|}}{CH}—CH_3}$$

However, in the presence of a peroxide, the addition of HBr to an unsymmetrical alkene, proceeds in contrary to the Markovnikov's rule. This effect is known as **Kharasch effect** or **Peroxide effect**.

$$\underset{\text{Propene}}{CH_3CH{=}CH_2} + HBr \xrightarrow{\text{Peroxide}} \underset{\text{1-bromopropane}}{CH_3CH_2CH_2Br}$$

From Alcohols

Most common method for preparation of haloalkanes is the replacement of —OH group of an alcohol by required halogen atom. Reaction of alcohols with different reagents like halogen acids or (PX_5, PX_3) or $SOCl_2$ are given below

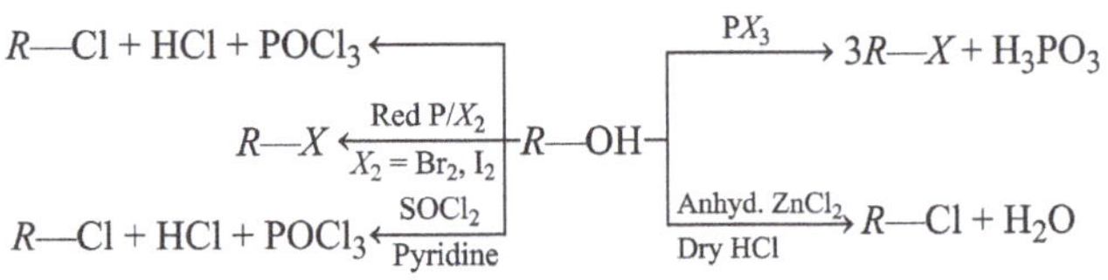

From Silver Salt of Fatty Acid

$$CH_3COO^-Ag^+ + Br_2 \xrightarrow{CCl_4} CH_3Br + CO_2\uparrow + AgBr\downarrow$$

From Halogen Exchange

(i) Finkelstein reaction

$$R—X + NaI \xrightarrow{\text{Dry acetone}} R—I + NaX$$

(ii) Swarts reaction

$$R—X + AgF \longrightarrow RF + AgX \ (X = Cl, Br)$$

2. For Haloarenes

Preparation of haloarenes are shown in the flowchart.

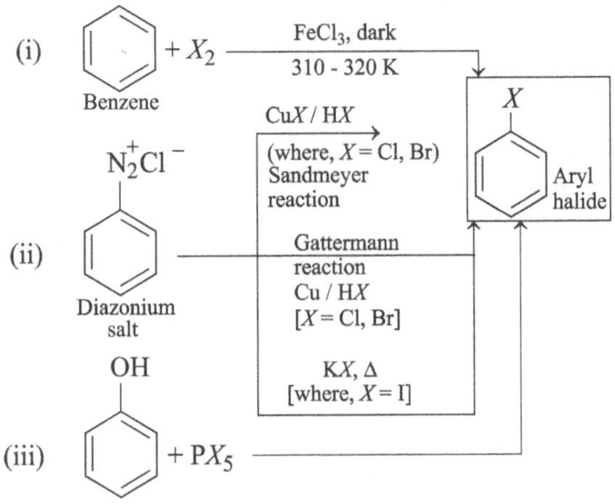

PYQs Previous Years' Questions

1 Mark Questions

Exams' Questions

1. **Assertion** (A) Haloalkanes when treated with alcoholic KCN forms alkane nitrile as a major product.

   Reason (R) Potassium cyanide is a covalent compound.

   ISC Specimen 2021-22 (Sem-I)

   (a) Both (A) and (R) are correct and (R) is the correct explanation for (A).

   (b) Both (A) and (R) are correct but (R) is not the correct explanation for (A).

   (c) (A) is correct but (R) is incorrect.

   (d) (A) is incorrect but (R) is correct.

2. Give the balanced equation for the following reaction. 1-butanol and hydrogen chloride (in presence of $ZnCl_2$).

   ISC 2012

3. The reaction of chlorine with methane is a .... reaction which involves .... fission of the C—H bond.

   ISC 2007, 2000

Important Questions

4. Write the structure of 2, 4-dinitrochlorobenzene.

5. Out of 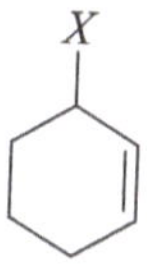 and 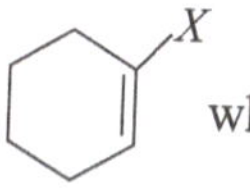 which one is an example of allylic halide?

6. Write the structure of 1-bromo-4-chlorobut-2-ene.

7. Write the structure of 3-bromo-2-methylprop-1-ene.

8. Draw the structure of 2-bromopentane.

9. Write the IUPAC name of $(CH_3)_2CH \cdot CH(Cl)CH_3$.

10. Write the IUPAC name of

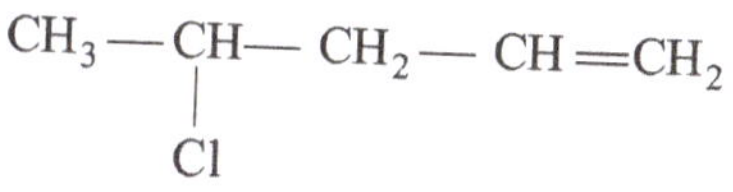

11. Write the IUPAC name of

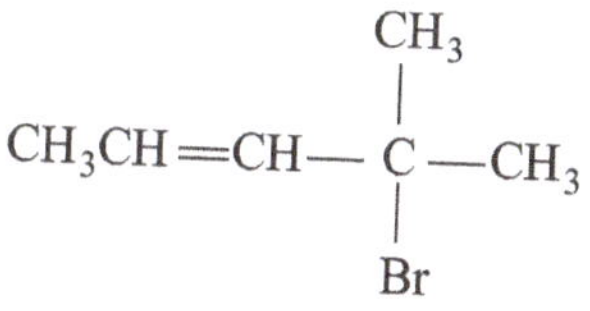

12. Write the IUPAC name of the following compound.

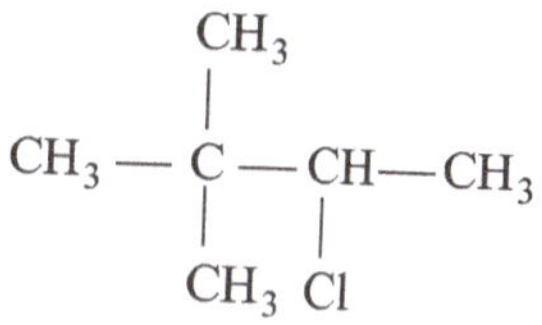

13. Write the IUPAC name of the following compound:

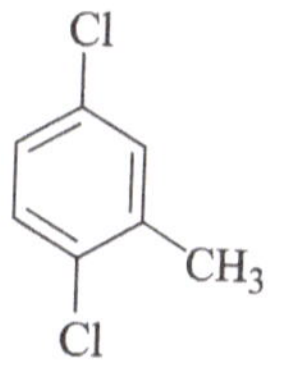

14. Write the IUPAC name of the following compound.

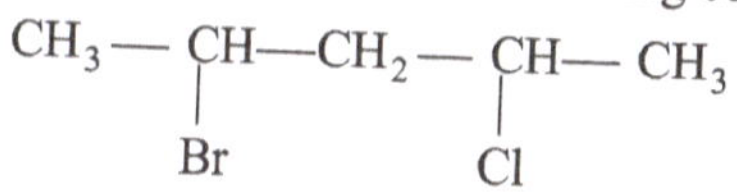

15. A hydrocarbon C_5H_{12} gives only one monochlorination product. Identify the hydrocarbon.

16. Give the IUPAC name of the following compound.

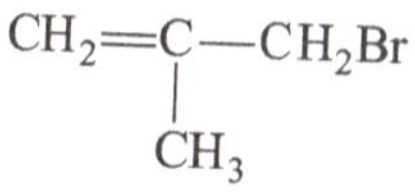

17. What happens when bromine attacks $CH_2=CH-CH_2-C \equiv CH$?

18. Write the IUPAC name of the following compound $(CH_3)_3CCH_2Br$.

19. Write the IUPAC name of the following compound $CH_2=CHCH_2Br$.

20. Draw the structure of 1,4-dibromobut-2-ene.

21. Draw the structure of 2-(2-bromophenyl) butane.

22. Draw the structure of 2-(2-chlorophenyl)-1-iodooctane.

23. Draw the structure of the following compound: 1-bromo-4-*sec*-butyl-2-methylbenzene

24. Draw the structure of the following organic compound: 2-chloro-3-methylpentane.

25. Draw the structure of the following compound: 3-(4-chlorophenyl)-2-methylpropane

26. Write the IUPAC name of the following compound.

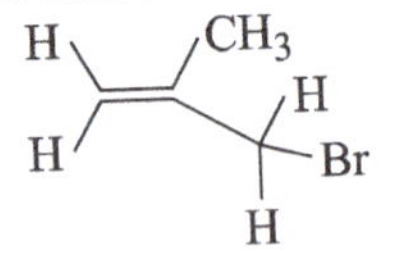

27. Give the IUPAC name of the following compound.

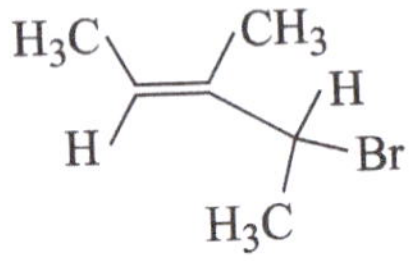

28. Draw the structure of the compound, 4-*tert*-butyl-3-iodoheptane.

29. Write the IUPAC name of the following compound:

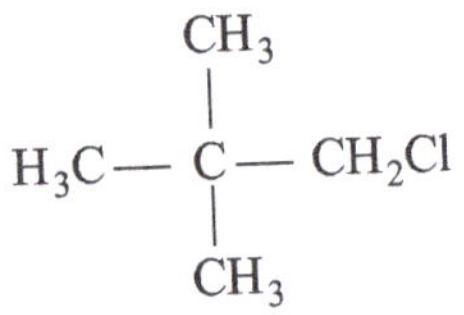

30. Draw the structure of the compound, 1-chloro-4-ethylcyclohexane.

> **KEY IDEA**
> Cyclic arrangement of 6C- atoms; Cl at C-1 and C_2H_5 at C-4.

31. Draw the structure of the following compound 4-bromo-3-methylpent-2-ene.

32. Write a chemical reaction in which the iodide ion replaces the diazonium group in a diazonium salt.

33. Complete the following chemical equation,

$$CH_3CH_2CH{=}CH_2 + HBr \xrightarrow{\text{Peroxide}}$$

34. Write the IUPAC name of $ClCH_2C{\equiv}CCH_2Br$.

2 Marks Questions

Exams' Questions

35. Silver acetate refluxed with bromine in carbon tetrachloride. **ISC 2021-22 (Sem-I)**
   (i) What are the products formed?
      (a) Ethane, silver bromide and water
      (b) Ethanoyl bromide and silver
      (c) Ethanoic acid and silver bromide
      (d) Bromomethane, silver bromide and carbon dioxide
   (ii) What is the above reaction known as?
      (a) Finkelstein reaction (b) Swarts reaction
      (c) Hunsdiecker reaction (d) Sandmeyer's reaction

Important Questions

36. Write the mechanism of the following reaction.

$$CH_3CH_2OH \xrightarrow{HBr} CH_3CH_2Br + H_2O$$

37. Draw the structure of major monohalo product in each of the following reactions.

(i) 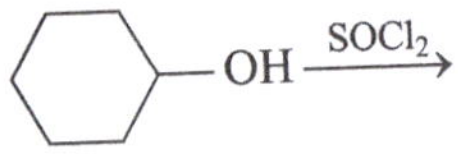

(ii) 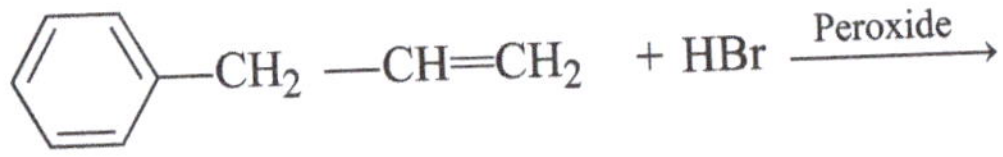

38. Draw the structures of the following organic halogen compounds.
   (i) *p*-bromochlorobenzene
   (ii) 1-chloro-4-ethylcyclohexane

39. Draw the structures of the following organic halogen compounds:
   (i) 4-*tert*-butyl-3-iodoheptane
   (ii) 4-bromo-3-methylpent-2-ene

40. Write the IUPAC names of the following compounds :
   (i) $CH_2{=}CHCH_2Br$ (ii) $(CCl_3)_3CCl$

41. Complete the following reactions:

(i) 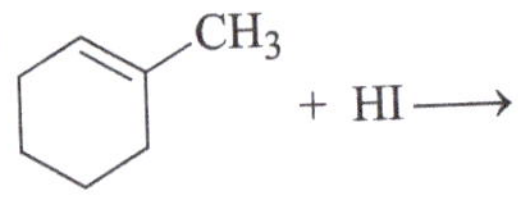

(ii) $CH_3CH_2CH{=}CH_2 + HBr \longrightarrow$

> **KEY IDEA**
> In case of non-symmetric unsaturated compounds, addition of HI and HBr takes place according to Markovnikov's rule, i.e. I and Br add to less substituted double bonded C-atoms.

42. Complete the following reactions.
   (i) $C_6H_5N_2Cl + KI \longrightarrow$ (ii) 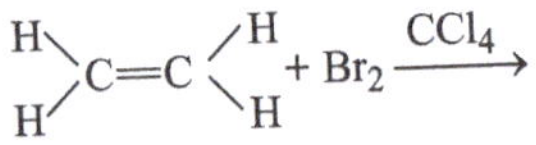

3 Marks Question

Important Questions

43. Give the IUPAC names of the following compounds:
   (i) $CH_3—CH(Br)—CH_2—CH_3$
   (ii) 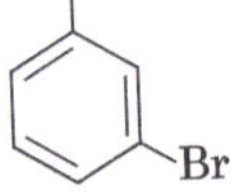
   (iii) $CH_2{=}CH—CH_2—Cl$

Explanations

1. (b) Assertion is correct but reason is incorrect.

   Correct reason is potassium cyanide is an ionic compound and provides cyanide ions in solution.

2. $ZnCl_2$ is dehydrating agent, i.e. remove water molecule.

   When alcohols are treated with halogen acid in the presence of dehydrating agent $ZnCl_2$ —OH group is replaced by halogen followed by dehydration.

$$\underset{\text{Butanol}}{CH_3CH_2CH_2CH_2—OH} + \underset{\text{Hydrogen chloride}}{HCl} \xrightarrow{ZnCl_2} \underset{\text{Chlorobutane}}{Cl—CH_2CH_2CH_2CH_3} + H_2O$$

3. The reaction of chlorine with methane is a **substitution** reaction which involves **homolytic** fission of the C—H bond.

$$CH_4 + Cl_2 \xrightarrow{\text{Sunlight}} CH_3Cl + HCl$$

   H-atom is substituted by Cl-atom. It follows free radical mechanism.

4. The structure of 2,4-dinitrochlorobenzene is

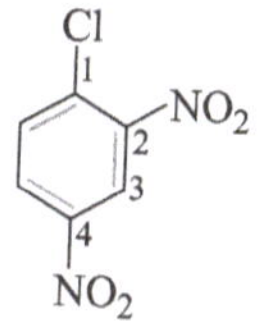

5. In allylic halides, the halogen is bonded to the sp^3-hybridised carbon atom next to a carbon-carbon double bond.

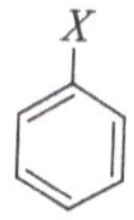

3-halocyclohex-1-ene

   Thus, is an allylic halide.

6. The structure of 1-bromo-4-chlorobut-2-ene is

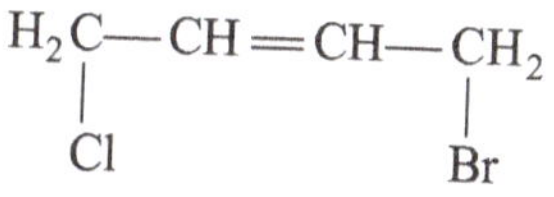

7. The structure of 3-bromo-2-methylprop-1-ene is

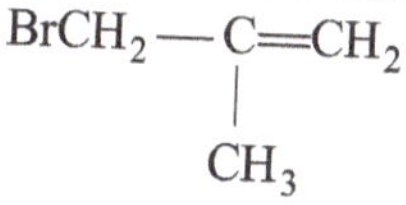

8.

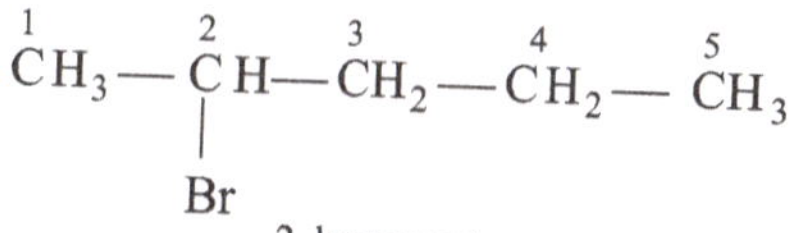

2-bromopentane

9.

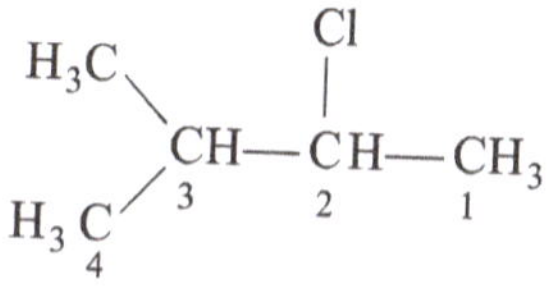

2-chloro-3-methylbutane

10.

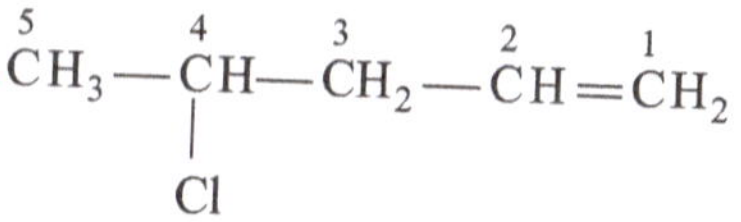

4-chloropent-1-ene

(As double bond is given preference over halogen)

11.

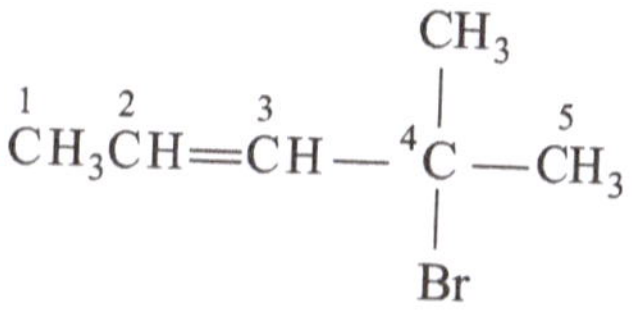

4-bromo-4-methylpent-2-ene

12.

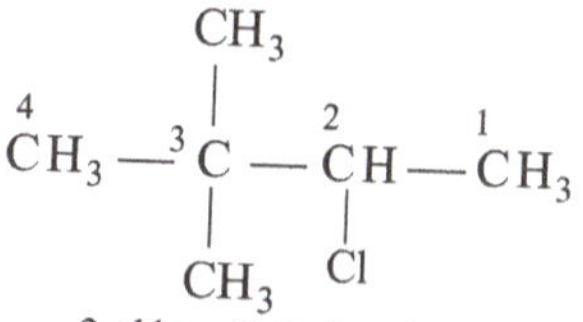

2-chloro-3, 3-dimethylbutane

13.

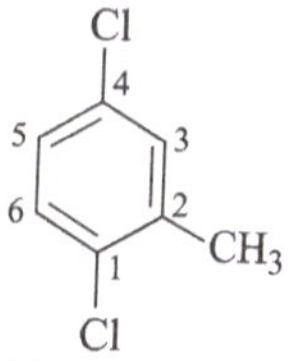

1, 4-dichloro-2-methylbenzene

14.

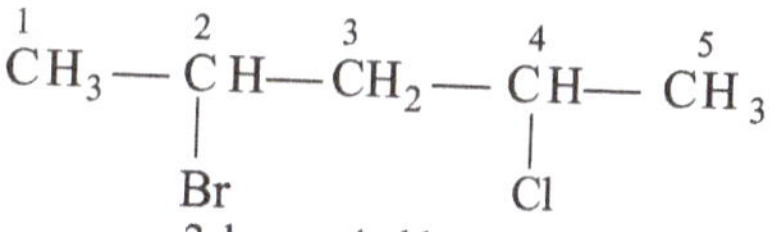

2-bromo-4-chloropentane

Numbering will be done in alphabetically manner.

15. Hydrocarbon which gives only one monochlorination product is

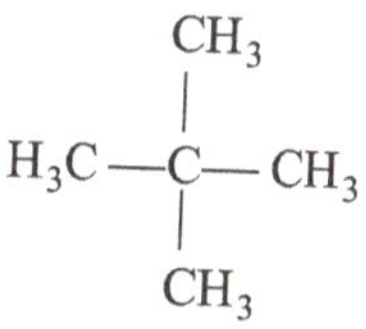

16.

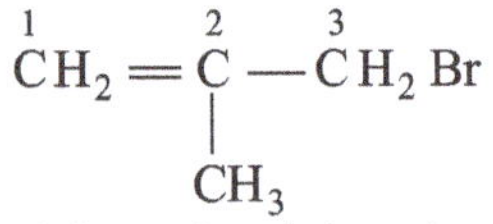

3-bromo-2-methylprop-1-ene

17. $CH_2=CH-CH_2-C\equiv CH \xrightarrow{Br_2}$

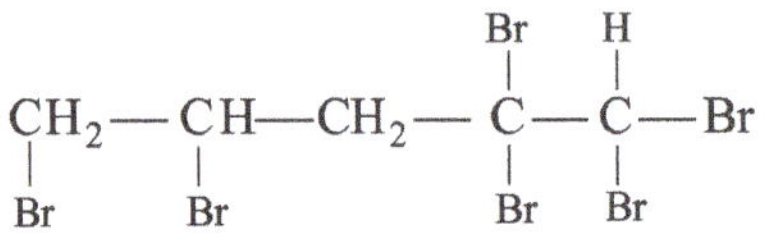

This product is formed when Br_2 is used in excess. But if only one mole of Br_2 is used, the following product will be formed.

$CH_2=CH-CH_2-C\equiv CH \xrightarrow[\text{(1 mol)}]{Br_2}$

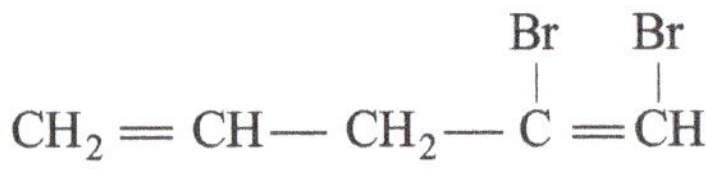

18.

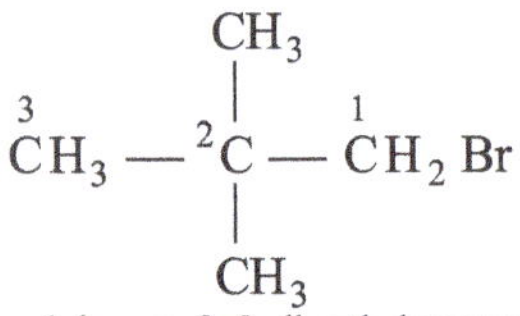

1-bromo-2, 2-dimethylpropane

19. $\overset{1}{C}H_2=\overset{2}{C}H\overset{3}{C}H_2Br$

3-bromoprop-1-ene

20.

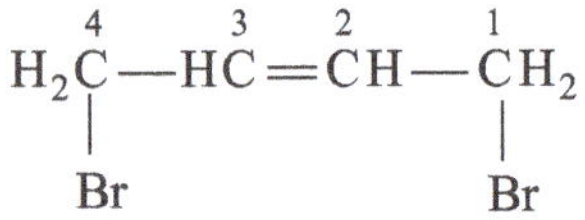

1,4-dibromobut-2-ene

21.

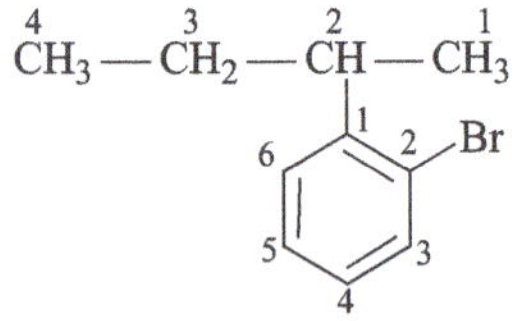

2-(2-bromophenyl) butane

22.

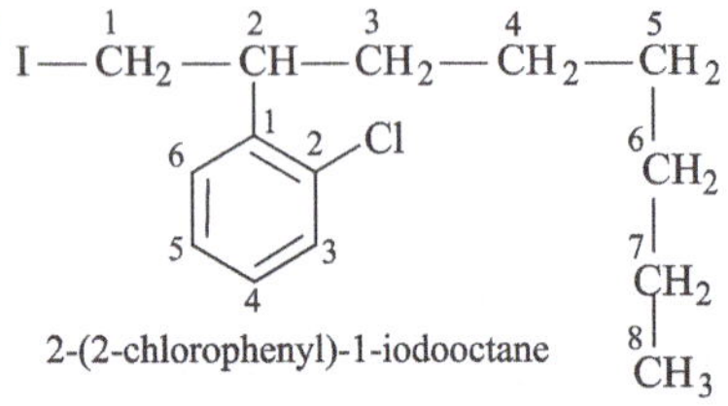

2-(2-chlorophenyl)-1-iodooctane

23.

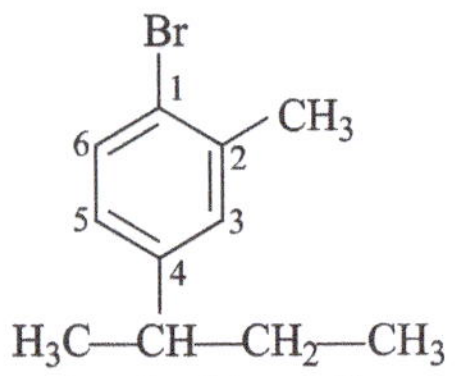

1-bromo-4-*sec*-butyl-2-methylbenzene

24.

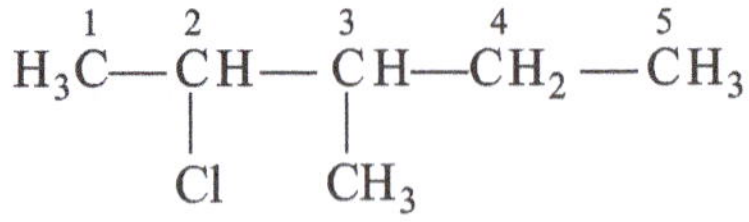

2-chloro -3-methylpentane

25.

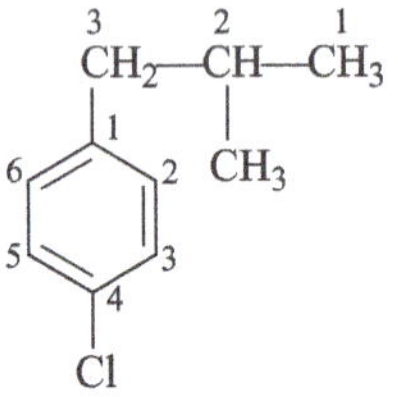

3-(4-chlorophenyl)-2-methylpropane

26.

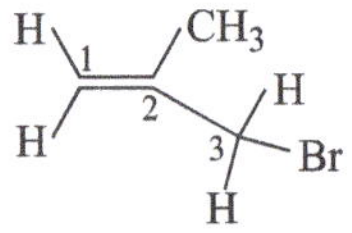

3-bromo-2-methylprop-1-ene

27.

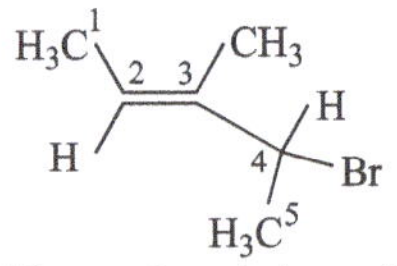

4-bromo-3-methylpent -2-ene

28.

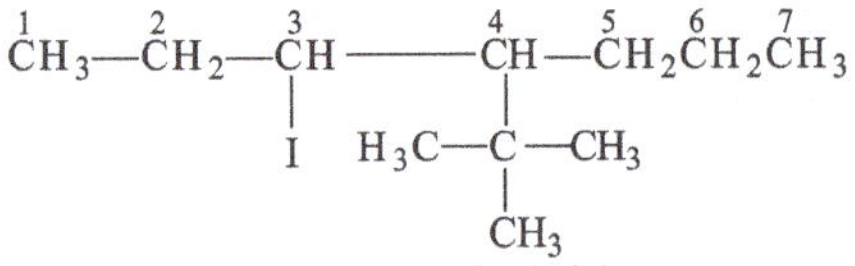

4-*tert*-butyl-3-iodoheptane

29.

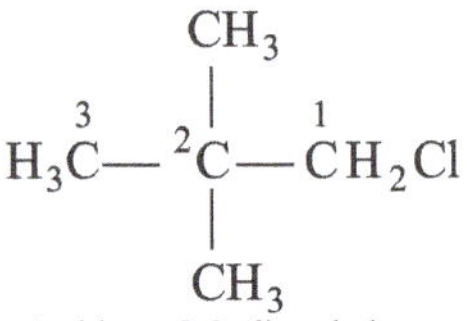

1-chloro-2,2-dimethylpropane

30.

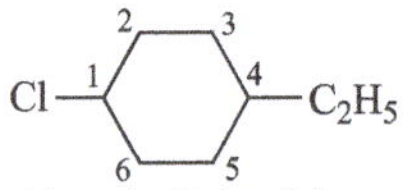

1-chloro-4-ethylcyclohexane

31.

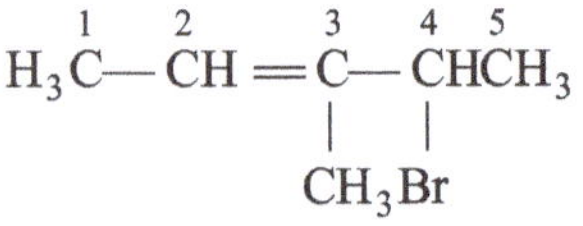

4-bromo-3-methylpent -2-ene

32.

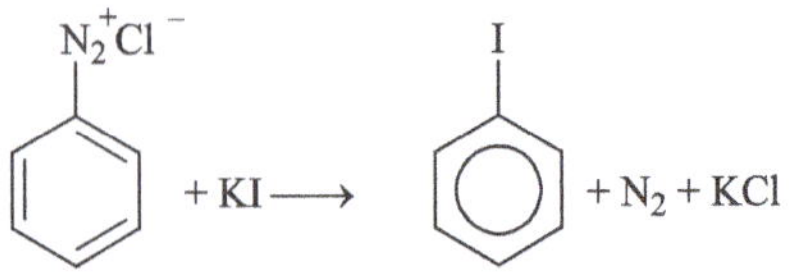

Benzene diazonium chloride (Diazonium salt) Iodobenzene

33. $CH_3CH_2CH{=}CH_2 + HBr \xrightarrow{\text{Peroxide}}$

$$CH_3-CH_2-CH_2-CH_2Br$$
1-bromobutane (Major)

$$+CH_3-CH_2-CH(Br)CH_3$$
(Minor)

> **Concept Enhancer** When halogen acid treated with alkenes (unsymmetrical) they follow Markownikoff's rule. However, in the presence of peroxide, product will form according to Anti-Markownikoff rule.

34. $\overset{4}{Cl-CH_2}-\overset{3}{C}\equiv\overset{2}{C}-\overset{1}{CH_2}-Br$

1-bromo-4-chlorobut-2-yne

35. (i) (d) $CH_3COO^-Ag^+ + Br_2 \xrightarrow{CCl_4} CH_3Br + CO_2\uparrow + AgBr\downarrow$

Silver acetate; Bromomethane; Carbon dioxide; Silver bromide

(ii) (c) This reaction is known as Borodine-Hunsdiecker reaction.

36. The mechanism of the given reaction is as follows

***Step* I** $HBr \longrightarrow H^+ + Br^-$

***Step* II** Protonation of alcohol

$$CH_3-CH_2-OH + H^+ \longrightarrow CH_3-CH_2-\overset{+}{O}H_2$$
Protonated alcohol

***Step* III** Nucleophilic attack of Br^-

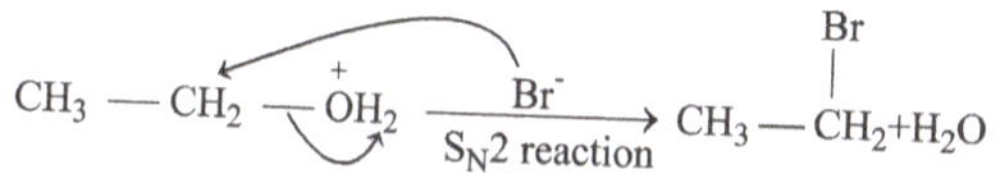

37. (i)

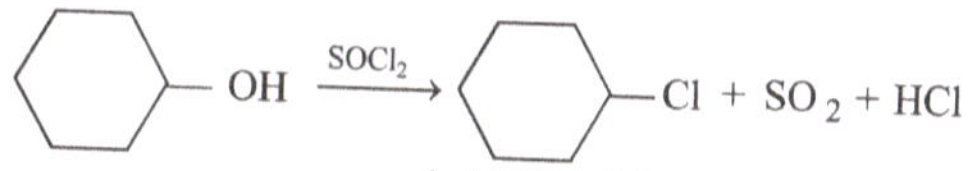

1-chlorocyclohexane

(ii)

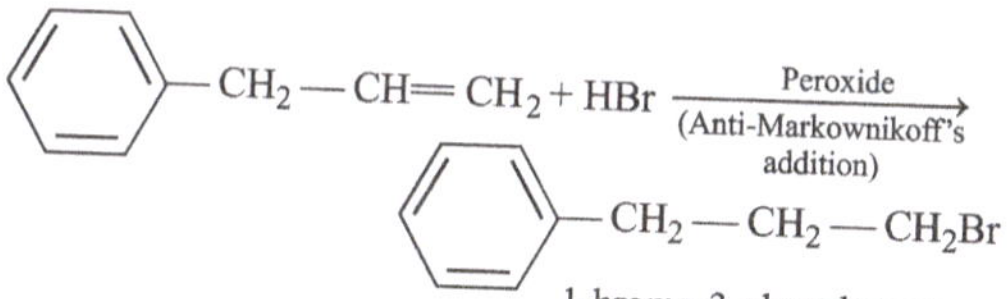

1-bromo-3-phenylpropane

38. (i)

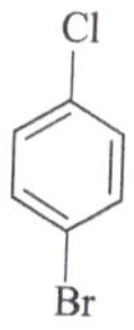

p-bromochlorobenzene

(ii)

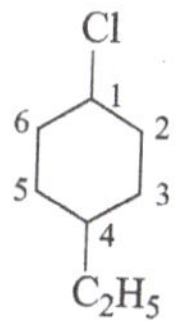

1-chloro-4-ethylcyclohexane

39. (i)

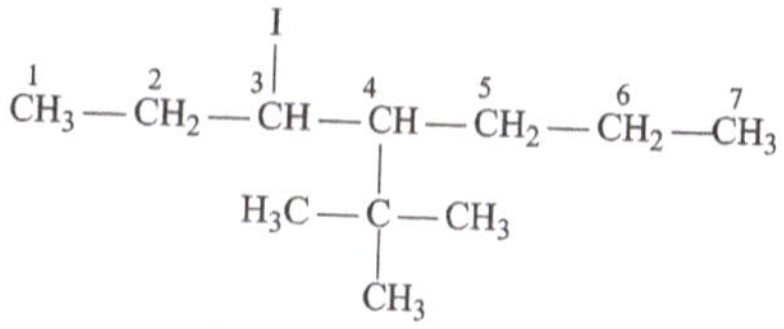

4-*tert*-butyl-3-iodoheptane

(ii)

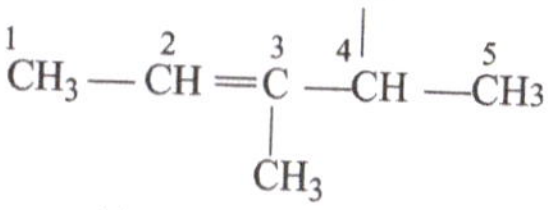

4-bromo-3-methylpent-2-ene

40. (i) $\overset{1}{CH_2}{=}\overset{2}{CH}\overset{3}{CH_2}Br$

3-bromoprop-1-ene

(ii) $(CCl_3)_3CCl$: The structure can be drawn as

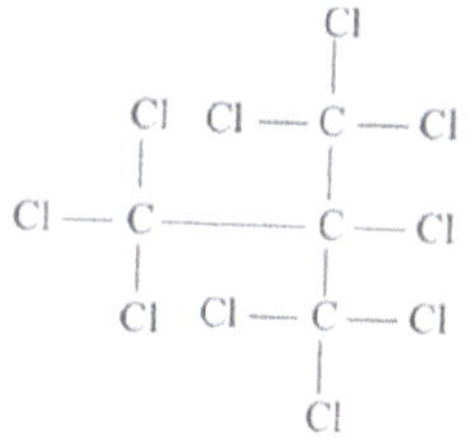

tris-(trichloromethyl) chloromethane

41. (i)

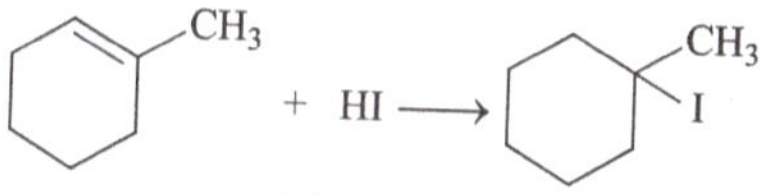

1-iodo-1-methylcyclohexane

(ii) $CH_3CH_2-CH{=}CH_2 + HBr \longrightarrow CH_3-CH_2-\underset{\displaystyle Br}{CH}-CH_3$

2-bromobutane

42. (i) $C_6H_5N_2^+Cl^- + KI \longrightarrow C_6H_5I + KCl + N_2\uparrow$

Iodobenzene

(ii) 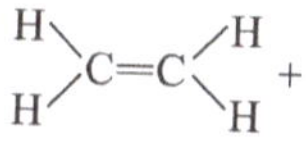 $+ Br_2 \xrightarrow{CCl_4} Br-CH_2-CH_2-Br$

1, 2-dibromoethane

43. (i) $\overset{1}{CH_3}-\underset{\displaystyle Br}{\overset{2}{CH}}-\overset{3}{CH_2}-\overset{4}{CH_3}$

2-bromobutane

(ii)

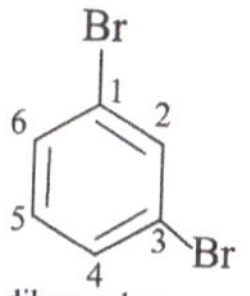

1,3-dibromobenzene

(iii) $\overset{1}{CH_2}{=}\overset{2}{CH}-\overset{3}{CH_2}-Cl$

3-chloroprop-1-ene

TOPIC 2

Properties of Haloalkanes and Haloarenes Including Polyhalogens Compounds

Physical Properties of Haloalkanes and Haloarenes

- For the same halogen atom, the boiling point of alkyl halides increase with increase in the size of alkyl group.
- For the same alkyl group, the boiling point decreases in the order

$$RI > RBr > RCl > RF$$

- Amongst isomeric dichlorobenzene, *p*-isomer has highest melting point due to symmetry. For isomeric alkyl halides, boiling point decreases with branching.
- Alkyl halides are slightly soluble in water because they do not form H-bonds with water.
- The stability of haloalkanes decreases down the group as the strength of C—*X* bond decreases, ($RF > RBr > RCl > RI$) due to increase in size of halogen atom.
- C—*X* bond in aryl halides is shorter (due to partial double bond character acquired by C—*X* bond because of resonance), stronger and less polar than in alkyl halides.

Nucleophilic Substitution Reactions

These reactions involve substitution that begins with nucleophilic attack. The atom which departs with its bonding pair of electrons is called **leaving group**.

$$R\text{—}\underset{\substack{\uparrow \\ \text{Leaving group}}}{X} + Nu^- \longrightarrow R\text{—}Nu + X^-$$

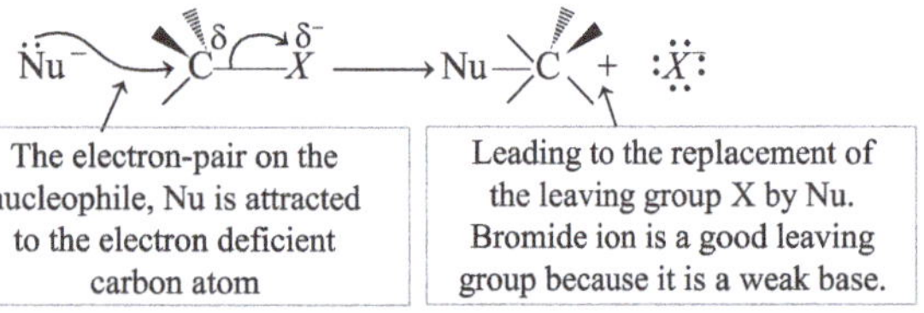

The halide ions are particularly good leaving groups, thus an alkyl halide is the most common substrate for nucleophilic substitution reactions.

There are following two types of nucleophilic substitution reactions.

S_N2 Type

(Bimolecular Nucleophilic Substitution)

The term bimolecular means that rate of a reaction depends upon the concentration of two molecules, i.e. on substrate and nucleophile. It follows second order kinetics. These reactions are commonly seen in primary alkyl halides and alcohols. This reaction takes place in one step.

$$\text{Rate} \propto \underset{\substack{\downarrow \\ RX}}{[A]}\ \underset{\substack{\downarrow \\ Nu^-}}{[B]}$$

Mechanism

These reactions take place through a transition state in which both the reactants are partially bonded to each other.

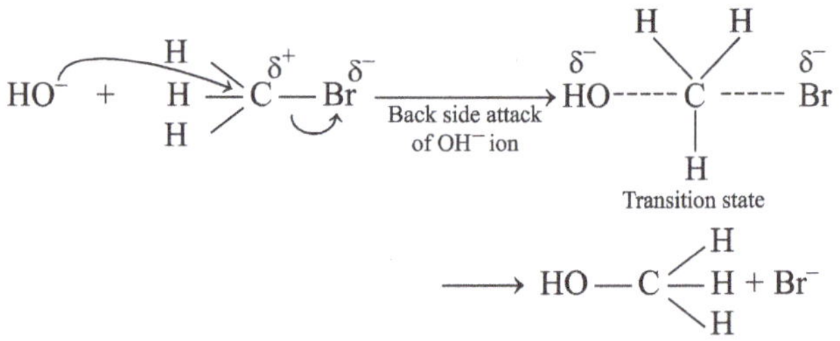

As the hydroxide ion approaches, the molecule from the back side, an effective collision takes place, the —OH bond is formed and the —Br bond is broken simultaneously with the liberation of bromide ion.

Factors Affecting S_N2 Reaction

- **Steric effect** Due to this, the reactivity order towards S_N2 reaction is $3° < 2° < 1° <$ methyl halide.
- Nucleophilicity
- Leaving group ability $\xrightarrow[\text{Reactivity order}]{F^- < Cl^- < Br^- < I^-}$ (Order of leaving group).
- Effect of solvent.

Note These solvents form H-bonding with the reactants. This reaction can also proceed through polar protic solvents. More H-bonding takes place with smallest anion (F^- ion) that leads to lesser reactivity. So, the order is $I^- > Br^- > Cl^- > F^-$.

S_N1 Type

(Unimolecular Nucleophilic Substitution)

The term unimolecular means that rate of nucleophilic substitution reaction depends upon the concentration of the substrate and not on the nucleophile. It follows first order kinetics.

The reaction takes place in two steps.

$$\text{Rate} \propto [\text{Substrate}]$$

Mechanism

These reactions take place in two steps through carbocation as the intermediate.

Step I $R—X \underset{\text{step}}{\overset{\text{Slowest}}{\rightleftharpoons}} R^+ + X^-$

Step II $R^+ + \underset{\text{(Nucleophile)}}{OH^-} \xrightarrow[\text{step}]{\text{Fast}} R—OH$

Factors Affecting S_N1 Reactions

Various factors affecting S_N1 reactions are as follows :

(i) **Nucleophilicity** S_N1 reactions does not depend on the concentration of nucleophile.

(ii) **Leaving group ability** Good leaving groups such as Cl^-, Br^-, I^- help in proceeding the S_N1 reactions faster.

(iii) **Solvent effect** Reaction by S_N1 is favoured by solvents of high ionising power, i.e. by polar protic solvents that help to pull the leaving group out of the molecule.

Relative Reactivity of Haloalkanes and Haloarenes towards Substitution Reactions

Alkyl halides are more reactive than aryl halides towards nucleophilic substitution reactions. It is due to the following reasons.

- In haloalkanes, there is single bond between *R—X*, which needs less bond dissociation energy, hence they are more reactive towards nucleophiles.
- In haloarenes, there is double bond character between C—*X* bond due to resonance, therefore, has more bond dissociation energy.
- Carbon attached to halogen is sp^3-hybridised in haloalkane and sp^2-hybridised in haloarene.
- It is difficult for electron rich nucleophiles to approach electron rich benzene ring in haloarenes. There is no such thing occurs in haloalkane.
- The phenyl cation formed as a result of self ionisation in haloarenes is not stabilised by resonance. Thus, it doesn't undergo S_N1 mechanism.

Elimination Reactions

Haloalkanes having β-hydrogen atom undergoes β-elimination when heated with alcoholic solution of KOH. These reactions are governed by **Saytzeff's rule** which state that dehydrohalogenation occurs in such a way that the major product is highly substituted product.

$$CH_3CH_2—CH_2—\underset{\displaystyle Br}{\underset{|}{CH}}—CH_3 \xrightarrow[-KBr,\ -H_2O]{\text{Alc.KOH}} \begin{cases} \underset{\text{Pent-2-ene (Major)}}{CH_3CH_2CH=CH—CH_3} \\ \underset{\text{Pent-1-ene (Minor)}}{CH_3CH_2CH_2CH=CH_2} \end{cases}$$

Flowchart of Some Chemical Properties of Alkyl Halides

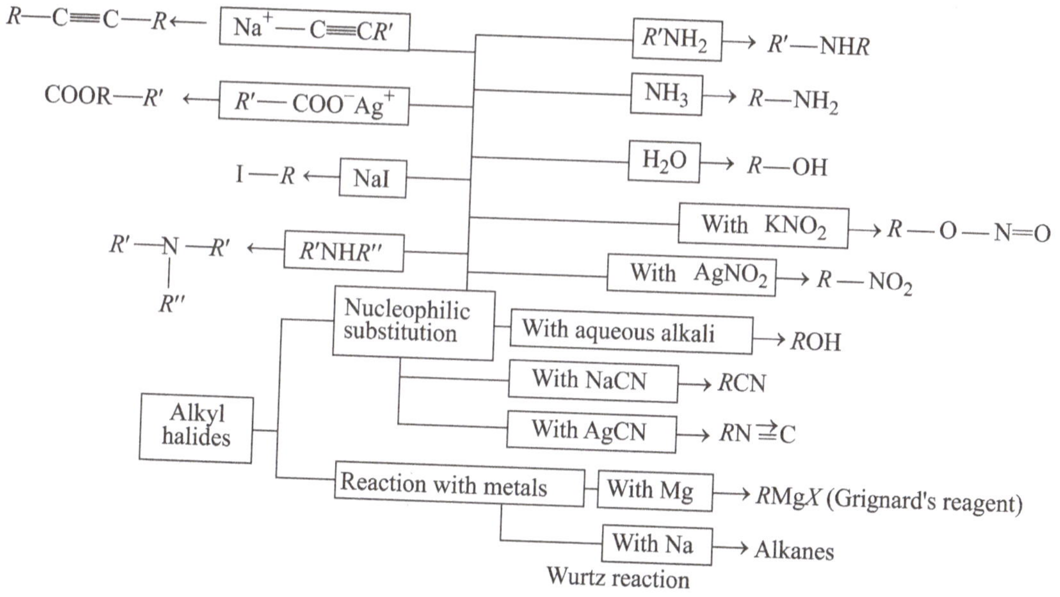

Aryl Halides Undergo Electrophilic Substitution Reactions

Chlorine is *o*-, *p*-directing in electrophilic substitution reactions as, electron density is maximum at *o* and *p*-positions due to $+R$-effect. Flowchart for some chemical properties of aryl halides are given below.

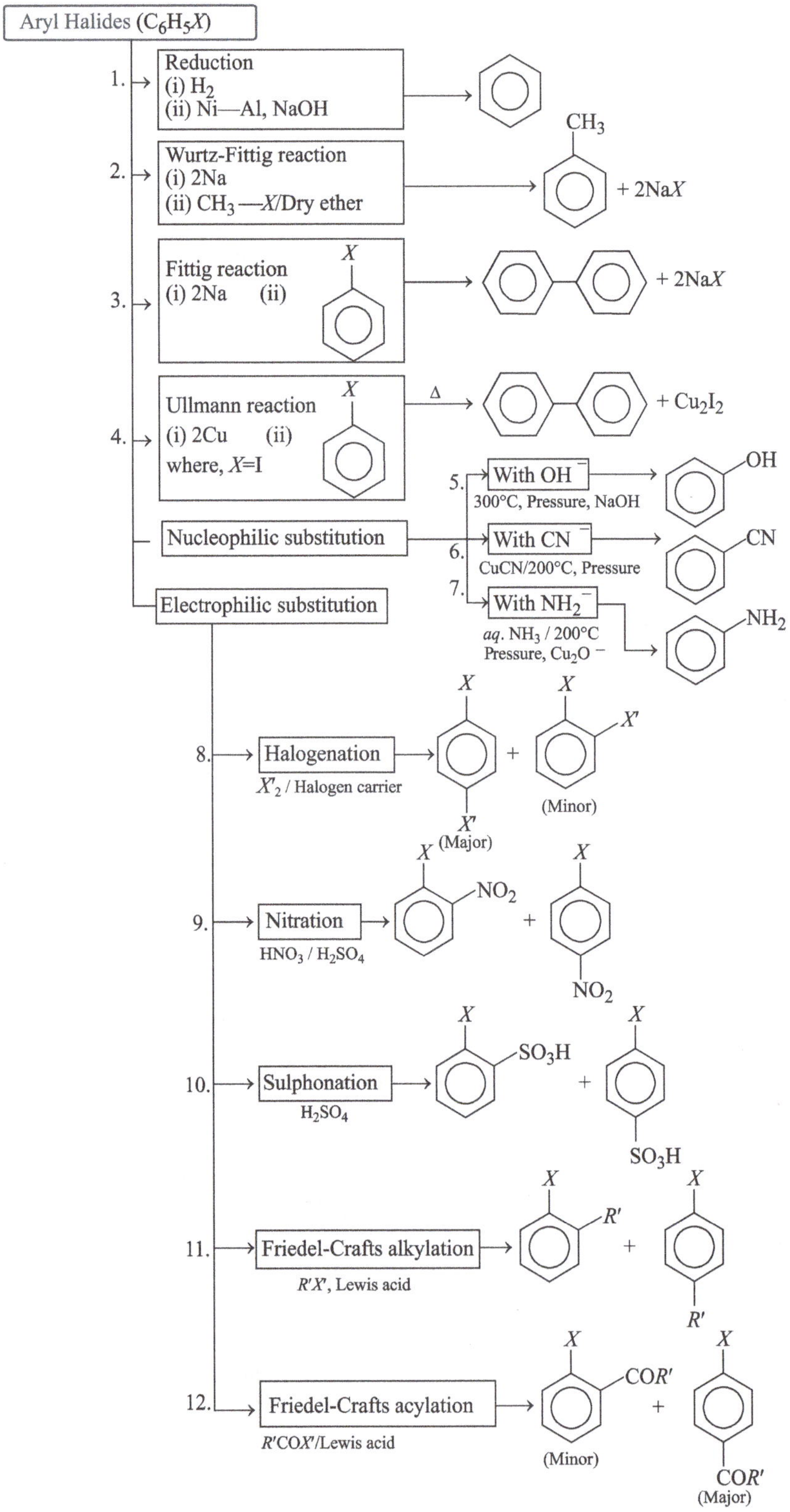

Uses

- Synthesis of a large variety of organic compounds.
- Ethyl chloride is used as a local anaesthetic and as refrigerant.
- Ethyl bromide is used for the preparation of barbiturate drugs.

Polyhalogen Compounds

Carbon compounds having more than one halogen atom are usually referred to as **polyhalogen compounds.**

Some important polyhalogen compounds are described as follows:

1. Trichloromethane [Chloroform, $CHCl_3$]

Trichloromethane is the trichloro derivative of methane, commonly known as chloroform.

Preparation

Preparation method of chloroform are as follows

(i) **From methane**

$$CH_4 + Cl_2 \xrightarrow[-HCl]{Light/675\ K} CH_3Cl \xrightarrow[-HCl]{+Cl_2}$$

$$CH_2Cl_2 \xrightarrow[-HCl]{+Cl_2} \underset{Chloroform}{CHCl_3}$$

(ii) **Partial reduction of carbon tetrachloride**

$$CCl_4 + 2H \xrightarrow{Fe+steam} CHCl_3 + HCl$$

(iii) **Bleaching powder on ethanol and from acetone** (Lab method)

$$\underset{Bleaching\ powder}{CaOCl_2} + H_2O \longrightarrow Ca(OH)_2 + Cl_2 \quad (\text{Liberation of } Cl_2)$$

$$C_2H_5OH + Cl_2 \longrightarrow CH_3CHO + 2HCl\ (\text{Oxidation})$$

$$CH_3CHO + 3Cl_2 \longrightarrow CCl_3CHO + 3HCl\ (\text{Chlorination})$$

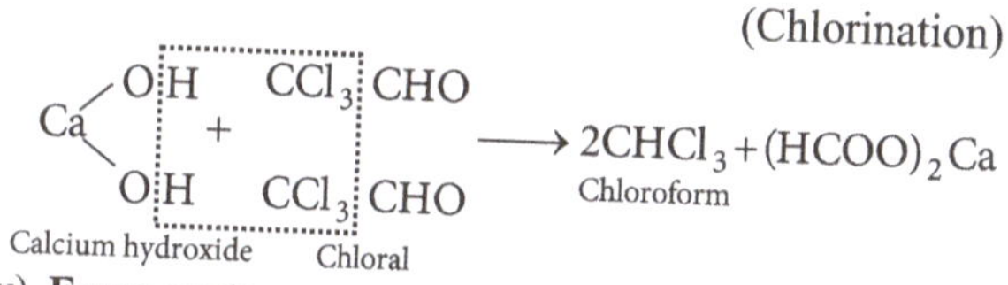

(iv) **From acetone**

$$CaOCl_2 + H_2O \longrightarrow Cl_2 + Ca(OH)_2$$

$$\underset{Acetone}{CH_3-\overset{\overset{O}{\|}}{C}-CH_3} + 3Cl_2 \longrightarrow CCl_3-\overset{\overset{O}{\|}}{C}-CH_3 + 3\ HCl$$

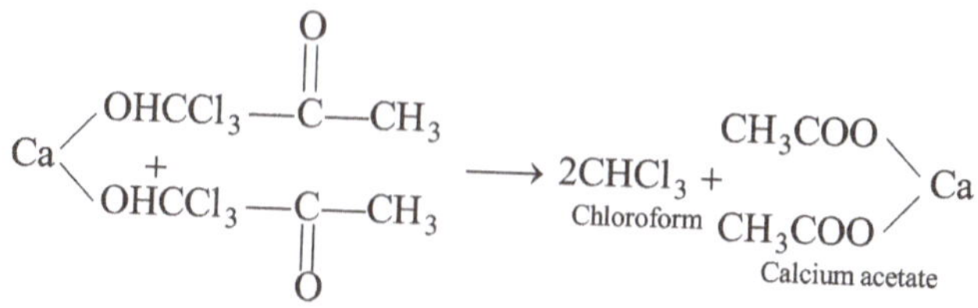

Physical Property

Colourless heavy liquid causes temporary unconsciousness.

Chemical Properties

The important chemical reactions of chloroform are given as follows

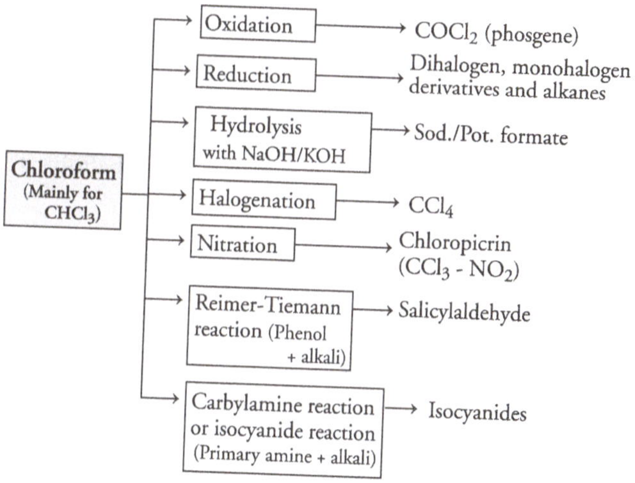

Uses

- It is used as an anaesthetic, solvent for oils, fats and medicines.
- It is used as a laboratory reagent.

Effects Chronic exposure to chloroform damages liver and kidney due to the formation of phosgene gas inside the body.

2. Triiodomethane [Iodoform, CHI_3]

Triodomethane is the triiodo derivative of methane and commonly known as **iodoform**.

Preparation (Haloform Reaction)

Some of the preparation methods of iodoform are as follows

(i) **From ethanol** Ethanol on heating with I_2/NaOH form iodoform.

$$\underset{Ethanol}{CH_3CH_2OH} + 4I_2 + 6NaOH \xrightarrow{Heat}$$

$$\underset{\substack{Iodoform\\ [Yellow\ ppt.]}}{CHI_3\downarrow} + \underset{Sodium\ formate}{HCO\overset{-}{O}\overset{+}{Na}} + 5NaI + 5H_2O$$

(ii) **From acetone** Acetone on heating with I_2 and NaOH form iodoform.

$$\underset{\text{Acetone}}{CH_3-\overset{\overset{O}{\|}}{C}-CH_3} + 3I_2 + 4NaOH \xrightarrow{\text{Heat}}$$

$$\underset{\substack{\text{Iodoform}\\\text{(Yellow ppt.)}}}{CHI_3\downarrow} + 3NaI + \underset{\text{Sodium acetate}}{CH_3-\overset{\overset{O}{\|}}{C}-\overset{-}{O}\overset{+}{Na}} + 3H_2O$$

Sodium hypoiodite can also be used in place of sodium hydroxide.

$$\underset{\text{Propanone}}{CH_3COCH_3} + \underset{\substack{\text{Sodium}\\\text{hypoiodite}}}{3NaOI} \longrightarrow \underset{\text{1,1,1-triiodopropan-2-one}}{CH_3COCI_3} + 3NaOH$$

(Iodination)

$$CH_3COCI_3 + NaOH \longrightarrow \underset{\text{Sodium acetate}}{CH_3CO\overset{-}{O}\overset{+}{Na}} + \underset{\text{Iodoform}}{CHI_3}$$

(Hydrolysis)

Physical Properties

- It is a yellow crystalline solid and insoluble in water.
- On heating, it decomposes to give iodine vapours.

Chemical Properties

The important chemical reactions of iodoform are given as follows

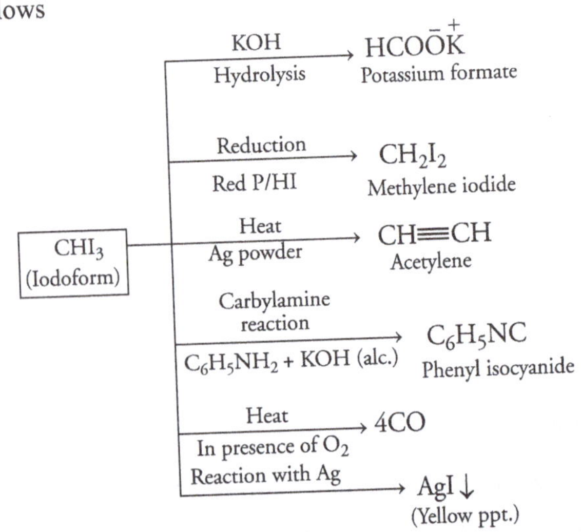

Uses

- It is used as an antiseptic due to liberation of iodine. But due to its unpresant smell, it has been replaced by other formulations containing iodine.
- It is also used in the manufacture of pharmaceuticals.
- **Environmental effects of iodoform** High amounts of iodoform exposure can cause nausea and dizziness.

3. Freons

Chlorofluorocarbon compounds of methane and ethane are collectively known as **freons**. They are extremely stable, unreactive, non-toxic, non-corrosive and easily liquefiable gases.

Freon 12 (dichlorodifluoromethane, CCl_2F_2) is one of the most common freons in industrial use. It is manufactured from tetrachloromethane by **Swarts reaction.**

$$3\,CCl_4 + 2\,SbF_3 \xrightarrow{SbCl_5} 2\,SbCl_3 + \underset{\substack{\text{Freon-12}\\\text{Dichlorodifluoromethane}}}{3CCl_2F_2}$$

Uses

- Freons are used as refrigerants in refrigerators and air conditioning.
- These are used as propellants for aerosols and foams to spray out deodrants, cleansers, shaving cream, hair sprays and insecticides.

Harmful Effect (Physiological Effects)

Most freon makes its way into the atmosphere where it undergoes photochemical decomposition and initiate radical chain reactions for depletion of the ozone layer.

Therefore, the use of freons as propellants and refrigerants has been drastically discouraged.

4. DDT

[2, 2-*bis*-(*p* -chlorophenyl)-1, 1, 1-trichloroethane] or (*p*, *p*′- dichlorodiphenyltrichloroethane)

Preparation

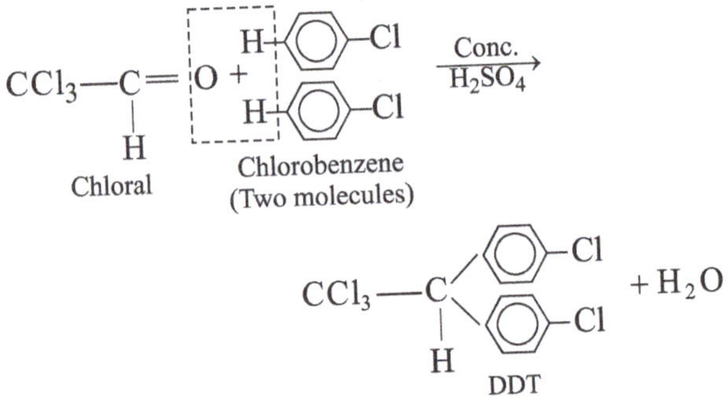

Uses

- It is cheap but powerful insecticide.
- It is popularly very effective against anopheles mosquitoes and lices which carry typhus.

Harmful Effect

- It is non-biodegradable and extremely stable compound which acts as water pollutant and kills aquatic animals, thus imbalance the water ecosystem.
- It get stored in fat tissues of animal and increase in amount over the time. It causes cancer and other harmful disease.

4. Dichloromethane [CH_2Cl_2]

- Uses of dichloromethane
  (i) It is used as a solvent in food technology.
  (ii) It is also used in aerosols as a propellant.
- Environment effects of dichloromethane
  (i) Exposure to high concentrations may cause unconsciousness and death.
  (ii) The substance is irritating to the eyes, skin and respiratory tract.

5. Tetrachloromethane (CCl_4)

Uses

It is used as follows

- CCl_4 is used as a fire extinguisher under the name **pyrene**. It is used in medicines as helmenthicide and as a solvent for fats, oils, waxes, greases etc.
- It is also used in the manufacture of refrigerants and propellants for aerosol cans.

Harmful Effects

The presence of CCl_4 produced the following harmful effects

- Exposure to CCl_4 may cause irregular heart beat or heart failure. It may irritate the eyes on contact.
- It causes dizzines, light-headedness, nausea, vomiting which can cause permanent damage to nerve cells.
- Subsequently, these effects may lead to stupor, coma, unconsciousness or death.

PYQs Previous Years' Questions

1 Mark Questions

Exams' Questions

1. The addition of small quantity of ethanol to chloroform prevents the formation of .... and converts it into the harmless compound .... *ISC 2024*

2. Haloalkenes undergo both nucleophilic and electrophilic reactions due to the presence of .... bond and the .... atom. *ISC Specimen 2024*

3. **Assertion** (A) Addition of bromine water to 1-butene gives two optical isomers. *ISC 2023*

   Reason (R) The product formed contains two asymmetric carbon atoms.

   (a) Both (A) and (R) are correct and (R) is the correct explanation of (A).
   (b) Both (A) and (R) are correct but (R) is not the correct explanation of (A).
   (c) (A) is correct and (R) is incorrect.
   (d) (A) is incorrect and (R) is correct.

4. **Assertion** (A) Nitration of chlorobenzene leads to the formation of *m*-nitrochlorobenzene. *ISC Specimen 2021*

   Reason (R) Nitro (—NO_2) group is *m*-directing group.

   (a) Both (A) and (R) are correct and (R) is the correct explanation of (A).
   (b) Both (A) and (R) are correct but (R) is not the correct explanation of (A).
   (c) (A) is correct and (R) is incorrect.
   (d) (A) is incorrect and (R) is correct.

5. The optically active compound is *ISC Specimen 2021-22 (Sem-I)*

   (a) butan-1-ol
   (b) butan-2-ol
   (c) propan-1-ol
   (d) 2-methylpropan-1-ol

6. The gas obtained on heating iodoform with silver powder is *ISC Specimen 2021-22 (Sem-I)*

   (a) propane (b) ethane
   (c) ethyne (d) ethene

7. During the course of S_N1 reaction, the intermediate species formed is *ISC Specimen 2021-22 (Sem-I), 2018*

(a) a carbocation (b) a free radical
(c) a carbanion (d) an intermediate complex

8. Write the balanced chemical equation for ethyl chloride treated with alcoholic potassium hydroxide. *ISC 2019*

9. Which among the following reacts fastest by S_N2 reaction? *ISC Specimen 2018*

(a) $(CH_3)_3C—Br$ (b) $(CH_3)_2CHBr$
(c) $CH_3—CH_2—Br$ (d) $CH_3—Br$

10. Give the balanced equation for the following name reaction. *ISC 2016*

Wurtz-Fittig reaction

11. How can the following conversions be brought about ? Chlorobenzene to phenol *ISC 2015*

12. What will be the product formed when chlorobenzene is heated with sodium metal in the presence of dry ether? *ISC 2015*

13. The product formed when aniline is warmed with chloroform and caustic potash. *ISC 2010, 2002*

(a) Phenyl chloride (b) Methyl isocyanide
(c) Phenyl isocyanide (d) Nitrophenol

14. A ……… precipitate is obtained on adding iodine and sodium hydroxide to……… *ISC 2012, 2008, 2006*

15. Write the balanced equation for the preparation of DDT. *ISC 2008*

16. Correct the following statement.

When acetone is treated with bleaching powder, chloroform is obtained. *ISC 2007*

17. Write the chemical equation for the following reaction Acetone with sodium hypoiodite. *ISC 2005*

Important Questions

18. Out of ethyl bromide and ethyl chloride, which has higher boiling point and why?

19. Write the structure of an isomer of compound C_4H_9Br which is most reactive towards S_N1 reaction.

20. Out of $CH_3—CH(CH_3)—CH_2—Cl$ and $CH_3—CH_2—CH(CH_3)—Cl$, which is more reactive towards S_N1 reaction and why?

21. Which would undergo S_N1 reaction faster in the following pair?

$CH_3—CH_2—CH_2—Br$ and $CH_3—CH(Br)—CH_3$

22. Which would undergo S_N2 reaction faster in the following pair and why?

$CH_3—CH_2—Br$ and $CH_3—C(CH_3)(Br)—CH_3$

23. Which would undergo S_N2 reaction faster in the following pair and why?

$CH_3—CH_2—Br$ and $CH_3—CH_2—I$

24. Identify the chiral molecule in the following pair :

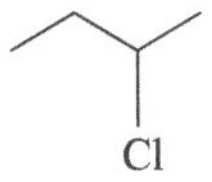 and 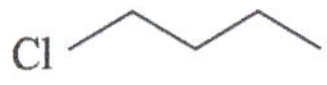

25. What happens when $CH_3—Br$ is treated with KCN?

26. What happens when ethyl chloride is treated with aqueous KOH ?

27. Which compound in the following pair undergoes faster towards S_N1 reaction?

(I)  (II) 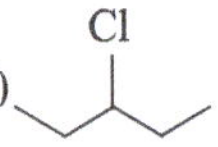

28. How methyl bromide be preferentially converted to methyl isocyanide?

29. Predict the order of reactivity of four isomeric bromobutanes in S_N1 reaction.

30. Which will react faster towards S_N2 displacement, 1-bromopentane or 2-bromopentane and why?

31. A solution of KOH hydrolyses $CH_3CHClCH_2CH_3$ and $CH_3CH_2CH_2CH_2Cl$. Which one of these is more easily hydrolysed?

2 Marks Questions

Exams' Questions

32. How will you bring the following conversions? *ISC 2024*

(i) Benzene to biphenyl (ii) Iodoform to acetylene

33. Give balanced chemical equations to convert the following: *ISC Specimen 2024*

(i) Benzene to biphenyl
(ii) Propene to propan -1-ol

34. Two compounds, D-2-chlorobutane and L-2-chlorobutane, are enantiomers of each other. *ISC Specimen 2024*

Name one physical property that is:

(i) same for D-2-chlorobutane and L-2-chlorobutane.

(ii) different for D-2-chlorobutane and L-2-chlorobutane.

35. Given chemical equations for each of the following.

(i) Ethyl chloride is treated with aqueous KOH solution.

(ii) Chlorobenzene is treated with ammonia at 573 K and high pressure. *ISC 2023*

36. Ethyl alcohol when reacts with PCl_5 gives a compound (*A*). When compound (*A*) is treated with alc. KOH, compound (*B*) is formed alongwith KCl and H_2O.

(i) The compound (*A*) is *ISC 2021-22 (Sem I)*

(a) $C_2H_4Cl_2$ (b) CH_3CHO

(c) C_2H_5Cl (d) CH_3OH

(ii) The compound (*B*) is

(a) C_2H_2 (b) C_2H_4

(c) C_2H_6 (d) C_2H_5OH

37. The reaction $CH_3Br + OH^- \longrightarrow CH_3OH + Br^-$ *[2]*

(i) The expected mechanism of the above reaction is *ISC Specimen 2021-22 (Sem-I)*

(a) S_N1 mechanism (b) S_N2 mechanism

(c) S_E1 mechanism (d) S_E2 mechanism

(ii) The above reaction is

(a) elimination reaction

(b) nucleophilic addition reaction

(c) nucleophilic substitution reaction

(d) electrophilic substitution reaction

38. How will you convert the following? *ISC 2020*

(i) Chlorobenzene to biphenyl

(ii) Propene to 1-bromopropane

39. What will be the major product obtained when 2-bromobutane reacts with alcoholic potassium hydroxide? State the type of reaction involved in it. *ISC Specimen 2018*

40. How can the following conversion be brought about methyl chloride to acetone. *ISC 2016*

41. Complete the following reaction and name the reaction.

$$C_3H_7NH_2 + CHCl_3 + 3KOH\,(alc.) \xrightarrow{\Delta} \ldots + 3KCl + 3H_2O$$ *ISC 2012, 2007*

42. Suggest a possible mechanism for the following reaction

$$n\text{-}BuBr + KCN \xrightarrow{EtOH,\ H_2O} n\text{-}BuCN$$

ISC 2009, 2008

KEY IDEA

(i) Write the resonating structures of KCN.

(ii) Due to the presence of polar solvent, find the possibility, which product will be formed preferentially.

43. Draw the resonating structures of chlorobenzene. *2008*

Important Questions

44. Explain the following reactions with an example: Friedel-Crafts reaction.

45. (i) Which alkyl halide from the following pair is chiral and which one can undergoes faster towards S_N2 reactions?

(a) 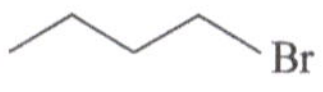 (b) 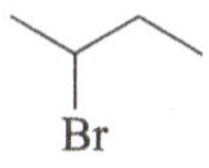

(ii) Out of S_N1 and S_N2, which reaction occurs with (a) inversion of configuration? (b) racemisation?

46. Write chemical equations when

(i) ethyl chloride is treated with aqueous KOH.

(ii) chlorobenzene is treated with CH_3COCl in the presence of anhydrous $AlCl_3$.

47. (i) Which alkyl halide from the following pair would you expect to react more rapidly by an S_N2 mechanism and why?

$CH_3—CH_2—CH(Br)—CH_3$;

$CH_3—CH_2—CH_2—CH_2—Br$

(ii) Racemisation occurs in S_N1 reactions. Why?

48. Which compound in each of the following pairs will react faster towards S_N2 reaction with —OH? Why?

(i) CH_3Br or CH_3I

(ii) $(CH_3)_3CCl$ or CH_3Cl

49. Write the chemical equations when,

(i) methyl chloride is treated with $AgNO_2$.

(ii) bromobenzene is treated with CH_3Cl in the presence of anhydrous $AlCl_3$.

50. What are ambident nucleophiles? Give an example.

51. Account for the following.

(i) The C — Cl bond length in chlorobenzene is shorter than that in CH_3— Cl.

(ii) Chloroform is stored in closed dark brown bottles.

52. Chlorobenzene is extremely less reactive towards a nucleophilic substitution reaction. Give two reasons for the same.

53. Explain why

(i) alkyl halides though polar are immiscible with water?

(ii) Grignard's reagent should be prepared under anhydrous conditions?

> **KEY IDEA**
>
> (i) Strong intermolecular H-bonding is present among water molecules.
>
> (ii) Consider reactive nature of Grignard's reagent with water.

54. Which one in the following pairs of substances undergoes S_N2 substitution reaction faster and why?

(i) 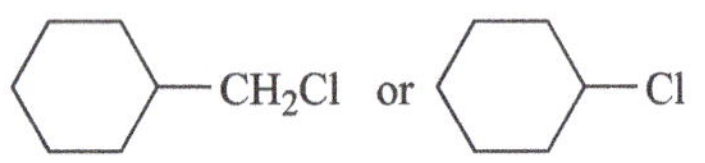

(ii) 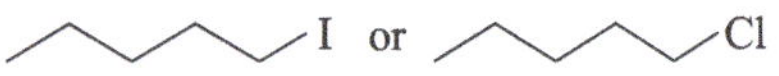

55. Which one in the following pairs undergoes S_N1 substitution reaction faster and why?

(i) 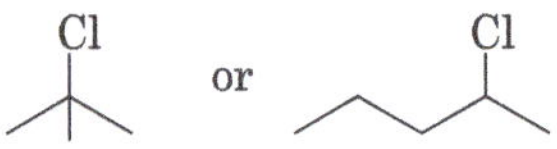

(ii) 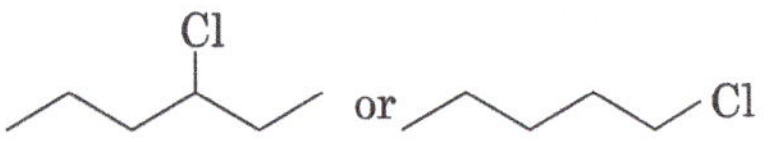

> **KEY IDEA**
>
> Reactivity of a halogen derivative towards S_N1 reaction depends upon the stability of the carbocation formed. So, compare the stability of carbocation formed.

56. Suggest a possible reason for the following observations.

(i) The order of reactivity of haloalkanes is $RI > RBr > RCl$.

(ii) *Neo*-pentyl chloride, $(CH_3)_3C—CH_2Cl$ does not follow S_N2 mechanism.

57. Discuss the mechanism of S_N1 reaction of haloalkanes.

58. (i) Why is it that haloalkanes are more reactive than haloarenes toward nucleophiles?

(ii) Which one of the following react faster towards S_N1 reaction and why?

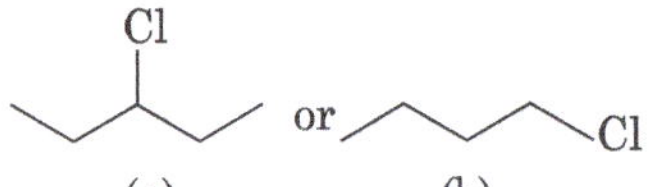

3 Marks Questions

Exams' Questions

59. Write the balanced chemical equations for the following name reactions. **ISC 2023**

(i) Sandmeyer's reaction (ii) Wurtz reaction

(iii) Finkelstein reaction

Important Questions

60. Following compounds are given to you.

2-bromopentane, 2-bromo-2-methylbutane, 1-bromopentane

(i) Write the compound which is most reactive towards S_N2 reaction.

(ii) Write the compound which is optically active.

(iii) Write the compound which is most reactive towards β-elimination reaction.

61. How do you convert the following?

(i) Chlorobenzene to biphenyl

(ii) Propene to 1-iodopropane

(iii) 2-bromobutane to but-2-ene

62. Write the major product(s) in the following.

(i) 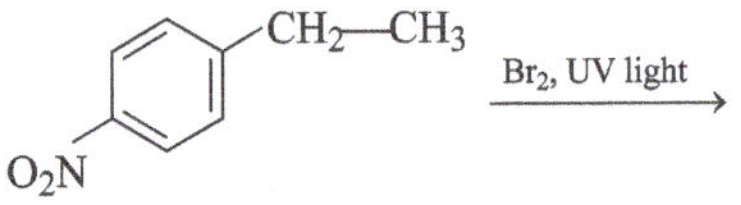

(ii) $2CH_3—\underset{\underset{Cl}{|}}{C}H—CH_3 \xrightarrow[\text{Dry ether}]{\text{Na}}$

(iii) $CH_3—CH_2—Br \xrightarrow{\text{AgCN}}$

63. Give reasons.

(i) C—Cl bond length in chlorobenzene is shorter than C—Cl bond length in CH_3— Cl.

(ii) The dipole moment of chlorobenzene is lower than that of cyclohexyl chloride.

(iii) S_N1 reactions are accompanied by racemisation in optically active alkyl halides.

64. How can the following conversions be carried out?

(i) Aniline to bromobenzene

(ii) Chlorobenzene to 2-chloroacetophenone

(iii) Chloroethane to butane

65. What happens when

(i) chlorobenzene is treated with Cl_2 / $FeCl_3$?

(ii) ethyl chloride is treated with $AgNO_2$?

(iii) 2-bromopentane is treated with alcoholic KOH?

Write the chemical equations in support of your answer.

66. Give reasons.

(i) *n*-butyl bromide has higher boiling point than *t*-butyl bromide.

(ii) Racemic mixture is optically inactive.

(iii) The presence of nitro group ($—NO_2$) at *o*/*p*-positions increases the reactivity of haloarenes towards nucleophilic substitution reactions.

67. Give reasons for the following.

(i) Ethyl iodide undergoes S_N2 reaction faster than ethyl bromide.

(ii) (±) 2-butanol is optically inactive.

(iii) C—*X* bond length in halobenzene is smaller than C—*X* bond length in $CH_3—X$.

68. Answer the following questions:

(i) What is meant by chirality of a compound? Give an example.

(ii) Which one of the following compounds is more easily hydrolysed by KOH and why?

$CH_3CHClCH_2CH_3$ or $CH_3CH_2CH_2CH_2Cl$

(iii) Which one undergoes S_N2 substitution reaction faster and why?

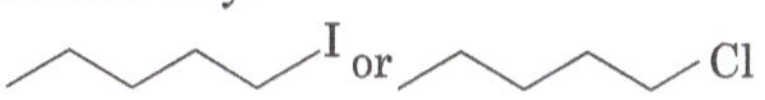

69. Answer the following.

(i) Haloalkanes easily dissolve in organic solvents. Why?

(ii) Iodoform has antiseptic properties. Give one reason to support it.

(iii) Of the two bromo derivatives, $C_6H_5CH(CH_3)Br$ and $(C_6H_5)CH(C_6H_5)Br$, which one is more reactive towards S_N1 substitution reaction and why?

70. Rearrange the compounds of each of the following sets in order of reactivity towards S_N2 displacement.

(i) 2-bromo-2-methylbutane, 1-bromopentane, 2-bromopentane.

(ii) 1-bromo-3-methylbutane, 2-bromo-2-methylbutane, 3-bromo-2-methylbutane.

(iii) 1-bromobutane, 1-bromo-2, 2-dimethylpropane, 1-bromo-2-methylbutane, 1-bromo-3-methylbutane.

> **KEY IDEA**
>
> S_N2 reactions depend upon steric hindrance. More the steric hindrance, slower is the reaction. So, order of reactivity is 1° > 2°>3°.

71. (i) Write a chemical test to distinguish between

(a) chlorobenzene and benzyl chloride

(b) chloroform and carbon tetrachloride

(ii) Why is methyl chloride hydrolysed more easily than chlorobenzene?

72. (i) State one use of DDT and iodoform.

(ii) Which compound in the following couples will react faster towards S_N2 displacement and why?

(a) 1-bromopentane or 2-bromopentane

(b) 1-bromo-2-methyl butane or 2-bromo-2-methyl butane

73. How would you differentiate between S_N1 and S_N2 mechanism of substitution reactions? Give one example of each.

Explanations

1. Phosgene; diethyl carbonate
2. Carbon; halogen
3. (c) Assertion is correct but reason is incorrect.
   The reaction is
   $$\underset{\text{1-butene}}{CH_2=CH-CH_2-CH_3} \xrightarrow{Br_2,\ water} \underset{\quad Br\qquad\ Br}{CH_2-\overset{*}{C}H-CH_2-CH_3}$$
   The product formed contains only 1 asymmetric carbon. Hence, number of optical isomers = 2
4. (d) Assertion is incorrect but Reason is correct as the chlorination of nitrobenzene. (not the nitration of chlorobenzene) leads to the formation of *m*-nitrochlorobenzene because —NO_2, group deactivates the ring because it is *meta*-directing.
5. (b) Butan-2-ol is optically active compound due to the presence of a chiral carbon.

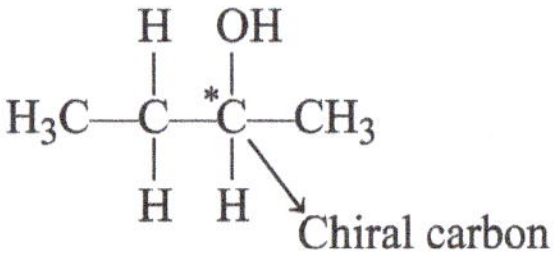

Concept Enhancer A compound that contains an asymmetric center is known as chiral atom or chiral center and thus, can occur in two non-superimposable mirror images of each other.

6. (c) When iodoform is heated with silver powder, acetylene is formed.
   $$2CHI_3 + 6Ag \longrightarrow \underset{\text{Ethyne (acetylene)}}{CH\equiv CH}$$
7. (a) **Carbocation** During S_N1 reaction, a carbocation is formed as an intermediate species. For example, in S_N1 reaction between *tert*-butyl bromide and hydroxide ion forms, carbocation intermediate.
8. When ethyl chloride is treated with alcoholic KOH, it undergoes elimination reaction to form ethene.
   $C_2H_5Cl + \text{alc. } KOH \longrightarrow C_2H_4 + KCl + H_2O$
9. (d) The order of reactivity of alkyl halides towards S_N2 reaction is as follows
   Methyl halide > Primary halide > Secondary halide > Tertiary halide
   Therefore, among the given options, CH_3Br reacts fastest by S_N2 reaction.
10. Wurtz-Fittig reaction

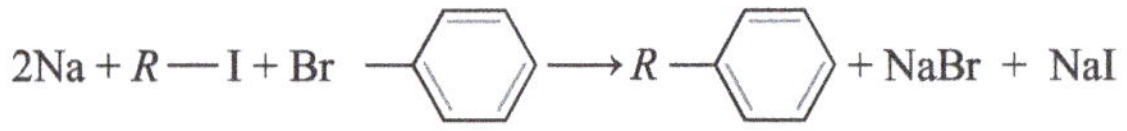

11.

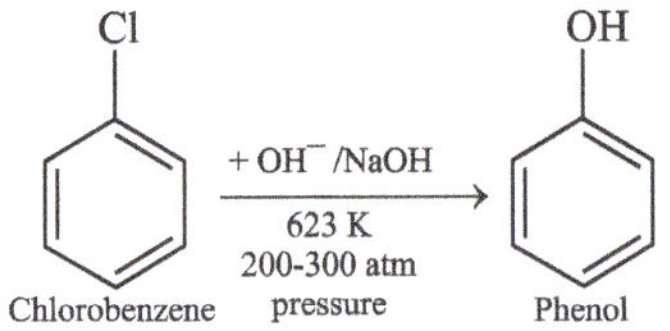

12. Chlorobenzene is heated with sodium metal in the presence of dry ether gives diphenyl compound.

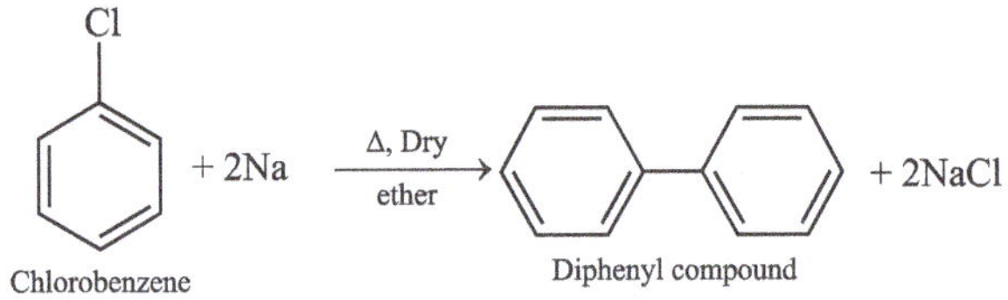

13. (c) **Phenyl isocyanide** In carbylamine reaction, when chloroform is warmed with aniline and alcoholic caustic potash, phenyl isocyanide is obtained which has an extremely offensive smell.
   $$C_6H_5-N\begin{matrix} H & & Cl \\ & + & \\ H & & Cl\end{matrix}\ C\begin{matrix} H \\ Cl\end{matrix} + \underset{(Alc.)}{3KOH} \xrightarrow{Warm} \underset{\text{Phenyl isocyanide}}{C_6H_5-N\overrightarrow{=}C} + 3KCl + 3H_2O$$
   Hence, option (c) is correct.
14. When acetone is heated with iodine and sodium hydroxide, a yellow precipitate of iodoform is formed.
   $$\underset{\text{Acetone}}{CH_3-\overset{O}{\overset{\|}{C}}-CH_3} + 3I_2 + 4NaOH \xrightarrow{Heat} \underset{\substack{\text{Iodoform}\\\text{(Yellow ppt.)}}}{CHI_3} + 3NaI + CH_3-\overset{O}{\overset{\|}{C}}-\overset{-}{O}\overset{+}{Na} + 3H_2O$$
15. DDT is prepared by heating chlorobenzene with chloral in the presence of concentrated sulphuric acid.

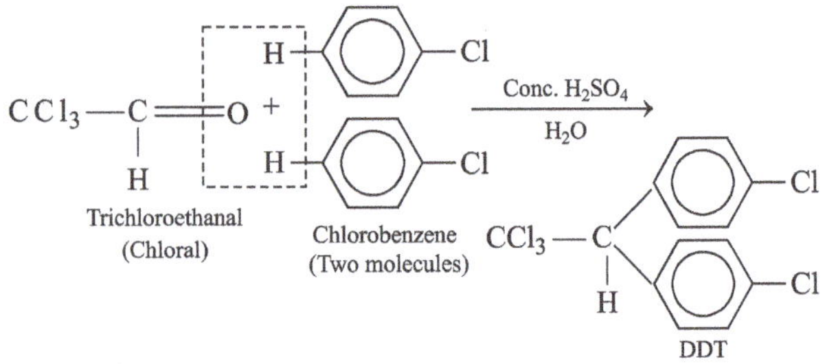

16. When acetone is treated with bleaching powder, **chloroform** is obtained.
[For more detail. Refer page 118]

17. In the preparation of iodoform, sodium hypoiodite can also be used in place of sodium hydroxide with acetone.

$$CH_3COCH_3 + 3NaOI \longrightarrow CH_3COCI_3 + 3NaOH$$
$$CH_3COCI_3 + NaOH \longrightarrow CH_3COONa + CHI_3$$

18. For the same alkyl group, boiling point increases with the size of the halogen atom. Thus, boiling point of ethyl bromide is higher than ethyl chloride.

19. Tertiary (3°) alkyl halides are most reactive towards S_N1 reaction followed by secondary (2°) and primary (1°) alkyl halides. C_4H_9 Br has four isomer among them. The isomer, $CH_3—C(CH_3)_2—Br$ (2-bromo -2-methylpropane) of compound C_4H_9Br is most reactive towards S_N1 reaction.

20. Among the given haloalkanes, $CH_3—CH_2—CH(CH_3)—Cl$ will undergo S_N1 reaction faster because it is a secondary alkyl halide and forms a secondary carbocation that can stabilise itself more than primary carbocation.

21. Secondary alkyl halides prefer to undergo S_N1 reaction than primary alkyl halides because of formation of more stable 2° carbocation.

Hence, out of the given pair

$$CH_3—CH(Br)—CH_3$$

would undergo S_N1 reaction faster.

22. On steric grounds, 1° alkyl halides are more reactive than *tert*-alkyl halides toward S_N2 reactions. Thus, $CH_3—CH_2—Br$ would undergo S_N2 reaction faster than $[(CH_3)_3CBr]$ because it is a primary halide, i.e. less hindered.

23. As I^- ion is a better leaving group than Br^- ion, therefore iodides are more reactive than bromides.

Therefore, $CH_3—CH_2—I$ is more reactive than $CH_3—CH_2—Br$ towards S_N2 reaction and hence, $CH_3—CH_2—I$ would undergo S_N2 reaction faster than $CH_3—CH_2—Br$.

24. 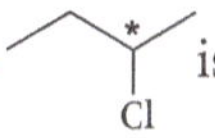

is chiral molecule as it contains an asymmetric carbon atom (which is denoted by *).

25. When $CH_3—Br$ is treated with KCN, methyl cyanide is obtained.

$$\underset{\text{Methyl bromide}}{CH_3—Br} + \underset{\text{Potassium cyanide}}{K^+—CN^-} \longrightarrow \underset{\text{Methyl cyanide}}{CH_3—CN} + \underset{\text{Potassium bromide}}{KBr}$$

It is a nucleophilic substitution reaction. Nucleophile CN^- substitutes Br^-.

26. Ethyl chloride undergoes hydrolysis to form ethyl alcohol (through S_N2 nucleophilic substitution).

$$\underset{\text{Ethyl chloride}}{C_2H_5Cl} + KOH(aq) \longrightarrow \underset{\text{Ethanol}}{C_2H_5OH} + KCl$$

27. The reactivity towards S_N1 reaction depends upon the stability of the intermediate carbocation which an alkyl halide gives on ionisation.

As 3° carbocations are more stable than 2° carbocations, therefore, 

will react faster than 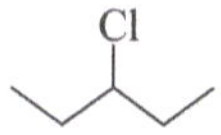

in S_N1 reaction.

28. It can be done by treating the methyl bromide with alcoholic silver cyanide.

$$CH_3Br + \underset{\text{(Alc.)}}{AgCN} \longrightarrow \underset{\text{Methyl isocyanide}}{CH_3NC} + AgBr$$

29. Order of reactivity of four isomeric bromobutanes in S_N1 reaction is

$$(CH_3)_3CBr > CH_3CH_2CH(Br)CH_3 > (CH_3)_2CHCH_2Br > CH_3CH_2CH_2CH_2Br$$

30. 1-bromopentane is a primary alkyl halide while 2-bromopentane is a secondary alkyl halide. Since, primary alkyl halides are sterically less hindered therefore, 1-bromopentane reacts faster towards S_N2 reaction as in S_N1 reactions, reactivity depends upon the stability of carbocation.

Common Mistake There is confusion in the order of reactivity of 1°, 2°, 3° towards S_N1 and S_N2 reactions.

31. The reaction of alkyl halide with aqueous KOH occurs by S_N1 mechanism. Further, the reactivity in S_N1 depends upon the stability of carbocation.

Since, $CH_3CHClCH_2CH_3$ forms more stable 2 °carbocation on ionisation than $CH_3CH_2CH_2CH_2Cl$, therefore, $CH_3CHClCH_2CH_3$ hydrolyses faster than $CH_3CH_2CH_2CH_2Cl$.

32. (i) **Benzene to biphenyl**

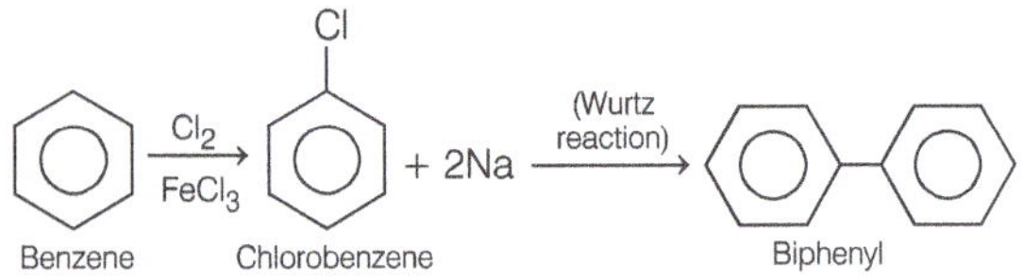

(ii) **Iodoform to acetylene**

$$\underset{\text{Iodoform}}{2CHI_3} + 6Ag \longrightarrow \underset{\text{Acetylene}}{CH{\equiv}CH} + \underset{\text{ppt.}}{6AgI\downarrow}$$

33. (i) Conversion of benzene to biphenyl is given as

Step 1 First of all benzene is treated with chlorine in the presence of $AlCl_3$ to form chlorobenzene.

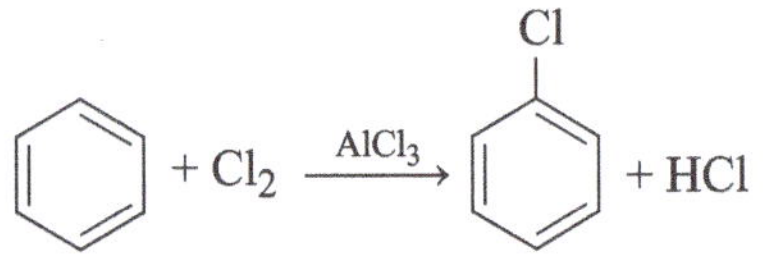

Step 2 Preparation of biphenyl from chlorobenzene is done by Fittig's reaction. In this reaction, chlorobenzene is treated with Na metal in the presence of dry ether to form biphenyl.

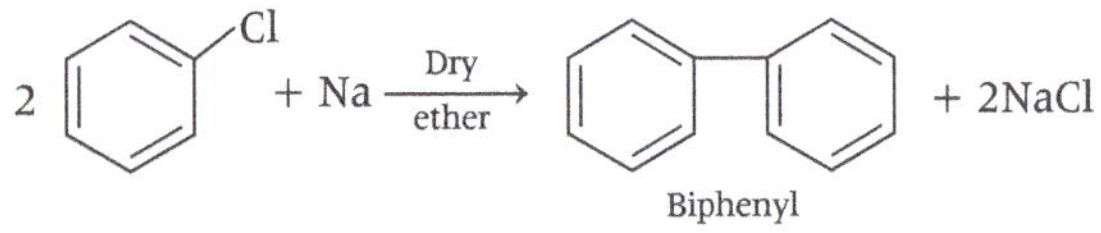

(ii) **Step 1** At first, propene reacts with hydrogen bromide in the presence of peroxide to form 1-bromopropane (anti-Markownikoff's product).

$$\underset{\text{(Propene)}}{CH_3CH{=}CH_2} + \underset{\text{Hydrogen bromide}}{HBr} \xrightarrow{\text{Peroxide}} \underset{\text{(1-bromopropane)}}{CH_3CH_2CH_2Br}$$

Step 2 The produced alkyl halide reacts with KOH followed by heating to propan-1-ol as the final product

$$CH_3CH_2CH_2Br + KOH(aq) \xrightarrow{\Delta} \underset{\text{(Propan-1-ol)}}{CH_3CH_2CH_2OH}$$

34. (i) Enantiomers have identical melting points, boiling points and density.

(ii) Enantiomers differ in optical rotation, as they rotate the plane of polarised light by equal amounts in opposite directions.

35. (i) Ethyl chloride undergoes hydrolysis to form ethyl alcohol (through S_N2 nucleophilic substitution)

$$\underset{\text{Ethyl chloride}}{C_2H_5Cl} + KOH(aq) \longrightarrow \underset{\text{Ethanol}}{C_2H_5OH} + KCl$$

> **Concept Enhancer** Ethyl chloride when reacts with alcoholic KOH undergoes dehydrohalogenation reaction whereas aqueous KOH undergoes hydrolysis.

(ii)

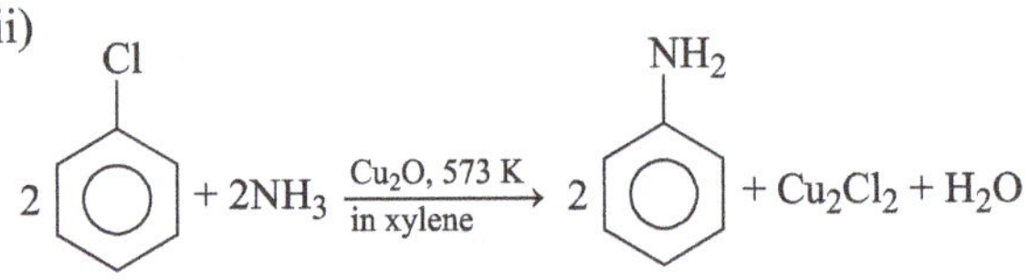

36. When ethyl alcohol reacts with PCl_5, it forms ethyl chloride.

(i) (c) $\underset{\text{Ethyl alcohol}}{C_2H_5OH} + PCl_5 \longrightarrow \underset{\text{(Ethyl chloride) (A)}}{C_2H_5Cl} + POCl_3 + HCl$

(ii) (b) When ethyl chloride reacts with alc KOH undergoes β-elimination reaction to form ethene as a product.

$$\underset{(A)}{C_2H_5Cl} \longrightarrow \underset{(B)}{C_2H_4}$$

37. (i) (b) S_N2 mechanism

Reason Since the given alkyl halide (CH_3Br) is a primary alkyl halide which usually undergoes substitution by S_N2 mechanism.

(ii) (c) $CH_3Br + OH^- \longrightarrow CH_3OH + Br^-$

is a nucleophilic reaction.

In this reaction, the nucleophile (OH^-) attacks on the positively charged carbon of haloalkane and the halogen leaves the group.

38. (i) **Chlorobenzene to biphenyl** Refer to text on page 126 (Fittig reaction).

(ii) **Propene to 1-bromopropane**

$$\underset{\text{Propene}}{CH_3CH{=}CH_2} + HBr \longrightarrow \underset{\text{(Minor)}}{\underset{\text{1-bromopropane}}{CH_3CH_2CH_2Br}} + \underset{\text{(Major)}}{\underset{\text{2-bromopropane}}{CH_3\underset{\underset{Br}{|}}{C}H{-}CH_3}}$$

39.

$$CH_3{-}CH_2{-}\underset{\underset{Br}{|}}{C}H{-}CH_3 + \underset{\text{(Alc.)}}{KOH} \longrightarrow$$

$$\underset{\text{(Minor)}}{\underset{\text{But-1-ene}}{CH_3CH_2{-}CH{=}CH_2}} + \underset{\text{(Major)}}{\underset{\text{But-2-ene}}{CH_3{-}CH{=}CHCH_3}}$$

The type of reaction involved in above case is β-elimination.

40. $CH_3Cl \xrightarrow[\text{Ether}]{\text{Mg}} CH_3MgCl$
Methyl chloride → Methyl magnesium chloride

$CH_3Cl \xrightarrow{KCN} CH_3CN \xrightarrow{CH_3MgCl} CH_3-\underset{}{\overset{CH_3}{\overset{|}{C}}}=NMgCl \xrightarrow{H_3O^+} CH_3-\overset{O}{\overset{||}{C}}-CH_3$
Methyl cyanide; Acetone

41. $C_3H_7NH_2 + CHCl_3 + 3KOH\ (alc.) \xrightarrow{\Delta}$
$C_3H_7N \rightleftarrows C + 3KCl + 3H_2O$ (Carbylamine reaction)
Propyl isocyanide

When chloroform is warmed with a suitable aromatic or aliphatic primary amine and alcoholic caustic potash, corresponding isocyanide is formed which has extremely offensive smell.

42. KCN is a reagent that gives CN^- ion as nucleophile in aqueous medium.

Resonating forms of KCN

$K^+ [\,:\bar{C}\equiv N:\,] \longleftrightarrow K^+[\,:C=\ddot{\bar{N}}:\,]$

$K^+CN^- + CH_3CH_2CH_2\overset{\delta+}{CH_2}\overset{\delta-}{Br} \longrightarrow CH_3CH_2CH_2CH_2CN + KBr$

or n-$BuBr + KCN \xrightarrow{C_2H_5OH,\ H_2O} n$-$BuCN + KBr$

CN^- is an ambident nucleophile therefore, it can attack either through C-atom or through N-atom. Since, C—C is a stronger bond than C—N bond, therefore it attacks through C to form *n*-butyl cyanide.

43. Chlorobenzene can be represented as a resonance hybrid of the following five canonical forms.

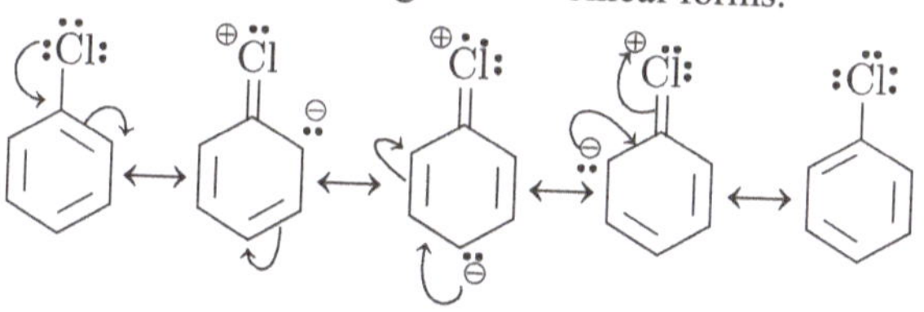

From the above canonical forms, it is clear that C—Cl bond in chlorobenzene acquires a partial double bond character. This shortens C—Cl bond length and imparts stability to the molecule.

44. Haloarenes in presence of Lewis acid react with alkyl halide or acid halide to give a mixture of *o*- and *p*-haloalkylbenzene (or haloacylbenzene)

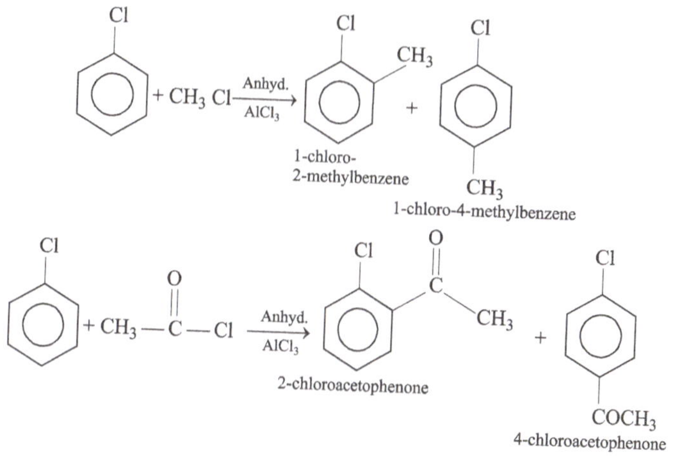

45. (i) (a)  undergoes faster towards S_N2 reaction as it is a primary halide.

(b) The alkyl halide 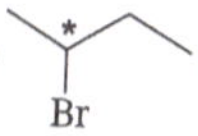 is chiral as it contains asymmetric carbon (*) atom.

(ii) (a) S_N2 reaction occurs with inversion of configuration.

(b) S_N1 reaction proceeds with racemisation.

46. (i) $CH_3-CH_2-Cl + KOH(aq) \longrightarrow CH_3CH_2OH + KCl$
Ethyl chloride; Ethanol

(ii)

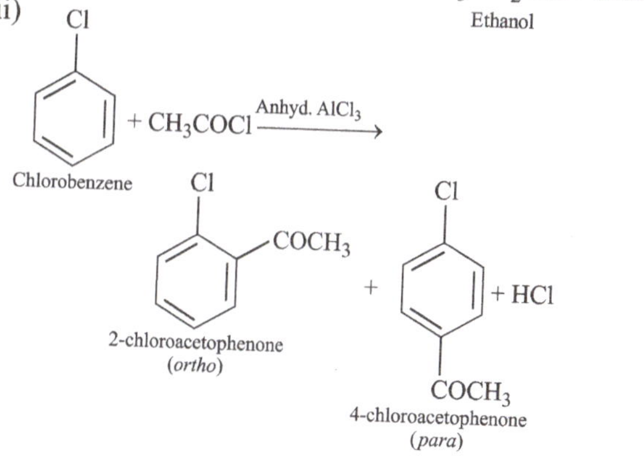

47. (i) In S_N2 reactions, reactivity depends upon the steric hindrance. $CH_3CH_2-CH_2-CH_2-Br$ is a primary alkyl halide while

$CH_3-CH_2-\underset{Br}{\underset{|}{C}H}-CH_3$ is a secondary alkyl halide. Since, primary alkyl halides are sterically less hindered therefore, $CH_3CH_2CH_2CH_2Br$ reacts faster towards S_N2 reaction.

(ii) In S_N1 reaction, there is a formation of carbocation as an intermediate in rate determining step. Since, carbocation is sp^2-hybridised and planar reactive intermediate, the nucleophile can attack from both sides (above and below) of carbocation with almost equal ease.

This gives rise to 50% product with *d*-isomer (+) and 50% product with *l*-isomer (–).

Hence, product formed is racemic mixture of equal proportions of two optically active enantiomers (±).

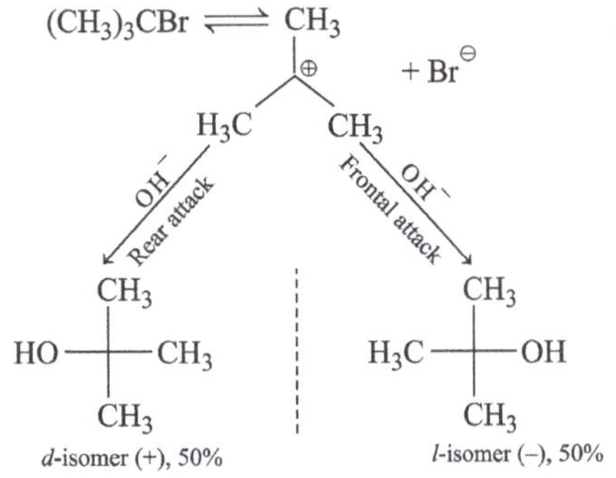

Racemic mixture

48. (i) CH_3I will react faster as compared to CH_3Br because CH_3I has lower bond dissociation energy and I^- is a better leaving group than Br^-. Thus, in the presence of nucleophile, iodide ion will be released at a faster rate.

(ii) CH_3Cl being a 1° halide will react faster as compared to $(CH_3)_3CCl$ which is a 3° halide because 1° halides undergo S_N2 mechanism faster than 3° halides.

49. (i) $\underset{\text{Methyl chloride}}{CH_3Cl} + AgNO_2 \longrightarrow CH_3NO_2 + AgCl$

(ii)

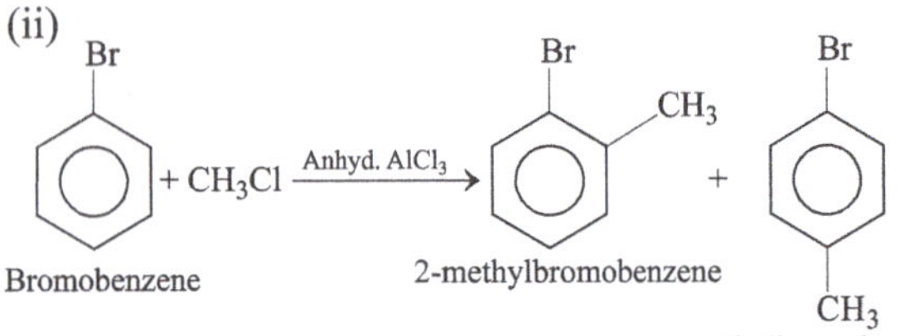

Bromobenzene 2-methylbromobenzene 4-methylbromobenzene

50. Ambident nucleophiles have two nucleophilic sites through which they can attack, e.g. nitrite ion is an ambident nucleophile. $[^-O—\ddot{N}=O]$

$$R—X + \bar{O}—N=O \longrightarrow \underset{\text{Alkyl nitrite}}{R—O—N=O} + X^-$$
Nitrite ion

It can attack through oxygen resulting in the formation of alkyl nitrites. Also, it can attack through nitrogen resulting in the formation of nitroalkanes.

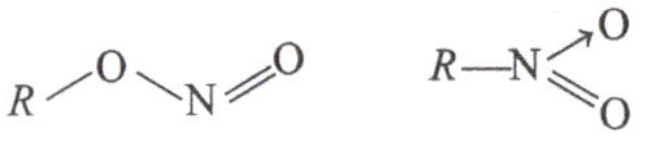

Alkyl nitrite Nitroalkane

51. (i) Due to partial double bond character of C — Cl bond (due to resonance in C_6H_5Cl), bond length of C — Cl (in chlorobenzene) is shorter than that in methyl chloride (CH_3Cl).

(ii) In the presence of air and sunlight, chloroform gets oxidised to phosgene (carbonyl chloride, $COCl_2$), a poisonous compound.

Thus, to prevent the formation of phosgene, chloroform is stored in dark brown bottles filled upto brim.

$$\underset{\text{Chloroform}}{CHCl_3} + \frac{1}{2}O_2 \xrightarrow{h\nu} \underset{\text{Carbonyl chloride (Phosgene)}}{COCl_2} + HCl$$

52. Two reasons for the less reactivity of chlorobenzene towards a nucleophilic substitution reaction are as follows

(i) **Resonance effect** The electron pair of chlorine atom is involved in conjugation with the π-electrons of the benzene ring and the following resonating structures are obtained.

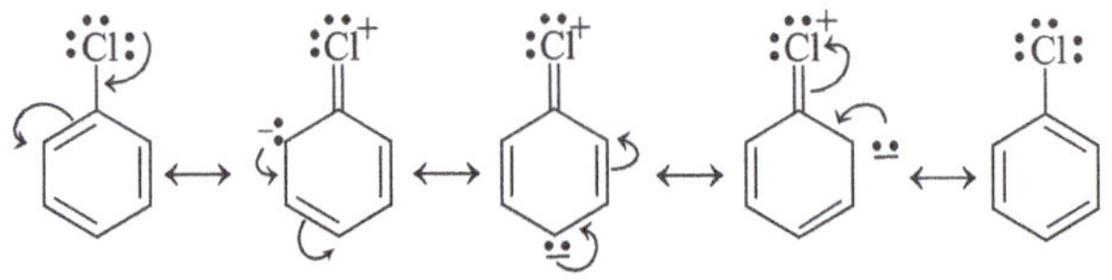

As a result, electrons of C—Cl bond get delocalised and a partial double bond character develops in the bond and hence, it becomes difficult for the nucleophile to cleave the C—Cl bond.

(ii) **Increased electron density** A repulsion is suffered by the nucleophile due to increased electron density on the benzene ring which prohibits the nucleophile to make a close access for the attack on the molecule.

53. (i) To be miscible with (or soluble in water) water, the solute-water force of attraction must be stronger than the solute-solute and water-water forces of attraction. Alkyl halides are polar molecules and so, held together by dipole-dipole interactions. Similarly, strong H-bonds exist between the water molecules.

The new forces of attraction between the alkyl halides and water molecules is weaker than the forces of attraction already existing between alkyl halide-alkyl halide and water-water molecules. Hence, alkyl halides (though polar) are immiscible with (or insoluble in) water.

(ii) Grignard's reagents are very reactive. In the presence of moisture, they react to give alkanes.

$$\underset{\text{Grignard's reagent}}{\overset{\delta-\ \delta+\ \delta-}{R\ Mg\ X}} + H—OH \longrightarrow \underset{\text{Alkane}}{R—H} + Mg(OH)X$$

Therefore, Grignard's reagents should be prepared under anhydrous conditions.

54. (i) 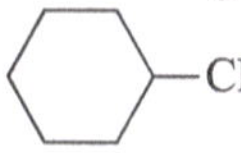 $—CH_2Cl$, it is a primary halide and therefore, undergoes, S_N2 reaction faster.

(ii)  , as iodide ion is a better leaving group because of its larger size therefore, it undergoes S_N2 reaction faster.

55. (i) 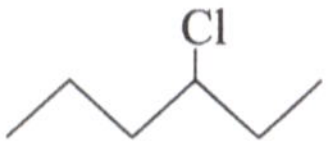 tertiary halide reacts faster than secondary halide towards S_N1 reactions because of the greater stability of tertiary carbocation intermediate.

(ii)  reacts faster because of greater stability of secondary carbocation than primary.

56. (i) When alkyl group is same, the reactivity of alkyl halide is decided by the halogen present. Greater the size of halogen atom, larger is the $R—X$ bond length, and weaker is the bond. Thus, more reactive is the alkyl halide. The order of size of halogen is

$$F < Cl < Br < I$$

Thus, the order of reactivity is

$$R—I > R—Br > R—Cl$$

(ii) Since, reactivity of S_N2 reactions depends upon steric hindrance and less sterically hindered molecules reacts faster in S_N2 reaction. As there is large steric hindrance in the case of *neo*-pentyl chloride so, it does not follow S_N2 mechanism.

57. S_N1 reactions are generally carried out in polar protic solvents (like water, alcohol, acetic acid, etc). The reaction between *tert*-butyl bromide and hydroxide ion yields *tert*-butyl alcohol and follows the first order kinetics.

$$(CH_3)_3CBr + OH^- \longrightarrow (CH_3)_3COH + Br^-$$

The steps involved are

(i) Formation of carbocation intermediate

$$(CH_3)_3\ C—Br \xrightarrow{\text{Slow}} \underset{\text{(Carbocation)}}{(CH_3)_3C^+} + Br^-$$

(ii) Attack of nucleophile on carbocation formed leading to formation of substituted product.

$$(CH_3)_3C^+ + \underset{\text{(Nucleophile)}}{OH^-} \xrightarrow{\text{Fast}} (CH_3)_3COH$$

58. (i) It is due to the following reasons.

(a) In haloalkanes, there is single bond between $R—X$, which needs less bond dissociation energy to break hence, they are more reactive towards nucleophiles. In haloarenes, there is partial double bond character between $C—X$ bond due to resonance, therefore $C—X$ bond in haloarenes are more stronger and requires more bond dissociation energy to break.

(b) Carbon attached to halogen is sp^3-hybridised in haloalkanes and sp^2-hybridised in haloarenes. sp^3-hybridised carbon is less electronegative than sp^2-hybridised carbon due to less *s*-character. Thus, $C—X$ bond in haloalkane releases more electrons to halogen.

(c) It is difficult for electron rich nucleophiles to approach electron rich benzene ring in haloarenes due to repulsion while there is no such thing in haloalkanes.

(ii) 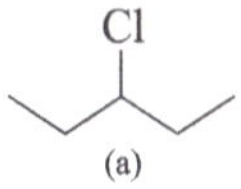 will react faster towards S_N1 reaction because (a) will form more stable 2° carbocation as compared to (b) 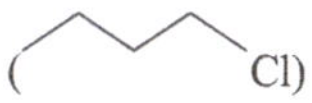 which forms 1° carbocation.

59. (i) **Sandmeyer's reaction** In this reaction, replacement of the diazonium group by chloride, bromide and cyanide takes place.

Nucleophiles such as CN^-, Cl^- and Br^- replace the diazonium group if appropriate cuprous salt is added to the solution containing diazonium group.

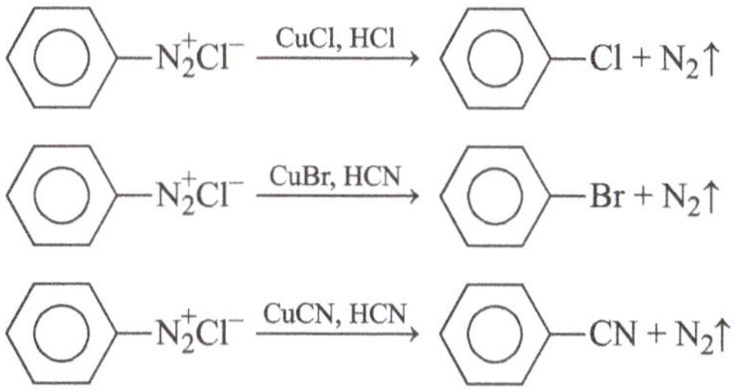

(ii) **Wurtz reaction** When two molecules of alkyl halides (same or different) reacts with metallic sodium in the presence of ether to form alkane

$$R—X + R—X \xrightarrow[\text{ether}]{\text{Na, Dry}} \underset{\text{Alkane}}{R—R}$$

(iii) **Finkelstein reaction** Alkyl iodide are often prepared by the reaction of chlorides/bromides with NaI in dry acetone.

$$R—X + \text{NaI} \xrightarrow[\text{Reflux}]{\text{Acetone}} R—\text{I} + \text{Na}X$$

60. (i) S_N2 reactions involve the formation of transition state. Higher the steric hinderance, lesser the stability of transition state and lower is their reactivity towards S_N2.

$$\underset{\substack{\text{1-bromopentane}\\(1^\circ)}}{CH_3CH_2CH_2CH_2CH_2Br} > \underset{\substack{\text{2-bromopentane}\\(2^\circ)}}{CH_3\underset{\substack{|\\Br}}{C}HCH_2CH_2CH_3} > \underset{\substack{\text{2-bromo-2-methylbutane}\\(3^\circ)}}{CH_3\overset{\substack{Br\\|}}{\underset{\substack{|\\CH_3}}{C}}CH_2CH_3}$$

(ii) Among the given compounds, 2-bromopentane is optically active due to presence of chiral carbon (*)

$$C_3H_7—\overset{\substack{H\\|}}{\underset{\substack{|\\Br}}{\overset{*}{C}}}—CH_3$$

Concept Enhancer A chiral carbon have four different groups or atoms attached separately to its four valencies.

(iii) 2-bromo-2-methylbutane is the most reactive towards β-elimination reaction because in this case more substituted alkene is the major product.

$$CH_3CH_2\overset{\substack{CH_3\\|}}{\underset{\substack{|\\Br}}{C}}—CH_3 \xrightarrow[-HBr]{} \underset{\text{2-methyl but-2-ene}}{CH_3CH{=}\overset{\substack{CH_3\\|}}{C}—CH_3}$$

61. (i) **Chlorobenzene to biphenyl**

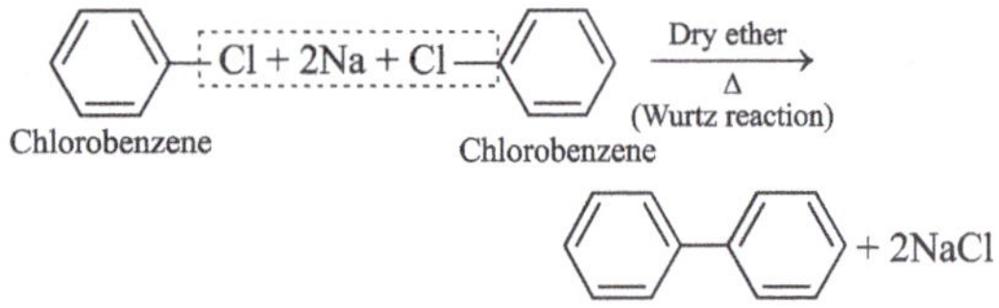

Chlorobenzene Chlorobenzene Biphenyl

(ii) **Propene to 1-iodopropane**

$$\underset{\text{Propene}}{CH_3—CH{=}CH_2} + HBr \xrightarrow[\text{(Anti-Markovnikov's addition)}]{(C_6H_5COO)_2}$$

$$\underset{\text{1-bromopropane}}{CH_3—CH_2CH_2Br} \xrightarrow{\text{Acetone / }\Delta\text{, NaI}} NaBr + \underset{\text{1-iodopropane}}{CH_3—CH_2CH_2I}$$

(iii) **2-bromobutane to but-2-ene**

$$\underset{\text{2-bromobutane}}{CH_3—CH_2—\underset{\substack{|\\Br}}{C}H—CH_3} \xrightarrow[-HBr]{\text{KOH(alc.)}/\Delta} \underset{\text{But-2-ene (Major product)}}{CH_3CH{=}CHCH_3}$$

Note In this reaction, another product, but-1-ene would also be formed as a minor product which being a less substituted product.

Common Mistake Generally, student missed the reaction condition like heating, reagents and temperature.

62. (i)

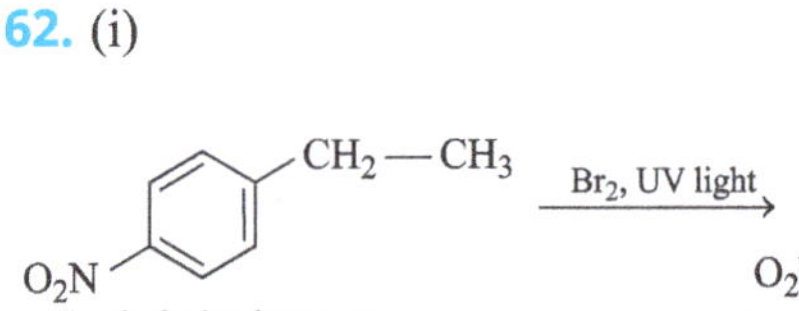

4-ethyl nitrobenzene 1-(1-bromoethyl)-4-nitrobenzene

(ii) $$2\underset{\text{2-chloropropane}}{CH_3—\underset{\substack{|\\Cl}}{C}H—CH_3} \xrightarrow[\text{Dry ether}]{\text{Na}} \underset{\text{2,3-dimethylbutane}}{CH_3—\underset{\substack{|\\CH_3}}{C}H—\underset{\substack{|\\CH_3}}{C}H—CH_3}$$

(iii) $$\underset{\text{1-bromoethane}}{CH_3—CH_2—Br} \xrightarrow{\text{AgCN}} \underset{\text{Ethyl isocyanide}}{CH_3—CH_2—N\overset{\rightarrow}{=}C} + AgBr$$

63. (i) In chlorobenzene, the lone pair of electrons present on Cl-atom are in conjugation with π-electrons of the benzene ring.

As a result, C — Cl bond acquires some double bond character while in CH_3 — Cl, bond is a pure single bond. Since, bond length of C — Cl single bond is greater than C — Cl partial double bond. Therefore, C — Cl bond in halobenzene is shorter than that in CH_3 — Cl.

(ii) Due to greater *s*-character, sp^2-hybridised carbon atom of chlorobenzene is more electronegative than a sp^3-hybridised carbon atom of cyclohexyl chloride.

Therefore, sp^2-hybridised carbon of C — Cl bond in chlorobenzene has less tendency to release electrons to Cl than a sp^3-hybrid carbon of cyclohexyl chloride. As a result, C — Cl bond in chlorobenzene is less polar than in cyclohexyl chloride.

[In other words, the magnitude of negative charge is less on Cl-atom of chlorobenzene than in cyclohexyl chloride. Further, due to delocalisation of lone pair of electrons of the Cl-atom over the benzene ring, C — Cl bond is shorter than C — Cl bond of cyclohexyl chloride.

Since, dipole moment is a product of charge and distance, therefore, chlorobenzene has lower dipole moment than cyclohexyl chloride due to lower magnitude of negative charge on the Cl-atom and shorter C — Cl distance.]

(iii) In S_N1 reactions, if the alkyl halide is optically active, the product obtained is a racemic mixture. The intermediate carbocation formed in slowest step being sp^2-hybridised is planar (achiral) species.

Therefore, the attack of the nucleophile on it, can occur from both the faces (front and back) with equal ease, forming a 50:50 mixture of two enantiomers, i.e. the products with opposite configuration. Thus, S_N1 reaction of optically active alkyl halides are accompanied by racemisation.

e.g.

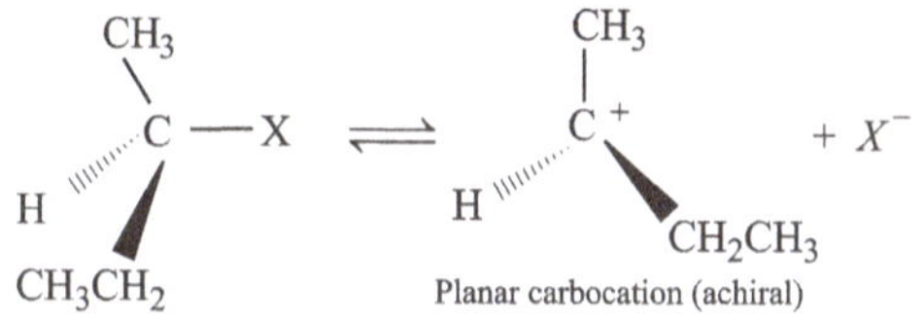

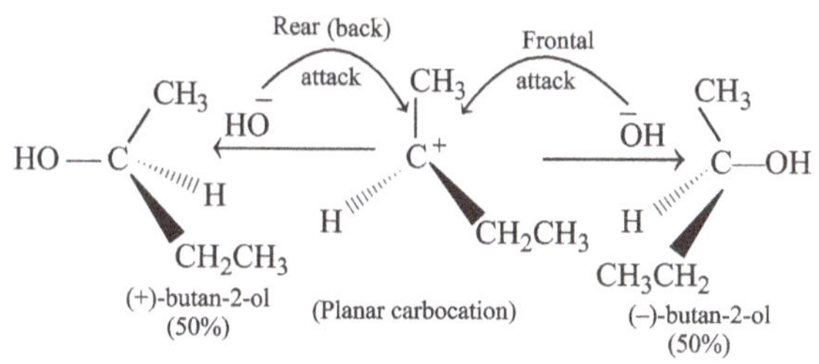

64. (i) **Aniline to bromobenzene**

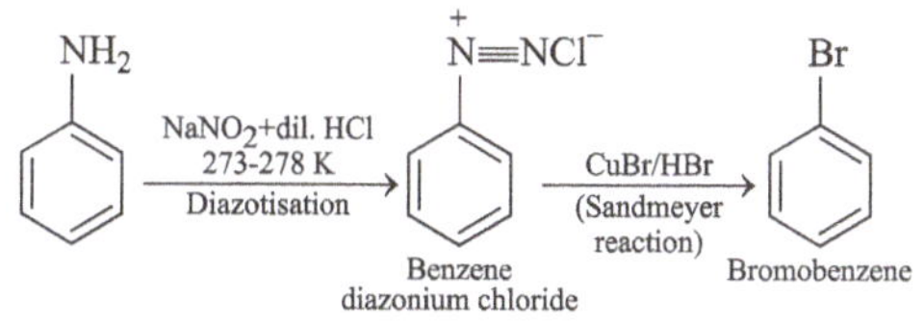

(ii) **Chlorobenzene to 2-chloroacetophenone**

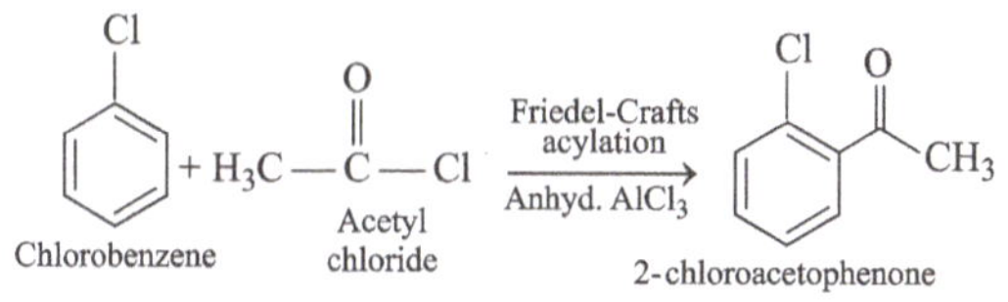

(iii) **Chloroethane to butane**

$$\underset{\text{Chloroethane}}{2\,CH_3CH_2Cl} + 2Na \xrightarrow[\text{Wurtz reaction}\ (-2NaCl)]{\text{Dry ether}} \underset{n\text{-butane}}{CH_3CH_2 — CH_2 — CH_3}$$

65. (i) When chlorobenzene is treated with $Cl_2/FeCl_3$, two types of products are formed as

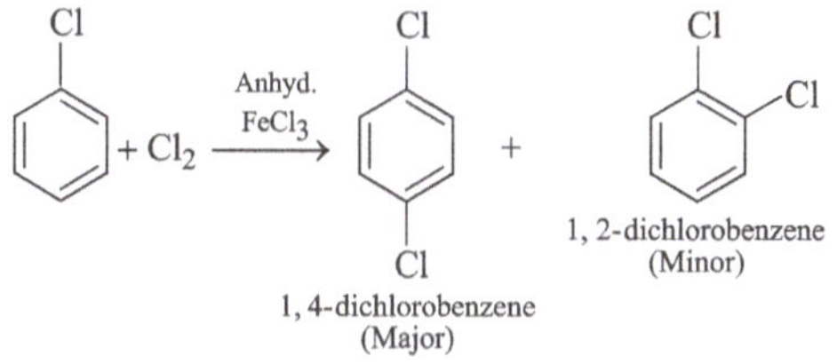

(ii) When ethyl chloride is treated with $AgNO_2$, nitroethane is formed.

$$CH_3CH_2Cl + AgNO_2 \longrightarrow CH_3CH_2NO_2 + AgCl$$

(iii) When 2-bromopentane is treated with alcoholic KOH, it undergoes dehydrohalogenation leading to the formation of two or more different products depending upon the number of different types of β-hydrogen available.

The more highly substituted alkene (i.e. having lesser number of hydrogen atoms on the doubly bonded carbon atoms) is the major product of dehydrohalogenation. This is in accordance to Saytzeff rule.

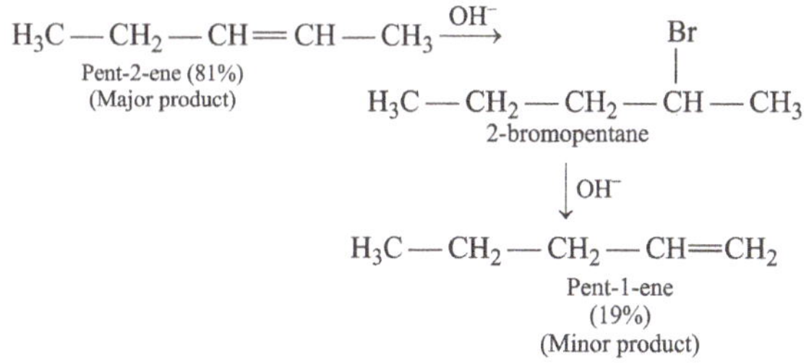

66. (i) Boiling point of a compound depends upon the surface area. Higher the surface area, higher will be the boiling point of a compound. Surface area decreases with increase in branching. If the compound has branching, its boiling point will be minimum. That's why, n-butyl bromide being (bp 375 K), a straight chain alkyl halide has higher boiling point than tertiary butyl bromide (346 K) which is a highly branched alkyl halide.

(ii) A mixture containing two enantiomers in equimolar amounts have zero optical rotation, as the rotation caused by the molecules of one isomer (enantiomer) is exactly cancelled by an equal and opposite rotation caused by the same number of molecules of other isomer (enantiomer).

Such a mixture is known as racemic mixture. Since, enantiomers have equal and opposite specific rotations, a racemic mixture exhibits no optical activity.

(iii) The reactivity of haloarenes towards nucleophilic substitution reactions can be increased by the presence of an electron withdrawing group ($—NO_2$) at *ortho* and *para*-positions. This is because NO_2 groups at *ortho* and *para*-positions withdraw electron density from the benzene ring and thus, facilitates the nucleophilic attack on haloarenes.

The mechanism can be shown as:

Attack at *p*-position

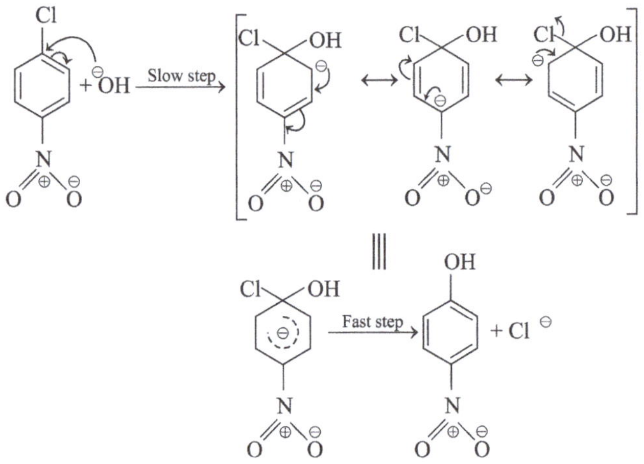

Attack at *o*-position

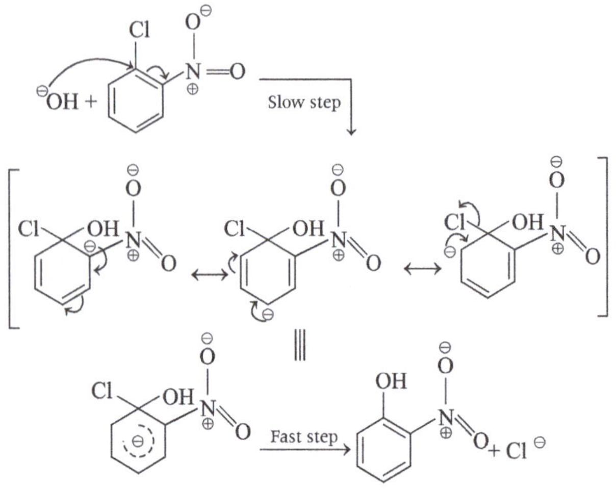

From the above resonating structures, it is very clear that electron density is rich at *ortho* and *para*-positions. So, presence of EWG will facilitate nucleophilic attack at *ortho* and *para*-positions.

67. (i) Iodide ion is a better leaving group because of its larger size than bromide ion, therefore ethyl iodide undergoes S_N2 reaction faster than ethyl bromide.

(ii) (±) 2-butanol is a racemic mixture. It is a mixture which contains two enantiomers in equal proportion and thus, have zero optical rotation. Therefore, it is optically inactive.

(iii) Refer to sol. 63 (i).

68. (i) An object or molecule which is non-superimposable on its mirror image is called chiral and the property of being chiral is known as chirality. e.g. Lactic acid, $CH_3CH(OH)COOH$

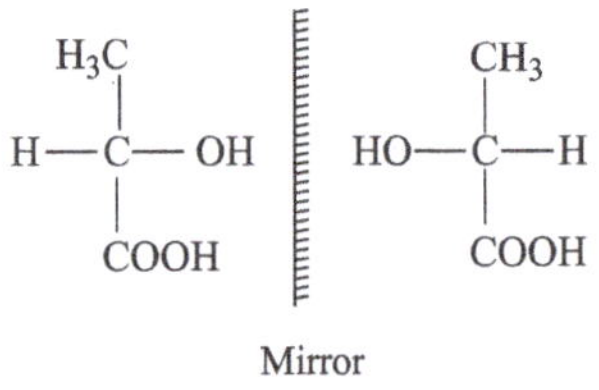

(ii) $CH_3—CH(Cl)—CH_2CH_3$ is more easily hydrolysed by KOH because this hydrolysis occurs through S_N1 mechanism and this alkyl halide forms a more stable 2° carbocation than $CH_3—CH_2—CH_2—CH_2Cl$ which forms a less stable 1° carbocation.

(iii) Refer to solution 54 (ii).

69. (i) Haloalkanes easily dissolve in organic solvents because both are covalent in nature (like dissolves like).

Also, the steric effect in haloalkanes is not more as seen in the case of haloarenes.

(ii) The antiseptic properties of iodoform is due to free I_2, which is liberated when iodoform comes in contact with skin.

$$4CHI_3 + 5O_2 \xrightarrow[\text{Air, }\Delta]{\text{Moisture}} 6I_2 + 4CO_2 + 2H_2O$$

(iii) The carbocation intermediate from $(C_6H_5)CH(C_6H_5)Br$ is more stable because it is stabilised by two phenyl groups due to resonance, so $(C_6H_5)CH(C_6H_5)Br$ is more reactive towards S_N1 reaction.

70. (i) 1-bromopentane > 2-bromopentane > 2- bromo-2-methylbutane

(ii) 1-bromo-3-methylbutane > 3-bromo-2-methylbutane > 2-bromo-2-methylbutane

(iii) 1-bromobutane > 1-bromo-3-methylbutane > 1-bromo-2-methylbutane > 1-bromo-2, 2 dimethylpropane

71. (i) (a) Benzyl chloride when treated with $AgNO_3$ solution, will give a white ppt. while chlorobenzene will not.

(b) Chloroform when treated with 1° amine and KOH, gives offensive smelling isocyanides while CCl_4 does not give this test.

(ii) Chlorobenzene is stabilised by resonance so, has a double bond character between C and Cl. Secondly, C is sp^2-hybridised so, more electronegative, thus Cl^- is not replaced easily.

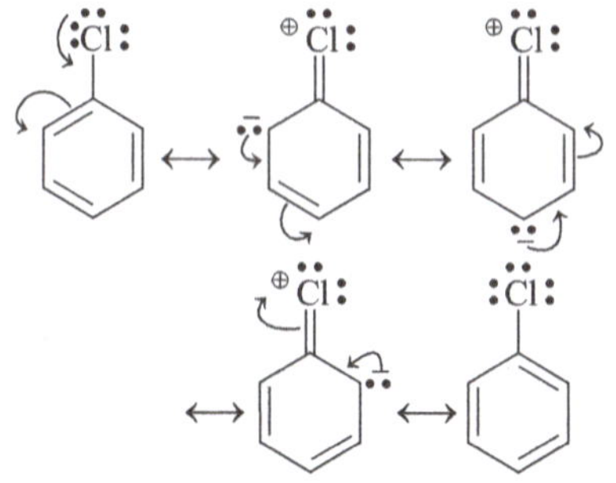

While in methyl chloride, C— Cl has a single bond character which can be cleaved easily and hence, it is hydrolysed more easily than chlorobenzene.

72. (i) DDT is used as an insecticide and iodoform is used as a mild antiseptic.

(ii) Reactivity of S_N2 reactions depends on steric hindrance. Therefore,

(a) 1-bromopentane will react faster because it is a primary alkyl halide and hence, less sterically hindered.

(b) 1-bromo-2-methyl butane, as it is a primary alkyl halide and less sterically hindered.

73. In S_N1 mechanism of substitution reaction, the rate of reaction depends upon the concentration of only one reactant, e.g. in the reaction between *tert*-butyl bromide and hydroxide ion to form *tert*-butyl alcohol, rate of reaction depends only on the concentration of *tert*-butyl bromide.

$$(CH_3)_3C—Br + OH^- \longrightarrow (CH_3)_3C—OH + Br^-$$

It involves the formation of carbocation intermediate and racemisation.

In S_N2 mechanism of substitution reaction, the rate of reaction depends upon the concentration of both the reactants. e.g. In the reaction between methyl chloride and hydroxide ion to form methanol, rate of reaction depends on the concentration of both the reactants.

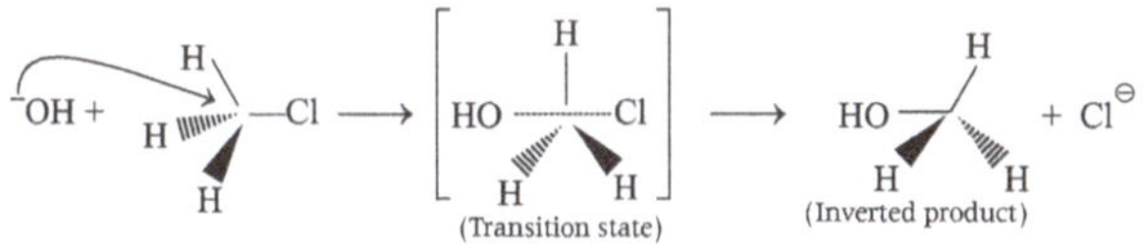

It involves the formation of transition state and inversion (Walden inversion) of configuration.

CHAPTER TEST

01 Marks Questions

1. Fill in the blanks by choosing the appropriate word(s) from those given in the brackets.

[higher, aromatic, dipole-dipole, light, aryl, aqueous KOH, substitution, phosgene, aliphatic, dark, carbon monoxide, lower, alc. KOH]

(i) The replacement of hydrogen atom(s) in .... hydrocarbon by halogen atom(s) results in the formation of .... halide.

(ii) Chloroform is stored away from .... and air to avoid the formation of ....

(iii) The boiling point of an alkyl halide is .... than that of the corresponding alkane because of .... interactions.

(iv) The alkyl halide is converted into an alcohol by .... in the presence of ....

2. Select and write the correct alternatives from the choices given below.

(i) Which of the following molecule most easily hydrolysed under S_N1 conditions?

(a) Benzyl chloride (b) Allyl chloride
(c) Ethyl chloride (d) Ethylidene chloride

(ii) Predict the main product in

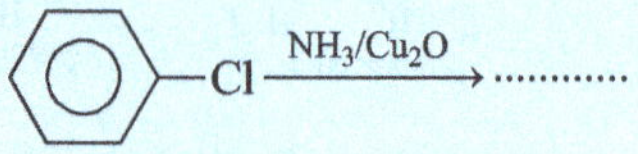

(a) phenyl cyanide
(b) aniline
(c) hydroxylamine
(d) nitrophenol

(iii) Which is the correct increasing order of boiling points of the following compounds?
1-bromoethane, 1-bromopropane, 1-bromobutane, bromobenzene

(a) Bromobenzene < 1-bromobutane < 1-bromopropane < 1-bromoethane
(b) Bromobenzene < 1-bromoethane < 1-bromopropane < 1-bromobutane
(c) 1-bromopropane < 1-bromobutane < 1-bromoethane < bromobenzene
(d) 1-bromoethane < 1-bromopropane < 1-bromobutane < bromobenzene

(iv) Which of the following reaction(s) is not given by haloalkanes?

(a) Nucleophilic substitution reactions
(b) Elimination reaction
(c) Reaction with metals
(d) Addition reactions

3. (i) **Assertion** (A) CH_4 does not react with Cl_2 in dark.
Reason (R) Chlorination of CH_4 takes place in sunlight.

(a) Both (A) and (R) are correct and (R) is the correct explanation of (A).
(b) Both (A) and (R) are correct but (R) is not the correct explanation of (A).
(c) (A) is correct but (R) is incorrect.
(d) (A) is incorrect but (R) is correct.

(ii) **Assertion** (A) Chlorine is an *ortho-para* directing group in electrophilic aromatic substitution reaction.
Reason (R) Chlorine is an electron withdrawing group.

(a) Both (A) and (R) are correct and (R) is the correct explanation of (A).
(b) Both (A) and (R) are correct but (R) is not the correct explanation of (A).
(c) (A) is correct but (R) is incorrect.
(d) (A) is incorrect but (R) is correct.

02 Marks Questions

4. Draw the structures of the following organic halogen compounds.

(i) 4-*tert*-butyl-3- iodoheptane
(ii) 1, 4-dibromobut-2- ene

5. What happens when

(i) chlorobenzene is treated with $Cl_2/FeCl_3$?
(ii) 2-bromopentane is treated with alcoholic KOH ?

6. State one use of chloroform and carbon tetrachloride.

7. Answer the following questions.

(i) What is meant by chirality of a compound ?
(ii) Haloalkanes easily dissolve in organic solvents. Why?

8. Give reasons.

(i) Why are alkyl halides insoluble in water?

(ii) Ethyl iodide undergoes S_N2 reaction faster than ethyl bromide.

9. Write the IUPAC names of the following compounds :

(i) $CH_3—\underset{\underset{Cl}{|}}{CH}—CH_2—CH=CH_2$

(ii) $CH_2=CH\,CH_2Br$

10. Draw the structure of major monohalo products in each of the following reactions.

(i) 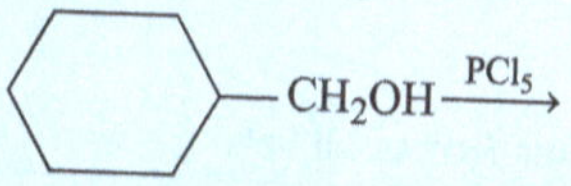

(ii) 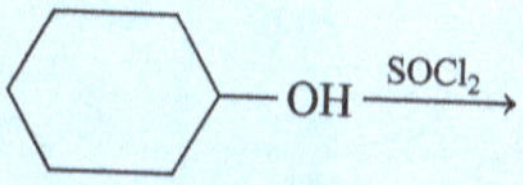

03 Marks Questions

11. How can the following conversions be carried out ?

(i) Chloroethane to butane

(ii) 2-bromobutane to but-2-ene

(iii) Chlorobenzene to biphenyl

12. Give reasons.

(i) Thionyl chloride method is preferred for preparing alkyl chloride from alcohols.

(ii) Ethyl iodide undergoes S_N2 reaction faster than ethyl bromide.

(iii) The dipole moment of chlorobenzene is lower than that of cyclohexyl chloride.

13. Answer the following questions.

(i) Write the mechanism of the following reaction.

$$CH_3CH_2OH \xrightarrow{HBr} CH_3CH_2Br + H_2O$$

(ii) Draw the structure of 2, 4-dinitrochlorobenzene.

14. Complete the following reactions.

(i) $CH_3CH_2CH=CH_2 + HBr \longrightarrow$

(i) $CH_3—Cl + KCN \longrightarrow$

(iii) $C_6H_5(Cl)COONa + NaOH \xrightarrow{Sodalime}$

15. Write the physical properties of chloroform.

05 Marks Questions

16. (i) Name of the following polyhalogen compounds.

(a) Compound that acts as fire extinguisher.

(b) Compound that acts as a propellant in aerosols.

(c) Compound that is used in the preparation of chloropicrin.

(ii) Write one use for each of the following.

(a) DDT

(b) Iodoform

17. (i) How can the following conversions be carried out?

(a) Aniline to bromobenzene

(b) Chlorobenzene to 2-chlorocetophenone

(c) Propene to 1-iodopropane

(ii) Identify the chiral molecule in the following pair and write their IUPAC name.

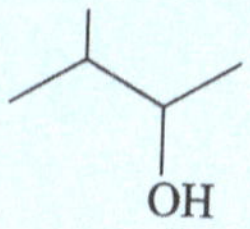
(I)

and

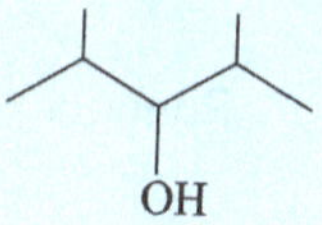
(II)

18. (i) Account for the following.

(a) Use of DDT was banned in United States in 1973.

(b) Alkyl halides prefer to undergo dehydrohalogenation in the presence of a strong base such as Na metal, instead of undergoing Wurtz reaction.

(c) Allyl chloride is more reactive than the *n*- propyl chloride towards nucleophilic substitution reaction. Explain why?

(ii) Why happens, when

(a) ethyl chloride is treated with aqueous KCN?

(b) chlorobenzene is subjected to hydrolysis?

Answers

1. (i) Aromatic/aryl (ii) Light/phosgene (iii) Higher/dipole-dipole
(iv) Substitution/aq. KOH

2. (i) (b), (ii) (b), (iii) (d), (iv) (d)

3. (i) (b), (ii) (c)

07

Alcohols, Phenols and Ethers

TREND ANALYSIS 4 YEARS

Topic	Types of Questions	2024	2023	2020	2019
		Average No. of Questions Across all Sets			
TOPIC 01 Alcohols	1 Mark	1	1	—	2
	2 Marks	1	—	2	—
	3 Marks	1	—	—	—
	5 Marks	—	—	—	—
TOPIC 02 Phenols	1 Mark	—	—	2	—
	2 Marks	2	—	—	—
	3 Marks	1	—	—	—
	5 Marks	—	—	—	—
TOPIC 03 Ethers	1 Mark	—	—	—	—
	2 Marks	1	1	2	—
	3 Marks	—	1	—	—
	5 Marks	—	—	—	—

TOPIC 1

Alcohols

Hydroxy derivatives of aliphatic hydrocarbons are called alcohols. They possess the general formula *R*—OH, where *R* is an alkyl or substituted alkyl group.

Classification of Alcohols

Depending upon the number of —OH group directly attached to carbon atom(s) of an aliphatic system alcohols are classified as monohydric, dihydric, trihydric and polyhydric alcohols.

The compounds in which —OH group is attached to an aromatic ring are called aromatic alcohols, e.g. $C_6H_5CH_2OH$. According to the hybridisation of the carbon atom to which the hydroxyl group is attached as, monohydric alcohols may be further classified.

$$—CH_2—OH \qquad >CH—OH \qquad >C—OH$$

Primary   Secondary   Tertiary

Nomenclature of Alcohols

- In the IUPAC system, alcohols are named as alkanols,
  e.g. CH_3OH : Methane − e + ol = Methanol
  CH_3CH_2OH : Ethane − e + ol = Ethanol
- Select the longest carbon chain and is numbered from the end nearest to the hydroxyl group.

- The positions of the —OH group and other substituents are indicated by using the numbers of carbon atoms to which these are attached.
- For naming polyhydric alcohols, the 'e' of the alkane is retained and the ending 'ol' is added.
- The number of —OH groups is indicated by adding the multiplicative prefix, di, tri, etc.

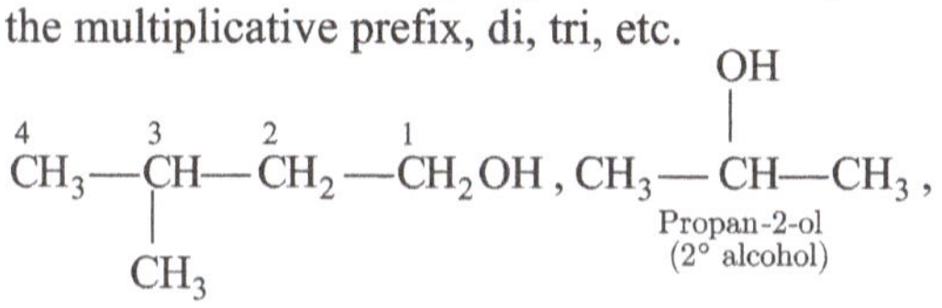

3-methylbutan-1-ol (1° alcohol)

Propan-2-ol (2° alcohol)

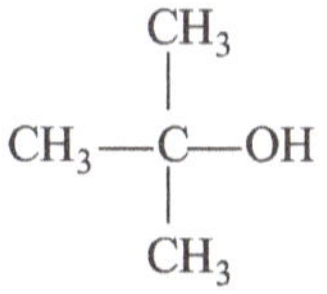

2-methylpropan-2-ol (3° alcohol)

Cyclic alcohols are named using the prefix cyclo and considering the —OH group attached to C-1.

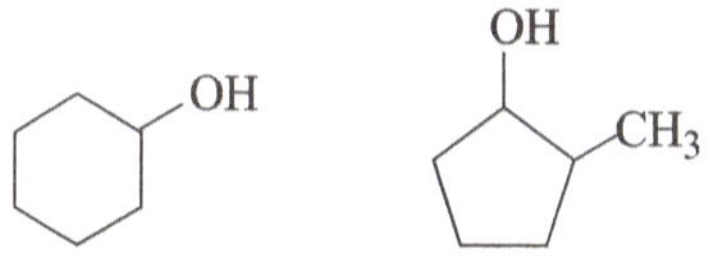

Cyclohexanol 2-Methylcyclopentanol

Structure of Alcohols

In alcohols, the oxygen of the —OH group is attached to carbon by sigma (σ) bond.

This bond is formed by the overlap of a sp^3-hybridised orbital of carbon with a sp^3-hybridised orbital of oxygen.

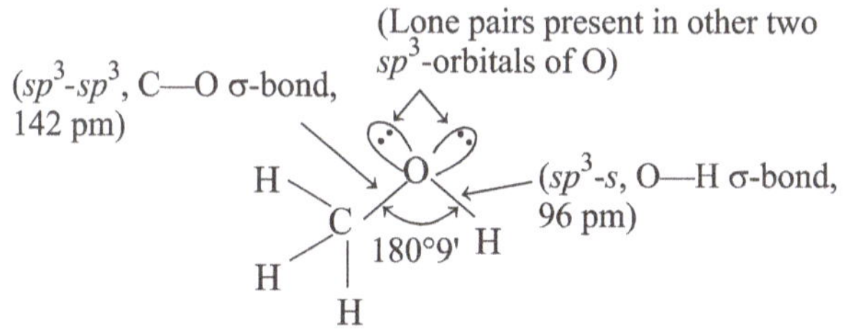

The C–Ö–H bond angle in alcohols is slightly less than the tetrahedral angle (109°28′). It is due to the repulsion between the unshared electron pairs of oxygen.

Isomerism in Alcohols

Alcohols show four types of isomerism. These are as follows

(i) Chain isomerism (ii) Position isomerism
(iii) Functional isomerism (iv) Optical isomerism

Methods of Preparation

These are prepared by following methods

(i) **Hydrolysis of alkylhalide**

$$\underset{\text{Haloalkane}}{R—X} + KOH(aq) \longrightarrow \underset{\text{Alcohol}}{R—OH} + KX$$

(ii) **Reduction of aldehyde and ketones**

$$RCHO + H_2 \xrightarrow{Pd} RCH_2OH$$

$$RCOR' \xrightarrow{NaBH_4} R—\underset{\underset{OH}{|}}{CH}—R'$$

(iii) **Reduction of carboxylic acids**

$$RCOOH \xrightarrow[H_2O]{LiAlH_4} RCH_2OH$$

$$RCOOH \xrightarrow[H^+]{ROH} RCOOR' \xrightarrow[\text{Catalyst}]{H_2} RCH_2OH + R'OH$$

(iv) **From Grignard reagent** Alcohols can also be prepared by the use of Grignard's reagent, such as

(a) $HCHO + RMgX \longrightarrow RCH_2\overset{-}{O}\overset{+}{Mg}X \xrightarrow{H_2O} \underset{(1°\text{ alcohol})}{RCH_2OH + Mg(OH)X}$

(b) $RCHO + R'MgX \xrightarrow{H_2O} R—\overset{\overset{R'}{|}}{CH}—OMgX \xrightarrow{H_2O} \underset{(2°\text{ alcohol})}{R—\overset{\overset{R'}{|}}{CH}—OH + Mg(OH)X}$

(c) $RCOR + R'MgX \longrightarrow R—\overset{\overset{R'}{|}}{\underset{\underset{R}{|}}{C}}—OMgX \xrightarrow{H_2O} \underset{(3°\text{ alcohol})}{R—\overset{\overset{R'}{|}}{\underset{\underset{R}{|}}{C}}—OH + Mg(OH)X}$

(v) **Hydration of alkenes**

$$>C=C< + H_2O \underset{}{\overset{H^+}{\rightleftharpoons}} >\underset{H}{C}-\underset{OH}{C}<$$

In case of unsymmetrical alkenes, the addition reaction takes place in accordance with Markownikoff's rule.

(vi) Alcohols can also be prepared by

(a) **Oxymercuration-reduction process**

$$\underset{\text{Prop-1-ene}}{CH_3-CH=CH_2} \xrightarrow[\text{THF}/H_2O \text{ (Oxymercuration)}]{(CH_3COO)_2Hg}$$

$$CH_3-\underset{OH}{CH}-CH_2HgOOCCH_3 \xrightarrow[\text{Reduction}]{NaBH_4/OH^-} \underset{\text{Propan-2-ol}}{CH_3-\underset{OH}{CH}-CH_3}$$

(b) **Hydroboration-oxidation process** .

$$3CH_3-CH=CH_2 \xrightarrow[\text{Ether (Hydroboration)}]{H-BH_2(B_2H_6)}$$

$$(CH_3-CH_2-CH_2)_3B \xrightarrow[\text{(Oxidation)}]{OH^-/H_2O_2} \underset{\text{Propan-1-ol}}{3CH_3CH_2CH_2OH} + H_3BO_3$$

The addition of borane to the double bond takes place in such a manner that the boron atom gets attached to the sp^2 carbon carrying greater number of hydrogen atoms.

The alcohol so formed looks as if it has been formed by the addition of water to the alkene in a way opposite to the Markownikoff's rule.

(vii) **From aliphatic primary amines**

$$NaNO_2 + HCl \xrightarrow{0\text{-}3^\circ C} \underset{\text{Nitrous acid}}{HNO_2} + NaCl$$

$$R-NH_2 + HNO_2 \xrightarrow{0\text{-}3^\circ C} R-OH + N_2\uparrow + H_2O$$

But this is not a good method for the preparation of 1° alcohols because a mixture of alkenes, alkyl halides aldehydes are also produced along with alcohols, e.g. methylamine gives ether and methylnitrite.

Physical Properties of Alcohols

- In general alcohols are colourless, volatile toxic liquids having characteristic alcoholic odour and burning taste.
- Alcohols are polar in nature and capable of forming intermolecular hydrogen bonding.
- Alcohols are soluble in water. The solubility of alcohols in water decreases with increase in molecular mass.
- The boiling point of alcohols are considerably higher than those of corresponding hydrocarbons, haloalkanes, ethers, etc., due to strong hydrogen bonding between their molecules.
- The boiling points of isomeric alcohols follow the order 1°> 2°> 3°.

Chemical Properties of Alcohols

Alcohols react with both electrophiles and nucleophiles.

(i) **Acidic behaviour** Alcohols behave as weak acids and ionise to a very small extent. Acidic strength of alcohols is even less than that of water.

Relative acidic strength of alcohols : 1°> 2°> 3°

The acidic character of alcohols is due to the polar nature of O — H bond.

An electron-releasing group ($-CH_3, -C_2H_5$) increases electron density on oxygen, tending to decrease the polarity of O — H bond. This effect decreases the acid strength.

(ii) **Reaction with active metals**

$$2R-OH + 2Na \longrightarrow \underset{\text{Sodium alkoxide}}{2R\overset{-}{O}\overset{+}{Na}} + H_2\uparrow$$

(iii) **Reaction with metal hydrides**

$$CH_3OH + NaH \longrightarrow CH_3\overset{-}{O}\overset{+}{Na} + H_2\uparrow$$

(iv) **Reaction with Grignard's reagent**

$$\underset{\text{Alcohol}}{R-O-H} + \underset{\text{Grignard's reagent}}{R'-Mg-X} \longrightarrow \underset{\text{Alkane}}{R'-H} + \underset{\text{Alkoxy magnesium halide}}{Mg\begin{matrix}OR\\X\end{matrix}}$$

(v) **Reaction with carboxylic acid** (Esterification)

$$\underset{\text{Acid}}{R-\overset{O}{\overset{\|}{C}}-OH} + \underset{\text{Alcohol}}{HOR'} \underset{H_2SO_4}{\overset{\text{Conc.}}{\rightleftharpoons}} \underset{\text{Ester}}{R-\overset{O}{\overset{\|}{C}}-OR'} + H_2O$$

Mechanism

The reaction is said to proceed through **"nucleophilic addition elimination"** and gives best result in the presence of mineral acids.

The nucleophilic addition-elimination pathway with acid catalysed condition for esterification can be said to proceed as follows

***Step* I** Initially the H^+ of mineral acid attacks on O-atom of carbonyl part of —COOH group.

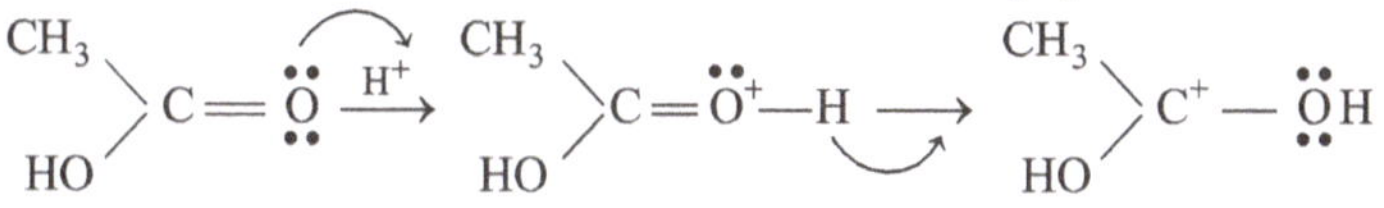

***Step* II** Now, the oxygen of alcohol donates its lone pair to positively charged C-atom of carbonium ion as

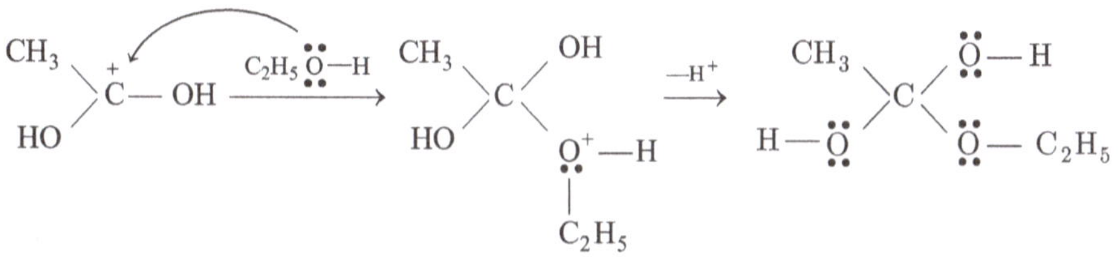

***Step* III** The H^+ liberated in step II attacks on the oxygen of —OH group, taking the lone pair from it, thus

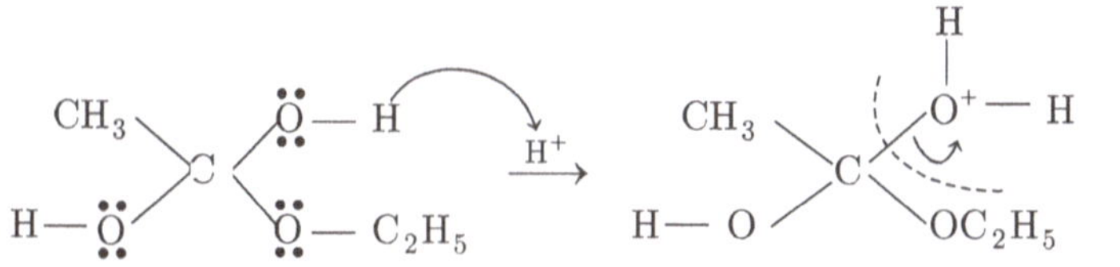

This results in liberation of water molecule and formation of another carbonium ion as

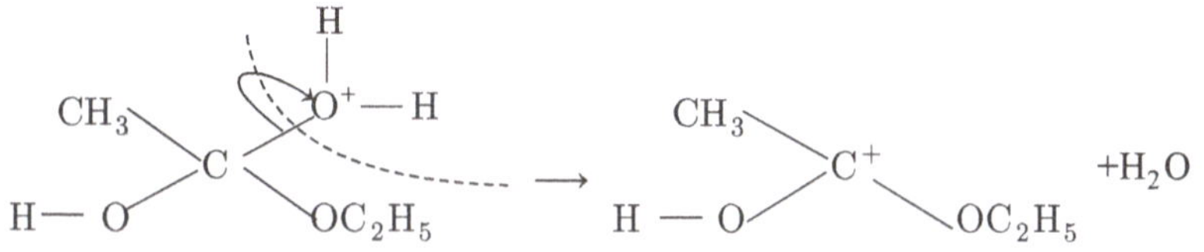

This carbonium ion stabilises itself as

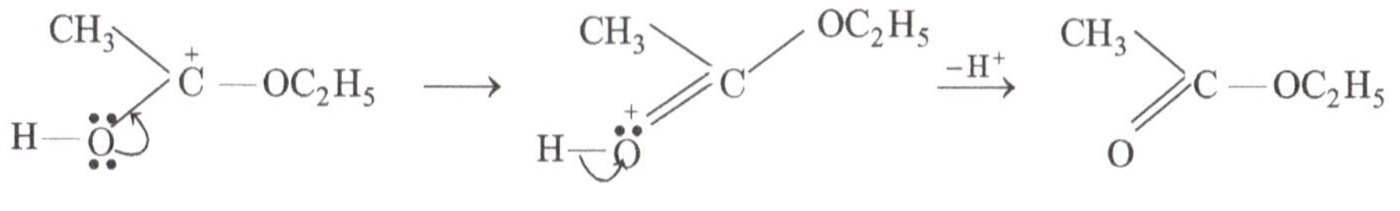

(vi) **Reaction with acid chlorides and acid anhydrides** (Acylation)

$$\underset{\text{Acid chloride}}{R-\overset{\overset{\displaystyle O}{\|}}{C}-Cl} + \underset{\text{Alcohol}}{H-O-R'} \xrightarrow[\text{base}]{\text{Pyridine}} \underset{\text{Ester}}{R-\overset{\overset{\displaystyle O}{\|}}{C}-O-R'} + HCl$$

$$\underset{\text{Acid anhydride}}{R-\overset{\overset{\displaystyle O}{\|}}{C}-O-\overset{\overset{\displaystyle O}{\|}}{C}-R} + \underset{\text{Alcohol}}{H-O-R'} \xrightarrow{\text{Pyridine}} \underset{\text{Ester}}{R-\overset{\overset{\displaystyle O}{\|}}{C}-O-R'} + \underset{\text{Acid}}{R-\overset{\overset{\displaystyle O}{\|}}{C}-OH}$$

(vii) **Reaction with hydrogen halides**

$$R-OH + HX \longrightarrow \underset{\text{Haloalkane}}{R-X} + H_2O$$

(viii) **Reaction with phosphorus halides**

$$CH_3CH_2OH + PCl_5 \longrightarrow \underset{\text{Chloroethane}}{CH_3CH_2Cl} + \underset{\text{Phosphorus oxychloride}}{POCl_3} + HCl\downarrow$$

$$3CH_3CH_2OH + PCl_3 \longrightarrow \underset{\text{Chloroethane}}{3CH_3CH_2Cl} + \underset{\text{Phosphorus acid}}{H_3PO_3}$$

(ix) **Reaction with thionyl chloride**

$$R{-}OH + \underset{\text{Thionyl chloride}}{SOCl_2} \xrightarrow{\text{Pyridine}} \underset{\text{Chloroalkane}}{R{-}Cl} + SO_2\uparrow + HCl\uparrow$$

(x) **Reaction with NH_3**

$$CH_3{-}OH + HNH_2 \xrightarrow[633\text{ K}]{Al_2O_3} \underset{(1^\circ\text{amine})}{CH_3NH_2} + H_2O$$

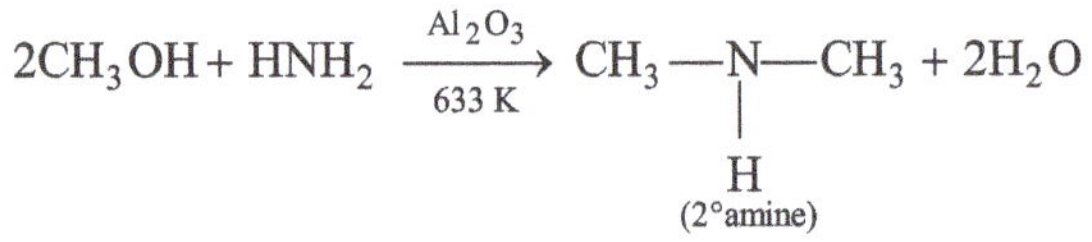

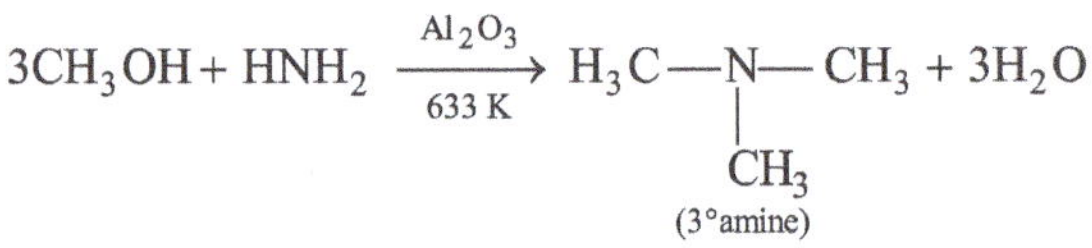

Note The order of reactivity of different types of alcohols in the reaction involving cleavage of C— OH bond is 3° > 2° > 1°.

(xi) **Dehydration**

$$CH_3{-}CH_2{-}OH \xrightarrow[433\text{ K}]{\text{Conc. }H_2SO_4} \underset{\text{Ethene}}{CH_2{=}CH_2} + H_2O$$

$$2CH_3CH_2OH \xrightarrow[413\text{ K}]{\text{Conc. }H_2SO_4} \underset{\text{Diethyl ether}}{CH_3{-}CH_2{-}O{-}CH_2{-}CH_3} + H_2O$$

The ease of dehydration of alcohols is in the order of

3° > 2° > 1°

Mechanism of dehydration of alcohols to alkenes

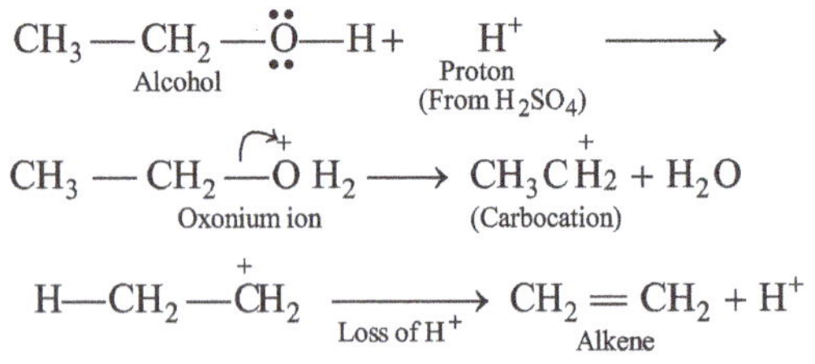

Mechanism of dehydration of alcohols to ethers

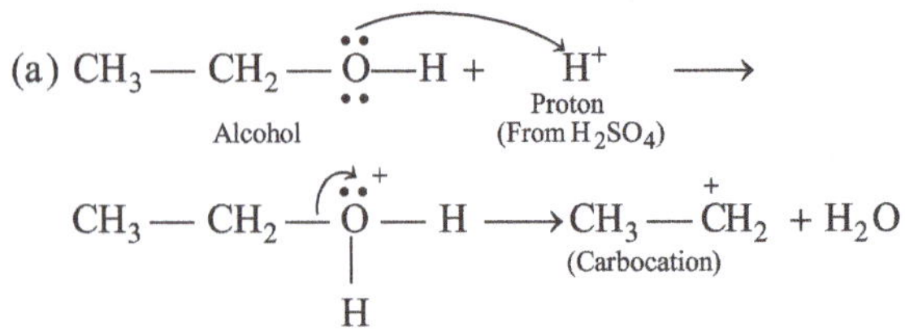

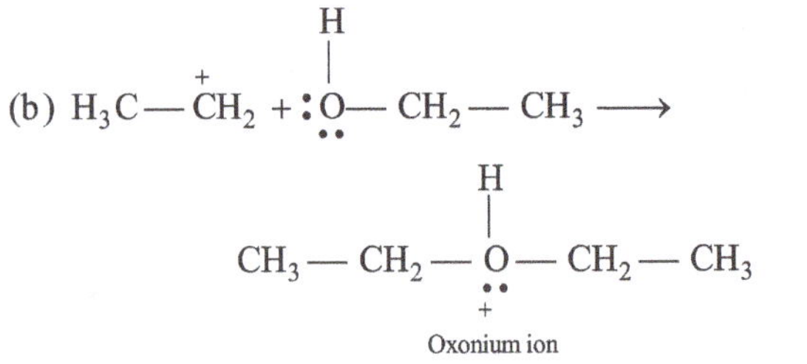

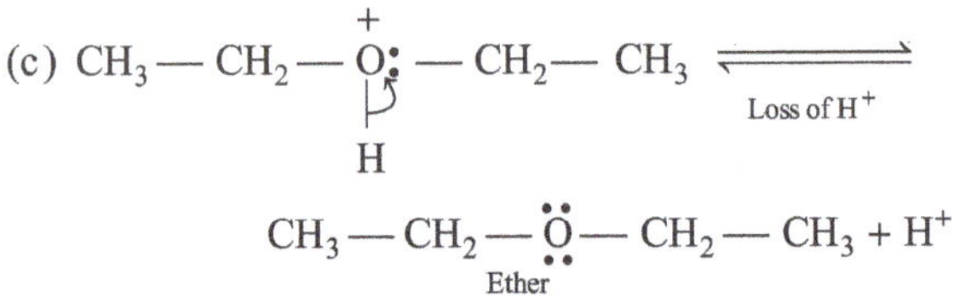

(xii) **Oxidation**

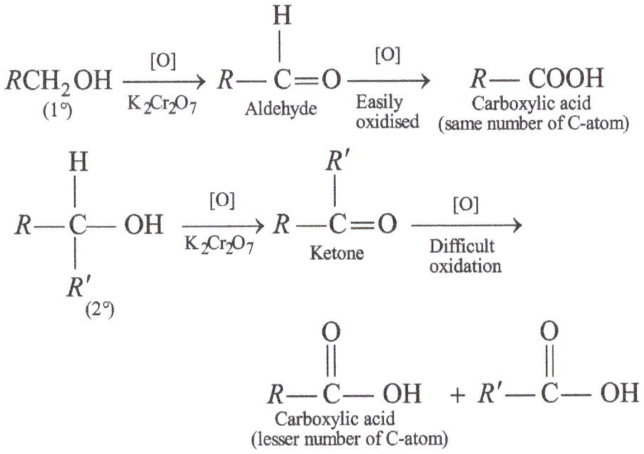

Tertiary alcohols, when subjected to vigorous oxidation with nitric acid give ketone containing lesser number of carbon atoms.

e.g.

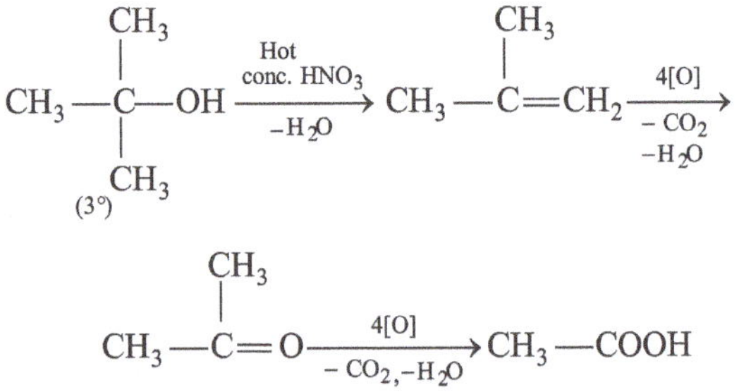

(xiii) **Reaction with copper** When vapours of alcohols are passed over heated copper at 573 K, primary and secondary alcohols undergo dehydrogenation to give aldehydes and ketones respectively while tertiary alcohols undergo dehydration to give alkenes.

e.g. $$\underset{(1^\circ)}{CH_3{-}CH_2OH} \xrightarrow[573\text{ K}]{Cu} \underset{\text{Aldehyde}}{CH_3{-}CHO} + H_2\uparrow$$

$$\underset{(2^\circ)}{(CH_3)_2\text{—}CHOH} \xrightarrow[573\text{ K}]{Cu} \underset{\text{Ketone}}{CH_3\text{—}C(CH_3){=}O} + H_2\uparrow$$

$$\underset{(3^\circ)}{CH_3\text{—}C(CH_3)_2\text{—}OH} \xrightarrow[573\text{ K}]{Cu} \underset{\text{Alkene}}{CH_3\text{—}C(CH_3){=}CH_2} + H_2O$$

Distinction Tests between Primary, Secondary and Tertiary Alcohols

There are two major test to distinguish between primary, secondary and tertiary alcohols.

These are as follows

(i) **Lucas test** A small quantity of unknown alcohol is added to Lucas reagent (anhyd. $ZnCl_2$ + conc. HCl) at room temperature and the mixture is shaken.

$$R_3COH \xrightarrow[\text{Anhyd. }ZnCl_2]{\text{Conc. HCl +}} \underset{\text{Turbidity appears immediately}}{R_3CCl} + H_2O$$

$$R_2CHOH \xrightarrow[\text{Anhyd. }ZnCl_2]{\text{Conc. HCl +}} \underset{\text{Turbidity appears in 5 min}}{R_2CHCl}$$

$$R\,CH_2OH \xrightarrow[\text{Anhyd. }ZnCl_2]{\text{Conc. HCl +}} \text{No reaction}$$

(ii) **Victor Meyer's test** The given alcohol is treated with red phosphorus and iodine to convert it into the corresponding alkyl iodide which is then further treated with $AgNO_2$ to form nitroalkane, which is finally treated with nitrous acid and the resulting solution is made alkaline.

Following observation takes place

Primary (1°) alcohol	Secondary (2°) alcohol	Tertiary (3°) alcohol
CH_3CH_2OH	$(CH_3)_2CHOH$	$(CH_3)_3COH$
↓ P/I_2	↓ P/I_2	↓ P/I_2
CH_3CH_2I	$(CH_3)_2CH\text{—}I$	$(CH_3)_3C\text{—}I$
↓ $AgNO_2$	↓ $AgNO_2$	↓ $AgNO_2$
$CH_3CH_2NO_2$	$(CH_3)_2CHNO_2$	$(CH_3)_3C\text{—}NO_2$
↓ HNO_2	↓ HNO_2	↓ HNO_2
$R\text{—}C(NO_2){=}N\text{—}OH$ (Nitrolic acid)	$(CH_3)_2C(NO_2)\text{—}N{=}O$	(No reaction) No colour
↓ NaOH	↓ NaOH	
Blood red colouration	Blue colouration	

Conversion of Alcohols

Some important conversions are as follows

(i) **Conversion of a lower alcohol into a higher alcohol**

$$\underset{\text{Lower alcohol}}{R\text{—}OH} \xrightarrow[-H_2O]{HI} RI \xrightarrow[-KI]{KCN} RCN \xrightarrow[\text{Reduction}]{4[H]} RCH_2NH_2 \xrightarrow{HNO_2} \underset{\text{Higher alcohol}}{RCH_2OH}$$

(ii) **Conversion of higher alcohol into a lower alcohol**

$$\underset{\text{Higher alcohol}}{RCH_2OH} \xrightarrow[K_2Cr_2O_7]{[O]} RCHO \xrightarrow{[O]} RCOOH \xrightarrow{NaOH}$$

$$R\overset{-\;+}{COONa} \xrightarrow[\text{Heat}]{NaOH + CaO} Na_2CO_3 + RH \xrightarrow{Cl_2} R\text{—}Cl \xrightarrow{Aq.\ KOH} \underset{\text{Lower alcohol}}{R\text{—}OH} + Na_2CO_3$$

(iii) **Conversion of primary alcohol to a secondary alcohol**

$$\underset{1^\circ\text{alcohol}}{R\text{—}CH_2\text{—}CH_2\text{—}OH} \xrightarrow{SOCl_2}$$

$$RCH_2CH_2Cl \xrightarrow{\text{KOH (alc.)}} RCH{=}CH_2 \xrightarrow{HBr} R\text{—}CH(Br)\text{—}CH_3 \xrightarrow{Aq.\ KOH} \underset{2^\circ\text{ alcohol}}{R\text{—}CH(OH)\text{—}CH_3}$$

(iv) **Conversion of secondary alcohol to a tertiary alcohol**

$$\underset{2^\circ\text{ alcohol}}{R_1\text{—}C(H)(R_2)\text{—}OH} \xrightarrow[K_2Cr_2O_7]{[O]} R_1\text{—}C(R_2){=}O \xrightarrow{R_3MgBr}$$

$$R_1\text{—}C(R_3)(R_2)\text{—}OMgBr \xrightarrow[-MgBr(OH)]{H_2O} \underset{3^\circ\text{ alcohol}}{R_1\text{—}C(R_3)(R_2)\text{—}OH}$$

(v) **Conversion of primary alcohol to a tertiary alcohol**

$$\underset{1^\circ\text{ alcohol}}{R\text{—}CH_2\text{—}CH_2OH} \xrightarrow[433\text{ K}]{\text{Conc. }H_2SO_4} R\text{—}CH{=}CH_2$$

$$\xrightarrow{HBr} R\text{—}CH(Br)\text{—}CH_3 \xrightarrow[-KBr]{Aq.\ KOH}$$

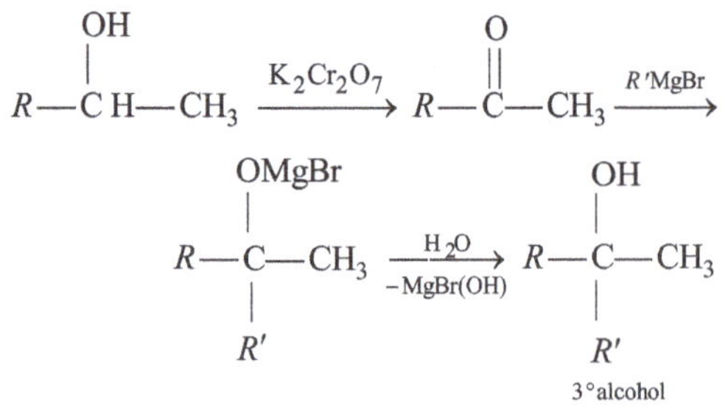

Some Commercially Important Alcohols

These are as follows

Methanol (CH_3OH)

It is also known as '**wood spirit**', as it was produced by the destructive distillation of wood.

Now-a-days, methanol is produced by **Bosch process**.

$$CO + 2H_2 \xrightarrow[\substack{200-300\text{ atm} \\ 575-673\text{ K}}]{ZnO-Cr_2O_3} \underset{\text{Methyl alcohol or Methanol}}{CH_3-OH}$$

Ethanol (C_2H_5OH)

It is obtained commercially by the fermentation of sugar present in molasses, sugarcane or fruits like grapes.

$$\underset{\text{Sucrose}}{C_{12}H_{22}O_{11}} + H_2O \xrightarrow{\text{Invertase}} \underset{\text{Glucose}}{C_6H_{12}O_6} + \underset{\text{Fructose}}{C_6H_{12}O_6}$$

$$\underset{\text{Glucose or Fructose}}{C_6H_{12}O_6} \xrightarrow{\text{Zymase}} \underset{\text{Ethanol}}{2C_2H_5OH} + 2CO_2\uparrow$$

PYQs Previous Years' Questions

1 Mark Questions

1. The dehydration of ethyl alcohol with conc. H_2SO_4 at 140°C mainly yields .... while at 170°C the main product formed is .... **ISC 2024**

2. In case of alcohols, as the carbon chain length increases, the boiling point .... and the solubility in water .... **ISC Specimen 2024**

3. The primary alcohols are easily oxidised first into ...... and then into .... **ISC 2023**

4. Haloform reaction does not take place with which of the following compounds? **ISC Specimen 2021-22 (Sem-I)**
   (a) Propanone (b) 2-propanol
   (c) Ethanol (d) Methanol

5. Reaction between acetone and methyl magnesium chloride, followed by hydrolysis will give **ISC Specimen 2021-22 (Sem-I)**
   (a) *tert*-butyl alcohol (b) *iso*-butyl alcohol
   (c) *iso*-propyl alcohol (d) *sec*-butyl alcohol

6. A liquid is mixed with ethanol and few drops of conc. H_2SO_4 is added. A compound with a fruity smell is formed. The liquid is **ISC Specimen 2021-22 (Sem-I)**
   (a) HCHO (b) CH_3CHO
   (c) CH_3COOH (d) CH_3COCH_3

7. A mixture of conc. HCl and anhydrous $ZnCl_2$ is called ... which shows maximum reactivity with ..... alcohol. **ISC 2019**

8. How will you obtain the following? (Give balanced chemical equations) **ISC 2019**
   Propan -2- ol from Grignard's reagent

9. Propan-2-ol on reaction with iodine and sodium hydroxide gives .... precipitate and the reaction is called .... test. **ISC 2018**

10. In the dehydration of alcohols to alkenes by heating with concentrated sulphuric acid, the initiation step is **ISC 2018**
    (a) formation of carbocation (b) formation of an ester
    (c) protonation of alcohol molecule (d) elimination of water

11. When acetaldehyde is treated with Grignard reagent followed by hydrolysis, the product formed is **ISC 2015, 2018**
    (a) primary alcohol (b) secondary alcohol
    (c) carboxylic acid (d) tertiary alcohol

12. How can the following conversions be brought about? Acetaldehyde to propan-2-ol **ISC 2017**

13. Why do alcohols possess higher boiling points as compared to those of corresponding alkanes? **ISC 2017**

    KEY IDEA
    Compare the polar nature and presence of H-bonding in alcohol and alkane and answer accordingly.

14. Glycerol (propane-1, 2, 3-triol) is more viscous than ethylene glycol (ethane-1, 2-diol). Explain. **ISC 2016**

15. How can the following conversions be brought about? Glycerol to formic acid **ISC 2015**

16. Complete the following statement by selecting the correct alternative from the choices given below. **ISC 2013**
The compound which is optically active
(a) 1-butanol (b) 2-butanol
(c) 1-propanol (d) 2-methyl-1-propanol

17. Name the type of isomerism exhibited by the following pairs of compounds.
1-butanol and 2-methyl-1-propanol **ISC 2013**

18. Give balanced equation for the following reaction.
1-butanol and hydrogen chloride **ISC 2012**

19. ......is an example of trihydric alcohol and ...... is an example of dihydric alcohol. **ISC 2011**

20. Give balanced equation for the following.
Glycerol is heated with oxalic acid at 110°C (383 K). **ISC 2011**

21. Draw a pair of isomers for $C_4H_{10}O$ and name the type of isomerism. **ISC 2011**

22. ......and ......are functional isomers. **ISC 2009**

23. Write chemical equation for the given reaction and name the main product. Oxalic acid with glycerol at 260°C. **ISC 2005**

2 Marks Questions

24. An organic compound [*A*] having molecular formula $C_4H_{10}O$ forms a compound [*B*] with molecular formula C_4H_8O on oxidation. Compound [*B*] gives a positive iodoform test. The reaction of compound [*B*] with CH_3MgBr followed by hydrolysis gives compound [*C*] with molecular formula $C_5H_{12}O$.
Identify the compounds [*A*], [*B*] and [*C*]. Write the reaction for the conversion of compound [*A*] and compound [*B*]. **ISC 2024**

25. Write the chemical equation for the dehydration of ethanol of with conc. H_2SO_4 at 140° and 170° C. **ISC Specimen 2023**

26. An unknown alcohol is treated with Lucas reagent to determine whether the alcohol is primary, secondary or tertiary. **ISC Specimen 2021-22 (Sem-I)**
(i) Which alcohol reacts fastest and by what mechanism?
(a) Tertiary alcohol by S_N2
(b) Secondary alcohol by S_N1
(c) Tertiary alcohol by S_N1
(d) Secondary alcohol by S_N2
(ii) What is the chemical composition of the Lucas reagent used above?
(a) Anhydrous zinc chloride in concentrated HCl
(b) Anhydrous aluminium chloride in concentrated HCl
(c) Anhydrous lead chloride in concentrated HCl
(d) Anhydrous barium chloride in concentrated HCl

27. (i) Give balanced chemical equations when ethyl alcohol is treated with thionyl chloride.
(ii) Give one chemical test to distinguish between the following pair of compound.
Propan-1-ol and propan-2-ol **ISC 2020**

28. (i) Write chemical equation to illustrate the following name reaction.
Esterification reaction
(ii) Identify the compounds *A* and *B* in the given reaction.

$$C_2H_5OH \xrightarrow[\Delta]{Cu} A \xrightarrow{\text{Dil. NaOH}} B$$

ISC 2020

29. Write the mechanism of acid dehydration of ethanol to yield ethene. **ISC 2018**

30. Give chemical test to distinguish:
Ethyl alcohol and *sec*-propyl alcohol. **2017**

Or

Give one chemical test to distinguish between the following pairs of compounds.
Ethanol and propan-2-ol **ISC 2014**

31. Name the two organic compounds which have the same molecular formula C_2H_6O. Will they react with PCl_5? If they react, what are the products formed? **ISC 2017**

32. How is iodoform prepared from ethanol? Give the balanced equation. **ISC 2015**

33. Carry out the following conversion :
Ethanol to acetone **ISC 2011**

KEY IDEA
Follow the following steps
(i) Oxidation with $K_2Cr_2O_7/H_2SO_4$
(ii)Product formed in step (i) reacted with CH_3MgBr.
(iii)Then hydrolysis of product of (ii).
(iv) Oxidation of product of (iii) by using $K_2Cr_2O_7/H_2SO_4$.

34. How can the following conversion be brought about?
Propan-2-ol to acetoxime **ISC 2010**

35. Give one good chemical test to distinguish between the following pair of compounds.
Propan-1-ol and propan-2-ol **ISC 2010**

36. How will you bring about the following conversion?
Diethyl ether to ethanol **ISC 2008**

37. How will you convert acetaldehyde to *iso*-propyl alcohol? **ISC 2002, 2000**

38. Give balanced equations and explain what happen when glycerol reacts with conc. H_2SO_4? **ISC 2000**

39. Explain what happens when ethanol is heated with acetic acid in presence of conc. H_2SO_4? **ISC 2000**

3 Marks Question

40. Give a chemical test to distinguish between the following pairs of compounds. **ISC 2024**

(a) Ethanol and methanol
(b) Ethanol and ethanal
(c) Propan-2-ol and 2-methyl propan-2-ol

41. Explain the mechanism of acid catalysed dehydration of ethanol to yield the corresponding alkene. **ISC Specimen 2024**

42. Write the names and structures of three isomers which have the same molecular formula C_3H_8O. **2008**

Explanations

1. Diethylether; ethene

2. Increases; decreases

3. aldehyde, carboxylic acid

4. (d) Methanol

5. (a) *tert*-butyl alcohol

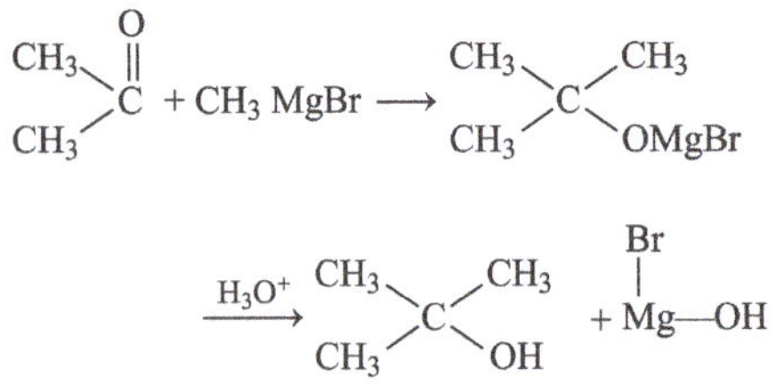

2-methyl-propan-2-ol
(*tert*-butyl alcohol)

6. (c)

$$\underset{\substack{\text{(Taken liquid)}\\(A)}}{CH_3COOH} + \underset{\text{(Ethanol)}}{C_2H_5OH} \xrightarrow{\text{Conc. } H_2SO_4} \underset{\substack{\text{(Fruity smell)}\\\text{[Ethyl acetate]}}}{CH_3-\overset{\overset{O}{\|}}{C}-OC_2H_5} + H_2O$$

Thus, the compound (A) is acetic acid.

7. Lucas reagent, tertiary

8. Propan-2-ol from Grignard's reagent

$$CH_3CHO \xrightarrow[\text{(ii) } H_2O/H^+]{\text{(i) } CH_3MgX} \underset{\text{Propan-2-ol}}{CH_3\underset{\underset{CH_3}{|}}{C}HOH} + Mg(OH)$$

9. Propan-2-ol on reaction with iodine and sodium hydroxide gives **yellow** precipitate and the reaction is called **iodoform** test.

10. (c) The initiation of step in dehydration of alcohols is protonation of alcohol molecule by heating with conc. H_2SO_4.

11. (b) $\underset{\text{Acetaldehyde}}{CH_3-CHO} + RMgX \xrightarrow[\text{(ii) } H_2O/H^+]{\text{(i) Dry ether}}$

$$\underset{\substack{\text{Secondary alcohol}\\(2^\circ)}}{H_3C-\overset{\overset{H}{|}}{\underset{\underset{R}{|}}{C}}-OH} + Mg(OH)X$$

12. $\underset{\text{Acetaldehyde}}{CH_3CHO} \xrightarrow{CH_3MgBr} \left[\underset{\text{Addition product}}{CH_3-\overset{\overset{OMgBr}{|}}{CH}-CH_3}\right] \xrightarrow[-Mg(OH)\,Br]{H^+/H_2O}$

$$\underset{\text{Propan-2-ol}}{CH_3-\overset{\overset{OH}{|}}{CH}-CH_3}$$

13. Due to the presence of strong hydrogen bonding between alcohol molecules, they possess higher boiling point as compared to their corresponding alkanes.

14. Glycerol (propane-1, 2, 3- triol) has three —OH groups per molecules, while ethylene glycol (ethane-1, 2-diol) has two—OH groups. The viscosity depends on the amount of hydrogen bonding between molecules and the more number of —OH bonds. There is greater hydrogen bonding in glycerol than ethylene glycol. So, glycerol is more viscous than ethylene glycol.

15. 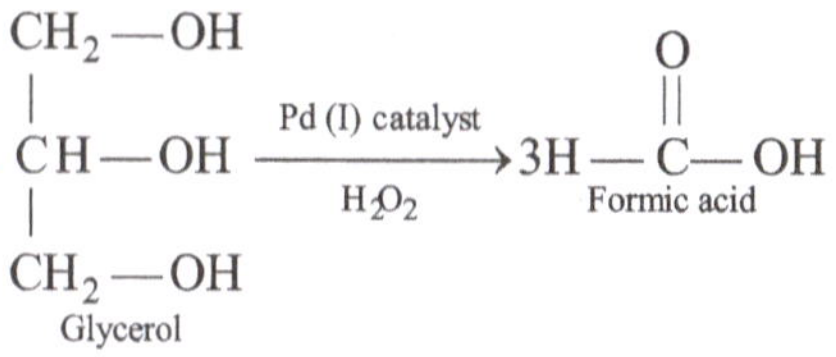

16. (b)

(a) 1-butanol, $CH_3CH_2CH_2CH_2OH$

Here, no chiral carbon is present, so it is optically inactive.

(b) Butan-2-ol, $H_3C-CH_2-\overset{*}{C}H(OH)-CH_3$

Here, the second carbon is chiral carbon and thus, the molecule is optically active.

(c) 1-propanol, $CH_3CH_2CH_2OH$

Again no chiral carbon atom is present, so it is optically inactive.

(d) 2-methyl-1-propanol, $H_3C-CH(CH_3)-CH_2OH$

Here, again no chiral carbon is present and thus, the compound is optically inactive.

Hence, option (b) is correct.

> **Concept Enhancer** When all the four substituents attached to the carbon atom in a compound are different then such a carbon is called **chiral carbon** and the compounds containing chiral carbon are called **optically active compounds**.

17. The given two compounds will show chain isomerism. The structural formula of the two compounds are

$$\underset{\text{Butan-1-ol}}{CH_3-CH_2-CH_2-CH_2-OH};$$

$$\underset{\text{2-methyl-propan-1-ol}}{CH_3-CH(CH_3)-CH_2-OH}$$

The two compounds have the same molecular formula but different number of carbon atoms present in their parent chain.

18. Alcohol (butan-1-ol) reacts with hydrogen chloride to form chloroalkane (chlorobutane).

$$\underset{\text{Butan-1-ol}}{CH_3-CH_2-CH_2-CH_2-OH}+HCl\xrightarrow{\text{Anhyd. }ZnCl_2}\underset{\text{Chlorobutane}}{CH_3-CH_2-CH_2-CH_2-Cl}+H_2O$$

19. **Glycerol** is an example of trihydric alcohol and **glycol** is an example of dihydric alcohol.

> **Concept Enhancer** Dihydric alcohols contain two hydroxyl ($-OH$) groups while trihydric alcohols contain three hydroxyl ($-OH$) groups. The structural formula of glycerol and glycol are respectively.
>
> $HO-CH_2-CH(OH)-CH_2OH$; $HO-CH_2-CH_2-OH$

20. When glycerol is heated with crystalline oxalic acid at 110°C, it yields glycerol monoformate which on hydrolysis gives glycerol and formic acid.

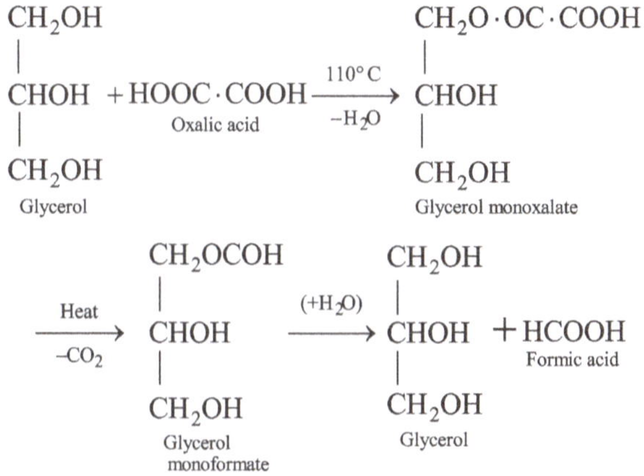

21. The two isomers of $C_4H_{10}O$ are

$$\underset{\text{Butan-1-ol}}{H_3C-CH_2-CH_2-CH_2-OH};\quad \underset{\text{Butan-2-ol}}{CH_3-CH_2-CH(OH)-CH_3}$$

These two isomers have the same molecular formula, i.e. $C_4H_{10}O$ but they differ in the position of $-OH$ group. Thus, the two compounds are showing position isomerism.

22. Ethanol, dimethyl ether

23. When glycerol is heated with oxalic acid at 260°C, glyceryl dioxalate is formed. It decomposes at once into CO_2 and allyl alcohol.

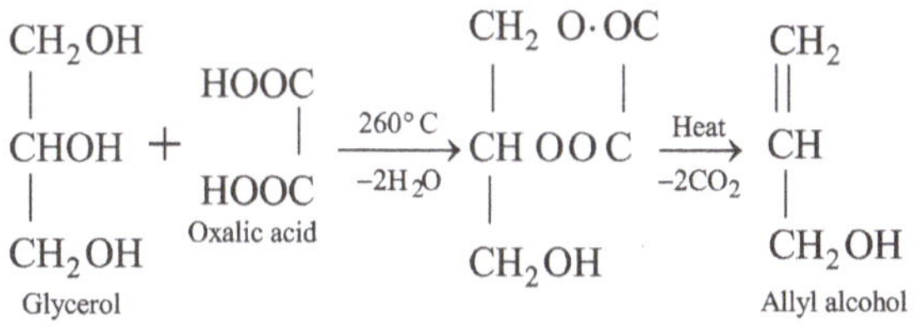

24. According to the given question compound B, i.e. C_4H_8O gives positive iodoform test. Thus, it is a ketone containing $CH_3-\overset{O}{\overset{||}{C}}-$ group. As only one

aldehyde, i.e. acetaldehyde gives positive iodoform test, hence, the formula of B may be

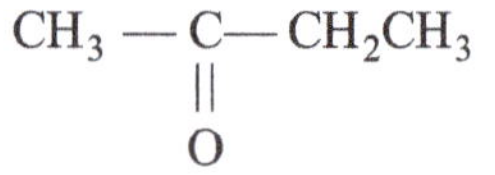

As B is formed by the oxidation of A, thus A must be an alcohol.

Thus, the formula of alcohol forming B is

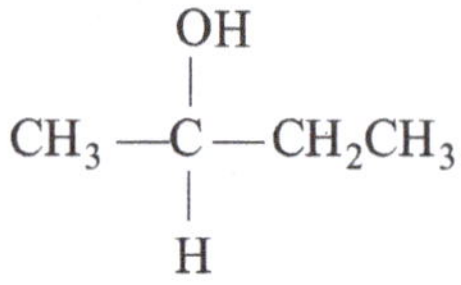

i.e. butanol.

The reaction involve is

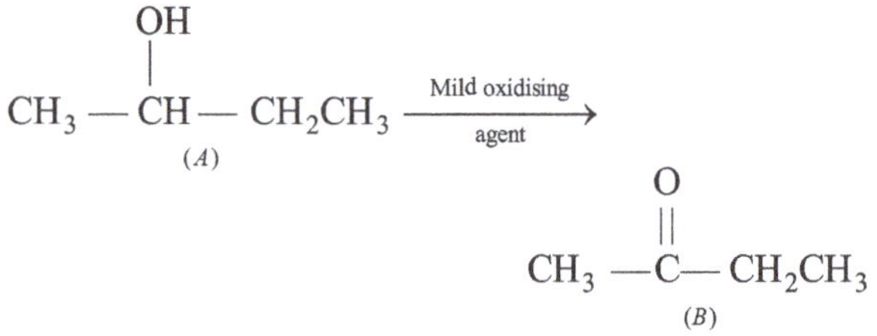

The reaction of (B) with CH_3MgBr followed by hydrolysis gives (C).

The reaction is given as

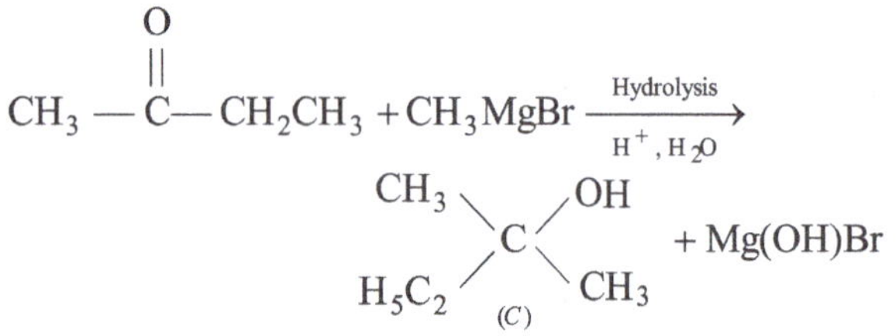

Thus, compounds A, B and C are butanol, butan-2-one and 2-methylbutan-2-ol respectively.

25. Ethanol can be dehydrated to give ethene by heating it with an excess of concentrated H_2SO_4 at 170° C.

$$\underset{\text{Ethanol}}{C_2H_5OH} + \underset{\text{Sulphuric acid}}{\text{Conc. } H_2SO_4} \xrightarrow{170^\circ C} \underset{\text{Ethene}}{C_2H_4} + H_2O$$

At 140° C, ethanol on reacting with conc. H_2SO_4 gives diethyl ether.

$$2C_2H_5OH \xrightarrow{\text{Conc. at } 140^\circ C\ (411 K)} C_2H_5—O—C_2H_5 + H_3O$$

At 110°C, ethanol on reacting with conc. H_2SO_4 gives ethyl hydrogen sulphate

$$CH_3CH_2OH \xrightarrow[110^\circ C]{\text{Conc. } H_2SO_4} CH_3CH_2OSO_3H$$

26. (i) (c) Tertiary alcohol reacts fastest and by S_N1 mechanism. **(1)**

(ii) (a) Anhydrous zinc chloride in concentrated HCl is used as Lucas reagent. **(1)**

27. (i) Refer to text on page 150 (Reaction with thionyl chloride). **(1)**

(ii) Propan-1-ol and propan-2-ol can be distinguished by Lucas test. When Lucas reagent (solution of HCl and $ZnCl_2$) is added to propan-2-ol, cloudiness (turbidity) appears within 5 min.

When Lucas reagent is added to propan-1-ol, no turbidity appears at room temperature and solution remains clear. **(1)**

$$\underset{\text{Propan-1-ol}}{CH_3CH_2CH_2—OH} \xrightarrow[ZnCl_2]{\text{Conc. HCl}} \text{No turbidity appears at room temperature}$$

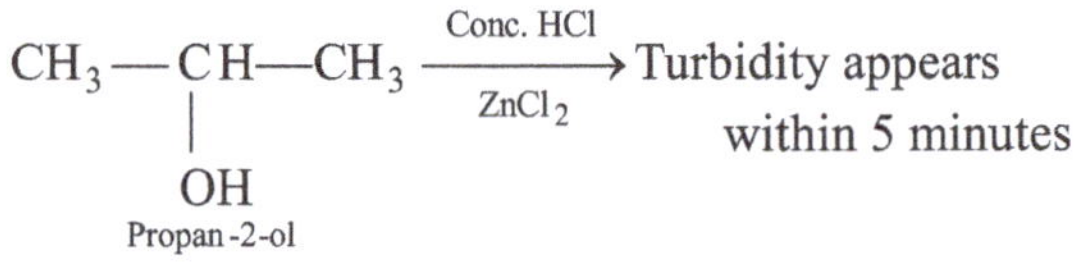

28. (i) Refer to text on page 148 (Esterification). **(1)**

(ii)

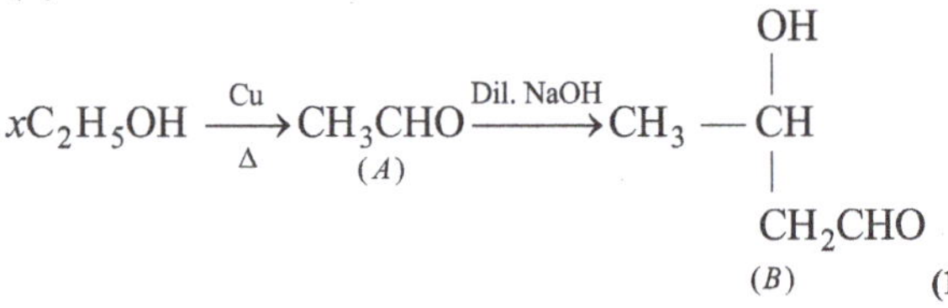

(1)

29. The mechanism of dehydration of ethanol involves the following steps

***Step* I Formation of protonated alcohol**

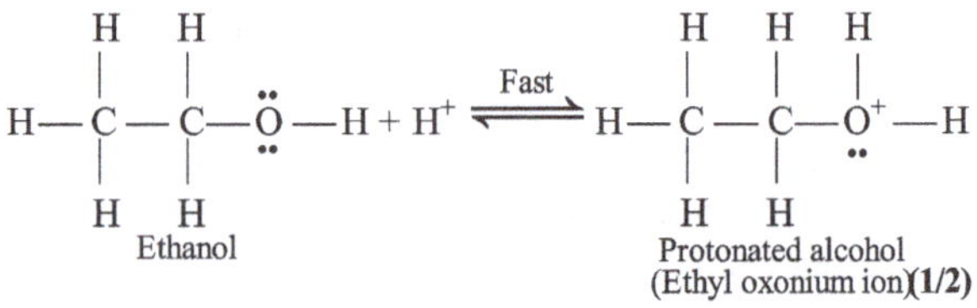

(1/2)

***Step* II Formation of carbocation** It is the slowest step and hence, the rate determining step of the reaction.

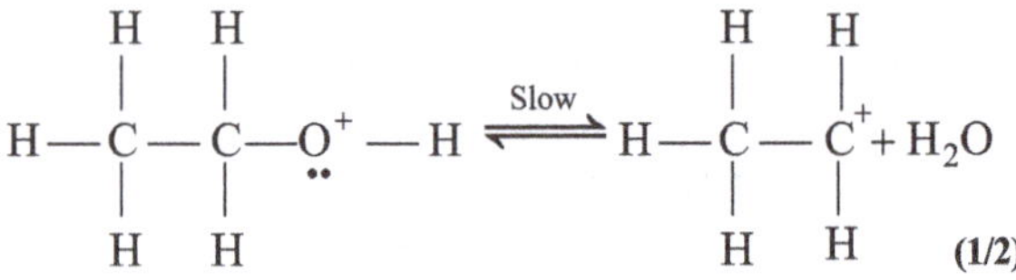

(1/2)

***Step* III Formation of ethene by the elemination of a proton**

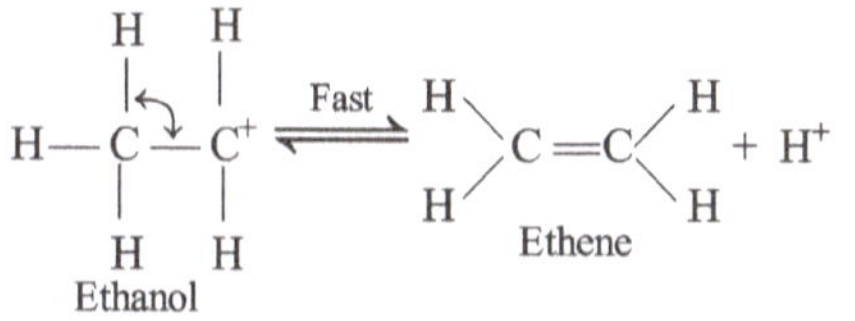

The acid used in step I is released in step III. To drive the equilibrium to the right, ethene is removed as it is formed. **(1)**

Common Mistake Sometime students make mistake by showing the incorrect shifting of electron in the mechanism.

30. Ethanol is primary alcohol while propan-2-ol is secondary alcohol. So, the two can be distinguished by Victor Meyer's test. **(1)**

The reactions involved for the two alcohols are as follows

$$\underset{\text{Ethanol (1°)}}{CH_3CH_2OH} \xrightarrow{P_4 + I_2} \underset{\text{Ethyl iodide}}{CH_3CH_2I} \xrightarrow{AgNO_2} \underset{\text{Nitroethane}}{CH_3CH_2NO_2} \xrightarrow{HNO_2}$$

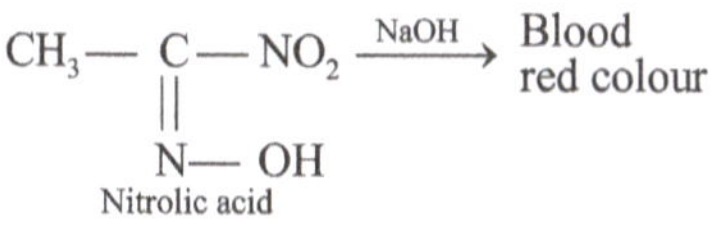

(1/2)

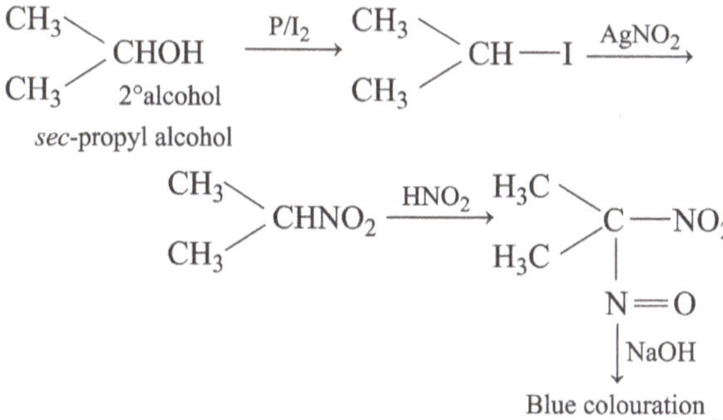

(1/2)

31. Ethanol (CH_3CH_2OH) and dimethyl ether ($CH_3—O—CH_3$) have the same molecular formula, i.e. C_2H_6O. **(1)**

Yes, only CH_3CH_2OH react with PCl_5.

$$CH_3CH_2OH + PCl_5 \longrightarrow CH_3CH_2Cl + POCl_3 + HCl \quad \textbf{(1)}$$

32. $$\underset{\text{Ethanol}}{CH_3—CH_2—OH} + 4I_2 + 6NaOH \xrightarrow{\Delta} \underset{\text{Iodoform}}{CHI_3\downarrow} + HCO\overset{-}{O}\overset{+}{Na} + 5NaI + 5H_2O \quad \textbf{(2)}$$

33. The reactions involved to convert ethanol into acetone are as follows

$$\underset{\text{Ethanol}}{CH_3CH_2OH} + O_2 \xrightarrow[H_2SO_4]{K_2Cr_2O_7} \underset{\text{Acetaldehyde}}{CH_3CHO} + H_2O$$

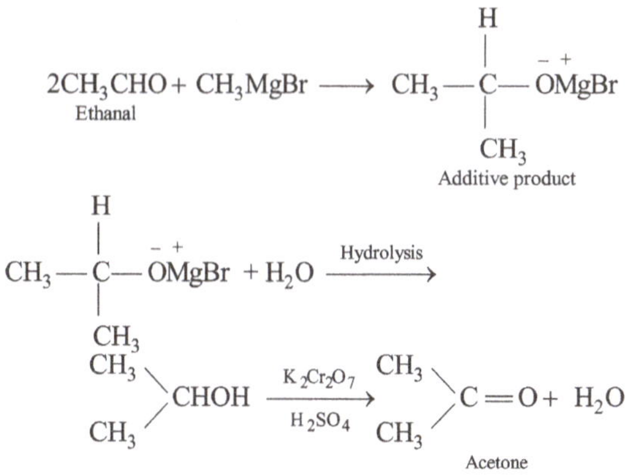

34. Conversion of propan-2-ol into acetoxime.

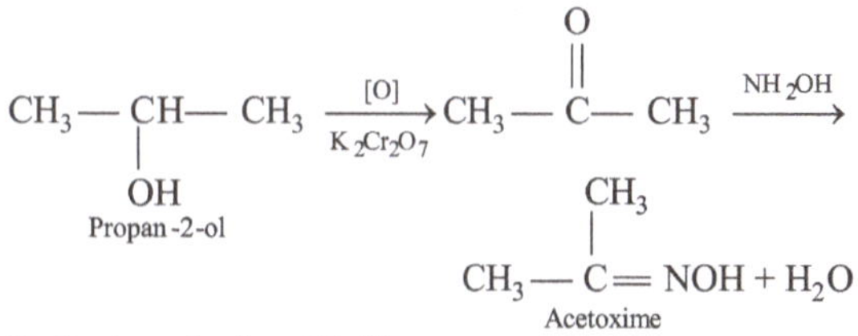

35. Refer to solution 27 (ii).

36. Diethyl ether ($C_2H_5—O—C_2H_5$) can be converted into ethanol by boiling it with water under pressure.

$$\underset{\text{Diethyl ether}}{C_2H_5—O—C_2H_5} + HOH \xrightarrow{\text{Boiling}} \underset{\text{Ethanol}}{2C_2H_5OH}$$

37. First of all acetaldehyde reacts with Grignard's reagent to form an addition product, which on hydrolysis gives *iso*-propyl alcohol.

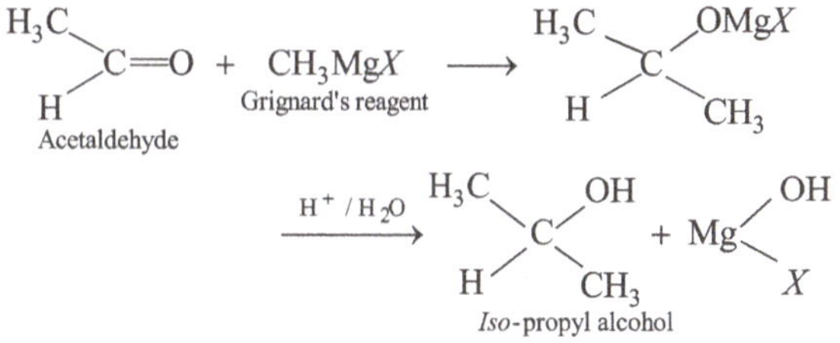

38. When glycerol is heated with conc. H_2SO_4, it eliminates two molecules of water and form acrolein.

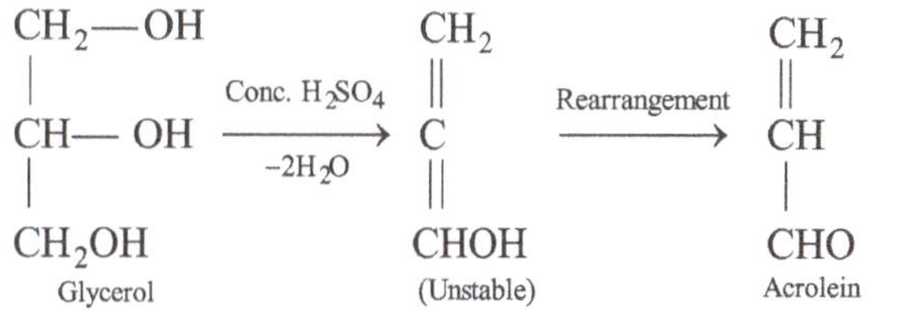

39. When ethanol is heated with acetic acid in presence of conc. sulphuric acid, it forms ester.

$$\underset{\text{Ethanol}}{C_2H_5OH} + \underset{\text{Acetic acid}}{HOOC\cdot CH_3} \xrightarrow[\Delta]{\text{Conc. } H_2SO_4} \underset{\text{Ethyl acetate}}{CH_3COOC_2H_5} + H_2O$$

40. (a) **Ethanol and methanol** Ethanol gives positive iodoform test when warmed with iodine in presence of NaOH while methanol does not.

$$CH_3CH_2OH \xrightarrow{3I_2 + 4\,NaOH} CHI_3 + HCOO^-Na^+ + 5NaI + 5H_2O$$

$$CH_3—OH \xrightarrow{NaOH,\,I_2} \text{No reaction}$$

(b) **Ethanol and ethanal** Ethanal gives positive Tollen's test while ethanol does not.

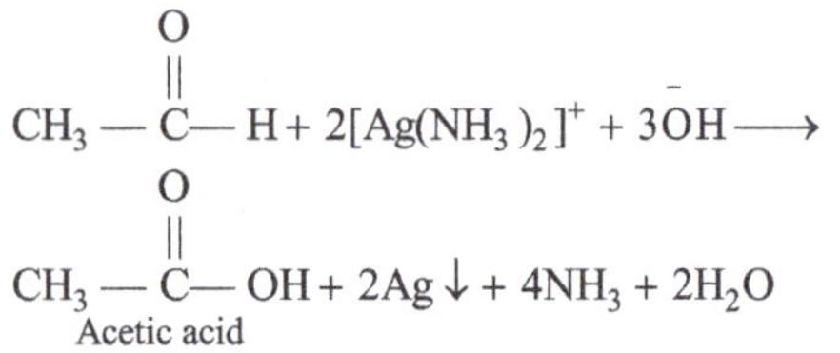

$$CH_3CH_2—OH + 2[Ag(NH_3)_2]^+ + 3\bar{O}H \longrightarrow \text{No reaction}$$

(c) **Propan-2-ol and 2-methylpropan-2-ol:** Propan-2-ol when passed over heated copper at 573 K, a ketone is formed.

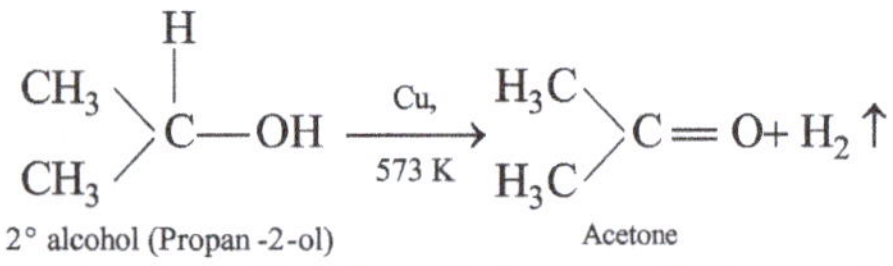

whereas, when 2-methylpropan-2-ol passed over heated copper at 573 K, it gives an alkene.

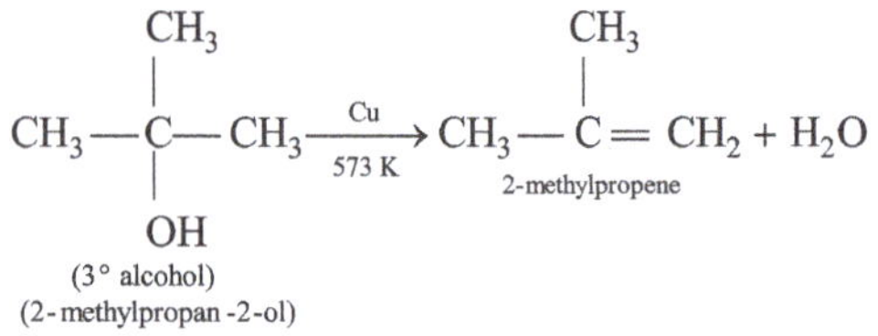

41. First step is the protonation of oxygen atom of —OH group. Second step is the loss of a molecule of water to form carbonium ion.

Last step is deprotonation to form carbon carbon double bond.

$$2CH_3CH_2OH \xrightarrow[\text{Conc. } H_2SO_4]{} 2CH_2=CH_2 + 2H_2O$$

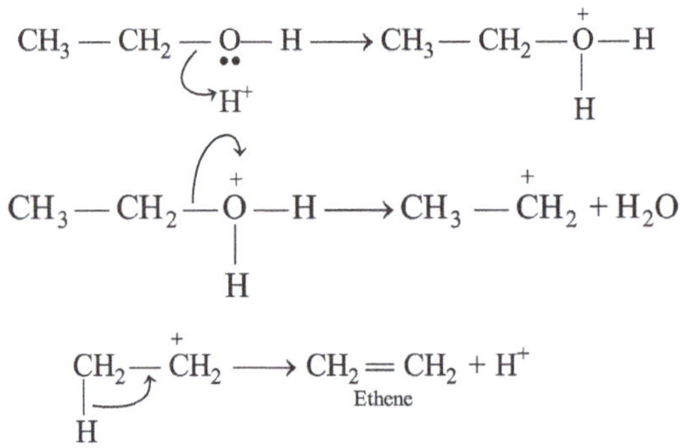

42. Three isomers which have the same molecular formula C_3H_8O are as follows.

(i) $CH_3—CH_2—CH_2—OH$
Propan-1-ol

(ii) 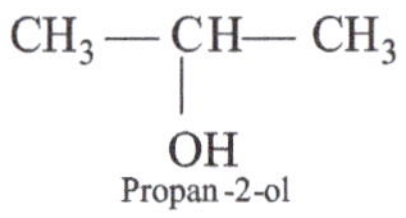
Propan-2-ol

(iii) $CH_3—CH_2—O—CH_3$
Methoxyethane **(1× 3)**

Structures (i) and (ii) are the position isomers. Structures (ii) and (iii) or structures (i) and (iii) are the functional isomers of each other.

TOPIC 2

Phenols

These organic compounds enols are the hydroxy derivatives of arenes in which one or more —OH groups are directly attached to the carbon atoms of an aromatic ring.

Nomenclature of Phenols

The simplest hydroxy derivative of benzene is phenol. As the structure of phenol involves a benzene ring in its substituted compounds the terms *ortho* (1, 2-disubstituted), *meta* (1,3-disubstituted) and *para* (1,4-disubstituted) are often used in the common names.

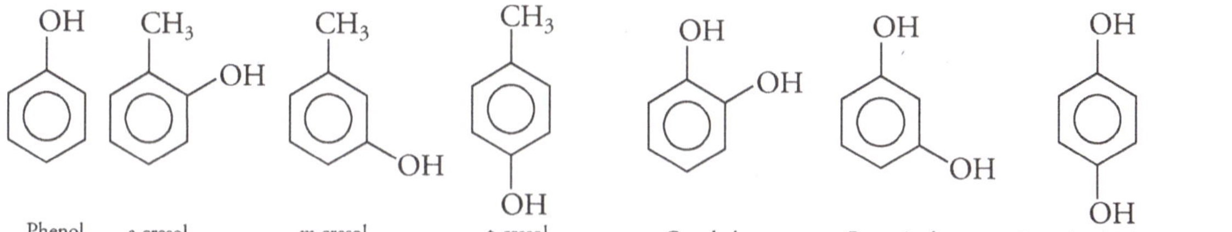

Common name	Phenol	*o*-cresol	*m*-cresol	*p*-cresol	Catechol	Resorcinol	Quinol or hydroquinone
IUPAC name	Phenol	2-methylphenol	3-methylphenol	4-methylphenol	Benzene-1, 2-diol	Benzene-1, 3-diol	Benzene-1, 4-diol

Preparation of Phenols

Various methods are as follows

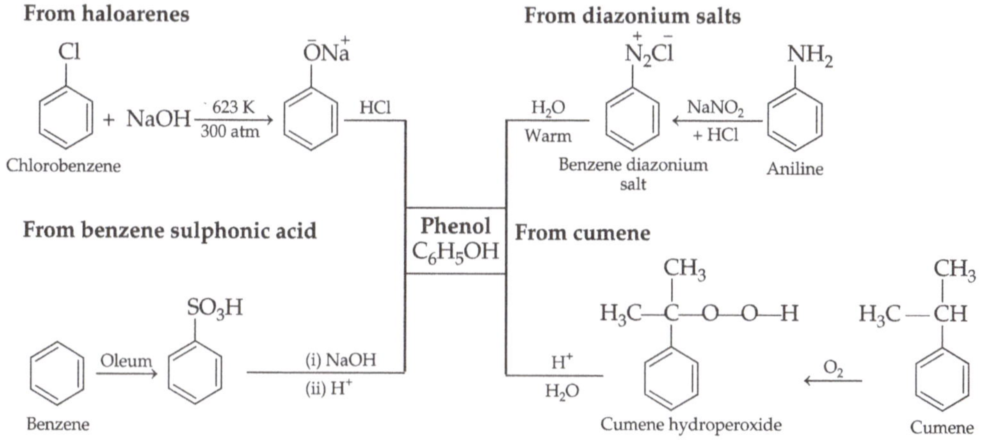

Physical Properties

Phenols are either colourless liquids or colourless crystalline solids with low melting points. They are slightly soluble in water.

They also possess higher boiling points as compared to those of the corresponding aromatic hydrocarbons and haloarenes.

Chemical Properties

Acidic character of phenol Phenols behave as weak acids. They react with alkali metals and their hydroxides to form salts.

The acidic character of phenols is mainly due to the presence of polar —OH group and resonance stabilisation of phenoxide ion.

$$2C_6H_5OH + 2Na \longrightarrow 2C_6H_5\overset{-}{O}\overset{+}{Na} + H_2$$

$$C_6H_5OH + NaOH \longrightarrow C_6H_5\overset{-}{O}\overset{+}{Na} + H_2O$$

Phenoxide ion is resonance stabilised which makes the phenol more acidic than alcohols. An electron withdrawing group increases the acidic strength of phenol.

The effect is more pronounced at *o*- and *p*-positions while the presence of an electron releasing group decreases the acidic strength of phenol.

Some other important reactions of phenol are

(a) **Carboxylation of phenol** (Kolbe's reaction)

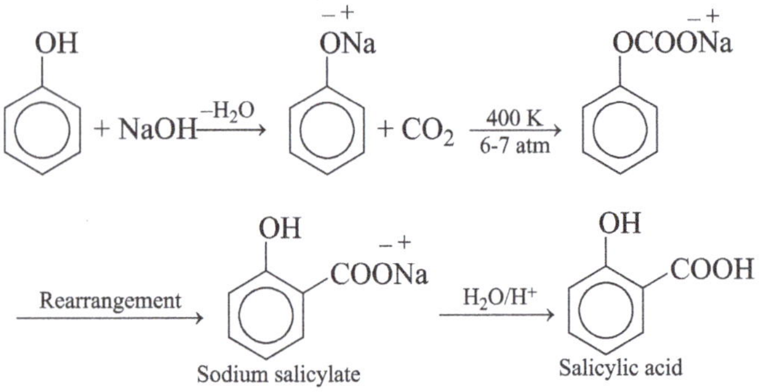

(b) **Reimer-Tiemann reaction**

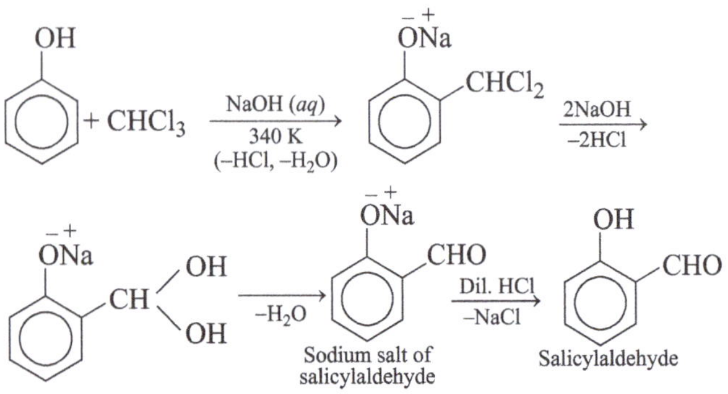

(c) **Coupling reaction**

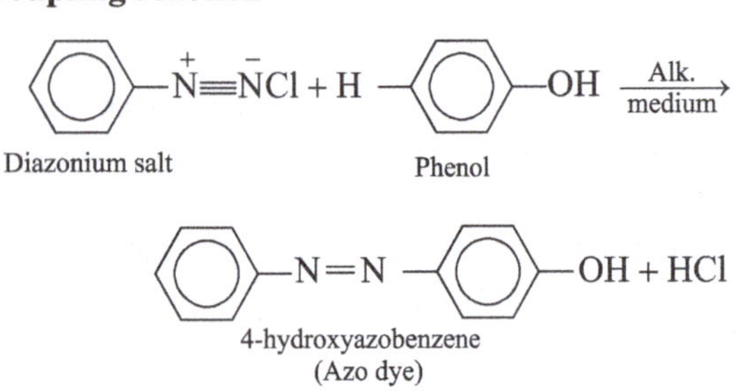

Phenol reading undergo following reactions

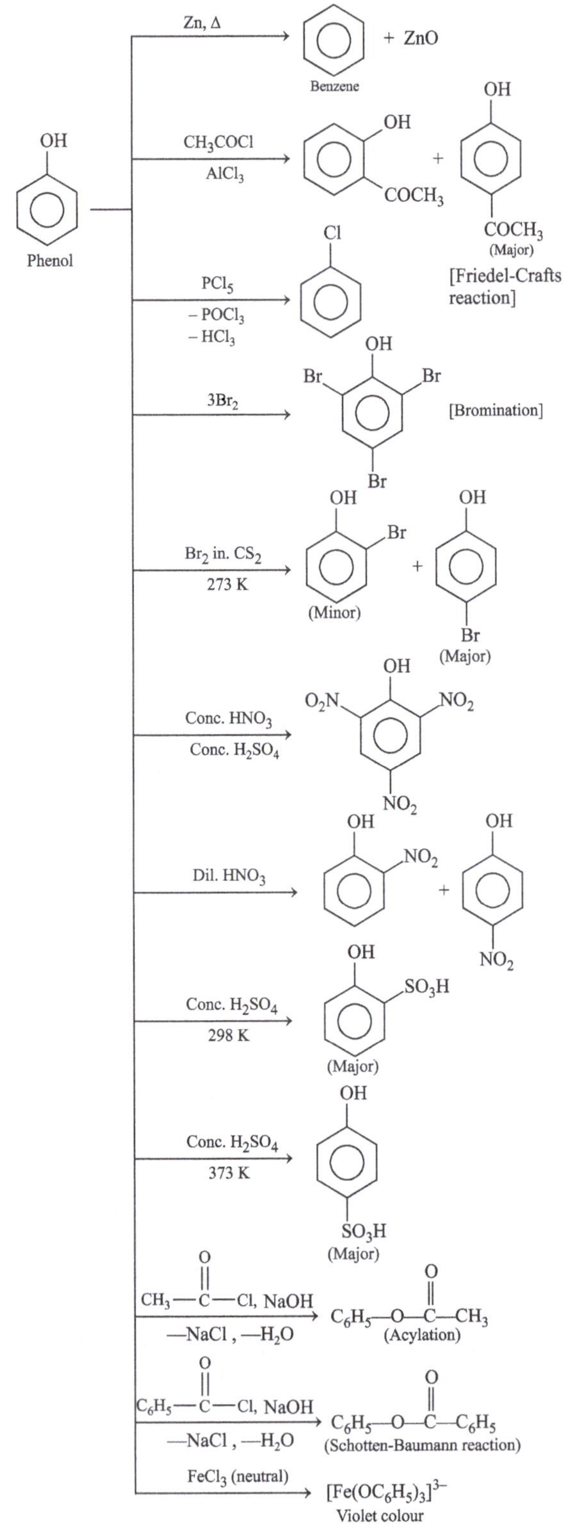

Test for Phenols

- Aqueous solution of phenol gives a violet colouration with a drop of ferric chloride.
- Phenol undergoes coupling with benzene diazonium chloride and forms azo dye while alcohols does not form any dye.

Uses

- It is used in perfumery.
- It is widely used in the manufacture of dyes, plastics, etc.

PYQs Previous Years' Questions

1 Mark Questions

1. When phenol is treated with excess of bromine water, a white precipitate is formed. The compound formed is
   (a) *m*-bromophenol **ISC 2021-22 (Sem-I)**
   (b) *o*- and *p*-bromophenol
   (c) 3,5-dibromophenol
   (d) 2,4,6-tribromophenol

2. When phenol is treated with zinc dust, it gives **ISC 2021-22 (Sem-I)**
   (a) benzoic acid (b) benzaldehyde
   (c) benzene (d) toluene

3. **Assertion** (A) Phenol reacts with neutral ferric chloride ($FeCl_3$) and gives violet colour solution.
   Reason (R) The violet colour solution is due to the formation of $[Fe(OC_6H_5)_6]^{3-}$ complex ion.
   (a) Both (A) and (R) are correct and (R) is the correct explanation of (A).
   (b) Both (A) and (R) are correct but (R) is not the correct explanation of (A).
   (c) (A) is correct and (R) is incorrect.
   (d) (A) is incorrect and (R) is correct. **ISC 2021-22 (Sem-I)**

4. Give balanced chemical equations for the following reaction. Phenol is treated with ice cold alkaline solution of benzene diazonium chloride. **ISC 2020**

5. Write chemical equations to illustrate the following name reaction.
   Reimer-Tiemann reaction **ISC 2020**
   Or Give the balanced equation for the following name reaction.
   Reimer–Tiemann reaction **ISC 2015**
   Or Give balanced equation for the preparation of salicylaldehyde from phenol. **ISC 2013**
   Or Give an example (equation) for the following name reaction.
   Reimer-Tiemann reaction **ISC 2011**
   Or Give balanced chemical equation when phenol is heated with chloroform and sodium hydroxide. **ISC 2009**

6. Identify the compounds *A* and *B* in the given reaction.

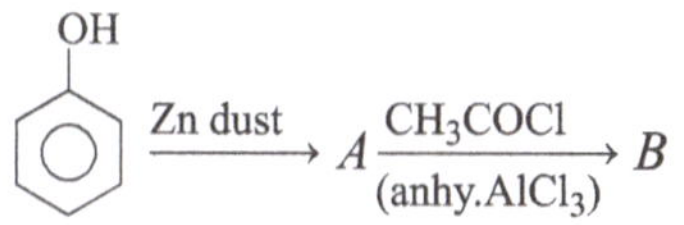

7. The acidic strength of phenol is ...... ethyl alcohol but ...... nitrophenol. **ISC Specimen 2018**

8. Write the equation and name the following reaction.
   Phenol with acetyl chloride in the presence of $AlCl_3$. **ISC 2004**

> **KEY IDEA**
> Acetylation of phenol occurs at *o*- and *p*- position of phenol.

9. How will you convert phenol to picric acid? Write the relevant equation. **ISC 2003**

2 Marks Questions

10. (i) Write a chemical test to distnguish between ethanol and phenol.
    (ii) Give a chemical reaction to convert acetaldehyde into secondary propyl alcohol. **ISC 2024**

11. Convert the following by giving chemical equations for each. **ISC 2024**
    (i) Ethyl bromide to diethyl ether
    (ii) Phenol to salicylaldehyde

12. (i) Arrange the following alcohols in order of decreasing activity towards Lucas' reagent.
    2-butanol, 2-methyl-2-propanol and 1-butanol **ISC Specimen 2024**
    (ii) Ethanol has a higher boiling point than methoxymethane. Justify the statement.

13. An organic compound [*A*] having molecular formula C_6H_6O gives a characteristic colour with aqueous $FeCl_3$ solution. [*A*] on treatment with CO_2 and NaOH at 400 K under pressure gives [*B*] which on acidification gives compound [*C*]. [*C*] reacts with acetyl chloride to give [*D*] which is a popular pain killer. Identify the compounds [*A*], [*B*], [*C*] and [*D*].
ISC Specimen 2023

14. How will the following be obtained? (Give chemical equations) ***ISC Specimen 2023***

(i) Picric acid from phenol

(ii) Ethanol from formaldehyde

15. Chlorobenzene is fused with aqueous sodium hydroxide at 623 K and 300 atm followed by hydrolysis with dil. HCl. ***ISC 2021-22 (Sem-I)***

(i) The organic product formed is

(a) phenol (b) sodium phenoxide
(c) benzene (d) cyclohexyl chloride

(ii) What is the name of the above reaction?

(a) Williamson's synthesis
(b) Dow's process
(c) Rosenmund's reduction
(d) Kolbe's reaction

16. Phenol and ethyl alcohol can be distinguished by a single chemical test. ***ISC 2021-22 (Sem-I)***

(i) Which of the following is the reagent used to distinguish phenol from ethyl alcohol?

(a) Solid PCl_5
(b) Dry sodium metal
(c) Neutral $FeCl_3$
(d) Acetyl chloride in presence of pyridine

(ii) Which colour is developed in the solution due to the addition of the above reagent to phenol?

(a) Blue (b) Green
(c) Red (d) Violet

17. Phenol is heated with alcoholic KOH and chloroform. ***ISC 2021-22 (Sem-I)***

(i) What is the name of the reaction?

(a) Cannizzaro reaction
(b) Gattermann reaction
(c) Reimer - Tiemann reaction
(d) Kolbe reaction

(ii) What is the main product formed in this reaction?

(a) Salicylaldehyde
(b) Salicylic acid
(c) Aniline
(d) Phenyl isocyanide

18. Conversion of chlorobenzene into phenol.

(i) Which of the following statements is correct for the above conversion? ***ISC 2021-22 (Sem-I)***

(a) Heating it with alc. KOH at room temperature.
(b) Heating it with aqueous NaOH at 623 K under pressure followed by acidificatioin with dilute HCl.
(c) Heating it with CuCN followed by acidification with dilute HCl.
(d) Heating it with sodium metal in the presence of dry ether.

(ii) What is the name of the above reaction?

(a) Dow process (b) Wurtz reaction
(c) Sandmeyer's reaction (d) Kolbe's reaction

19. How will you obtain the following? (Give balanced chemical equations)

(i) Benzene from phenol ***ISC 2019***

(ii) Salicylaldehyde from phenol ***ISC 2019***

20. How is phenol converted to benzoic acid? Explain with the help of balanced chemical equations.
ISC Specimen 2018

21. Give one chemical test to distinguish between the following pairs of compounds.
Acetone and phenol ***ISC 2013***

22. How can you convert benzene to phenol? ***ISC 2012***

23. How will you bring about the following conversion?
Phenol to benzoic acid ***ISC 2009***

24. How will you obtain the following? (Give balanced equation)

(i) Picric acid from phenol

(ii) Anisole form phenol

KEY IDEA

(i) Write the reaction of phenol with conc. H_2SO_4 followed by conc. HNO_3 with heating.
(ii) Write the reaction of phenol with NaOH and CH_3Br.

25. Give one test to distinguish between phenol and benzoic acid. ***ISC 2004***

26. How will you convert phenol to salicylic acid? ***ISC 2004***

27. Give reason why phenol is more easily nitrated than benzene? ***ISC 2001***

28. Give balanced equation and explain what happens when phenol is treated with bromine water? ***ISC 2000***

3 Marks Questions

29. Identify the compounds [*A*], [*B*] and [*C*] in each of the following reactions. *ISC 2024*

(a) $C_2H_5OH \xrightarrow{PCl_5} [A] \xrightarrow{KCN} [B] \xrightarrow{H_3O^+} C_2H_5COOH \xrightarrow[\Delta]{NH_3} [C]$

(b) $C_6H_5OH \xrightarrow{Zn/Dust} [A] \xrightarrow[\text{Anhy. } AlCl_3]{CH_3Cl} [B] \xrightarrow[K_2Cr_2O_7 + H_2SO_4]{[O]} [C]$

30. How will the following be obtained? (Give chemical equation) *ISC Specimen 2024*

(a) Picric acid from Phenol (b) Ethyl acetate from ethanol (c) Anisole from sodium phenoxide

Explanations

1. (d) Refer to text on page 160 (Bromination).

2. (c) Refer to text on page 160 (Reaction with zinc dust).

3. (a) Both (A) and (R) are correct and (R) is the correct explanation of the (A).

4. Refer to text on page 160 (Coupling reaction)

5. Reimer-Tiemann reaction

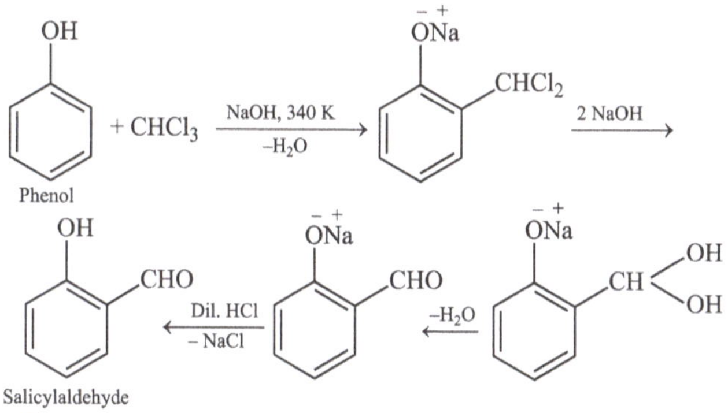

6.

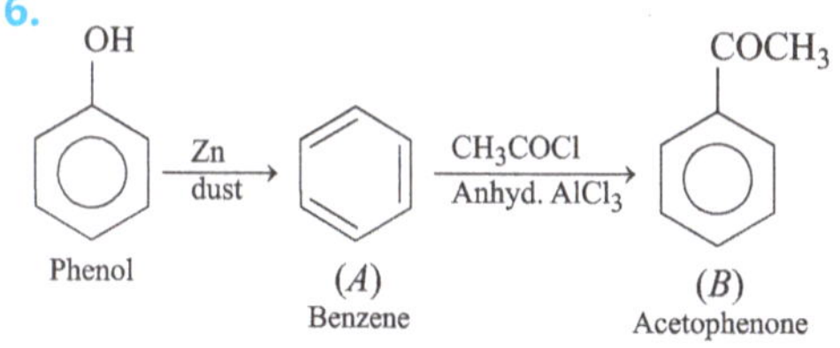

7. greater than, less than.

8. Phenol when treated with acetyl chloride in the presence of $AlCl_3$ to give the mixture of *o* - and *p* -derivatives.

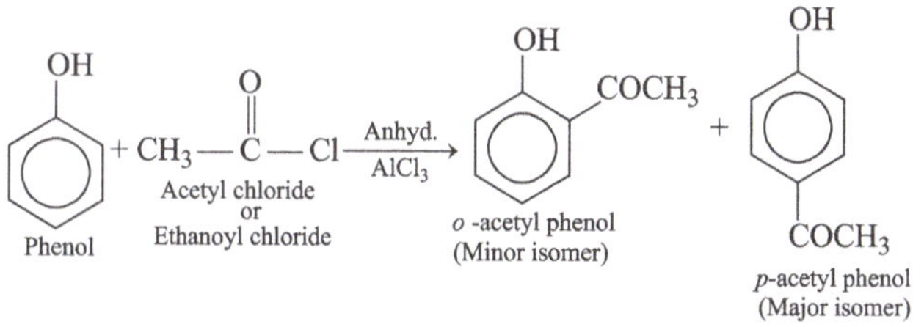

9. Refer to sol. 24 (i).

10. (i) Iodoform test can be used distinguish between ethanol and phenol.

- $\underset{\text{Ethanol}}{CH_3CH_2OH} + 4NaOI \longrightarrow \underset{\substack{\text{Iodoform}\\\text{(Yellow ppt.)}}}{CHI_3} + HCOONa + NaI + H_2O + 2NaOH$

- $\underset{\text{Phenol}}{C_6H_5OH} + NaOH \longrightarrow$ No yellow ppt.

(ii) Conversion of acetaldehyde to secondary propyl alcohol.

$$\underset{\text{(Acetaldehyde)}}{CH_3-\overset{\overset{\large H}{|}}{C}=O} + CH_3MgBr \longrightarrow CH_3-\underset{\underset{\large CH_3}{|}}{\overset{\overset{\large H}{|}}{C}}-OMgBr \xrightarrow[\text{Hydrolysis}]{H_2O/H^+}$$

$$\underset{\text{(Secondary propyl alcohol)}}{CH_3-\underset{\underset{\large CH_3}{|}}{\overset{\overset{\large H}{|}}{C}}-OH} + Mg\langle^{OH}_{Br}$$

11. (i) **Ethyl bromide to diethyl ether**

$$\underset{\text{Ethyl bromide}}{CH_3CH_2Br} + \underset{\text{Sodium ethoxide}}{NaO-C_2H_5} \longrightarrow \underset{\text{Diethyl ether}}{CH_3CH_2-O-CH_2CH_3}$$

(ii) **Phenol to salicylaldehyde**

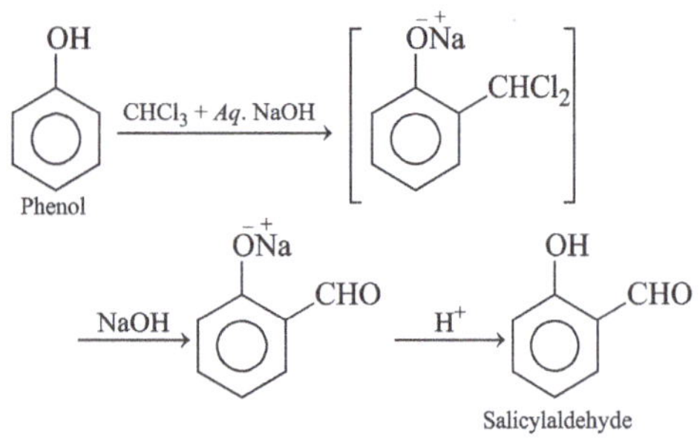

12. (i) The order of reactivity of alcohols towards Lucas reagent follows the sequence :

$$3° > 2° > 1°$$

Thus, the correct sequence of reactivity is:

2-methyl-2-propanol (3°) > 2-butanol (2°) > 1-butanol (1°).

(ii) Ethanol undergoes intermolecular H-bonding due to the presence of a hydrogen attached to the electronegative oxygen atom. As a result, ethanol exists as associated molecules.

Consequently, a large amount of energy is required to break these hydrogen bonds. Therefore, the boiling point of ethanol is higher than that of methoxymethane which does not form H-bonds.

13.

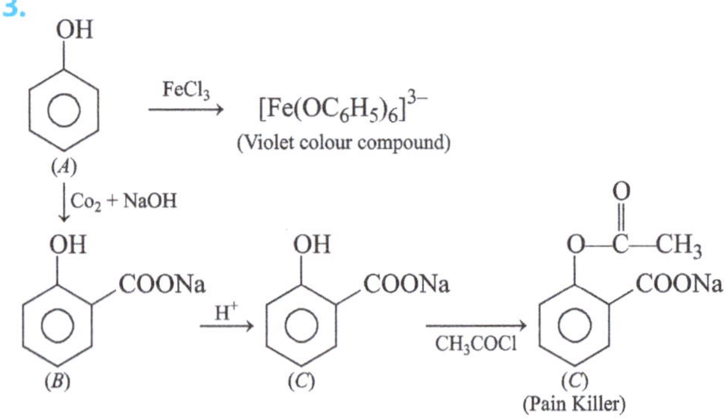

14. (i) Refer to sol. 24 (i). **(1)**

(ii) Formaldehyde is converted to ethanol by adding Grignard's reagent.

$$\underset{\text{Formaldehyde}}{HCHO} + CH_3MgBr \longrightarrow \underset{\text{Ethanol}}{CH_3CH_2OH}$$ **(1)**

15. (i) (a)

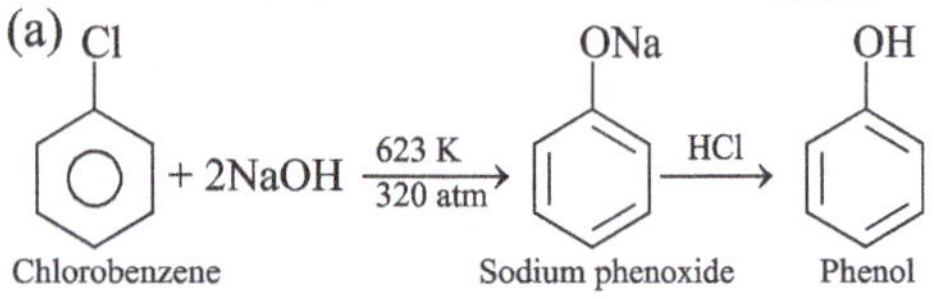

(1)

(ii) (b) The name of this reaction is Dow's process. **(1)**

16. (i) (c) Phenol react with Fe^{3+} ion in a ferric chloride ($FeCl_3$) solution to give complex ions with strong colours from red to purple. Ethanol doesn't undergo such reaction. **(1)**

(ii) (d) Violet colour is developed in solution due to addition of phenol to $FeCl_3$. **(1)**

17. (i) (c) The name of given reaction is Reimer-Tiemann reaction. **(1)**

(ii) (a)

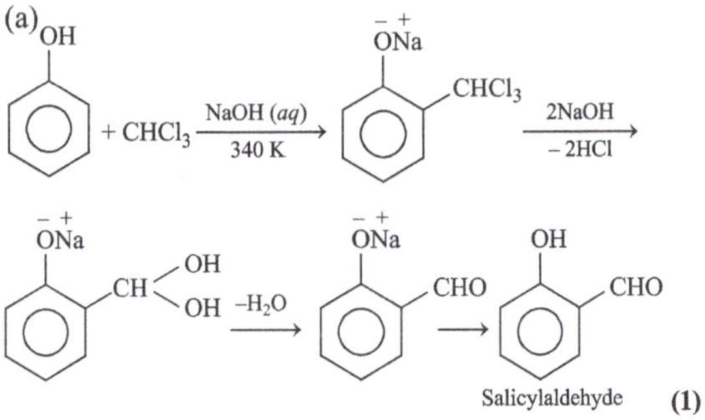

(1)

18. (i) (b) The conversion given in option (b) is incorrect.

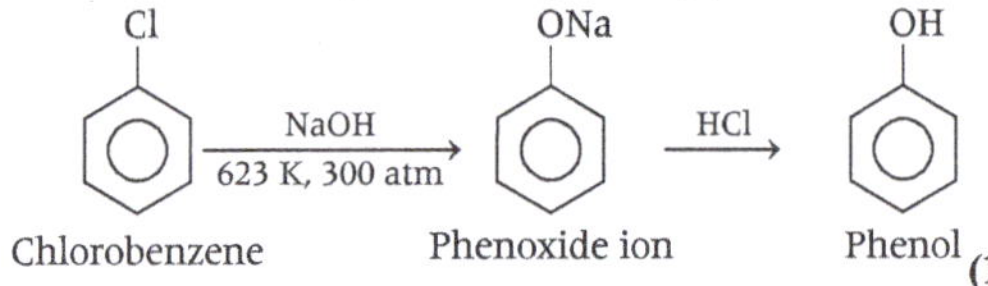

(1)

(ii) (a) The name of given reaction is Dow's process. **(1)**

19. (i) Reaction involve for the formation of benzene from phenol is as follows

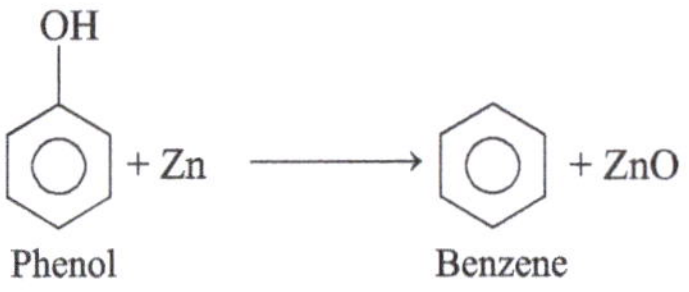

(1)

(ii) Reaction involve for the formation of salicylaldehyde from phenol is as follows

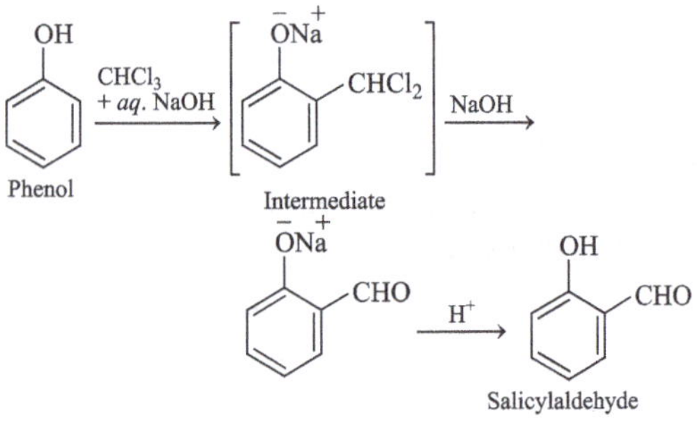

(1)

20.

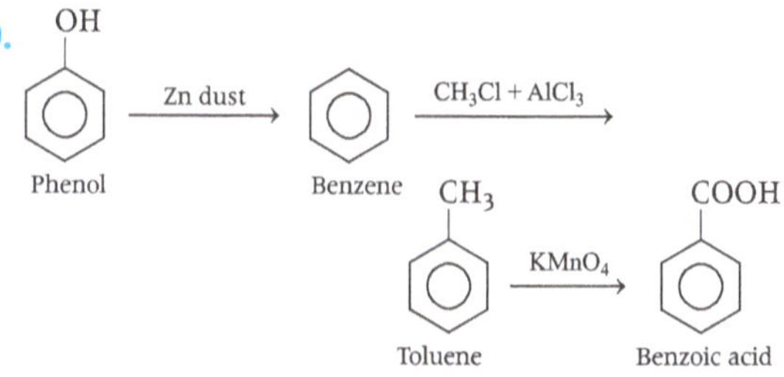

21. Phenol gives violet colour with neutral $FeCl_3$ solution while acetone does not give this test.

$$C_6H_5OH + FeCl_3 \longrightarrow \text{Violet colour}$$

$$CH_3COCH_3 + FeCl_3 \longrightarrow \text{No reaction}$$

Concept Enhancer Acetone has methyl group linked to the carbonyl carbon atom which is oxidised by sodium hypohalite to sodium salt of ethanoic acid and iodoform while phenol does not give this test.

$$CH_3-\overset{\overset{O}{||}}{C}-CH_3 \xrightarrow{3NaOI} CH_3CO\overset{-}{O}\overset{+}{Na} + CHI_3\downarrow + 3NaOH$$

$$C_6H_5OH \xrightarrow{NaOI} \text{No reaction}$$

22. Conversion of benzene to phenol is as follows

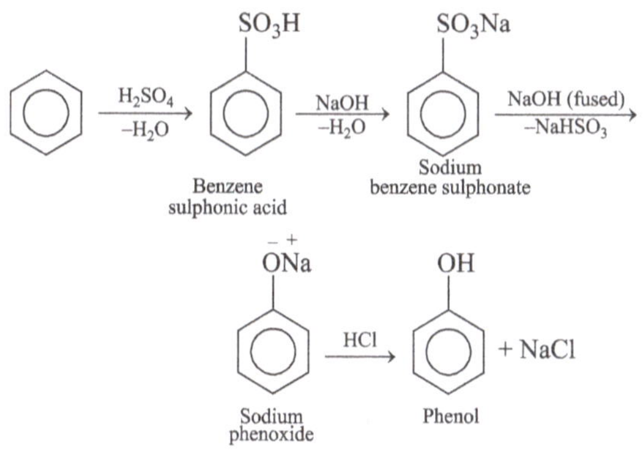

23. Conversion of phenol to benzoic acid is as follows

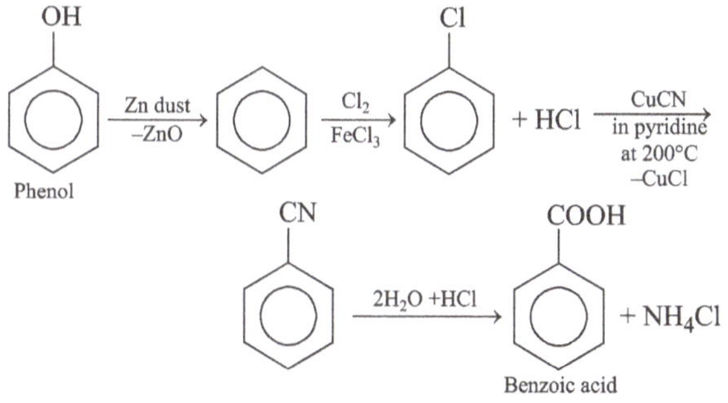

24. (i) **Picric acid from phenol** Phenol is treated with conc. HNO_3 and conc. H_2SO_4 to yield 2,4,6- trinitrophenol (picric acid.)

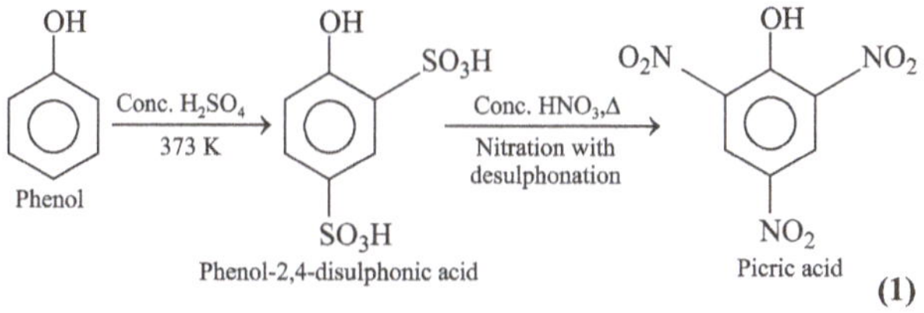

(1)

(ii) **Anisole from phenol** Phenol reacts with aqueous NaOH to form sodium phenoxide which on reaction with methyl bromide forms anisole.

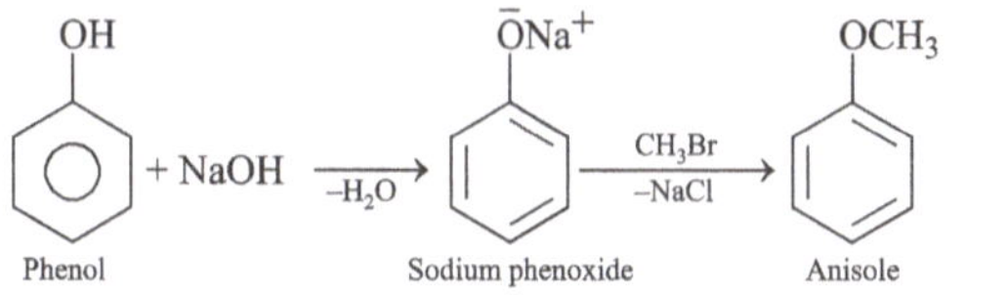

(1)

25. **$FeCl_3$ test** Phenol gives violet colour with neutral $FeCl_3$ solution while benzoic acid gives buff coloured ppt.

$$3C_6H_5OH + FeCl_3 \longrightarrow \underset{\text{(Violet colour)}}{[(C_6H_5O)_3\ Fe]^{3-}} + 3\ HCl$$

$$3\ C_6H_5COOH + FeCl_3 \longrightarrow \underset{\text{(Buff coloured ppt.)}}{Fe\ (C_6H_5COO)_3} + 3\ HCl$$

Concept Enhancer Benzoic acid reacts with sodium hydrogen carbonate to evolve brisk effervesence of CO_2 while phenol does not give this reaction.

$$C_6H_5COOH + NaHCO_3 \longrightarrow C_6H_5CO\overset{-}{O}\overset{+}{Na} + H_2O + CO_2\uparrow$$

26. Conversion of phenol to salicylic acid is as follows

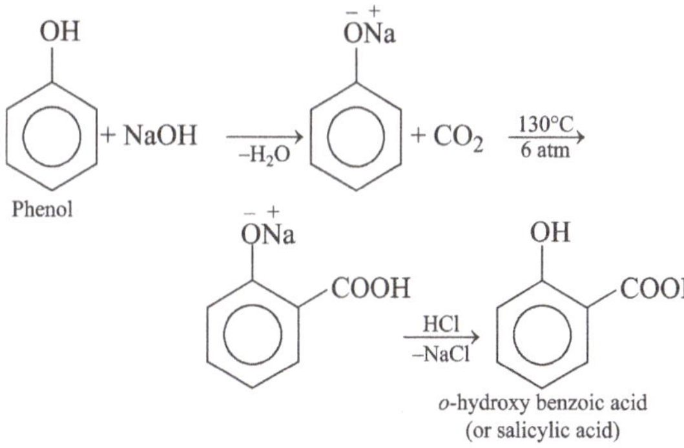

This reaction is named as Kolbe's reaction.

27. In phenol, — OH group activates the benzene ring and increases the electron density at *ortho* and *para*-positions. Hence, nitration (an electrophilic substitution) can be carried out easily.

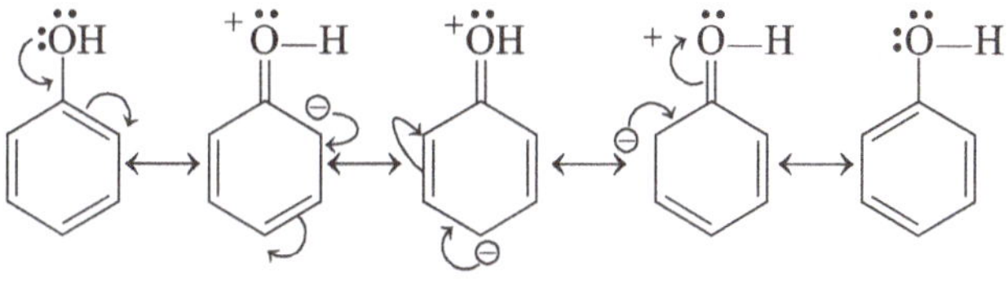

While in benzene, no such activating group is present, thus nitration is carried out under only in special conditions.

28. Reaction of phenol with bromine water produces white ppt. of 2, 4, 6-tribromophenol.

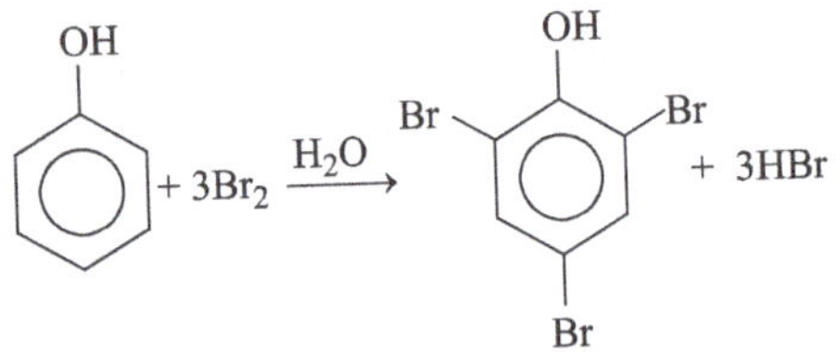

2, 4, 6-tribromophenol

29. (a) $C_2H_5OH \xrightarrow{PCl_5} \underset{(A)}{C_2H_5Cl} \xrightarrow{KCN}$

$\underset{(B)}{C_2H_5—CN} \xrightarrow{H_3O^+} C_2H_5COOH \xrightarrow[\Delta]{NH_3}$

$\underset{(C)}{CH_3—CH_2—\overset{\overset{\large O}{||}}{C}—NH_2}$

(b) 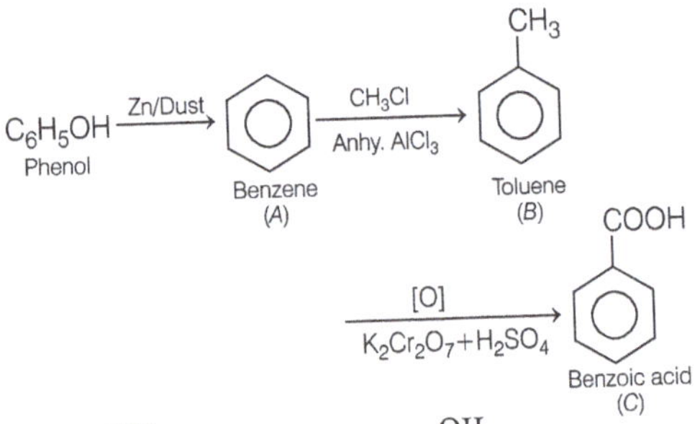

30. (a) 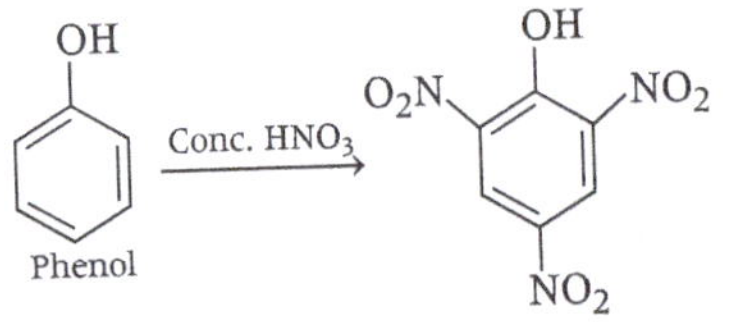

2, 4, 6-trinitrophenol
(Picric acid)

(b) $\underset{\text{Ethanol}}{C_2H_5OH} \xrightarrow[KMnO_4]{[O]} \underset{\text{Ethanoic acid}}{CH_3COOH}$

$\underset{\text{Ethanol}}{C_2H_5OH} + CH_3COOH \xrightarrow[H_2SO_4]{[H^+]} \underset{\text{Ethyl acetate}}{CH_3COOC_2H_5}$

(c) Anisole can be prepared by the action of methyl iodide on sodium phenoxide.

$C_6H_5—ONa \xrightarrow{CH_3—I} \underset{\text{Anisole}}{C_6H_5—O—CH_3}$

TOPIC 3

Ethers

These are the organic compounds having general formula $C_nH_{2n+2}O$ and are represented by general structure $R—O—R'$.

They are dialkyl derivatives of water or monoalkyl derivatives of alcohols.

Structure of Ethers

O-atom in ethers is sp^3-hybridised. Ethers have a bent or angular structure.

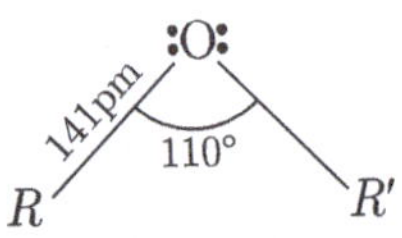

Classification of Ethers

On the basis of nature of R and R' groups in the general structure of ethers ($R—O—R'$), they are classified as **symmetrical** (simple), and **unsymmetrical** (mixed) ethers.

Depending upon the aliphatic and aromatic nature of R and R' groups they are divided as **aliphatic ethers** and **aromatic ethers**, i.e. alkyl, aryl or phenolic ethers (Ethers with one alkyl and one aryl group) and diaryl ethers (ethers with both aryl groups).

Nomenclature of Ethers

- In the common system, the two alkyl groups attached to the oxygen atom are named in alphabetic order and the word ether is added, e.g. are $CH_3—O—CH_2CH_3$ (ethylmethyl ether), $C_6H_5—O—C_2H_5$ (ethyl phenyl ether) (i.e. mixed ether).
- If two alkyl groups are same (i.e. simple ethers), the prefix di- is used, e.g. $CH_3—O—CH_3$ (dimethyl ether).
- In the **IUPAC system**, an ether is named as alkoxy alkane, e.g. CH_3OCH_3 (methoxy methane) and $CH_3OCH_2CH_3$ (methoxy ethane).

Note (i) The isomerism commonly exhibited by ethers is metamerism.
(ii) Ethanol and diethyl ether are functional isomers.

Preparation of Aliphatic Ethers

(i) **From alcohols** (By dehydration of 2 moles of alcohols)

(a) **Acid catalysed dehydration** Alcohols undergo dehydration in the presence of protic acids such as H_2SO_4, H_3PO_4.

Formation of the reaction product, alkene or ether depends upon the reaction conditions.

$$R\text{—O—H} + \text{H—O—}R \xrightarrow[413\text{ K}]{\text{Conc. } H_2SO_4} \underset{\text{Ether}}{R\text{—O—}R} + H_2O$$

The order of dehydration of alcohols leading to the formation of ethers is primary > secondary > tertiary

At **443 K**, ethene is the main product.

$$CH_3CH_2OH \xrightarrow[443\text{K}]{H_2SO_4} \underset{\text{Ethene}}{CH_2{=}CH_2} + H_2O$$

(b) **Catalytic dehydration** Alcohol on catalytic dehydration give ether.

$$R\text{—O—H} + \text{H—O—}R \xrightarrow[525\text{ K}]{Al_2O_3} \underset{\text{Ether}}{R\text{—O—}R} + H_2O$$

(ii) **By Williamson's synthesis** This is one of the best method for the preparation of ethers.

In this method, alkyl halide is treated with a suitable sodium (or potassium) alkoxide.

$$\underset{\text{Sodium alkoxide}}{R\text{—}O^-Na^+} + \underset{\text{Alkyl halide}}{R'X} \longrightarrow \underset{\text{Ether}}{R\text{—O—}R'} + NaX$$

Note This method is not applicable when the alkyl halide used in this synthesis is tertiary.

Physical Properties

The important physical properties of ether are as follows

(i) Dimethyl ether and ethylmethyl ethers are gases at ordinary temperature whereas higher ones are liquids with characteristic smell.

(ii) The C—O bonds in ethers are **polar**, therefore ethers have a net dipole moment.

(iii) **Boiling points** of ethers are much lower than those of isomeric alcohols. The large difference in boiling points of alcohols and ethers is due to the presence of H-bonding in alcohols. The boiling points of ethers are close to alkanes of comparable molecular masses due to their low polarity.

(iv) **Solubility** Lower ethers (up to three carbon atoms) are soluble in water and their miscibility with water resembles those of alcohols of the same molecular masses. This is due to the fact that just like alcohols, oxygen of ethers can also form H-bonds with water molecule as shown below.

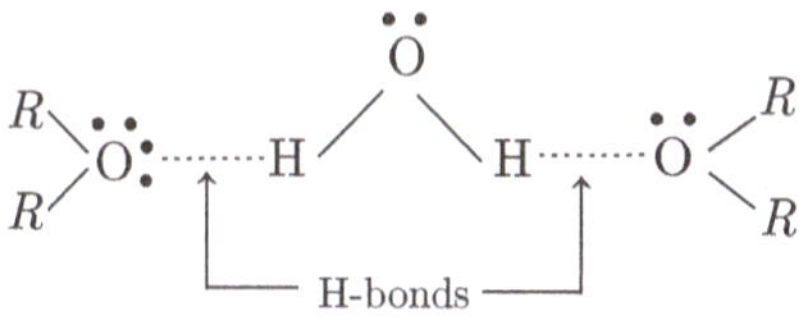

Chemical Properties

Important chemical properties of ethers are as follows

(i) **Reactions with chlorine** (Halogenation) When ethers react with Cl_2 or Br_2 in dark, substitution takes place mainly at α - C atom.

$$\underset{\text{Ether}}{R'CH_2\text{—O—}R} + Cl_2 \xrightarrow{\text{Dark}} \underset{\text{Chloroether}}{R'CHCl\text{—O—}R} + HCl$$

In the presence of light and excess of Cl_2, all H-atoms of ether are substituted by halogen atom to form perchlorodialkyl ether.

$$CH_3\text{—}CH_2\text{—O—}CH_2\text{—}CH_3 + \underset{\text{Excess}}{10\,Cl_2} \xrightarrow[-10HCl]{\text{Light}} \underset{\text{Perchlorodiethyl ether}}{CH_3\text{—}\underset{|}{\overset{}{CH}}(Cl)\text{—O—}\underset{|}{CH}(Cl)\text{—}CH_3}$$

(ii) **Oxidation** (Formation of peroxides) In contact with air or O_2, ethers form peroxides which are unstable compounds.

$$CH_3CH_2OCH_2CH_3 \xrightarrow[\text{Light}]{O_2\text{(air)}} \underset{\text{1-ethoxyethylhydroperoxide}}{CH_3\text{—}CH(O\text{—}O\text{—}H)\text{—O—}CH_2CH_3}$$

(iii) Reactions involving the cleavage of C — O Bond in ethers.

(a) **Reaction with halogen acids** (HX)

In cold, alkyl halide and alcohol are formed.

$$\underset{\text{Ether}}{R\text{—O—}R} + \underset{(X = \text{I or Br})}{HX} \xrightarrow{\text{Cold}} \underset{\text{Alcohol}}{ROH} + \underset{\text{Alkyl halide}}{RX}$$

With excess of halogen acids, 2 molecules of alkyl halides are formed.

$$R\text{—O—}R + \underset{\text{Excess}}{2HX} \xrightarrow{\Delta} 2RX + H_2O$$

(b) **Reaction with PCl_5** Alkyl chlorides are formed by the cleavage of C—O bond.

$$R\text{—O—}R + PCl_5 \xrightarrow{\Delta} \underset{\text{Alkyl chloride}}{2R\text{—Cl}} + POCl_3$$

Aryl Ethers

Aryl ethers have either one or both R and R' are aryl groups, i.e. $C_6H_5OCH_3, C_6H_5OC_6H_5$.

Physical Properties

(i) **Physical state** Generally aromatic ethers are liquids with characteristic smell called ethereal smell.

(ii) **Solubility** Aromatic ethers are almost immiscible with water.

Preparation of Anisole

The best method for the laboratory preparation of both simple and mixed ethers and involves the action of sodium phenoxide on a suitable alkyl halide (CH_3Cl). This method is known as **Williamson's synthesis.**

$$\underset{\text{Sodium phenoxide}}{C_6H_5\overset{-+}{ONa}} + CH_3Cl \longrightarrow \underset{\text{Methylphenyl ether}}{C_6H_5OCH_3} + NaCl$$

Chemical Properties

Reactions involving benzene ring (Electrophilic Substitution Reaction)

Alkoxy group(—OR) is *ortho, para*-directing and activates the aromatic ring towards electrophilic substitution reaction and directs the incoming electrophile at *o*- and *p*- positions (because of the negative charge at *o*- and *p*- positions indicates the more electron density at these positions due to resonance).

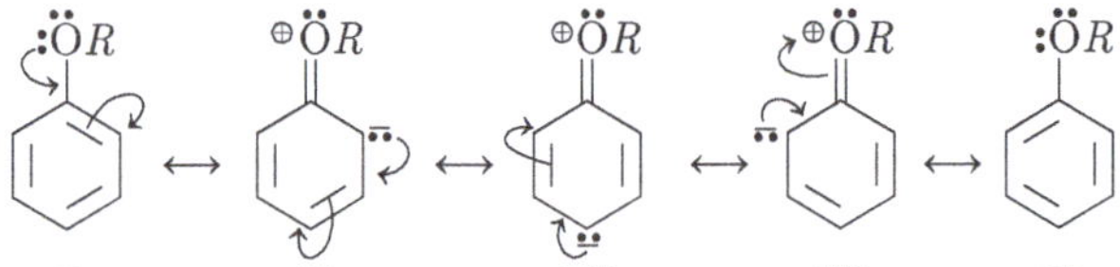

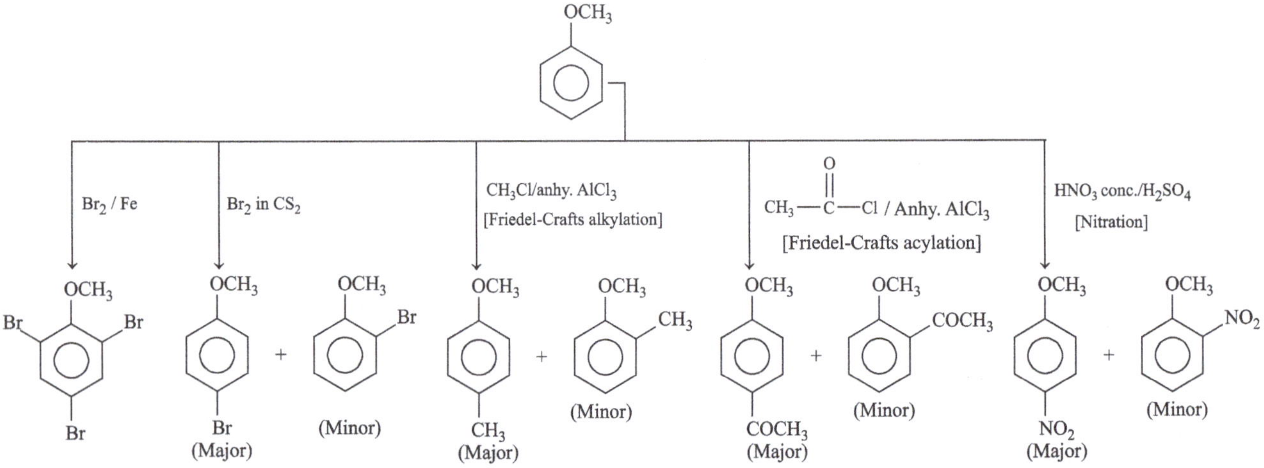

Uses of Ethers

- Dimethyl ether is used as a refrigerant and as a solvent at low temperatures.
- Used as an industrial solutions for oils, resins, gums, etc.
- As an extracting solvent in laboratory and industry because of their almost inert nature and good dissolving power.
- Diphenyl ether is used as heat transfer medium because of its high boiling point.

PYQs Previous Years' Questions

1 Mark Questions

1. Sodium phenoxide reacts with methyl chloride to give ...... The reaction is known as.... **ISC Specimen 2023**

2. Acetyl chloride on heating with diethyl ether in the presence of anhydrous $ZnCl_2$ gives **ISC 2021-22 (Sem-I)**
   (a) ethyl alcohol and acetic acid
   (b) methyl chloride and methyl alcohol
   (c) methyl acetate and methyl alcohol
   (d) ethyl acetate and ethyl chloride

3. When excess of ethanol is heated with conc. H_2SO_4 at 413 K, which compound is obtained? **ISC 2021-22 (Sem-I)**
   (a) Diethyl sulphate (b) Ethyl hydrogen sulphate
   (c) Ethoxy ethane (d) Ethene

4. Boiling point of ethyl alcohol is greater than diethyl ether due to **ISC Specimen 2021-22 (Sem-I)**
   (a) van der Waals' forces (b) London forces
   (c) polarity (d) hydrogen bonding

5. **Assertion** (A) Ethers are more volatile than alcohols having the same molecular formula.
   Reason (R) Alcohols have intermolecular hydrogen bond. **ISC Specimen 2021-22 (Sem-I)**
   (a) Both (A) and (R) are correct and (R) is the correct explanation of (A).
   (b) Both (A) and (R) are correct but (R) is not the correct explanation of (A).
   (c) (A) is correct and (R) is incorrect.
   (d) (A) is incorrect and (R) is correct.

6. The reaction
   Sodium alkoxide + alkyl halide $\longrightarrow$ ether + sodium halide is called **ISC Specimen 2021-22 (Sem-I)**
   (a) Wurtz reaction (b) Kolbe's reaction
   (c) Perkin's reaction (d) Williamson's synthesis

7. Benzene diazonium chloride on hydrolysis gives **ISC Specimen 2021-22 (Sem-I)**
   (a) benzene (b) phenol
   (c) chlorobenzene (d) benzyl alcohol

8. Give one chemical test each to distinguish between the following pairs of compounds :
   Ethanol and dimethyl ether **ISC 2020, 2016**

9. Give the balanced equation for the following reaction : Diethyl ether with phosphorus pentachloride. **ISC 2020, 2016**

10. Give the chemical equation for the following.
    Williamson's synthesis **ISC 2015**

11. Give the balanced equation for the following reaction. Sodium ethoxide is treated with ethyl bromide. **ISC 2014**

12. Give the balanced equation for the following reaction. Chlorine is passed through diethyl ether. **ISC 2010**

13. ...... and ...... are functional isomers. **ISC 2009**

14. Give the name of the following reaction. **ISC 2009**
    $C_2H_5Br + C_2H_5ONa \longrightarrow C_2H_5OC_2H_5 + NaBr$

15. Write the structures of the isomeric ethers with the formula $C_4H_{10}O$. **ISC 2001**

2 Marks Questions

16. Convert the following by giving chemical equations for each. **ISC 2024**
    (i) Ethyl bromide to diethyl ether
    (ii) Phenol to salicylaldehyde

17. What happens when (write chemical reactions only) **ISC Specimen 2024**
    (i) Diethyl ether is treated with phosphorous pentachloride.
    (ii) Ethyl alcohol is treated with methyl magnesium bromide.

18. How will the following be obtained? (Give chemical equation) **ISC 2023**
    (i) Ethanol form Grignard's reagent.
    (ii) Diethyl ether form sodium ethoxide.

19. When ethene reacts with HBr, a compound (*X*) is formed. When compound (*X*) reacts with sodium ethoxide then compound (*Y*) is formed along with sodium bromide. **ISC 2021-22 (Sem-I)**
    (i) Identify the compound (*X*).
    (a) C_2H_6 (b) C_2H_5Br (c) CH_3Br (d) $C_2H_4Br_2$
    (ii) Identify the compound (*Y*).
    (a) CH_3OH (b) C_2H_5OH
    (c) CH_3OCH_3 (d) $C_2H_5OC_2H_5$

20. How will you obtain the following? (Give balanced equation)
    (i) Ethyl chloride from diethyl ether
    (ii) Ethyl acetate from ethanol **ISC 2018**

21. Write the structure of three ethers with molecular formula $C_4H_{10}O$. **ISC 2016**

22. Complete the following reactions.
   (i) Chlorobenzene to phenol
   (ii) Diethyl ether to ethanol **ISC 2015**

3 Marks Question

23. According for the following. **ISC 2023**
   (i) Phenol is a stronger acid than aliphatic alcohols.
   (ii) Ethanol gives iodoform reaction whereas methanol does not give iodoform reaction.
   (iii) Ethers should not be distilled to dryness.

Explanations

1. anisole, Williamson's synthesis

2. (d) $\underset{\text{Acetyl chloride}}{CH_3COCl} + \underset{\text{Ethyl ether}}{C_2H_5OC_2H_5} \xrightarrow[\Delta]{\text{Anhyd. } ZnCl_2} \underset{\text{Ethyl chloride}}{C_2H_5Cl} + \underset{\text{Ethyl acetate}}{CH_3COOC_2H_5}$

3. (d) $\underset{\text{Ethanol (Excess)}}{CH_3CH_2OH} \xrightarrow[443\text{ K}]{\text{Conc. } H_2SO_4} \underset{\text{Ethene}}{CH_2{=}CH_2} + H_2O$

4. (d) The boiling point of ethyl alcohol is greater than diethyl ether due to hydrogen bonding.

5. (b) Both (A) and (R) are correct but (R) is not the correct explanation of (A).

6. (d) The given reaction is Williamson's synthesis.

7. (b)

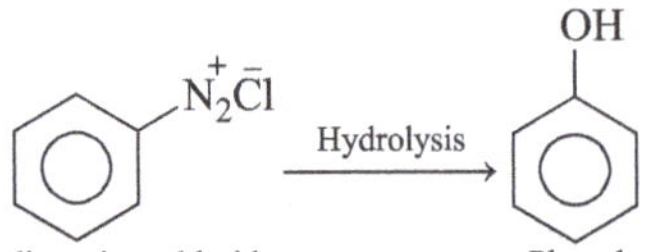

Benzene diazonium chloride Phenol

8. Ethyl alcohol gives yellow precipitate during iodoform test, while dimethyl ether does not give such test.

$$\underset{\text{Ethyl alcohol}}{CH_3CH_2OH} + 6NaOH + 4I_2 \longrightarrow CHI_3(\downarrow) + HCO\overset{-}{O}\overset{+}{Na} + 5NaI + 5H_2O$$

$$\underset{\text{Dimethyl ether}}{CH_3 - O - CH_3} + 6NaOH + 4I_2 \longrightarrow \text{No reaction}$$

9. $\underset{\text{Diethyl ether}}{C_2H_5 - O - C_2H_5} + PCl_5 \xrightarrow{\Delta} \underset{\text{Ethyl chloride}}{2C_2H_5Cl} + \underset{\text{Phosphoryl chloride}}{POCl_3}$

10. In this method, alkyl halide is treated with a suitable sodium (or potassium) alkoxide.

$$\underset{\text{Sodium alkoxide}}{R - O^-Na^+} + \underset{\text{Alkyl halide}}{R'X} \longrightarrow \underset{\text{Ether}}{R - O - R'} + NaX$$

> **Common Mistake** Generally students are not clear about the suitable condition for this reaction. For a better yield alkyl halide must be primary and sodium alkoxide can be primary, secondary or tertiary.

11. $\underset{\text{Sodium ethoxide}}{C_2H_5\overset{-}{O}\overset{+}{Na}} + \underset{\text{Ethyl bromide}}{C_2H_5Br} \longrightarrow \underset{\text{Diethyl ether}}{C_2H_5OC_2H_5} + NaBr$

12. With Cl_2, substitution takes place at α-C atom.

$$\underset{\text{Diethyl ether}}{CH_3CH_2 - O - CH_2CH_3} \xrightarrow[-HCl]{+Cl_2} \underset{\alpha\text{-chlorodiethyl ether}}{CH_3CHClOCH_2CH_3} \xrightarrow[-HCl]{+Cl_2} \underset{\alpha,\alpha'\text{-dichlorodiethyl ether}}{CH_3CHCl \cdot OCHClCH_3}$$

13. The isomer which differs by the presence of functional group are called functional isomerism.
Ethanol and **diethyl ether** are functional isomers.

14. The given reaction is Williamson's synthesis used for the preparation of ether.

15. Isomeric ethers with formula $C_4H_{10}O$ are as

$$\underset{\text{Methyl propyl ether}}{\begin{matrix} CH_3 \\ CH_3CH_2CH_2 \end{matrix}\!>\!O} + \underset{\text{Diethyl ether}}{\begin{matrix} C_2H_5 \\ C_2H_5 \end{matrix}\!>\!O} \longrightarrow \underset{\text{Methyl iso-propyl ether}}{CH_3 - O - CH\!<\!\begin{matrix} CH_3 \\ CH_3 \end{matrix}}$$

16. (i) Alcohols react with active metals like Na to produce corresponding alkoxides with the evolution hydrogen gas. This show that alcohols are acidic in nature (and can donate a proton to a stronger base). Whereas diethyl ether does not contain any ionic functional groups nor can deprotonate readily. Thus, in the absence of available hydrogen atoms or other ionic species, the sodium ions will not react.
   (ii) In case of unsymmetrical ethers having two different alkyl groups, the alcohol and the alkyl halide formed depends on the nature of the alkyl group. In ethoxy ethane, alkyl groups are present, thus, lower alkyl group forms alkyl iodide (CH_3I) and higher alkyl group forms alcohol, i.e. C_2H_5OH. This is an example of S_N2 reaction.

17. (i) Diethyl ether reacts with phosphorus pentachloride on heating to form ethyl chloride.

$$C_2H_5—O—C_2H_5 + PCl_5 \longrightarrow 2C_2H_5Cl + POCl_3$$

(ii) When ethyl alcohol is treated with methyl magnesium bromide it forms methane.

$$CH_3MgBr + CH_3—CH_2—OH \longrightarrow \underset{\text{Methane}}{CH_4} + CH_3CH_2O^{\ominus}Mg^{\oplus}Br$$

18. (i) When methanal reacts with methyl magnesium bromide in the presence of dry ehter to give a complex which on hydrolysis gives ethanol.

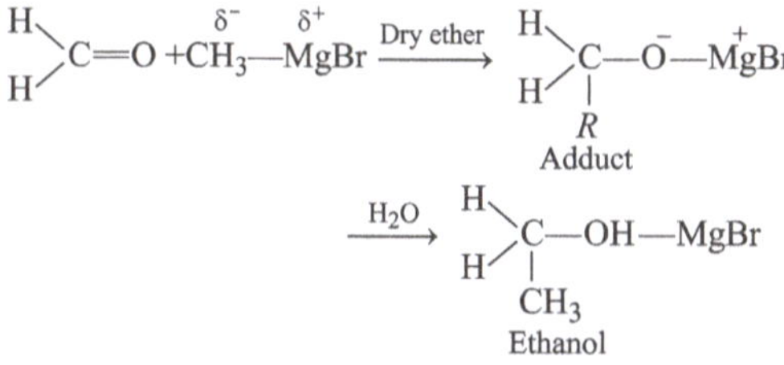

(1)

(ii) **Williamson's synthesis**

$$\underset{\text{Sodium ethoxide}}{CH_3—CH_2—ONa} + \underset{\text{Ethyl bromide}}{Br—CH_2—CH_3} \xrightarrow{\Delta} \underset{\text{Diethyl ether}}{CH_3—CH_2—O—CH_2—CH_3} + NaBr \quad (1)$$

19. $$\underset{\text{Ethene}}{CH_2=CH_2} + HBr \longrightarrow \underset{(X)}{CH_3—CH_2—Br} \xrightarrow{C_2H_5ONa} \underset{(Y)}{C_2H_5OC_2H_5} + NaBr$$

Therefore, (i)-(b) and (ii)-(d) are correct. (1 + 1)

20. (i) **Ethyl chloride from diethyl ether** Diethyl ether reacts with phosphorus pentachloride to give ethyl chloride and phosphoryl chloride.

$$\underset{\text{Diethyl ether}}{C_2H_5—O—C_2H_5} + PCl_5 \longrightarrow \underset{\text{Ethyl chloride}}{2C_2H_5Cl} + POCl_3 \quad (1)$$

(ii) **Ethyl acetate from ethanol** Ethyl acetate is an ester formed by reaction between ethanol and ethanoic acid. Ethanol is first oxidised to ethanoic acid, which further react with ethanol to form ethyl acetate

$$\underset{\text{Ethanol}}{CH_3CH_2OH} \xrightarrow{\text{Alkaline } KMnO_4} \underset{\text{Ethanoic acid}}{CH_3COOH}$$

$$CH_3COOH + CH_3CH_2OH \xrightarrow{\text{Conc. } H_2SO_4} \underset{\text{Ethyl acetate}}{CH_3COOCH_2CH_3} + H_2O \quad (1)$$

21. The three ethers with molecular formula $C_4H_{10}O$ are diethylether, methoxypropane and methyl *iso*-propyl ether.

(i) 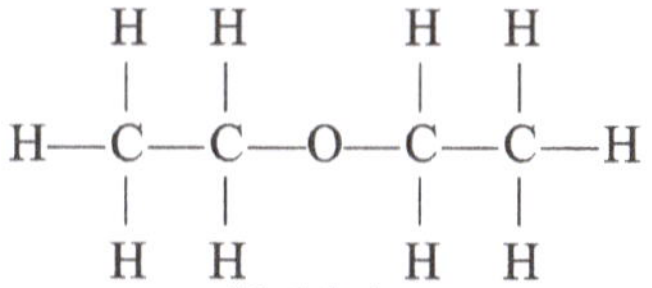

Diethyl ether

(ii) 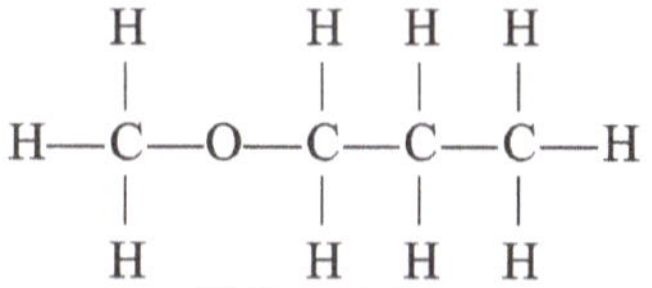

Methoxy propane

(iii) 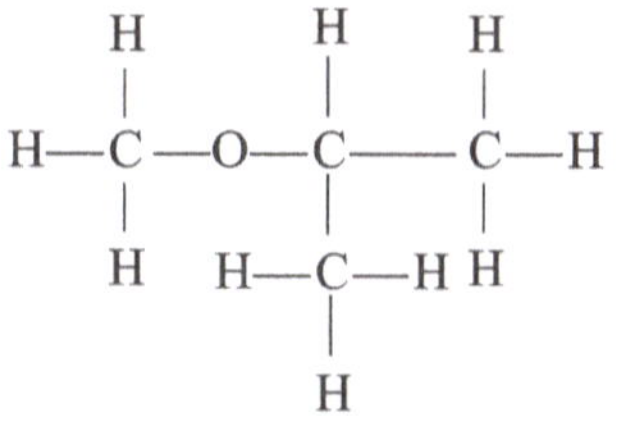

Methyl *iso*-propyl ether

(2)

22. (i) **Conversion of chlorobenzene to phenol**

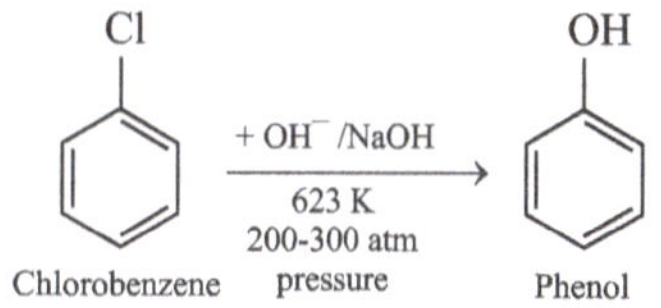

(1)

(ii) **Conversion of diethyl ether to ethanol**

$$\underset{\text{Diethyl ether}}{C_2H_5—O—C_2H_5} + HI \xrightarrow[\Delta]{} \underset{\text{Ethanol}}{C_2H_5OH} + C_2H_5I \quad (1)$$

23. (i) Phenol is a stronger acid due to the presence of polar —OH group and resonance stabilisation of phenoxide ion. This resonance stabilisation of phenoxide ion makes phenol more acidic than aliphatic alcohols. (1)

(ii) Compounds that can be oxidised to methyl ketone or having methyl group attached to carbonyl carbon can gave haloform reaction. Thus, ethyl alcohol (ethanol) can be oxidised to ethanal which contains methyl keto group but methyl alcohols do not, as it cannot oxidised to methyl keto group.

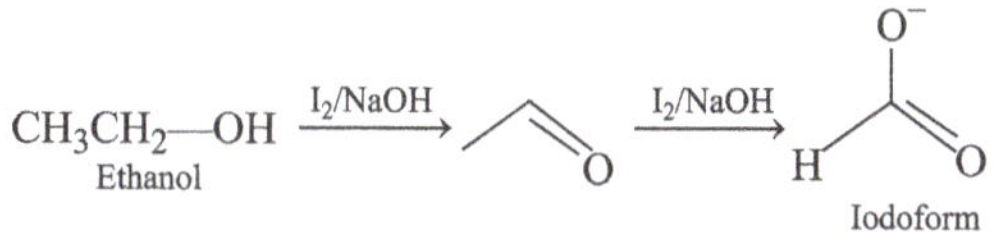

(1)

(iii) Ethers are not distilled to dryness for the fear of explosion due to formation of peroxides. Peroxides are highly explosive and are less volatile than ethers. (1)

CHAPTER TEST

01 Marks Questions

1. Fill in the blanks by choosing the appropriate word(s) from those given in the bracket.

[acidic, basic, orange, green, soluble, insoluble, absolute alcohol, rectified alcohol, primary, *tert*-butoxide, no reaction, reaction in 5 minutes]

(i) Phenol reacts with diazonium salts in weakly .... solution to form .... coloured azo dyes.

(ii) Primary alcohols give .... while secondary alcohols give .... with Lucas reagent.

(iii) 100% ethanol is .... and 95% ethanol is ....

(iv) To obtain best yield of *tert*-butyl ether by Williamson's synthesis, the alkyl halide should be .... and alkoxide should be ....

2. Select and write the correct alternatives from the choices given below.

(i) The alcohol obtained by the hydrolysis of oils and fats is

(a) glycol (b) glycerol
(c) propanol (d) pentanol

(ii) Upon treatment with I_2 and aqueous NaOH which of the following compounds will form iodoform ?

(a) $CH_3CH_2CH_2CH_2CHO$
(b) $CH_3CH_2COCH_2CH_3$
(c) $CH_3CH_2CH_2CH_2CH_2OH$
(d) $CH_3CH_2CH_2CH(OH)CH_3$

(iii) The reaction of phenol with excess of bromine water gives

(a) *m*-bromophenol (b) *o*- and *p*-bromophenol
(c) 2, 4-dibromophenol (d) 2, 4, 6- tribromophenol

(iv) Anisole is the product obtained from phenol by the reaction known as

(a) coupling (b) etherification
(c) oxidation (d) esterification

3. (i) **Assertion** (A) The density of glycerol is higher than propanol.

Reason (R) Propanol has intramolecular hydrogen bonding.

(a) Both (A) and (R) are correct and (R) is the correct explanation of (A).
(b) Both (A) and (R) are correct but (R) is not the correct explanation of (A).
(c) (A) is correct and (R) is incorrect.
(d) (A) is incorrect and (R) is correct.

(ii) **Assertion** (A) Phenol is more acidic than alcohol.

Reason (R) Due to resonance the phenoxide ion is more stable as compare to alcohol.

(a) Both (A) and (R) are correct and (R) is the correct explanation of (A).
(b) Both (A) and (R) are correct but (R) is not the correct explanation of (A).
(c) (A) is correct and (R) is incorrect.
(d) (A) is incorrect and (R) is correct.

02 Marks Questions

4. (i) Arrange the following compounds in the increasing order of their acidic strength.

p-cresol, *p*-nitrophenol, phenol

(ii) Write the mechanism (using the curved arrow rotation) of the following reaction.

$$CH_2{=}CH_2 \xrightarrow{H_3O^+} CH_3{-}\overset{+}{C}H + H_2O$$

5. Explain why?

(i) The boiling points of *p*-alcohol decreases with increase in branching of the alkyl chain.

(ii) *o*- nitrophenol is more acidic than *o*-methoxy phenol.

6. Account the following.

(i) *o*-nitrophenol is more steam valatile than *p*-nitrophenol.

(ii) *tert*-butyl chloride on heating with sodium methoxide gives 2-methylpropene instead of *tert*-butyl methyl ether.

7. Describe the chemical test to distinguish between ethanol and phenol.

8. (i) Write the IUPAC name of the following compound.

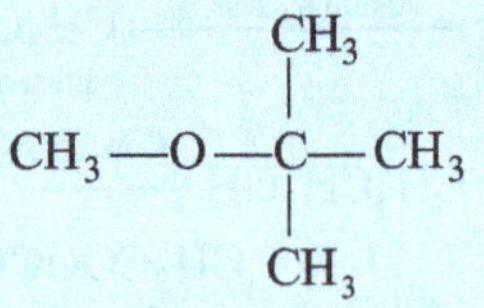

(ii) Phenyl methyl ether reacts with HI to give phenol and methyl iodide and not iodobenzene and methyl alcohol. Why ?

9. (i) Draw the structural formula of 2-methyl propan-2-ol molecule.

(ii) How would you obtain ethane - 1, 2-diol from ethanol?

10. How are following conversion carried out ?

(i) Propene to propan-2-ol

(ii) Ethyl chloride to ethanol

03 Marks Questions

11. Write the product(s) of the following reactions.

(i) 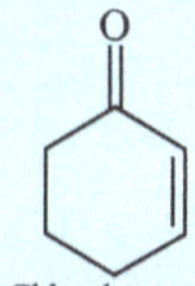 $\xrightarrow{PCC}$

Chlorobenzene

(ii) 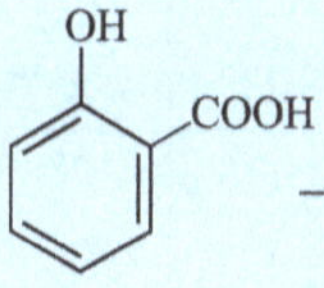 $\xrightarrow[CH_3COOH]{(CH_3CO)_2O}$

(iii) 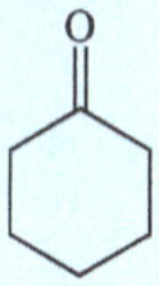 $+ CH_3MgBr \xrightarrow{H_3O^+}$

12. (i) Butanol has a higher boiling point than diethyl ether. Why ?

(ii) Write the mechanism of the following reaction.

$$2CH_3CH_2OH \xrightarrow[143K]{H^+} CH_3CH_2—O—CH_2CH_3$$

13. How can you convert the following ?

(i) Phenol to *o*-hydroxybenzaldehyde

(ii) Methanal to ethanol

(iii) Phenol to phenyl ethanoate

14. (i) Give one chemical test to distinguish between the following pairs of compounds.

(a) Phenol and benzoic acid

(b) 1-propanol and 2-propanol

(ii) Write the IUPAC name of the given compound ?

$$HO—CH_2—CH{=}\underset{\large CH_3}{\underset{|}{C}}—CH_3$$

15. Predict the product of the following reactions.

(i) $CH_3—CH{=}CH_2 \xrightarrow[(b)\,3H_2O/\bar{O}H]{(a)\,B_2H_6}$

(ii) $C_6H_5OH \xrightarrow{Br_2\,(aq)}$

(iii) $CH_3CH_2OH \xrightarrow{Cu/573\ K}$

05 Marks Questions

16. (i) How are the following conversion carried out ?

(a) Benzyl chloride to benzyl alcohol

(b) Ethyl magnesium chloride to propan -1-ol

(c) Propene to propan-2-ol

(ii) Why phenol undergoes electrophilic substitution more easily than benzene ?

(iii) Write the equations involved in the Reimer-Tiemann reaction.

17. (i) How would you obtained the following?

(a) Benzoquinone from phenol

(b) 2- methylpropan -2-ol from methyl magnesium bromide

(c) Propan -2-ol from propene

(ii) Write the Kolbe's reaction with an example.

(iii) Explain why O=C=O is polar while *R*—O—*R* is polar ?

18. (i) Predict the products of the following reactions

(a) $CH_3—CH_2—CH_2—O—CH_3 + HBr \longrightarrow$

(b) 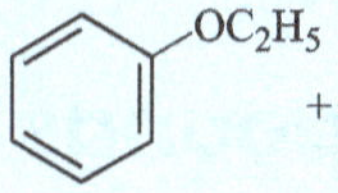 $+ HBr \longrightarrow$

(c)  $\xrightarrow{Conc.\ H_2SO_5/Conc.\ HNO_3}$

(ii) Give reasons.

(a) Phenols boil at higher temperature than haloarenes of comparable molecular mass.

(b) The C—O—H bond angle in alcohols is slightly less than the tetrahedral angle (109°28′).

Answers

1. (i) basic, orange (ii) no reaction, reaction in 5 minutes
(iii) absolute alcohol, rectified alcohol (iv) primary alkyl halide, *t*-alkyl halide

2. (i) (b), (ii) (d), (iii) (d), (iv) (b)

3. (i) (c), (ii) (a)

08

Aldehydes, Ketones and Carboxylic Acids

TREND ANALYSIS 4 YEARS

Topic	Types of Questions	2024	2023	2020	2019
	Average No. of Questions Across all Sets				
TOPIC 01 Carbonyl compounds (Aldehydes and Ketones)	1 Mark	—	—	2	2
	2 Marks	1	—	—	1
	3 Marks	1	—	1	2
	5 Marks	1	—	—	—
TOPIC 02 Carboxylic Acids	1 Mark	—	—	—	—
	2 Marks	—	2	2	1
	3 Marks	—	—	—	—
	5 Marks	—	1	—	—

TOPIC 1

Carbonyl Compounds
(Aldehydes and Ketones)

The $>C{=}O$ group is known as the **carbonyl group** and the compounds containing $>C{=}O$ group are known as carbonyl compounds. In aldehydes, the carbonyl group is bonded to carbon and hydrogen, while in ketones it is bonded to two carbon atoms.

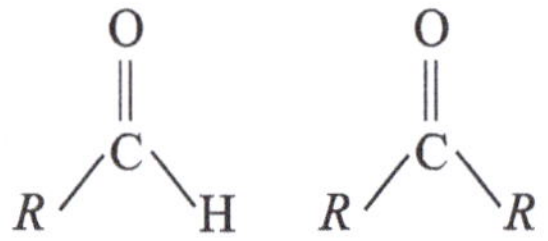

Aldehyde   Ketone

Aldehydes and ketones have molecular formula, $C_nH_{2n}O$ and are functional isomers of each other.

Nomenclature of Aldehydes and Ketones

(i) Common Names

The common names of aldehydes are derived from the common names of corresponding carboxylic acids just by replacing the ending 'ic' of carboxylic acid with aldehyde.

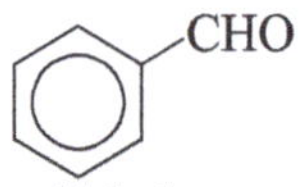

Benzaldehyde

Common names of aliphatic and aromatic ketones are derived by writing the names of alkyl groups attached to the C=O group in alphabetical order and adding the word ketone.

e.g. $CH_3-\overset{\overset{\large O}{||}}{C}-C_2H_5$ (Ethyl methyl ketone)

(ii) IUPAC Names

The word 'al' and 'one' replaces the ending 'e' of corresponding alkanes, while naming the open chain aliphatic aldehydes and ketones, respectively.

Structure and Nature of Carbonyl Group

In carbonyl group, the C-atom is in a state of sp^2-hybridisation.

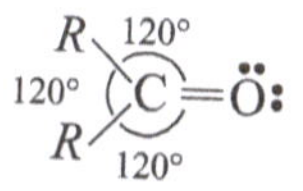

The carbon-oxygen double bond present in a carbonyl group is different from an ordinary C=C bond (in alkenes). Carbonyl group is polar in nature.

Methods of Preparation of Aliphatic Aldehydes and Ketones

Some important methods of preparation of aliphatic aldehydes and ketones are as follows

(i) From Alcohols

(a) By oxidation of alcohols with $K_2Cr_2O_7 / H_2SO_4$ or $KMnO_4 / KOH$.

$$\underset{1^\circ \text{alcohol}}{RCH_2OH} + [O] \xrightarrow{K_2Cr_2O_7/H_2SO_4} \underset{\text{Aldehyde}}{R-CHO} + H_2O$$

$$\underset{2^\circ \text{ alcohol}}{R_2CHOH} + [O] \xrightarrow{K_2Cr_2O_7/H_2SO_4} \underset{\text{Ketone}}{R_2C=O} + H_2O$$

(b) By catalytic dehydrogenation of alcohols with Cu at 573 K.

$$\underset{1^\circ \text{alcohol}}{R-CHOH} \xrightarrow{Cu/573\text{ K}} \underset{\text{Aldehyde}}{R-CHO} + H_2\uparrow$$

$$\underset{2^\circ \text{ alcohol}}{R_2CHOH} \xrightarrow{Cu/573\text{ K}} \underset{\text{Ketone}}{R_2C=O} + H_2\uparrow$$

(ii) From Alkenes (Ozonolysis)

By reductive ozonolysis of alkenes

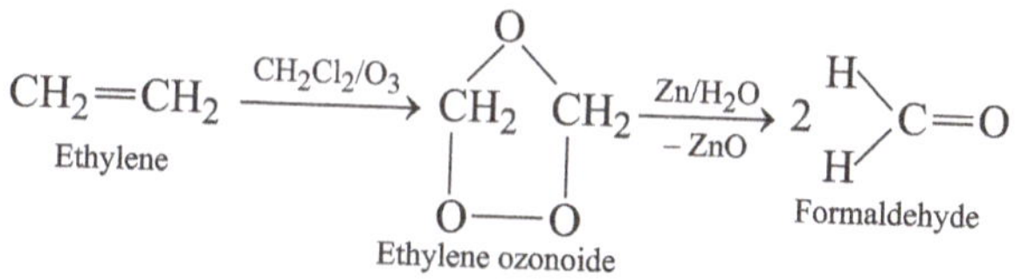

(iii) From Alkynes (Hydration)

By hydration of alkynes

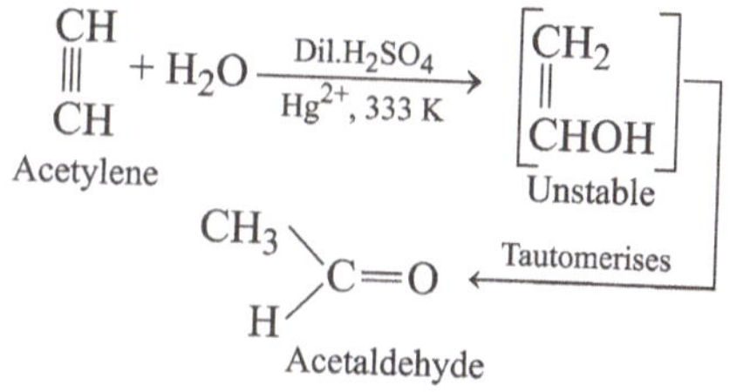

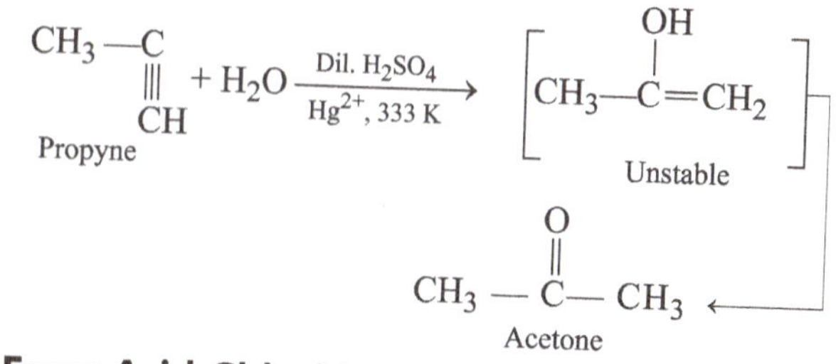

(iv) From Acid Chlorides

Aldehydes can be obtained from acid chlorides by the catalytic hydrogenation known as **Rosenmund reduction.**

$$\underset{\text{Acid chloride}}{R-\overset{\overset{\large O}{||}}{C}-Cl} + H_2 \xrightarrow[\text{Boiling xylene}]{Pd/BaSO_4, S} \underset{\text{Aldehyde}}{RCHO} + HCl$$

Formaldehyde cannot be prepared by this method, as formyl chloride (HCOCl) is unstable at room temperature.

Note Catalyst is poisoned in order to avoid further reduction of aldehydes into alcohols.

Ketones cannot be prepared by Rosenmund reduction. They are prepared by treating acid chlorides with dimethyl cadmium in the presence of dry ether.

$$2R'-\underset{\underset{\large O}{||}}{C}-Cl + R_2Cd \xrightarrow{\text{Dry ether}} 2R'-\underset{\underset{\large O}{||}}{C}-R + CdCl_2$$

(v) From Nitriles (Stephen Reaction)

(a) **Stephen reaction**

$$\underset{\text{Nitrile}}{RCN} + SnCl_2 + HCl \longrightarrow \underset{\text{Imine}}{RCH=NH} \xrightarrow{H_3O^+} RCHO$$

(b) **Reaction of nitrile with Grignard's reagent**

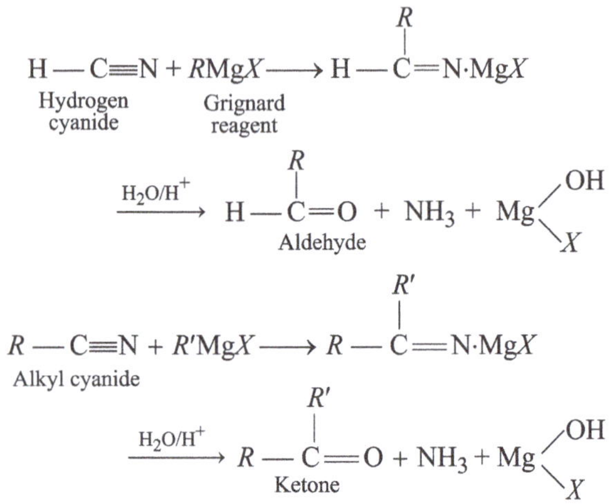

(vi) From Calcium Salts of Carboxylic Acids

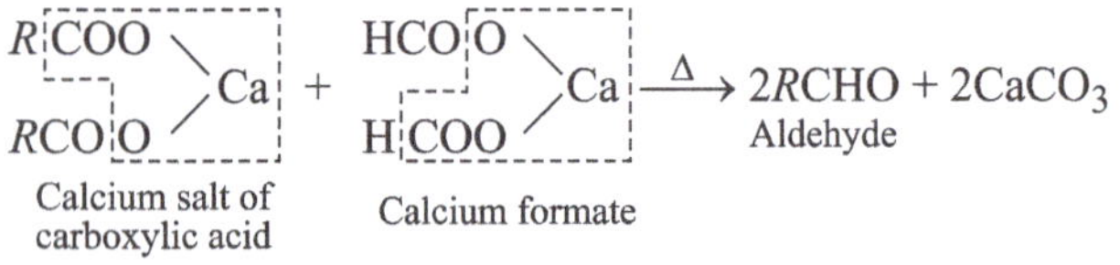

Note Instead of Ca salts, Mg, Ba and Th salts may also be used in the above method.

(vii) From Esters

Esters can also be reduced to aldehydes with DIBAL-H.

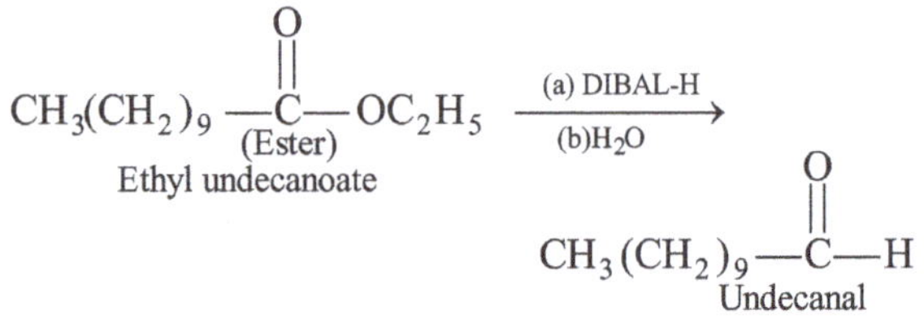

Physical Properties of Aldehydes and Ketones

- Methanal is a gas while ethanal is a volatile liquid at room temperature.
- Boiling points of aldehydes and ketones are higher than hydrocarbons and ethers of comparable molecular masses, because both compounds contain polar carbonyl group, therefore they have strong intermolecular dipole-dipole interactions between the opposite ends of C=O dipoles.
- The boiling points of aldehydes and ketones are much lower than those of corresponding alcohols and carboxylic acids which possess intermolecular H-bonding.
- Lower members (upto four C-atoms) are miscible with water in all proportions, because they form hydrogen bond with water.
- In water, solubility of aldehydes and ketones decreases with increase in the size of alkyl group.
- All aldehydes and ketones are fairly soluble in organic solvents like benzene, ether, methanol, chloroform, etc.

Chemical Properties of Aldehydes and Ketones

Chemical properties of aldehydes and ketones are as follows

1. Nucleophilic Addition Reactions

Aldehydes are more reactive towards nucleophilic addition reactions than ketones due to the following reasons.

(a) Inductive effect (b) Steric effect

- In general, aromatic aldehydes and ketones are less reactive than the corresponding aliphatic analogues.
- Aromatic aldehydes are more reactive than alkyl aryl ketones which in turn are more reactive than diaryl ketones.

$$\underset{\text{Benzaldehyde}}{C_6H_5CHO} > \underset{\text{Acetophenone}}{C_6H_5COCH_3} > \underset{\text{Benzophenone}}{C_6H_5COC_6H_5}$$

Examples of Some Important Nucleophilic Addition Reactions

(i) **Addition of hydrogen cyanide** (HCN)

e.g.

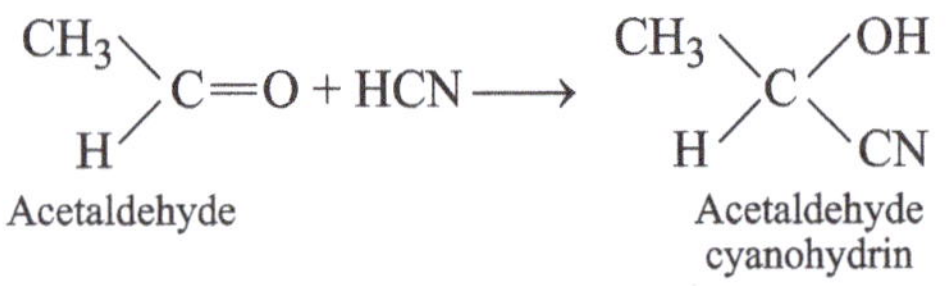

(ii) **Addition of sodium hydrogen sulphite** ($NaHSO_3$)

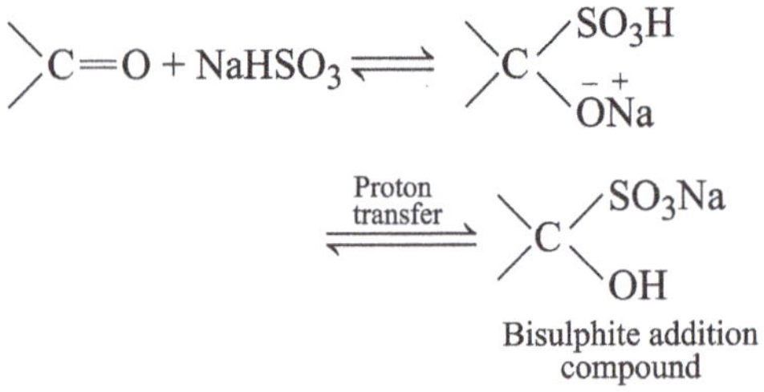

(iii) **Addition of Grignard reagent** Aldehydes and ketones on reaction with Grignard reagent give addition products which upon hydrolysis with water or dilute mineral acids gives alcohol. The type of alcohol formed depends upon the aldehyde or ketone used.

Note (formaldehyde $\rightarrow 1°$ alcohol, aldehydes $\rightarrow 2°$ alcohols and ketones $\rightarrow 3°$ alcohols).

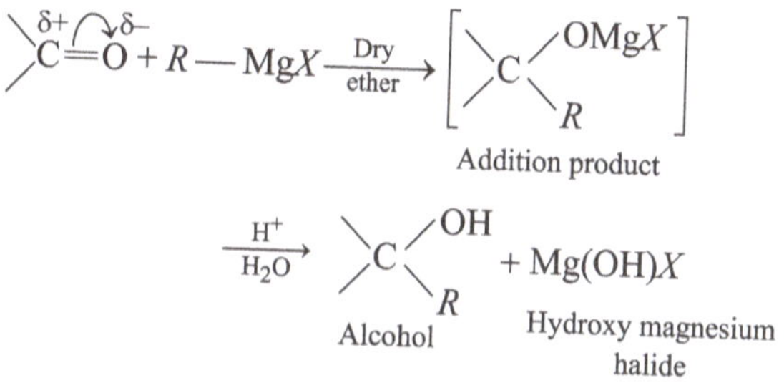

(iv) **Addition of alcohols**

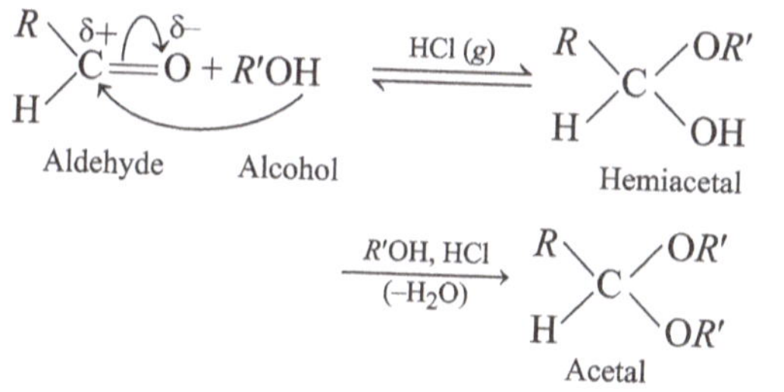

Ketones, however, do not react with monohydric alcohols but they react with dihydric alcohols such as ethylene glycol to give cyclic ketals.

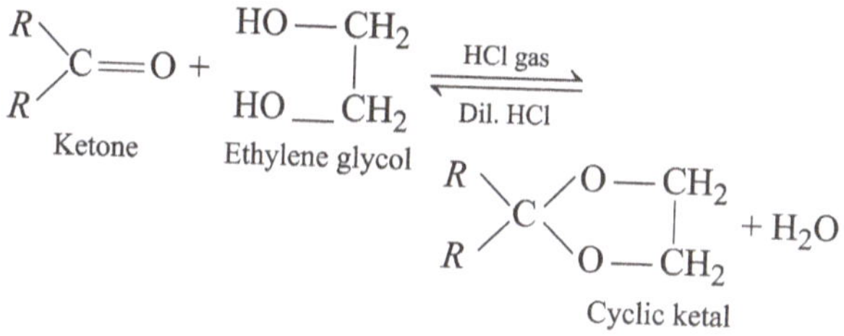

Note **Acetals** and **ketals** are hydrolysed by dilute acids and generate original aldehydes and ketones.

(v) Addition of ammonia and its derivatives

- **Addition of ammonia** Aldehydes react with NH_3 to form aldehyde ammonia.

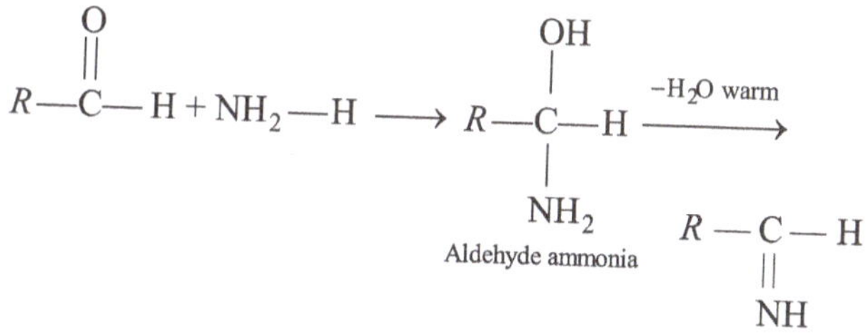

Ketones react with NH_3 to form ketone ammonia or ketonic amine complex which cannot be isolated.

e.g.

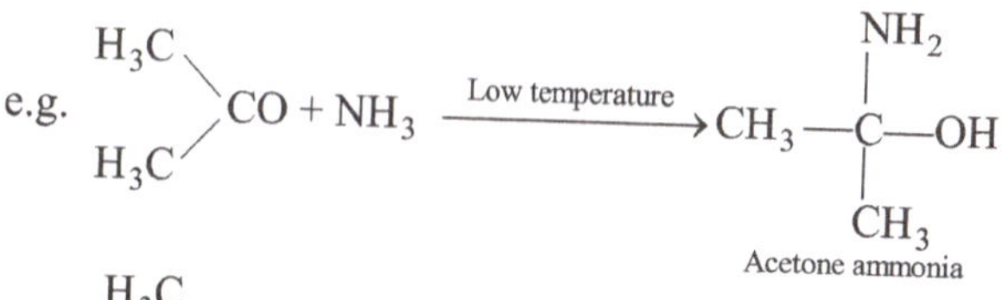

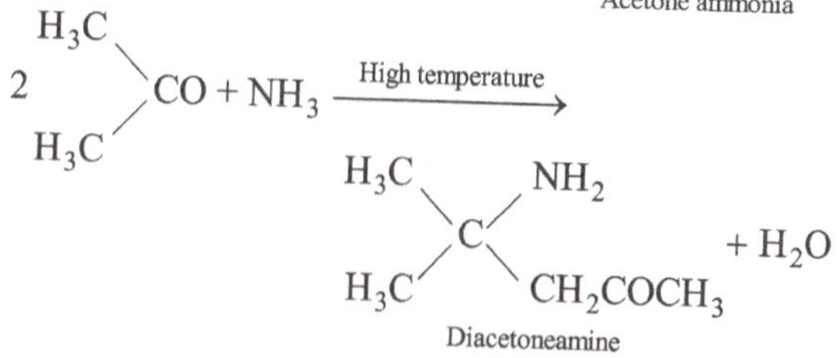

- **Addition of ammonia derivatives** Different reactions are as follows

Reaction with hydroxyl amine Oximes are formed.

$$R{-}CH{=}O + \underset{\text{Hydroxyl amine}}{NH_2OH} \longrightarrow \underset{\text{Aldoxime}}{R{-}CH{=}NOH} + H_2O$$

Reaction with hydrazine Hydrazones are formed.

$$>C{=}O + \underset{\text{Hydrazine}}{NH_2NH_2} \longrightarrow \underset{\text{Hydrazone}}{>C{=}N{\cdot}NH_2} + H_2O$$

Reaction with phenyl hydrazine Phenyl hydrazones are formed.

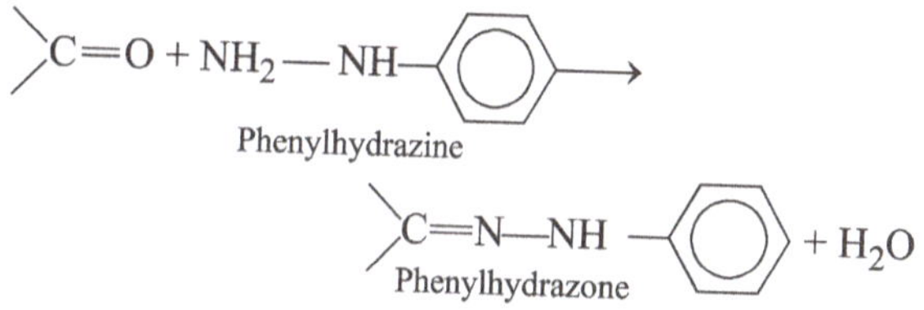

Reaction with 2,4-dinitrophenyl hydrazine

2, 4-dinitrophenyl hydrazine is **Brady's reagent.** Aldehydes and ketones react with it to form yellow, orange or red ppt. of 2, 4-dinitrophenylhydrazone. These are useful for characterisation of aldehydes and ketones.

Reaction with semicarbazide Semicarbazones are formed.

$$>C{=}O + \underset{\text{Semicarbazide}}{NH_2{-}NH{-}\overset{\overset{O}{\|}}{C}{-}NH_2} \longrightarrow \underset{\text{Semicarbazone}}{>C{=}N{-}NH{-}\overset{\overset{O}{\|}}{C}{-}NH_2} + H_2O$$

2. Oxidation Reactions

Oxidation of Aldehydes

$$R{-}CHO + [O] \xrightarrow[\text{or } KMnO_4/H_2SO_4]{K_2Cr_2O_7/H_2SO_4} \underset{\text{Carboxylic acid}}{R{-}COOH}$$

(i) **Reaction with Tollen's reagent**

$$RCHO + \underset{\text{Tollen's reagent}}{2[Ag(NH_3)_2]^+ OH^-} \longrightarrow \underset{\text{Ammonium salt of the acid}}{RCO\overset{-}{O}\overset{+}{N}H_4} + \underset{\text{Silver mirror}}{2Ag\downarrow} + 3NH_3 + H_2O$$

Ketones do not give this test. So, this reaction is used to test the presence of an aldehydic group in a compound and is known as **silver mirror test**.

(ii) **Reaction with Fehling solution**

When an aldehyde is heated with Fehling reagent, a reddish brown precipitate of cupric oxide is obtained.

$$\underset{\text{Aldehyde}}{RCHO} + \underset{\text{Fehling solution}}{2Cu^{2+}} + 5OH^- \xrightarrow{\Delta} RCOO^- + \underset{\text{Red brown ppt.}}{Cu_2O} + 3H_2O$$

(iii) **Reaction with Benedict's solution and Benedict's test** Benedict's solution reacts in the same way as Fehling's solution.

Note **Benedict's solutions** and **Fehling solutions** are very weak oxidising agents. They can oxidise only aliphatic aldehydes. Benzaldehyde and ketones cannot be oxidised by these solutions.

Oxidation of Ketones

$$\underset{\text{Pentan-2-one}}{RCH_2{-}\overset{\overset{O}{\|}}{C}{-}CH_2R'}$$

$$\xrightarrow[H_2SO_4]{K_2Cr_2O_7} \begin{cases} \xrightarrow[\text{Cleavage}]{C_1{-}C_2 \text{ bond}} R{-}COOH + R'CH_2COOH \\ \xrightarrow[\text{Cleavage}]{C_2{-}C_3 \text{ bond}} R{-}CH_2COOH + R'COOH \end{cases}$$

Note In case of unsymmetrical ketones (e.g. pentan-2-one) the keto group stays preferentially with smaller alkyl group (Popoff's rule).

Haloform Reaction

$$R{-}\overset{\overset{O}{\|}}{C}{-}CH_3 + 3X_2 + 4NaOH \longrightarrow \underset{\text{Haloform}}{CHX_3} + R{-}\overset{\overset{O}{\|}}{C}{-}\overset{-}{O}\overset{+}{Na} + 3NaX + 3H_2O$$

This reaction is called **iodoform reaction.**

- Among aldehydes, the iodoform reaction is given by only **acetaldehyde** because other aldehydes do not possess $CH_3{-}\overset{\overset{O}{\|}}{C}{-}$ group.
- Among ketones, the reaction is given by almost all methyl ketones.

3. Reduction

Aldehydes and ketones can be reduced to a variety of compounds under different conditions.

(i) **Reduction to hydrocarbons**

$$>C{=}O \xrightarrow{4[H]} \begin{cases} \xrightarrow{\text{Zn-Hg/conc.HCl}} >CH_2 + H_2O \quad \text{(Clemmensen's reduction)} \\ \xrightarrow[\text{455-475K}]{NH_2{-}NH_2/KOH} >CH_2 + H_2O + N_2 \quad \text{(Wolff-Kishner reduction)} \\ \xrightarrow{\text{4HI\textbackslash P\textbackslash 423K}} >CH_2 + H_2O + 2I_2 \end{cases}$$

(ii) **Reduction to alcohols**

$$\underset{\text{Aldehyde}}{R{-}CHO} + 2[H] \xrightarrow[\text{or } NaBH_4]{LiAlH_4} \underset{1^\circ \text{ alcohol}}{R{-}CH_2{-}OH}$$

$$\underset{\text{Ketone}}{\begin{matrix}R\\R'\end{matrix}\!\!>C{=}O} + H_2 \xrightarrow{\text{Ni or Pt}} \underset{2^\circ \text{ alcohol}}{\begin{matrix}R\\R'\end{matrix}\!\!>CH{-}OH}$$

Note (i) $LiAlH_4$ is more powerful reducing agent than $NaBH_4$ as it can also reduce esters, acids and nitriles and even $C{=}C$ bond also if present in the compound.

(ii) In contrast to it, $NaBH_4$ is so specific that it reduces only $C{=}O$ bond but not $C{=}C$ bond.

$$CH_3CH{=}CHCHO \begin{cases} \xrightarrow{LiAlH_4} CH_3CH_2CH_2CH_2OH \\ \xrightarrow{NaBH_4} CH_3CH{=}CHCH_2OH \end{cases}$$

4. Base Catalysed Reactions

Aldol Condensation

Aldehydes and ketones containing α-H atoms undergo aldol condensation in presence of dilute alkali as catalyst.

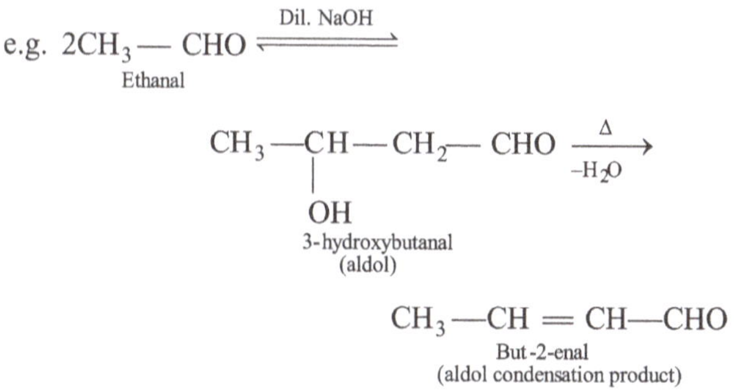

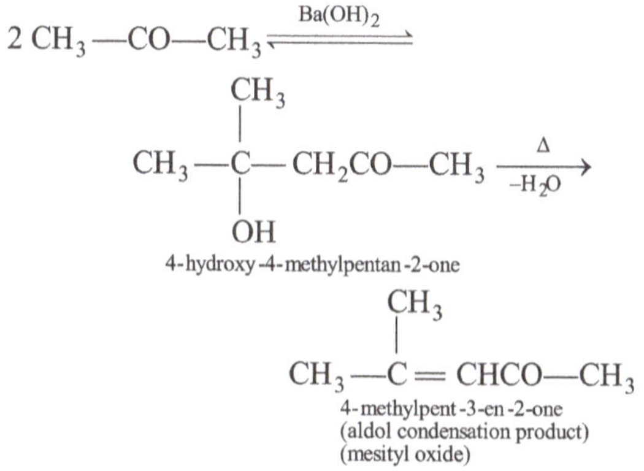

Note Formaldehyde (HCHO), benzaldehyde (C_6H_5CHO) and benzophenone ($C_6H_5COC_6H_5$) do not undergo aldol condensation as they do not contain α-H atoms.

Crossed Aldol Condensation`

Aldol condensation may also occur between the molecules of different aldehydes or different ketones or one aldehyde and one ketone provided they contain α-H atoms. Such aldol condensation is called crossed aldol condensation or mixed aldol condensation.

When two different aldehydes each containing α-H atoms undergo crossed aldol condensation, several products are obtained.

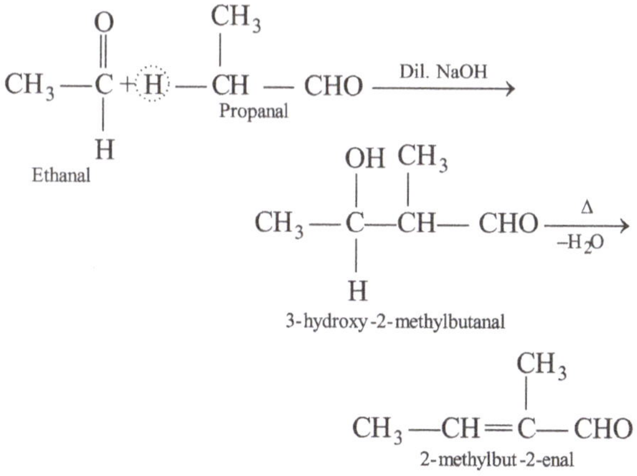

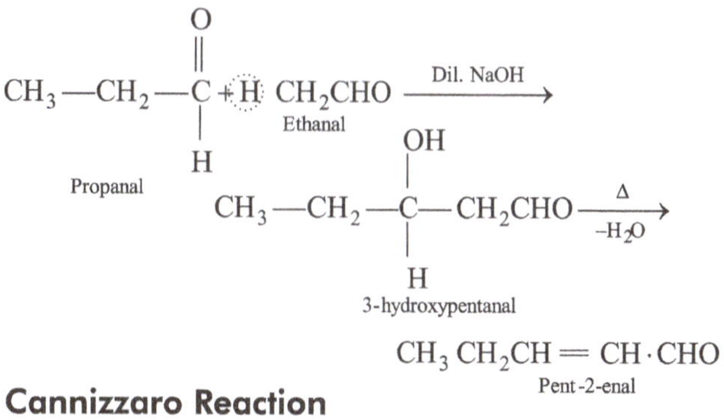

Cannizzaro Reaction

Aldehydes which do not have α-H atoms undergo self oxidation and reduction (disproportionation) on treatment with conc. alkali.

In this reaction, one molecule of aldehyde is reduced to alcohol while another molecule is oxidised to salt of carboxylic acid.

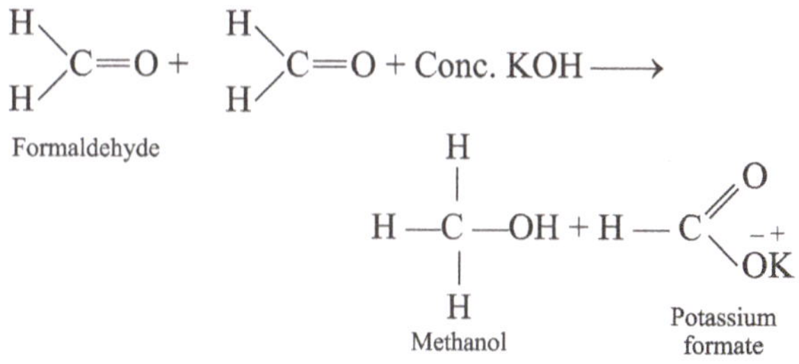

Note When crossed Cannizzaro reaction involves formaldehyde and some other aldehyde, it is the formaldehyde that undergoes oxidation.

Uses of Aldehydes and Ketones

- Formaldehyde is used as disinfectant and as a germicide, 40% aqueous solution of formaldehyde is called **formalin**.
- Formaldehyde is used in the manufacture of bakelite, resin, and other polymers.
- Formaldehyde is used in making urotropine, a medicine for urine infections.
- Paraldehyde is used in medicine as a hypnotic.
- Acetone is used as a constituent of liquid nail polish.

Difference between Formaldehyde and Acetaldehyde

Acetaldehyde gives a yellow precipitate iodoform test while formaldehyde does not respond to this test

$$\underset{\text{Acetaldehyde}}{CH_3CHO} + 4NaOH + 3I_2 \xrightarrow{\Delta} \underset{\substack{\text{Iodoform} \\ \text{(yellow ppt.)}}}{CHI_3} + HCO\overset{-}{O}\overset{+}{Na} + 3NaI + 3H_2O$$

Difference between aldehydes and ketones

Test	Aldehydes	Ketones
Tollen's reagent test	Give silver mirror	No response
Fehling solution test	Give red precipitate	No response
Schiff's reagent test	Restore pink colour	No response, (acetone restore the pink colour but very slowly)
Reaction with $LiAlH_4$	Form primary alcohols	Form secondary alcohols

Aromatic Aldehyde

[Benzaldehyde (C_6H_5CHO)]

It is commercially known as **oil of bitter almonds.**

Preparation

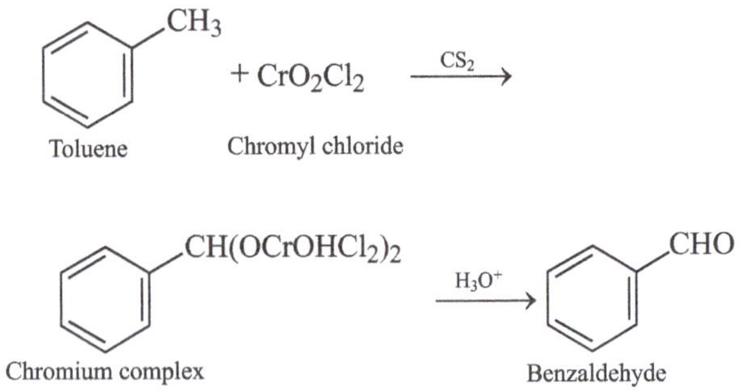

This reaction is called **Etard reaction.**

Physical Properties

- Benzaldehyde is a colourless liquid with bitter almond-like odour.
- It is soluble in organic solvents like ethanol, diethyl ether etc.
- It is steam volatile.
- It's boiling point is 179°C.

Chemical Properties

Different chemical properties of benzaldehyde are as follows

(i) Oxidation

It gets oxidised to benzoic acid in the presence of dil. HNO_3 or alkaline $KMnO_4$.

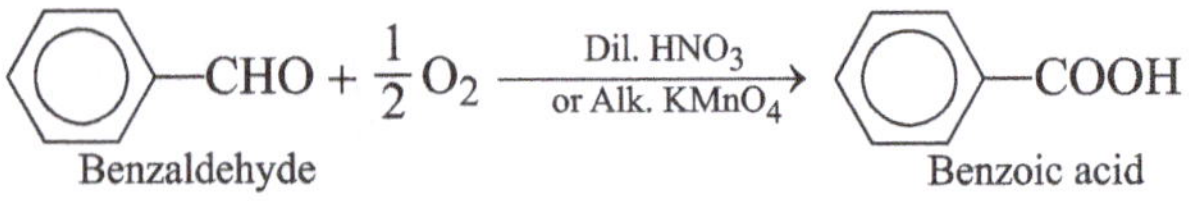

(ii) Reduction

It is reduced to benzyl alcohol.

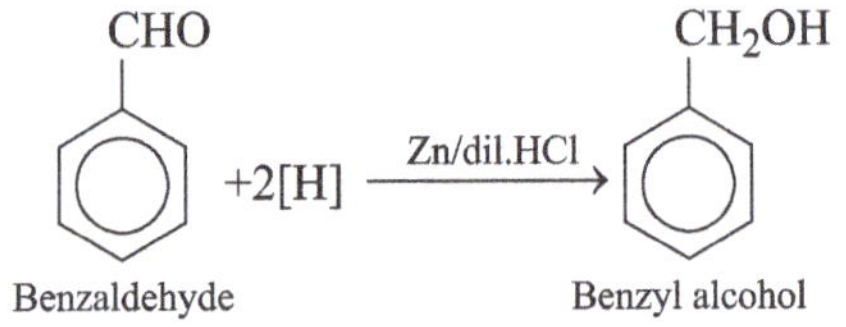

(iii) Nucleophilic Addition Reaction

(a) **With HCN** it gives benzaldehyde cyanohydrin.

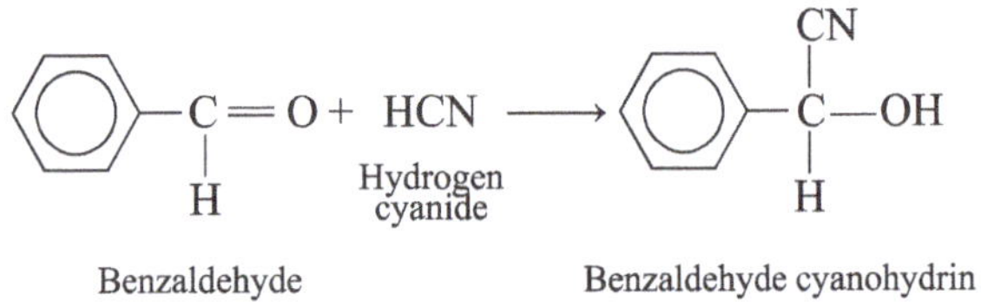

(b) **With $NaHSO_3$** it gives benzaldehyde bisulphite.

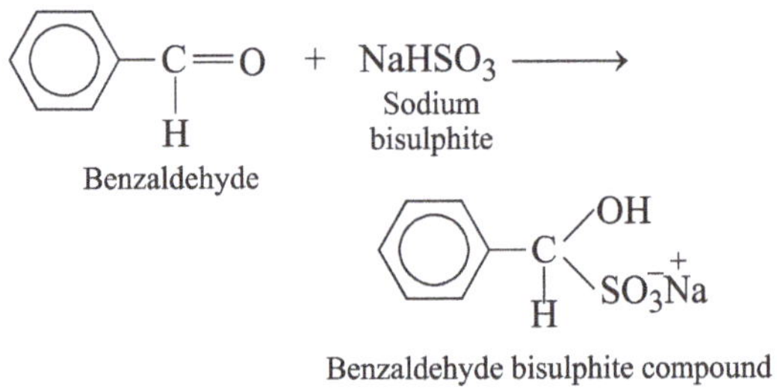

(iv) Nucleophilic Addition followed by Elimination Reaction

These are two steps reactions involving addition followed by elimination of some small molecules. Their first step is similar to nucleophilic addition reaction.

Some examples are given below.

Addition of Ammonia and its Derivatives

(a) **With ammonia** It reacts with NH_3 to form complex product called **hydrobenzamide.**

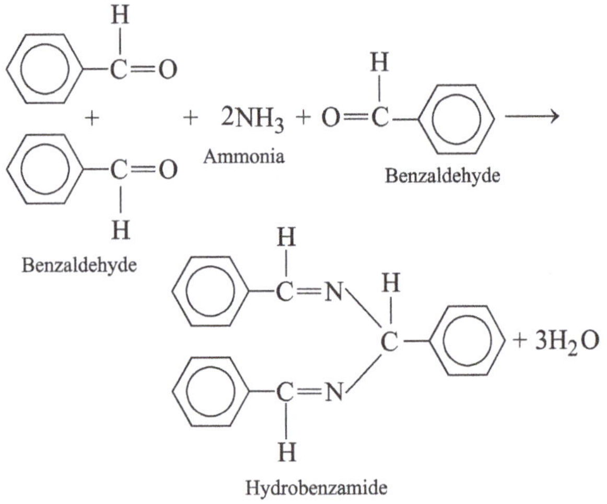

(b) **With hydroxyl amine**

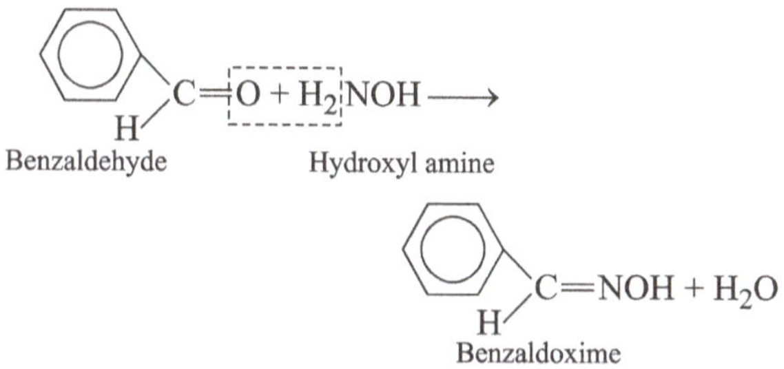

(c) **With hydrazine**

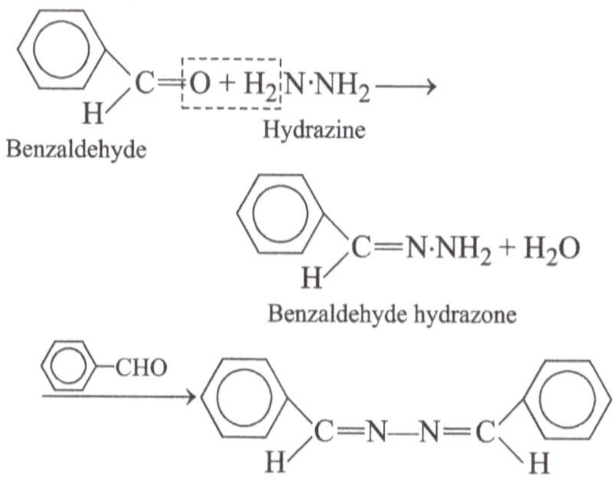

(d) **With phenyl hydrazine**

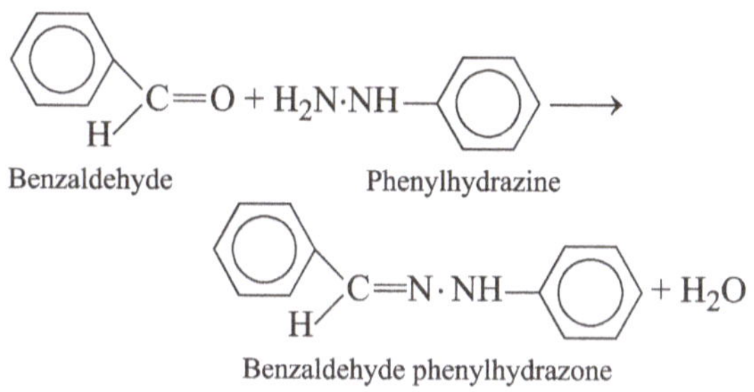

(v) Reaction with PCl_5

Benzal chloride is formed.

$$\underset{\text{Benzaldehyde}}{C_6H_5CHO} + PCl_5 \longrightarrow \underset{\text{Benzal chloride}}{C_6H_5CHCl_2} + POCl_3$$

(vi) Cannizzaro Reaction

$$\underset{\text{Benzaldehyde}}{2C_6H_5CHO} + \underset{\text{Conc.}}{NaOH} \longrightarrow$$

$$\underset{\text{Benzyl alcohol}}{C_6H_5CH_2OH} + \underset{\text{Sodium benzoate}}{C_6H_5CO\overset{-}{O}\overset{+}{Na}}$$

(vii) Benzoin Condensation

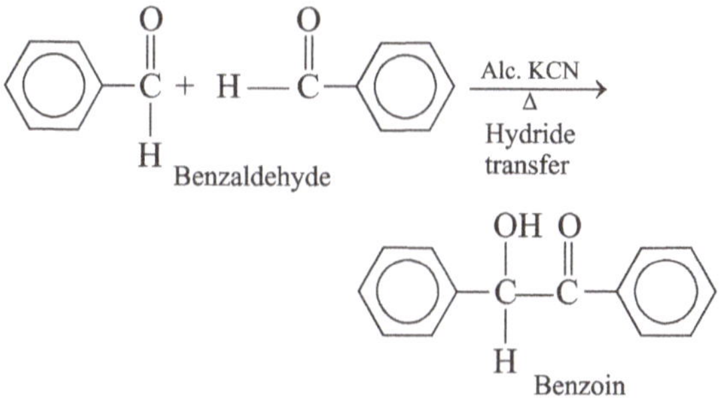

This reaction is called benzoin condensation.

(viii) Perkin's Reaction

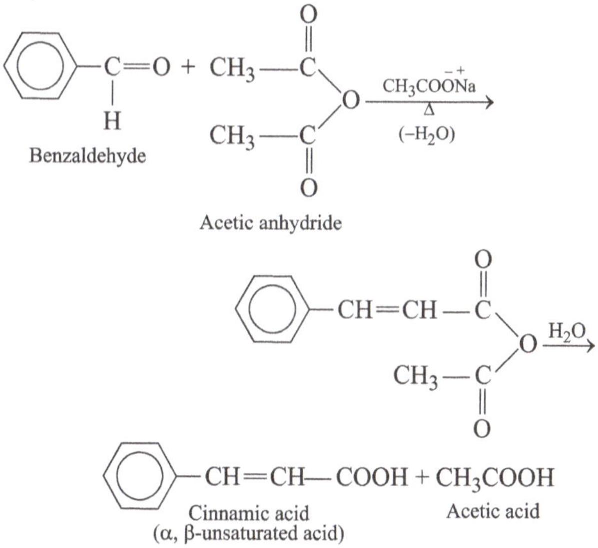

(ix) Electrophilic Substitution Reactions

— CHO group is deactivating *m*-directing group.

(a) **Halogenation**

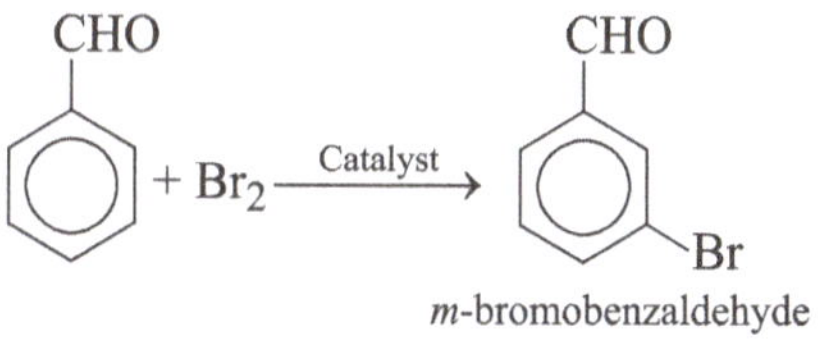

(b) **Nitration**

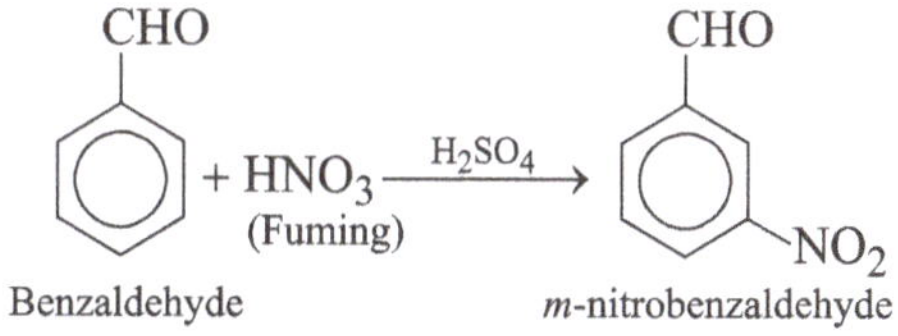

(c) **Sulphonation**

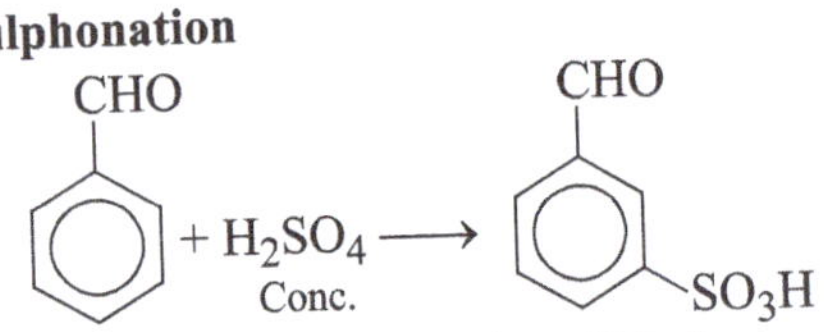

m-benzaldehyde sulphonic acid

Distinction between Benzaldehyde and Acetaldehyde

Acetaldehyde gives a yellow precipitate to iodoform test while benzaldehyde does not respond to this test.

$$CH_3CHO + 4NaOH + 3I_2 \xrightarrow{\Delta} \underset{\text{Iodoform (Yellow ppt.)}}{CHI_3} + H\overset{-}{COO}\overset{+}{Na} + 3NaI + 3H_2O$$

Uses of Benzaldehyde

- as a flavouring essence in perfumery.
- in the manufacture of dyes.
- in the synthesis of cinnamic acid, cinnamaldehyde etc.

PYQs Previous Years' Questions

1 Mark Questions

1. Calcium acetate on dry distillation gives……which gives……on heating with iodine and alkali. **ISC Specimen 2023**

2. Benzaldehyde undergoes ……… substitution at ……… position. **ISC 2021-22 (Sem-II)**

3. Benzaldehyde when heated with alcoholic solution of potassium cyanide gives **ISC 2021-22 (Sem-II)**
   (a) $C_6H_5CH(OH)CN$ (b) $C_6H_5CH(OH)COC_6H_5$
   (c) $C_6H_5CH(OH)COOH$ (d) $C_6H_5CH(OH)C_6H_5$

4. How will the following be converted ?
   Acetone to iodoform. **ISC 2021-22 (Sem-II)**

5. Give one test to distinguish between acetaldehyde and formaldehyde. **ISC 2021-22 (Sem-II), 2016**

6. Formaldehyde when reacts with CH_3MgI forms an additional product, which on hydrolysis gives **ISC 2022 (Sem-II)**
   (a) ethyl iodide (b) methyl alcohol
   (c) methyl iodide (d) ethyl alcohol

7. When acetone is treated with Grignard reagent, followed by hydrolysis, the product formed is **ISC 2020**
   (a) secondary alcohol (b) tertiary alcohol
   (c) primary alcohol (d) aldehyde

8. How will you convert benzoyl chloride to benzaldehyde? **ISC 2020**

9. Give balanced equations for aldol condensation. **ISC 2019, 2017**

10. Give one example each of the following name reaction.
    Benzoin condensation **ISC 2019, 2008**

11. When acetaldehyde is treated with Grignard reagent followed by hydrolysis, the product formed is **ISC Specimen 2018**
    (a) primary alcohol (b) secondary alcohol
    (c) carboxylic acid (d) tertiary alcohol

12. Calcium acetate on heating gives ....'*A*'.... which gives ....'*B*'.... on heating with iodine and sodium hydroxide solution. In the above sentence, '*A*' and '*B*' are
    (a) aldehyde, chloroform
    (b) acetone, iodoform
    (c) aldehyde, iodoform
    (d) acetone, iodine tincture **ISC 2017**

13. Give balanced equation for the reaction of acetaldehyde with hydroxylamine. **ISC 2017**

14. How can the following conversion be brought about acetaldehyde to propan-2-ol? **ISC 2017**

15. Benzaldehyde undergoes ….'*A*'... reaction due to …. '*B*'… of α-hydrogen atom.
    In the above sentence, '*A*' and '*B*' respectively are
    (a) Cannizzaro, absence
    (b) Rosenmund, presence
    (c) Cannizzaro, presence
    (d) Rosenmund, absence **ISC 2016**

    Or Benzaldehyde undergoes ....'*A*'........ reaction on treatment with concentrated sodium hydroxide because it has .....'*B*'....... atom. **ISC 2015**

    In the above sentence, '*A*' and '*B*' respectively are
    (a) Cannizzaro, α-hydrogen
    (b) Cannizzaro, no α-hydrogen
    (c) Clemmensen, α-hydrogen
    (d) Clemmensen, no α-hydrogen

16. Give the balanced equation for the following name reaction.
Benzoin condensation **ISC 2016**

17. Write the reaction to prepare acetaldehyde from hydrogen gas and an acid chloride. **ISC 2016**

18. When acetaldehyde is treated with Grignard reagent, followed by hydrolysis the product formed is
(a) primary alcohol (b) secondary alcohol
(c) carboxylic acid (d) tertiary alcohol **ISC 2015**

19. Give one chemical test to distinguish between the following pairs of compounds.
Acetaldehyde and benzaldehyde **ISC 2015**

20. Give one test to distinguish between the following pair. Write the relevant equation.
Acetophenone and benzophenone **ISC 2014**

21. How can the following conversions be brought about?
Acetaldehyde to formaldehyde **ISC 2014**

22. Give the balanced equation for the following name reaction.
Clemmensen reduction **ISC 2014, 2010**

23. Benzaldehyde when treated with an alcoholic solution of ... forms .... . **ISC 2013**

24. Write balanced chemical equation for the following reaction and name the reaction.
Benzaldehyde is treated with 50% sodium hydroxide solution. **ISC 2013, 2002**

25. Give one chemical test to distinguish between the following pair of compounds.
Acetone and phenol **ISC 2013**

26. Iodoform test is given by
(a) formaldehyde (b) benzaldehyde
(c) methyl ketones (d) All of these **ISC 2012**

27. Give one good chemical test to distinguish between the following pair of compounds.
Methanal and ethanal **ISC 2012**

28. When acetic acid reacts with calcium hydroxide and the product is distilled dry, the compound formed is
(a) calcium acetate (b) acetone **ISC 2012**
(c) acetaldehyde (d) acetic anhydride

29. Write the formula of the product formed when formaldehyde reacts with ammonia and name the product. **ISC 2012**

Or Write the balanced equation for the formation of urotropine. **ISC 2007**

30. Complete the following reaction and name the reaction.
$$\ldots\ldots + 3I_2 + 4KOH \longrightarrow CHI_3 + CH_3\overset{-}{CO}\overset{+}{OK} + 3KI + 3H_2O$$ **ISC 2012**

31. Give the balanced equations for the following reactions.
Benzaldehyde and hydroxylamine **ISC 2012**

32. Carry out the following conversions.
Ethanol to acetone **ISC 2011**

33. Give the balanced equations for the following.
Acetone reacts with hydrogen in the presence of heated copper. **ISC 2011**

34. Give one good chemical test to distinguish between the following pair of organic compounds :
Benzaldehyde and acetone **ISC 2011**

35. How can the following conversion be brought about?
2-propanol to acetoxime **ISC 2010**

> **KEY IDEA**
> Following steps will be taken.
> (i) First convert 2-propanol to acetone by catalytic dehydrogenation with Cu at 573 K.
> (ii) Then, convert acetone to acetoxime by addition of hydroxylamine.

36. Give the balanced equation for the following reaction.
Benzaldehyde treated with hydrogen cyanide. **ISC 2010**

37. How will you bring about the following conversion?
Acetaldehyde to acetamide **ISC 2009**

38. Name the following reaction.
$$CH_3CHO + CH_3COCH_3 \xrightarrow{OH^-} CH_3CH(OH)CH_2COCH_3$$ **ISC 2009**

39. Acetaldehyde reacts with HCN to give ......which on hydrolysis gives .... **ISC 2008**

40. Write the balanced equation of the following reaction.
Acetone and phosphorus pentachloride **ISC 2008**

41. The compound which gives a positive haloform test and a positive Fehling solution test is
(a) acetone (b) acetaldehyde
(c) formaldehyde (d) diethyl ether **ISC 2007**

42. Benzaldehyde when heated with an alcoholic solution of potassium cyanide, forms **ISC 2007**
(a) benzyl alcohol (b) benzoin
(c) hydrobenzamide (d) benzoic acid

43. Give a chemical test to distinguish between acetaldehyde and acetone. **ISC 2007, 2000**

44. Explain the following with at least one example :
Haloform reaction **ISC 2007**

45. Acetaldehyde in the presence of dilute alkali gives …… and the reaction is called ……. **ISC 2005**

46. Write chemical equation for the following reaction and name the main product :
Formaldehyde with ammonia **ISC 2005**

Or

How will you carry out the following conversion? Write the relevant equation
Formaldehyde to urotropine **ISC 2003**

47. Name the following reaction and write balanced equation :
Acetaldehyde with dilute sodium hydroxide **ISC 2002**

48. How will you carry out the following conversion?
Acetaldehyde to *iso*-propyl alcohol **ISC 2002, 2000**

49. How will you carry out the following reaction? Write the relevant balanced equations and name the reaction.
Acetyl chloride to acetaldehyde **ISC 2001**

50. Benzaldehyde undergoes …… reaction on treatment with concentrated sodium hydroxide because it has ……. . **ISC 2001**

2 Marks Questions

51. (i) Benzaldehyde is less reactive than propionaldehyde. Why? **ISC 2024**

(ii) In the preparation of ethanal by the oxidation of ethanol, ethanal should be removed immediately as it is formed. Why?

52. (i) Aromatic aldehydes do not give a reddish-brown precipitate on heating with Fehling solution. Give a reason. **Latest Specimen 2024**

(ii) Why is benzaldehyde less reactive to electrophilic substitution reactions than benzene?

53. Give one chemical test for each to distinguish between the following pairs of compound. **ISC 2021-22 (Sem-II)**

(i) Acetaldehyde and benzaldehyde
(ii) Acetone and acetic acid

54. Write chemical equations to illustrate each of the following name reactions. **ISC 2021-22 (Sem-II)**

(i) Rosenmund reduction
(ii) Clemmensen reduction

55. Identify the compounds A, B, C and D in the given reaction.

$$HC\equiv CH \xrightarrow[Hg^{2+}/H_2SO_4]{H_2O} [A] \xrightarrow[K_2Cr_2O_7 + H_2SO_4]{[O]} [B] \xrightarrow{Ca(OH)_2} [C] \xrightarrow[\text{Dry distillation}]{\text{Heat}} [D]$$

ISC 2019

56. Give the balanced equations for the following name reactions.

(i) Rosenmund reaction
(ii) Formaldehyde is treated with ammonia. **ISC 2015**

57. Give an example (equation) for each of the following name reactions. **ISC 2011, 2007**

(i) Aldol condensation (ii) Rosenmund reduction

58. Give the balanced equations for the following reactions.

(i) Phenol heated with chloroform and sodium hydroxide.
(ii) Acetaldehyde reacted with phenyl hydrazine. **ISC 2009**

59. Correct the following statements by changing the underlined part of the sentence. (Do not change the whole sentence)

(i) Acetone gives a white precipitate on <u>treatment with sodium chloride.</u>
(ii) Acetaldehyde undergoes <u>Cannizzaro reaction</u> on treatment with dilute alkali. **ISC 2008**

60. Give one reason each for the following.
Acetone reacts with hydroxylamine to form only one product which has no geometrical isomer, but acetaldehyde reacts with hydroxylamine to form a product which has two geometrical isomers. **ISC 2007**

61. Write the structures of three compounds which have the same molecular formula of C_4H_8O but have different functional groups. **ISC 2006**

62. Write balanced chemical equations for the following and name the reactions occurring in each case :

(i) Benzaldehyde reacts with an alcoholic solution of potassium cyanide.
(ii) Propanone is treated with iodine and excess of alkali and warmed. **ISC 2006**

3 Marks Questions

63. An organic compound C_2H_4O gives red precipitate when heated with Fehling solution. It also undergoes aldol condensation in the presence of dilute NaOH. **ISC 2024**

(i) Identify the organic compound and write its IUPAC name.

(ii) Which compound will be formed when this organic compound reacts with hydroxylamine?

(iii) What is observed when the compound, referred to in subpart (i), is heated with ammoniacal silver nitrate?

64. A ketone *A* (C_4H_8O) which undergoes iodoform reaction gives compound *B* on reduction. *B* on heating with conc. H_2SO_4 at 443 K gives a compound *C* which forms ozonide *D*. *D* on hydrolysis with Zn dust gives only *E*. Identify the compounds *A* to *E*. Write the iodoform reaction with compound *A*. ***ISC 2020***

65. (i) Write chemical equations to illustrate the following name reaction. ***ISC 2019***

Cannizzaro reaction

(ii) Identify the compounds *A* and *B* in the given reactions.

(a)  $\xrightarrow[\text{AlCl}_3\text{(anhyd.)}]{\text{CH}_3\text{Cl}} [A] \xrightarrow[\text{K}_2\text{Cr}_2\text{O}_7+\text{H}_2\text{SO}_4]{[O]} [B]$

Benzene

(b) $CH_3COCH_3 \xrightarrow[\text{HNO}_3\text{(conc.)}]{[O]} [A] \xrightarrow{\text{PCl}_5} [B]$

66. (i) Give balanced chemical equations for the following reactions. ***ISC 2019***

(a) Acetaldehyde reacts with hydrogen cyanide.

(b) Acetone reacts with phenyl hydrazine.

(ii) Give one chemical test to distinguish between acetone and benzaldehyde. ***ISC 2019***

67. (i) Give balanced equations for the following reactions. : ***ISC 2018***

(a) Benzaldehyde reacts with hydrazine.

(b) Acetone reacts with sodium bisulphite.

(ii) Give one chemical test to distinguish between acetaldehyde and benzaldehyde.

68. (i) Write chemical equations to illustrate the following name reactions. ***ISC 2018***

(a) Clemmensen reduction

(b) Rosenmund reduction

(ii) Explain, why acetaldehyde undergoes aldol condensation, but formaldehyde does not?

69. Give balanced equations for the following reactions :

(i) Acetaldehyde is heated with hydroiodic acid in the presence of red phosphorus.

(ii) Calcium acetate is subjected to dry distillation.

(iii) Benzaldehyde is treated with sodium bisulphite.

ISC 2014

70. An organic compound *A* with molecular formula C_7H_8 on oxidation by chromylchloride in the presence of CCl_4 gives a compound *B* which gives positive Tollen's test. The compound *B* on treatment with NaOH followed by acid hydrolysis gives two products *C* and *D*. *C* on oxidation gives *B* which on further oxidation gives *D*.

The compound *D* on distillation with sodalime gives a hydrocarbon *E*. Below 60°C, concentrated nitric acid reacts with *E* in the presence of concentrated sulphuric acid forming a compound *F*. Identify the compounds *A*, *B*, *C*, *D*, *E* and *F*. ***ISC 2014***

71. Write the balanced equations for the reaction of ammonia with formaldehyde, acetaldehyde and acetone. ***ISC 2001***

72. What is Cannizzaro reaction? Name a compound which undergoes this reaction. Name the products formed when this compound undergoes the reaction.

ISC 2000

73. (i) An organic compound [*A*], having a specific smell forms two compounds [*B*] and [*C*] by reacting with conc. sodium hydroxide. The molecular formula of compound [*B*] is C_7H_8O, which forms compound [*A*] again on oxidation. Compound [*C*] forms benzene on heating with soda lime.

Write the structures of compounds [*A*], [*B*] and [*C*]. Also, write the reactions involved. ***ISC 2024***

(ii) Identify the compounds [*A*] and [*B*] in the reactions given below.

(a) $C_6H_6 \xrightarrow[\text{AlCl}_3\text{ (anhy.)}]{\text{CH}_3\text{Cl}} [A] \xrightarrow[\text{KrCr}_2\text{O}_7+\text{H}_2\text{SO}_4]{[O]} [B]$

(b) $CH_3—CHOH—CH_3 \xrightarrow[\text{K}_2\text{Cr}_2\text{O}_7+\text{H}_2\text{SO}]{[O]} [A] \xrightarrow{\text{NH}_2\text{OH}} [B]$

74. (i) Give a reason for each of the following:

Latest Specimen 2024

(a) Formaldehyde does not undergo aldol condensation, but acetaldehyde does.

(b) Chloroacetic acid is stronger acid than acetic acid.

(c) Both aldehydes and ketones undergo a number of nucleophilic addition reactions.

(ii) An organic compound with the molecular formula C_7H_6O gets oxidised by Tollen's reagent. It does not respond to Fehling test but can undergo the Cannizzaro reaction. Identify the compound. Show how you used the above information to identify the compound.

Explanations

1. acetone, iodoform
2. electrophilic, *meta*
3. (b)

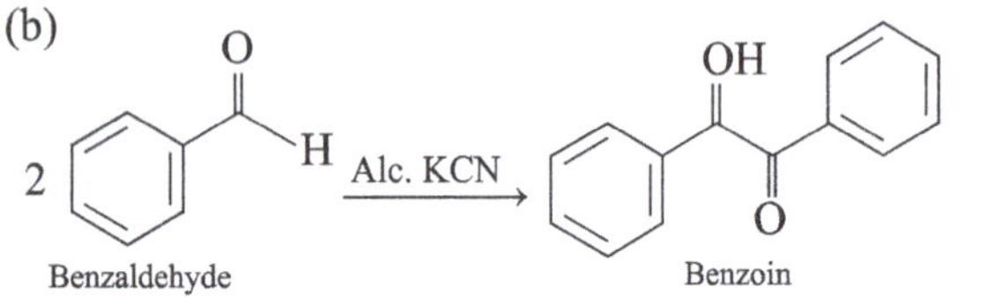

4. $\underset{\text{Acetone}}{CH_3{-}COCH_3} \xrightarrow{I_2/Na_2CO_3} \underset{\text{Triodoacetone}}{I_3CCOCH_3} \xrightarrow{NaOH} \underset{\text{Iodoform}}{CHI_3} + \underset{\text{Sodium acetate}}{CH_3CO\overset{-}{O}\overset{+}{Na}}$

5. Refer to text on page 179.

6. (d) $\underset{\text{Formaldehyde}}{HCHO} + CH_3MgI \xrightarrow{\text{Hydrolysis}} \underset{\text{Ethyl alcohol}}{CH_3CH_2OH}$

7. (b) Refer to text on page 177.

8.

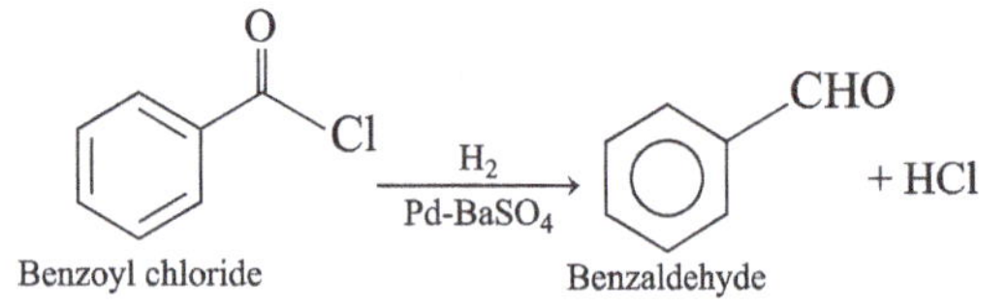

9. Aldehydes and ketones containing α-H-atoms undergo aldol condensation in presence of dilute alkali as catalyst.

e.g. $\underset{\text{Ethanal}}{2CH_3{-}CHO} \xrightarrow{\text{Dil. NaOH}} \underset{\substack{\text{3-hydroxybutanal} \\ \text{(Aldol)} \\ \text{(Aldol condensation product)}}}{CH_3{-}\underset{\substack{| \\ OH}}{CH}{-}CH_2{-}CHO}$

10. Refer to text on page 181.

11. (b) $\underset{\text{Acetaldehyde}}{CH_3{-}CHO} + RMgX \xrightarrow[\text{(ii) } H_2O/H^+]{\text{(i) Dry ether}} \underset{\substack{\text{(Secondary alcohol)} \\ (2°)}}{H_3C{-}\overset{\substack{H \\ |}}{\underset{\substack{| \\ R}}{C}}{-}OH} + Mg(OH)X$

12. (b) (*A*) acetone, (*B*) iodoform

13. $\underset{\text{Acetaldehyde}}{CH_3CHO} + \underset{\text{Hydroxylamine}}{NH_2OH} \longrightarrow CH_3{-}CH{=}NOH + H_2O$

14. $\underset{\text{Acetaldehyde}}{CH_3CHO} \xrightarrow{CH_3MgBr} \underset{\text{Addition product}}{\left[CH_3{-}\overset{\substack{OMg \\ |}}{CH}{-}CH_3\right]} \xrightarrow[-Mg(OH)Br]{H^+/H_2O} \underset{\text{Propan-2-ol}}{CH_3{-}\overset{\substack{OH \\ |}}{CH}{-}CH_3}$

15. (a) Benzaldehyde undergoes **Cannizzaro reaction** on treatment with concentrated sodium hydroxide because it has no α- hydrogen (or **absence** of α-hydrogen) atom. Hence, option (a) is correct.

Note Option (b) is correct for or part.

16. Refer to text on page 181.

17. Acid chloride (e.g. acetyl chloride) can be reduced to aldehyde (e.g. acetaldehyde) with hydrogen gas in boiling xylene using palladium as catalyst supported by $BaSO_4$ and partially poisoned by the addition of sulphur.

$$\underset{\text{Acetyl chloride}}{CH_3{-}\overset{\substack{O \\ \|}}{C}{-}Cl} + H_2 \xrightarrow[\text{Boiling xylene}]{Pd/BaSO_4,\ S} \underset{\text{Acetaldehyde}}{CH_3{-}\overset{\substack{O \\ \|}}{C}{-}H} + HCl \quad \textbf{(1)}$$

18. (b) $\underset{\text{Acetaldeyde}}{(H_3C)_2\overset{\delta+}{C}{=}\overset{\delta-}{O}} + \underset{\text{[Grignard reagent]}}{R{-}MgX} \longrightarrow$

$$CH_3{-}\underset{\substack{| \\ R}}{CH}{-}OMgX \xrightarrow[H_3O^+]{} \underset{\text{Secondary alcohol}}{CH_3{-}\underset{\substack{| \\ R}}{CH}{-}OH}$$

19. **Acetaldehyde and benzaldehyde** Acetaldehyde reacts as reducing agent which reduces Fehling solution and itself gets oxidised to carboxylate ion and Cu^{2+} is reduced to cuprous oxide.

$$\underset{\text{Acetaldehyde}}{CH_3{-}\underset{\substack{\| \\ O}}{C}{-}H} + 2\,Cu^{2+} + 5OH^- \longrightarrow \underset{\text{Carboxylate ion}}{\left[CH_3{-}\overset{\substack{O \\ \|}}{C}{-}O\right]^-} + Cu_2O$$

- Benzaldehyde is not oxidised by Fehling solution.

20 **Acetophenone and benzophenone** These can be distinguished by the iodoform test.

Acetophenone ($C_6H_5COCH_3$) due to the presence of $CH_3\overset{\overset{O}{\|}}{C}$— group gives yellow ppt. of iodoform on treatment with NaOI. While benzophenone ($C_6H_5COC_6H_5$) does not respond to this test.

$$C_6H_5COCH_3 + 3NaOI \longrightarrow \underset{\text{Sodium benzoate}}{C_6H_5CO\overset{-}{O}\overset{+}{N}a} + \underset{\substack{\text{Iodoform}\\\text{(Yellow ppt.)}}}{CHI_3\downarrow} + 2NaOH$$

$$C_6H_5COC_6H_5 \xrightarrow{NaOI} \text{No yellow ppt. of } CHI_3$$

21. $\underset{\text{Acetaldehyde}}{CH_3CHO} \xrightarrow[K_2Cr_2O_7 + H_2SO_4]{[O]} CH_3COOH \xrightarrow{NH_3} CH_3COONH_4 \xrightarrow{\Delta} CH_3CONH_2 \xrightarrow{Br_2 + KOH} CH_3NH_2 \xrightarrow{HNO_2} CH_3OH \xrightarrow[\Delta, (573\ K)]{Cu} \underset{\text{Formaldehyde}}{HCHO}$

22. Reduction of acetaldehyde to ethane using Zn/Hg and HCl as reducing agent is an example of Clemmensen's reduction. The reaction involve is as follows

$$\underset{\text{Ethanal}}{CH_3—\overset{\overset{O}{\|}}{C}—H} + 4[H] \xrightarrow[HCl]{Zn/Hg} \underset{\text{Ethane}}{CH_3—CH_3} + H_2O$$

23. Benzaldehyde when treated with an alcoholic solution of **potassium cyanide** forms **benzoin.**

24. $\underset{\text{Benzaldehyde}}{C_6H_5CHO + C_6H_5CHO} \xrightarrow{50\%\ NaOH} \underset{\text{Benzyl alcohol}}{C_6H_5CH_2OH} + \underset{\text{Sodium benzoate}}{C_6H_5COO^-\overset{+}{Na}}$

This reaction is known as **Cannizzaro reaction.**

25. Acetone gives iodoform test while phenol does not. Acetone gives a yellow ppt. of iodoform when heated with I_2 in the presence of an alkali, while phenol does not contain $CH_3—\overset{\overset{O}{\|}}{C}$— group, so do not give this test.

$$CH_3COCH_3 \xrightarrow{I_2/Na_2CO_3} \underset{\text{Triiodoacetone}}{I_3CCOCH_3} \xrightarrow{NaOH} \underset{\text{Sodium acetate}}{CH_3CO\overset{-}{O}\overset{+}{Na}} + \underset{\text{Iodoform}}{CHI_3}$$

26. (c) Methyl ketones

27. **Methanal and ethanal** Ethanal when heated with I_2 and NaOH, it gives a yellow ppt. of iodoform.

$$\underset{\text{Ethanal}}{CH_3CHO} + 3I_2 + 4NaOH \longrightarrow \underset{\substack{\text{Iodoform}\\\text{(Yellow ppt.)}}}{CHI_3\downarrow} + HCO\overset{-}{O}\overset{+}{N}a + 3NaI + 3H_2O$$

$$\underset{\text{Methanal}}{HCHO} + 3I_2 + 4NaOH \longrightarrow \text{No reaction}$$

(Due to absence of CH_3CO—group)

28. (b) When (CH_3COOH) is treated with calcium hydroxide [$Ca(OH)_2$] and product is distilled dry, the compound formed is acetone.

$$2CH_3COOH + Ca(OH)_2 \longrightarrow \underset{\text{Calcium acetate}}{(CH_3COO)_2Ca} + 2H_2O$$

$$\underset{\text{Calcium acetate}}{(CH_3COO^-)_2Ca^{2+}} \xrightarrow{\Delta} \underset{\text{Acetone}}{(CH_3)_2C{=}O} + CaCO_3$$

Hence, the option (b) is correct.

29. Formaldehyde reacts with ammonia to form hexamethylene tetraamine. Also, known as urotropine.

$$\underset{\text{Formaldehyde}}{6HCHO} + 4NH_3 \xrightarrow{\Delta} \underset{\substack{\text{(Urotropine)}\\\text{Hexamethylenetetraamine}}}{(CH_2)_6N_4} + 6H_2O$$

30. $CH_3COCH_3 + 3I_2 + 4KOH \longrightarrow CHI_3 + CH_3CO\overset{-}{O}\overset{+}{K} + 3KI + 3H_2O$

This reaction is called **iodoform reaction.**

31.

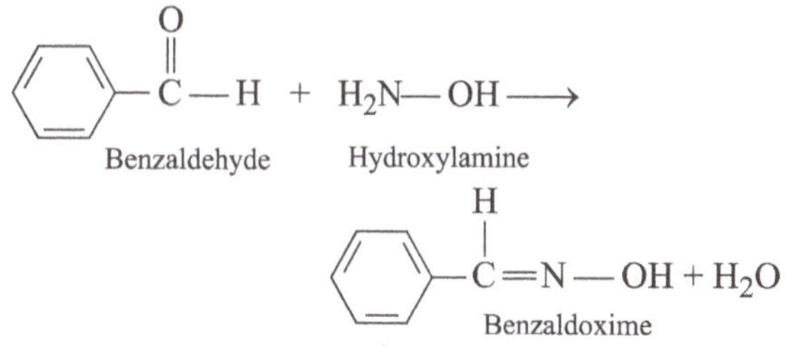

32. **Ethanol to acetone**

$$\underset{\text{Ethanol}}{2CH_3CH_2OH} \xrightarrow[K_2Cr_2O_7 + H_2SO_4]{[O]} \underset{\text{Acetaldehyde}}{2CH_3CHO} \xrightarrow[K_2Cr_2O_7 + H_2SO_4]{[O]} \underset{\text{Acetic acid}}{2CH_3COOH} \xrightarrow{Ca(OH)_2} \underset{\text{Calcium acetate}}{(CH_3COO)_2Ca} \xrightarrow{\Delta} \underset{\text{Acetone}}{CH_3—\overset{\overset{O}{\|}}{C}—CH_3} + CaCO_3\downarrow$$

33. $$\underset{\text{Acetone}}{(CH_3)_2CO} + H_2 \xrightarrow[573\text{ K}]{\text{Heated Cu}} \underset{\text{Iso-propyl alcohol}}{(CH_3)_2CHOH}$$

34. Due to the presence of CH_3CO— group acetone gives iodoform test, i.e. it gives a yellow ppt. of iodoform when heated with iodine in the presence of an alkali while benzaldehyde does not give this test.

35. 2-propanol to acetoxime

$$\underset{\text{2-Propanol}}{CH_3CHOHCH_3} \xrightarrow[O_2,\ 573\text{ K}]{\text{Cu}} \underset{\text{Acetone}}{CH_3COCH_3} \xrightarrow{+NH_2OH} \underset{\text{Acetoxime}}{(CH_3)_2C{=}NOH} + H_2O$$

36. $$\underset{\text{Benzaldehyde}}{C_6H_5CHO} + \underset{\text{Hydrogen cyanide}}{HCN} \longrightarrow \underset{\text{Benzaldehyde cyanohydrin}}{C_6H_5-CH(OH)(CN)}$$

37. Acetaldehyde to acetamide

$$\underset{\text{Acetaldehyde}}{CH_3CHO} \xrightarrow[K_2Cr_2O_7 + H_2SO_4]{[O]} \underset{\text{Acetic acid}}{CH_3COOH} \xrightarrow{+NH_3}$$

$$\underset{\text{Ammonium acetate}}{CH_3COONH_4} \xrightarrow[-H_2O]{\Delta} \underset{\text{Acetamide}}{CH_3CONH_2}$$

38. The given reaction is **crossed aldol condensation** as it occurs between one aldehyde and one ketone having α-H atom.

39. Acetaldehyde reacts with HCN to give **acetaldehyde cyanohydrin** which on hydrolysis gives **lactic acid.**

$$\underset{\text{Acetaldehyde}}{CH_3(H)C{=}O} \xrightarrow{HCN} \underset{\text{Acetaldehyde cyanohydrin}}{CH_3(H)C(OH)(CN)} \xrightarrow{H_3O^+} \underset{\text{Lactic acid}}{CH_3(H)C(OH)(COOH)}$$

40. $$(H_3C)_2C{=}O + PCl_5 \longrightarrow \underset{\text{2, 2-dichloropropane}}{(H_3C)_2CCl_2} + POCl_3$$

41. (b) The compounds which have $CH_3-\overset{O}{\overset{\|}{C}}-$ group, give iodoform (haloform test).

The compounds which have —CHO group (aldehyde) give Fehling solution test.

Among the given options, the compound which gives a positive haloform test and a positive Fehling solution test is acetaldehyde, because it has both

$CH_3-\overset{O}{\overset{\|}{C}}-$ group and —CHO group.

Hence, option (b) is correct.

42. (b) Benzaldehyde when heated with alcoholic solution of potassium cyanide, forms benzoin. This reaction is benzoin condensation.

Hence, option (b) is correct.

43. Acetaldehyde and acetone Acetaldehyde gives a silver mirror test when heated with Tollen's reagent.

$$\underset{\text{Acetaldehyde}}{CH_3CHO} + \underset{\text{Tollen's reagent}}{2[Ag(NH_3)_2]^+OH^-} \longrightarrow CH_3COONH_4 + \underset{\text{Silver miror}}{2Ag} + 3NH_3 + H_2O$$

Acetone does not give this test as it is a ketone.

44. Aldehydes and ketones having

$CH_3-\overset{O}{\overset{\|}{C}}-$ group can be oxidised with sodium hypohalite [NaOX] to give a haloform (CHX_3) and the salt of carboxylic acid. This reaction is called **haloform reaction**.

e.g. $$CH_3-\overset{O}{\overset{\|}{C}}-CH_3 + 3I_2 + 4NaOH \longrightarrow \underset{\text{Yellow ppt.}}{CHI_3\downarrow} + CH_3-\overset{O}{\overset{\|}{C}}-\overset{-}{O}\overset{+}{Na} + 3NaI + 3H_2O$$

45. Acetaldehyde in the presence of dilute alkali gives **aldol** and the reaction is called **aldol condensation.**

46. $$\underset{\text{Formaldehyde}}{6HCHO} + 4NH_3 \xrightarrow{\Delta} \underset{\text{Urotropine}}{(CH_2)_6N_4} + 6H_2O$$ Urotropine is formed.

Concept Enhancer Chemical name of urotropin is hexamethylene tetramine. It acts as an anti-infective agent which is most commonly used to treat urinary tract infections.

47. $2\,CH_3-\overset{\overset{O}{\|}}{C}-H + \text{Dil. NaOH} \longrightarrow$
Acetaldehyde

$$CH_3-\underset{\underset{H}{|}}{\overset{\overset{OH}{|}}{C}}-CH_2CH_2OH$$
3-hydroxybutanol (aldol)

This reaction is called aldol condensation.

48.
$$\underset{\text{Acetaldehyde}}{CH_3-\overset{\overset{O}{\|}}{C}-H} \xrightarrow{CH_3MgI} CH_3-\underset{\underset{CH_3}{|}}{\overset{\overset{OMgI}{|}}{C}}-H \xrightarrow{H_2O}$$
$$\underset{\textit{Iso}\text{-propyl alcohol}}{CH_3-\underset{\underset{CH_3}{|}}{\overset{\overset{OH}{|}}{C}}-H} + Mg\begin{matrix}OH\\I\end{matrix}$$ **(1)**

49. Acetyl chloride is converted to acetaldehyde by reduction with hydrogen in the presence of a palladium catalyst supported over barium sulphate.

$$CH_3COCl + H_2 \xrightarrow[BaSO_4]{Pd} CH_3CHO + HCl$$ **(1)**

50. Benzaldehyde undergoes **Cannizzaro** reaction on treatment with concentrated sodium hydroxide because it has **no α-hydrogen atoms**.

$$\underset{\text{Benzaldehyde}}{2C_6H_5CHO} + \underset{\text{Conc.}}{NaOH} \longrightarrow \underset{\text{Benzyl alcohol}}{C_6H_5CH_2OH} + \underset{\text{Sodium benzoate}}{C_6H_5COONa}$$ **(1)**

51. (i) The carbon atom of carbonyl group of benzaldehyde is less electrophilic than carbon atom of the carbonyl group present in propionaldehyde. As the polarity of $>C=O$ group is reduced in benzaldehyde due to resonance hence, it is less reactive.

(ii) In oxidation of ethanol to ethanal, is the formed ethanal is readily oxidised to carboxylic acid if allowed to remain in the reaction mixture. Therefore, ethanal should be removed immediately as it is formed.

52. (i) Aldehydes such as benzaldehyde, lacks in alpha hydrogens and cannot form an enolate and thus, do not give a positive test with Fehling solution.

(ii) Benzaldehyde is less reactive to electrophilic substitution reactions than benzene because the aldehyde group is an electron withdrawing group and destabilises the intermediate carbocation formed in electrophilic substitution reactions.

53. (i) **Acetaldehyde and benzaldehyde** Fehling solution test is used to distinguish between acetaldehyde and benzaldehyde as benzaldehyde does not have α-hydrogen.

Acetaldehyde gives red precipitate of cuprous oxide while benzaldehyde does not.

$$\underset{\text{Acetaldehyde}}{CH_3CHO} + 5OH^- + 2Cu^{2+} \longrightarrow CH_3COO^- + \underset{\text{Red ppt.}}{Cu_2O\downarrow} + 3H_2O$$ **(1)**

(ii) **Acetone and acetic acid** Acetic acid on heating with ethyl alcohol in presence of H_2SO_4 gives a fruity smell of an ester, while acetone does not give this test.

$$\underset{\text{Acetic acid}}{CH_3COOH} + \underset{\text{Ethanol}}{C_2H_5OH} \xrightarrow[\text{Conc. } H_2SO_4]{\Delta} \underset{\text{Ester}}{CH_3COOC_2H_5} + H_2O$$ **(1)**

54. (i) **Rosenmund reduction** Acyl chloride or acid chloride is hydrogenated in the presence of palladium catalyst supported over and partially poisoned by the addition of sulphur or barium sulphate. This reaction is called Rosenmund reduction.

$$\underset{\text{Acetyl chloride}}{CH_3-\overset{\overset{O}{\|}}{C}-Cl} \xrightarrow[Pd/BaSO_4,S]{H} \underset{\text{Acetaldehyde}}{CH_3-\overset{\overset{O}{\|}}{C}-Cl}$$

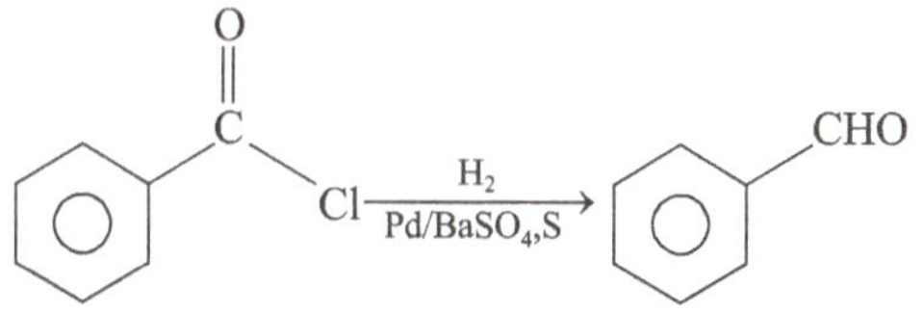

Benzoyl chloride Benzaldehyde **(1)**

(ii) **Clemmensen reduction** It involves reduction of carbonyl group of an aldehyde or ketone to methylene group to form a hydrocarbon.

Clemmensen reduction is carried out in presence of Zn amalgam and conc. HCl.

$$>C=O + 4\,[H] \xrightarrow{\text{Zn–Hg/conc.HCl}} \underset{\text{Hydrocarbon}}{>CH_2} + H_2O$$ **(1)**

55. $$HC \equiv CH \xrightarrow[Hg^{2+}/H_2SO_4]{H_2O} \left[\begin{matrix} CH_2 \\ \| \\ CHOH \end{matrix}\right] \xrightarrow{\text{Tautomerises}} \begin{matrix} CH_3 \\ H \end{matrix} \!\!> C{=}O$$
(Acetaldehyde) (*A*)

$$\underset{(A)}{CH_3{-}CHO} \xrightarrow[K_2Cr_2O_7 + H_2SO_4]{[O]} \underset{\substack{\text{(Acetic acid)} \\ (B)}}{CH_3COOH}$$

$$\underset{(B)}{CH_3COOH} \xrightarrow{Ca(OH)_2} \underset{(C)}{(CH_3COO)_2Ca}$$

$$\underset{(C)}{(CH_3COO)_2Ca} \xrightarrow[\text{Dry distillation}]{\Delta} \underset{\substack{\text{(Acetone)} \\ (D)}}{\begin{matrix} CH_3 \\ CH_3 \end{matrix} \!\!> C{=}O} + CaCO_3$$

∴ (*A*) = $CH_3{-}CHO$ (Acetaldehyde)

(*B*) = CH_3COOH (Acetic acid)

(*C*) = $(CH_3COO)_2Ca$ (Calcium acetate)

(*D*) = $\begin{matrix} CH_3 \\ CH_3 \end{matrix} \!\!> C{=}O$ (Acetone)

56. (i) Refer to solution 54 (i). **(1)**

(ii) Refer to solution 29. **(1)**

57. (i) Refer to text on pages 178 and 179. **(1)**

(ii) Refer to solution 54 (i). **(1)**

58. (i)

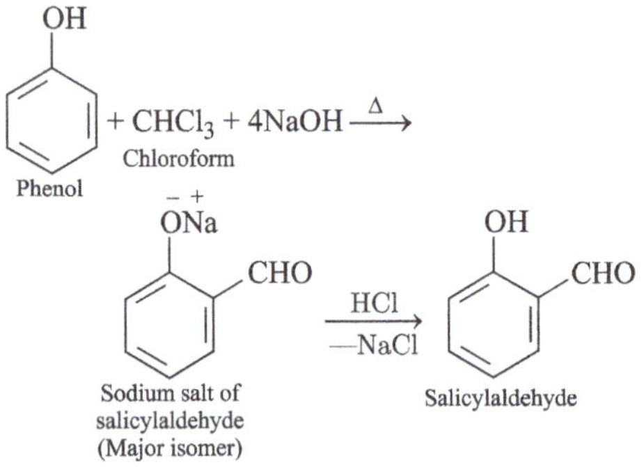

(1)

(ii) $$\underset{\text{Acetaldehyde}}{CH_3CHO} + \underset{\text{Phenyl hydrazine}}{H_2N \cdot NHC_6H_5} \longrightarrow \underset{\text{Phenyl hydrazone}}{CH_3CH{=}N \cdot NHC_6H_5} + H_2O$$ **(1)**

59. (i) Acetone gives a white precipitate on treatment with **sodium bisulphate**. **(1)**

(ii) Acetaldehyde undergoes **aldol condensation** on treatment with dilute alkali. **(1)**

60. This is because when acetone reacts with $-NH_2OH$, acetoxime formed has two identical groups, $-CH_3$ attached to carbon with which N forms a double bond. This does not fulfill conditions for geometrical isomerism.

But when acetaldehyde reacts with NH_2OH, acetaldoxime is formed which has two different groups attached to C forming double bond with nitrogen.

Therefore, it exhibits geometrical isomerism. **(1)**

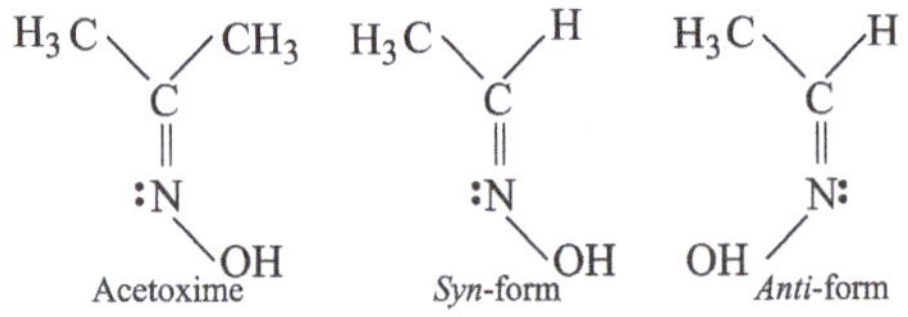

61. (i) Butanal $CH_3CH_2CH_2CHO$, (An aldehyde)

(ii) Butanone $CH_3COCH_2CH_3$, (A ketone)

(iii) An unsaturated alcohol, i.e. butanol $CH_2{=}CH{-}CH_2{-}CH_2OH$.

62. (i)

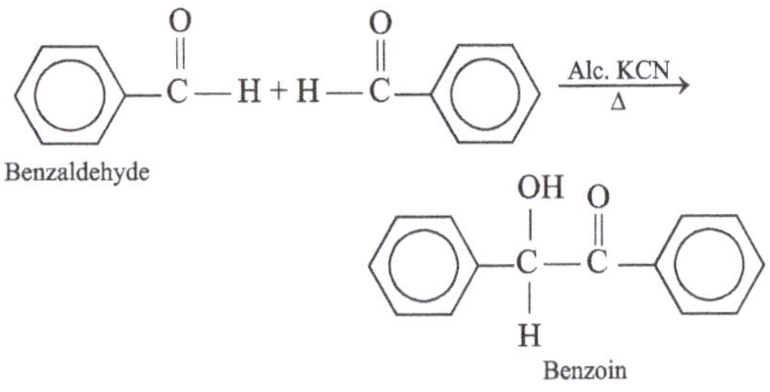

This reaction is **benzoin condensation.** **(1)**

(ii) $$\underset{\text{Propanone}}{CH_3COCH_3} + 3I_2 + 4NaOH \xrightarrow{\Delta} \underset{\text{Iodoform}}{CHI_3} \downarrow + CH_3CO\overset{-}{O}\overset{+}{Na} + 3NaI + 4H_2O$$

This reaction is **iodoform reaction.** **(1)**

63. (i) According to the given information that C_2H_4O gives red ppt. with Fehling solution and undergoes aldol condensation in presence of dil. NaOH. This means C_2H_4O is an aldehyde having an α-H atom. Thus, it can be $CH_3{-}CHO$. Its IUPAC name is ethanal.

$$\underset{\text{Ethanal}}{CH_3CHO} + \underset{\text{Fehling solution}}{2Cu^{2+}} + 4\overset{-}{O}H \xrightarrow{\Delta} \underset{\text{Acetic acid}}{CH_3{-}\overset{\overset{O}{\|}}{C}{-}OH} + \underset{\text{Red ppt.}}{Cu_2O} \downarrow + 2H_2O$$

$$2CH_3-\overset{O}{\overset{\|}{C}}-H \xrightarrow[(H_2O)]{\text{Dil. NaOH}} CH_3-\overset{OH}{\overset{|}{C}H}-CH_2-\overset{O}{\overset{\|}{C}}-H$$

Ethanol — 3-hydroxybutanal

(ii) Reaction of ethanal with hydroxylamine.

$$CH_3-\overset{O}{\overset{\|}{C}}-H + \underset{\text{Hydroxylamine}}{H_2N-OH} \xrightarrow{H^+} \underset{\text{Acetaldoxime}}{CH_3-\underset{H}{\underset{|}{C}}=N-OH} + H_2O$$

(iii) Reaction of ethanal with ammoniacal silver nitrate.

$$CH_3-\overset{O}{\overset{\|}{C}}-H + \underset{\text{(Tollen's reagent)}}{2[Ag(NH_3)_2]^+} + 2\bar{O}H \xrightarrow{\Delta} \underset{\text{Acetic acid}}{CH_3-\overset{O}{\overset{\|}{C}}-OH} + 2Ag\downarrow + 4NH_3 + H_2O$$

64. The road map of the given equation is as follows

The only possible ketone formed from the given formula which gives iodoform reaction is 2-butanone i.e.

$CH_3CH_2-\overset{O}{\overset{\|}{C}}-CH_3$. This is compound *A*.

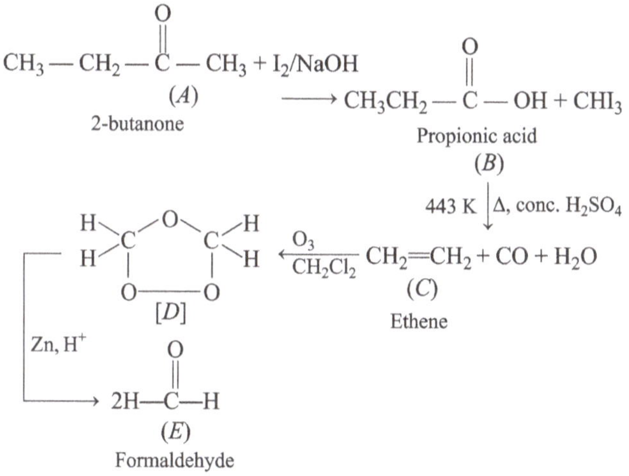

Iodoform reaction with compound *A* is as follows

$$CH_3-CH_2-\overset{O}{\overset{\|}{C}}-CH_3 + I_2/NaOH \longrightarrow CH_3-CH_2-\overset{O}{\overset{\|}{C}}-ONa + CHI_3\downarrow + NaI + H_2O$$

65. (i) **Cannizzaro reaction**

Refer to text on page 179.

(ii) (a)

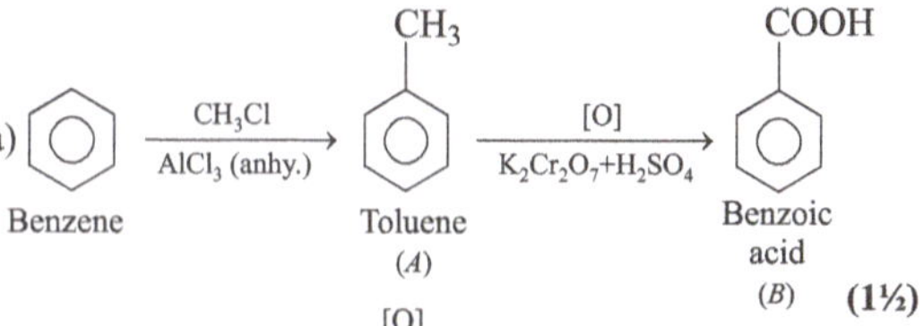

(1½)

(b) $CH_3-CO-CH_3 \xrightarrow[HNO_3(conc.)]{[O]} \underset{\text{Formic acid}}{HCOOH} + \underset{\text{Acetic acid}}{CH_3COOH}$

$\downarrow PCl_3$

$\underset{\text{Formyl chloride}}{HCOCl} + \underset{\text{Acid chloride}}{CH_3COCl}$ (1½)

If *A* is formic acid then *B* is formyl chloride. While if *A* is acetic acid then*B* is acid chloride.

66. (i)(a) Acetaldehyde reacts with hydrogen cyanide to give ethane cyanohydrin.

$$\underset{\text{Acetaldehyde}}{\overset{CH_3}{H}\!\!>C=O} + \underset{\text{Hydrogen cyanide}}{HCN} \longrightarrow \underset{\text{Ethane cyanohydrin}}{\overset{CH_3}{H}\!\!>C<\!\!\overset{OH}{CN}}$$

Above reaction is a nucleophilic addition reaction.

(b) Acetone reacts with phenyl hydrazine to give phenyl hydrazone.

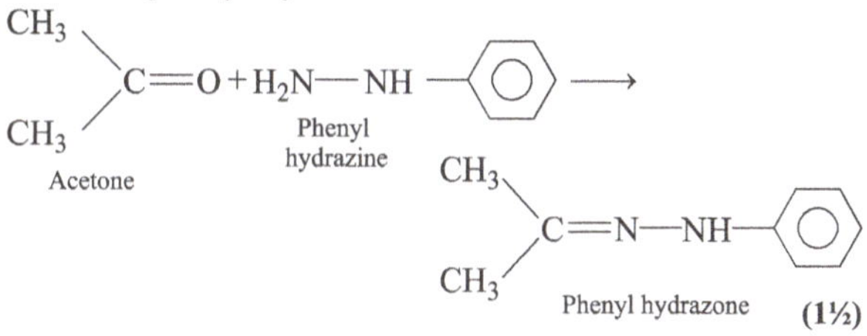

(1½)

(ii) Refer to solution 34. (1½)

67. (i)(a) **Benzaldehyde reacts with hydrazine**

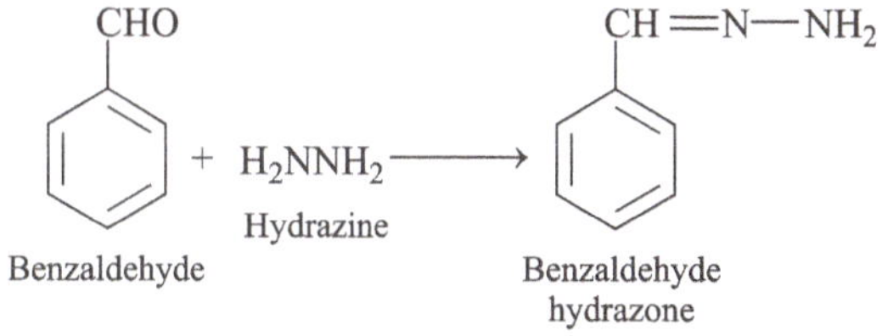

(b) **Acetone reacts with sodium bisulphite**

$$\underset{\text{Acetone}}{\overset{CH_3}{CH_3}\!\!>C=O} + NaHSO_3 \rightleftharpoons \overset{CH_3}{CH_3}\!\!>C<\!\!\overset{OH}{SO_3^-Na^+}$$

Acetone sodium bisulphite (addition product) (2)

(ii) **Acetaldehyde and benzaldehyde** Refer to solution 53 (i). **(1)**

68. (i) (a) **Clemmensen reduction**

Refer to solution 54 (ii). **(1)**

(b) **Rosenmund reduction**

Refer to solution 54 (i). **(1)**

(ii) The basic requirement of aldol condensation reaction is that the compound should have α-hydrogens.

Acetaldehyde undergoes aldol condensation but formaldehyde do not undergo aldol condensation because it does not have α-hydrogen atom.

[α-hydrogen is the hydrogen atom present on the carbon atom next to carbonyl group].

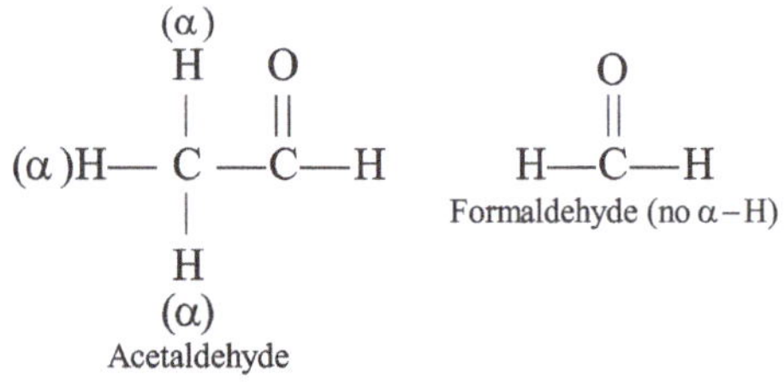

(2)

69. (i) $CH_3CHO + 4HI \xrightarrow[423\text{ K}]{\text{Red P}} CH_3{-}CH_3 + H_2O$ **(1)**

Acetaldehyde, Ethane

(ii)

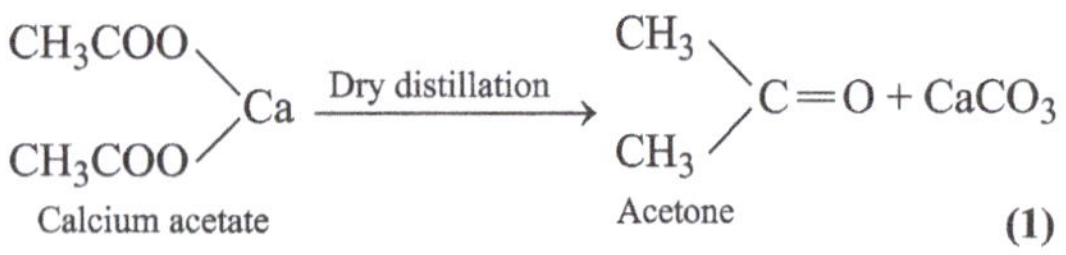

(1)

(iii)

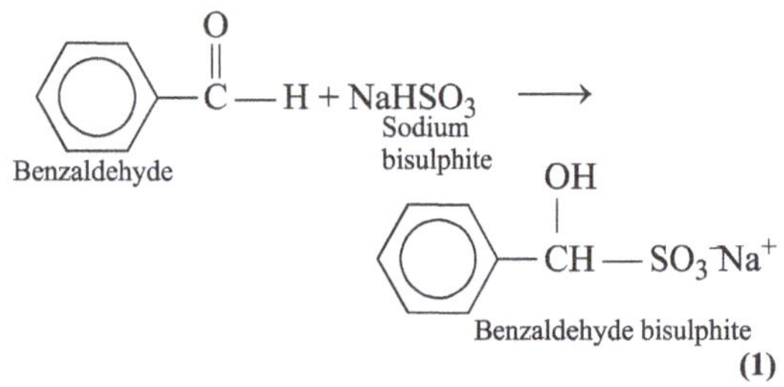

(1)

70. Compound A must be toluene and B should be benzaldehyde (as it gives positive Tollen's test).

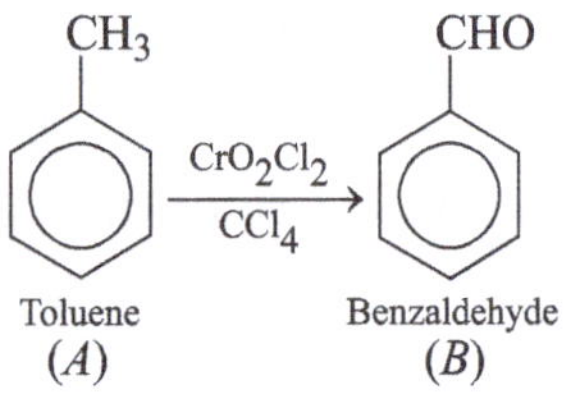

(1)

Compound B (C_6H_5CHO) on treatment with NaOH followed by acid hydrolysis gives two products, benzyl alcohol (C), and sodium benzoate (D). This is **Cannizzaro reaction.**

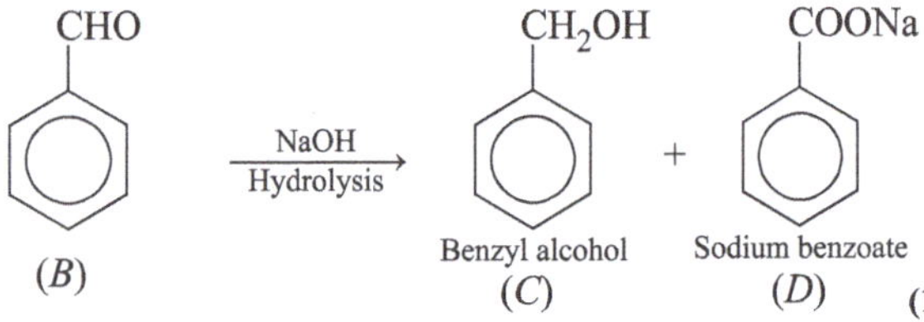

(1)

Compound C on oxidation gives B, which on further oxidation gives D, i.e.

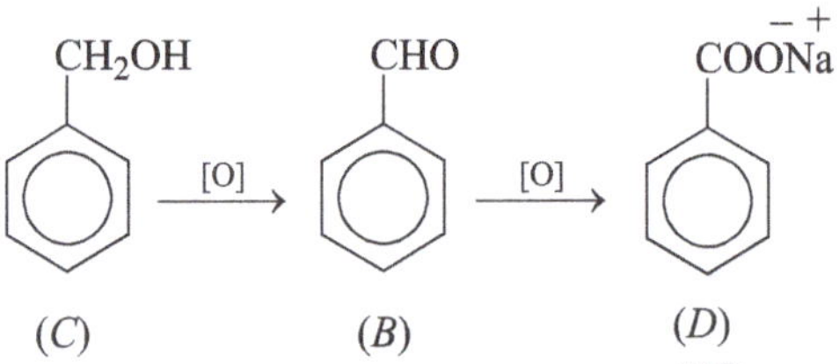

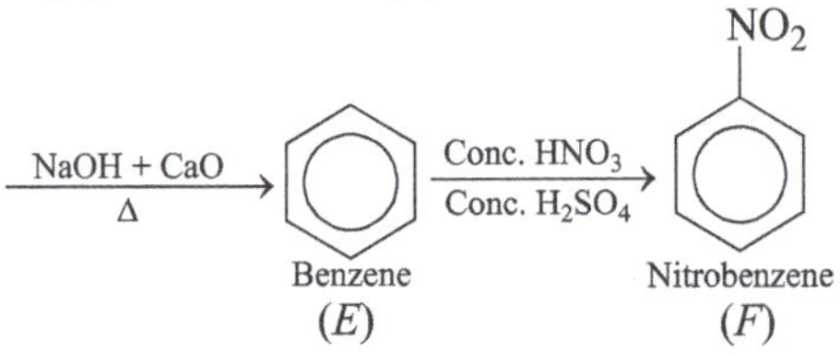

Therefore, E is benzene and F is nitrobenzene. **(1)**

71. Ammonia with formaldehyde

$$6HCHO + 4NH_3 \longrightarrow 6H_2O + (CH_2)_6N_4$$

Formaldehyde; Hexamethylene tetraamine (Urotropine)

Ammonia with acetaldehyde

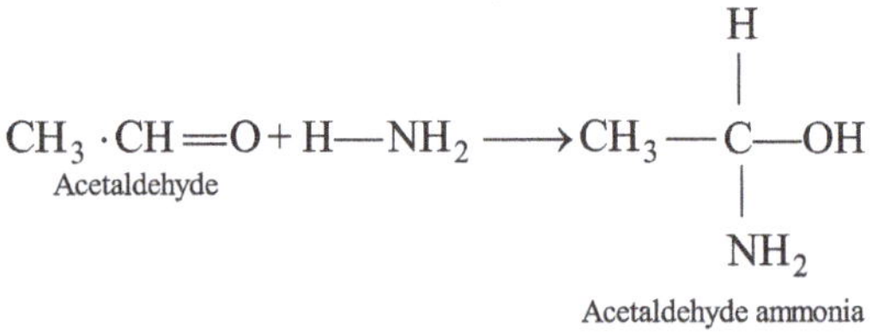

Ammonia with acetone

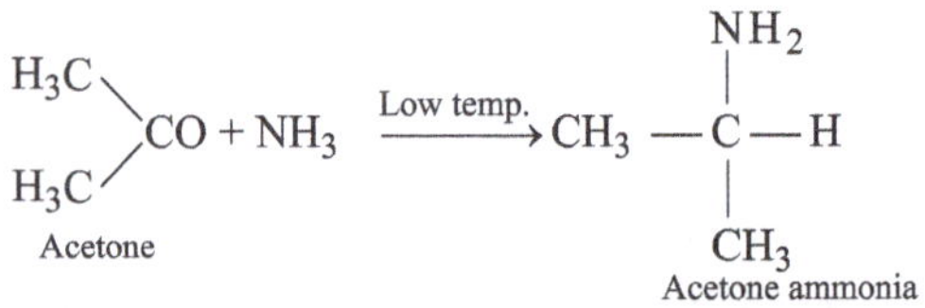

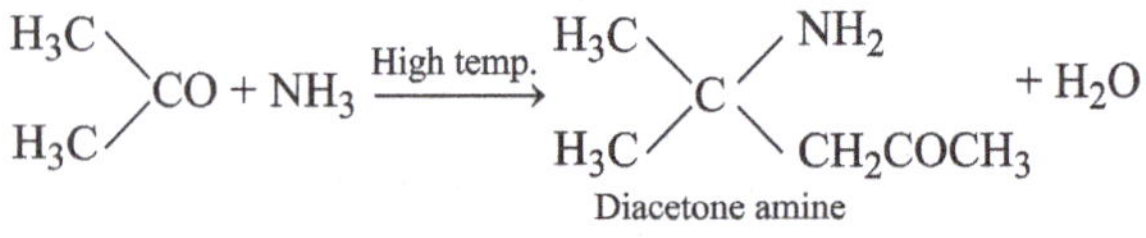

72. Cannizzaro reaction Aldehydes which do not have α-hydrogen atom, when treated with concentrated solution of NaOH or KOH undergoes simultaneous oxidation and reduction forming salts of carboxylic acid and alcohol.

e.g. Formaldehyde undergoes Cannizzaro reaction to form product sodium formate and methyl alcohol. The reaction can be represented as follows

$$\underset{\text{Formaldehyde}}{2HCHO} + \underset{\text{(Conc.)}}{NaOH} \longrightarrow \underset{\text{Sodium formate}}{HCO\overset{-}{O}\overset{+}{N}a} + \underset{\text{Methyl alcohol}}{CH_3OH}$$

Common Mistake Generally, students gets confused between aldol condensation and Cannizzaro reaction. It should be noted that aldol condensation involve the reactant molecule (either aldehydes or ketones containing atleast one α-H atom) undergo a reaction in the presence of dilute alkali as catalyst to form β-hydroxy aldehyde, whereas, Cannizzaro reaction involve aldehyde which do not have α-H atom undergo self oxidation and reduction, when treated with concentrated solution of NaOH or KOH.

73. (i) It is given that the molecular formula of B is C_7H_8O. The possible compound having this molecular formula may be benzyl alcohol ($C_6H_5CH_2OH$), anisole ($C_6H_5OCH_3$), *ortho*, *meta* or *para*-cresol ($CH_3—C_6H_4OH$).

- *o*-, *m*-, *p*-cresol on oxidation give complex products and anisol cannot be easily oxidised. Thus, the compound (B) must be benzyl alcohol.
- It is given that compound (B) forms compound (A) on oxidation, which has characteristic smell, that means compound (D) should be benzaldehyde.
- Benzaldehyde (A) on treatment with NaOH undergoes Cannizzaro reaction to give compounds (B) and (C). We know that compound (B) is benzyl alcohol, therefore compound (C) may be sodium benzoate ($C_6H_5CO\overset{-}{O}\overset{+}{N}a$).

Also, it is given that compound (C) forms benzene on heating with soda lime. Thus, it confirm that compounds (C) must be sodium benzoate ($C_6H_5CO\overset{-}{O}\overset{+}{N}a$).

The chemical equation of all the reactions involved are as follows

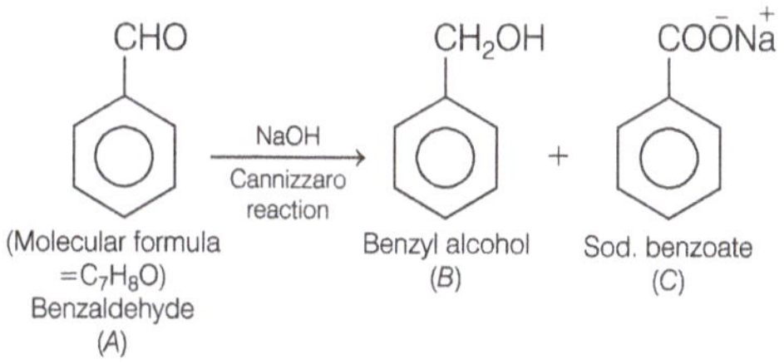

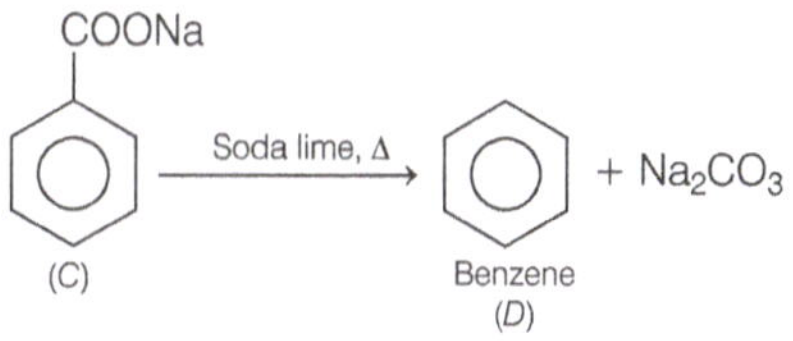

Thus, A = C_6H_5CHO, Benzaldehyde
$B = C_6H_5CH_2OH$, Benzyl alcohol
$C = C_6H_5COONa$, Sodium benzoate
$D = C_6H_5$, Benzene

(ii) (a)

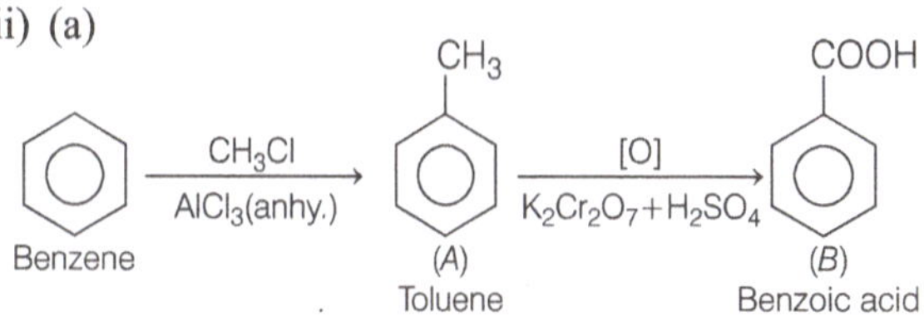

(b)

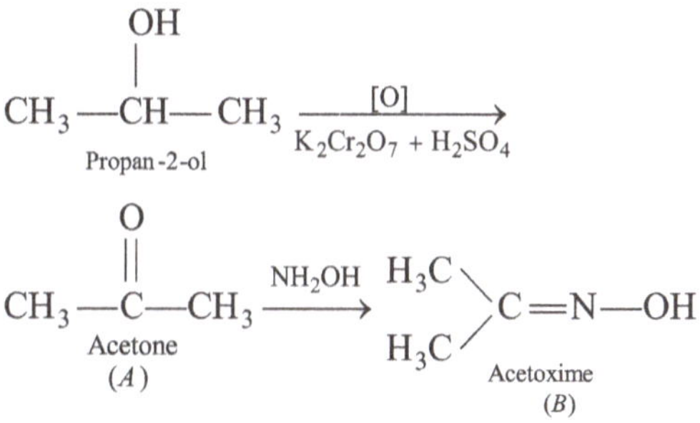

$+H_2O$

74. (i) (a) Aldehydes having atleast one α-H undergo aldol condensation in the presence of a base to give α-hydroxyaldehydes (aldol).
Since, acetaldehyde CH_3CHO has α-H whereas, formaldehyde HCHO has no α-H, therefore HCHO do not undergo aldol condensation.

(b) Chloroacetic acid $Cl—CH_2—COOH$ is strongest acid than acetic acid $CH_3—COOH$. —Cl is electron withdrawing group. It increases the acidity of acetic acid by dispersing negative charge by inductive effect and stabilise the acetate anion.

(c) Carbon, the C atom of the $C=O$ group acquires a partial positive charge in aldehydes and ketones and hence readily undergo nucleophilic addition reactions.

(ii) An organic compound (A) is not reduced by Fehling solution but undergoes Cannizzaro reaction (A) is benzaldehyde.

$$C_6H_5CHO + C_6H_5CHO \xrightarrow{NaOH} C_6H_5COONa + C_6H_5CH_2OH$$

TOPIC 2

Carboxylic Acids

The organic compounds which contain the carboxyl group

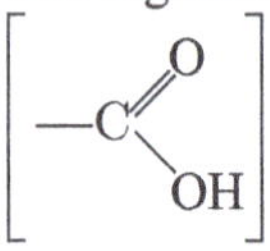

as the functional group are known as **carboxylic acids.**

Structure of —COOH Group

In carboxylic acids, the bonds attached to the carboxyl carbon are coplanar and are separated by about 120°. The carboxylic carbon is less electrophilic than carbonyl carbon because of the following possible resonance structures

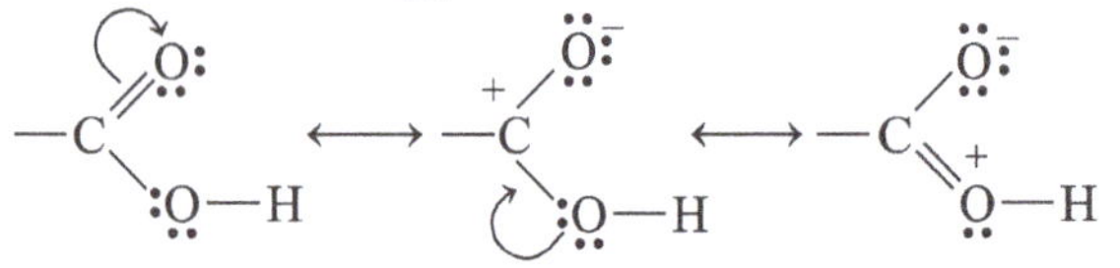

I II III

In structures (I) and (III), carboxyl carbon is electrically neutral. As a result, the carboxyl carbon of resonance hybrid is less positive. However, like carbonyl group, carboxyl group is also polar due to the resonance structures (II) and (III).

Classification of Carboxylic (*R*—COOH) Acids

Classification Based on Nature of Group Attached to the Carboxyl group

It is of two types.

(i) **Aliphatic carboxylic acids**, e.g. acetic acid (CH_3COOH) and formic acid (HCOOH).

(ii) **Aromatic carboxylic acids**, e.g. benzoic acid (C_6H_5COOH).

Classification Based on Number of Carboxyl Groups

It includes both aliphatic and aromatic acids and may be classified as follows

(i) **Monocarboxylic acids**, e.g. acetic acid (CH_3COOH), *n*-butyric acid ($CH_3CH_2CH_2COOH$).

(ii) **Dicarboxylic acids**, e.g. oxalic acid

$$\left[\begin{array}{c} COOH \\ | \\ COOH \end{array}\right], \text{ malonic acid } \left[CH_2\begin{array}{l} \diagup COOH \\ \diagdown COOH \end{array}\right].$$

(iii) **Tricarboxylic acids**, e.g. citric acid

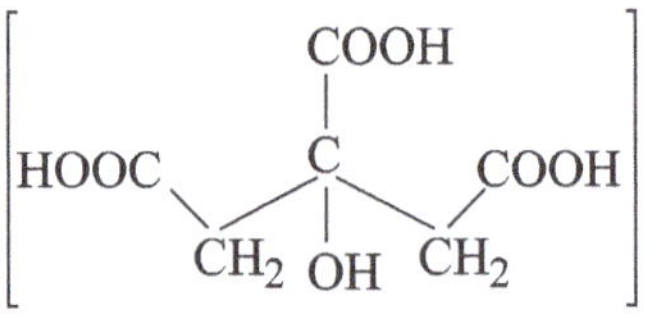

Nomenclature of Carboxylic Acids

In the IUPAC system of nomenclature, the monocarboxylic acids are named as alkanoic acids, i.e. name of the parent alkane – e + oic acid = alkanoic acid.

e.g. $\underset{\text{Ethanoic acid}}{CH_3COOH}$ and $\underset{\text{Butanoic acid}}{CH_3CH_2CH_2COOH}$

In the IUPAC system, the dicarboxylic acids are referred as alkanedioic acids.

Preparation of Carboxylic Acids

Some important methods of preparation are as follows

(i) From Oxidation of Primary Alcohols and Aldehydes

$$\underset{\substack{\text{Primary}\\\text{alcohol}}}{RCH_2OH} \xrightarrow[\substack{KMnO_4 \text{ or } K_2Cr_2O_7\\ \text{(in acidic or}\\ \text{alkaline medium)}}]{[O]} \underset{\text{Aldehyde}}{RCHO} \xrightarrow{[O]} \underset{\substack{\text{Carboxylic}\\\text{acid}}}{RCOOH}$$

(ii) From Hydrolysis of Nitriles

$$\underset{\text{Nitrile}}{RC{\equiv}N} + 2H_2O \xrightarrow[\Delta]{H^+ \text{ or } OH^-} \underset{\substack{\text{Carboxylic}\\\text{acid}}}{RCOOH} + NH_3\uparrow$$

[where, R = alkyl and C_6H_5-group]

(iii) From Grignard's Reagents (*RMgX*)

$$\underset{\substack{\text{Grignard's}\\\text{reagent}}}{RMgX} + \underset{\substack{\text{Carbon}\\\text{dioxide}}}{CO_2} \xrightarrow[\text{ether}]{\text{Dry}} \left[\underset{\substack{\text{(Addition}\\\text{product)}}}{R{-}\overset{\overset{\large O}{\|}}{C}{-}OMgX}\right] \xrightarrow{H_2O/H^+} \underset{\substack{\text{Carboxylic}\\\text{acid}}}{R{-}\overset{\overset{\large O}{\|}}{C}{-}OH} + Mg\begin{array}{l}\diagup OH\\ \diagdown X\end{array}$$

[where, R = alkyl and C_6H_5-group]

Physical Properties of Carboxylic Acids

The physical properties of carboxylic acids are described below

(i) Aliphatic carboxylic acids upto three carbon atoms are colourless pungent smelling liquids, next six members (C_4-C_9) are oily liquids at room temperature with unpleasant odour while higher carboxylic acids are wax like solids and odourless due to their low volatility.

(ii) **Solubility** Simple aliphatic carboxylic acids having upto four carbon atoms are miscible in water because of hydrogen bond formation with water.

Solubility decreases with increase in the number of carbon atoms which is due to increased hydrophobic interaction of hydrocarbon part. Carboxylic acids are also soluble in less polar organic solvents like benzene, ether, alcohol, chloroform, etc.

(iii) **Boiling points** As compared to hydrocarbons, aldehydes and ketones, carboxylic acids have higher boiling points because they have high extent of hydrogen bonding with water due to which they exists as associated molecules.

(iv) **Melting points** The melting points of aliphatic carboxylic acids do not show a regular pattern rather they show oscillation or alteration effect, i.e. melting point of an acid containing even number of carbon atoms is higher than the next member containing odd number of carbon atoms.

Chemical Properties of Carboxylic Acids

Chemical properties of carboxylic acid are as follows

(i) Reaction Due to H-atom of the Carboxyl Group

(a) **Acidic nature of carboxylic acids**

$$\underset{\text{Carboxylic acid}}{R-\overset{O}{\overset{\|}{C}}-OH} + H_2O \rightleftharpoons \underset{\text{Carboxylate ion}}{R-\overset{O}{\overset{\|}{C}}-O^-} + \underset{\text{Hydronium ion}}{H_3O^+}$$

Greater the extent of ionisation, greater is the strength of the acid.

Presence of an electron releasing substituent ($+I$ effect) decreases the acidic strength of the carboxylic acid.

Presence of an electron withdrawing substituent ($-I$ effect) increases the acidic strength of the carboxylic acid.

(b) **Reactions showing acidic character of carboxylic acids**

- **Reaction with active metals**

$$2RCOOH + 2Na \longrightarrow 2RCO\overset{-}{O}\overset{+}{N}a + H_2\uparrow$$

- **Reaction with alkalis**

$$RCOOH + NaOH \longrightarrow RCO\overset{-}{O}\overset{+}{N}a + H_2O$$

- **Reaction with carbonates and bicarbonates**

$$2RCOOH + \underset{\text{Sodium carbonate}}{Na_2CO_3} \longrightarrow 2RCO\overset{-}{O}\overset{+}{N}a + CO_2\uparrow + H_2O$$

$$RCOOH + \underset{\text{Sodium bicarbonate}}{NaHCO_3} \longrightarrow RCO\overset{-}{O}\overset{+}{N}a + CO_2\uparrow + H_2O$$

(ii) Reactions Involving —OH Part of the Carboxyl Group

(a) **Formation of acid chlorides** Carboxylic acids can be converted into the corresponding acid chlorides by treating with PCl_5, PCl_3 or $SOCl_2$.

- **Reaction with phosphorus pentachloride**

$$\underset{\text{Carboxylic acid}}{R-\overset{O}{\overset{\|}{C}}-OH} + \underset{\text{Phosphorus pentachloride}}{PCl_5} \longrightarrow \underset{\text{Acid chloride}}{R-\overset{O}{\overset{\|}{C}}-Cl} + \underset{\text{Phosphorus oxychloride}}{POCl_3} + HCl$$

- **Reaction with phosphorus trichloride**

$$3\underset{\text{Carboxylic acid}}{R-\overset{O}{\overset{\|}{C}}-OH} + \underset{\text{Phosphorus trichloride}}{PCl_3} \longrightarrow 3\underset{\text{Acid chloride}}{R-\overset{O}{\overset{\|}{C}}-Cl} + \underset{\text{Phosphorus acid}}{H_3PO_3}$$

- **Reaction with thionyl chloride**

$$\underset{\text{Carboxylic acid}}{R-\overset{\overset{\displaystyle O}{\|}}{C}-OH} + \underset{\text{Thionyl chloride}}{SOCl_2} \longrightarrow \underset{\text{Acid chloride}}{R-\overset{\overset{\displaystyle O}{\|}}{C}-Cl} + SO_2\uparrow + HCl$$

(b) **Formation of esters**

$$\underset{\text{Carboxylic acid}}{R-\overset{\overset{\displaystyle O}{\|}}{C}-OH} + \underset{\text{Alcohol}}{R'-OH} \underset{\text{or dry HCl gas}}{\overset{\text{Conc. } H_2SO_4}{\rightleftharpoons}} \underset{\text{Ester}}{R-\overset{\overset{\displaystyle O}{\|}}{C}-OR'} + H_2O$$

This reaction is reversible in nature and is called **esterification**.

(c) **Formation of amides**

$$\underset{\text{Carboxylic acid}}{R-\overset{\overset{\displaystyle O}{\|}}{C}-OH} + \underset{\text{Ammonia}}{NH_3} \longrightarrow \underset{\text{Ammonium carboxylate}}{R-\overset{\overset{\displaystyle O}{\|}}{C}-O^-NH_4^+} \xrightarrow{\text{Heat}} \underset{\text{Acid amide}}{R-\overset{\overset{\displaystyle O}{\|}}{C}-NH_2} + H_2O$$

(d) **Formation of acid anhydrides**

$$2R-\overset{\overset{\displaystyle O}{\|}}{C}-OH \underset{\text{Heat}}{\xrightarrow{P_2O_5}} \underset{\text{Acid anhydride}}{(R-CO)_2O} + H_2O$$

(iii) Reactions Involving Carboxyl Group

(a) **Decarboxylation** (Removal of $-CO_2$ Group)

- By heating sodium salt of the acid with sodalime

$$\underset{\text{Sodium salt of carboxylic acid}}{R-\overset{\overset{\displaystyle O}{\|}}{C}-\overset{-\ +}{ONa}} + NaOH \underset{\text{Heat}}{\xrightarrow{\text{CaO}}} \underset{\text{Alkane}}{R-H} + Na_2CO_3$$

- By electrolysis of aqueous solution of sodium or potassium salt

$$2R\overset{-\ +}{COONa} \longrightarrow \underset{\text{Carboxylate ion}}{2RCOO^-} + 2Na^+$$

At anode,

$$\underset{\text{Carboxylate ion}}{2RCOO^-} \longrightarrow \underset{\text{Alkane}}{R-R} + 2CO_2 + 2e^-$$

At cathode,

$$2H_2O \rightleftharpoons 2H^+ + 2OH^-, \quad (2H^+ + 2e^- \longrightarrow H_2)$$

This process is known as **Kolbe's electrolysis.**

(b) **Reduction**

- **Partial reduction to alcohols**

$$\underset{\text{Carboxylic acid}}{RCOOH} + 2H_2 \underset{(\text{or } LiAlH_4)}{\xrightarrow{\text{Copper chromite}}} \underset{\text{Alcohol}}{RCH_2OH} + H_2O$$

- **Complete reduction to alkanes**

$$\underset{\text{Carboxylic acid}}{RCOOH} + 6HI \underset{\text{Heat}}{\xrightarrow{\text{Red P}}} \underset{\text{Alkane}}{RCH_3} + 3I_2 + 2H_2O$$

(iv) Reactions Involving Alkyl Group of Carboxylic Acid

Halogenation

$$\underset{\text{Acetic acid}}{CH_3COOH} \underset{(-HCl)}{\xrightarrow{Cl_2,\ \text{Red P}}} \underset{\text{Monochloro acetic acid}}{CH_2ClCOOH} \underset{(-HCl)}{\xrightarrow{Cl_2,\ \text{Red P}}}$$

$$\underset{\text{Dichloro acetic acid}}{CHCl_2COOH} \underset{-HCl}{\xrightarrow{Cl_2,\ \text{Red P}}} \underset{\text{Trichloro acetic acid}}{CCl_3COOH}$$

This reaction is called **Hell-Volhard-Zelinsky** (HVZ) **reaction.**

(v) Reactions Due to Benzene Ring Present in Aromatic Carboxylic Acids

(a) **Nitration**

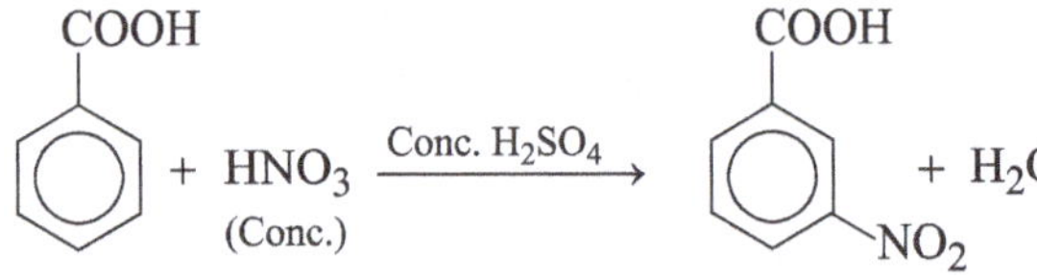

m-nitrobenzoic acid

(b) **Sulphonation**

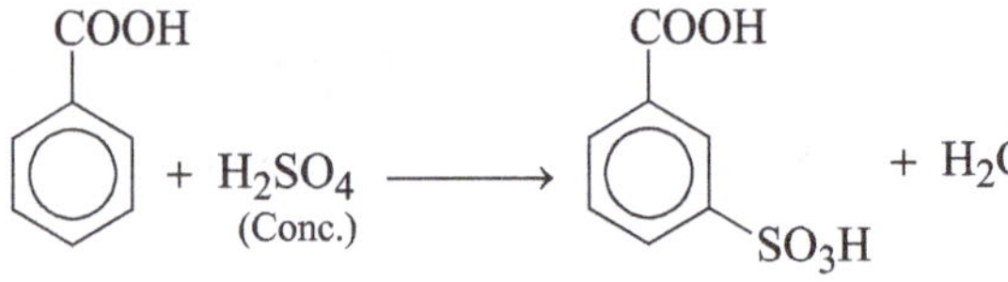

m-sulphobenzoic acid

Tests for Formic Acid

- It gives silver mirror or black precipitate with Tollen's reagent.
- It gives red precipitate with Fehling solution.
- It decolourises pink colour of acidified $KMnO_4$.

Uses of Formic Acid

It is used

- as an antiseptic.
- for dye baths in textiles.
- as a coagulating agent in rubber industry.

Tests for Acetic Acid

- It liberates carbon dioxide gas with bicarbonates and carbonates.
- With ferric chloride, it produces wine red colour.
- When warmed with ethyl alcohol and conc. H_2SO_4, a pleasant fruity odour of ethyl acetate is formed.

Uses of Acetic Acid

- As a solvent for resins, cellulose, etc.
- In the production of dyes, perfumes, esters, acetone, etc.
- For the manufacture of cellulose acetate which is used for making packaging materials, varnishes, rayon, etc.

Tests for Benzoic Acid

- It dissolves in water on boiling but separates out in the form of white shining leaflets on cooling.
- Benzoic acid (neutral solution) gives buff coloured precipitate with $FeCl_3$.
- On warming it with a little alcohol and conc. H_2SO_4, a fragrant odour of ethyl benzoate is obtained.

Uses of Benzoic Acid

- As a food preservative either in the pure form or mostly in the form of sodium benzoate.
- As urinary antiseptic in medicine.
- In the manufacture of antiseptics and dyes.

PYQs Previous Years' Questions

1 Mark Questions

1. Give one chemical test to distinguish following pairs of compounds.
   Benzaldehyde and acetic acid. *ISC 2021-22 (Sem-II)*
2. Give chemical test to distinguish acetaldehyde and acetic acid. *ISC 2017*
3. An aqueous solution of $CH_3CO\overset{-}{O}\overset{+}{N}a$ is ......'A'...... due to .....'B'...... . *ISC 2017*

   In the above sentence, 'A' and 'B' are
   (a) acidic, anionic hydrolysis
   (b) basic, cationic hydrolysis
   (c) acidic, cationic hydrolysis
   (d) basic, anionic hydrolysis
4. In the equation, $CH_3COOH + Cl_2 \xrightarrow[-HCl]{\text{Red P}} A$,

   The compound A is
   (a) CH_3CH_2Cl (b) $ClCH_2COOH$
   (c) CH_3Cl (d) CH_3COCl *ISC 2016*
5. Starting with Grignard's reagent, how will you prepare propanoic acid? *ISC 2016*
6. The aqueous solution of sodium acetate is basic. Explain. *ISC 2015*
7. Give the balanced equations for the following reaction:
   Kolbe's electrolytic reaction *ISC 2014*
8. How can the following conversion be brought about?
   Propanoic acid to ethylamine. *ISC 2013*

   KEY IDEA
   To convert propanoic acid to ethylamine, following steps are applied.
   (i) Propanoic acid is converted into amide through a suitable catalyst such as NH_4OH and heat.
   (ii) Amide is converted into primary amine through Br_2/KOH (Hofmann bromamide reaction)
9. How can the following conversion be brought about?
   Benzoic acid to benzaldehyde. *ISC 2013*
10. Give one chemical test to distinguish between the following pair of compounds.
    Formic acid and acetic acid *ISC 2013*
11. Give the balanced equation for the following reaction.
    Benzoic acid and phosphorus pentachloride. *ISC 2012*

12. Carry out the following conversion:
Methyl chloride to acetic acid. **ISC 2011**

13. Carry out the following conversion:
Benzene to benzoic acid. **ISC 2011, 2007**

14. Give one good chemical test to distinguish between the following pair of compounds:
Oxalic acid and benzoic acid. **ISC 2010**

15. Give one example for the following name reaction:
Hell-Volhard-Zelinsky (HVZ) reaction. **ISC 2010**

16. When oxalic acid is heated with glycerol, we get **ISC 2009**
(a) formic acid (b) acetic acid
(c) lactic acid (d) tartaric acid

17. Give the balanced equation for the following reaction:
Formic acid is heated with Tollen's reagent. **ISC 2009**

18. How will you distinguish between the following pair of compounds? Give one good chemical test.
Oxalic acid and acetic acid. **ISC 2009**

19. How will you bring about the following conversion?
Formic acid to oxalic acid. **ISC 2008, 2003**

> **KEY IDEA**
>
> Formic acid is first treated with NaOH solution to get sodium formate which is then heated at 390°C to form sodium oxalate. Formed sodium oxalate when reacted with $CaCl_2$ followed by reaction with dil. H_2SO_3 gives oxalic acid.

20. Correct the following statement:
Chloroacetic acid is more acidic than acetic acid because of the $-M$ effect. **ISC 2007**

21. Give the balanced equation for the following reaction.
Sucrose is warmed with concentrated nitric acid. **ISC 2007, 2000**

22. Give one test to distinguish between acetone and acetic acid. **ISC 2006**

23. Write the relevant equations to convert :
Acetic acid to acetone. **ISC 2006**

24. Write the chemical equation for the following reaction and name the main product:
Oxalic acid with glycerol at 260°C. **ISC 2005**

25. Write the equation and name of the following reaction:
Acetic acid with red phosphorus and chlorine. **ISC 2004**

26. Effervescence takes place when sodium carbonate solution is added to **ISC 2003**
(a) formaldehye (b) acetaldehyde
(c) acetic acid (d) phenol

27. ...... is more acidic than acetic acid because of ...... effect. **ISC 2003**

28. How will you carry out the following conversion?
Acetic acid to methane **ISC 2002**

2 Marks Questions

29. An aromatic carboxylic acid [*A*] which readily sublimes on heating, produces compound [*B*] on treatment with PCl_5. Compound [*B*], when reduced in the presence of Pd catalyst over $BaSO_4$ poisoned by sulphur in xylene solution gives compound [*C*].When compound [*C*] is condensed in the presence of alcoholic KCN, it gives compound [*D*]. (Molecular formula of compound [*D*] is $C_{14}H_{12}O_2$). Identify the compounds [*A*], [*B*], [*C*] and [*D*]. **ISC 2023**

30. An organic compound [*A*] C_2H_6O, on heating with conc. H_2SO_4 at 413 K gives a neutral compound [*B*] $C_4H_{10}O$. Compound [*B*] on treatment with PCl_5 gives a product, which on subsequent treatment with KCN yields compound [*C*] C_3H_5N. Compound [*C*] on hydrolysis gives an acid [*D*] $C_3H_6O_2$. Identify the compounds [*A*], [*B*], [*C*] and [*D*]. **ISC 2023**

31. Give one chemical test for each to distinguish between the following pair of compounds. **ISC Specimen 2023**
(i) Formaldehyde and acetic acid
(ii) Acetaldehyde and acetone

32. How will you bring about the following conversions? (Give equation). **ISC Specimen 2021-22 (Sem-II)**
(i) Acetic acid to acetone
(ii) Formaldehyde to urotropine

33. (i) Write the chemical equations to illustrate following name reactions. HVZ reaction.
(ii) How will the following the converted? (Give chemical equation)
Acetic acid to methane **ISC 2021-22 (Sem-II)**

34. Identify the compounds *A*, *B*, *C* and *D*. **ISC 2020**

$$C_6H_5COOH \xrightarrow{SOCl_2} [A] \xrightarrow{NH_3} [B] \xrightarrow{Br_2/KOH} [C] \xrightarrow[0\text{-}5°C]{NaNO_2 + HCl} [D]$$

35. How will you convert the following ? (Give balanced equation). **ISC 2020**
(i) Methyl chloride to acetic acid
(ii) Acetic acid to methane

36. (i) Give balanced chemical equations for the following reactions.
Acetic acid reacts with phosphorus pentachloride
(ii) Give one chemical test to distinguish between the following pairs of compounds.
Phenol and benzoic acid **ISC 2019**

37. (i) Give balanced equations for the following reactions.
Acetic acid reacts with phosphorus pentachloride
(ii) Give one chemical test to distinguish between the following pairs of compounds
Ethanol and acetic acid **ISC 2018**

38. (i) Write chemical equations to illustrate the following name reaction :
HVZ reaction
(ii) Explain, why acetic acid is a weaker acid as compared to formic acid ? **ISC 2018**

39. Identify the products *A*, *B* and *C*.

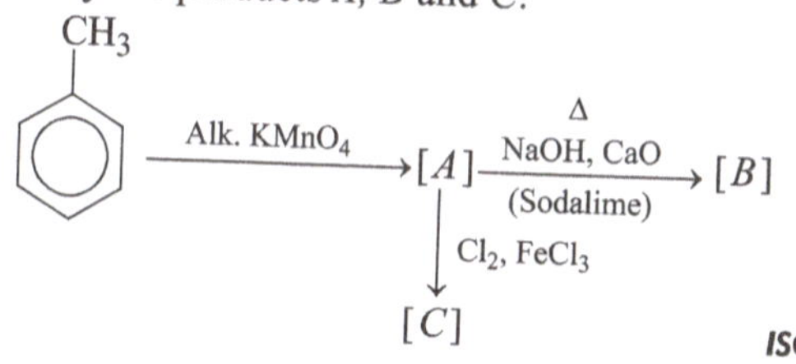

ISC 2012

3 Marks Questions

40. Identify the compounds [*A*], [*B*] and [*C*].

(i) $C_6H_5COOH \xrightarrow{PCl_5} [A] \xrightarrow{+H_2,\ Pd/BaSO_4} [B] \xrightarrow{KCN\ (alc.),\ distil} [C]$

(ii) $H-C\equiv C-H + H_2O \xrightarrow{Hg^{2+}/H_2SO_4} [A] \xrightarrow[K_2Cr_2O_7/H_2SO_4]{[Oxidation]} [B] \xrightarrow[(b)\ Dry\ distillation]{(a)\ Ca(OH)_2} [C]$

Latest Specimen 2024

41. Write the chemical equation for the following named organic reactions. **ISC Specimen 2023**
(i) Haloform reaction
(ii) Reimer - Tiemann reaction
(iii) Kolbe - Schmidt reaction or Kolbe reaction

42. Identify the compounds *A*, *B* and *C*.

(i) $C_6H_5COOH \xrightarrow{PCl_5} [A] \xrightarrow{H_2-Pd/BaSO_4} [B] \xrightarrow[distillation]{KCN\ (alc.)} [C]$

(ii) $H-C\equiv C-H \xrightarrow[Dil.\ H_2SO_4 + HgSO_4]{H_2O} [A] \xrightarrow[[Ni]]{H_2} [B] \xrightarrow[Conc.\ H_2SO_4]{140°C} [C]$ **ISC 2017**

43. How can the following conversions be brought about ?
(i) Acetaldehyde to acetaldehyde phenyl hydrazone.
(ii) Methyl chloride to acetone. **ISC 2016**

44. Identify the compounds *A*, *B* and *C*.

(i) $C_2H_5OH \xrightarrow{PCl_5} [A] \xrightarrow{KCN} [B] \xrightarrow{H_3O^+} C_2H_5COOH \xrightarrow[\Delta]{NH_3} [C]$

(ii) $C_6H_5COOH \xrightarrow{SOCl_2} [A] \xrightarrow{NH_3} [B] \xrightarrow{Br_2/KOH} [C]$ **ISC 2016**

45. Write the balanced chemical equation for the following reaction.
(i) Oxalic acid is treated with acidified potassium permanganate solution.
(ii) Benzoic acid is treated with a mixture of concentrated nitric acid and concentrated sulphuric acid.
(iii) Methyl magnesium iodide is treated with carbon dioxide and the product hydrolysed in acidic medium. **ISC 2013**

46. Identify *A* to *F*.

$[A] \xrightarrow{LiAlH_4} C_2H_5OH \xrightarrow{PBr_3} [B] \xrightarrow{KCN} [C] \xrightarrow{D} C_3H_7NH_2 \xrightarrow{HNO_2} [E] \xrightarrow[K_2Cr_2O_7/H^+]{[O]} [F]$ **ISC 2011**

4 Marks Questions

47. An aliphatic unsaturated hydrocarbon [A] when treated with $HgSO_4$ / H_2SO_4 yields a compound [B] having molecular formula C_3H_6O. [B] on oxidation with concentrated HNO_3 gives two compounds [C] and [D]. Compound [C] when treated with PCl_5 gives compound [E]. [E] when reacts with ethanol gives a sweet smelling liquid [F]. Compound [F] is also formed when [C] reacts with ethanol in the presence of concentrated H_2SO_4.

(i) Identify the compound *A*, *B*, *C*, *D*, *E* and *F*.
(ii) Give the chemical equation for the reaction of (*C*) with chlorine in the presence of red phosphorus and name the reaction. **ISC 2017**

48. An organic compound A has the molecular formula C_7H_6O. When A is treated with NaOH followed by acid hydrolysis, it gives two products, B and C. When B is oxidised, it gives A. When A and C are each treated separately with PCl_3, they give two different organic products D and E.

(i) Identify A to E.

(ii) Give the chemical reaction when A is treated with NaOH and name the reaction. *ISC 2016, 2011*

49. How will you carry out the following conversion?
Acetic acid to propionic acid *ISC 2002*

5 Marks Questions

50. (i) Write the chemical equations to illustrate the following name reactions. *ISC 2023*

(a) Cannizzaro reaction
(b) HVZ reaction
(c) Aldol condensation

(ii) How will the following be converted ? (Give chemical equations)

(a) Acetaldehyde to acetone
(b) Formaldehyde to urotropine

51. (i) Starting with methyl magnesium bromide, how will the following compounds be synthesised? *ISC Specimen 2023*

(a) Acetaldehyde (b) Acetone (c) Acetic acid

(ii) Explain the following.

(a) Chloroacetic acid is stronger acid than acetic acid.

(b) Formic acid reduces Tollens' reagent but acetic acid does not.

52. (i) Write the product(s) of the following reactions.

(a) $CH_3COCH_3 + H_2NOH \longrightarrow$ *ISC Specimen 2018*

(b) $2C_6H_5CHO + \text{Conc. NaOH} \longrightarrow$

(c) $CH_3COOH \xrightarrow{Cl_2/P}$

(ii) Give one chemical test each to distinguish between the following pairs of compounds.

(a) Benzaldehyde and benzoic acid
(b) Propanal and propanone

53. (i) Write the chemical equations to illustrate the following name reactions. *ISC Specimen 2018*

(a) Wolff-Kishner reduction
(b) Aldol condensation
(c) Cannizzaro reaction

(ii) Account for the following.

(a) CH_3CHO is more reactive with HCN than CH_3COCH_3.

(b) Carboxylic acids are stronger acids thanphenol.

Explanations

1. Benzaldehyde reduces Tollen's reagent to give shining silver mirror but acetic acid does not.

$$\underset{\text{Benzaldehyde}}{C_6H_5CHO} + \underset{\text{Tollen's reagent}}{2[Ag(NH_3)_2]^+} + 3OH^- \longrightarrow C_6H_5COO^- + \underset{\text{Silver mirror}}{2Ag\downarrow} + 2H_2O + 4NH_3$$

$$CH_3COOH \xrightarrow{\text{Tollen's reagent}} \text{No reaction}$$ **(1)**

Concept Enhancer Tollen's reagent is a colourless, basic, aqueous solution containing silver ions coordinated to ammonia. It's IUPAC name is ammoniacal solution of silver nitrate.

2. Tollen's test Acetaldehyde reduces Tollen's reagent to give shining silver mirror but acetic acid does not.

$$\underset{\text{Acetaldehyde}}{CH_3CHO} + \underset{\text{Tollen's reagent}}{2[Ag(NH_3)_2]^+} + 3OH^- \longrightarrow \underset{\text{Acetate ion}}{CH_3COO^-} + \underset{\text{Silver mirror}}{2Ag\downarrow} + 2H_2O + 4NH_3$$

$$\underset{\text{Tollen's reagent}}{CH_3COOH \longrightarrow} \text{No reaction}$$

3. (d) basic, anionic hydrolysis

4. (b) $ClCH_2COOH$

5. $$\underset{\text{Grignard's reagent}}{C_2H_5—MgCl} \xrightarrow[\text{(ii) } H_3O^+]{\text{(i) } CO_2} \underset{\text{Propanoic acid}}{C_2H_5—\overset{\overset{\large O}{||}}{C}—OH}$$

Concept Enhancer Grignard reagents are strong bases and will react with protic compounds which makes them exceedingly valuable tools for organic synthesis.

6. Because, when it reacts with water, it produces strong base, i.e. NaOH which makes the solution basic.

7. Kolbe's electrolytic reaction can be proceed as follows Let us take an example

$$\underset{\text{Sodium acetate}}{2CH_3\overset{-}{CO}\overset{+}{ONa}} \longrightarrow \underset{\text{Acetate ion}}{2CH_3COO^-} + 2Na^+$$

At anode,

$$\underset{\text{Acetate ion}}{2CH_3COO^-} \longrightarrow \underset{\text{Ethane}}{CH_3—CH_3} + 2CO_2 + 2e^-$$

At cathode, $2H_2O \rightleftharpoons 2H^+ + 2OH^-$

$$2H^+ + 2e^- \longrightarrow H_2$$

$$2Na^+ + 2OH^- \longrightarrow 2NaOH$$

8.

$$\underset{\text{Propanoic acid}}{CH_3CH_2COOH} \xrightarrow{NH_4OH} CH_3CH_2COONH_4$$

$$\xrightarrow{\Delta} CH_3CH_2CONH_2 \xrightarrow[\text{Hofmann bromamide reaction}]{Br_2/KOH} \underset{\text{Ethylamine}}{CH_3CH_2NH_2}$$

9. Benzoic acid is converted into benzaldehyde through the following steps.

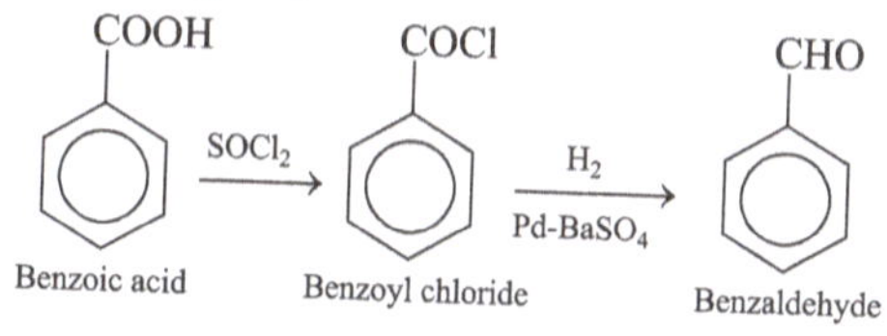

10. Formic acid gives silver mirror test with Tollen's reagent while acetic acid does not give this test.

$$\underset{\text{Formic acid}}{HCOOH} + 2[Ag(NH_3)_2]^+NO_3^- + H_2O \longrightarrow$$

$$2NH_4NO_3 + (NH_4)_2CO_3 + \underset{\text{Silver mirror}}{2Ag\downarrow}$$

$$\underset{\text{Acetic acid}}{CH_3COOH} + \underset{\text{Tollen's reagent}}{2[Ag(NH_3)_2]^+NO_3^-} + H_2O$$

$$\longrightarrow \text{No reaction}$$

11. The balanced chemical equation is

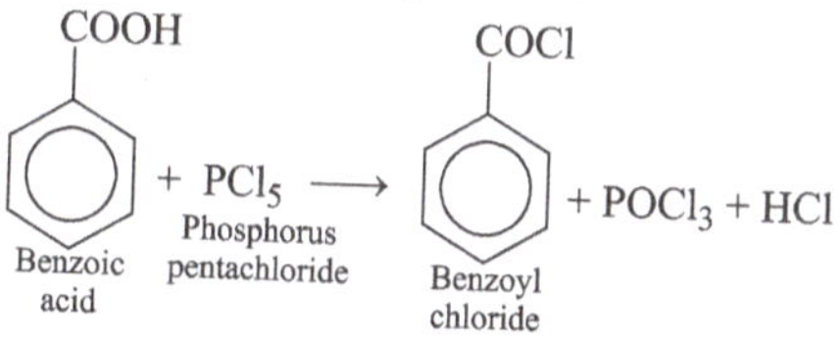

12. The conversion of methyl chloride to acetic acid have the following steps.

$$\underset{\text{Methyl chloride}}{CH_3Cl} + 2Na + Cl\cdot CH_3 \longrightarrow CH_3\cdot CH_3 + 2NaCl$$

$$CH_3\cdot CH_3 + Cl_2 \xrightarrow{h\nu} C_2H_5Cl + HCl$$

$$C_2H_5Cl + KOH\ (aq) \longrightarrow C_2H_5OH + KCl$$

$$C_2H_5OH + O_2 \xrightarrow[H_2SO_4]{K_2Cr_2O_7} \underset{\text{Acetic acid}}{CH_3COOH} + H_2O$$

13. The conversion of benzene to benzoic acid have the following steps.

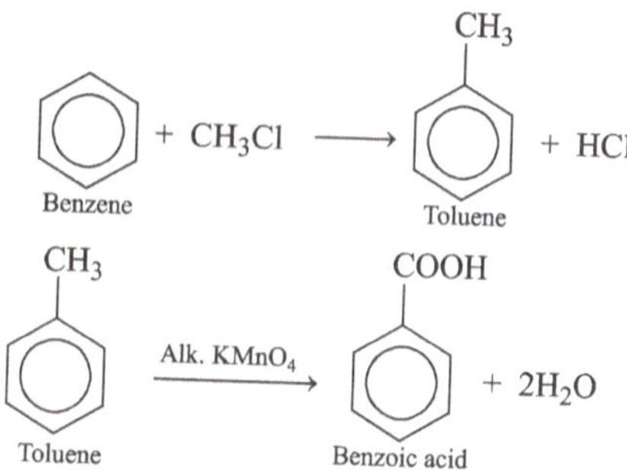

14. Oxalic acid decolourised hot solution of acidified $KMnO_4$ whereas benzoic acid does not give this test.

15. Refer to text on page 196.

16. (a) When oxalic acid is heated with glycerol then we get formic acid.

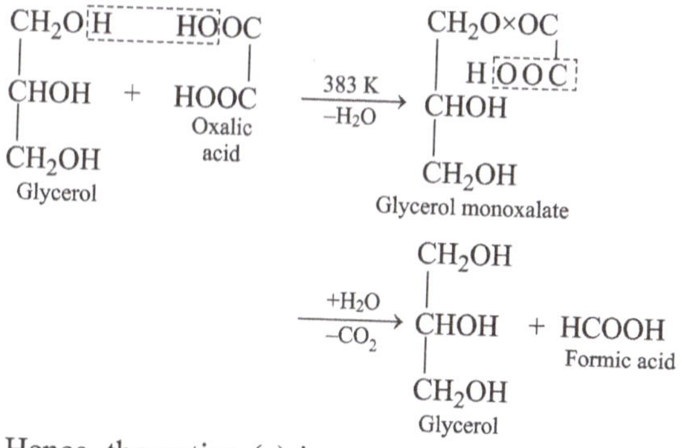

Hence, the option (a) is correct. **(1)**

17.

$$\underset{\text{Formic acid}}{HCOOH} + 2[Ag(NH_3)_2]^+NO_3^- + H_2O \longrightarrow$$

$$2NH_4NO_3 + (NH_4)_2CO_3 + \underset{\text{Silver mirror}}{2Ag\downarrow}$$

Tollen's reagent $= [Ag(NH_3)_2]\overset{+}{N}O_3^-$

18. Oxalic acid decolourises acidified potassium permanganate solution while acetic acid does not. **(1)**

$$2MnO_4 + 16H^+ + 5C_2O_4^{2-} \longrightarrow Mn^{2+} + 8H_2O + 10CO_2$$

19.

$$\underset{\text{Formic acid}}{HCOOH} + NaOH \longrightarrow HCO\overset{-}{O}\overset{+}{Na} + H_2O$$

$$\underset{\text{Sodium formate}}{2HCO\overset{-}{O}\overset{+}{Na}} \xrightarrow{390°C} (COONa)_2 + H_2\uparrow$$

$$\underset{\text{Sodium oxalate}}{(COONa)_2} + CaCl_2 \longrightarrow \underset{\text{Calcium oxalate}}{(COO)_2Ca} + 2NaCl$$

$$(COO)_2Ca + \underset{\text{(Dil.)}}{H_2SO_4} \longrightarrow \underset{\text{Oxalic acid}}{(COOH)_2} + CaSO_4\downarrow$$

(1)

20. The correct statement is chloroacetic acid is more acidic than acetic acid because of the $-I$ effect of Cl group. **(1)**

21. The balanced chemical equation is

$$\underset{\text{Sucrose}}{C_{12}H_{22}O_{11}} \xrightarrow[\text{Conc. }HNO_3,\ V_2O_5]{18[O]} 6\ \underset{\text{Oxalic acid}}{\begin{matrix}COOH\\|\\COOH\end{matrix}} + 5H_2O$$ **(1)**

22. Acetic acid when heated with ethyl alcohol in the presence of conc. H_2SO_4, it gives a fruity smell of an ester, ethyl ethanoate.

$$\underset{\text{Acetic acid}}{CH_3COOH} + \underset{\text{Ethyl alcohol}}{C_2H_5OH} \xrightarrow[\text{Conc. }H_2SO_4]{\Delta\text{ with}} \underset{\text{Ethyl ethanoate}}{CH_3COOC_2H_5} + H_2O$$

while acetone does not give this test. **(1)**

23. The relevant chemical equations are

$$\underset{\text{Acetic acid}}{2CH_3COOH} + Ca(OH)_2 \longrightarrow \underset{\text{Calcium acetate}}{(CH_3COO)_2Ca} + 2H_2O$$

$$(CH_3COO)_2Ca \xrightarrow{\Delta} \underset{\text{Acetone}}{CH_3COCH_3} + CaCO_3\downarrow$$ **(1)**

24. Allyl alcohol is formed as

$$\underset{\text{Glycerol}}{\begin{matrix}CH_2OH\\|\\CHOH\\|\\CH_2OH\end{matrix}} + \underset{\text{Oxalic acid}}{\begin{matrix}HOOC\\|\\HOOC\end{matrix}} \xrightarrow[-2H_2O]{260^\circ C} \underset{\text{Glycerol dioxalate}}{\begin{matrix}CH_2OOC\\|\quad\ \ |\\CHOOC\\|\\CH_2OH\end{matrix}} \xrightarrow{-2CO_2} \underset{\text{Allyl alcohol}}{\begin{matrix}CH_2\\||\\CH\\|\\CH_2OH\end{matrix}}$$ **(1)**

25. Refer to text on page 196. **(1)**

26. (c) Effervescence takes place when sodium carbonate solution is added to acetic acid.

Hence, the option (c) is correct. **(1)**

27. **Benzoic acid** is more acidic than acetic acid because of **negative inductive effect** ($-I$-effect is due to the presence of benzene ring). **(1)**

28. When acetic acid is treated with caustic soda, it produces sodium salt of acetic acid.

When it is refluxed in the presence of slaked lime, hydrocarbon is produced.

$$\underset{\text{Acetic acid}}{CH_3COOH} \xrightarrow{NaOH} CH_3-\overset{\overset{\displaystyle O}{||}}{C}-\overset{-}{O}\overset{+}{Na} \xrightarrow[\Delta]{NaOH/CaO} \underset{\text{Methane}}{CH_4}$$ **(1)**

29.

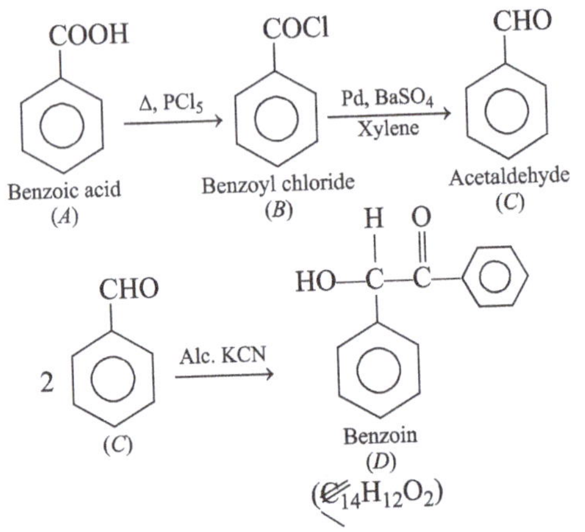

30. Organic compound having formula C_2H_6O is alcohol (CH_3CH_2OH) (A).

When ethyl alcohol is heated with conc. H_2SO_4 at 413 K it gives an ester $(C_4H_{10}O)$.

$$\underset{\text{Ethanol}}{2CH_3-CH_2-OH} \xrightarrow[413\text{ K}]{\text{Conc. }H_2SO_4} \underset{\text{Diethyl ether }(B)}{CH_3-CH_2-O-CH_2-CH_3}$$

$$\xrightarrow{PCl_5} CH_3-CH_2-Cl + \underset{\text{Ethyl chloride}}{CH_3-CH_2-Cl}$$

$$\xrightarrow{KCN} \underset{\text{Ethyl cyanide }(C)}{CH_3-CH_2-CN} \xrightarrow{H^{\oplus}} \underset{\text{Propanoic acid }(D)}{CH_3CH_2COOH}$$

31. (i) **Formaldehyde and acetic acid** Aldehyde reduces Tollen's reagent to give shining silver mirror but acetic acid does not.

$$\underset{\text{Formaldehyde}}{HCHO} + \underset{\text{Tollen's reagent}}{2[Ag(NH_3)_2]^+} + 3OH^- \longrightarrow HC\begin{matrix}O\\O^-\end{matrix} + \underset{\text{Silver mirror}}{2Ag\downarrow} + 2H_2O$$

$$CH_3COOH \xrightarrow[\text{Tollen's reagent}]{} \text{No reaction}$$ **(1)**

(ii) **Acetaldehyde and acetone** Acetaldehyde gives a silver mirror test with Tollen's reagent but acetone gives no such test with Tollen's reagent. **(1)**

$$\underset{\text{Acetaldehyde}}{CH_3-\overset{\overset{\displaystyle O}{||}}{C}-H} + 2[Ag(NH_3)_2]^+ \longrightarrow CH_3-\overset{\overset{\displaystyle O}{||}}{C}-O^- + 2Ag + H_2O$$

$$\underset{\text{Acetone}}{CH_3-\overset{\overset{\displaystyle O}{||}}{C}-CH_3} \xrightarrow{[Ag(NH_3)_2]^+} \text{No reaction}$$

32. (i) **Acetic acid to acetone**

$$\underset{\text{Acetic acid}}{2\,CH_3COOH} \xrightarrow{Ca(OH)_2} \underset{\text{Calcium acetate}}{(CH_3COO)_2Ca^{2+}} \xrightarrow[\text{distillation}]{\text{Dry}} \underset{\text{Acetone}}{CH_3-\overset{O}{\overset{||}{C}}-CH_3} + CaCO_3$$

(1)

(ii) **Formaldehyde to urotropine**

$$\underset{\text{Formaldehyde}}{6HCHO} + \underset{\text{Ammonia}}{4NH_3} \xrightarrow{50°\text{-}70°C}$$

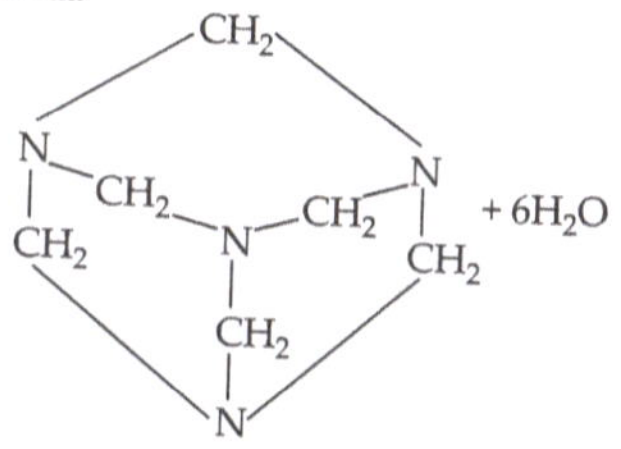

Urotropine (1)

33. (i) Refer to text on page 196.

(ii) $\underset{\text{Acetic acid}}{CH_3COOH} \xrightarrow{NaOH} CH_3COO^-Na^+ \xrightarrow[\Delta]{NaOH/CaO} \underset{\text{Methane}}{CH_4}$

34.

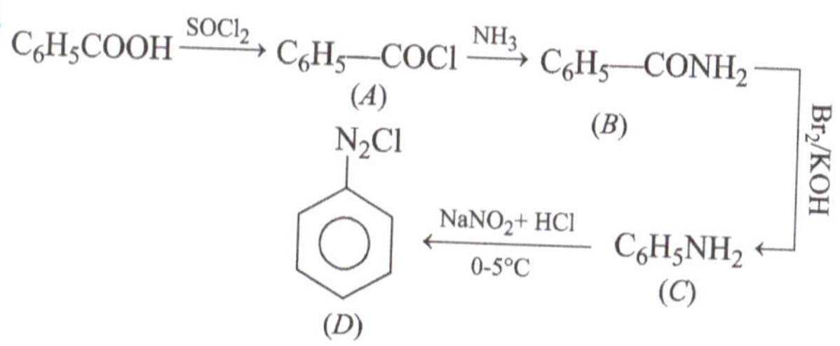

35. (i) $\underset{\text{Methylchloride}}{CH_3-Cl} \xrightarrow{Mg/Ether} CH_3MgCl \xrightarrow[\text{(b) Water}]{\text{(a) } CO_2} \underset{\text{Acetic acid}}{CH_3COOH}$ (1)

(ii) Refer to solution 33 (ii).

36. (i) Refer to text on page 195. (1)

(ii) Phenol and benzoic acid can be distinguish by sodium bicarbonate test.

Benzoic acid reacts with sodium bicarbonate to produce effervescence of carbon dioxide, whereas phenol does not.

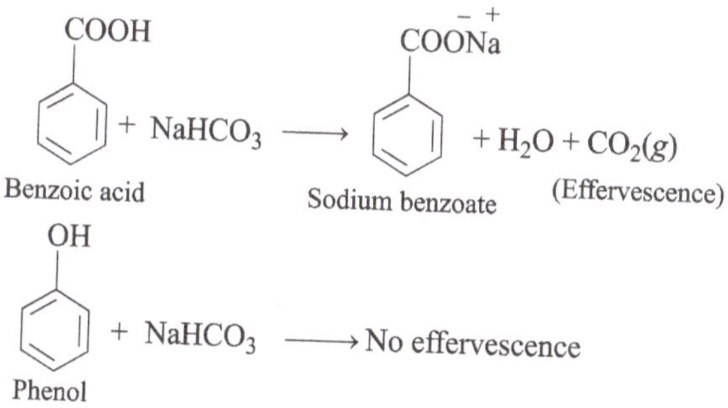

(1)

37. (i) Refer to text on page 195. (1)

(ii) **Ethanol and acetic acid** These can be distinguished by reaction with sodium bicarbonate.

Acetic acid reacts with sodium bicarbonate producing CO_2 gas, whereas ethanol does not show any reaction with sodium bicarbonate.

$$\underset{\text{Acetic acid}}{CH_3COOH} + NaHCO_3 \longrightarrow \underset{\text{Sodium acetate}}{CH_3\overset{-}{COO}\overset{+}{Na}} + \underset{\text{Effervescence}}{CO_2\uparrow} + H_2O$$

$$\underset{\text{Ethanol}}{CH_3CH_2OH} + NaHCO_3 \longrightarrow \text{No reaction}$$ (1)

38. (i) **Hell-Volhard-Zelinsky** (HVZ) **reaction**

Refer to text on page 196. (1)

(ii) Acetic acid is a weaker acid as compared to formic acid because in acetic acid $-CH_3$ group acts as electron donating group. It decreases the stability of carboxylate ion by intensifying the negative charge and hence, decreases the acidity of carboxylic acid.

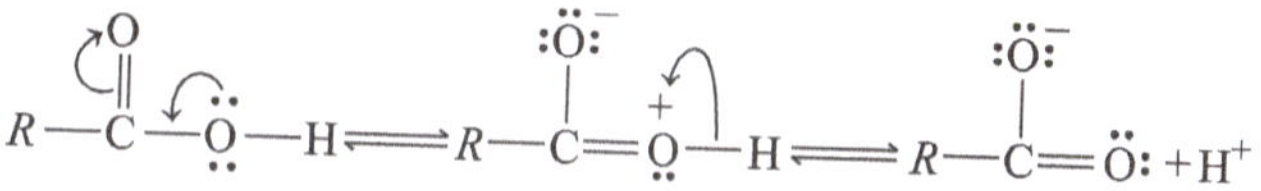

Carboxylate ion (1)

39. The products are

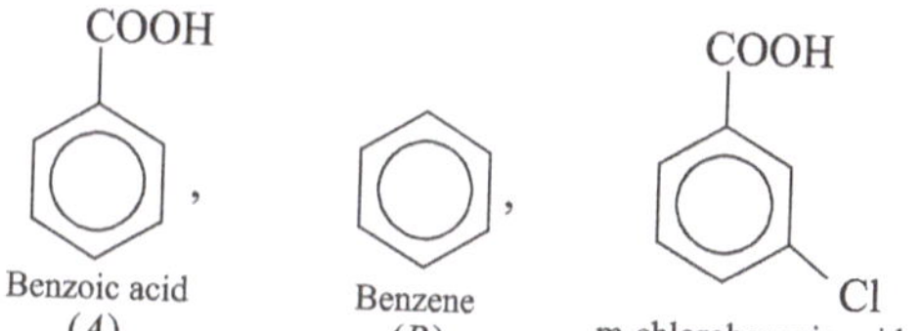

Benzoic acid (*A*), Benzene (*B*), m-chlorobenzoic acid (*C*)

(½+ ½+ 1)

40. (i) Benzoic acid reacts with PCl_5 to form benzyl chloride and reduction with H_2 - Pd / $BaSO_4$ gives benzaldehyde.

Reaction with alcoholic KCN gives cyanohydrin.

$$C_6H_5COOH \xrightarrow{PCl_5} \underset{(A)}{C_6H_5COCl} \xrightarrow{H_2\text{-}Pd/BaSO_4}$$

$$\underset{(B)}{C_6H_5CHO} \xrightarrow{\text{KCN (Alc.) distil.}} \underset{(C)}{C_6H_5\underset{OH}{\underset{|}{C}}-C\equiv N}$$

(ii) Hydration of ethyne with $H_2O/HgSO_4$/ H_2SO_4 gives acetaldehyde. Moreover, oxidation of acetaldehyde gives ethanoic acid. It is reacted with

$Ca(OH)_2$ and the product is distilled dry and form acetone.

$$H-C\equiv C-C \xrightarrow[\text{Dil. } H_2SO_4 + HgSO_4]{H_2O} \underset{(A)}{CH_3CHO}$$

$$\xrightarrow[H^+]{K_2Cr_2O_7/} \underset{(B)}{CH_3COOH} \xrightarrow{Ca(OH)_2} Ca(OCOCH_3)_3$$

$$+2H_2O \xrightarrow[\text{distillation}]{\text{Dry}} \underset{(C)}{CH_3-CO-CH_3} + CaCO_3$$

41. (i) **Haloform reaction** It is reaction of methyl ketone with chlorine, bromine, or iodine in the presence of hydroxide ions to give a carboxylate ion and a haloform.

The formed carboxylate ion on hydrolysis gives benzoic acid

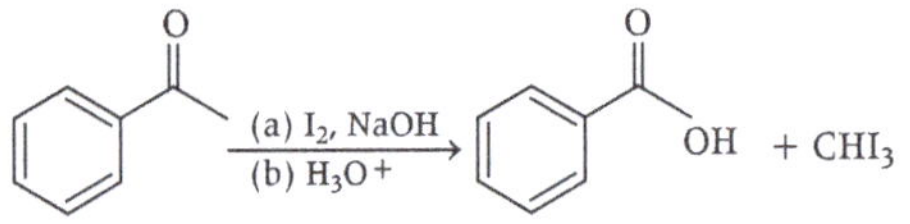

(1)

(ii) **Reimer-Tiemann reaction** is an organic chemical reaction where phenol is converted into an *ortho*-hydroxy benzaldehyde using chloroform, a base and acid workup.

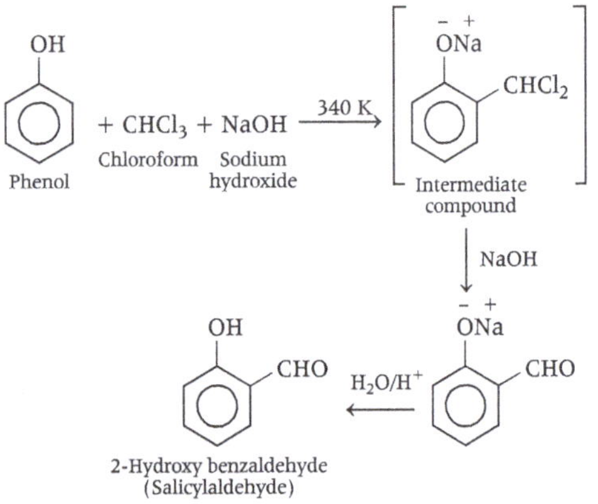

(1)

(iii) **Kolbe-Schmidt reaction or Kolbe reaction** When phenol is treated with sodium hydroxide, sodium phenoxide is produced. This sodium phenoxide when treated with carbon dioxide, followed by acidification undergoes electrophilic substitution to give *ortho*-hydroxy benzoic acid as the main product.

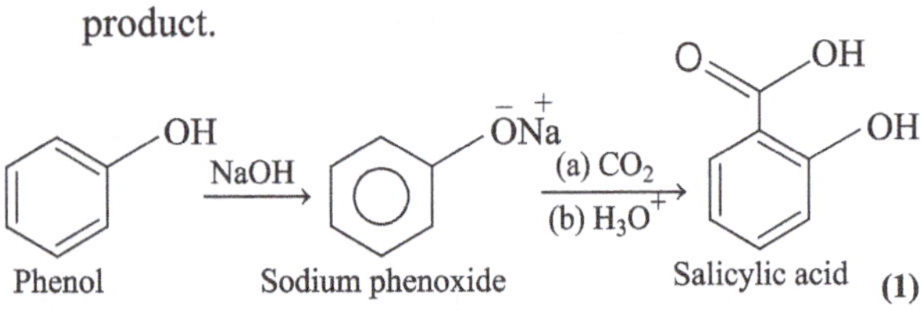

(1)

42. (i) $\underset{\text{Benzoic acid}}{C_6H_5COOH} \xrightarrow{PCl_5} \underset{\substack{\text{Benzoyl chloride}\\(A)}}{C_6H_5COCl} \xrightarrow[Pd/BaSO_4]{H_2}$

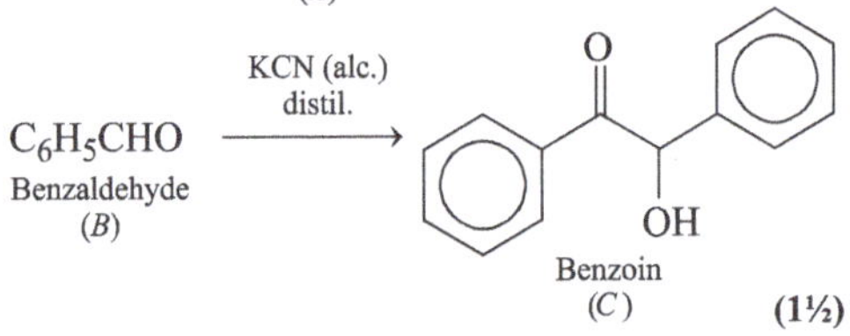

(1½)

(ii) $\underset{\text{Ethyne}}{H-C\equiv C-H} \xrightarrow[\text{Dil. } H_2SO_4 + HgSO_4]{H_2O} \underset{\substack{\text{Acetaldehyde}\\(A)}}{CH_3-\overset{\overset{O}{\|}}{C}-H}$

$$\xrightarrow[Ni]{H_2} \underset{\substack{\text{Ethanol}\\(B)}}{CH_3CH_2OH} \xrightarrow[\text{Conc. } H_2SO_4]{140°C} \underset{\substack{\text{Ethene}\\(C)}}{CH_2=CH_2}$$

(1½)

43. (i) Acetaldehyde reacts with phenyl hydrazine in acidic medium to form an addition compound, which undergoes elimination of a water molecule to form acetaldehyde phenyl hydrazone.

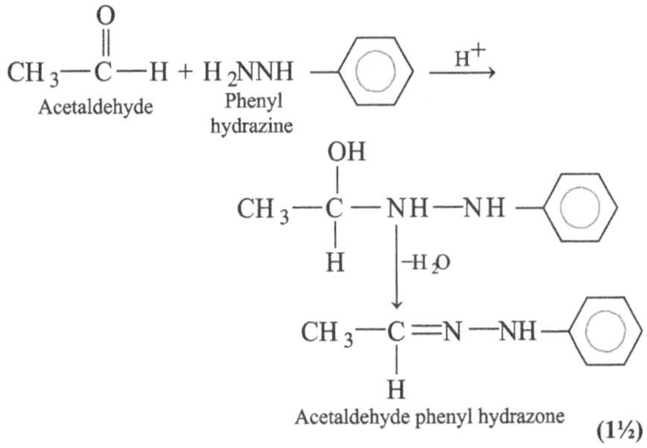

(1½)

(ii) $\underset{\substack{\text{Methyl}\\\text{chloride}}}{CH_3Cl} \xrightarrow[\text{Ether}]{Mg} \underset{\substack{\text{Methyl magnesium}\\\text{chloride}}}{CH_3MgCl}$

$$CH_3Cl \xrightarrow{KCN} \underset{\substack{\text{Methyl}\\\text{cyanide}}}{CH_3CN} \xrightarrow{CH_3MgCl} CH_3-\overset{\overset{CH_3}{|}}{C}=NMgCl$$

$$\xrightarrow{H_3O^+} \underset{\text{Acetone}}{CH_3-\overset{\overset{O}{\|}}{C}-CH_3}$$

(1½)

44. (i) $C_2H_5OH \xrightarrow{PCl_5} \underset{(A)}{C_2H_5Cl} + POCl_3 + HCl$

$$C_2H_5Cl \xrightarrow{KCN} \underset{(B)}{C_2H_5CN} \xrightarrow{H_3O^+} C_2H_5COOH$$

$$C_2H_5COOH \xrightarrow[\Delta]{NH_3} \underset{(C)}{C_2H_5COONH_4}$$

(1½)

(ii) $C_6H_5COOH \xrightarrow{SOCl_2} C_6H_5COCl + HCl + SO_2\uparrow$
Benzoic acid → Benzoyl chloride (*A*)

$C_6H_5COCl \xrightarrow{NH_3} C_6H_5CONH_2 \xrightarrow{KOH/Br_2} C_6H_5NH_2$
Benzamide (*B*) → Aniline (*C*)

(1½)

45. The balanced chemical equations for the given reactions are as follows

(i) $5\,\begin{matrix}COOH\\|\\COOH\end{matrix} + 2KMnO_4 + 3H_2SO_4 \longrightarrow K_2SO_4 + 2MnSO_4 + 10CO_2 + 8H_2O$

Oxalic acid, Potassium permanganate; (Colourless) **(1)**

(ii)

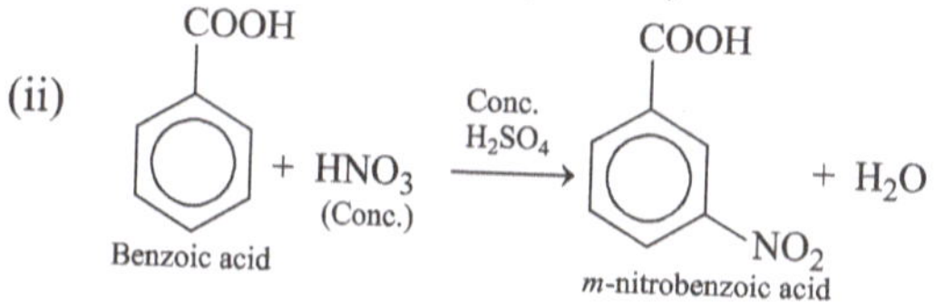

(1)

(iii) $O{=}C{=}O + CH_3{-}Mg{-}I \longrightarrow$
Carbon dioxide, Methyl magnesium iodide

$O{=}\underset{}{\overset{CH_3}{\overset{|}{C}}}{-}OMgI \xrightarrow{H_2O/H^+} CH_3{-}\overset{O}{\overset{||}{C}}{-}OH + Mg\begin{matrix}OH\\I\end{matrix}$

Acetic acid, Hydroxy magnesium iodide **(1)**

46. Substances from *A* to *F* are

- *A* is acetic acid (CH_3COOH). **(½)**
- *B* is ethyl bromide (C_2H_5Br). **(½)**
- *C* is ethyl cyanide (C_2H_5CN). **(½)**
- *D* is H_2/Pt or $LiAlH_4$. **(½)**
- *E* is propyl alcohol (C_3H_7OH). **(½)**
- *F* is propionic acid (C_2H_5COOH). **(½)**

47. The reaction takes place as follows

$CH_3{-}C{\equiv}CH \xrightarrow[H_2SO_4]{HgSO_4} CH_3{-}\overset{O}{\overset{||}{C}}{-}CH_3$
Propyne (*A*) → Acetone (*B*)

$\xrightarrow{Conc.\ HNO_3} CH_3{-}\overset{O}{\overset{||}{C}}{-}OH + H\overset{O}{\overset{||}{C}}{-}OH$
Acetic acid (*C*), Formic acid (*D*)

- $CH_3{-}\overset{O}{\overset{||}{C}}{-}OH \xrightarrow{PCl_5} CH_3{-}\overset{O}{\overset{||}{C}}{-}Cl \xrightarrow{Ethanol} CH_3{-}\overset{O}{\overset{||}{C}}{-}O{-}CH_2CH_3$
  Acetyl chloride (*E*), Ethyl acetate (*F*)

  $CH_3{-}\overset{O}{\overset{||}{C}}{-}OH \xrightarrow[Conc.\ H_2SO_4]{Ethanol} CH_3{-}\overset{O}{\overset{||}{C}}{-}OCH_2CH_3$ (*F*)

- $CH_3{-}\overset{O}{\overset{||}{C}}{-}OH \xrightarrow[(HVZ)]{Cl_2/Red\ P} H_2\underset{Cl}{\underset{|}{C}}\overset{O}{\overset{||}{C}}{-}OH \xrightarrow{Cl_2/Red\ P} Cl_2H{-}C{-}\overset{O}{\overset{||}{C}}{-}OH$
  (*C*), Monochloro acetic acid, Dichloro acetic acid **(3)**

48. (i) The organic compound *A*, C_7H_6O is benzaldehyde,

i.e. C_6H_5CHO or 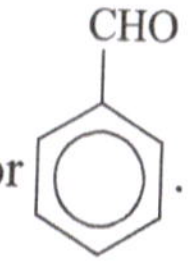.

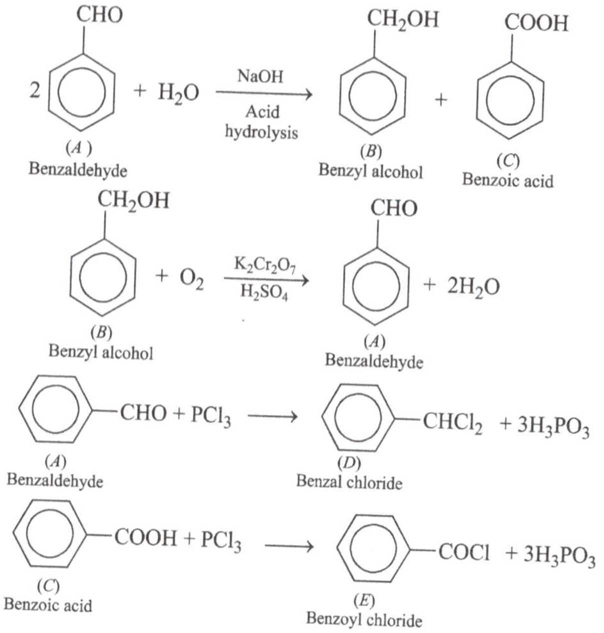

Thus, *A* is benzaldehyde.
B is benzyl alcohol. *C* is benzoic acid.
D is benzal chloride. *E* is benzoyl chloride.

(½×4 = 2)

(ii) When benzaldehyde reacts with sodium hydroxide then the benzyl alcohol and sodium benzoate are formed. This reaction is known as **Cannizzaro reaction**.

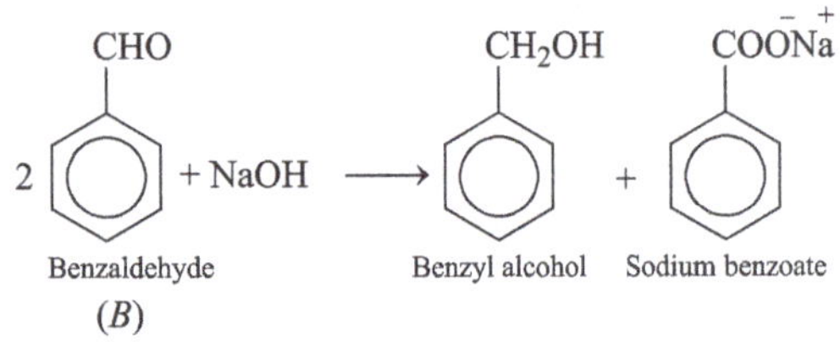

(1)

Note Cannizzaro reaction is given by aldehydes which do not have α-hydrogen atom. It is disproportionation (self oxidation reduction) reaction in which half of the molecules of aldehydes are oxidised and other half reduced.

49.

$$\underset{\text{Acetic acid}}{2CH_3COOH} \xrightarrow{Ca(OH)_2} \underset{\text{Calcium acetate}}{(CH_3COO)_2Ca} \xrightarrow[\text{with }(HCOO)_2Ca]{\text{Distillation}}$$

$$\underset{\text{Acetaldehyde}}{CH_3CHO} \xrightarrow[\text{Reduction}]{LiAlH_4} \underset{\text{Ethyl alcohol}}{CH_3CH_2OH} \xrightarrow{P+I_2}$$

$$\underset{\text{Ethyl iodide}}{CH_3CH_2I} \xrightarrow{KCN} \underset{\text{Ethyl nitrile}}{CH_3CH_2CN} \xrightarrow[\text{Hydrolysis}]{H^+/H_2O} \underset{\text{Propionic acid}}{CH_3CH_2COOH}$$

50. (i) (a) Refer to text on page 179. (1)

(b) Refer to text on page 196. (1)

(c) Refer to text on pages 178 and 179. (1)

(ii) (a) $\underset{\text{Acetaldehyde}}{CH_3CHO} \xrightarrow[{[O]}]{K_2Cr_2O_7/H^+} \underset{\text{Acetic acid}}{CH_3COOH} \xrightarrow{Ca(OH)_2}$

$$(CH_3COO)_2Ca \xrightarrow{\text{Heat}} \underset{\text{Acetone}}{CH_3COCH_3}$$ (1)

(b) Formaldehyde reacts with ammonia to form hexamethylene tetraamine (urotropine).

$$6HCHO + 4NH_3 \longrightarrow (CH_2)_6N_4 + 6H_2O$$ (1)

51. (i) (a) **Methyl magnesium bromide to ethanol**

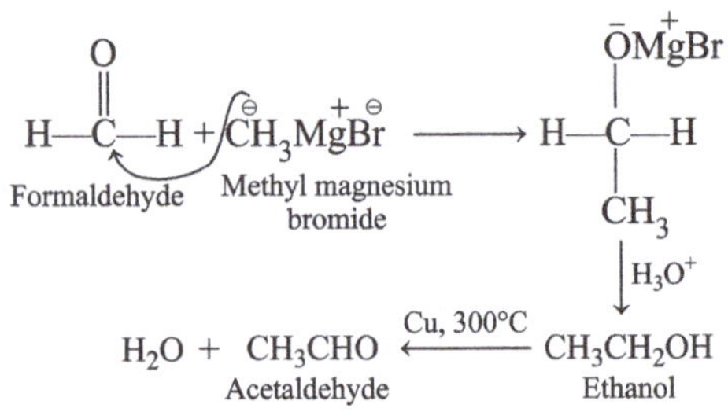

(1)

(b) **Methyl magnesium bromide to acetone**

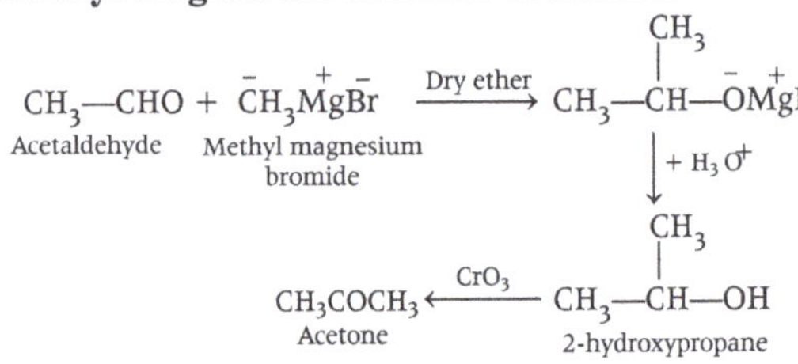

(1)

(c) **Methyl magnesium bromide to acetic acid**

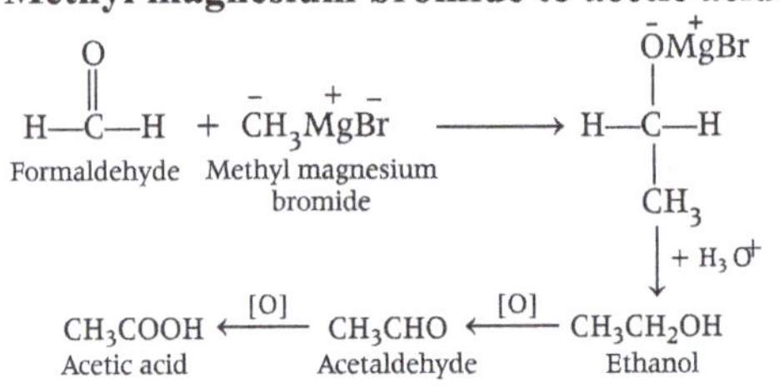

(1)

(ii) (a) Cl-group in chloroacetic acid ($Cl—CH_2COOH$) is a electron withdrawing group. It increases the acidity of acetic acid by dispersing negative charge by inductive effect and stabilizing the acetate anion. Hence, chloroacetic acid is stronger acid than acetic acid. (1)

(b) Formic acid is unique because it contain both aldehyde carboxylic group.

Hence, it can act as reducing agent.It reduces Tollen's reagent. While acetic acid has no aldehyde group hence, it does not reduces Tollen's reagent. (1)

52. (i) (a)

$$CH_3COCH_3 + H_2NOH \xrightarrow[-H_2O]{} (CH_3)_2C{=}NOH$$

(1)

(b)

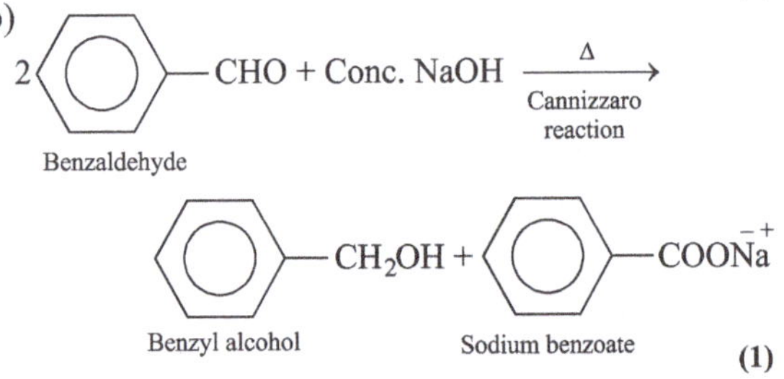

(1)

(c) $CH_3COOH \xrightarrow[\text{HVZ reaction}]{Cl_2/P} \underset{\alpha\text{-chloroacetic acid}}{CH_2(Cl)—COOH}$ (1)

(ii) (a) **Benzaldehyde and benzoic acid** $NaHCO_3$ **test** is used to distinguish between the two molecules. Benzoic acid being an acid reacts with $NaHCO_3$ solution to produce brisk effervescence due to evolution of CO_2 while benzaldehyde does not give this test.

$$C_6H_5COOH + NaHCO_3 \longrightarrow C_6H_5CO\overset{-}{O}\overset{+}{N}a + CO_2\uparrow + H_2O$$

$$C_6H_5CHO \xrightarrow{NaHCO_3 \text{ solution}} \text{No effervescence}$$ **(1)**

(b) **Propanal and propanone** Propanone responds to iodoform test whereas propanal (CH_3CH_2CHO) due to the absence of CH_3CO— group does not.

$$\underset{\text{Propanone}}{CH_3COCH_3} + \underset{\text{Sodium hypoiodite}}{3NaOI} \xrightarrow[\text{Heat}]{NaOH,\ I_2} \underset{\substack{\text{(Yellow ppt.)}\\ \text{Iodoform}}}{CHI_3}\downarrow + \underset{\substack{\text{Sodium}\\ \text{acetate}}}{CH_3CO\overset{-}{O}\overset{+}{N}a} + 2NaOH$$ **(1)**

53. (i) (a) Refer to text on page 178. **(1)**

(b) Refer to text on pages 178 and 179. **(1)**

(c) Refer to text on page 179. **(1)**

(ii) (a) CH_3CHO (aldehyde) is more reactive with HCN than CH_3COCH_3 (ketone) towards nucleophilic addition reactions. It can be explain by the following facts:

Inductive effect Since, an alkyl group has electron donating ($+I$) inductive effect. Hence, greater the number of alkyl groups attached to carbonyl group, greater the electron density on carbonyl carbon. Thus, it lowers the attack of nucleophile and hence, reactivity decreases. Hence,

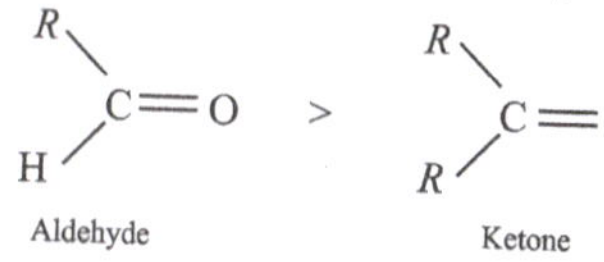

Steric effect As the number of alkyl group attached to carbonyl carbon increases, the attack of nucleophile on carbonyl group becomes more and more difficult due to steric hindrance. Therefore, due to the presence of two bulky alkyl (or R) groups, the attack of nucleophile is hindered and hence, ketones are less reactive than aldehydes. **(½)**

(b) Phenoxide ion has non-equivalent resonance structures in which the negative charge is less effectively delocalised overless electronegative carbon atom and one oxygen atom. While in carboxylate ion, the negative charge is delocalised over two electronegative oxygen atoms. Thus, carboxylate ion is much more resonance stabilised than phenoxide ion. Since, more stable the conjugate base of an acid, stronger is the acid.

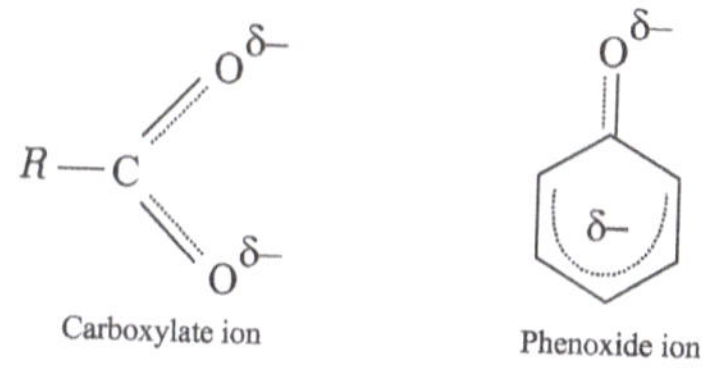

(1)

CHAPTER TEST

01 Mark Questions

1. Fill in the blanks by choosing the appropriate word(s) from those are given in the bracket.
[sp^3, aldehyde, two, three, sp^2, reduction, aldol condensation, formaldehyde, $+I$, benzoic acid, Cannizzaro, $-I$, acetaldehyde, Tollen's]

(i) The carbon atom in carbonyl group is .... hybridised and forms .... sigma bonds.

(ii) Aldehydes which have α - H atom undergo .... reaction while aldehyde which have no α - H atom undergo .... reaction.

(iii) .... gives a yellow precipitate to iodoform test while .... does not response to this test.

(iv) .... is more acidic than acetic acid because of .... effect.

2. Select and write the correct alternatives from the choices given below.

(i) Consider the following reaction,

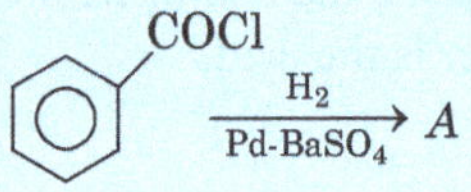

The product A is
(a) C_6H_5CHO (b) C_6H_5OH (c) $C_6H_5COCH_3$ (d) C_6H_5Cl

(ii) Which of the following reactions convert acetone into hydrocarbon having same number of carbon atoms?
(a) Wolff-Kishner reaction (b) Hofmann reaction
(c) Grignard reaction (d) Reduction with $LiAlH_4$

(iii) Benzaldehyde reacts with ammonia to form
(a) benzaldehyde ammonia (b) urotropine
(c) hydrobenzamide (d) ammonium chloride

(iv) Give IUPAC name of the product, when acetamide is heated with anhydrous phosphorus pentoxide.
(a) Ethylamine (b) Propane nitrile
(c) Cyanomethane (d) Ethane nitrile

3. (i) **Assertion** (A) Aromatic aldehydes and formaldehyde undergo Cannizzaro reaction.
Reason (R) Aromatic aldehydes are almost as reactive as formaldehyde.
(a) Both (A) and (R) are correct and (R) is the correct explanation of (A).
(b) Both (A) and (R) are correct but (R) is not the correct explanation of (A).
(c) (A) is correct and (R) is incorrect.
(d) (A) is incorrect and (R) is correct.

(ii) **Assertion** (A) Aldehydes and ketones both react with Tollen's reagent to form silver mirror.
Reason (R) Both aldehydes and ketones contain a carbonyl group.
(a) Both (A) and (R) are correct and (R) is the correct explanation of (A).
(b) Both (A) and (R) are correct but (R) is not the correct explanation of (A).
(c) (A) is correct and (R) is incorrect.
(d) (A) is incorrect and (R) is correct.

02 Marks Questions

4. Arrange the following compounds in the increasing order of their reactivity towards nucleophilic addition reactions.
(i) Ethanol, propanol, propanone, butanone
(ii) Benzaldehyde, *p*-tolualdehyde, *p*-nitrobenzaldehyde, acetophenone.

5. How do you convert the following?
(i) Benzene to *m*-nitroacetophenone
(ii) Toluene of benzoic acid

6. Give reasons.
(i) Electrophilic substitution in benzoic acid takes place at *meta*-position.
(ii) Carboxylic acids are higher boiling liquids than aldehyde, ketones and alcohols of comparable molecular masses.

7. Give the simple chemical tests to distinguish between the following pairs of compounds.
(i) Ethanal and propanal
(ii) Acetophenone and benzophenone

8. (i) Name any two reagents which are used to distinguish between aldehydes and ketones.
(ii) pK_a of chloroacetic acid is lower than pK_a of acetic acid. Why ?

9. Complete the following reaction.

(i) $HCOOH \xrightarrow[H_2SO_4]{Conc.}$

(ii) $CH_3COOH + CH_3OH \xrightarrow[H_2SO_4]{Conc.}$

10. How will you bring about the following conversion?
   (i) Ethanol to 3-hydroxybutanol
   (ii) Benzoic acid to benzyl alcohol

03 Marks Questions

11. Write the main product(s) in each of the following.

(i) 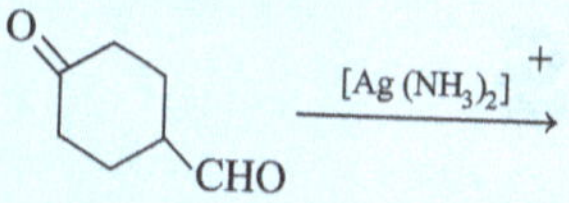

(ii) 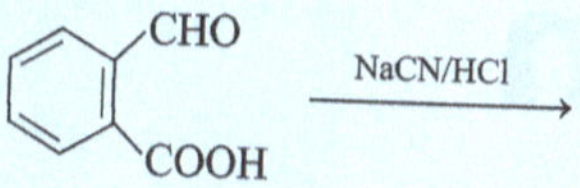

(iii) 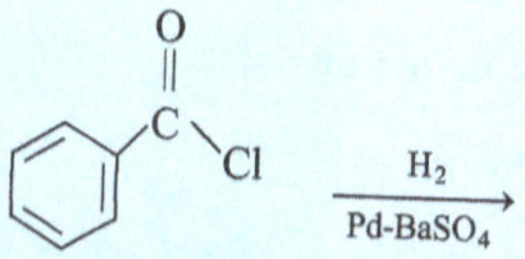

12. Write down the IUPAC and common name of the following.

(i) 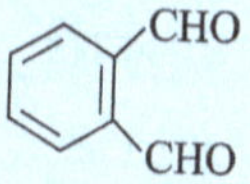

(ii) 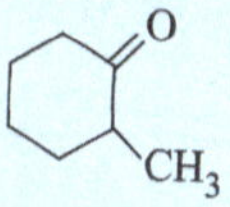

(iii) $CH_2{=}CHCH_3$

13. Write the reaction for following conversions.
   (i) Acetaldehyde to formaldehyde
   (ii) Propanal to butanone
   (iii) Benzonitrile to acetophenone

14. Account for the following.
   (i) Aromatic carboxylic acids do not undergo Friedel-Crafts reaction.
   (ii) Carboxylic acids do not give characteristic reactions of carbonyl group.
   (iii) C—O bond in RCOOH is shorter than in RCHO ?

15. (i) Give simple chemical tests to distinguish between the following pair of compounds. Benzoic acid and phenol.
   (ii) Draw the structural formula of hex-2-en-ynoic acid.
   (iii) Illustrate the decarboxylation reaction giving a suitable example.

05 Marks Questions

16. (i) Write the products of the following reactions.

(a) 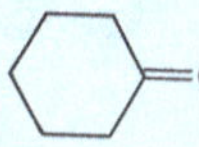 $=O + NH_2—NH—\overset{O}{\overset{\|}{C}}—NH_2 \xrightarrow{H^+}$

(b) $CH_3MgBr + CO_2 \xrightarrow[H_3O^+]{\text{Dry ether}}$

(c) $CH_3CH_2COOH + Br_2 \xrightarrow{\text{Red phosphorus}}$

   (ii) Write a simple chemical test to distinguish between the following pairs of compounds.
   (a) Propanal and propaone
   (b) Benzaldehyde and benzoic acid

17. (i) Write the products of the following reactions :

(a) 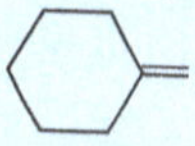 $=O + H_2N—OH \xrightarrow{H^+}$

(b) $2C_6H_5CHO +$ Conc. NaOH $\longrightarrow$

(c) $CH_3COOH \xrightarrow{Cl_2/P}$

   (ii) Give simple chemical tests to distinguish between the following pairs of compounds.
   (a) Benzaldehyde and benzoic acid
   (b) Propanal and propanone

18. (i) Write the products formed when CH_3CHO reacts with the following reagents.
   (a) HCN
   (b) $H_2N—OH$
   (c) CH_3CHO is the presence of dilute NaOH.
   (ii) Write the chemical equations to illustrate the following name reactions.
   (a) Rosenmund reduction
   (b) Cannizzaro reaction
   (iii) Out of $CH_3CH_2—CO—CH_2—CH_3$ and $CH_3CH_2—CH_2—CO—CH_3$, which gives iodoform test?

Answers

1. (i) sp^2, nucleophilic
   (ii) aldol condensation, Cannizzaro
   (iii) acetaldehyde, formaldehyde
   (iv) benzoic acid, $-I$

2. (i) (a), (ii) (a), (iii) (c), (iv) (d)

3. (i) (c), (ii) (d)

09

Organic Compounds Containing Nitrogen

TREND ANALYSIS 4 YEARS

Average No. of Questions Across all Sets

Topic	Types of Questions	2024	2023	2020	2019
TOPIC 01 Amines	1 Mark	2	1	1	1
	2 Marks	1	1	1	1
	3 Marks	1	—	—	—
	5 Marks	—	—	—	—
TOPIC 02 Cyanides, Isocyanides and Diazonium Salts	1 Mark	—	—	1	1
	2 Marks	—	—	—	1
	3 Marks	2	2	—	—
	5 Marks	—	—	—	—

TOPIC 1

Amines

Amines can be considered as derivatives of ammonia obtained by the replacement of hydrogen atoms of $—NH_2$ group by alkyl or aryl groups.

Aliphatic Amines

When one of the hydrogen atoms in ammonia is replaced by an alkyl group, it is called aliphatic amines. Its general formula is C_nH_{2n+3}.

Nomenclature of Aliphatic Amines

In common system, they are named as alkylamines or aminoalkanes. In the IUPAC system, they are named as alkanamines, derived by the replacement of 'e'of alkane by the word amines.

e.g.	CH_3NH_2	$C_2H_5NH_2$	$C_3H_7NH_2$
IUPAC name	Methanamine	Ethanamine	Propanamine
Common name	*n*-methylamine	*n*-ethylamine	*n*-propylamine

Classification of Amines

They are classified as primary (1°), secondary (2°) and tertiary (3°) amines according to the number of alkyl groups attached directly with N-atom.

e.g. $CH_3—NH_2$ (Primary amine); $CH_3—N(CH_3)—H$ (Secondary amine); $CH_3—N(CH_3)—CH_3$ (Tertiary amine)

The compounds having general formula $R_4N^+X^-$ are called quaternary ammonium compounds.

Structure of Amines

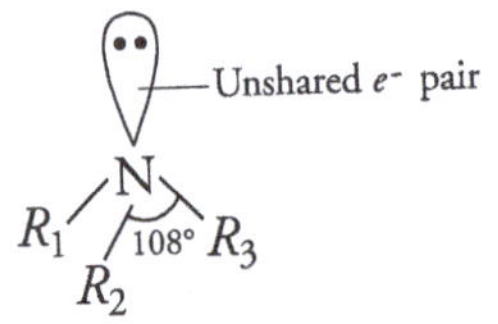

Pyramidal shape of tertiary amine

Preparation of Amines

(i) **Ammonolysis**

$NH_3 + R—X \xrightarrow{373\ K}$ (Mixture of 1°, 2°, 3° amines are obtained)

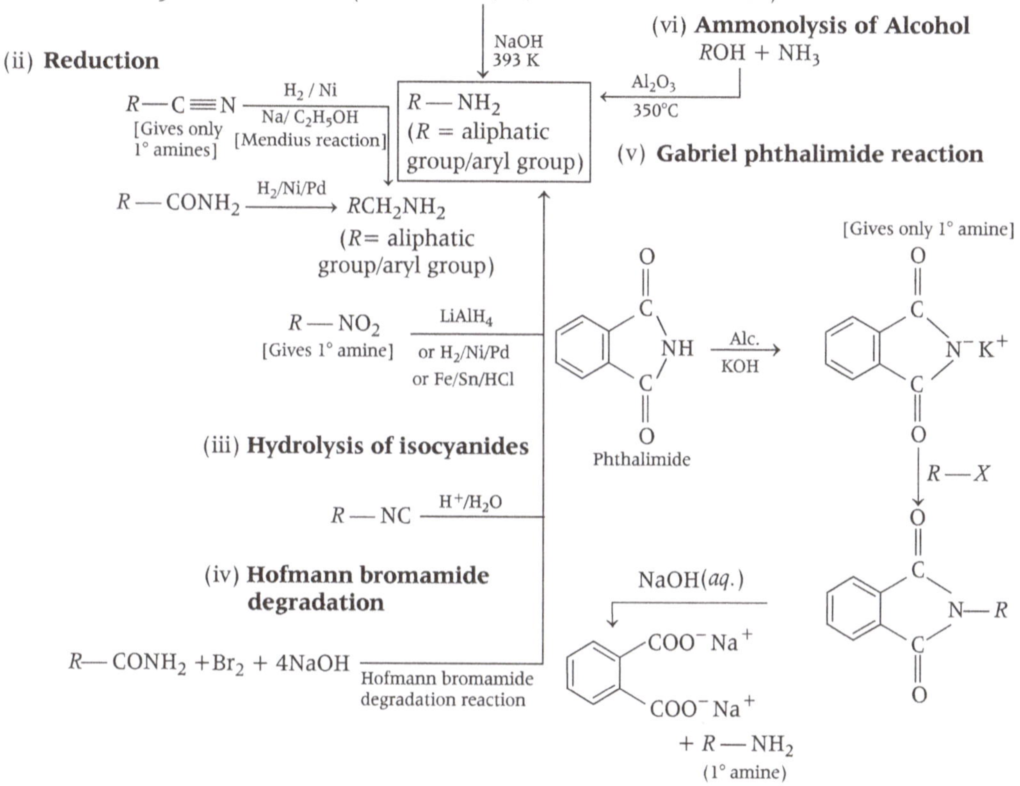

Note
- Gabriel phthalimide synthesis cannot be used for the preparation of 2° and 3° amines. Also, aromatic primary amines cannot be prepared by this method because aryl halides do not undergo nucleophilic substitution with the anion formed by phthalimide.
- Hofmann bromamide reaction gives 1° amine having one carbon atom less than parent primary amide.

Physical Properties of Amines

Physical properties of amines are as follows

Physical State

Pure amines are colourless but develop colour on keeping in air or on storage due to atmospheric oxidation. The lower aliphatic amines are gases and smell like ammonia.

Primary amines with three or more carbon atoms are liquids with fishy odours and higher ones are solid. Aromatic amines are toxic in nature.

Solubility

Lower aliphatic amines can form hydrogen bonds with water molecules and hence are soluble in water.

Solubility of amines decreases with increase in molar mass due to increase in the hydrophobic part which retard the formation of H-bonds and hence, aromatic amines are insoluble in water.

Boiling Point

The order of boiling point of amines is

1° amines > 2° amines > 3° amines.

Alcohols and carboxylic acids have high polarity than amines and hence, amines form weaker H-bonds than alcohols and carboxylic acids.

Thus, amines have low boiling point as compared to them.

Chemical Properties of Amines

The chemical properties of amines are as follows

(i) Basic Character of Amines

All aliphatic amines are more basic than ammonia.

- $NH_3 < R_3N < RNH_2 < R_2NH$ in aqueous solution (due to steric effect).
- $NH_3 < RNH_2 < R_2NH < R_3N$ in gaseous state.
  (1°) (2°) (3°)
- Aliphatic amines are more basic than aromatic amines because in aromatic amines, lone pair of electrons present on nitrogen takes part in resonance, hence not available for donation whereas in aliphatic amines, it is available.
- Electron donating group increases the basicity while electron withdrawing group decreases the basicity.

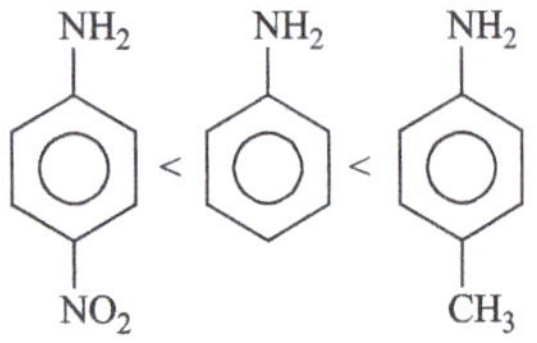

- *o*-substituted amines are usually weaker base than aniline due to *ortho*-effect which is due to steric hindrance and electronic factors.

(ii) Alkylation

H-atoms of amine get replaced one by one by alkyl group of alkyl halide.

$$\underset{1°\text{amine}}{RNH_2} \xrightarrow[-HX]{RX} \underset{2°\text{amine}}{R_2NH} \xrightarrow[-HX]{RX} \underset{3°\text{ amine}}{R_3N} \xrightarrow[-HX]{RX} \underset{\text{Quaternary salt}}{[R_4N]^+ X^-}$$

(iii) Acylation

It is the addition of acyl group [RCO—] to an amine. In this reaction, 1° amines give N-substituted amide, while 2° amine give N, N-disubstituted amides.

$$R\text{—}NH_2 + R'COCl \longrightarrow R\text{—}NH\text{—}COR' + HCl$$

$$\underset{\text{Ethylamine}}{CH_3CH_2NH_2} + \underset{\text{Acetic anhydride}}{(CH_3CO)_2O} \longrightarrow \underset{\text{N-ethyl ethanamide}}{CH_3\text{—}\overset{\overset{\displaystyle O}{\|}}{C}\text{—}NHCH_2CH_3} + CH_3COOH$$

$$R_2NH + R'COCl \longrightarrow R_2N \cdot COR' + HCl$$

In aromatic amines, acylation occurs in the presence of base such as pyridine as catalyst.

(iv) Reaction with Nitrous Acid

Aliphatic amine $\xrightarrow{HNO_2}$
- → H_2 gas
- → Yellow oily layer
- → Water soluble salt

(v) Carbylamine Reaction

$$RNH_2 + CHCl_3 + 3KOH(alc.) \longrightarrow RNC + 3KCl + 3H_2O$$

Note Only 1° amine (aliphatic / aromatic give this reaction).

Distinction between Primary, Secondary and Tertiary Amines

Amines can be differentiated by the following test.

Hinsberg's Test

- Primary amine when reacts with benzene sulphonyl chloride (Hinsberg reagent), it yields N-ethylbenzene sulphonamide.
- Hydrogen attached to nitrogen is strongly acidic due to the presence of strong electron withdrawing sulphonyl group, hence it is soluble in alkali.

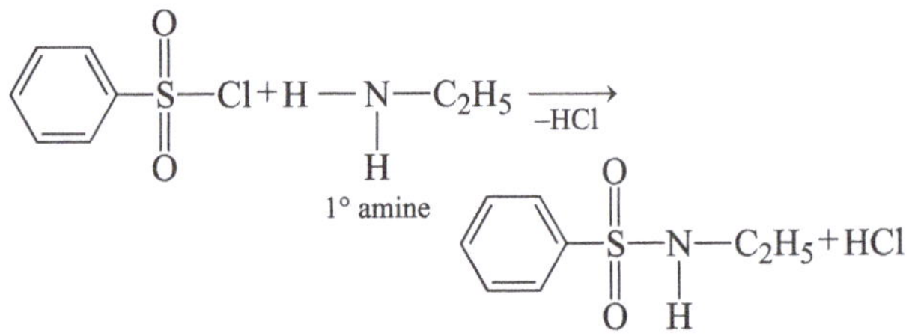

N-ethylbenzene sulphonamide (soluble in alkali)

- Secondary amine when reacts with benzene sulphonyl chloride, it yields N,N-diethylbenzene sulphonamide. It does not have any H-atom attached to N-atom. Thus, it is not acidic and hence insoluble in alkali.

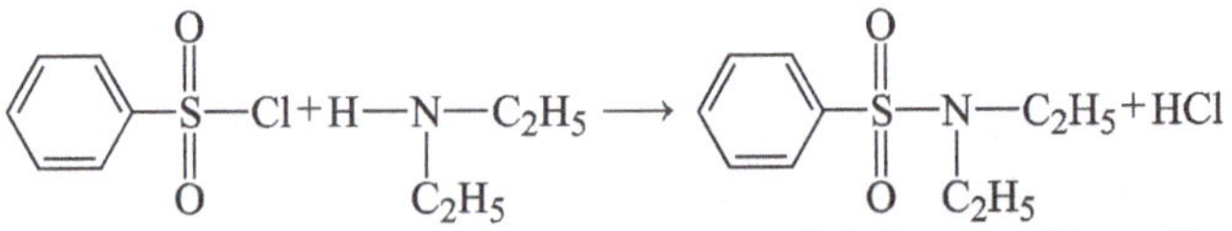

N,N-diethylbenzene sulphonamide (insoluble in alkali)

- Tertiary amines do not react with benzene sulphonyl chloride.

Stepping Up and Down Conversion for Amine Series

(i) Conversion of Methylamine to Ethylamine

$$\underset{\text{Methylamine}}{CH_3NH_2} \xrightarrow{\text{HONO}} \underset{\text{Methanol}}{CH_3OH} \xrightarrow{PI_3} \underset{\text{Methyl iodide}}{CH_3I}$$

$$\xrightarrow{\text{NaCN}} \underset{\text{Methyl cyanide}}{CH_3CN} \xrightarrow[4[H]]{LiAlH_4} \underset{\text{Ethylamine}}{CH_3CH_2NH_2}$$

(ii) Conversion of Ethylamine to Methylamine

$$\underset{\text{Ethylamine}}{CH_3CH_2NH_2} \xrightarrow{\text{HONO}} \underset{\text{Ethanol}}{CH_3CH_2OH} \xrightarrow[\text{Cu/573 K}]{\Delta}$$

$$\underset{\text{Acetaldehyde}}{CH_3CHO} \xrightarrow{KMnO_4} \underset{\text{Acetic acid}}{CH_3COOH} \xrightarrow[\text{or } PCl_5]{SOCl_2}$$

$$\underset{\text{Acetyl chloride}}{CH_3COCl} \xrightarrow{NH_3} \underset{\text{Acetamide}}{CH_3CONH_2} \xrightarrow[\text{NaOH}]{Br_2}$$

$$\underset{\substack{\text{Methylamine} \\ \text{[Hofmann degradation]}}}{CH_3NH_2}$$

Aniline [$C_6H_5NH_2$]

Aniline is simplest aromatic amine with the formula $C_6H_5NH_2$ consist of a phenyl ring attached to amino group.

Preparation of Aniline

Aromatic nitro compounds can be reduced to corresponding aromatic amine, i.e. aniline by metal/acid reducing agent combination.

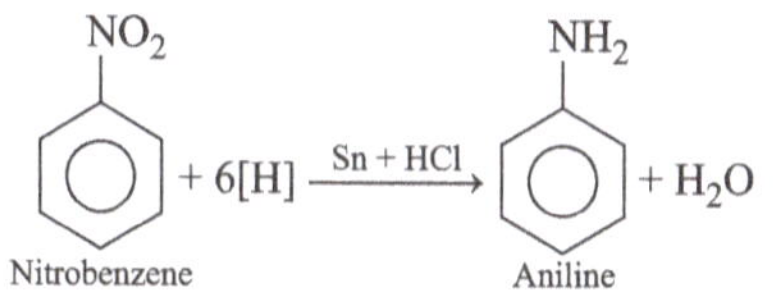

Physical Properties of Aniline

It is steam volatile and toxic in nature.

Note Physical properties of aniline has already been discussed alongside those of aliphatic amines.

Chemical Properties of Aniline

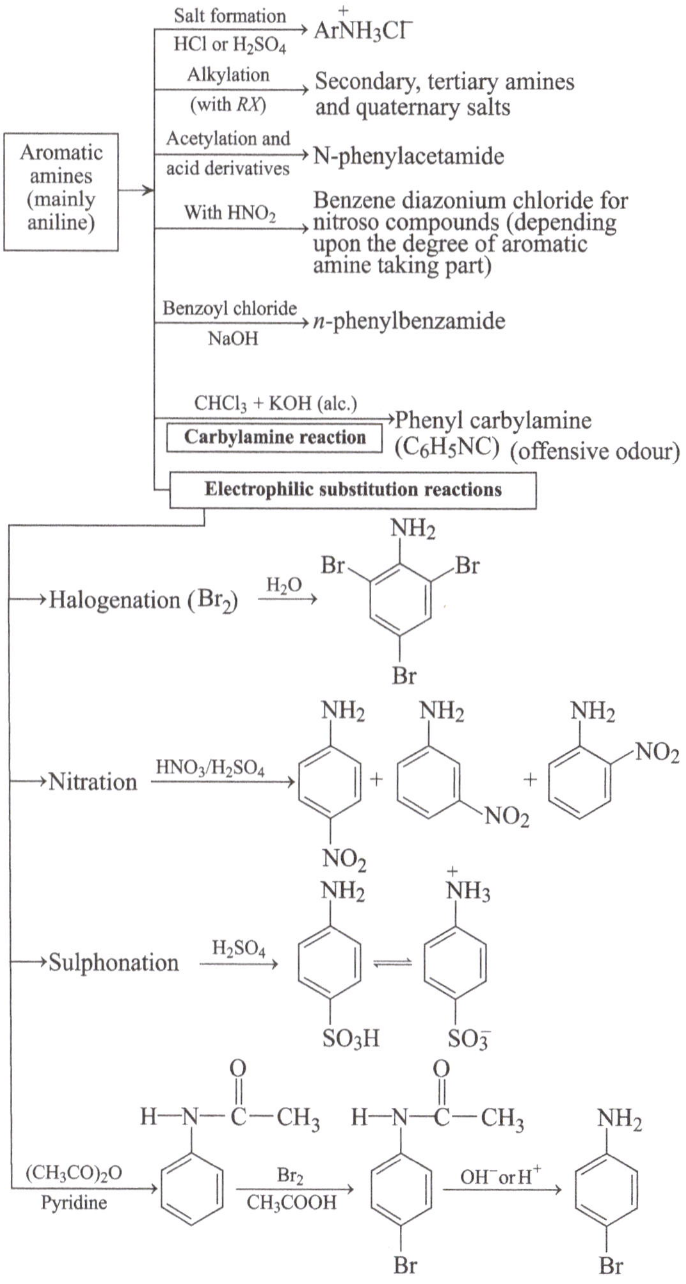

Test for Aniline

(i) Nitrous Acid Test

Aromatic primary amines also react with nitrous acid but at low temperatures.

$$C_6H_5—NH_2 \xrightarrow[273\text{-}278\ K]{NaNO_2 + 2HCl} C_6H_5—\overset{+}{N}_2\overset{-}{Cl} + NaCl + 2H_2O$$

Secondary and tertiary aromatic amines also react with nitrous acid in different manner.

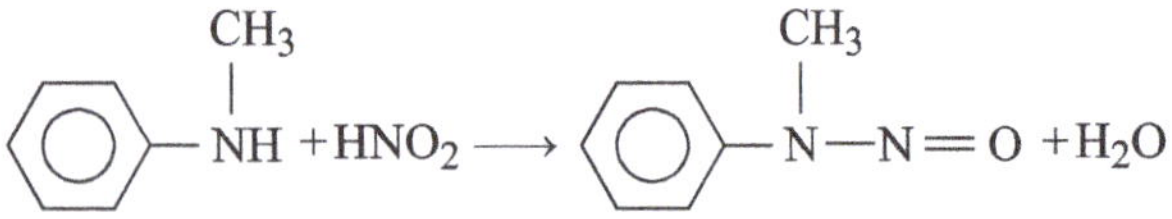

N-methylaniline N-nitroso methylaniline (yellow oil)

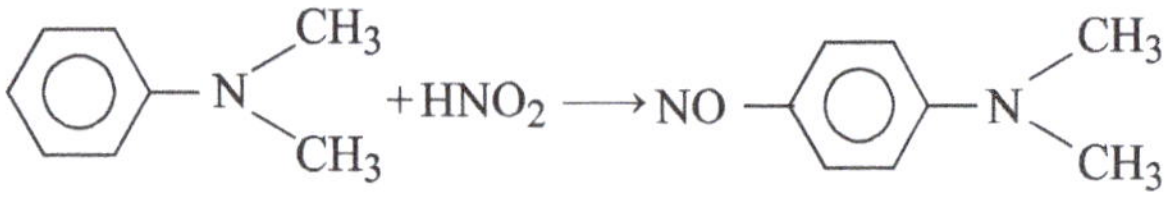

N, N-dimethylaniline *p*-nitroso-N, N-dimethylamine

(ii) Azo Dye Test

This test is used to distinguish aromatic primary (1°) amines from aliphatic 1° amines. Aniline on treatment with HNO_2 ($NaNO_2$ + dil. HCl) followed by the treatment with alkaline solution of β -naphthol forms an orange or red dye.

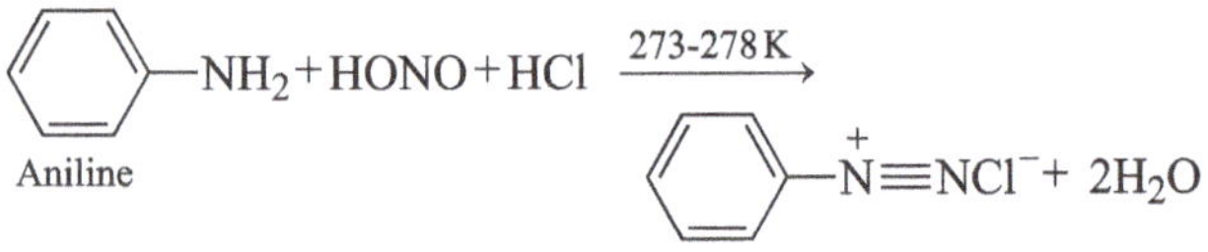

Benzene diazonium chloride

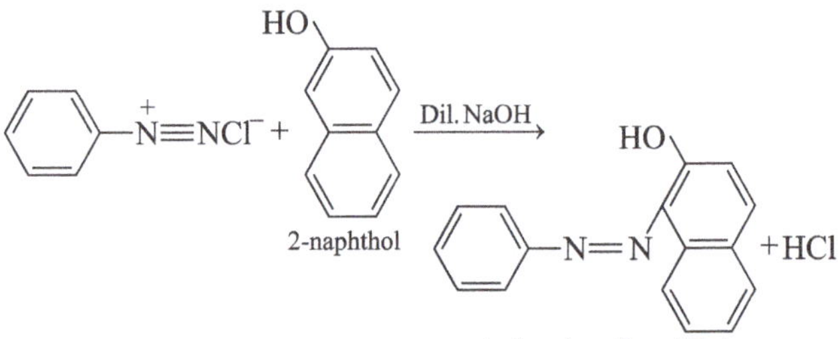

1-phenylazo-2-naphthol (orange-red dye)

Aliphatic amine, i.e. ethylamine does not form dye. It gives brisk effervescence due to evolution of N_2.

Uses of Aniline

- It is used in the preparation of benzene diazonium chloride.
- It is used in the preparation of Schiff's bases, sulpha drugs etc.
- It is used as solvent in rubber industry.

PYQs Previous Years' Questions

1 Mark Questions

1. The reaction of ethanamide with alcoholic sodium hydroxide and bromine gives **ISC 2024**
   (a) ethylamine (b) methylamine
   (c) propylamine (d) aniline

2. **Assertion** Ammonolysis of alkyl halides involves the reaction between alkyl halides and alcoholic ammonia.
   Reason Ammonolysis of alkyl halides produces secondary amines only. **ISC 2024**
   (a) Both Assertion and Reason are true and Reason is the correct explanation for Assertion.
   (b) Both Assertion and Reason are true but Reason is not the correct explanation for Assertion.
   (c) Assertion is true but Reason is false.
   (d) Assertion is false but Reason is true.

3. **Assertion** (A) Aniline is soluble in HCl, while it is only slightly soluble in water. **ISC Specimen 2024**
   Reason (R) Aniline cannot make hydrogen bonds with water but gets protonated easily by acids.
   (a) Both Assertion and Reason are true and Reason is the correct explanation of Assertion.
   (b) Both Assertion and Reason are true but Reason is not the correct explanation for Assertion.
   (c) Assertion is true but Reason is false.
   (d) Assertion is false but Reason is true.

4. The reaction of a primary amine with chloroform and ethanolic KOH is called **ISC 2023**
   (a) carbylamine reaction
   (b) Kolbe's reaction
   (c) Reimer-Tiemann reaction
   (d) Wurtz-Fittig reaction

5. Ethylamine ($C_2H_5NH_2$) reacts with nitrous acid (HNO_2) to form ISC 2021-22 (Sem-II)
(a) methyl alcohol
(b) ethyl alcohol
(c) ethane
(d) ethyl nitrite

6. **Assertion** (A) Nitration of chlorobenzene leads to the formation of *m*-nitrochlorobenzene.
Reason (R) Nitro ($—NO_2$) group is *m*-directing group. ISC 2021-22 (Sem-II)
(a) Both (A) and (R) are correct and (R) is the correct explanation of (A).
(b) Both (A) and (R) are correct but (R) is not the correct explanation of (A).
(c) (A) is correct and (R) is incorrect.
(d) (A) is incorrect and (R) is correct.

7. Convert chlorobenzene to aniline. ISC 2020

8. Write a chemical equation of chlorobenzene treated with ammonia in the presence of Cu_2O at 475 K and 60 atm. ISC 2019

9. Arrange the following in the increasing order of their basic strength.
$C_2H_5NH_2, C_6H_5NH_2, (C_2H_5)_2NH$ ISC 2018

KEY IDEA
Presence of electron donating *R* group increases the basicity of amines. However, alkylamine are more basic than aryl amines.

10. How will you distinguish between primary, secondary and tertiary amines by Hinsberg test?

11. Convert benzoic acid to aniline. ISC 2016

12. Give the balanced equation for carbylamine reaction. ISC 2016

13. Give the balanced equation for Hofmann's degradation reaction. ISC 2015

14. Give a chemical test to distinguish between ethylamine and diethylamine. ISC 2014

15. Write the equation for the preparation of acetanilide from aniline. ISC 2014

16. Write the balanced chemical equation for the following reaction and name the reaction.
Acetamide is heated with bromine and sodium hydroxide solution. ISC 2013

17. Complete the following reaction and name the reaction. ISC 2012
$$C_3H_7NH_2 + CHCl_3 + 3KOH(alc.) \xrightarrow{\Delta} \ldots\ldots + 3KCl + 3H_2O$$

18. When acetamide is treated with bromine and caustic soda, it gives ...... as the main product and the reaction is called .... ISC 2011

19. Give the balanced equation for the following.
Acetamide is heated with sodium hydroxide. ISC 2011

20. The product formed when aniline is warmed with chloroform and caustic potash is ISC 2010
(a) phenyl chloride
(b) methyl isocyanide
(c) phenyl isocyanide
(d) nitrophenol

21. Give the balanced equation for the following reaction.
Aniline is treated with benzoyl chloride. ISC 2009

22. Give one example of the following name reaction.
Hofmann's degradation ISC 2008

23. Explain the following with at least one example:
Carbylamine reaction ISC 2007

24. How would you convert the following?
Methylamine to ethylamine ISC 2007

25. Dehydration of an amide with phosphorus pentoxide yields ISC 2006
(a) ammonia
(b) alkyl cyanide
(c) alkyl isocyanide
(c) alkyl amine

26. Write the balanced chemical equation for the following and name the reaction.
Aniline is warmed with chloroform and alcoholic potassium hydroxide. ISC 2006, 2002

27. How will you convert the acetic anhydride to methylamine? ISC 2004

28. Methylamine is more ...... than ammonia because of ...... effect. ISC 2002

29. Name the following reaction and write balanced equation.
Acetamide with bromine in the presence of potassium hydroxide. ISC 2002

30. Basicity of aniline is ...... than that of ammonia because of .... ISC 2000

2 Marks Questions

31. State one reason for each of the following. ISC 2023
(i) Alkylamine is soluble in water, whereas arylamine is insoluble in water.
(ii) Methylamine is a stronger base than methyl alcohol.

32. Give balanced chemical equation for each of the following.
(i) Aniline and bromine water
(ii) Ethylamine and ethyl bromide
ISC 2021-22 (Sem-II), 2019

33. State reasons for the following.
(i) Ethylamine is soluble in water, whereas aniline is insoluble in water.
(ii) Aliphatic amines are stronger bases than aromatic amines. *ISC Specimen 2023, 2020*

> **KEY IDEA**
> Solubility of compound in water depends on H-bonding. Bulkiness of the group attached to such bond decreases the extent of H-bonding.

34. Give balanced equation for each of the following.
ISC Specimen 2021-22 (Sem-II), 2016
(i) Ethylamine and nitrous acid
(ii) Aniline and acetyl chloride

35. Complete and balance the following equations.
(i) $C_6H_5NH_2 + CH_3COCl \longrightarrow \ldots + \ldots$
(ii) $C_2H_5NH_2 + HNO_2 \longrightarrow \ldots + \ldots + \ldots$ *ISC 2020*

36. An aromatic organic compound [*A*] on heating with NH_3 and Cu_2O at high pressure gives [*B*]. The compound [*B*] on treatment with ice cold solution of $NaNO_2$ and HCl gives [*C*] which on heating with Cu/HCl gives compound [*A*] again. Identify the compounds [*A*], [*B*] and [*C*]. Write the name of the reaction for the conversion of [*B*] to [*C*]. *ISC 2018*

37. Arrange the following compounds in the ascending order of their basic strength and give reasons for your answer.
Methylamine, Aniline, Ethylamine, Diethyl ether
ISC 2015

38. Give the balanced equations for following reactions.
(i) How will you convert ethylamine to methylamine?
(ii) Aniline is treated with nitrous acid and HCl at low temperature. *ISC 2016*

39. Give the chemical test to distinguish between the following pair of compounds.
Aniline and ethylamine *ISC 2014*

40. How can the following conversion be brought about?
Nitrobenzene to 2, 4, 6-tribromoaniline *ISC 2014*

41. Acetamide is amphoteric in nature. Give two equations to support this statement. *ISC 2013*

42. Identify the reagents, *X*, *Y* and *Z*.

$$C_2H_5Cl \xrightarrow{[X]} C_2H_5CN \xrightarrow{[Y]} C_2H_5CH_2NH_2 \xrightarrow{Z} C_2H_5CH_2NHCOCH_3$$ *ISC 2012*

43. Give one good chemical test to distinguish between the following pair of organic compounds.
Methylamine and dimethylamine *ISC 2011*

44. How will you distinguish between the following pair of compounds? Give one chemical test.
Ethylamine and acetamide *ISC 2009*

45. Give reason.
Direct nitration of aniline is not possible. *ISC 2007*

46. How will you carry out the following conversion?
Acetamide to ethylamine *ISC 2003*

47. Give two tests to distinguish between aniline and dimethyl aniline. *ISC 2003*

48. How will you carry out the following conversion? Write the balanced equation and name the reaction.
Acetamide to methylamine *ISC 2001, 2000*

3 Marks Questions

49. (i) Illustrate the following reactions by giving one suitable example in each case. *ISC 2024*
(a) Coupling reaction
(b) Acetylation of ethylamine
(ii) Aniline does not give Friedel - Crafts reaction. Give a reason.

50. Arrange the following compounds: *ISC Specimen 2024*
$C_6H_5NH_2$, $(C_2H_5)_2NH$, $(C_2H_5)_3N$, $C_2H_5NH_2$
(i) in the increasing order of their basic strength in water.
(ii) in a decreasing order of their basic strength in gas phase.

51. Identify the compounds *A*, *B* and *C* in the following reactions. *ISC Specimen 2023*

(i) $C_6H_5NO_2 \xrightarrow{Sn + HCl} [A] \xrightarrow[273\,K-278K]{NaNO_2 + HCl} [B] \xrightarrow{H_2O} [C]$

(ii) $CH_3CN \xrightarrow{H_2O / H^+} [A] \xrightarrow{NH_3/Heat} [B] \xrightarrow{Br_2 + KOH} [C]$

52. Arrange the following as directed.
(i) Increasing order of basic strength.
Aniline, *p*-nitroaniline and *p*-toluidine.

(ii) Decreasing order of basic strength in gas phase.
$C_2H_5NH_2$, $(C_2H_5)_2NH$, $(C_2H_5)_3N$ and NH_3.

(iii) Increasing order of solubility in water.
$C_6H_5NH_2$, $(C_2H_5)_2NH$, $C_2H_5NH_2$

53. An organic compound [*A*] with molecular formula C_2H_7N on reaction with nitrous acid gives a compound [*B*]. [*B*] on controlled oxidation gives compound [*C*]. [*C*] reduces Tollen's reagent to give silver mirror and [*D*]. [*B*] reacts with [*D*] in the presence of concentrated sulphuric acid to give sweet smelling compound [*E*]. Identify [*A*], [*B*], [*C*], [*D*] and [*E*]. Give the reaction of [*C*] with ammonia. **ISC 2015**

54. How can the following conversion be brought about?
Ethylamine to methylamine **ISC 2010, 2000**

55. How can the following conversion be brought about?
Benzene to acetanilide **ISC 2010**

56. Write the balanced equations of the following reactions.
(i) Aniline and bromine water
(ii) Ethylamine and nitrous acid
(iii) Acetic anhydride and ammonia **ISC 2008**

57. How can primary, secondary and tertiary aliphatic amines be distinguished by reaction with HNO_2 ($NaNO_2$ + Dil. H_2SO_4)? **ISC 2005**

58. Identify *A*, *B* and *C*.

$$CH_3CONH_2 \xrightarrow[\Delta]{P_2O_5} [A] \xrightarrow{H_2/Pt} [B] \xrightarrow[HCl]{NaNO_2} [C]$$ **ISC 2002**

59. Give the structures of various amines with molecular formula C_3H_9N. State whether they are primary, secondary or tertiary amines? **ISC 2002**

Explanations

1. (b) $\underset{\text{(Ethanamide)}}{CH_3CONH_2} \xrightarrow[Br_2]{NaOH/Ethanol} \underset{\text{(Methyl amine)}}{CH_3NH_2}$

2. (c) Assertion is true but Reason is false.
The correct Reason is : Ammonolysis of alkyl halides produces primary amines only.

3. (a) Aniline does not undergo hydrogen bonding because of the presence of the benzene which is highly hydrophobic therefore aniline is insoluble in water. In the HCl the amine group becomes protonated ($—NH_3^+$) and the ionic hence soluble in HCl.
Hence, both Assertion and Reason are true and Reason is the correct explanation of Assertion.

4. (a) **Carbylamine reaction** Amine reacts with chloroform in the presence of base to give isocyanide which have foul smell. This reaction is only given by the primary amine.

$$RNH_2 + CHCl_3 + 3KOH \longrightarrow RN{\equiv}C + 3KCl + 3H_2O$$

5. (b) $\underset{\text{Ethylamine}}{H_3C—CH_2—NH_2} \xrightarrow{NaNO_2+HCl}$

$$\underset{\text{Ethyl diazonium salt}}{\left[H_3C—CH_2—\overset{\oplus}{N}{\equiv}N\right]\overset{\ominus}{Cl}} \xrightarrow[-N_2\uparrow]{H_2O} \underset{\text{Ethyl alcohol}}{H_3C—CH_2—OH} + HCl$$

Nitrous acid is used to distinguish between primary, secondary and tertiary amines

- with 1° amine, it liberates N_2 gas.
- with 2° amine, it forms a yellow green oily layer.
- with 3° amine, it forms water soluble salt.

6. (d) (A) is incorrect but (R) is correct as the chlorination of nitrobenzene leads to the formation of *m*-nitrochlorobenzene because $—NO_2$ group deactivates the ring as it is *meta*-directing.

7.

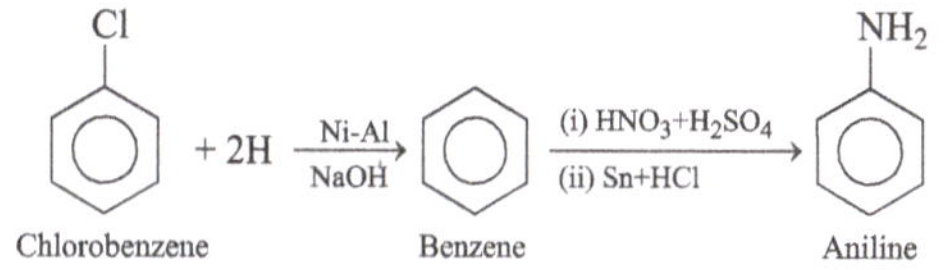

8. Chlorobenzene when treated with ammonia in the presence of Cu_2O at 475 K and 60 atm pressure form aniline.

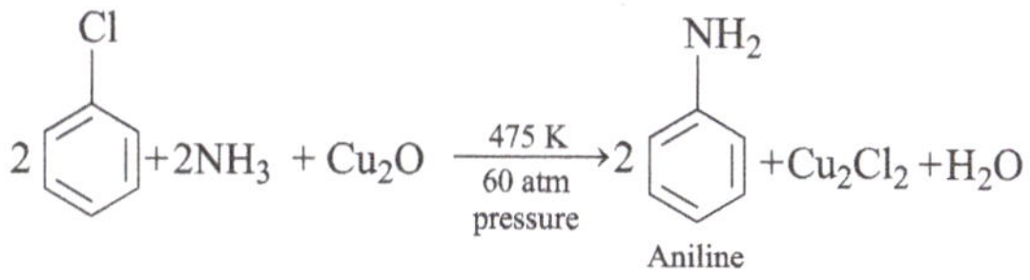

9. Basic character of amines depends upon the availability of lone pair of electrons on nitrogen for donation.
Presence of electron releasing group increases the electron density over nitrogen, thus lone pair of nitrogen are available for donation. Hence, basic character increases. Due to resonance in aniline, lone pair of electron gets delocalised inside the benzene ring, thus it is less available for protonation.

Thus, the correct increasing order of basic strength is

$$C_6H_5NH_2 < C_2H_5NH_2 < (C_2H_5)_2NH$$

10. Refer to text on page 212.

11.

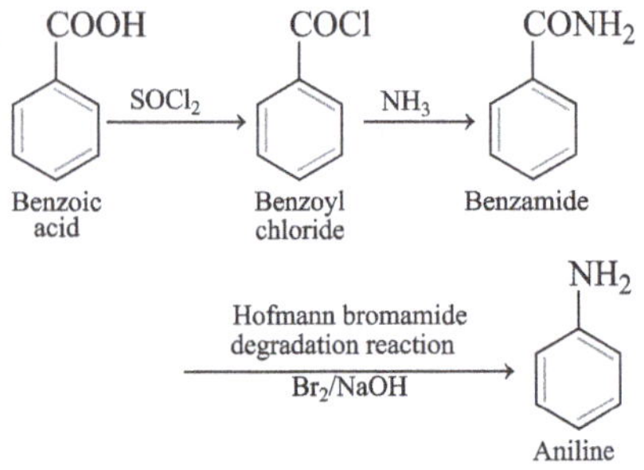

12. Carbylamine reaction

$$RNH_2 + CHCl_3 + 3KOH \longrightarrow RNC + 3KCl + 3H_2O$$

13. Hofmann's degradation reaction

$$CH_3—\overset{\overset{\large O}{||}}{C}— NH_2 + Br_2 + 4NaOH \xrightarrow{\Delta} 2NaBr + \underset{\text{Methylamine}}{CH_3—NH_2} + Na_2CO_3 + 2H_2O$$

14. Hinsberg's test can distinguish between (1°) ethylamine and (2°) diethylamine.

15.

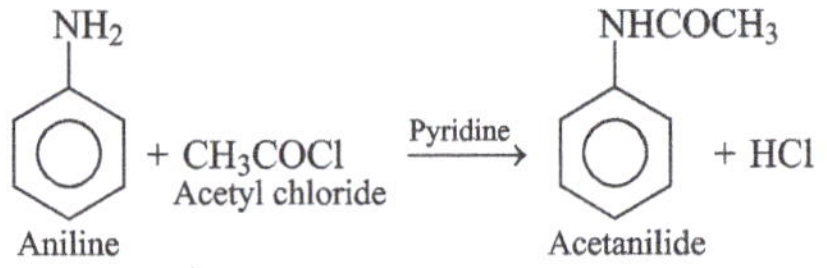

This reaction is known as acetylation.

16. $\underset{\text{Acetamide}}{CH_3CONH_2} + Br_2 + 4NaOH \longrightarrow \underset{\text{Methylamine}}{CH_3NH_2} + 2NaBr + Na_2CO_3 + 2H_2O$

This reaction is known as Hofmann- bromamide reaction.

17. $C_3H_7NH_2 + CHCl_3 + 3KOH(alc.) \xrightarrow{\Delta} C_3H_7NC + 3KCl + 3H_2O$

This reaction is called **carbylamine reaction.**

18. When acetamide is treated with bromine and caustic soda, it gives methylamine as the main product and the reaction is called Hofmann's degradation.

19. $\underset{\text{Acetamide}}{CH_3CONH_2} + NaOH \xrightarrow{\text{Boil}} \underset{\text{Sodium acetate}}{CH_3CO\overset{-}{O}\overset{+}{N}a} + NH_3$

This reaction is called hydrolysis of amide in alkaline conditions.

20. (c) When aniline is warmed with chloroform and caustic potash, phenyl isocyanide is formed.

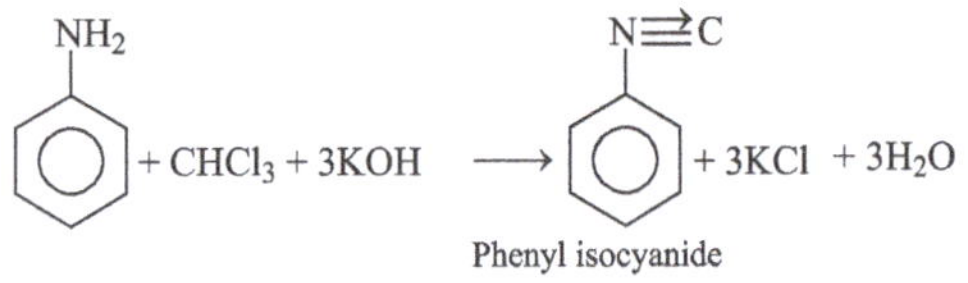

Hence, option (c) is correct.

21.

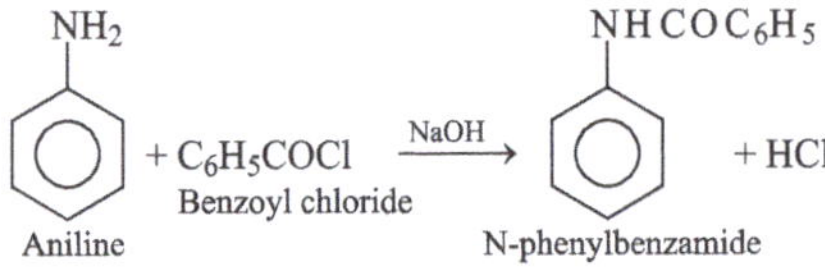

22. Refer to solution 13.

23. Refer to solution 12.

24. Methylamine to ethylamine

$$\underset{\text{Methylamine}}{CH_3NH_2} \xrightarrow{HNO_2} CH_3OH \xrightarrow{PCl_5} CH_3Cl \xrightarrow{NaCN} CH_3CN \xrightarrow{LiAlH_4} \underset{\text{Ethylamine}}{CH_3CH_2NH_2}$$

25. (b) Dehydration of an amide with phosphorus pentaoxide yields alkyl cyanide.

$$R—\overset{\overset{\large O}{||}}{C}—NH_2 \xrightarrow[\Delta]{P_2O_5 \text{ or } SOCl_2} R— C \equiv N + H_2O$$

Hence, option (b) is correct.

26. $\underset{\text{Aniline}}{C_6H_5NH_2} + CHCl_3 + \underset{\text{(Alc.)}}{3KOH} \longrightarrow \underset{\text{Phenyl isocyanide}}{C_6H_5NC} + 3KCl + 3H_2O$

The reaction is **carbylamine reaction.**

27. Acetic anhydride to methylamine

$$\underset{\text{Acetic anhydride}}{(CH_3CO)_2O} \xrightarrow[-CH_3COOH]{NH_3} \underset{\text{Ethanamide}}{CH_3—\overset{\overset{\large O}{||}}{C}—NH_2} \xrightarrow[\text{Hofmann bromamide reaction}]{Br_2 + KOH} \underset{\text{Methylamine}}{CH_3NH_2}$$

28. Methylamine is more basic than NH_3 (ammonia) because of inductive (+*I*) effect.

29. This reaction is Hofmann's degradation.

$$\underset{\text{Acetamide}}{CH_3CONH_2} + Br_2 + 4KOH \longrightarrow \underset{1° \text{ amine}}{CH_3NH_2} + 2KBr + K_2CO_3 + 2H_2O$$

30. Basicity of aniline is **less** than that of ammonia because of **inductive** ($-I$) effect.

> **Concept Enhancer** Inductive effect is the phenomenon in which a partial displacement of σ-electrons towards a more electronegative atom of σ-bond.

31. (i) Alkylamine forms intermolecular hydrogen bonding with water molecules when mixed with water.

Hence, it is soluble in water.

On the other hand, arylamine has large hydrophobic C_6H_5 group which do not allow to form H-bonds to greater extent.

Therefore, it is insoluble in water. **(1)**

(ii) In methylamine ($MeNH_2$), nitrogen is less electronegative than oxygen in methyl alcohol. So, methylamines can easily donate a lone pair of electrons to a proton of an acid and hence are stronger base than methyl alcohol. **(1)**

32. (i)

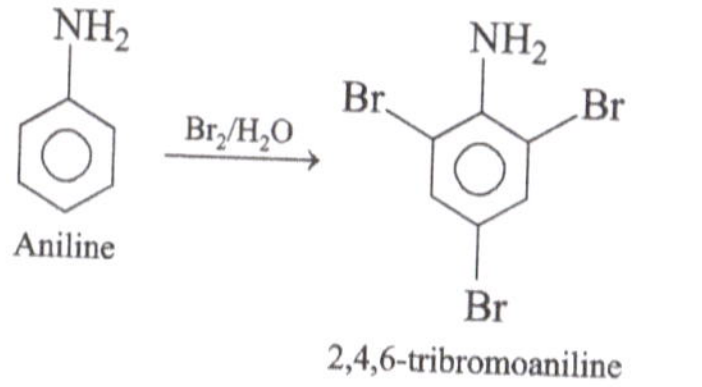

(1)

(ii) $\underset{\text{Ethylamine}}{CH_3CH_2-NH_2} + Br-CH_2CH_3 \xrightarrow{-HBr} \underset{\text{N, N-diethylamine}}{H_3C-CH_2-NH-CH_2CH_3}$ **(1)**

33. (i) Refer to text on page 211 (Solubility).

(ii) Refer to text on page 212 (Chemical properties of amines). **(1+1)**

34. (i) Reaction between ethylamine and nitrous acid

$$\underset{\text{Ethylamine}}{CH_3CH_2NH_2} + \underset{\text{Nitrous acid}}{HNO_2} \longrightarrow \underset{\text{Ethanol}}{CH_3CH_2OH} + H_2O + N_2\uparrow$$

(ii) Reaction between aniline and acetyl chloride

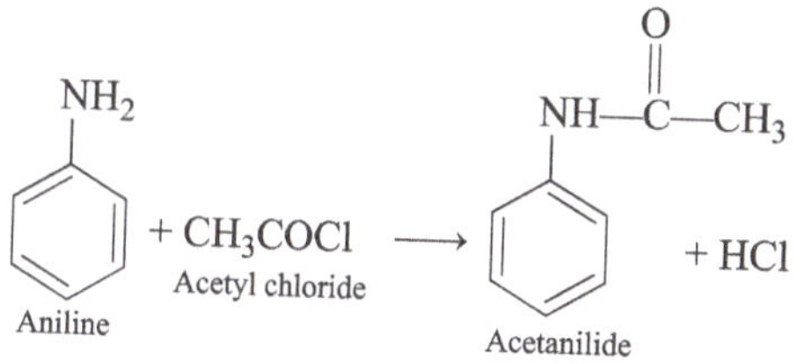

(1+1)

35. (i)

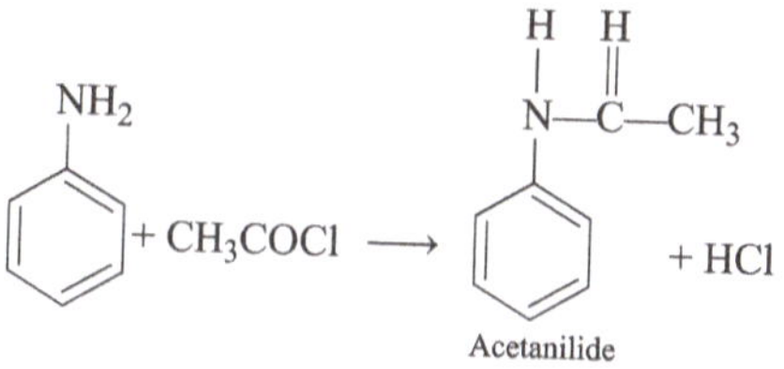

(ii) $C_2H_5NH_2 + HNO_2 \longrightarrow C_2H_5OH + N_2\uparrow + HCl$

(1+1)

36. According to given information

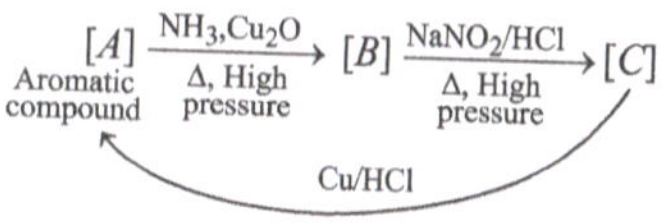

The compound [*B*] on treatment with ice cold solution of $NaNO_2$ and HCl gives [*C*], which is most probably benzene diazonium chloride because compound [*A*] is aromatic.

∴ Compound [*C*] is 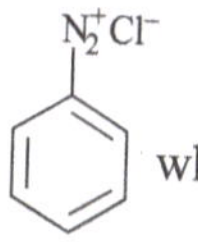 which on reaction with Cu / HCl forms compound [*A*], i.e. chlorobenzene (Sandmeyer reaction).

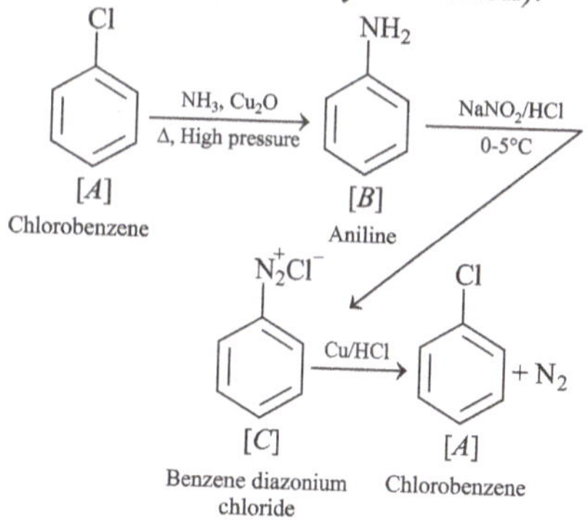

> **Concept Enhancer** Sandmeyer reaction is a chemical reaction used to synthesise aryl halides from aryl diazonium salt.

37. Basic strength order :

diethyl ether < aniline < methylamine < ethylamine.

In aliphatic amines, due to the presence of electron donating alkyl group, electron density on nitrogen increases. Hence, lone pair is easily available for protonation.

In aniline, the lone pair of nitrogen is in conjugation with benzene and less available for protonation hence, aniline is less basic than aliphatic amine and ethers are inert in nature due to stable C— O— C bond.

38. (i) $$\underset{\text{Ethylamine}}{CH_3-CH_2-NH_2} + HNO_2 \xrightarrow{\text{Cold}} CH_3-CH_2-OH + N_2\uparrow + H_2O$$

$$CH_3-CH_2-OH + [O] \xrightarrow[\text{Dil. } H_2SO_4, \Delta]{K_2Cr_2O_7} CH_3COOH + H_2O$$

$$CH_3COOH \xrightarrow{SOCl_2} CH_3COCl \xrightarrow{NH_3} CH_3CONH_2 \xrightarrow{Br_2+NaOH} \underset{\text{Methylamine}}{CH_3NH_2} \quad \textbf{(1)}$$

(ii) When aniline is treated with nitrous acid and HCl at 0-5°C temperature, then benzene diazonium salt is formed.

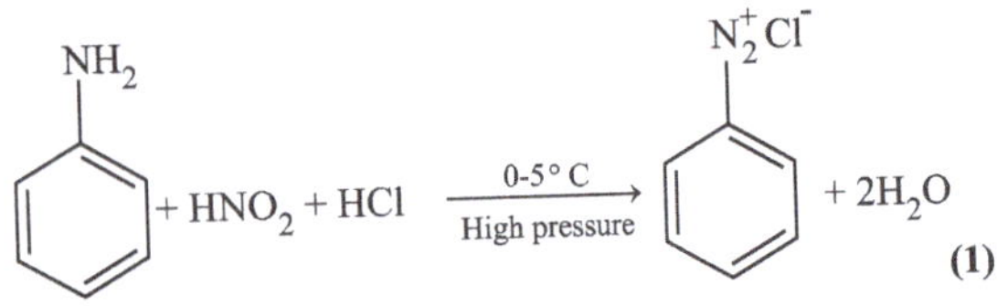

(1)

39. Aniline and ethylamine are distinguished by azo-dye test which are as follows

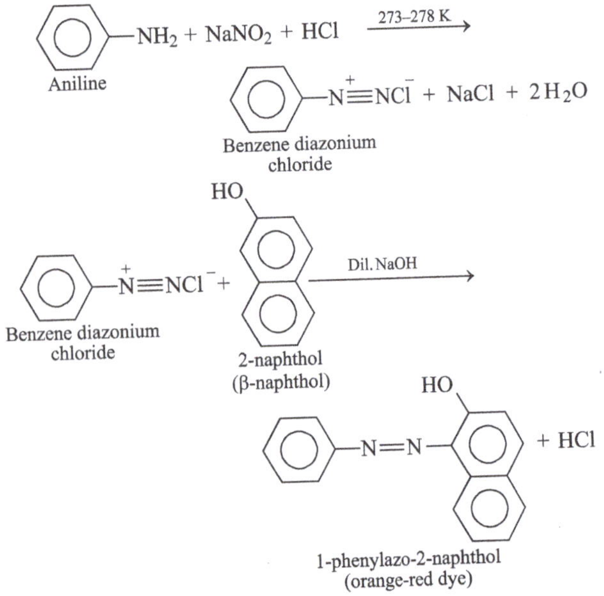

Ethylamine does not form any dye and therefore, does not show any colour when treated with β-naphthol. **(1)**

40. Nitrobenzene to 2, 4, 6-tribromoaniline

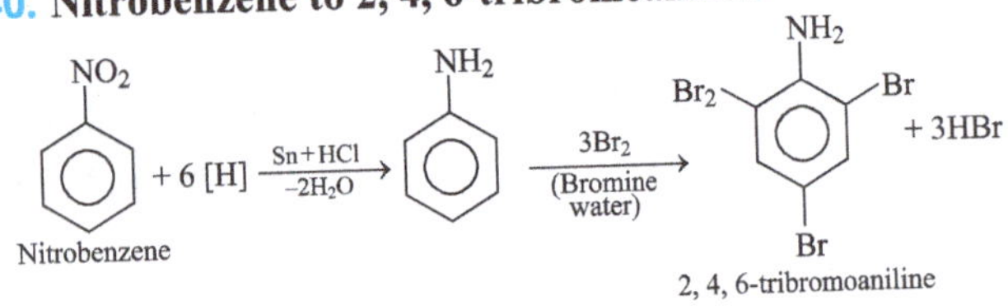

41. Acetamide is formed from weak acid (CH_3COOH) and a weak base (NH_3).

Basic nature

$$CH_3CONH_2 + HCl \longrightarrow CH_3CON\overset{+}{H}_3Cl^-$$

Acidic nature

$$2CH_3CONH_2 + HgO \longrightarrow (CH_3CONH)_2Hg + H_2O$$

42. $$C_2H_5Cl \xrightarrow[[X]]{KCN} C_2H_5CN \xrightarrow[[Y]]{Na/C_2H_5OH} C_2H_5CH_2NH_2 \xrightarrow[[Z]]{(CH_3CO)_2O} C_2H_5CH_2NHCOCH_3$$

$X = KCN$, $Y = Na/C_2H_5OH$, $Z = (CH_3CO)_2O$

43. Methylamine(1°) and dimethyl amine(2°) can be distinguished by carbylamine test.

Methylamine when heated with chloroform and alcoholic potassium hydroxide, it forms methyl isocyanide commonly known as carbylamine which can be recognised once by its offensive odour but this test is not responded by dimethylamine because it is secondary amine.

$$\underset{\text{Methylamine}}{CH_3NH_2} + CHCl_3 + 3KOH(alc.) \xrightarrow{\Delta} CH_3NC + 3KCl + 3H_2O$$

44. Ethylamine (1° amine) when heated with chloroform and alcoholic KOH it forms ethyl carbylamine which has peculiar offensive smell.

Acetamide (acid amide) does not give this test.

$$CH_3CH_2NH_2 + CHCl_3 + KOH(alc.) \xrightarrow{\Delta} \underset{\text{(Foul smell)}}{CH_3CH_2NC} + 3KCl + 3H_2O$$

45. Direct nitration of aniline gives oxidation products alongwith some nitro derivatives therefore, direct nitration is not possible.

> **Concept Enhancer** In strongly acidic medium, aniline on nitration gives a mixture of *ortho, para* and significant amount of *meta*-nitroaniline. This *m*- nitroaniline formation is that, under strongly acidic conditions aniline is protonated to form anilinium ion which is a *m*-directing group.

46. Acetamide to ethylamine

$$\underset{\text{Acetamide}}{CH_3-\overset{\overset{O}{\|}}{C}-NH_2} \xrightarrow[P_2O_5]{\Delta} CH_3C\equiv N + H_2O \xrightarrow[LiAlH_4]{+4[H]} \underset{\text{Ethylamine}}{CH_3CH_2NH_2}$$

47. (i) **Carbylamine reaction**

Aniline [1°amine]	**Dimethyl aniline** [2°amine]
Aniline gives foul smell of phenyl isocyanide, when heated with chloroform and KOH. $C_6H_5NH_2 + CHCl_3 + 3KOH \longrightarrow C_6H_5NC + 3KCl + 3H_2O$	No characteristic observation.
(ii) **Dye test**	
On diazotisation and coupling with alkaline β-naphthol, aniline forms an orange red dye.	No characteristic observation.

48. Acetamide can be converted to methylamine by the reaction of acetamide with bromine in the presence of alkali solution.

Reaction

$$CH_3CONH_2 + Br_2 + 4KOH \longrightarrow CH_3NH_2 + 2KBr + K_2CO_3 + 2H_2O$$

Name of the reaction is **Hofmann bromamide reaction.**

49. (i) (a) **Example of Coupling reaction**

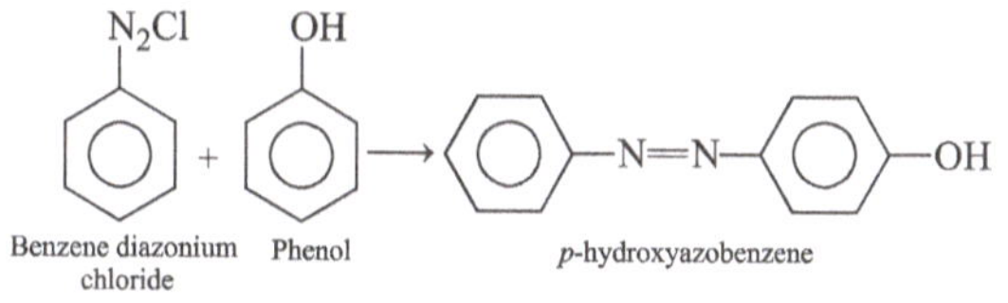

(b) **Example of acetylation of ethylamine**

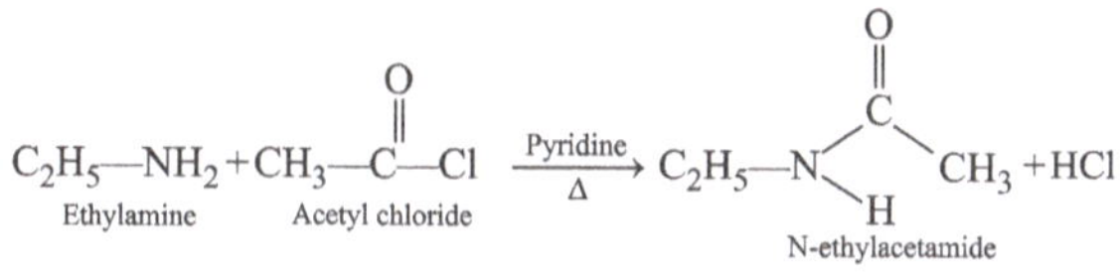

(ii) Aniline does not undergo Friedel-Craft's reaction it is due to salt formation with aluminium chloride which is used as Lewis acid catalyst.

$$\underset{\text{Aniline (Lewis base)}}{C_6H_5NH_2} + \underset{\text{(Lewis acid)}}{AlCl_3} \longrightarrow \underset{\text{(Complex)}}{[C_6H_5NH_2]^+ [AlCl_3]^-}$$

50. (i) In aliphatic amines, the $—NH_2$ group is attached to an alkyl group which is an electron donating group, i.e. they have $+I$-effect. So, the lone pair of electrons on nitrogen are readily available.

Therefore, aliphatic amines are more basic than aromatic amines.

The presence of alkyl groups increases the basicity of 2° amine in water phase in comparison to 1° amine due to increased $+I$-effect.

3° amine leads to steric hindrance due to presence of 3 alkyl groups. Hence, the order is

$C_6H_5NH_2 < C_2H_5NH_2 < (C_2H_5)_3N < (C_2H_5)_2NH$

(ii) The decreasing order of basic strength in gaseous phase is

$(C_2H_5)_3N > (C_2H_5)_2NH > C_2H_5NH_2 > C_6H_5NH_2$

The $+I$ effect of alkyl groups increases electron density on N-atoms and hence the basic character of amine.

51. (i)

$$\underset{\text{Nitrobenzene}}{C_6H_5NO_2} \xrightarrow{Sn+HCl} \underset{\text{Aniline } (A)}{C_6H_5NH_2} \xrightarrow[273\text{-}278K]{NaNO_2+HCl} \underset{\text{Benzene diazonium chloride } (B)}{C_6H_5N_2^+Cl^-} \xrightarrow{H_2O} \underset{\text{Phenol } (C)}{C_6H_5OH}$$ **(1½)**

(ii)

$$\underset{\text{Acetonitrile}}{CH_3CN} \xrightarrow{H_2O/H^+} \underset{(A)}{CH_3CH_2OH} \xrightarrow[Heat]{NH_3/} \underset{\text{Ethanamide } (B)}{CH_3CONH_2} \xrightarrow{Br_2+KOH} \underset{\text{Methanamine } (C)}{CH_3NH_2}$$ **(1½)**

52. (i) Increasing order of basic strength is as follows

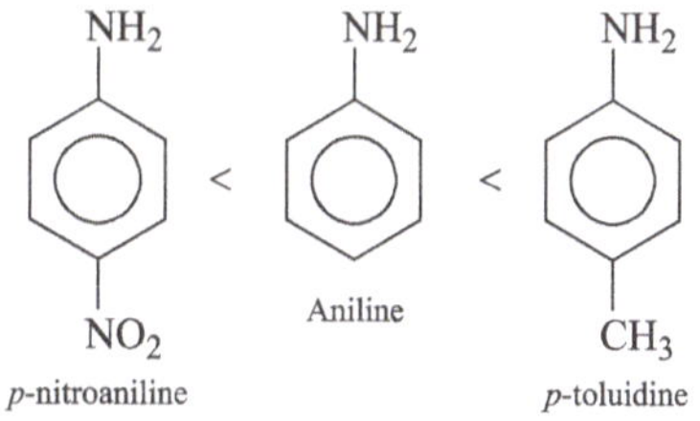

Reason More is the availability of electron density over N-atom, more is the basic strength. Electron releasing group increases while electron withdrawing group decreases the basicity (or basic strength). **(1)**

(ii) Decreasing order of basic strength in gas phase is as follows

$$(C_2H_5)_3N > (C_2H_5)_2NH > C_2H_5NH_2 > NH_3$$

Reason Due to electron releasing nature of alkyl group, it pushes electron towards nitrogen and makes the unshared electron pair more available for sharing with the proton of the acid.

Basic nature of amine increases with increase in the number of alkyl group. **(1)**

(iii) Increasing order of solubility of given compound in water is $C_6H_5NH_2 < (C_2H_5)_2NH < C_2H_5NH$.

Reason Lower aliphatic amines can form hydrogen bonds with water molecule and hence are soluble in water.

Solubility of amines decreases with increase in molar mass due to increase in the hydrophobic part which retard the formation of H-bonds and hence aromatic amines are insoluble in water. **(1)**

53. $\underset{[A]}{CH_3—CH_2—NH_2} + HNO_2 \longrightarrow \underset{[B]}{CH_3—CH_2—OH} + N_2\uparrow + H_2O$

$\underset{[B]}{CH_3—CH_2—OH} + [O] \xrightarrow[\text{Oxidation}]{\text{Controlled}} \underset{[C]}{CH_3—CHO} + H_2O$

$\underset{[C]}{CH_3—CHO} + 2[Ag(NH_3)_2]^+ + 3OH^- \xrightarrow{\Delta} \underset{[D]}{CH_3COOH} + 2Ag + 4NH_3 + 2H_2O$

$\underset{[D]}{CH_3COOH} + \underset{[B]}{HO—CH_2—CH_3} \underset{}{\overset{\text{Conc. } H_2SO_4}{\rightleftharpoons}} \underset{\text{Ethyl acetate } [E]}{CH_3—COOC_2H_5} + H_2O$

$\underset{[C]}{CH_3—CHO} + NH_3 \longrightarrow CH_3—CH(OH)(NH_2) \xrightarrow{\Delta} CH_3—CH{=}NH$

54. Ethylamine to methylamine

$\underset{\text{Ethylamine}}{CH_3CH_2 \cdot NH_2} \xrightarrow[-NH_2, -H_2O]{+HNO_2} \underset{\text{Ethanol}}{CH_3CH_2OH} \xrightarrow[\Delta]{Cu/573K}$

$\underset{\text{Acetaldehyde}}{CH_3CHO} \xrightarrow[KMnO_4]{\text{Alkaline}} \underset{\text{Acetic acid}}{CH_3COOH} \xrightarrow{SOCl_2}$

$\underset{\text{Acetyl chloride}}{CH_3COCl} \xrightarrow[-H_2O]{NH_3/\Delta} \underset{\text{Acetamide}}{CH_3CONH_2}$

$\xrightarrow[\Delta]{Br_2+NaOH} \underset{\text{Methylamine}}{CH_3NH_2} + 2NaBr + Na_2CO_3 + 2H_2O$

(Hofmann bromamide reaction)

55. Benzene to acetanilide

Following steps will be taken

$\underset{\text{Benzene}}{C_6H_6} \xrightarrow[-H_2O]{HNO_3/H_2SO_4} \underset{\text{Nitrobenzene}}{C_6H_5NO_2} \xrightarrow[(Sn + HCl), -2H_2O]{4[H]}$

$\underset{\text{Aniline}}{C_6H_5NH_2} \xrightarrow[-HCl]{CH_3COCl} \underset{\text{Acetanilide}}{C_6H_5NHCOCH_3}$

56. (i)

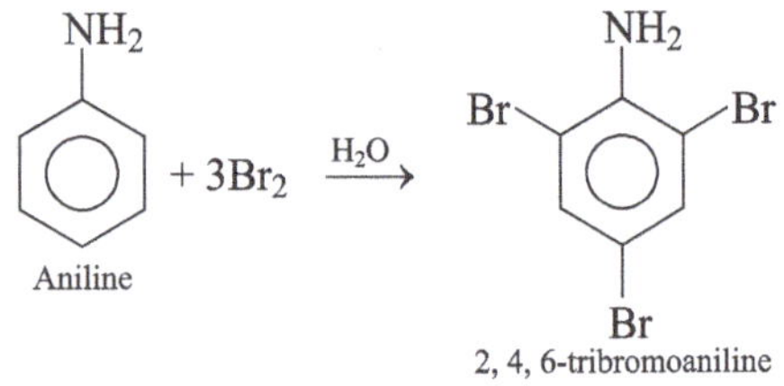

Aniline 2, 4, 6-tribromoaniline

(ii) $\underset{\text{Ethylamine}}{C_2H_5NH_2} + HNO_2 \longrightarrow \underset{\text{Ethanol}}{C_2H_5OH} + N_2\uparrow + H_2O$

(iii) $\underset{\text{Acetic anhydride}}{(CH_3CO)_2O} + NH_3 \longrightarrow \underset{\text{Acetic acid}}{CH_3COOH} + \underset{\text{Acetamide}}{CH_3CONH_2}$

57. Primary amines form alcohols with HNO_2.

$RNH_2 + HONO \longrightarrow \underset{\text{Alcohol}}{R—OH} + N_2\uparrow + H_2O$

Secondary amines form nitrosoamines with HNO_2.

$R_2NH + HONO \longrightarrow \underset{\text{Nitrosoamine}}{R_2N—N{=}O} + H_2O$

Tertiary amines form trialkyl ammonium nitrite salt with HNO_2.

$R_3N + HONO \longrightarrow \underset{\text{Trialkyl ammonium nitrite}}{R_3N \cdot HNO_2} \xrightarrow{\Delta} \underset{\text{N-nitrosoamine}}{R_2N—N{=}O} + \underset{\text{Alcohol}}{ROH}$

58. $CH_3CONH_2 \xrightarrow[\Delta]{P_2O_5} \underset{[A]}{CH_3CN} + H_2O$

$\underset{[A]}{CH_3CN} \xrightarrow[\Delta]{H_2/Pt} \underset{[B]}{CH_3CH_2NH_2}$

$CH_3CH_2NH_2 \xrightarrow[HCl]{NaNO_2} \underset{[C]}{CH_3CH_2OH} + N_2\uparrow + H_2O$

$A \rightarrow$ Methyl cyanide, $B \rightarrow$ Ethylamine,

$C \rightarrow$ Ethyl alcohol.

59. Molecular formula of amine is C_3H_9N.

(i) $\underset{\text{Ethyl methylamine (secondary)}}{CH_3—NH—CH_2CH_3}$ (ii) $\underset{\text{2-propanamine (primary)}}{CH_3—CH(CH_3)—NH_2}$

(iii) $\underset{\text{Trimethylamine (tertiary)}}{CH_3—N(CH_3)—CH_3}$

TOPIC 2

Cyanides, Isocyanides and Diazonium Salts

Cyanides and Isocyanides

The cyanide group is an ambident group and can attach itself to H through both C as well as N-atom. HCN exists in the following two tautomeric forms

$$\underset{\text{Hydrogen cyanide}}{H—C\equiv N} \rightleftharpoons \underset{\text{Hydrogen isocyanide}}{H—N\overset{\rightarrow}{=}C}$$

The functional group in cyanides is —C≡N and is called **cyano** or **nitrile** group, while that in isocyanides is $—N\overset{\rightarrow}{=}C$ and is called **isocyano** or **isonitrile** or **carbylamine** group.

General Methods for the Preparation of Cyanides and Isocyanides

(i) Cyanides

(a) **From alkyl halides**

$$RX + K^+CN^- \text{(alc.)} \xrightarrow{\Delta} R—C\equiv N + K^+X^-$$

(b) **From acid amides**

$$R—\overset{\overset{O}{||}}{C}—NH_2 \xrightarrow[\Delta]{P_2O_5 \text{ or } SOCl_2} R—C\equiv N + H_2O$$

(ii) Isocyanides

(a) **From alkyl halides**

$$RX + AgCN\text{(alc.)} \longrightarrow R—N\overset{\rightarrow}{=}C + AgX$$

(b) **From primary amines** (carbylamine reaction)

$$\underset{\text{Primary amine}}{R—NH_2} + CHCl_3 + 3KOH\text{(alc.)} \xrightarrow{\Delta} \underset{\text{Alkyl isocyanide}}{R—N\overset{\rightarrow}{=}C} + 3KCl + 3H_2O$$

Diazonium Salts

Diazonium salts have the general formula $RN_2^+X^-$, where X^- ion may be Cl^-, Br^-, HSO_4^-, NO_3^-, etc.

Preparation of Diazonium Salts

$$C_6H_5NH_2 + NaNO_2 + 2HCl \xrightarrow{273\text{-}278\text{ K}} C_6H_5\overset{+}{N_2}Cl^- + NaCl + 2H_2O$$

This process of conversion of a primary aromatic amines into their diazonium salts is called **diazotisation.**

The stability of arene diazonium salts is due to the dispersal of the positive charge over the benzene ring, as shown below.

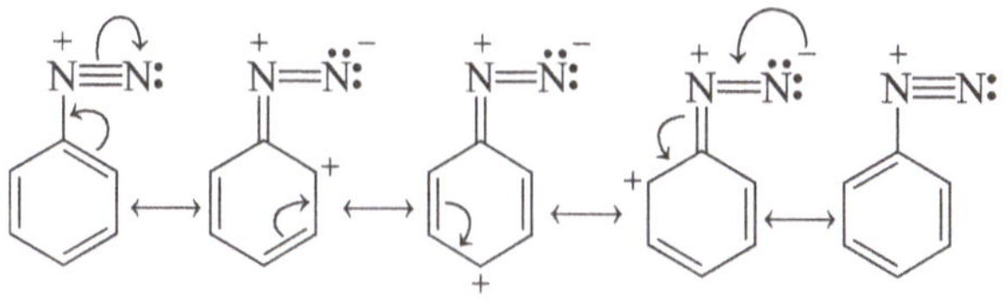

Resonating structures of benzene diazonium salt

Chemical Properties of Diazonium Salts

The reactions of diazonium salts can be divided into two categories.

(i) Reactions Involving Displacement of Nitrogen

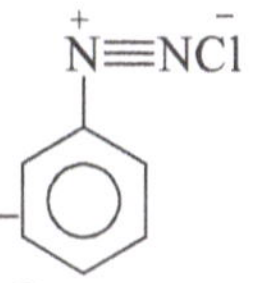

Benzene diazonium chloride ($C_6H_5\overset{+}{N}\equiv N\overset{-}{Cl}$)

- $\xrightarrow[\text{(Sandmeyer reaction)}]{CuCl/HCl} C_6H_5Cl + N_2\uparrow$
- $\xrightarrow[\text{(Sandmeyer reaction)}]{CuBr/HBr} C_6H_5Br + N_2\uparrow$
- $\xrightarrow[\text{(Sandmeyer reaction)}]{CuCN/KCN} C_6H_5CN + N_2\uparrow$
- $\xrightarrow[\text{(Gattermann reaction)}]{Cu/HCl} C_6H_5Cl + N_2\uparrow + CuCl$
- $\xrightarrow[\text{(Gattermann reaction)}]{Cu/HBr} C_6H_5Br + N_2\uparrow + CuBr$
- $\xrightarrow{KI/\Delta} C_6H_5I + KCl + N_2\uparrow$
- $\xrightarrow[\text{(Balz-Schiemann reaction)}]{HBF_4,\,\Delta} C_6H_5F + BF_3 + N_2\uparrow + HCl$
- $\xrightarrow{H_3PO_2 + H_2O} C_6H_6 + N_2\uparrow + H_3PO_3 + HCl$
- $\xrightarrow{CH_3CH_2OH} C_6H_6 + N_2\uparrow + CH_3CHO + HCl$
- $\xrightarrow[H_2SO_4\text{(Boil)}]{H_2O} C_6H_5OH + N_2\uparrow + HCl$
- $\xrightarrow[-HCl]{HBF_4} C_6H_5\overset{+}{N_2}\overset{-}{BF_4} \xrightarrow[Cu/\Delta]{NaNO_2} C_6H_5NO_2 + N_2\uparrow + NaBF_4$

(ii) Coupling Reactions with Phenol and Aniline

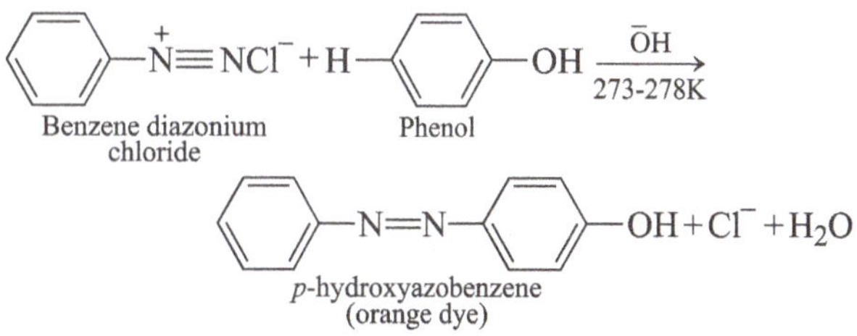

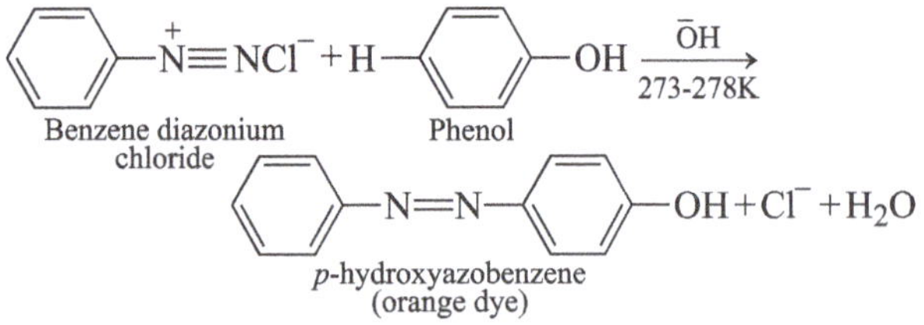

Importance of Diazonium Salts in the Synthesis of Aromatic Compounds

Diazonium salts are important in synthesis of aromatic compounds due to the following facts.

- Diazonium salts are very good intermediates for the introduction of —F, — Cl, — OH, — CN, — NO_2, etc., into the aromatic ring.
- Aryl fluorides and iodides cannot be prepared by direct halogenation. Cyano group cannot be introduced by nucleophilic substitution but cyanobenzene can be prepared from diazonium salts.
- Replacement of diazo group by other group is helpful in preparing those aromatic compounds which cannot be prepared by direct substitution in benzene.

PYQs Previous Years' Questions

1 Mark Questions

1. Which of the following product is formed when benzene diazonium chloride is reduced by hypophosphorous acid (H_3PO_2) in the presence of cuprous ion as catalyst? **ISC Specimen 2024**
(a) Phenol (b) Aniline
(c) Benzene (d) Benzene cyanide

2. An alkyl isocyanide on complete reduction gives **ISC Specimen 2023**
(a) primary amine (b) secondary amine
(c) tertiary amine (d) carboxylic acid

3. Primary amine when warmed with chloroform and alc. KOH yields **ISC Specimen 2021-22 (Sem-II)**
(a) cyanide (b) isocyanide
(c) benzene diazonium chloride (d) secondary amine

4. On heating an aliphatic primary amine with chloroform and alc. potassium hydroxide, the organic compound formed is an **ISC 2020**
(a) alkyl isocyanide (b) alkanol
(c) alkanal (d) alkyl cyanide

5. Give balanced equation when ethylamine is heated with chloroform and alcoholic solution of potassium hydroxide. **ISC 2019**

6. Which of the following undergoes diazotisation?
(a) Aniline (b) Methylamine
(c) Ethylamine (d) All of these **ISC 2017**

7. Convert benzene to benzene diazonium chloride. **ISC 2016**

> **KEY IDEA**
> Nitration, i.e. introduction of —NO_2 group on benzene, reduction by Sn/HCl to convert —NO_2 to —NH_2 followed by diazotisation.

8. Give balanced equation for the following name reaction:
Balz-Schiemann's reaction **ISC 2014**

9. How can the following conversion be brought about?
Acetic acid to methyl cyanide **ISC 2014**

10. How can the following conversion be brought about?
Nitrobenzene to benzene diazonium chloride **ISC 2013**

> **KEY IDEA**
> - Reduction of nitrobenzene to aniline.
> - Diazotisation to form benzene diazonium chloride.

11. Give balanced equation for the following reaction given below.
Aniline is treated with a mixture of $NaNO_2$ and excess of HCl at low temperature. **ISC 2007**

12. Complete the following reaction and name the intermediate products *A*, *B* and *C*. **ISC 2006**

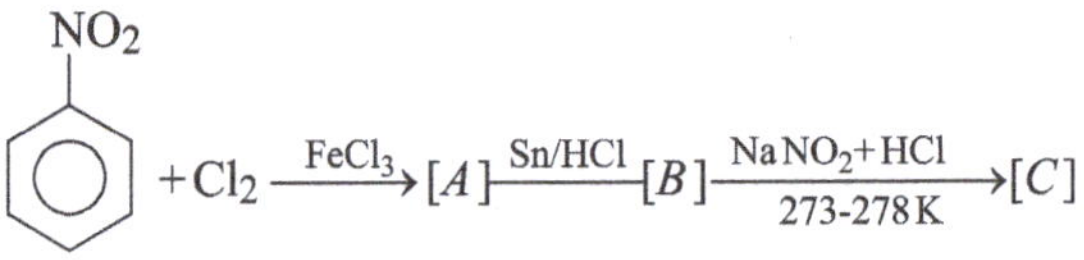

2 Marks Questions

13. Identify compounds [*A*] and [*B*] in the following reactions. **ISC Specimen 2023**

(i) $CH_3Br + KCN(alc.) \longrightarrow [A] \xrightarrow[\text{(Complete hydrolysis)}]{+HOH/H^+} [B]$

(ii) $C_6H_5NH_2 + HNO_2 + HCl \xrightarrow{0\text{-}5°C} [A] \xrightarrow{Cu_2Cl_2/HCl} [B]$

14. (i) What are the products formed when benzene diazonium chloride reacts with aniline in weakly acidic medium, at very low temperature? (Give equation) **ISC 2021-22 (Sem-II)**

Or

Give balanced equation when benzene diazonium chloride is treated with ice cold solution of aniline in acidic medium. **ISC 2019**

(ii) $CH_3NH_2 + CHCl_3 + 3KOH\ (alc.) \xrightarrow{Heat}$ .... $3KCl + 3H_2O$

(a) Complete the reaction given above.

(b) Name the reaction given above. **ISC 2022 (Sem-II)**

15. (i) Arrange the following in the increasing order of their basic strength; $C_2H_5NH_2, C_6H_5NH_2, (C_2H_5)_2NH$.

(ii) What are the products formed when benzene diazonium chloride reacts with phenol in weak alkaline medium? (Give equation). **ISC Specimen 2021-22 (Sem-II)**

16. Identify the compounds *A*, *B*, *C* and *D*.

$$CH_3CN \xrightarrow{H_2O/H^+} [A] \xrightarrow{NH_3} [B] \xrightarrow{Heat} [C]$$
$$\xrightarrow{Br_2/KOH} [D]$$ **ISC 2018**

17. (i) Give a balanced chemical equation to convert methyl cyanide to ethyl alcohol. **ISC 2018**

(ii) What happens when benzene diazonium chloride reacts with phenol in weak alkaline medium? (Give balanced equation).

18. Write balanced chemical equations for carbylamine reaction and diazotisation reaction. **ISC 2018**

19. State the reagents for the following conversion.

$$\text{Benzene} \xrightarrow{[A]} \text{Nitrobenzene} \xrightarrow{[B]} \text{Aniline} \xrightarrow{[C]}$$
$$\text{Aniline hydrochloride} \xrightarrow{[D]} \text{Benzene diazonium chloride}$$ **ISC 2008**

3 Marks Questions

20. How will the following be converted? (Give chemical equation) **ISC 2023**

(i) Ethyl bromide to ethyl isocyanide

(ii) Aniline to benzene diazonium chloride

(iii) Benzene diazonium chloride to phenol

21. Identify the compounds [*A*], [*B*] and [*C*] in the following reactions. **ISC 2023**

(i) $CH_3COOH \xrightarrow[\Delta]{NH_3} [A] \xrightarrow{Br_2 + KOH} [B] \xrightarrow{CHCl_3 + NaOH(alc.)} [C]$

(ii) $CH_3Br \xrightarrow{KCN} [A] \xrightarrow{LiAlH_4} [B] \xrightarrow[273\ K]{HNO_2} [C]$

22. How will the following be converted? (Give chemical equations) **ISC Specimen 2023**

(i) Benzene diazonium chloride to benzene

(ii) Ethylamine to ethyl alcohol

(iii) Methylamine to methyl isocyanide

23. An organic compound '*A*' on treatment with *aq*. KCN produces compound '*B*'. Compound '*B*' on reduction with Na/C_2H_5OH gives compound '*C*' with molecular formula C_2H_5N. Compound '*C*' reacts with $NaNO_2$ and HCl to form compound '*D*' on treatment with acetic acid in the presence of conc. H_2SO_4 produces a sweet smelling compound '*E*'.

(i) Identify the compounds '*A*' to '*E*'.

(ii) Name the reaction for the formation of compound '*E*' from the compound '*D*'. **ISC Specimen 2023**

24. How can the following conversion be brought about

(i) acetic acid to methylamine?

(ii) aniline to benzene?

25. Identify the compounds *A*, *B*, *C*, *D*, *E* and *F* required for the following conversion. **ISC 2014**

$$C_6H_5NO_2 \xrightarrow{[A]} C_6H_5NH_2 \xrightarrow{[B]} C_6H_5\overset{+}{N_2}Cl^- \xrightarrow{[C]}$$
$$C_6H_5Cl \xrightarrow{[D]} C_6H_5OH \xrightarrow{H_2SO_4} [E] + [F]$$

26. How will you carry out the following conversion? Aniline to chlorobenzene **ISC 2002**

> **KEY IDEA**
> Aniline to chlorobenzene will be carried by
> (i) Diazotisation (ii) Gattermann reaction

27. Identify *A*, *B* and *C*. **ISC 2003**

$$C_6H_5CONH_2 \xrightarrow{Br_2/KOH} [A]$$
$$\xrightarrow[\text{(ii) Steam}]{\text{(i) } NaNO_2/HCl} [B] \xrightarrow[\text{ice cold}]{C_6H_5N_2Cl} [C]$$

5 Marks Question

28. Identify *A*, *B*, *C*, *D* and *E*, **ISC 2001**

$$\text{Benzoic acid} \xrightarrow[Heat]{NH_3} [A] \xrightarrow{Br_2/KOH} [B] \xrightarrow[\text{Ice cold}]{NaNO_2 + HCl} [C]$$
$$\xrightarrow[HCl]{CuCl} [D]$$

Explanations

1. (c) Benzene is the product when benzene diazonium chloride is reduced by hypophosphorus acid in the presence of cuprous ion as catalst.

   This reaction is known as sandmeyer reaction.

2. (b) Reduction of isocyanide gives secondary amine. i.e.

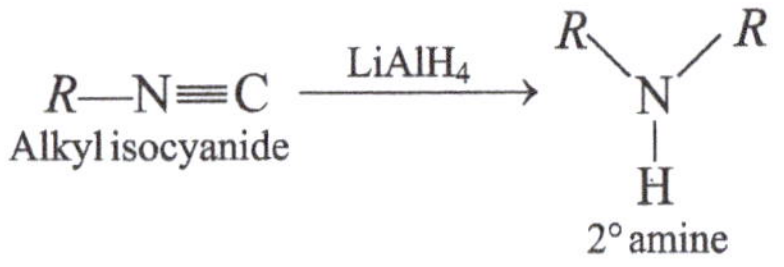

3. (b) Isocyanide is formed. It is the example of carbylamine reaction.

   e.g. $CH_3CH_2NH_2 + CHCl_3 + 3KOH(alc.) \longrightarrow CH_3CH_2NC + 3KCl + 3H_2\uparrow$

   Ethylamine (1° amine) ... Isocyanide

4. (a) $RNH_2 + CHCl_3 + 3KOH(alc.) \xrightarrow{\Delta} RN \rightleftharpoons C + 3KCl + H_2O$

   Alkyl isocyanide

5. $CH_3CH_2NH_2 + CHCl_3 + 3KOH(Alc.) \xrightarrow{\Delta} CH_3CH_2—N \rightleftharpoons C + 3KCl + 3H_2O$

   Ethylamine, Chloroform, Ethyl isocyanide

6. (a) Aniline undergoes diazotisation reaction.

7.

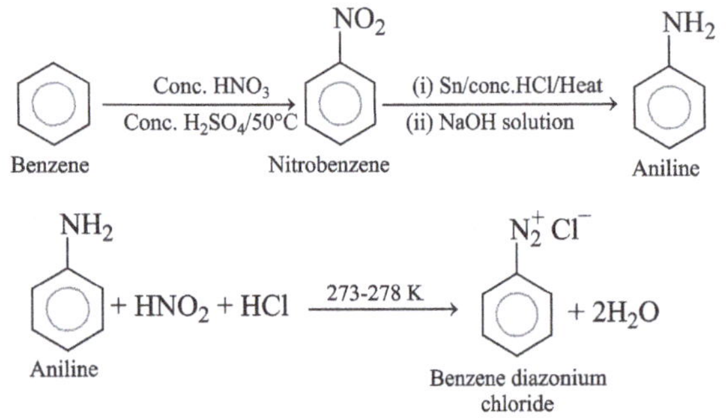

8. **Balz-Schiemann's reaction**

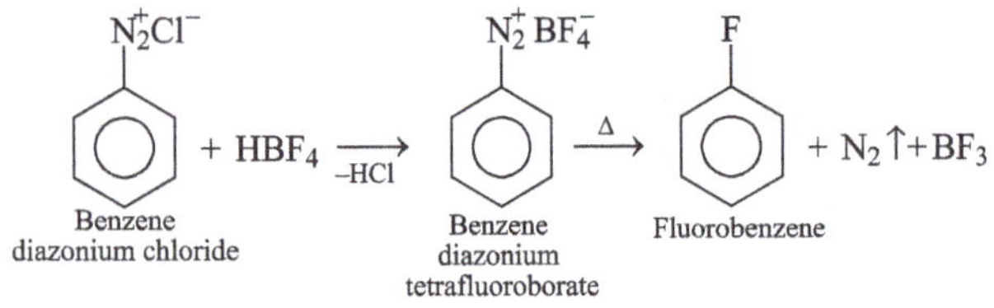

9. $CH_3COOH \xrightarrow[\text{(ii) Heat}]{\text{(i) } NH_3} CH_3CONH_2 \xrightarrow{P_2O_5, \Delta} CH_3CN$

   Acetic acid, Methyl cyanide

10.

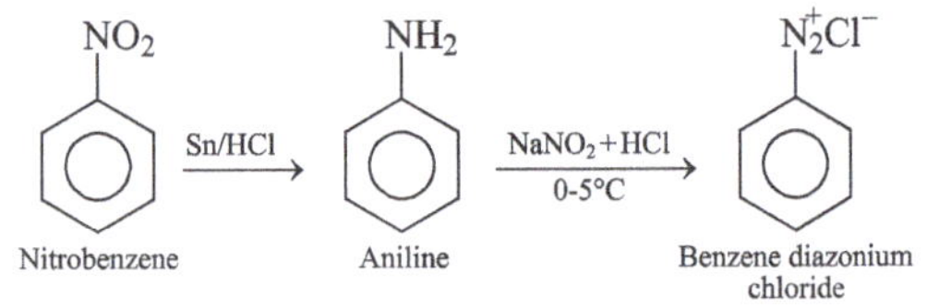

11. $C_6H_5NH_2 + HNO_2 + HCl \xrightarrow[\text{HCl at low temperature}]{NaNO_2} C_6H_5\overset{+}{N} \equiv N\overset{-}{Cl} + 2H_2O$

12.

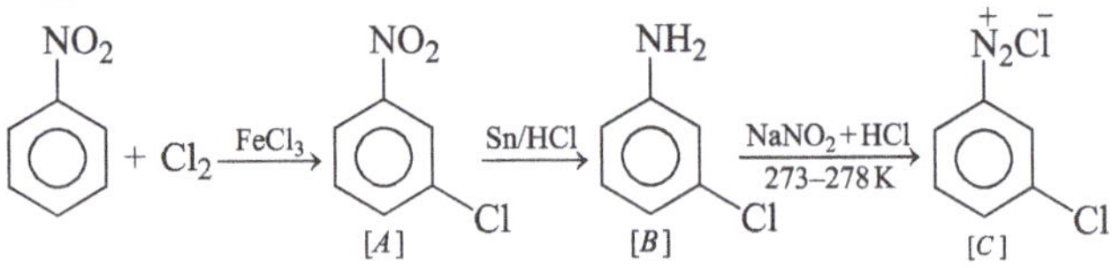

   A is *m*-chloronitrobenzene. *B* is *m*-chloroaniline.

   C is *m*-chlorobenzene diazonium chloride.

13. (i) When an alkyl halide is heated with an alc. solution of KCN alkylcyanides are formed which on further hydrolysis carboxylic acid is obtained.

   $CH_3KCN\ (alc.) \xrightarrow{\Delta} CH_3—C \equiv N + KX \xrightarrow{H_2O/H^+} CH_3COOH$ **(1)**

   (A) ... (B)

   (ii) When amide is treated with acid, diazonium salt is formed and on further treatment with copper chloride, the chlorobenzene is obtained.

   $C_6H_5NH_2 + HNO_2 + HCl \xrightarrow{0\text{-}5°C} C_6H_5N_2^+Cl^-\ [A]$

   Aniline, Nitric acid, Benzene diazonium chloride salt

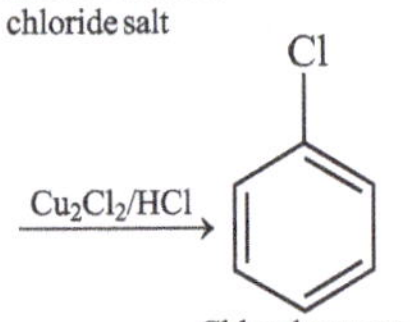

Chlorobenzene [*B*] **(1)**

Common Mistake Generally, temperature conditions 0 - 5°is not written while writing this chemical equation.

14. (i)

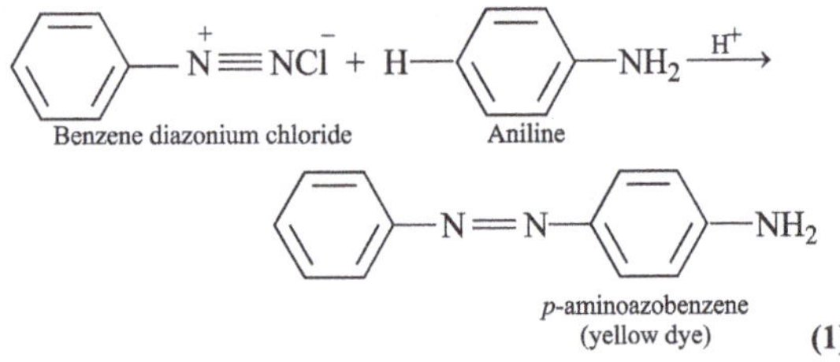

(1)

> **Concept Enhancer** p-aminoazobenzene is used to synthesise azodyes, disperse dyes and used to make paints and pigments.

Or

(ii) (a) $CH_3NH_2 + CHCl_3 + 3KOH(alc.) \xrightarrow{\Delta} CH_3-N \overrightarrow{=} C + 3KCl + 3H_2O$ **(1/2)**

(b) This reaction is called as carbylamine reaction. **(1/2)**

15. (i) Due to $-I$-effect of C_6H_5 group, the electron density of N-atom in $C_6H_5NH_2$ is lower than that of $C_2H_5NH_2$. So, $C_6H_5NH_2$ is least basic while in case of $C_2H_5NH_2$ and $(C_2H_5)_2NH$, considering the inductive effect and steric hindrance of alkyl group.

The increasing order of basic strength is
$C_6H_5CH_2 < C_2H_5NH_2 < (C_2H_5)_2NH.$ **(1)**

(ii) When benzene diazonium chloride reacts with phenol in weak alkaline medium results in the formation of *p*-hydroxy azobenzene.

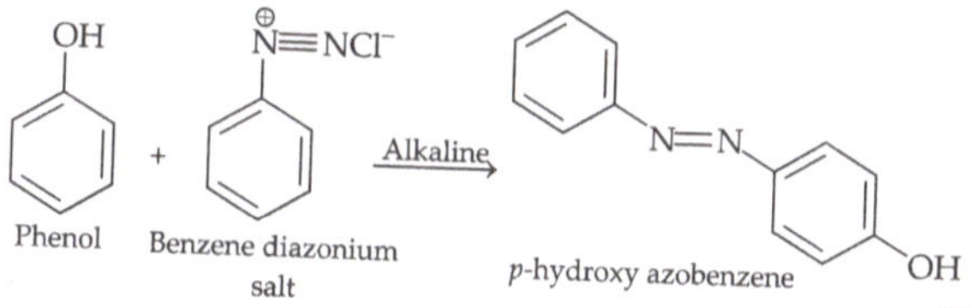

(1)

> **Concept Enhancer** p- hydroxyazobenzene is an orange colour dye which is used in varnish, grease, resin and soap kind of colouring.

16. $\underset{\text{Methyl cyanide}}{CH_3CN} \xrightarrow{H_2O/H^+} \underset{\substack{\text{Ethanoic acid}\\(A)}}{CH_3CO\overset{-}{O}\overset{+}{H}} \xrightarrow{NH_3} \underset{\substack{\text{Ammonium ethanoate}\\(B)}}{CH_3COOH}$

$\xrightarrow{\text{Heat}} \underset{\substack{\text{Ethanamide}\\(C)}}{CH_3CONH_2} \xrightarrow[\text{Hofmann bromamide reaction}]{Br_2/KOH} \underset{\substack{\text{Methylamine}\\(D)}}{CH_3NH_2}$ **(2)**

17. (i) $\underset{\text{Methyl cyanide}}{CH_3CN} \xrightarrow[\text{Hydrolysis}]{H^+/H_2O} \underset{\text{Acetic acid}}{CH_3COOH}$

$\xrightarrow[H_3O^+]{LiAlH_4/\text{ether or } B_2H_6} \underset{\text{Ethanol}}{CH_3CH_2OH}$

(ii)

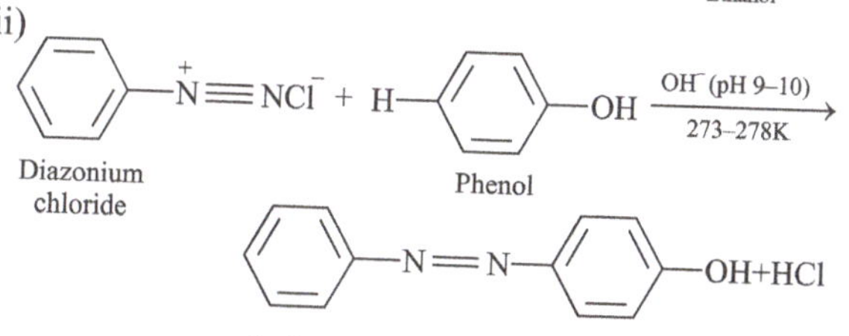

p-hydroxy azobenzene (Orange)

Benzene diazonium chloride reacts with phenol at its *para*-position to form *p*-hydroxy azobenzene, which is used as a dye. **(1+1)**

18. Carbylamine reaction Aliphatic or aromatic amines on heating with chloroform and alcoholic KOH forms isocyanides or carbylamines which are foul smelling substances.

$$\underset{\text{Amine}}{R-NH_2} + \underset{\text{Chloroform}}{CHCl_3} + 3KOH \xrightarrow{\Delta} \underset{\text{Alkyl or aryl isocyanide}}{R-NC} + 3KCl + 3H_2O$$

Diazotisation reaction Diazonium salts can be prepared by diazotisation. In this reaction, ice-cold solution of HNO_3 $(NaNO_2 + HCl + NaNO_2 + H_2SO_4)$ is added to ice-cold solution of primary aromatic amine dissolved in acid to form diazonium salt.

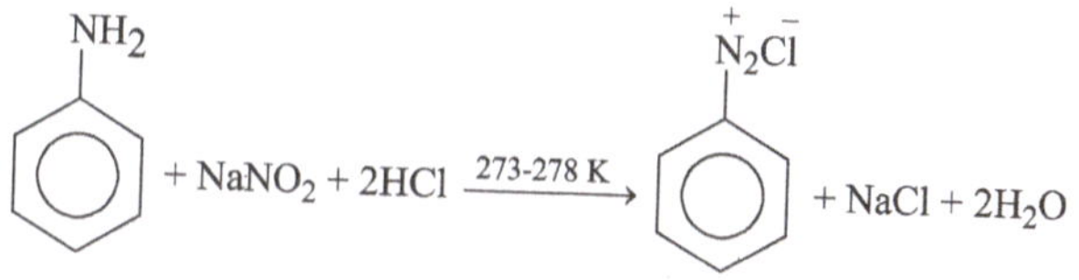

19. Benzene $\xrightarrow[\substack{\text{Conc. } H_2SO_4\\(A)}]{\text{Conc. } HNO_3 \text{ and}}$ Nitrobenzene $\xrightarrow[[B]]{Sn/HCl}$ Aniline

$\xrightarrow[[C]]{HCl}$ Aniline hydrochloride $\xrightarrow[[D]\ 5°C]{NaNO_2+HCl}$ Benzene diazonium chloride

20. (i) Ethylbromide will react with alcoholic AgCN to give ethyl isocyanide (C_2H_5-NC)

$$C_2H_5-Br + AgCN \xrightarrow{Aq.\ EtOH} C_2H_5-NC + AgBr$$

(ii) When aniline reacts with dil. HCl and *aq*. solution of sodium nitrite $(NaNO_2)$ at 273-278 K, it will form benzene diazonium chloride called diazotisation reaction.

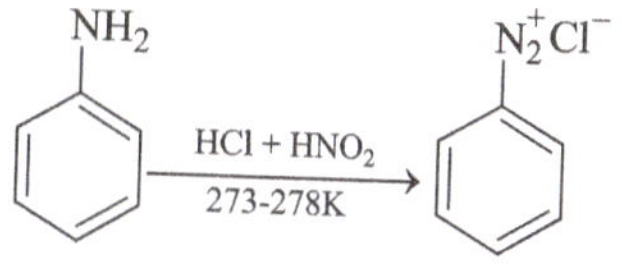

(iii) When diazonium salts are hydrolysed in the presence of dil. H_2SO_4, its gives phenols.

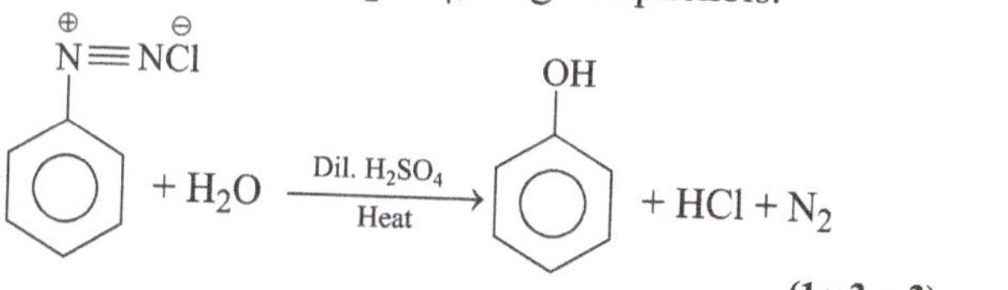

(1 × 3 = 3)

21. (i) $\underset{}{CH_3COOH} \xrightarrow[\Delta]{NH_3} \underset{[A]}{CH_3CONH_2} \xrightarrow[273\,K]{HNO_2} \underset{[B]}{CH_3NH_2}$

$\xrightarrow{CHCl_3 + NaOH} \underset{[C]}{CH_3NC}$ **(1½)**

(ii) $CH_3Br \xrightarrow{KCN} \underset{[A]}{CH_3CN} \xrightarrow{LiAlH_4} \underset{[B]}{CH_3CH_2NH_2}$

$\xrightarrow[273\,K]{HNO_2} \underset{[C]}{CH_3CH_2OH}$ **(1½)**

22. (i) **Benzene diazonium chloride to benzene**

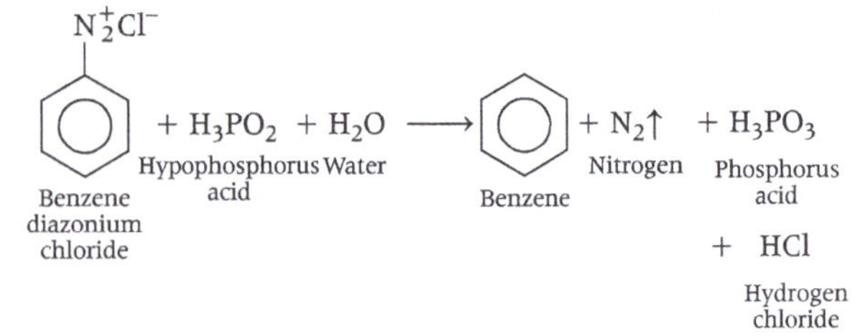

(ii) **Ethylamine to ethyl alcohol**

$\underset{\text{Ethylamine}}{CH_3CH_2NH_2} \xrightarrow[0\text{-}5^\circ C]{NaNO_2 + HCl} CH_3CH_2-\overset{+}{N}\equiv N\overset{-}{Cl}$

$\longrightarrow CH_3\overset{+}{C}H_2 \xrightarrow{\text{Hydrolysis}} \underset{\text{(Ethanol)}}{CH_3CH_2OH}$

(iii) **Methylamine to methyl isocyanide**

$\underset{\text{Methylamine}}{CH_3NH_2} + \underset{\text{Chloroform}}{CHCl_3} + \underset{\text{(alc.)}}{3KOH} \longrightarrow$

$\underset{\text{Methyl isocyanide}}{CH_3NC} + \underset{\text{Potassium chloride}}{3KCl} + \underset{\text{Water}}{3H_2O}$

It is an example of **carbylamine reaction.** **(1 × 3 = 3)**

23. $\underset{\substack{\text{Ethyl bromide}\\(A)}}{CH_3CH_2Br} \xrightarrow{Aq.\ KCN} \underset{\substack{\text{Ethyl cyanide}\\(B)}}{CH_3CH_2CN} \xrightarrow{Na/C_2H_5OH}$

$\underset{\substack{\text{Ethylamine}\\(C)}}{CH_3CH_2NH_2} \xrightarrow{NaNO_2+HCl} \underset{\substack{\text{Ethanol}\\(D)}}{CH_3CH_2-OH} \xrightarrow[\substack{\text{Conc. } H_2SO_4\\\text{(Esterification)}}]{CH_3COOH}$

$\underset{\substack{\text{Methyl ethyl ester}\\\text{(Sweet smelling compound)}\\(D)}}{CH_3CH_2COOCH_3}$

24. (i) $\underset{\text{Acetic acid}}{CH_3COOH} \xrightarrow{NH_3} \underset{\text{Ammonium acetate}}{CH_3\overset{-}{C}OO\overset{+}{N}H_4} \xrightarrow[-H_2O]{\Delta}$

$\underset{\text{Acetamide}}{CH_3CONH_2} \xrightarrow{Br_2/KOH} \underset{\text{Methylamine}}{CH_3NH_2}$ **(1½)**

(ii)

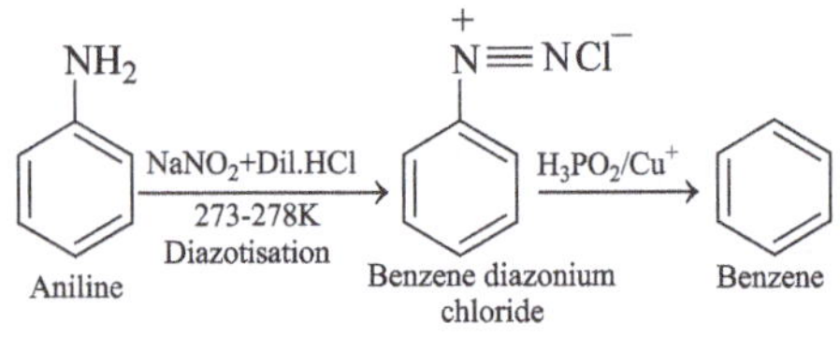

(1½)

25.

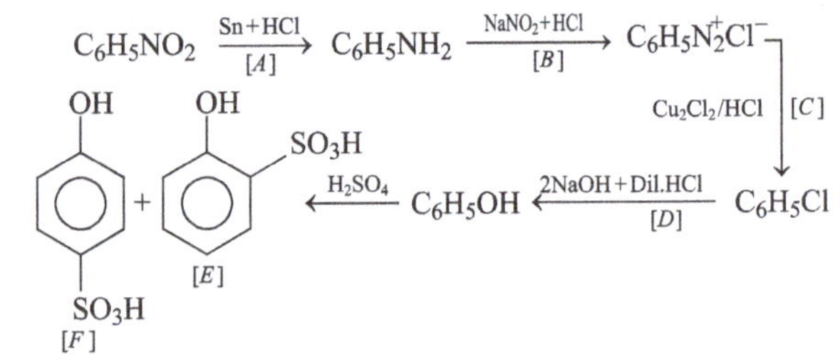

26. Aniline to chlorobenzene

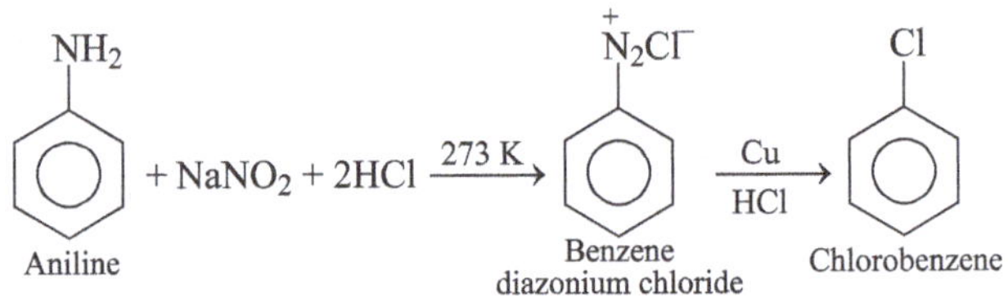

This reaction is known as **diazotisation reaction**.

27.

$C_6H_5CONH_2 \xrightarrow{Br_2/KOH} \underset{[A]}{C_6H_5NH_2} \xrightarrow{CHCl_3+KOH} \underset{[D]}{C_6H_5NC}$

$\underset{[A]}{C_6H_5NH_2} \xrightarrow{\text{(i) } NaNO_2/HCl \quad \text{(ii) Steam}} \underset{[B]}{C_6H_5OH}$

$\underset{[E]}{CH_3COOC_6H_5} \xleftarrow{CH_3COOH} \underset{[B]}{C_6H_5OH} \xrightarrow[\text{Ice cold}]{C_6H_5N_2Cl}$

$C_6H_5-N{=}N-C_6H_5OH$

p-hydroxyazobenzene
(an azo dye)
[C]

28.

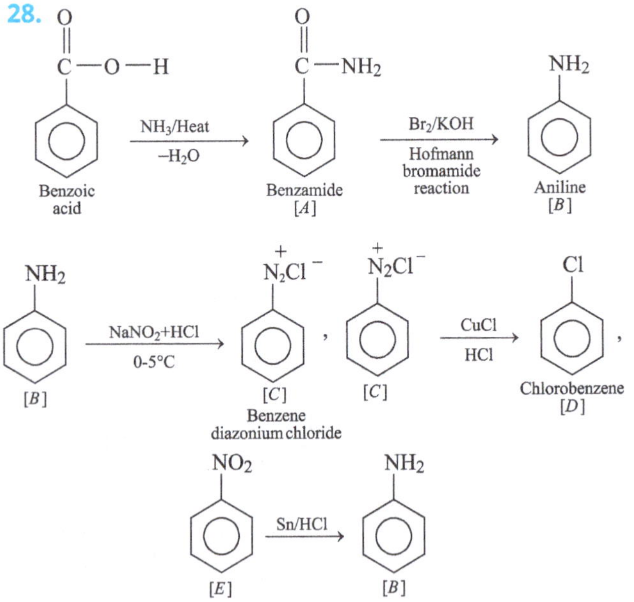

Since, *E* on reduction, gives aniline, hence it must be nitrobenzene, i.e. $C_6H_5NO_2$.

CHAPTER TEST

01 Marks Questions

1. Fill in the blanks by choosing the appropriate word(s) from those given in the bracket.

[1° amine, alkyl alcohol, Mendius reaction, Hofmann's degradation, soluble, insoluble, phenyl isocyanide, $CHCl_3$, CH_2Cl_2, phenol, amine, dye]

(i) When alkyl cyanides is treated with sodium and alcohol, it gives .... and the reaction is called ....

(ii) Ethylamine is .... in water whereas aniline is .... in water.

(iii) Aniline gives foul smell of .... when heated with .... and KOH.

(iv) Benzene diazonium chloride reacts with .... at its *para*-position to form *p*-hydroxy azobenzene which is used as a ....

2. Select and write the correct alternatives from the choices given below.

(i) The reagent that is used to distinguish between secondary and tertiary amine is

(a) *p*-toluene sulphonyl chloride
(b) Bosch's reagent
(c) $CHCl_3$ and alc. KOH
(d) Bromine water

(ii) Which reactant is used to prepare aniline using Fe/HCl as reagent ?

(a) Benzene
(b) Nitrobenzene
(c) Phenol
(d) Anisole

(iii) Which of the following reaction is used for the preparation of amine having one C-atom more than the starting amine?

(a) Reduction of nitriles
(b) Reduction of amides
(c) Reduction of nitro compounds
(d) All of the above

(iv) N-methylbenzamide is formed when methanamine reacts with benzoyl chloride. This reaction is known as

(a) benzoylation
(b) Hinsberg test
(c) Schmidt reaction
(d) Curtius reaction

3. (i) **Assertion** (A) The angle of C—N—C in trimethylamine is 108°.

Reason (R) There is unshared pair of electron in trimethylamine which makes the angle less than 109.5°.

(a) Both (A) and (R) are correct and (R) is the correct explanation of (A).
(b) Both (A) and (R) are correct but (R) is not the correct explanation of (A).
(c) (A) is correct and (R) is incorrect.
(d) (A) is incorrect and (R) is correct.

(ii) **Assertion** (A) Aniline does not undergo Friedel-Crafts alkylation and acetylation.

Reason (R) Nitrogen of aniline acquires positive charge in the presence of $AlCl_3$.

(a) Both (A) and (R) are correct and (R) is the correct explanation of (A).
(b) Both (A) and (R) are correct but (R) is not the correct explanation of (A).
(c) (A) is correct and (R) is incorrect.
(d) (A) is incorrect and (R) is correct.

02 Marks Questions

4. Give reason for the following.

(i) Aniline is a weaker base than cyclohexyl amine.

(ii) Ethylamine is soluble in water, whereas aniline is not soluble in water.

5. Write balanced chemical equation.

(i) Sandmeyer's reaction

(ii) Hofmann bromamide reaction

6. Complete and balance the following equations.

(i) $C_6H_5N_2Cl + CH_3CH_2OH \longrightarrow$

(ii) $C_6H_5N_2Cl + C_6H_5NH_2 \longrightarrow$

7. How will you convert

(i) aniline to benzonitrile?

(ii) methylamine into iodomethane?

9. Give the product formed when benzene diazonium chloride reacts with aniline in weakly acidic medium at very low temperature? Give equation.

10. Give a chemical test to distinguish between.

(i) Ethylamine and aniline

(ii) Ethylamine and dimethylamine

11. Account for the following.

(i) Aniline does not undergo Friedel-Crafts reaction.

(ii) Primary aromatic amines can not prepared by Gabriel phthalimide synthesis.

03 Marks Questions

12. Complete in the following reactions.

(i) $C_6H_5—NO_2 \xrightarrow{Sn/HCl}$

(ii) $C_6H_5—SO_2Cl \xrightarrow{(CH_3)_2NH}$

(iii) $C_6H_5NH_2 + Br_2(aq) \longrightarrow$

13. Identify the compounds *A*, *B* and *C* in the following reactions.

(i) $C_6H_5N_2^+BF_4^- \xrightarrow[\Delta]{NaNO_2/Cu} [A] \xrightarrow{Fe/HCl} [B] \xrightarrow{CH_3COCl/Pyridine} [C]$

(ii) $CH_3—Cl \xrightarrow{KCN} [A] \xrightarrow{LiAlH_4} [B] \xrightarrow{CHCl_3,\ Alc.\ KOH} [C]$

14. Give reason for the following.

(i) Benzene diazonium chloride is not stored and used immediately after its preparation.

(ii) Methylamine has lower pK_b value than aniline.

(iii) Aromatic diazonium salts are more stable than aliphatic diazonium salts.

15. Identify the compounds *A*, *B* and *C* in the following reactions.

(i) $CH_3COOH \xrightarrow[\Delta]{NH_3} [A] \xrightarrow{NaOBr} [B] \xrightarrow{NaNO_2/HCl} [C]$

(ii) $CH_3CH_2I \xrightarrow{NaCN} [A] \xrightarrow[\text{Partial hydrolysis}]{OH^-} [B] \xrightarrow{NaOH+Br_2} [C]$

16. An aromatic compound '*A*' on reaction with aqueous ammonia and on heating from compound '*B*' which on further heating with Br_2 and KOH gives a compound '*C* of molecular formula C_6H_7N. Write the structure and IUPAC names of compounds *A*, *B* and *C*.

05 Marks Questions

17. (i) Write the structure of main products when aniline reacts with the following reagents.

(a) Br_2 water

(b) HCl

(c) $(CH_3CO)_2O$/ pyridine

(ii) Write the product(s) in the following reactions.

(a) $C_6H_5N_2Cl^- \xrightarrow{Cu/HCl} [A] \xrightarrow{Cl_2/FeCl_3} [B]$

(b) $C_6H_5NO_2 \xrightarrow{Sn+HCl} [A] \xrightarrow[273]{NaNO_2+HCl} [B]$

18. (i) Why aliphatic primary amines can only be prepared by Grabriel phthalinide synthesis. Explain with an example.

(ii) Outline a synthesis of *p*-bromonitrobenzene from benzene in two steps.

19. (i) How will the following be converted?

(a) Methanol to ethanoic acid.

(b) Hexane nitrile to 1-aminopentane.

(c) Nitromethane to dimethylamine.

(ii) Give one chemical test to distinguish between the following pair of compounds.

(a) Aniline and benzylamine.

(b) Secondary and tertiary amines.

Answers

1. (i) 1° amine, Mendius reaction (ii) soluble, insoluble
(iii) phenyl isocyanide, $CHCl_3$ (iv) phenol dye

2. (i) (a) (ii) (c) (iii) (a) (iv) (a)

3. (i) (a) (ii) (a)

10

Biomolecules

TREND ANALYSIS 4 YEARS

Average No. of Questions Across all Sets

	Types of Questions	2024	2023	2020	2019
TOPIC 01 Carbohydrates	1 Mark	—	—	1	—
	2 Marks	—	—	—	—
	3 Marks	—	—	—	—
	5 Marks	—	—	—	—
TOPIC 02 Proteins and Enzymes	1 Mark	—	—	1	—
	2 Marks	—	—	—	—
	3 Marks	—	—	—	—
	5 Marks	—	—	—	—
TOPIC 03 Vitamins, Nucleic Acids and Hormones	1 Mark	—	—	—	—
	2 Marks	—	—	—	1
	3 Marks	1	1	—	—
	5 Marks	—	—	—	—

TOPIC 1

Carbohydrates

Carbohydrates are polyhydroxy aldehydes or polyhydroxy ketones or large polymeric molecules which on hydrolysis yield such units.

Classification of Carbohydrates

I. On the basis of behaviour on hydrolysis these are classified as

Monosaccharides

These cannot be further hydrolysed to simpler molecule where, $n = 3$ -7. These are of two types, **aldoses** and **ketoses**. e.g. Glucose, fructose, ribose etc.

Oligosaccharides

The carbohydrates which upon hydrolysis give (2-10) number of monosaccharides units are called oligosaccharides. Further categorised as di, tri, tetrasaccharides etc, depending on monosaccharide they provide on hydrolysis.

Polysaccharides

On hydrolysis give large number of monosaccharides. General formula $(C_6H_{10}O_5)_n$ where, $n = 100\text{-}3000$, e.g. starch, cellulose.

II. On basis of reducing activity sugars are classified as

Reducing Sugars

These are carbohydrates which are capable of reducing Tollen's reagent and Fehling's solution. e.g. Glucose, fructose, ribose etc.

Non-reducing Sugars

These are carbohydrates which are unable to reduce Tollen's reagent and Fehling's solution, e.g. sucrose.

Structure of Glucose and Fructose

Glucose is an aldohexose whereas fructose is a ketohexose with six carbon atoms.

Open Chain Structure

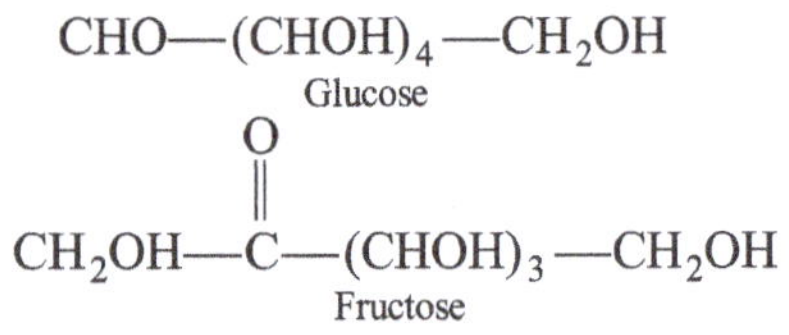

Bromine Water Test : Tests for Glucose and Fructose

When glucose is treated with bromine water, red colour of bromine water disappears as —CHO group changes to —COOH group whereas fructose does not decolourise the red colour of bromine water.

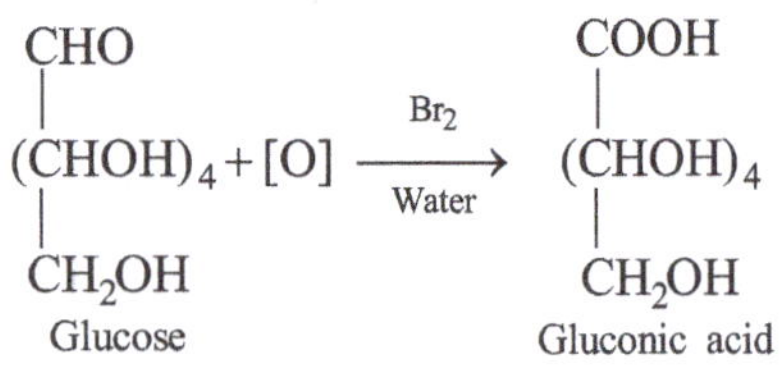

Properties of Carbohydrates

The following are properties of carbohydrates

(i) Glucose and fructose are functional isomers. Glucose has aldehyde group (—CHO) whereas fructose has ketone ($>C=O$) group at second carbon atom.

(ii) Due to presence of 1° alcoholic group, when glucose is oxidised with **nitric acid** it yield saccharic acid indicating the presence of a primary alcoholic group.

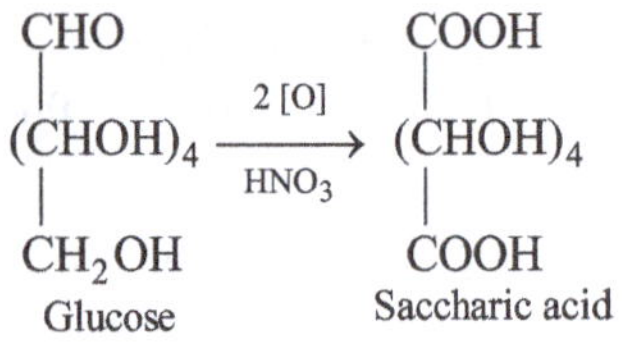

(iii) Glucose condenses with **hydroxylamine** to form oxime called **D-glucose oxime**.

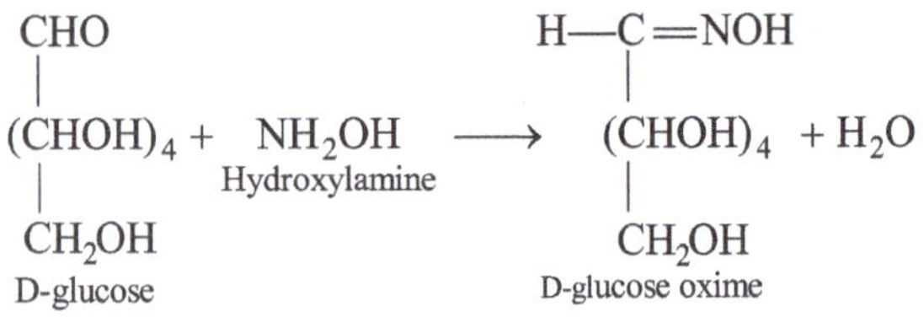

(iv) When heated with HI for a long time, it forms *n*-hexane which shows that all six carbon atoms are linked in a straight chain.

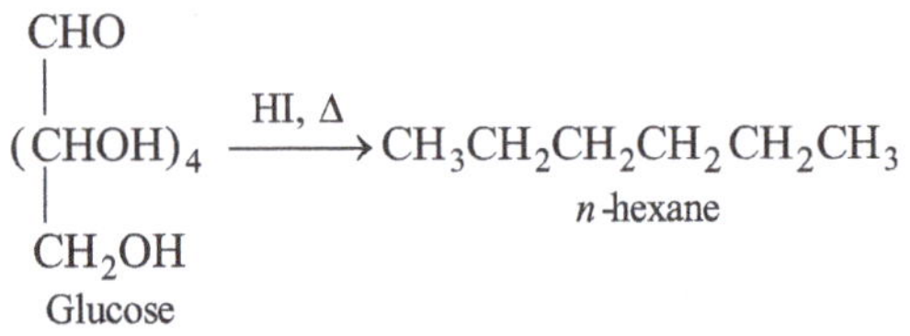

(v) Acetylation of glucose with **acetic anhydride** gives glucose pentaacetate which confirms the presence of five —OH groups.

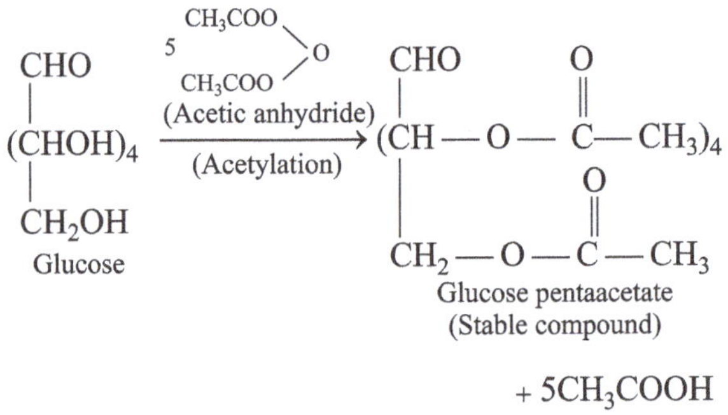

(vi) Both glucose and fructose react with **phenylhydrazine** to form osazone.

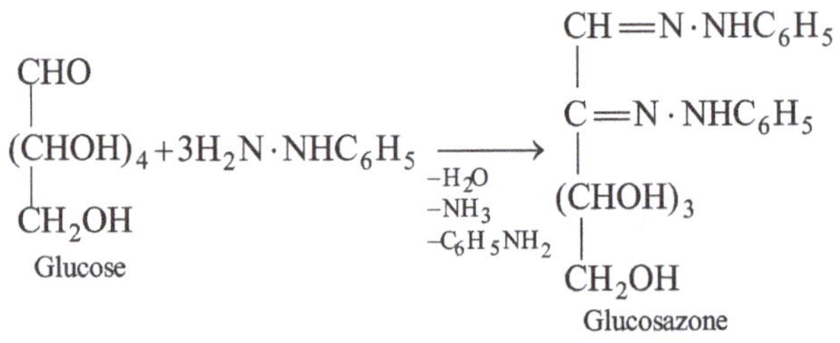

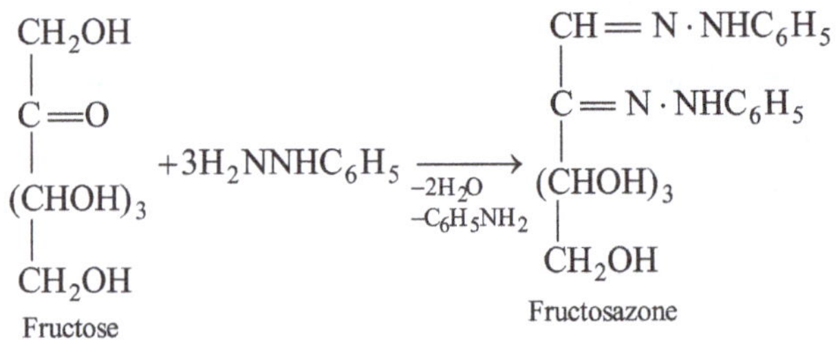

(vii) On reduction with $NaBH_4$ or $Na-Hg/H_2O$, fructose forms a mixture of sorbitol and mannitol.

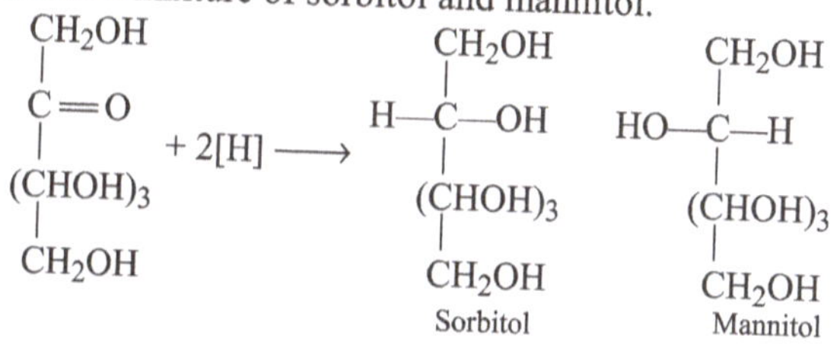

(viii) Fructose is not oxidised by mild oxidising agent like Br_2 water. However, it oxidises with nitric acid. The reaction is as follows

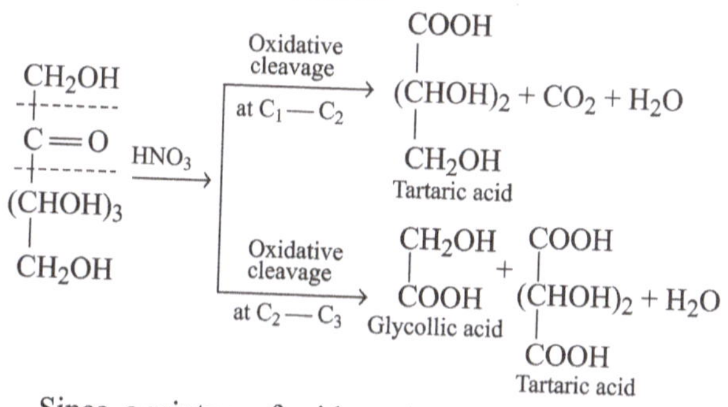

Since, a mixture of acids each containing fewer carbon atoms than fructose is obtained, the carbonyl group in fructose must be a ketonic group.

(ix) Unlike ketones, fructose can reduce Fehling's solution and Tollen's reagent.

Note Above properties number (ii), (iii), (iv), (v) and bromine water test gives structural evidence for open structure of glucose while properties number (vii), (viii), (ix) gives structural evidence for fructose open structure.

D and L-Notations

D and L before the name of any compound commonly indicates the relative configuration of a particular stereoisomer. e.g. Glyceraldehyde contains one asymmetric carbon atom and exists in two enantiomeric forms as given below.

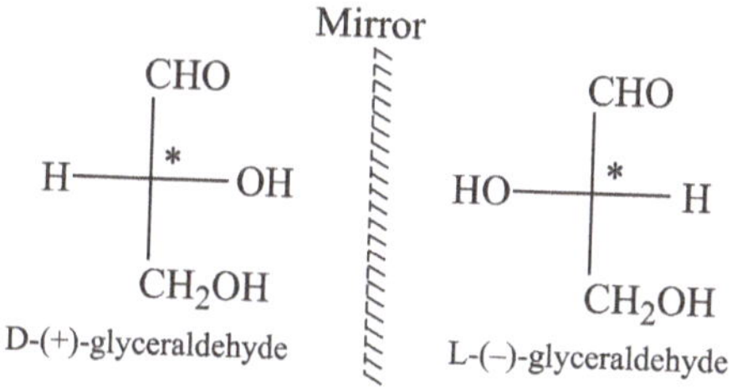

Compounds which can be chemically correlated to (+) -isomer of glyceraldehyde are said to have D-configuration whereas those which can be correlated to (–)-isomer of glyceraldehyde are said to have L-configuration.

Evidence Against Open Structure of Glucose

Glucose has assigned structure on basis of following evidences.

- Even though an aldehyde group is present the glucose does not react with $NaHCO_3$, NH_3, 2, 4-DNP and Grignard reagent.
- Does not response to Schiff's test.
- Glucose penta-acetate does not react with hydroxylamine.
- Glucose exist in two stereoisomerism forms, i.e. α and β.
- An aqueous solution of glucose show **mutarotation**.

Cyclic Structure of Glucose

It was found that glucose forms a six membered ring in which —OH at C-5 is involved in the ring formation. This explains the absence of —CHO group and existence of glucose in two forms as shown.

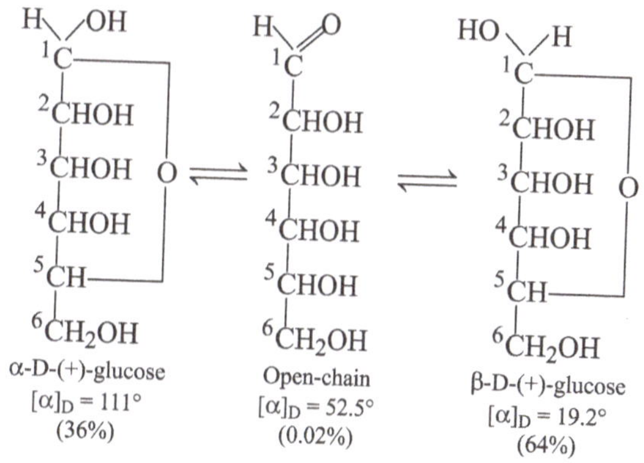

The cyclic structure of glucose is more correctly represented by the structure as given below.

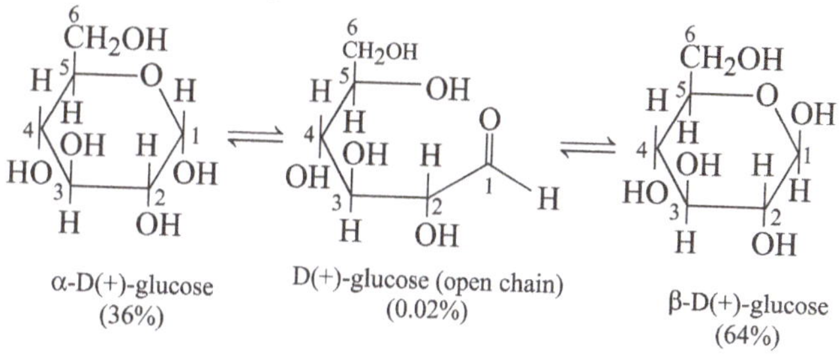

Cyclic Structure of Fructose

Fructose also has a cyclic structure in aqueous solution, i.e. intramolecular hemiketal. It also exhibit **mutarotation**.

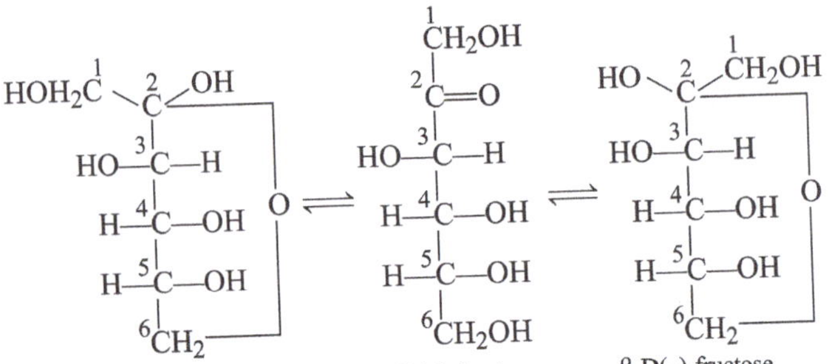

α-D(–)-fructose $[\alpha]_D = -21°$ α-D(–)-fructose $[\alpha]_D = -92°$ β-D(–)-fructose $[\alpha]_D = -133°$

The cyclic structure of two anomers of fructose are more correctly represented as given below.

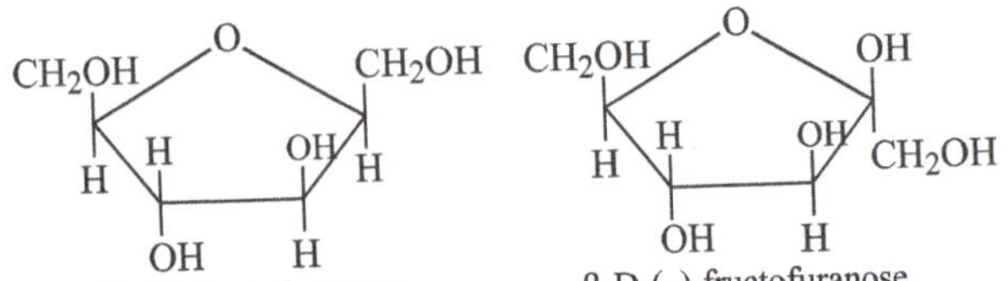

α-D-(–)-fructofuranose β-D-(–)-fructofuranose

Disaccharides

Disaccharides on hydrolysis with dilute acids or enzymes gives two molecules of monosaccharides. These molecules may be either same or different monosaccharides.

The linkage between two monosaccharide units through an oxygen atom is called **glycosidic linkage**. Some important disaccharides are

Sucrose

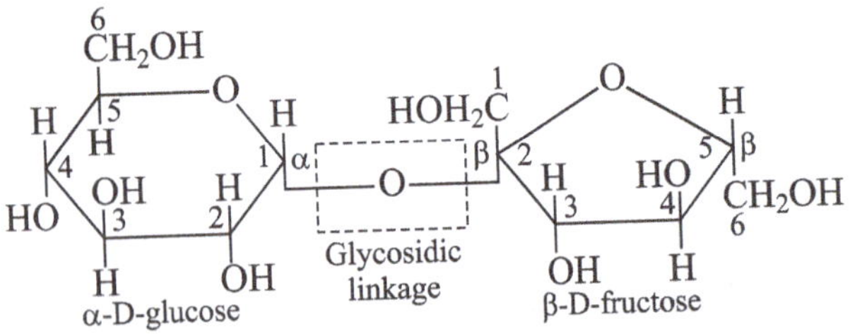

α-D-glucose β-D-fructose

Haworth structure of sucrose

Maltose

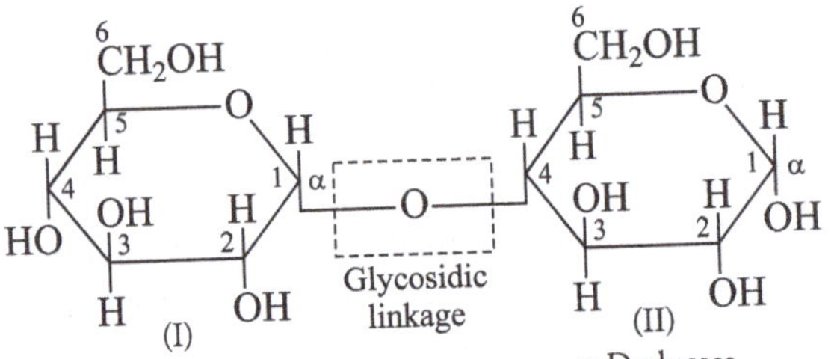

(I) α-D-glucose (II) α-D-glucose

Haworth structure of maltose

Lactose

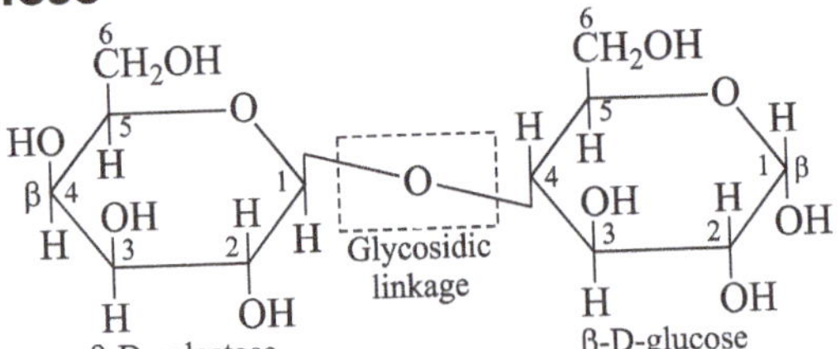

β-D-galactose β-D-glucose

Haworth structure of lactose

Polysaccharides

These are formed when large number of monosaccharide units joined together by glycosidic linkages. Some important polysaccharides are

Starch

It is an important storage polysaccharide of plants and the most important dietary source of carbohydrate for human beings. It is a polymer of α-glucose and consists of two components, i.e. **amylose** and **amylopectin.** Amylose is soluble in water and constitutes 15-20% of starch. While amylopectin is insoluble in water and constitutes about 80-85% of starch.

Cellulose

It is a straight chain polysaccharide composed only of β-D-glucose units that are linked together by glycosidic linkage between C-1 of one glucose unit and C-4 of the next glucose unit.

Glycogen

It is known to be the storage material of animals. Its structure is similar to amylopectin and is highly branched that is why it is also known as animal starch. It is found in liver, muscles and brain. When body requires energy, it breaks down to glucose by the action of enzymes.

Importance of Carbohydrates

These are very important and essential for life in both plants and animals. Few important roles of carbohydrates are listed below

- They form a major portion of our food.
- They are used as storage materials like starch in plants and glycogen in animals.
- Cellulose in the form of wood is used to build furniture and clothes in the form of cotton fibres.
- They provide raw materials for many industries like textiles, papers and lacquers.
- They act as a biofuels to provide energy for the functioning of living organisms.

PYQs Previous Years' Questions

1 Mark Questions

1. Write the chemical equation for the reaction of glucose with bromine water. *ISC 2020*

2. Fill in the blanks.
   Sucrose is a .... and yields upon hydrolysis, a mixture of .... and fructose. *ISC 2017*

3. What do you observe when glucose solution is heated with Tollen's reagent? *ISC 2016*

4. Which of the following is an example of disaccharide?
   (a) Glucose (b) Fructose
   (c) Sucrose (d) Cellulose *ISC 2015*

5. (i) What type of isomers glucose and fructose are?
   (ii) Name the functional group common to both glucose and fructose. *ISC 2012*

6. Correct the following statement.
   Oxidation of sucrose with concentrated nitric acid yields glycerol. *ISC 2006*

7. Give a test to distinguish between starch and cellulose. *ISC 2006*

8. Glucose on treatment with NH_2OH undergoes
   (a) condensation (b) reduction
   (c) hydrolysis (d) oxidation *ISC 2004*

> **KEY IDEA**
> $>C{=}O + H_2N{-}OH \longrightarrow\ >C{=}N{-}OH$

9. How will you convert glucose to gluconic acid? *ISC 2003*

10. The pair of sugars which give the same product with excess of phenylhydrazine are *ISC 2002*
    (a) starch and cellulose (b) cellulose and sucrose
    (c) sucrose and glucose (d) glucose and fructose

11. Classify the following into monosaccharides and disaccharides.
    Ribose, 2-deoxyribose, Maltose, Galactose, Fructose and Lactose.

12. Which one of the following is a disaccharide?
    Starch, Maltose, Fructose and Glucose

13. Which one of the following is a polysaccharide?
    Starch, Maltose, Fructose and Glucose

14. Name the two components of starch.

15. Which of the two components of starch is water soluble?

16. Which component of starch is a branched polymer of α-glucose and insoluble in water?

17. Write the two main functions of carbohydrate in plants.

2 Marks Questions

18. How will you distinguish between glucose and sucrose?

> **KEY IDEA**
> Tollen's reagent reacts with only aldehyde groups.

19. Write relevant equation to convert fructose to osazone.

20. How will you convert glucose to osazone?

21. Give one test to distinguish between glucose and fructose with relevant equation.

22. Carbohydrates are essential for life in both plants and animals.
    Name the carbohydrates that are used as storage molecules in plants and animals. Also, name the carbohydrate which is present in wood or in the fibre of cotton cloth.

3 Marks Questions

23. How will you convert glucose to saccharic acid? *ISC 2009*

24. What is glycogen? How is it different from starch?

5 Marks Question

25. How will you chemically convert glucose to fructose? *ISC 2001*

> **KEY IDEA**
> Conversion of glucose into fructose can be carried in three steps.
> (i) Heating glucose with excess of phenylhydrazine to give glucosazone.
> (ii) Glucosazone on hydrolysis with hydrochloric acid yields glucosazone and phenylhydrazine.
> (iii) Glucosazone when reduced with zinc dust and acetic acid changes into fructose.

Explanations

1. Refer to text on page 232 (Oxidation).
2. disaccharide, glucose
3. When glucose solution is heated with Tollen's reagent, silver mirror on the inner surface of the reaction vessel is observed.

Concept Enhancer Tollen's reagent is an alkaline solution of ammoniacal silver nitrate and is used to test for aldehydes.

4. (c) Sucrose, as it gives glucose and fructose upon hydrolysis.
5. (i) Glucose and fructose are functional isomers.
   (ii) Alcoholic (—OH) group is common in both, glucose and fructose.

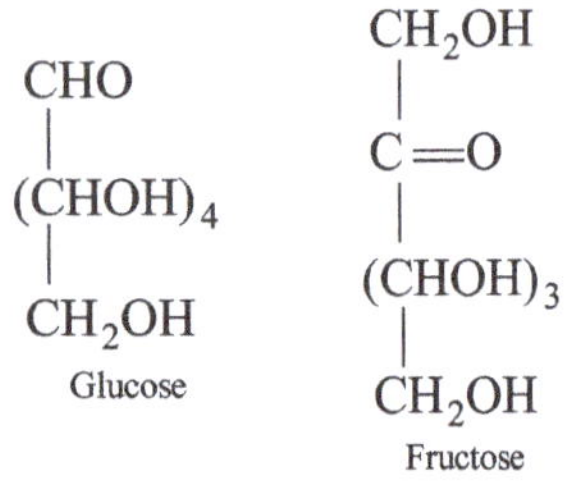

6. Oxidation of sucrose with concentrated nitric acid yields oxalic acid.

$$\underset{\text{Sucrose}}{C_{12}H_{22}O_{11}} + 9O_2 \xrightarrow{\text{Conc.}HNO_3} \underset{\text{Oxalic acid}}{6\,(COOH)_2} + 5H_2O$$

7. To distinguish between starch and cellulose, iodine test is done starch converts yellow coloured iodine to blue black whereas cellulose does not.
8. (a) Condensation.

Glucose condenses with hydroxylamine to form an oxime called D-glucose oxime.

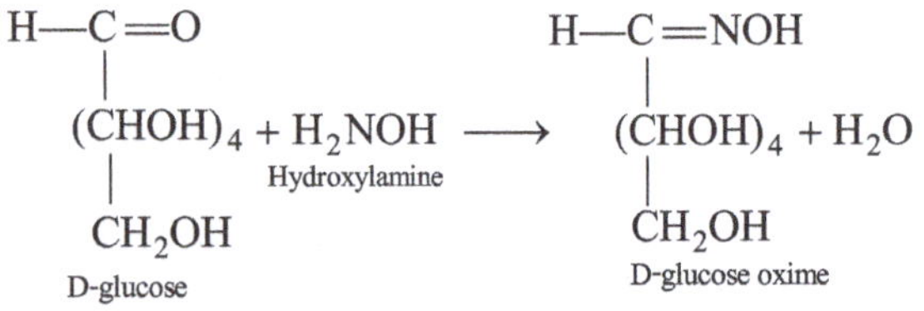

Hence, option (a) is correct.

9. Glucose with bromine water form gluconic acid.

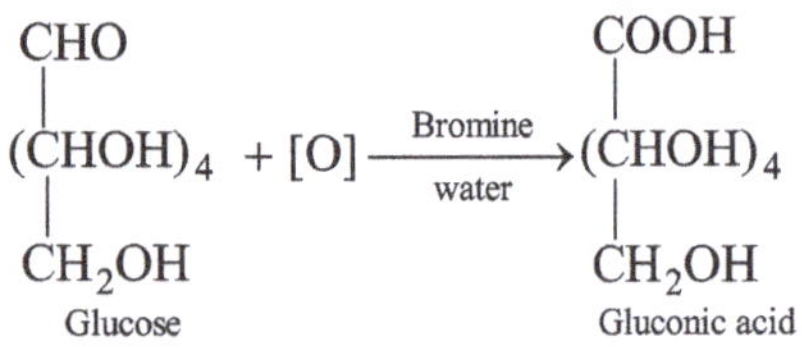

10. (d) Glucose and fructose both form same product (osazone) with excess of phenylhydrazine.

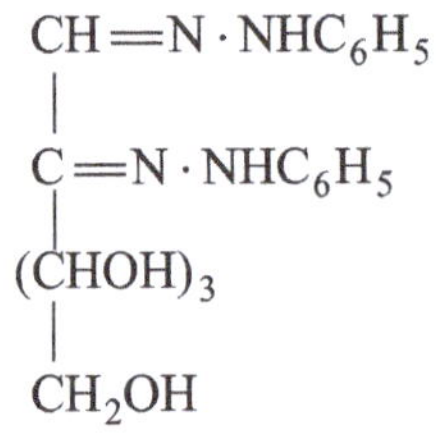

Hence, option (d) is correct.

Concept Enhancer Galactose and maltose which are epimers of glucose also give osazone.

11. **Monosaccharides** Ribose, 2-deoxyribose, galactose, and fructose.

    Disaccharides Maltose and lactose.

12. Maltose is a disaccharide. It is composed of two α-D-glucose molecules.
13. Starch is a polysaccharide. It gives the large number α-D-glucose molecules on hydrolysis.
14. Starch is composed of amylose and amylopectin.
15. Starch consists of amylose and amylopectin. Among them amylose is a water soluble component of starch.
16. Amylopectin is a branched polymer of α-glucose and insoluble in water.
17. (i) Carbohydrates are used as storage molecules like starch in plants.
    (ii) Cell wall of bacteria and plants is made up of cellulose.
18. With Tollen's reagent glucose give silver mirror test whereas sucrose does not.
19. 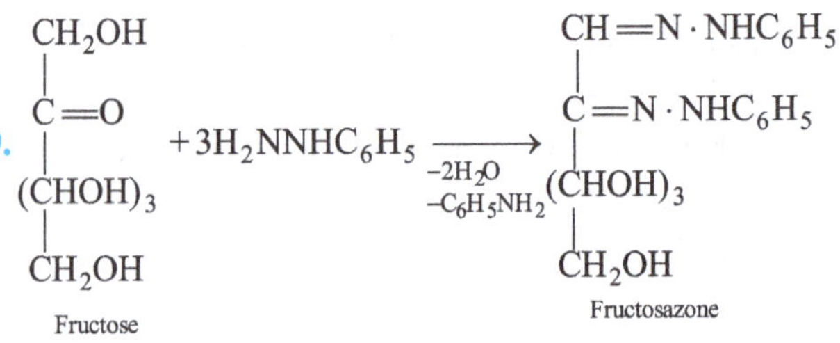

20. 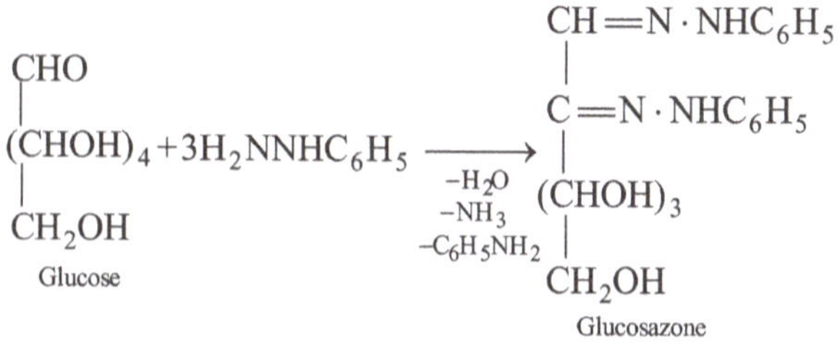

21. Glucose decolourises red colour of bromine water due to —CHO group whereas fructose does not.

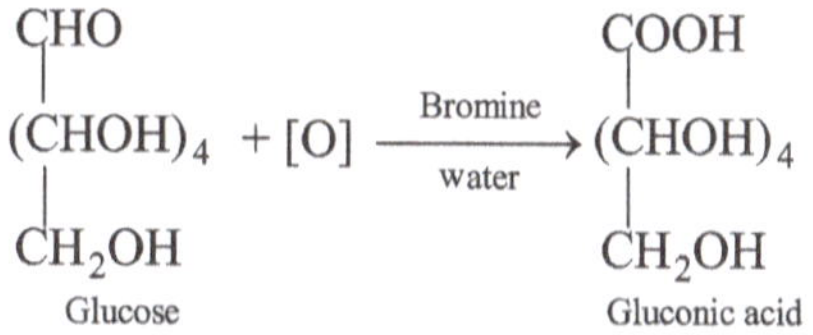

22. In plants, carbohydrates are stored in the form of starch while in animals, these are stored in the form of glycogen.

Cellulose, a carbohydrate is present in wood or in the fibre of cotton cloth.

23. When glucose is oxidised with nitric acid, glucose yield a dicarboxylic acid known as saccharic acid.

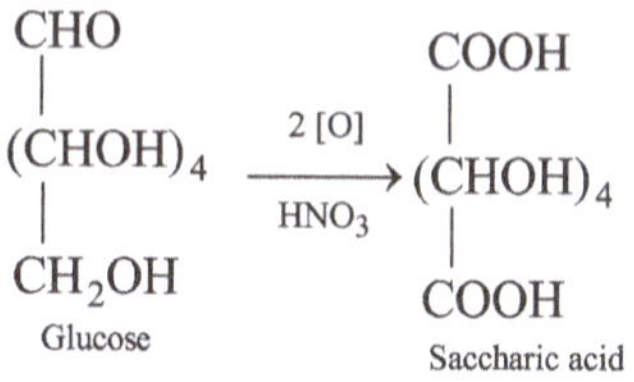

24. Glycogen is a highly chain condensation polymer of α-D-glucose. It is stored in the form of glucose in liver and muscles of human beings. **(1)**

In contrast, starch is a chief storage polysaccharide of plants and consists of a mixture of two components, amylose (water soluble component 15-20%) and amylopectin (water insoluble component 80-85%).

Amylose is a linear polymer of α-D-glucose, while amylopectin is a highly branched polymers of α-D-glucose.

Thus, both glycogen and amylopectin are branched chain condensation polymer of α-D-glucose.

The only difference is that amylopectin chain consists of 20-25 glucose units whereas glycogen chain consists of 10-14 glucose units.

25. The reaction that convert glucose into fructose is

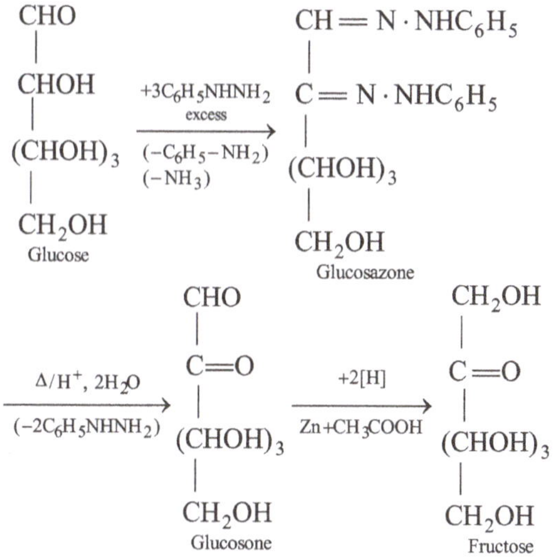

(4)

TOPIC 2

Proteins and Enzymes

Proteins are highly complex nitrogenous organic compounds of very high molecular masses.

Amino Acids

Amino acids are the basic building units of proteins. Their molecules contain amino ($-NH_2$) and carboxylic ($-COOH$) group.

Structure and Classification

The α-amino acids (contain α-carbon atoms) are asymmetric and exist in two stereoisomeric form D and L. On the basis of relative number of amino and carboxyl group in their molecule. They are of three types, i.e. neutral, acidic and basic.

Zwitter Ion

In neutral aqueous solution, the amino acid forms a dipolar ion structure called Zwitter ion structure.

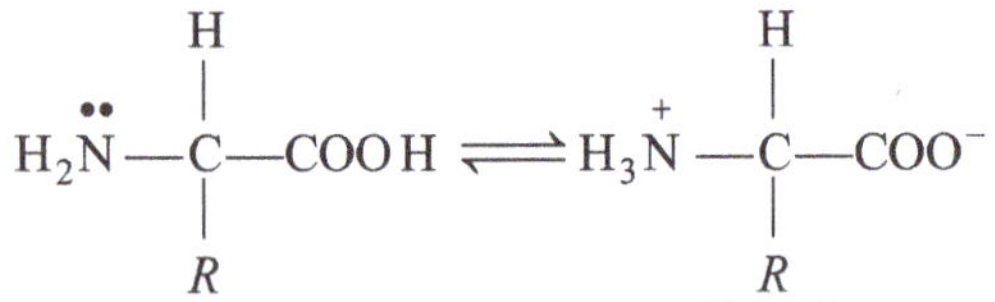

Amino acid   Zwitter ion

[If R = H then glycine, if $R = CH_3$ then alanine, etc.]

Isoelectric Point

The point (pH range) at which the amino acid molecule has equal positive and negative charges is called the isoelectric piont. At this point, the amino acids do not migrate in an electric field.

Peptide Bond

When two α-amino acids combine, $-COOH$ group of one amino acid condense with $-NH_2$ group of second amino acid with elimination of water molecule, forming $-\overset{O}{\overset{\|}{C}}-NH-$ bond or peptide linkage. These form proteins which are condensed polymer of amino acids.

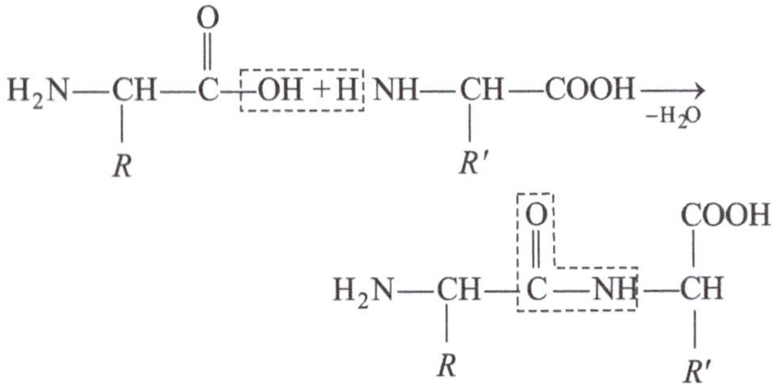

Dipeptide

Classification of Proteins

On the basis of molecular structure.

(i) **Fibrous proteins** Linear thread like molecules tend to lie side by side to form fibres. The polypeptides chain are held at many points by H— bonds, e.g. keratin in skin and hair.

(ii) **Globular proteins** Polypeptide chains is folded into compact units to give a spheroidal shape, e.g. haemoglobin, insulin, albumin etc.

Structure of Proteins

(i) **Primary structure** The specific sequence in which various amino acids are linked to one another by peptide linkage to form a peptide is called its primary structure.

(ii) **Secondary structure** Refers to the arrangement of polypeptide chains that arises as a result of H-bonding.

They are of two types

(a) α-helix   (b) β-pleated sheet

(iii) **Tertiary structure** The further folding of the secondary structure of proteins is known as tertiary structure. It gives rise to two major molecular shapes, fibrous and globular.

(iv) **Quaternary structure** Although many proteins exist as a single polypeptide chain, but some of the proteins are composed of two or more polypeptide chains called **subunits**.

The spatial arrangement of these subunits with respect to each other is known as quaternary structure.

Denaturation of Proteins

A change in physical and biological properties of a protein without affecting its chemical composition is called denaturation of protein. It is due to temperature and pH change.

Enzymes

They are the **biocatalysts** which are needed to catalyse biochemical reactions. These are very specific for a particular reaction and for a particular substrate. These are needed only in small quantities for the progress of a reaction. They are said to reduce the magnitude of activation energy.

PYQs Previous Years' Questions

1 Mark Questions

1. Write the Zwitter ion structure of glycine. ***ISC 2020***
2. Proteins are made up of ……… units held together by ……… linkages. ***ISC 2004***
3. Proteins are ……… polymers of ……… ***ISC 2001***
4. Correct the following statement.

   Glycine exists as a Zwitter ion at any pH. ***ISC 2000***

2 Marks Questions

5. What is peptide bond? Illustrate its formation with an example. ***ISC 2021-22 (Sem-II)***
6. What is a Zwitter ion? Represent the Zwitter ion of glycine. ***ISC Specimen 2021-22 (Sem-II)***
7. Explain the amphoteric behaviour of amino acids. ***ISC Specimen 2018***

> **KEY IDEA**
> Amphoteric compounds react with both acids and bases.

8. Write two differences between globular and fibrous proteins. ***ISC 2017***
9. Give one example of fibrous protein. Name the final product of hydrolysis of proteins. What is denaturation of proteins? ***ISC 2010, 2000***
10. Answer the following questions.
    (i) Give one example of an α-amino acid.
    (ii) Write the structure of the dipeptide using this example. ***ISC 2000***

Explanations

1. Refer to text on page 238 (Zwitter ion).
2. α-amino acid, peptide linkages
3. condensed, amino acid
4. Glycine exists as a Zwitter ion at a particular pH known as isoelectric point.

> **Concept Enhancer** The pH at which concentration of cation and anion form of glycine becomes equal is called isoelectric point. The glycine will exist as Zwitter ion at this pH.

5. A peptide bond is a chemical bond that is formed by joining the carbonyl group of one amino acid to the amino group of other.

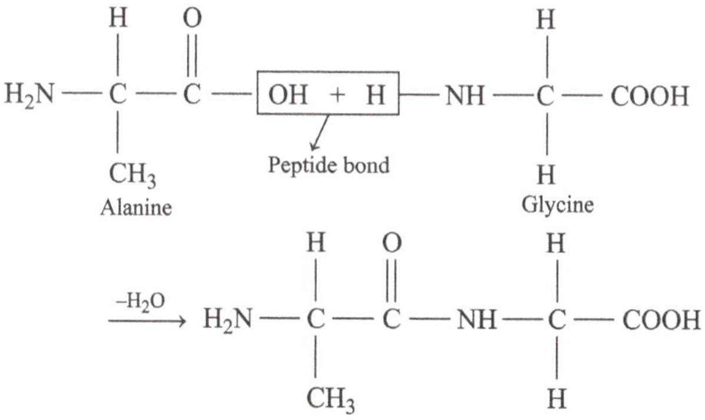

6. The Zwitter ion is a molecule that equal number of positive and negative charged function group.

Structure of glycine

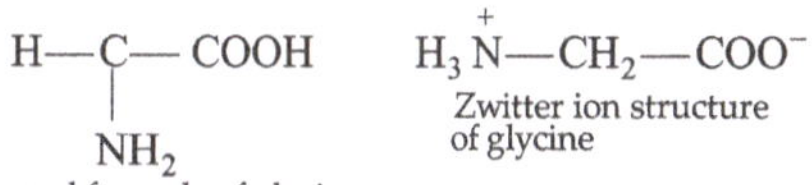
General formula of glycine

Zwitter ion structure of glycine

7. Amino acids contain both an acidic carboxyl group and a basic amino group.

In aqueous solution, they neutralise each other involving transfer of a proton from the carboxylic group to the amino group, giving rise to a dipolar ion known as 'Zwitter ion'. It is neutral but contains both positive and negative charges.

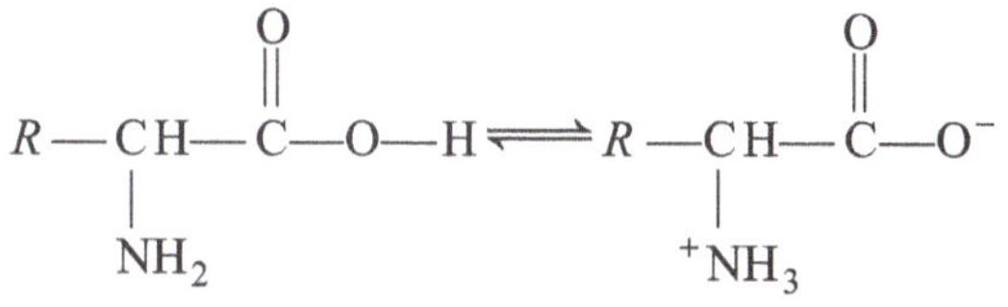

In Zwitter ionic form, amino acids shows amphoteric behaviour as they can react with both acids and bases.

8. (i) **Fibrous proteins** They have thread or fibre like structures in which polypeptide chains run parallel. These proteins are insoluble in water, e.g. keratin (found in hair, skin, nails, wool, silk) and myosin (present in muscles). **(1)**

(ii) **Globular proteins** They have spherical shape in which chains of polypeptides coil around. These are soluble in water, e.g. insulin and albumins. **(1)**

9. Keratin is a fibrous protein. The final product of hydrolysis of a protein is a mixture of amino acids. Change in physical and biological properties of a protein without affecting its chemical composition is called **denaturation of proteins**.

It may be caused by heating, reaction with alcohol, acid radiation etc. It changes only secondary and tertiary structures of proteins.

10. (i) Alanine, $H_2N—CH(CH_3)—COOH$ **(½)**

(ii) When two α-amino acids combine, a dipeptide is formed with the loss of a water molecule.

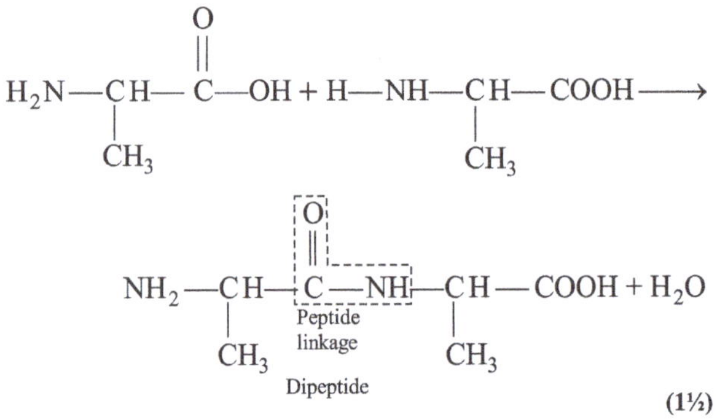

(1½)

TOPIC 3

Vitamins, Nucleic Acids and Hormones

Vitamins

Vitamins are the organic compounds required in small amounts in our diet but their deficiency causes specific diseases.

Classification of Vitamins

Depending upon their solubility in water or fat.

(i) **Fat soluble vitamins** These are vitamins A,D,E and K. These are stored in liver and adipose (fat storing) tissues.

(ii) **Water soluble vitamins** B group vitamins and vitamin C are soluble in water.

Water soluble vitamins must be supplied regularly in diet because they are readily excreted in urine and cannot be stored (except vitamin B_{12}) in our body.

Some important vitamins, their sources and their deficiency diseases

Name of vitamins	**Sources**	**Deficiency diseases**
Vitamin A (Retinol)	Fish, cod liver oil, carrots, butter and milk	Xerophthalmia (hardening of cornea of eye), Night blindness
Vitamin B_1 (Thiamine)	Yeast, milk, green vegetables and cereals	Beri-beri (loss of appetite, retarded growth)
Vitamin B_2 (Riboflavin)	Milk, egg yolk, liver, kidney	Cheilosis (fissuring at corners of mouth and lips), digestive disorders and burning sensation of the skin.
Vitamin B_6 (Pyridoxine)	Yeast, milk, egg yolk, cereals and rice bran	Convulsions, microcytic anaemia
Vitamin B_{12}	Meat, fish, egg and curd	Pernicious anaemia (RBC deficient in haemoglobin)
Vitamin C (Ascorbic acid)	Citrus fruits, amla and green leafy vegetables	Scurvy (bleeding of gums)
Vitamin D	Exposure to sunlight, fish and egg yolk	Rickets (bone deformities in children) and osteomalacia (soft bones and joint pain in adults)
Vitamin E	Vegetable oils, wheat, milk, sunflower oil etc.	Increased fragility of RBCs and muscular weakness
Vitamin K	Green leafy vegetables	Increased blood clotting time, haemorrhage

Nucleic Acids

Nucleic acids are biomolecules found in the nuclei of all living cells in the form of nucleoproteins (long chain polymers). The monomeric units of nucleic acids are called nucleotides.

Each nucleotide consists of three components.

1. A pentose sugar is D(−) ribose or 2-deoxy-D(−) ribose.
2. A heterocyclic base – These are of two types
   (i) **Purines** Adenine (A) and guanine (G).
   (ii) **Pyrimidines** Uracil (U), thymine (T) and cytosine (C).
3. **Phosphoric acid**

Nucleic acids are of two types deoxyribonucleic acid (DNA) and ribonucleic acid (RNA).

DNA consists adenine (A) and guanine (G) as purine bases and cytosine (C) and thymine (T) as pyrimidine bases.

While in RNA, purine bases are adenine (A) and guanine (G) and pyrimidine bases are cytosine (C) and uracil (U).

Structure of DNA

Structure of nucleic acid like DNA, can be studied at two levels; primary and secondary.

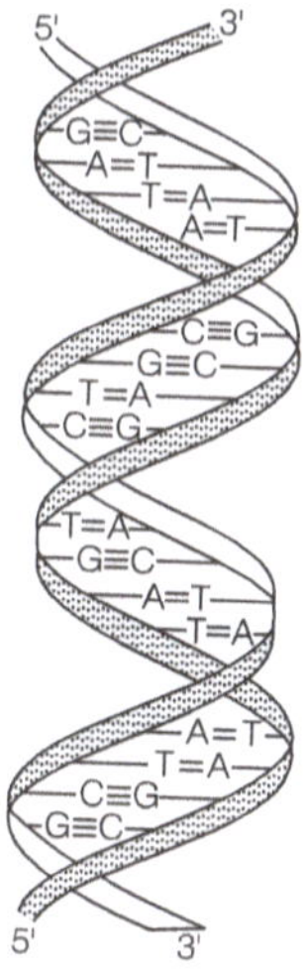

Primary Structure

A nucleoside phosphate linkage provides backbone structure to nucleic acids bearing purine and pyrimidine bases at regular intervals.

The manner in which the sugar, phosphate and nitrogen bases are linked with one another in the nucleic acids is known as **primary structure of nucleic acids**.

Secondary Structure

James Watson and **Francis Crick** proposed a double helical structure of DNA. According to this model, DNA consists of two separate polynucleotide strands leading in opposite directions (3′ or 5′).

The polynucleotide chains of the double helix are held together at definite intervals through hydrogen bonds.

The two strands are complementary, i.e. adenine of one strand is hydrogen bonded to thymine of the other (through two hydrogen bonds) whereas cytosine of one strand is hydrogen bonded with guanine of the other (through three hydrogen bonds).

i.e. A=T (↓ 2 hydrogen bonds) and C≡G (↓ 3 hydrogen bonds)

RNA

RNA consists of a single strand (as a secondary structure) but sometimes they fold back on themselves to form a double helix structure. RNA molecules are of three types namely, **messenger RNA** (*m*-RNA), **ribosomal RNA** (*r*-RNA) and **transfer RNA** (*t*-RNA), they perform different functions.

Hormones

These are molecules that act as intercellular messengers. These are produced by endocrine glands in the body and are poured directly in the blood steam which transports them to the site of action.

They help to maintain the balance of biological activities in the body.

Various types of hormones are steroids (estrogen and androgens), polypeptide (insulin and endorphins), amino acid derivative (epinephrine and norepinephrine).

PYQs Previous Years' Questions

1 Mark Questions

1. The deficiency of which vitamin will cause haemorrhage. **ISC 2014**
2. The deficiency of vitamin D causes **ISC 2013, 2001**
   (a) rickets (b) gout (c) scurvy (d) night blindness
3. The base present in both DNA and RNA are … and …. **ISC 2003**
4. Correct the following statement.
   The base not present in DNA is guanine. **ISC 2002**

2 Marks Questions

5. Name two water soluble vitamins and the diseases caused by their deficiency in the diet of an individual. **ISC 2019**
6. Name the purine bases and pyrimidine bases present in RNA and DNA. **ISC 2018**
7. Deficiency of what vitamins cause following disease.
   (i) Night blindness (ii) Scurvy **ISC 2017, 2014, 2011**

3 Marks Questions

8. (i) Aradhana visits a physician as she is suffering from rickets and joint pain. Which fat-soluble vitamin should the physician prescribe to her? **ISC 2024**
   (ii) Somesh put few drops of vinegar in milk. What change do you think he observed in the milk after some time? What is this phenomenon known as?
   (iii) Name the product of hydrolysis of sucrose. Is it a reducing sugar or a non-reducing sugar?
9. (i) What products are obtained when sucrose is subjected to acid hydrolysis? **ISC Specimen 2024**
   (ii) Why are vitamin B and vitamin C essential for us?
   (iii) On being heated, egg white becomes solid and opaque. Give a reason.
10. (i) Give an example each of reducing sugar and non-reducing sugar. **ISC 2023**
    (ii) What is denaturation of proteins?
    (iii) Give an example each of water soluble vitamin and fat soluble vitamin.

> **KEY IDEA**
> On heating, secondary and tertiary structures of protein are destroyed and hence protein is denatured.

11. (i) Name the four bases present in DNA. Which one of these is not present in RNA? **ISC Specimen 2023**
    (ii) Deficiency of which vitamin causes the following diseases.
    (a) Scurvy (b) Night blindness

Explanations

1. Deficiency of vitamin K causes haemorrhage.
   Vitamin K is obtained from leafy green vegetables.
2. (a) The deficiency of vitamin D causes rickets.
   Hence, option (a) is correct.

> **Concept Enhancer** Vitamin C causes scurvy, vitamin A causes night blindness and vitamin B_5 causes gout.

3. The base present in both DNA and RNA are **adenine** and **guanine**.
4. The base not present in DNA is uracil. In DNA thymine, instead of uracil, is found.
5. Vitamin-B and vitamin-C are water soluble and by the deficiency of vitamin-B and C in the diet beri-beri and scurvy diseases occurs, respectively.
6. Purine bases present in DNA and RNA are adenine (A) and guanine (G).
   Pyrimidine bases present in DNA are thymine (T) and cytosine (C). Uracil (U) and cytosine (C) are present only in RNA.
7. Deficiency of vitamin A causes night blindness and deficiency of vitamin C causes scurvy. Vitamin C is obtained from citrus fruits while the main sources of vitamin A are milk, fish, yellow ripe fruit and green vegetables.
8. (i) Vitamin D (fat soluble vitamin) should be prescribed to Aradhana by her physician.
   (ii) When Somesh put few drops of vinegar in milk, small white chunks or curds become visible in the mixture.
   This phenomenon is known as denaturation of protein.

(iii) • On hydrolysis with acids or enzyme, sucrose gives equimolar mixture of D-(+)-glucose and D-(–)-fructose.

• Sucrose is a non reducing sugar.

9. (i) The products obtained on hydrolysis of sucrose are two monosaccharides, glucose and fructose.

$$C_{12}H_{22}O_{11} + H_2O \xrightarrow{H^+} \underset{\text{(Glucose)}}{C_6H_{12}O_6} + \underset{\text{(Fructose)}}{C_6H_{12}O_6}$$

(ii) Vitamin B and vitamin C are essential for human health because they play important roles in many of our body functions.

Vitamin B is a group of water soluble vitamins that play a key role in energy metabolism, nervous system and the formation of red blood cells.

Vitamin C also acts as antioxidant and helps to protect the body against the damaging effects of free radicals.

(iii) As the egg gets hotter, the spliced proteins form a mesh with water filling in the spaces within the mesh.

As more protein molecules unfold and connect to each other, the mesh gets stronger and the egg becomes more solid.

10. (i) Glucose, fructose and ribose are reducing sugar. Sucrose and Raffinose are non-reducing sugar

(ii) **Denaturation of proteins** A change in physical and biological properties of a protein without affecting its chemical composition is called denaturation of protein. It may be affected by the action of heat, alcohol, acid, radiation etc.

Denaturation changes only the secondary and tertiary structures of protein, the primary structure remains unchanged. This process is irreversible in most cases. However, in some cases, it may be reversed and is termed as renaturation.

Coagulation of egg and curdling of milk are common example of denaturation of proteins.

(iii) Water soluble vitamin–vitamin C and B group vitamins. Fat soluble vitamins–These are vitamins A, D, E and K.

11. (i) The bases present used in DNA are adenine (A), cytosine (C), guanine (G) and thymine (*T*). In RNA, alongwith adenine (A), cytosine (C), guanine (G) and the base uracil (U) is presence in place of thymine.

(ii) (a) Scurvy is caused due to deficiency to vitamin C.

(b) Night blindness is caused due to deficiency of vitamin A.

CHAPTER TEST

01 Mark Questions

1. Fill in the blanks by choosing the appropriate word(s) from those given in the brackets.

[optically active, optically inactive, $C_x(H_2O)_y$, $C_x(HO)_y$ reducing, non-reducing, free, bind, α, β, protein, α-glucose, β- glucose, amylose]

(i) Carbohydrates are ……… polyhydroxy aldehyde or ketones having general formula ……… .

(ii) ……… sugars reduce Fehling solution because of ……… ketone or aldehyde part.

(iii) ……… are polymers of ……… amino acids.

(iv) Starch is a polymer of ……… and consists of two components ……… and amylopectin.

2. Select and write the correct alternatives from the choices given below.

(i) Which of the following disease is caused by the deficiency of vitamin D ?

(a) Beri-beri
(b) Rickets
(c) Haemorrhage
(d) Anaemia

(ii) Which of the following is not an example of monosaccharides?

(a) Glucose (b) Fructose
(c) Hexoses (d) Cellulose

(iii) Which of the following statement is not true about RNA?

(a) It controls the synthesis of protein.
(b) It has always double stranded α-helix structure.
(c) It usually does not replicate.
(d) It is present in the nucleus of the cell.

(iv) Which of the following is/are example(s) of denaturation of protein?

(a) Coagulation of egg white
(b) Clotting of blood
(c) Curdling of milk
(d) Both (a) and (c)

3. (i) **Assertion** (A) Vitamins B and C must be supplied regularly in the diet.

Reason (R) Vitamins B and C are soluble in water which are readily excreted through urine and cannot be stored (except vitamin B_{12}) in our body.

(a) Both (A) and (R) are correct and (R) is the correct explanation of (A).
(b) Both (A) and (R) are correct but (R) is not the correct explanation of (A).
(c) (A) is correct and (R) is incorrect.
(d) (A) is incorrect and (R) is correct.

(ii) **Assertion** (A) The two strands of DNA are complementary to each other.

Reason (R) Adenine forms hydrogen bonds with guanine and thymine forms hydrogen bonds with cytosine.

(a) Both (A) and (R) are correct and (R) is the correct explanation of (A).
(b) Both (A) and (R) are correct but (R) is not the correct explanation of (A).
(c) (A) is correct and (R) is incorrect.
(d) (A) is incorrect and (R) is correct.

02 Marks Questions

4. Answer the following questions.

(i) Write the functional differences between DNA and RNA.

(ii) Write the name of disease caused by the deficiency of vitamin B_{12}.

5. Explain the meaning of the following terms.

(i) Polypeptide
(ii) Proteins

6. (i) What are sugars and non-sugars?

(ii) Mention one main function of carbohydrates.

7. (i) Write one chemical test for the identification of glucose.

(ii) Which one of the following is a disaccharide ?
Starch, maltose, fructose, glucose

8. Answer the following questions.

(i) Write the defination of Zwitter ion.

(ii) How fructose is obtained from inulin ?

9. (i) What type of linkage is present in nucleic acid ?

(ii) Why vitamin C cannot be stored in our body ?

10. What happens when D-glucose is treated with the following reagents?

(i) Br_2 water (ii) HI

03 Marks Questions

11. Define the following terms.
(i) Oligosaccharides
(ii) Invert sugar
(iii) Polysaccharides

12. Answer the following.
(i) The two strands of DNA are complementary to each other.
(ii) Give one example each for fibrous protein and globular protein.
(iii) Name the base that is found in nucleotide of RNA only.

13. (i) Write the name of the vitamin responsible for the coagulation of blood.
(ii) Write the name of two monosaccharides obtained on hydrolysis of lactose sugar.
(iii) What is glycogen ?

14. (i) Differentiate between amylose and amylopectin.
(ii) Name the deficiency diseases resulting from lack of vitamins A and E in the diet.
(iii) Name the two components of starch.

15. (i) Classify the following into monosaccharides and disaccharides. Ribose, 2-deoxyribose, maltose, galactose, fructose and lactose.
(ii) What type of linkage is responsible for the formation of proteins ?
(iii) Why does nucleic acids are called polynucleotides ?

05 Marks Questions

16. (i) What is the essential difference between the α-form of glucose and β-form of glucose ? Explain.
(ii) Define the following as related to proteins.
(a) Denaturation
(b) Peptide bond
(c) Primary structure

17. (i) Answer the following questions.
(a) What is the difference between vitamins and hormones?
(b) What are enzymes ? Give examples.
(ii) (a) Write two main functions of carbohydrates in plants.
(b) Write the product formed when D-glucose is treated with conc. HNO_3.
(c) Which component of starch is a branched polymer of α-glucose and insoluble in water ?

18. (i) Define the following.
(a) Essential amino acids (b) Glycosidic linkage
(ii) What is the difference between a nucleoside and a nucleotide ?
(iii) What are the different types of RNA molecules which perform different functions ?
(iv) Why do amino acids show amphoteric behaviour?
(v) Write one difference between α-helix and β-pleated structures of proteins.

Answers

1. (i) optically active, $C_x(H_2O)_y$ (ii) reducing, free
(iii) proteins, α (iv) α-glucose, amylose

2. (i) (b), (ii) (d), (iii) (b), (iv) (d)

3. (i) (a), (ii) (c)

ISC Fully Solved

EXAMINATION PAPER 2025

Time : 3 hrs
Marks : 70

Chemistry

GENERAL INSTRUCTIONS

- This paper is divided into four sections A, B , C and D. Answer all questions.
- **Section A** has **fourteen subparts.** Each question carries 1 mark.
- While attempting **Multiple Choice Questions** in Section A, you are required to **write only ONE option as the answer.**
- **Section B** has **ten questions.** Each question carries 2 marks.
- **Section C** has **seven questions.** Each question carries 3 marks.
- **Section D** has **three questions.** Each question carries 5 marks.
- Internal choices have been provided in **one question each in Section B, Section C & Section D.**
- All working, including rough work, should be done on the same sheet as, and adjacent to the rest of the answer.
- The intended marks for questions are given in brackets [].
- Balanced equations must be given wherever possible and diagrams where they are helpful.
- When solving numerical problems, all essential working must be shown.
- In working out problems, use the following data :
  Gas constant R = 1.987 cal deg^{-1} mol^{-1} = 8.314 J K^{-1} mol^{-1} = 0.0821 dm^3 atm K^{-1} mol^{-1} 1 L atm = 1 dm^3 atm = 101.3 J.
  1 Faraday = 96500 coulombs. **Avogadro's number** = 6.023 × 10^{23}.

Section-A [14 Marks]

1. (A) Fill in the blanks by choosing the appropriate word(s) from those given in the brackets: [4 × 1]

[+2, ethane, tetrahedral, square planar, zero, dry cell, nickel-cadmium cell, propane Wolff-Kishner, Stephen, completely filled, incompletely filled, paramagnetic, diamagnetic]

(i) .... is an example of a primary cell but ...... is an example of a secondary cell.

(ii) The complex compound [Ni(CO_4)] is .... in shape and nickel is in .... oxidation state in this complex compound.

(iii) When acetaldehyde is treated with hydrazine and KOH in a high boiling solvent glycol, ... is formed and the reaction is known as .... reduction.

(iv) The transition metal ions having .... *d*-orbitals are colourless and ....in nature.

(B) Select and write the correct alternative from the choices given below. [7×1]

(i) Which one of the following can produce the foul smelling compound methyl isocyanide in presence of alcoholic KOH?

(a) Chloroform and aniline

(b) Chloroform and methanol

(c) Chloroform and dimethyl amine

(d) Chloroform and methyl amine

(ii) The osmotic pressure of a solution:

(P) increases with an increase in number of moles of solute.

(Q) decreases with an increase in number of moles of solute.

(R) increases at a higher temperature.

(S) is dependent on the nature of solute.

Which one of the following is correct?

(a) Only (P) and (Q) are correct.

(b) Only (P) and (R) are correct.

(c) Only (P) and (S) are correct.

(d) Only (Q) and (S) are correct.

(iii) Which one of the following alcohols is the strongest acid?

(a) Phenol (b) Methanol

(c) Ethanol (d) *t*-butyl alcohol

(iv) Which one of the following does not form a silver mirror on heating with Tollen's reagent?

(a) Glucose (b) Fructose

(c) Sucrose (d) Lactose

(v) The coordination number and the oxidation state of the central metal '*D*' in the complex $[D\,(en)_2(H_2O)_2]Cl_3$ are respectively.

(a) 6 and 2 (b) 4 and 2

(c) 3 and 6 (d) 6 and 3

(vi) Given below are two statements marked Assertion and Reason. Read the two statements carefully and select the correct option.

Assertion (A) The process of halogenation of benzene takes place in the presence of anhydrous $FeCl_3$.

Reason (R) Anhydrous $FeCl_3$ prepares nucleophile to attack the benzene ring.

(a) Both Assertion and Reason are true and Reason is the correct explanation for Assertion.

(b) Both Assertion and Reason are true but Reason is not the correct explanation for Assertion.

(c) Assertion is true and Reason is false.

(d) Both Assertion and Reason are false.

(vii) Given below are two statements marked Assertion and Reason. Read the two statements carefully and select the correct option.

Assertion (A) The Zr-Hf pair of elements has the same value of atomic radii though Zr and Hf are placed in different periods in the periodic table.

Reason (R) The lanthanoid contraction prevents the expected increase in atomic radii of Hf.

(a) Both Assertion and Reason are true and Reason is the correct explanation for Assertion.

(b) Both Assertion and Reason are true, but Reason is not the correct explanation for Assertion.

(c) Assertion is true and Reason is false.

(d) Both Assertion and Reason are false.

(C) Read the passage carefully and answer the questions that follow. [3 × 1]

The rate of a reaction depends on the concentration of reactants. The rate law for a hypothetical reaction $aA + bB \longrightarrow cC + dD$ is rate $= k[A]^x[B]^y$ where x and y are calculated experimentally and known as order of reaction. In most cases, the mechanism of a reaction is not straight forward but broken down in simple elementary steps. These steps represent the progress of overall reaction at the molecular level.

(i) What will be the order of reaction if the unit of k is $mol^{-2}\,L^2\,s^{-1}$?

(ii) State any one difference between order of reaction and molecularity of reaction.

(iii) For the reaction $2A \longrightarrow B + C$, the rate law is rate $= k[A]^{3/2}$.

What is the order and molecularity of the reaction?

Section-B [20 Marks]

2. Calculate the number of coulombs required to electroplate 4.75 g of aluminium when electrode reaction is $Al^{3+} + 3e^- \rightarrow Al$.

(Given: Atomic weight of Al = 27 g mol^{-1}, 1 Faraday = 96,500 C)

3. An organic compound [*A*] has molecular formula $C_7H_6O_2$. When compound [*A*] is treated with $SOCl_2$, it yields compound [*B*]. On heating with NH_3, compound [*B*] forms compound [C]. Compound [*C*] forms compound [*D*] on reaction with Br_2 / KOH. Compound [*D*] responds to carbylamine test.

Identify compounds [*A*], [*B*], [*C*] and [*D*].

4. In the reaction $2NO + O_2 \longrightarrow 2NO_2$, the rate law is rate $= k[NO][O_2]^2$.

(i) How will the rate of reaction change if [NO] concentration is doubled and $[O_2]$ concentration is halved at the same time?

(ii) Write the order of reaction if [NO] concentration is in large excess.

5. When an organic compound [*A*] having molecular formula C_4H_9Br is treated with aqueous KOH, the rate of reaction depends on concentration of compound [A] only. But when compound [*B*], with the same molecular formula, reacts with aqueous KOH, the rate of reaction depends on the concentration of compound [*B*] as well as of KOH. Compound (*B*) is a structural isomer of compound [*A*].

Identify compounds [*A*] and [*B*].

6. Write a balanced chemical equation for each of the following:

(i) Ethyl cyanide is reduced with $LiAlH_4$.

(ii) Aniline is treated with bromine water.

7. While conducting an experiment on coordination compounds, Shirin observed a white precipitate when $AgNO_3$, solution was added to the aqueous solution of the complex $[Co(NH_3)_3(en)SO_4]Cl$.
How can the ionisation isomer of this complex be detected by a chemical test? Write the structure and the IUPAC name of the ionisation isomer.

8. (i) Arrange the following in the increasing order of their acidic strength:

CH_3CH_2OH, CF_3CH_2OH, CCl_3CH_2OH

(ii) Arrange the following in the increasing order of their boiling points:

CH_3CH_2OH, $\underset{\displaystyle CH_2OH}{\underset{|}{C}H_2OH}$, CH_3CH_2Cl

9. (i) Identify the compounds [*A*], [*B*], [*C*] and [*D*] in the following reaction:

$$CH_3COOH + PCl_5 \longrightarrow [A] \xrightarrow[\text{Pd/BaSO}_4\text{, Boiling xylene}]{H_2} [B] \xrightarrow[\text{[O]}]{K_2Cr_2O_7 + H_2SO_4} [C] \xrightarrow{Ca(OH)_2,\ \text{heat}} [D]$$

Or

(ii) Write chemical equations to convert the following:

(a) Benzaldehyde to benzene

(b) Benzoic acid to benzaldehyde

10. Calculate the E°_{cell} of the following if the cell potential (E_{cell}) is 0.59 V.
(Given: Ni / Ni^{2+}(0.1 M) || Cu^{2+}(0.01 M / Cu)

11. Write the chemical test to distinguish between each of the following pairs of compounds.

(i) Ethanol and propan-1-al

(ii) Phenol and benzoic acid

Section-C [21 Marks]

12. Identify the compounds [*A*], [*B*] and [*C*] in each of the following reactions:

(i) $C_2H_5Br \xrightarrow{KCN} [A] \xrightarrow[\text{[4H]}]{LiAlH_4} [B] \xrightarrow[0^\circ\text{–}5^\circ C]{HNO_2} [C]$

(ii) $C_2H_5CONH_2 \xrightarrow{Br_2/KOH} [A] \xrightarrow{CHCl_3 + KOH} [B] \xrightarrow{Na/C_2H_5OH} [C]$

13. The scientist van't Hoff introduced a factor (*i*) to account for the extent of association or dissociation of solutes. It is mathematically expressed as:

$$i = \frac{\text{normal molecular mass}}{\text{experimental molecular mass}}$$

In case of association, $i < 1$ and in case of dissociation $i > 1$.

(i) In the calculation of molecular mass of $K_4[Fe(CN)_6]$ by using a colligative property, what will be the value of van't Hoff factor if the solute is 25% dissociated?

(ii) Find the value of van't Hoff factor for a dilute aqueous solution of benzoic acid in water when it is completely associated to form a dimer.

14. Write chemical equations to illustrate the following name reactions.

(i) Finkelstein reaction (ii) Williamson's synthesis

(iii) Reimer-Tiemann reaction

15. According to Crystal-Field Theory, the electronic configuration of complex compound [*A*] is $t_{2g}^4 e_g^2$ and that of complex compound [*B*] is $t_{2g}^6 e_g^0$.

(i) Which of the two complex compounds, [*A*] or [*B*], is a low spin complex?

(ii) Write the number of unpaired electrons in complex compounds [*A*] and [*B*].

(iii) Does complex [*A*] have strong field ligands or weak field ligands? Give a reason.

16. (i) Answer the following questions.

(a) By referring to electrochemical series, how can anode and cathode half cells be identified in a galvanic cell?

(b) What is the role of salt bridge in a galvanic cell?

(c) Write an advantage and a disadvantage of a fuel cell.

Or

(ii) Answer the following questions.

(a) Specific conductance of a solution decreases upon dilution. Why?

(b) The emf of a cell should be positive for a spontaneous reaction. Give a reason.

(c) Name the type of cell in which reaction occurs only in one direction and cannot be reversed by an external energy source. Write any one disadvantage of this type of cell.

17. (i) The structure of amino acid exists in the following two forms:

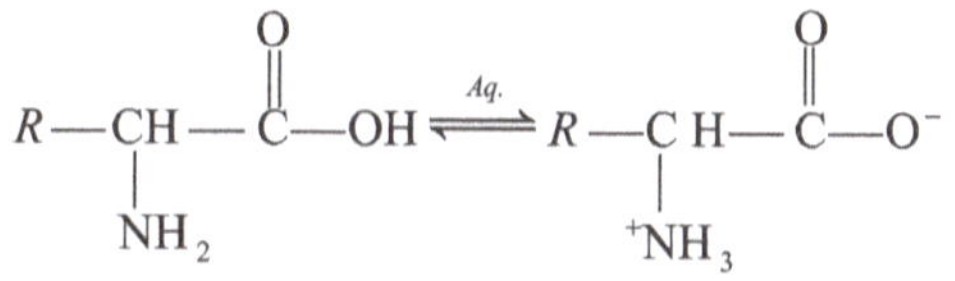

The above structure is an example of .... If the side chain R is replaced by hydrogen, the amino acid is known as ....

(ii) Janice notices that her gums bleed while brushing and eating food. Name the water soluble vitamin which she should consume to prevent bleeding of gums.

(iii) Which linkage holds two units of monosaccharides in a disaccharide?

18. The data given below is for the reaction between [NO] and [Cl_2] to form NOCl at 25°C.

S.No.	Conc. of [NO] mol L^{-1}	Conc. of [Cl_2] mol L^{-1}	Rate : mol L^{-1} sec^{-1}
1.	2.0	2.0	2.0×10^{-3}
2.	2.0	6.0	6.0×10^{-3}
3.	6.0	2.0	1.8×10^{-2}

Answer the following questions.

(i) What is the order of reaction with regard to NO and Cl_2?

(ii) Calculate the overall order of the reaction.

(iii) Find the value of rate constant (k).

Section-D [15 Marks]

19. Phenol is an aromatic alcohol that is used to prepare many important compounds such as picric acid. Phenol is widely used in household and industrial settings as a cleaner and disinfectant. It is also used as a primary chemical to make plastics. Phenol is less soluble in water as compared to aliphatic alcohol. Some aliphatic alcohols are toxic and can be addictive.

(i) How is the acid mentioned above prepared from phenol? Write the chemical reaction involved in this preparation.

(ii) 'Phenol is less soluble in water as compared to aliphatic alcohol'. Explain.

(iii) Write the chemical equation for the preparation of phenol from chlorobenzene.

(iv) An organic compound [A] having molecular formula $C_4H_{10}O$ gives positive Lucas test within five minutes at room temperature. Compound [A] upon oxidation with $K_2Cr_2O_7$ / H_2SO_4 forms compound [B] which does not respond to Tollen's test.

Identify compounds [A] and [B].

(v) In the above reaction, compound [B] gets reduced with Zn/Hg and HCl and forms compound [C]. Identify compound [C] and write the balanced reaction for the conversion of compound [B] to compound (C).

20. (i) Give a reason for each of the following:

(a) Ti^{3+} salts are coloured whereas Ti^{4+} salts are colourless.

[Given: Atomic number of Ti = 22]

(b) Transition elements form alloys.

(c) The pink coloured $KMnO_4$ solution turns colourless when reacted with Mohr's salt (Fe^{2+}) in acidic medium.

(ii) Complete and balance the following reactions:

(a) $KMnO_4 + H_2SO_4 + H_2C_2O_4 \longrightarrow$ ...... + ... + ... + ...

(b) $K_2Cr_2O_7 + H_2SO_4 + H_2S \longrightarrow$ ...... + ... + ... + ...

21. (i) Osmotic pressure is the external pressure which should be applied to stop the flow of solvent into the solution when the two are separated by a semipermeable membrane. The osmotic pressure is a colligative property. Two solutions having the same osmotic pressure are called isotonic.

If there are two solutions and one of them is of lower osmotic pressure, it is called hypotonic while the other is called hypertonic.

Answer the questions given below.

(a) What will happen if red blood corpuscles are placed in a 5% NaCl solution, which is a hypertonic solution?

(b) Show that osmotic pressure (π) is a colligative property.

(c) Calculate the amount of pressure required to stop osmosis of a solution, when 40 g of Na_2SO_4 is added to 1 L of water at 298 K.

(Given: Na = 23, O = 16, S = 32 and $R = 0.821$ L atm K^{-1} mol^{-1})

(d) Briefly discuss the process of reverse osmosis followed to desalinate sea water and convert it into drinking water.

Or

(ii) (a) An aqueous solution is made by dissolving 10 g of glucose ($C_6H_{12}O_6$) in 90 g of water at 300 K. If the vapour pressure of pure water at 300K is 32.8 mm Hg, what would be the vapour pressure of the solution?

(Given: C = 12, H = 1, and O = 16)

(b) A solution containing 12.5 g of a non-electrolyte solute in 175 g of water gave boiling point of 100.70°C. Calculate the molecular mass of the solute.

(Given: K_b for water = 0.52 K kg mol^{-1})

(c) Why are soda water bottles sealed under high pressure?

Solutions

1. (A) (i) Dry cell, nickel-cadmium cell

(ii) Tetrahedral, zero

(iii) Ethane, Wolff-kishner

(iv) Completely filled, diamagnetic

(B) (i) (d) Primary amines on heating with chloroform and alcoholic KOH form isocyanides or carbylamines which have foul smell.

$$\underset{\text{Amine}}{R\text{—}NH_2} + \underset{\text{Chloroform}}{CHCl_3} + 3KOH \xrightarrow{\Delta} \underset{\text{Alkyl or aryl isocyanide}}{R\text{—}NC} + 3KCl + 3H_2O$$

(ii) (b) Osmotic pressure of a solution increases with an increase in number of moles of solute and according to the Charles van't Hoff law it is directly proportional to the temperature, therefore, it increases at a higher temperature.

(iii) (a) Phenol is the strongest acid among the listed alcohols because, after losing a proton, the negative charge on the phenoxide ion is stabilised through resonance with the benzene ring.

(iv) (c) Sucrose does not form a silver mirror on heating with Tollen's reagent because sucrose is a non-reducing sugar, so it lacks a free aldehyde group which is necessary for the reaction, while the other three are reducing sugars and they give positive silver mirror test.

(v) (d) Since, *en* is a bidentate ligand, so two *en* in complex binds with the metal atom through four binding sites, and H_2O is a unidentate ligand, so two H_2O in the given complex binds to the metal atom through two binding sites. Therefore, the coordination number of the central metal '*D*' in the complex is 6.

Let the oxidation state of *D* in the complex is *x*.

$$\therefore \quad x + 2(0) + 2(0) = +3$$

$$x = +3$$

Thus, the oxidation state of the central metal '*D*' is 3.

(vi) (c) The process of halogenation of benzene takes place in the presence of anhydrous $FeCl_3$. The $FeCl_3$ reacts with the halogen to form a complex, which further dissociates to form the electrophile (Cl^+) which then attacks on the benzene ring to undergo electrophilic substitution reaction.

(vii) (a) Zr and Hf have nearly same value of atomic radii despite being in different periods due to the lanthanoid contraction. The ineffective shielding by 4*f* electrons in Hf increases the nuclear attraction, counteracting the expected increase in size and making their atomic radii almost same.

(C) (i) Unit of k = (mol L^{-1})$^{1-n}$s^{-1}.

For $n = 3$ (third order reaction)

Unit of k = (mol L^{-1})$^{1-3}$s^{-1} = L^2 mol^{-2} s^{-1}.

Thus, for the given unit of k (mol^{-2}L^{2}s^{-1}) the order of reaction is three.

(ii) Refer to text on Pg. 66. (Difference between molecularity and order of reaction).

(iii) Since, the order of reaction is the sum of the exponents of the concentration term in the rate law, thus in the given rate law order of the reaction is $\frac{3}{2}$. And from the given balanced equation, 2 molecules of *A* are reacting in a single step, hence the molecularity of reaction is 2.

2. Electrode reaction, $Al^{3+} + 3e^- \longrightarrow Al$

For 27g (1 mol) of Al required = 3×96500 C

$$\therefore \text{ 1g of Al required} = \frac{3 \times 96500 \text{ C}}{27}$$

$$\therefore \text{ 4.75 g of Al required} = \frac{3 \times 96500}{27} \times 4.75 = 50930.5 \text{ C}$$

Thus, the number of coulombs required to deposit 4.75 g of Al is 50930.5 C.

3.

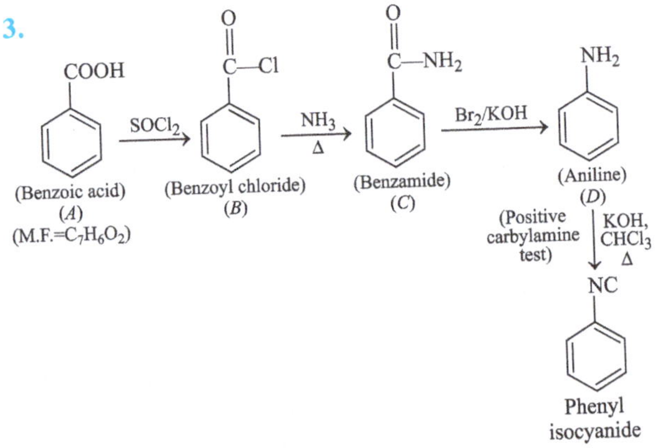

$\therefore$ *A* = Benzoic acid, *B* = Benzoyl chloride,

C = Benzamide and *D* = Aniline.

4. (i) Rate = $r = k[NO][O_2]^2$

$$r' = k\,[2NO]\left[\frac{1}{2}O_2\right]^2$$

$$= k[2NO]\cdot\frac{1}{4}[O_2]^2 = \frac{1}{2}k[NO][O_2]^2$$

$$r' = \frac{1}{2}r$$

∴ rate of reaction will reduce to half, if [NO] concentration is doubled and $[O_2]$ concentration is halved.

(ii) If [NO] is in large excess then, $[NO] \approx 1$.

∴ rate equation becomes, rate $= k[O_2]^2$.

Thus, the reaction becomes second order.

5. Since, the nucleophilic substitution reaction of [*A*] depends only on concentration of compound [*A*], therefore, this is a S_N1 reaction (unimolecular substitution reaction).

So, [*A*] must be a tertiary alkyl halide, as S_N1 favours the formation of 3° carbocation.

Thus, [*A*] can be 2-bromobutane.

```
      Br
      |
H3C—CH—CH2—CH3
      [A]
```

While, the nucleophilic substitution reaction of [*B*] depends on both the concentration of [*B*] and nucleophile, thus, this is a S_N2 reaction (bimolecular substitution reaction). So, [*B*] must be a primary alkyl halide as S_N2 favours the primary halide due to less steric hindrance.

∴ [*B*] can be 1-bromobutane.

$H_3C—CH_2—CH_2—CH_2—Br$ [*B*]

6. (i) $CH_3CH_2CN + 4[H] \xrightarrow{LiAlH_4} CH_3CH_2CH_2NH_2$
(Ethyl cyanide) (Propan-1-amine)

(ii)
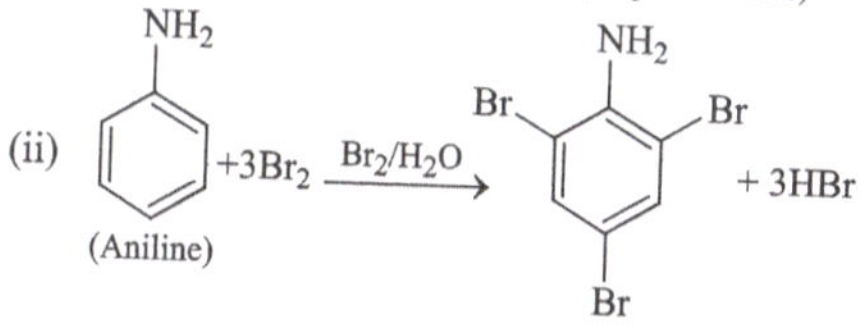

(Aniline) (2,4,6-tribromoaniline)

7. Shirin's observation of a white precipitate upon adding $AgNO_3$ solution to the complex, $[Co(NH_3)_3(en)(SO_4)]Cl$ indicates the presence of ionisable Cl^- ions outside the coordination sphere, leading to the formation of AgCl ppt.

The ionisation isomer of this complex, $[Co(NH_3)_3(en)(Cl)]SO_4$ would not produce a white ppt. with $AgNO_3$ as the Cl^- ion is inside the coordination sphere and is not ionisable. Thus, the ionisation isomer of the given complex can not be detected by $AgNO_3$ test. Therefore, we can perform $BaCl_2$ test to detect this ionisation isomers.

$$[Co(NH_3)_3(en)Cl]\,SO_4 + BaCl_2 \longrightarrow [Co(NH_3)_3(en)Cl]Cl_2 + \underset{\text{(white ppt.)}}{BaSO_4\downarrow}$$

Ionisation isomer $= [Co(NH_3)_3(en)(Cl)]SO_4$

Triamminechlorido (ethane-1, 2-diamine). cobalt (III) sulphate.

8. (i) The acidic character of alcohols is due to the polar nature of O—H bond. An electron withdrawing group decreases the electron density on oxygen, tending to decrease the polarity of O—H bond. Thus, this increases the acidic strength.

The order of electron withdrawing effect of substituents is : $—CF_3 > —CCl_3 > —CH_3$. Therefore, the increasing order of acidic character is:

$$CH_3CH_2OH < CCl_3CH_2OH < CF_3CH_2OH$$

(ii) Boiling point of alcohols are usually higher than haloalkanes of comparable molecular masses. The —OH group in alcohols is involved in intermolecular H-bonding, which is absent in haloalkanes. Also, ethylene glycol with two —OH groups has a higher boiling point than ethanol due to presence of more extensive intermolecular H-bonding.

Therefore, the increasing order of the boiling points is

```
CH3CH2Cl < CH3CH2OH < CH2—OH
                      |
                      CH2OH
```

9. (i) $\underset{\text{(Acetic acid)}}{CH_3COOH} + PCl_5 \longrightarrow \underset{\text{(Acetyl chloride)}}{\underset{[A]}{CH_3COCl}} \xrightarrow[\text{Pd/BaSO}_4\text{ Boiling xylene}]{H_2} \underset{\text{(Acetaldehyde)}}{\underset{[B]}{CH_3CHO}}$

$\xrightarrow{[O]\; K_2Cr_2O_7 + H_2SO_4} \underset{\text{(Acetic acid)}}{\underset{[C]}{CH_3COOH}} \xrightarrow{Ca(OH)_2\text{, heat}} \underset{\text{(Acetone)}}{\underset{[D]}{CH_3COCH_3}}$

Or

(ii) (a)
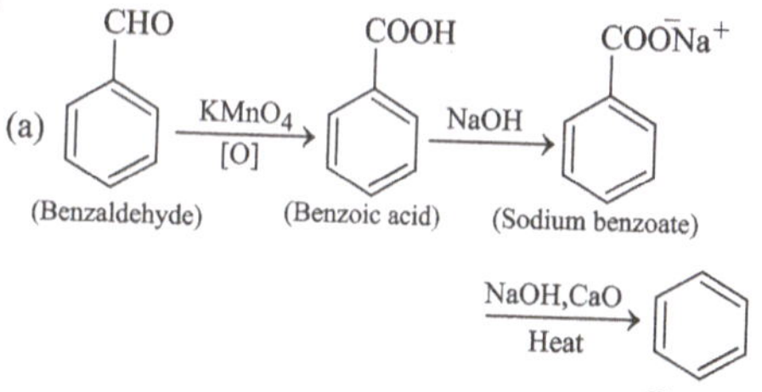

(Benzaldehyde) (Benzoic acid) (Sodium benzoate) (Benzene)

(b)
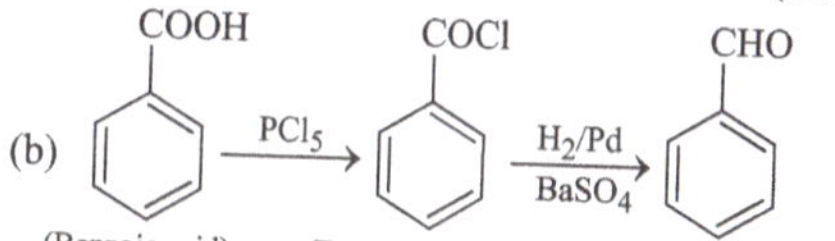

(Benzoic acid) (Benzoyl chloride) (Benzaldehyde)

10. By applying Nernst equation,

$$E_{cell} = E^\circ_{cell} - \frac{0.0591}{n}\log\frac{[Ni^{2+}]}{[Cu^{2+}]}$$

$$\Rightarrow \quad 0.59 = E^\circ_{cell} - \frac{0.0591}{2}\log\frac{(0.1)}{(0.01)}$$

$$\Rightarrow \quad E^\circ_{cell} = 0.59 + \frac{0.0591}{2}\log(10) = 0.61955\text{ V}$$

$$\Rightarrow \quad E^\circ_{cell} \approx 0.62\text{V}$$

11. (i) Ethanol and propan-1-al can be distinguished using the iodoform test. Ethanol gives a positive iodoform test, producing a yellow ppt. of iodoform (CHI_3). Propan-1-al does not give the iodoform test.

$$\underset{\text{(Ethanol)}}{CH_3CH_2OH} \xrightarrow[NaOH]{I_2} HCOO^-Na^+ + \underset{\text{(Yellow ppt.)}}{CHI_3\downarrow}$$

$$\underset{\text{(Propan-1-al)}}{CH_3CH_2CHO} \xrightarrow[NaOH]{I_2} \text{No reaction}$$

(ii) Phenol and benzoic acid can be distinguished by sodium bicarbonate test. Benzoic acid reacts with sodium bicarbonate to produce effervescence of carbon dioxide, whereas phenol does not.

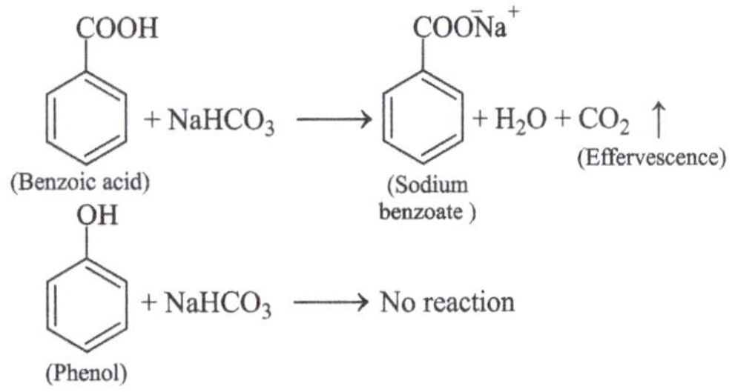

12. (i) $\underset{\text{Bromoethane}}{C_2H_5Br} \xrightarrow{KCN} \underset{\substack{\text{Propanenitrile}\\(A)}}{CH_3CH_2CN} \xrightarrow[\text{[4H]}]{LiAlH_4}$

$\underset{\substack{\text{Propan-1-amine}\\(B)}}{CH_3CH_2CH_2NH_2} \xrightarrow[0°-5°C]{HNO_2} \underset{\substack{\text{Propan-1-ol}\\(C)}}{CH_3CH_2CH_2OH}$

(ii) $\underset{\text{Propanamide}}{C_2H_5CONH_2} \xrightarrow{Br_2/KOH} \underset{\substack{\text{Ethylamine}\\(A)}}{CH_3CH_2NH_2}$

$\xrightarrow{CHCl_3+KOH} \underset{\substack{\text{Ethyl isocyanide}\\(B)}}{CH_3CH_2NC} \xrightarrow{Na/C_2H_5OH} \underset{\substack{\text{N-methylethan-1-amine}\\(C)}}{(CH_3CH_2NHCH_3)}$

13. (i) $K_4[Fe(CN)_6] \longrightarrow 4K^+ + [Fe(CN)_6]^-$

Here, $n = 5$ and $\alpha = 25\% = 0.25$.

$\therefore \quad \alpha = \dfrac{i-1}{n-1}$ [For dissociation]

$0.25 = \dfrac{i-1}{5-1} = \dfrac{i-1}{4}$

$1 = i - 1 \Rightarrow i = 2$

(ii) $\underset{\text{(Benzoic acid)}}{2C_6H_5COOH} \rightleftharpoons \underset{\text{(Dimer)}}{(C_6H_5COOH)_2}$

van't Hoff factor (i)

$= \dfrac{\text{Total number of moles of particles after association}}{\text{Total number of moles of particles before association}}$

Since, two molecules of benzoic acid dimerises into one molecule,

Therefore, $i = \dfrac{1}{2}$.

14. (i) Alkyl iodides are prepared by the reaction of alkyl chlorides/bromides with NaI in dry acetone.

$$R\text{—}X + NaI \xrightarrow{\text{Acetone}} R\text{—}I + NaX \quad (X = Cl, Br, I)$$

(ii) Refer to text on page-168.

(iii) Refer to text on page-160.

15. (i) Complex compound [B] has 6 electrons in t_{2g} orbital, which are paired and there are no electrons in e_g. orbitals. Therefore, complex compound [B] is a low spin complex as it can form d^2sp^3 hybridistion (by involving inner d-orbital).

(ii) In complex compound [A], $t_{2g}^4 e_g^2$, there are 2 unpaired electrons in t_{2g} and 2 unpaired electrons in e_g orbitals, therefore, there are total four unpaired electrons in [A].

While, in complex compound [B], $t_{2g}^6 e_g^0$, there are zero unpaired electrons as all six electrons in t_{2g} are paired.

(iii) Complex [A] have high spin state, i.e., electrons are filled in t_{2g} and e_g first, before getting paired, therefore, complex [A] have weak field ligands (as they do not cause pairing).

16. (i) (a) By referring to electrochemical series, we can identify the anode and cathode half cells in a galvanic cell. The negative sign of standard reduction potential indicates that the electrode when joined with standard hydrogen electrode (SHE) behave as anode and oxidation occurs at that electrode.

Similarly, positive sign of standard reduction potential indicates that the electrode behaves as a cathode when joined with SHE and reduction occurs at this electrode.

(b) In a galvanic cell, the salt bridge plays a crucial role in maintaining electrical neutrality and completing the circuit between the two half-cells, allowing for the continuous flow of electrons.

(c) An advantage of a fuel cell is that it is highly efficient (70%).

Whereas, the disadvantage of a fuel cell is its high cost.

Or

(ii) (a) Specific conductance of a solution decreases upon dilution because the number of ions that carry current in a unit volume of solution always decreases with decrease in concentration.

(b) For a spontaneous reaction, $\Delta_r G°$ is negative, i.e., $\Delta_r G° < 0$. According to the equation, $\Delta_r G° = -nFE°_{cell}$.

For $\Delta_r G°$ to be negative, $E°_{cell}$ needs to be positive.

Therefore, the emf of a cell should be positive for a spontaneous reactions.

(c) The type of cell in which reaction occurs only in one direction and cannot be reversed by an external energy source is primary cell. Its one disadvantage is that it is not reusable as it cannot be recharged.

17. (i) Zwitter ion, glycine

(ii) Janice should consume water soluble vitamin, vitamin C to prevent bleeding of gums.

(iii) Two units of monosaccharides are joined together through an oxide linkage, formed by the loss of water molecule. Such a linkage between two monosaccharide units to form a disaccharide is called a glycosidic linkage.

18. (i) Let the order w.r.t NO and Cl_2 be x and y.

Rate law expression can be written as;

Rate $= k[NO]^x[Cl_2]^y$

$\therefore \quad 2.0 \times 10^{-3} = k[2.0]^x[2.0]^y$ ...(i)

$6.0 \times 10^{-3} = [2.0]^x[6.0]^y$ ...(ii)

$1.8 \times 10^{-2} = [6.0]^x[2.0]^y$ ...(iii)

Dividing Equations (ii) by (i), we get

$\dfrac{6.0 \times 10^{-3}}{2.0 \times 10^{-3}} = \dfrac{[2.0]^x[6.0]^y}{[2.0]^x[2.0]^y}$

$(3)^1 = [3]^y$

$\therefore \quad y = 1$

Dividing (iii) by (i), we get

$$\frac{1.8\times10^{-2}}{2.0\times10^{-3}}=\frac{[6.0]^x[2.0]^y}{[2.0]^x[2.0]^y}$$

$$9=[3]^x \Rightarrow (3)^2=[3]^x$$

$$\therefore \quad x=2$$

Hence, the order of reaction with regard to NO and Cl_2 is 2 and 1, respectively.

(ii) Overall order of reaction $= x + y = 2 + 1 = 3$

(iii) Rate $= k[NO]^2[Cl_2]$

From expression (1), rate constant can be calculated as :

$$2.0\times10^{-3}=k[2.0]^2[2.0]$$

$$k=\frac{2\times10^{-3}\,\text{mol L}^{-1}\text{s}^{-1}}{(4\text{ mol}^2\text{L}^{-2})(2\text{ mol L}^{-1})}$$

$$=0.25\times10^{-3}\text{ L}^2\text{mol}^{-2}\text{ s}^{-1}$$

$$\Rightarrow \quad k=2.5\times10^{-4}\text{L}^2\text{mol}^{-2}\text{ s}^{-1}.$$

19. (i) Picric acid can be prepared from phenol by reacting phenol with conc. HNO_3, in the presence of conc. H_2SO_4.

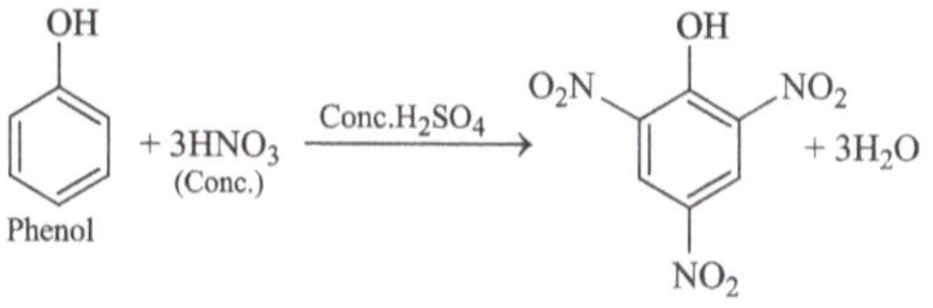

2,4,6-trinitrophenol (Picric acid)

(ii) Phenol is less soluble in water as compared to aliphatic alcohols because phenol has a bulky phenyl ring, (hydrophophic group) which decreases its solubility.

(iii) 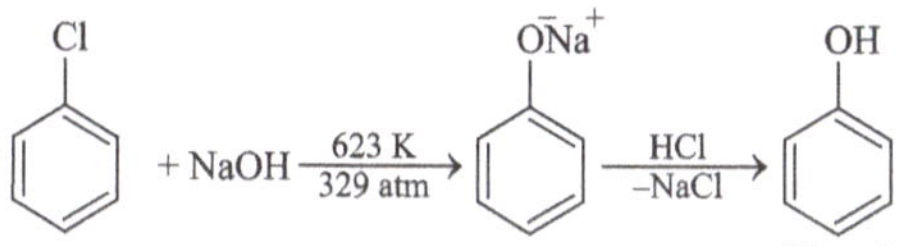

(Chlorobenzene) (Sodium phenoxide) (Phenol)

(iv) Since, compound [A] gives positive Lucas test within five minutes at room temperature, thus it is a secondary alcohol. Also, [A] on oxidation with $K_2Cr_2O_7$ /H_2SO_4 give [B], which does not respond to Tollen's test, thus, [B] is a ketone.

$$\underset{\text{(Butan -2-ol)}\ [A]}{CH_3-\underset{|}{\overset{OH}{}}CH-CH_2-CH_3}\xrightarrow[H_2SO_4]{K_2Cr_2O_7}\underset{\text{(Butan -2-one)}\ [B]}{CH_3-\overset{O}{\overset{\|}{C}}-CH_2-CH_3}$$

Thus, [A] = Butan-2-ol and [B] = butan-2-one.

(v) Compound [B] i.e., butan-2-one undergoes Clemmensen reduction to form butane (Compound [C]).

$$\underset{\text{(Butan - 2 - one)}\ [B]}{CH_3-\overset{O}{\overset{\|}{C}}-CH_2-CH_3}+4[H]\xrightarrow[\text{Conc. HCl}]{\text{Zn–Hg}}\underset{\text{(Butane)}\ [C]}{CH_3-CH_2-CH_2-CH_3}+H_2O$$

Thus, [C] = Butane.

20. (i) (a) Ti has an electronic configuration of $3d^24s^2$.

$Ti^{2+} = 3d^24s^0$

$Ti^{4+} = 3d^0$

Since, there are two unpaired electrons in Ti^{2+}, therefore Ti^{2+} salts are coloured due to d-d transition. Whereas, Ti^{4+} has no unpaired electrons, therefore, Ti^{4+} salts are colourless.

(b) The atomic radii of the transition elements in any series are not much different from each other. As a result, they can very easily replace each other in the lattice and form solid solutions over an appreciable composition range. Such solid solutions are called alloys.

(c) Mohr's salt contains Fe^{2+} ions, which are oxidised to Fe^{3+} ions by $KMnO_4$ solution in acidic medium. Thus, $KMnO_4$ is reduced to Mn^{2+} during this reaction and pink colour of $KMnO_4$ decolourises.

(ii) (a) $2KMnO_4 + 3H_2SO_4 + 5H_2C_2O_4 \longrightarrow 2MnSO_4 + 10CO_2 + K_2SO_4 + 8H_2O$

(b) $K_2Cr_2O_7 + 4H_2SO_4 + 3H_2S \longrightarrow K_2SO_4 + Cr_2(SO_4)_3 + 7H_2O + 3S$

21. (i) (a) If red blood corpuscles are placed in 5% NaCl solution (a hypertonic solution), then the cells will shrink as the water will move out of the cells from area of higher water concentration to lower water concentration *via* osmosis.

(b) Colligative properties are those which depends on the number of solute particles rather than the nature of solute particles.

Osmotic pressure $(\pi) = CRT = \frac{n}{V}RT\left[\because c=\frac{n}{V}\right]$

Since, osmotic pressure depends on the number of moles of solute (n), therefore, it is a colligative property.

(c) Osmotic pressure,

$$(\pi) = iCRT$$

Now, $Na_2SO_4 \longrightarrow 2Na^+ + SO_4^{2-}$

$\therefore \quad i = 3$

$$\pi = i\frac{n}{V}RT = \frac{i.W.R.T}{M\times V}$$

For Na_2SO_4, molecular weight

$$(M) = 2(23) + 32 + 4(16)$$

$$= 142\text{ g mol}^{-1}$$

Given, $W = 40$ g, $V = 1$ L, $R = 0.0821$ L atm K^{-1} mol^{-1} and $T = 298$ K.

$$\Rightarrow \pi = \frac{3\times40\text{ g}\times0.0821\text{ L atm K}^{-1}\text{mol}^{-1}\times298\text{K}}{142\text{g mol}^{-1}\times1\text{ L}}$$

$$\therefore \quad \pi = 20.675\text{ atm}$$

(d) Refer to text on page-9 (Reverse osmosis and water purification).

Or

(ii) (a) According to relative lowering of vapour pressure,

$$\frac{p_1^\circ - p_1}{p_1^\circ} = x_2 = \frac{n_2}{n_1+n_2}$$

[Here, 1 represents solvent and 2 represents solute]

where, p_1° = vapour pressure of pure solvent

p_1 = vapour pressure of solution

x_2 = mole fraction of solute.

Given, $W_2 = 10$ g, $M_2 = 180$ g mol^{-1}, $W_1 = 90$ g, $M_1 = 18$ g and $p_1^\circ = 32.8$ mm Hg.

$$\Rightarrow \quad n_1 = \frac{W_1}{M_1} = \frac{90\text{ g}}{18\text{ g mol}^{-1}} = 5\text{ mol}$$

$$\Rightarrow \quad n_2 = \frac{W_2}{M_2} = \frac{10\text{g}}{180\text{ g mol}^{-1}}$$

$$= 0.0556\text{ mol}$$

$$\therefore \quad \frac{32.8 - p_1}{32.8} = \frac{0.0556}{0.0556 + 5} = \frac{0.0556}{5.0556}$$

$$\Rightarrow \frac{32.8 - p_1}{32.8} = 0.011$$

$$\Rightarrow 32.8 - p_1 = 0.3608$$

$$p_1 = 32.4392\text{ mm Hg}$$

$$\Rightarrow \quad p_1 \approx 32.44\text{ mm Hg}$$

(b) Elevation in boiling point $(\Delta T_b) = K_b\, m$

(where, m = molality)

$$\Delta T_b = K_b \times \frac{\text{moles of solute}(n_2) \times 1000}{\text{weight of solvent }(W_1)(\text{in g})}$$

$$\Delta T_b = \frac{K_b \times W_2 \times 1000}{M_2 \times W_1} \quad \left[\because n_2 = \frac{W_2}{M_2}\right]$$

Also, $\Delta T_b = T_b - T_b^\circ$

[where, T_b = boiling point of solution, ΔT_b° = boiling point of water]

Given,

$T_b = 100.70°\text{C} = (100.70 + 273)\text{K} = 373.70$ K,

$T_b^\circ = 373$ K, $W_2 = 12.5$ g, $W_1 = 175$ g and

$K_b = 0.52$ K kg mol^{-1}

Now, $\Delta T_b = T_b - T_b^\circ = (373.70 - 373)\text{K} = 0.70$ K

$$\Delta T_b = 0.70\text{ K}$$

$$= \frac{0.52\text{ K kg mol}^{-1} \times 12.5\text{ g} \times 1000}{M_2 \times 175\text{ kg}}$$

$$\Rightarrow \quad M_2 = \frac{0.52\text{ K kg mol}^{-1} \times 12.5\text{g} \times 1000}{0.70\text{ K} \times 175\text{ kg}}$$

$$= 53.061\text{ g mol}^{-1}$$

$$\therefore \quad M_2 \approx 53.06\text{ g mol}^{-1}$$

(c) Soda water bottles are sealed under high pressure to increase the solubility of carbon dioxide (CO_2) in the drink, which is essential for maintaining its characteristic fizz and flavours.

ISC Fully Solved

LATEST SPECIMEN PAPER

Time : 3 hrs
Marks : 70

Chemistry

GENERAL INSTRUCTIONS

- This paper is divided into four sections-A, B, C and D. Answer all questions.
- **Section A** consists of **one** question **having sub-parts** of one mark each. **Section B** consists of **ten** questions of **two** marks each. **Section C** consists of **seven** questions of three marks each and **Section D** consists of **three** questions of **five** marks each.
- Internal choices have been provided in one question each in Section B, Section C and Section D.
- All working, including rough work, should be done on the same sheet as, and adjacent to the rest of the answer.
- The intended marks for questions or parts of questions are given in brackets [].
- Balanced equations must be given, wherever possible and diagrams where they are helpful.
  When solving numerical problems, all essential working must be shown.
- In working out problems, use the following data:
  Gas constant (R) = 1.987 cal deg^{-1} mol^{-1} = 8.314 JK^{-1} mol^{-1} = 0.0821 dm^3 atm K^{-1} mol^{-1} 1 L atm = 1 dm^3 atm = 101.3 J,
  1 Faraday = 96500 Coulombs. **Avogadro's number** (N_A) = 6.023×10^{23}.

Section-A [14 Marks]

1. (A) Fill in the blanks by choosing the appropriate word(s) from those given in the brackets: [4 × 1]
[four, three, remains same, propane, ns^{1-2}, increases, six, propan-2-ol, $(n-1)\,d^{1-10}$, two, decreases, Clemmensen's, Wolff-Kishner]

(i) The molar conductance of a solution .... on dilution but the specific conductance of a solution .... on dilution. • *Understanding*

(ii) In the complex ion $[CoCl(en)_2ONO]^+$, the coordination number and the oxidation number of the central metal ion are .... and .... • *Understanding*

(iii) Propanone on reaction with zinc amalgam in the presence of concentrated HCl gives .... and the reaction is called ...... reduction. • *Recall*

(iv) The variation and magnitude of oxidation state in coordination complexes is due to the participation of inner .... electrons in addition to outer .... electrons. • *Understanding*

(B) Select and write the correct alternative from the choices given below. [7 × 1]

(i) The correct order of the increasing basic nature of ammonia, methylamine and aniline is • *Analysis*

(a) Methylamine < aniline < ammonia
(b) Aniline < methylamine < ammonia
(c) Ammonia < aniline < methylamine
(d) Aniline < ammonia < methylamine

(ii) Colligative properties of a solution are • *Understanding*

(P) Independent of the nature of solute
(Q) Proportional to molecular mass of solute
(R) Proportional to concentration of solute
(S) Independent of the amount of solvent

(a) Only P and Q are correct
(b) Only P and R are correct
(c) Only P and S are correct
(d) Only Q and S are correct

(iii) According to Markownikoff's rule, "The negative part of the halogen acid attaches itself with that C-atom of an unsymmetrical alkene which has least number of H-atom."

Anti-Markownikoff's addition of HBr is not observed in • *Analysis*

(a) propene (b) but-2-ene

(c) but-1-ene (d) pent-2-ene

(iv) Most of the naturally occurring α-amino acids are optically active and have L-configuration. Which of the following amino acids is not asymmetric? • *Recall*

(a) Valine (b) Alanine

(c) Glycine (d) Leucine

(v) Which one of the following complex ions has geometrical isomers? • *Understanding*

(a) $[Ni(NH_3)_5Br]^+$ (b) $[Cr(NH_3)_4en]^{3+}$

(c) $[Co(NH_3)_2(en)_2]^{3+}$ (d) $[Co(NH_3)_6]^{3+}$

(vi) Given below are two statements marked Assertion and Reason. Read the two statements carefully and select the correct option.

Assertion (A) Tertiary butyl bromide undergoes Wurtz reaction to give 2,2,3,3 tetramethyl butane.

Reason (R) In Wurtz reaction, when same alkyl halides react with sodium in dry ether to give hydrocarbon; the hydrocarbon formed contains double the number of carbon atoms present in the alkyl halide. • *Analysis*

(a) Both Assertion and Reason are true and Reason is the correct explanation of Assertion.

(b) Both Assertion and Reason are true but Reason is not the correct explanation for Assertion.

(c) Assertion is true but Reason is false.

(d) Both Assertion and Reason are false.

(vii) Given below are two statements marked Assertion and Reason. Read the two statements carefully and select the correct option.

Assertion (A) There is a continuous increase in size among lanthanoids with an increase in atomic number.

Reason (R) Lanthanoids do not show lanthanoid contraction. • *Analysis*

(a) Both Assertion and Reason are true and Reason is the correct explanation of Assertion.

(b) Both Assertion and Reason are true but Reason is not the correct explanation for assertion.

(c) Assertion is true but Reason is false.

(d) Both Assertion and Reason are false.

(C) Read the passage carefully and answer the questions that follow. [3 × 1]

A plant or any other living being maintains a reasonable balance of C-14 (radioactive carbon) in its tissue during its lifetime. C-14 is used to determine the age of fossils. In the upper atmosphere, neutrons present in the cosmic rays are captured to produce the following nuclear reaction.

$${}_7N^{14} + {}_0n^1 \longrightarrow {}_6C^{14} + {}_1H^1$$

C-14 isotope is circulated in the atmosphere and gets absorbed by living organism during photosynthesis. The ratio of C-14 to C-12 in living being is $1:10^{12}$.

Once the living being dies, the level of C-14 in the dead being decreases due to the following reaction.

$${}_6C^{14} \longrightarrow {}_7N^{14} + {}_{-1}e^0 + \gamma \text{ rays}$$

The death of the plant brings an end to its tendency to take up C-14. The half-life period of C-14 is 5770 years. By knowing the concentration of C-14 in the living plant and the piece of dead material at a particular time, the age of the material (fossil) can be determined.

(i) Write the relation between the decay constant and half-life period. • *Recall*

(ii) In a piece of dead wood, the activity or concentration of C-14 is found to be one third of its initial activity. Calculate the age of the old wood. • *Application*

(iii) The half-life period ($t_{1/2}$) for a first order reaction is 30 minutes. Calculate the time taken to complete 87.5% of the reaction. • *Application*

Section-B [20 Marks]

2. The solution of two electrolytes A and B are diluted. Λ_m of B increases 1.5 times while that of A increases 25 times. Which of the two is a strong electrolyte? Give a reason. • *Understanding* [2]

3. An organic compound [A] which has characteristic odour, reacts with conc. NaOH to give two compounds [B] and [C]. Compound [B] has molecular formula C_7H_8O which upon oxidation gives back compound [A]. Compound [C] is the sodium salt of the acid and upon treatment with sodalime yields an aromatic hydrocarbon [D]. Identify the compounds [A], [B], [C] and [D]. [2] • *Understanding*

4. Devise a scheme for the synthesis of *n*-butane using CH_3I as the only source of carbon. Is it possible to obtain propane in pure state by applying this scheme? Give a reason for your answer. • *Evaluate* [2]

5. It is generally observed that the rate of a chemical reaction becomes double with every 10°C rise in temperature. If the generalisation holds true for a reaction in the temperature range of 298 K to 308 K, what would be the value of activation energy (E_a) for the reaction? • *Application* [2]

6. An organic compound [*X*] of molecular formula C_3H_5N, in one reaction produced a primary amine with $LiAlH_4$. In another case, the organic compound [*Y*] of same molecular formula C_3H_5N produced a secondary amine with $LiAlH_4$. Identify both the compounds [*X*] and [*Y*]. Why do these compounds form two different products? • *Understanding* [2]

7. During chemistry class, a teacher wrote $[Ni(CN)_4]^{2-}$ as a coordination complex ion on the board. The students were asked to find out the magnetic behaviour and shape of the complex. Pari, a student, wrote the answer paramagnetic and tetrahedral whereas another student Suhail wrote diamagnetic and square planer. • *Evaluate* [2]
Evaluate Pari's and Suhail's responses.

8. An organic compound '*X*' with molecular formula $C_4H_{10}O$ is found to be soluble in conc. H_2SO_4 and does not react with sodium metal or $KMnO_4$. Compound '*X*' when heated with excess of HI gives a single alkyl halide. Deduce the structure of the compound '*X*'. Explain all the reactions involved. [2] • *Understanding*

9. (i) Identify the compounds [*A*] and [*B*] in the following reactions. [2] • *Understanding*

(a) $C_6H_5CHO \xrightarrow[(2)\ SOCl_2]{(1)\ K_2Cr_2O_7/H_2SO_4} [A] \xrightarrow{C_6H_6\ (\text{anhy. } AlCl_3)} [B]$

(b) $CH_3—C\equiv CH \xrightarrow[(2)\ \text{Vigorous oxidation, conc. } HNO_3]{(1)\ H_2SO_4/HgSO_4}$

$[A] \xrightarrow[[\text{Conc. } H_2SO_4]]{C_2H_5OH} [B]$

Or (ii) Three organic compounds *A*, *B* and *C* are non-cyclic functional isomers of carbonyl compounds with molecular formula C_4H_8O. Isomers *A* and *C* give positive Tollen's test while compound *B* does not give positive Tollen's test but gives positive iodoform test. Compounds *A* and *B* on reduction with Zn amalgam and conc. HCl give the same product.

(a) Write the structures of the compounds *A*, *B* and *C*. • *Understanding*

(b) Out of the compounds *A*, *B* and *C*, which one will be the least reactive towards addition of HCN. • *Understanding*

10. Calculate the value of E°_{cell}, E_{cell} and ΔG that can be obtained from the following cell at 298 K.

$Al/Al^{3+}_{(0.01\ M)}\ //\ Sn^{2+}_{(0.015\ M)}/Sn$ • *Application* [2]

Given, $E^\circ_{Al^{3+}/Al} = -1.66\ V$, $E^\circ_{Sn^{2+}/Sn} = -0.14\ V$

11. Write the chemical test to distinguish between the following pairs of compounds. [2]

(i) Propan-1-ol and propan-2-ol

(ii) Phenol and ethanol • *Understanding*

Section-C [21 Marks]

12. Identify the compounds [*A*], [*B*] and [*C*] in the following reactions. [3]

(i) $C_6H_5NO_2 \xrightarrow[Sn/HCl]{6[H]} [A] \xrightarrow[273\ K-278\ K]{HNO_2 + HCl} [B] \xrightarrow{C_6H_5NH_2} [C]$ • *Understanding*

(ii) $CH_3CH_2NH_2 \xrightarrow[(2)\ P/Cl_2]{(1)\ HNO_2} [A] \xrightarrow[(2)\ H_2O/H^+]{(1)\ KCN} [B] \xrightarrow[(2)\ Br_2/KOH]{(1)\ NH_3/\text{heat}} [C]$ • *Understanding*

13. The molar mass calculated through colligative properties is sometimes different from that of experimentally determined molecular mass and is known as abnormal molecular mass. This difference is due to the solute particles that undergo association or dissociation. [3]
Consider the two cases given below and answer the questions that follow.

(A) The freezing point of a solution containing 5.85 of NaCl in 100 g of water is –3.348°C. (K_f of water = 1.86 K kg mol^{-1}, molecular mass of NaCl = 58.5)

(B) The freezing point of benzene solution decreases by 0.45°C when 0.2 g of acetic acid is added to 20 g of benzene. (K_f of benzene = 5.12 K kg mol^{-1}, molecular mass of acetic acid = 60)

Answer the following questions.

(i) Calculate the abnormal molecular mass of solute in both the cases. • *Application*

(ii) Inferring the value of van't Hoff factor in both the cases, find out which solution undergoes association and which solution undergoes dissociation. • *Analysis*

(iii) Given below is the increasing order of depression in freezing point of water observed for equimolar concentrations of the compounds, acetic acid < trichloro acetic acid < trifluoro acetic acid
Provide a reason to explain if the above ordered arrangement is correct or not. • *Understanding*

14. Write chemical equations to illustrate the following name reactions. • *Recall* [3]
(i) Rosenmund's reaction
(ii) Benzoin condensation
(iii) Perkin's reaction

15. (i) Assuming that cyanide is a strong ligand, write the formula of two coordination complex ions with cyanide and iron having coordination number six. Name the complex ions. • *Application* [3]

(ii) On the basis of Crystal Field Theory, write the electronic configuration of d^4 ion if: • *Application*
(a) $\Delta_o > P$ (b) $\Delta_o < P$

16. (i) Dry cells are commonly used in clocks, torches, calculators etc. They are the most familiar type of commercial cells. [3]
(a) What acts as anode and cathode in dry cell? • *Understanding*
(b) Which chemical compounds are filled between anode and cathode of this cell? • *Understanding*
(c) Why do dry cells not have a long life? • *Understanding*

Or (ii) Answer the following:
(a) What happens to the voltage when the salt bridge is removed from the two half cells and why? • *Understanding*
(b) Copper sulphate solution cannot be stored in a zinc pot. Why? • *Understanding*
(c) Why does the density of H_2SO_4 in a lead storage battery decrease as it is discharged? • *Understanding*

17. (i) The structures of glycine and alanine are given below. [3]
Show the peptide bond linkage in glycylalanine. • *Understanding* [3]

$H_2N—CH_2—COOH$
Glycine

$H_2N—CH(CH_3)—COOH$
Alanine

(ii) What products would be formed when a nucleotide from DNA containing thymine is hydrolysed? • *Understanding*

(iii) What are reducing sugars? Give an example. • *Recall*

18. Consider the data given below for the reaction
$A + B \longrightarrow \text{Product}$ [3]

S.No.	conc. of [A] mol L^{-1}	conc. of [B] mol L^{-1}	Rate; mol L^{-1} sec^{-1}
1.	0.1	0.1	4.0×10^{-4}
2.	0.2	0.2	1.6×10^{-3}
3.	0.5	0.1	1.0×10^{-2}
4.	0.5	0.5	1.0×10^{-2}

Answer the following questions.
(i) What is the order of reaction with respect to A and B? • *Application*
(ii) Calculate the rate constant. • *Application*
(iii) Determine the reaction rate when the concentration of A and B are 0.2 mol L^{-1} sec^{-1} and 0.35 mol L^{-1} sec^{-1} respectively. • *Evaluate*

Section-D [15 Marks]

19. Phenol, one of the deadliest acids, contains a hydroxyl group directly attached to the aromatic ring. A hydroxyl group attached to an aromatic ring is also referred to as a phenolic group. Due to the presence of —OH group, phenols show many reactions similar to those of alcohols.

The direct attachment of —OH group to the aromatic ring makes its behaviour very different from that of alcohols. That is why phenol behaves differently from alcohols in many reactions. The chemical reactions of phenol can be categorised as follows:
- Reactions involving —OH group
- Reactions involving benzene ring [5]

(i) Write the chemical equation for the preparation of phenol from benzene using H_2SO_4 and NaOH. • *Understanding*

(ii) What happens when phenol reacts with Br_2/CS_2 at low temperature? • *Recall*

(iii) What is observed when phenol is treated with neutral ferric chloride solution? • *Recall*

(iv) Write the reaction when phenol is treated with conc. HNO_3 in the presence of conc. H_2SO_4. • *Understanding*

(v) Write the reaction when phenol is treated with chloroform in the presence of aqueous NaOH at 340 K. • *Understanding*

20. (i) Give a reason for each of the following. [5]

(a) The purple colour of $KMnO_4$ disappears in the presence of acidified solution of oxalic acid. • *Understanding*

(b) Some transition metals and their compounds get attracted towards the magnetic field. • *Understanding*

(c) Why are Mn^{2+} compounds more stable than Fe^{2+} towards oxidation to the +3 state? (Atomic no. of Mn = 25 and Fe = 26) • *Understanding*

(ii) Complete and balance the following reactions. • *Recall*

(a) $KMnO_4 + H_2SO_4 + FeSO_4 \longrightarrow$ .... + ... + ...

(b) $K_2Cr_2O_7 + H_2SO_4 + KI \longrightarrow$ .... + ... + ...

21. Osmosis and osmotic pressure play a very significant role in biological processes. The osmotic pressure of human blood is 8.21 atm at 27°C. It is interesting to know that a 0.91% (mass/volume) solution of NaCl, known as saline water is isotonic with fluids inside the human red blood cells. In this solution, the blood corpuscles neither swell nor shrink. Therefore, medicines are mixed with saline water before being injected into the veins. [5]

Answer the following questions.

(i) What is an isotonic solution? • *Recall*

(ii) How much glucose should be used per 100 ml (aqueous solution) for intravenous injection that is isotonic with blood at 27°C? • *Application*

(iii) What would be the osmotic pressure of blood if the temperature is 37°C? • *Application*

(iv) A pure NaCl solution with salt concentration less than 0.91% (mass/volume) is hypertonic solution to human blood. Is this statement true or false? Give a reason. • *Understanding*

(v) Name the disease caused by taking a lot of salt or salty food, which results in water retention in tissue cells causing puffiness or swelling. • *Recall*

Or

(i) Calculate the boiling point of urea solution when 8.0 g of urea is dissolved in 250 g of water. Boiling point of pure water is 373 K. (K_b of water = 0.52 K kg mol^{-1}, molecular mass of urea = 60 g mol^{-1}) • *Application*

(ii) Ethylene glycol is used as an antifreeze agent. Calculate the amount of ethylene glycol to be added to four kilogram of water to prevent it from freezing at –6°C. (K_f of water = 1.86 K kg mol^{-1}) Assume that ethylene glycol ($CH_2OH \cdot CH_2OH$) does not dissociate or associate in aqueous solution. • *Application*

(iii) What will be the effect on the value of molality and molarity of a solution with change in temperature? • *Understanding*

Solutions

1. (A) (i) increases, decreases

(ii) six, three

(iii) propane, Clemmensen's

(iv) $(n-1)\,d^{1-10}$, ns^{1-2}

(B) (i) (d) Methylamine is a stronger base than ammonia due to +*I*-effect (electron-donating power) of alkyl group. On the other hand, aniline is a weaker base than ammonia due to electron withdrawing nature of aryl group. Thus, the correct order of the increasing basic nature is

Aniline < Ammonia < Methylamine

(ii) (b) Colligative properties of a solution depends only on the number of solute particles irrespective of their nature to the total number of particles present in the solution. Further, it is proportional to concentration of solute.

Thus, only statements (*P*) and (*R*) are correct.

(iii) (b) Anti-Markownikoff's addition of HBr is not observed in case of but-2-ene. This is because it a symmetrical alkene.

(iv) (c) The general formula of amino acid is

$$R\text{—}\underset{\substack{|\\ NH_2}}{CH}\text{—}COOH,$$

where, *R* represents side chain. The characteristic feature of *R* of given amino acids are follows

Glycine-H

Alanine- $—CH_3$

Valine- $—HC(CH_3)_2$
Leucine - $—(H_3C)_2CH—CH_2—$
Thus, glycine is not an asymmetric amino acid.

(v) (c) Geometrical isomerism is shown by $[Co(NH_3)(en_2)]^{3+}$ due to different possible geometric arrangements of the ligands. The structures of isomers are as follows

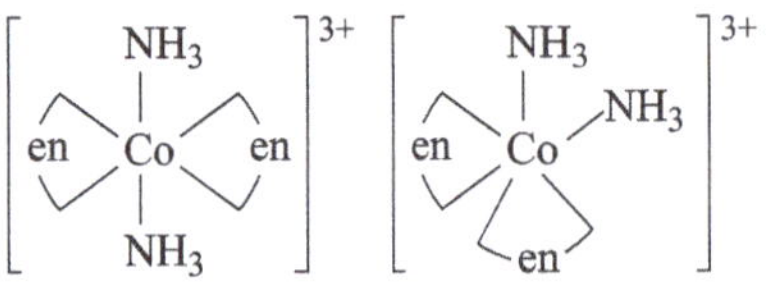

trans-isomer *cis*-isomer

(vi) (a) Tertiary butyl bromide undergoes Wurtz reaction to give 2, 2, 3, 3-tetramethyl butane. The reaction is as follows

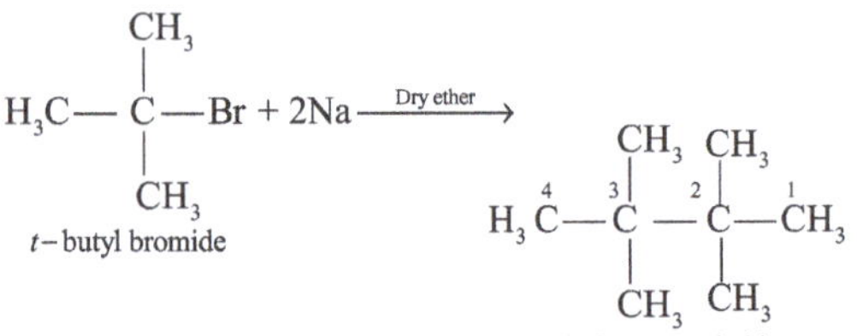

t−butyl bromide 2, 2, 3, 3-tetramethyl butane

Here, the hydrocarbon formed contain double the number of carbon atoms present in the alkyl halide. Thus, both Assertion and Reason are true and Reason is the correct explanation of Assertion.

(vii) (d) There is a gradual decrease in size among lanthanoids with an increase in atomic number. This is due to lanthanoid contraction. Thus, both Assertion and Reason are false.

(C) (i) The radioactive decay of C-14 takes place by first order kinetics. Therefore, the relation between the decay constant (k) and half-life period is given as

$$t_{\frac{1}{2}} = \frac{0.693}{k}$$

or $$k = \frac{0.693}{t_{\frac{1}{2}}}$$

(ii) Given, $t_{1/2} = 5770$ years

$$(a - x) = \frac{a}{3}$$

As we know that, for first order reaction

$$t = \frac{2303}{k} \log \frac{a}{(a-x)}$$

and, $$k = \frac{0.693}{t_{\frac{1}{2}}}$$

$\therefore$ $$t = \frac{2303 \times 5770}{0.693} \log \frac{a}{a/3}$$

$\Rightarrow$ $$t = \frac{2.303 \times 5770 \times \log 3}{0.693}$$

$$t = \frac{2.303 \times 5770 \times 0.4771}{0.693} \quad [\because \log 3 = 0.4771]$$

$\therefore$ $t = 9148.4$ years

(iii) Given, $t_{1/2} = 30$ minutes

If $a = 100, (a - x) = (100 - 87.5) = 12.5$

As we know that, for first order reaction,

$$t = \frac{2303}{k} \log \frac{a}{a-x} \quad \left[\because k = \frac{0.693}{t_{1/2}}\right]$$

$\therefore$ $$t = \frac{2.303 \times 30}{0.693} \times \log \frac{100}{12.5}$$

$\Rightarrow$ $$t = \frac{2.303 \times 30}{0.693} (\log 100 - \log 12.5)$$

or $$t = \frac{2.303 \times 30}{0.693} (2 - 1.097) \quad \left[\begin{array}{l}\because \log 100 = 2 \\ \log 12.5 = 1.097\end{array}\right]$$

$\therefore$ $t = 99.70 \times 0.903$ mins $= 90.03$ mins

2. B is a strong electrolyte as on dilution, Λ_m increases to a little extent. This is because in case of strong electrolyte, on dilution, number of ions remains almost the same and only inter ionic attraction decreases.

3. Compound $[A]$ has characteristic odour which means it can be benzaldehyde. It undergoes Cannizzaro reaction with NaOH to give alcohol and sodium salt of acid.

Compound $[B]$ can be benzyl alcohol as it contains only one oxygen atom, which on oxidation gives back compound $[A]$.

The reaction involved is

$$\underset{(B)}{C_6H_5CH_2OH} \xrightarrow{CrO_3} \underset{(A)}{C_6H_5CHO}$$

Compound 'C' can be sodium salt of benzoic acid which on heating with sodalime yields an aromatic compound 'D' which may be benzene.

Thus, $[A] = C_6H_5CHO$ (Benzaldehyde),

$[B] = C_6H_5CH_2OH$ (Benzyl alcohol)

$[C] = C_6H_5COONa$ (Sodium salt of benzoic acid)

$[D] = C_6H_6$ (Benzene)

4. The scheme/sequence of reactions for the synthesis of n-butane using CH_3I as the only source of carbon is as follows

$$\underset{\text{Methyl iodide}}{2CH_3I} \xrightarrow[\text{Wurtz reaction}]{\text{Na, dry ether}} \underset{\text{Ethane}}{CH_3 — CH_3} \xrightarrow{Cl_2/h\nu} \underset{\text{Ethyl chloride}}{CH_3CH_2Cl}$$

$$2CH_3CH_2Cl \xrightarrow[\text{Wurtz reaction}]{\text{Na, dry ether}} \underset{n\text{-butane}}{CH_3CH_2CH_2CH_3}$$

Propane cannot be obtained in pure state by the above scheme. This is because, Wurtz reaction between CH_3I and C_2H_5I will give three products, i.e., ethane, propane and butane.

5. Given, $T_1 = 298\text{ K}$ and $T_2 = 308\text{ K}$

$$\frac{k_2}{k_1} = 2,\ R = 8.314\ \text{J K}^{-1}\ \text{mol}^{-1}$$

According to Arrhenius equation,

$$\log\frac{k_2}{k_1} = \frac{E_a}{2.303\,R}\left[\frac{1}{T_1} - \frac{1}{T_2}\right]$$

$$\log 2 = \frac{E_a}{2.303 \times 8.314\ \text{J/K/mol}}\left[\frac{-1}{298} - \frac{1}{308}\right]$$

$$0.3010 = \frac{E_a}{2.303 \times 8.314} \times \frac{10}{298 \times 308}$$

$$E_a = \frac{0.3010 \times 2.303 \times 8.314 \times 298 \times 308}{10}\ (\text{J mol}^{-1})$$

$$E_a = 52897.78\ \text{J/mol or } 52.898\ \text{kJ/mol}$$

6. Since, compound $[X]$ having molecular formula C_3H_5N produces primary amine on reaction with $LiAlH_4$. Therefore, it must be propanenitrile or ethyl cyanide (C_2H_5CN).

However, compound $[Y]$ of same formula (C_3H_5N) produces secondary amine on reaction with $LiAlH_4$. Therefore, it must be ethyl isocyanide (C_2H_5NC). The reactions are as follows :

$$\underset{\substack{\text{Ethyl cyanide}\\[A]}}{CH_3CH_2C{\equiv}N} + LiAlH_4 \longrightarrow \underset{\substack{\text{Propanamine}\\\text{(Primary amines)}}}{CH_3CH_2CH_2NH_2}$$

$$\underset{\substack{\text{Ethyl isocyanide}\\[B]}}{CH_3CH_2{-}\overset{\oplus}{N}{\equiv}\overset{\ominus}{C}} \xrightarrow{LiAlH_4} \underset{\substack{\text{N-methyl ethanamine}\\\text{(Secondary amines)}}}{CH_3CH_2NHCH_3}$$

7. In the complex $[Ni(CN)_4]^{2-}$, the oxidation state of Ni is +2.

Ni (atom ($Z = 28$)

$= [Ar]3d^8 4s^2 =$ 3d: [⇅][⇅][⇅][↑][↑] 4s: [⇅] 4p: [ ][ ][ ]

$Ni^{2+} = [Ar]3d^8 =$ 3d: [⇅][⇅][⇅][↑][↑] 4s: [ ] 4p: [ ][ ][ ]

Since, CN^- is a strong field ligand, so pairing of electrons will take place.

$[Ni(CN)_4]^{2-} =$ 3d: [⇅][⇅][⇅][⇅][ ] [××][××][××][××]

dsp^2-hybridised

Thus, $[Ni(CN)_4]^{2-}$ is diamagnetic and the shape of the complex is square planar.

Therefore, out of Pari and Suhail's responses, Suhail's response was correct.

8. (i) As compound 'X' does not react with sodium metal or potassium permanganate, it cannot be an alcohol.

(ii) As compound 'X' dissolves in conc. H_2SO_4, it may be an ether.

(iii) As compound 'X' on heating with excess of HI, gives a single alkyl halide, therefore compound 'X' must be a symmetrical ether.

(iv) The only symmetrical ether having molecular formula $C_4H_{10}O$ is diethyl ether.

Thus, compound 'X' is diethyl ether,

$CH_3{-}CH_2{-}O{-}CH_2{-}CH_3$.

$$CH_3CH_2{-}O{-}CH_2CH_3 \xrightarrow{\text{Conc. } H_2SO_4} \underset{\text{Soluble oxonium salt}}{\left[CH_3{-}CH_2{-}\overset{+}{\underset{|\atop H}{O}}{-}CH_2{-}CH_3\right]HSO_4^-}$$

$$\underset{\substack{(X)\\\text{Diethyl ether}}}{CH_3CH_2OCH_2CH_3} \xrightarrow[\Delta]{HI} 2\underset{\text{Ethyl iodide}}{CH_3CH_2{-}I}$$

9. (i) (a) $\underset{\text{Benzladehyde}}{C_6H_5CHO} \xrightarrow[(2)\ SOCl_2]{(1)\ K_2Cr_2O_7/H_2SO_4} \underset{\substack{\text{Benzoyl}\\\text{chloride}\\(A)}}{C_6H_5COCl} \xrightarrow{C_6H_6\ (\text{Anhy. }AlCl_3)} \underset{\substack{\text{Benzophenone}\\(B)}}{C_6H_5COC_6H_5}$

(b) $\underset{\text{Propyne}}{CH_3{-}C{\equiv}CH} \xrightarrow[\substack{(2)\text{ Vigorous oxidation,}\\\text{conc. }HNO_3}]{(1)\ H_2SO_4/HgSO_4} \underset{\substack{\text{Acetic acid}\\(A)}}{CH_3COOH} \xrightarrow[\text{conc. }H_2SO_4]{C_2H_5OH} \underset{\substack{\text{Ethyl ethanoate}\\(B)}}{CH_3COOC_2H_5}$

Or

(ii) (a) The possible functional isomers of carbonyl compound with molecular formula, C_4H_8O are

$$CH_3{-}\overset{\overset{CH_3}{|}}{CH}{-}CHO,\ CH_3CH_2CH_2CHO,$$

$$CH_3CH_2{-}\overset{\overset{O}{\|}}{C}{-}CH_3$$

- Isomers (A) and (C) give positive Tollen's test, thus they must be aldehydes.

$$\underset{\text{Aldehyde}}{RCHO} + \underset{\text{Tollen's reagent}}{2[Ag(NH_3)_2]^+} + 3OH^- \xrightarrow{\Delta}$$

$$RCOO^- + \underset{\text{Silver mirror}}{2Ag\downarrow} + 2H_2O + 4NH_3\uparrow$$

$$CH_3{-}\underset{\underset{CH_3}{|}}{CH}{-}CHO \text{ and } CH_3CH_2CH_2CHO$$

- Isomer (B) does not give Tollen's test, but gives positive Iodoform test, thus it must be a ketone with

$$CH_3{-}\overset{\overset{O}{\|}}{C}{-}\text{ group.}$$

$$RCOCH_3 \xrightarrow{NaOX} RCOONa + CHX_3\ [X = Cl, Br, I]$$

Isomers (A) and (B) on reduction with Zn(Hg) / conc. HCl give same product.

$$CH_3-\underset{\underset{CH_3}{|}}{CH}-CHO + 4[H] \xrightarrow{\text{Zn-Hg/conc. HCl}} CH_3\underset{\underset{CH_3}{|}}{CH}-CH_3 + H_2O$$

$$CH_3-CH_2-CH_2-CHO + 4[H] \xrightarrow{\text{Zn-Hg/conc. HCl}} CH_3-CH_2-CH_2-CH_3 + H_2O$$

$$CH_3CH_2COCH_3 + 4[H] \xrightarrow{\text{Zn-Hg/conc. HCl}} CH_3CH_2CH_2CH_3 + H_2O$$

So, the structures of (*A*), (*B*) and (*C*) are

$$\underset{(A)}{CH_3CH_2CH_2CHO}, \underset{(B)}{CH_3CH_2COCH_3}, \underset{(C)}{CH_3\underset{\underset{CH_3}{|}}{CH}-CHO}$$

(b) The isomer (*B*) is least reactive towards addition of HCN.

Since, aldehydes are more reactive towards nucleophilic addition reactions than ketones due to inductive and steric effects.

10. Given, $E^\circ_{Al^{3+}/Al} = -1.66$ V

$E^\circ_{Sn^{2+}/Sn} = -0.14$ V

For the given cell,

$$Al/Al^{3+}\ (0.01\text{ M}) \,||\, Sn^{2+}\ (0.015\text{ M})/Sn$$

$$E^\circ_{cell} = E^\circ_{cathode} - E^\circ_{anode}$$
$$= -0.14\text{ V} - (-1.66)\text{ V}$$
$$= 1.52\text{ V}$$

The half-cell reactions are as follows

At anode

$$Al(s) \longrightarrow Al^{3+}(aq) + 3e^-] \times 2$$

At cathode

$$Sn^{2+}(aq) + 2e^- \longrightarrow Sn(s)] \times 3$$

Overall reaction

$$2Al(s) + 3Sn^{2+}(aq) \longrightarrow 2Al^{3+}(aq) + 3Sn(s)$$

$$E_{cell} = E^\circ_{cell} - \frac{0.0591}{n} \log \frac{[Al^{3+}]^2}{[Sn^{2+}]^3}$$

Here, n = number of electrons transferred, i.e., 6

$$\therefore \quad E_{cell} = 1.52 - \frac{0.0591}{6} \log \frac{[0.01]^2}{[0.015]^3}$$

$$E_{cell} = 1.52 - \frac{0.0591}{6} (\log (10)^5 - \log (15)^3)$$

$$\Rightarrow \quad E_{cell} = 1.52 - \frac{0.0591}{6} \times (5 - 3.528)$$

$$\therefore \quad E_{cell} = 1.5056\text{ V}$$

Now, $\Delta G = -nFE^\circ_{cell}$

$$\therefore \quad \Delta G = (-6\text{ mol}) \times (96500\text{ C mol}^{-1}) \times (1.5056\text{ V})$$
$$= -871742\text{ J}$$

11. (i) **Propan-1-ol and propan-2-ol**

Propan-1-ol and propan-2-ol can be distinguished by Lucas test.

$$\underset{\substack{\text{Propan-1-ol} \\ \text{(Primary alcohol)}}}{CH_3CH_2CH_2OH} + HCl \xrightarrow[\text{ZnCl}_2]{\text{Anhydrous}} \underset{\substack{\text{n-propyl chloride} \\ \text{(Do not produce turbidity} \\ \text{at room temperature)}}}{CH_3CH_2CH_2Cl} + H_2O$$

$$\underset{\substack{\text{Propan-2-ol} \\ \text{(Secondary alcohol)}}}{CH_3-\underset{\overset{|}{OH}}{CH}-CH_3} + HCl \xrightarrow{\text{Anhydrous ZnCl}_2} \underset{\substack{\text{2-chloropropane} \\ \text{(Produces turbidity after 5} \\ \text{mins at room temperature)}}}{CH_3-\underset{\overset{|}{Cl}}{CH}-CH_3} + H_2O$$

(ii) **Ethanol and phenol**

Phenol gives violet colouration complex with $FeCl_3$ solution but ethanol does not

$$\underset{\text{Phenol}}{6C_6H_5OH} + FeCl_3 \longrightarrow \underset{\text{Violet colour complex}}{[Fe(COC_6H_5)_6]^{3-}} + 3H^+ + 3HCl$$

12. (i) $\underset{\text{Nitrobenzene}}{C_6H_5NO_2} \xrightarrow[\text{Sn/HCl}]{6[H]} \underset{\substack{\text{Aniline} \\ (A)}}{C_6H_5NH_2} \xrightarrow[273-278\text{ K}]{HNO_2 + HCl}$

$$\underset{\substack{\text{Benzene diazonium} \\ \text{chloride} \\ (B)}}{C_6H_5N_2^+Cl^-} \xrightarrow[\text{(Coupling reaction)}]{C_6H_5NH_2} \underset{\substack{\text{p-aminoazobenzene} \\ (C)}}{C_6H_5N=NC_6H_4NH_2}$$

(ii) $\underset{\text{Ethanamine}}{CH_3CH_2NH_2} \xrightarrow[\text{(2) Red P/Cl}_2]{\text{(1) HNO}_2} \underset{\substack{\text{Ethyl chloride} \\ (A)}}{CH_3CH_2Cl} \xrightarrow[\text{(2) H}_2\text{O/H}^+]{\text{(1) KCN}}$

$$\underset{\substack{\text{Propanoic acid} \\ (B)}}{CH_3CH_2COOH} \xrightarrow[\text{(2) Br}_2\text{/KOH}]{\text{(1) NH}_3\text{/ heat}} \underset{\substack{\text{Ehanamine} \\ (C)}}{CH_3CH_2NH_2}$$

13. (i) For case *A*,

Given, $W_2 = 5.85$ g

$W_1 = 100$ g

$T_f = -3.348°C = 269.652$ K

$K_f = 1.86$ K Kg mol^{-1}

Molecular mass = 58.5 g/mol

As we know that,

$$\Delta T_f = T_f^\circ - T_f$$

$$\therefore \quad \Delta T_f = 273 - 269.652 = 3.348\text{ K}$$

$\because$ Observed molecular mass

$$M_2 = \frac{K_f \times W_2 \times 1000}{\Delta T_f \times W_1}$$

$$\therefore \quad M_2 = \frac{1.86 \times 5.85 \times 1000}{3.348 \times 100} = 32.5\text{ g/mol}$$

Now, For case *B*,

Given, $W_2 = 0.2$ g

$W_1 = 20$ g

$\Delta T_f = 0.45°C = 0.45$ K

$K_f = 5.12$ Kg mol^{-1}

Molecular mass = 60 g/mol

$\because$ Observed Molecular mass

$$M_2 = \frac{K_f \times W_2 \times 1000}{\Delta T_f \times W_1}$$

$$\therefore \quad M_2 = \frac{5.12 \times 0.2 \times 1000}{0.45 \times 20} = 113.78 \text{ g/mol}$$

(ii) As we know that,

$$\text{van't Hoff factor} = \frac{\text{Normal molecular mass}}{\text{Observed molecular mass}}$$

Therefore, [*A*] will undergo dissociation as its van't Hoff factor (*i*) value is 18. Whereas, [*B*] will undergo association as its van't Hoff factor (*i*) value is 0.53.

(iii) The given order of depression in freezing point is correct. This is because ΔT_f depends on the number of moles of solute molecules.

14. (i) **Rosenmund's reaction** Acyl chloride or acid chloride is hydrogenated in the presence of palladium catalyst supported over and partially poisoned by the addition of sulphur or barium sulphate.

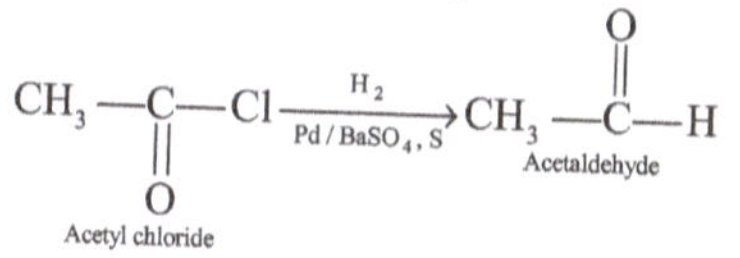

(ii) **Benzoin condensation** The addition reaction between two kinds of aromatic aldehydes especially benzaldehyde in presence of cyanide ions as a catalyst to form, α-hydroxy ketone.

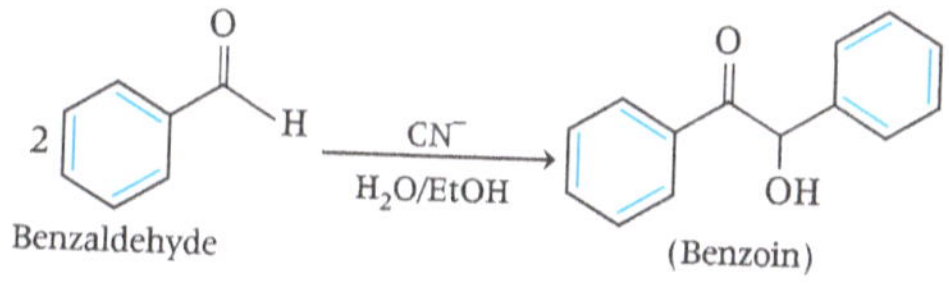

(iii) **Perkin's reaction** This reaction gives an α, β-unsaturated aromatic acid *via* Aldol condensation of aromatic aldehyde and an acid anhydride. It occurs in the presence of alkali, which acts as a base catalyst in the reaction.

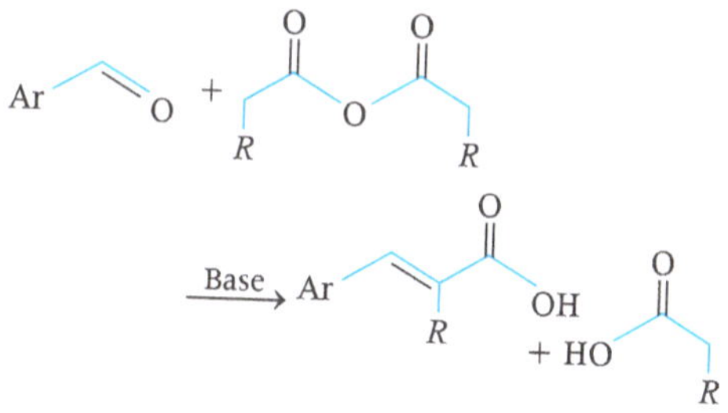

15. (i) The formula and IUPAC name of two coordination complex ions (C.N = 6) with cyanide ligand and iron as central metal atom is as follows

- $[Fe(CN)_6]^{4-}$

  IUPAC name — Hexacyanidoferrate (II) ion

- $[Fe(CN)_6]^{3-}$

  IUPAC name — Hexacyanidoferrate (III) ion

(ii) (a) If $\Delta_o > P$, then ligand will be a strong ligand. Therefore, it will become more energetically favourable for the fourth electron to occupy t_{2g} orbital with configuration $t_{2g}^4 e_g^0$.

(b) If $\Delta_o < P$, then ligand will be a weak field ligand. Therefore, the fourth electron will enter one of the e_g orbitals giving the configuration $t_{2g}^3 e_g^1$.

16. (i) (a) • Dry cell consists of a zinc container which acts as the anode.

• The cathode is a carbon (graphite) rod surrounded by a mixture of powdered manganese dioxide and carbon.

(b) The space between anode and cathode is filled with moist paste of ammonium chloride and zinc chloride.

(c) Dry cell do not have a long life because the acidic NH_4Cl corrodes the zinc container.

Or (ii) (a) If salt bridge is removed from the two half-cells, then cell will not function. This is because, electricity flow will stop after sometime as positive charge will accumulate at oxidation half-cell and negative at reduction half-cell which balance the redox free energy and thus, will stop the redox reaction.

(b) Copper sulphate solution cannot be stored in a zinc pot because zinc being more reactive than copper, displaces copper from its salt solution.

(c) The density of H_2SO_4 in a lead storage battery decreases as it is discharged. This is because sulphate is consumed from the electrolyte due to the formation of lead sulphate.

17. (i) The peptide bond linkage in glycylalanine is shown below.

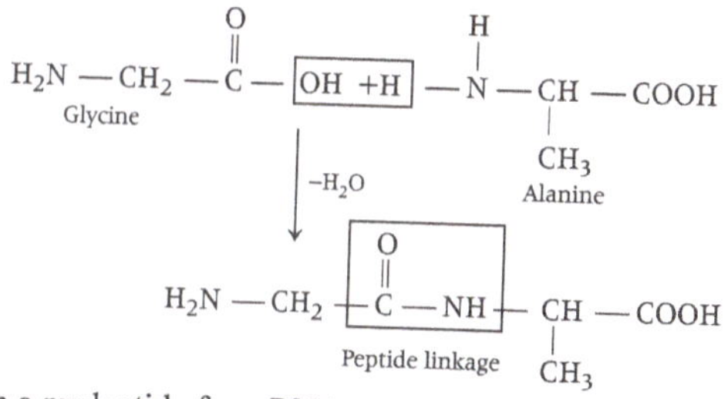

(ii) When a nucleotide from DNA containing thymine is hydrolysed, then β-D-2-deoxyribose (pentose sugar), phosphoric acid and thymine (nitrogenous base) are obtained as products.

(iii) Reducing sugars are the carbohydrates in which ketonic or aldehydic groups are free and are capable of reducing Fehling's solution or Tollen's reagent.
e.g. Glucose, fructose, ribose etc.

18. (i) Rate law for the given reaction

$A + B \rightarrow$ Product may be expressed as

$$\text{Rate} = k\,[A]^x[B]^y$$

$$(\text{Rate})_1 = 4.0 \times 10^{-4} = k\,(0.1)^x(0.1)^y \quad \ldots\text{(i)}$$

$$(\text{Rate})_2 = 1.6 \times 10^{-3} = k\,(0.2)^x(0.2)^y \quad \ldots\text{(ii)}$$

$(\text{Rate})_3 = 1.0 \times 10^{-2} = k\,(0.5)^x (0.1)^y$ ...(iii)

$(\text{Rate})_4 = 1.0 \times 10^{-2} = k\,(0.5)^x (0.5)^y$ ...(iv)

On dividing Eq^n (iii) by Eq^n (ii), we get

$$\frac{(\text{Rate})_3}{(\text{Rate})_1} = \frac{1.0 \times 10^{-2}}{4.0 \times 10^{-4}} = \frac{k\,(0.5)^x (0.1)^y}{k\,(0.1)^x (0.1)^y}$$

$\Rightarrow (5)^2 = (5)^x \quad \therefore \quad x = 2$

On dividing Eq^n (iv) by Eq^n (iii), we get

$$\frac{(\text{Rate})_4}{(\text{Rate})_3} = \frac{1.0\times 10^{-2}}{1.0\times 10^{-2}} = \frac{k\,(0.5)^x (0.5)^y}{k\,(0.5)^x (0.1)^y}$$

$(1)^0 = (5)^y$

$\therefore \quad y = 0$

Thus, order with respect A is 2 and with respect to B is 0.

(ii) Now, Rate $= k\,[A]^2[B]^0$

Putting values in Eq. (i), we get

$4.0 \times 10^{-4} = k\,[0.1]^2$

$\therefore \quad k = \dfrac{4.0 \times 10^{-4}}{0.1 \times 0.1} = 4 \times 10^{-2}\ \text{mol}^{-1}\ \text{L sec}^{-1}$

(iii) If $[A] = 0.2$ mol L^{-1}sec^{-1} and $[B] = 0.35$ mol L^{-1}sec^{-1}

Then, reaction rate can be calculated as

Rate $= k\,[A]^2[B]^0$

$\therefore$ Rate $= 4\times 10^{-2}\ [0.2]^2\ [0.35]^0$

$\Rightarrow$ Rate $= 4 \times 10^{-2} \times 4 \times 10^{-2}$

$= 1.6\times 10^{-3}$ mol L^{-1}sec^{-1}

19. (i)

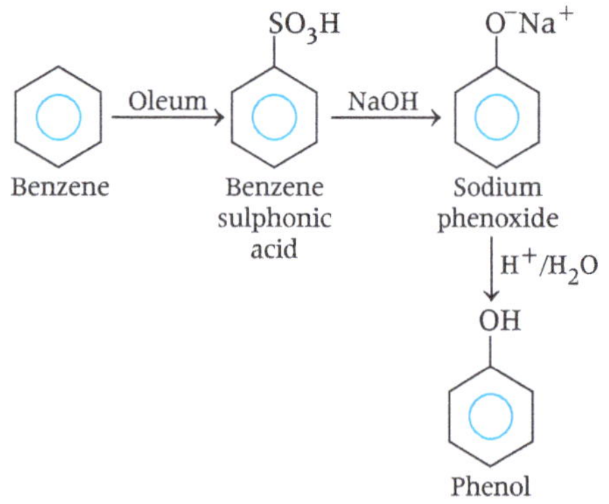

(ii) When phenol reacts with Br_2/CS_2 at low temperature, then monobromophenols are formed. The reaction is as follows

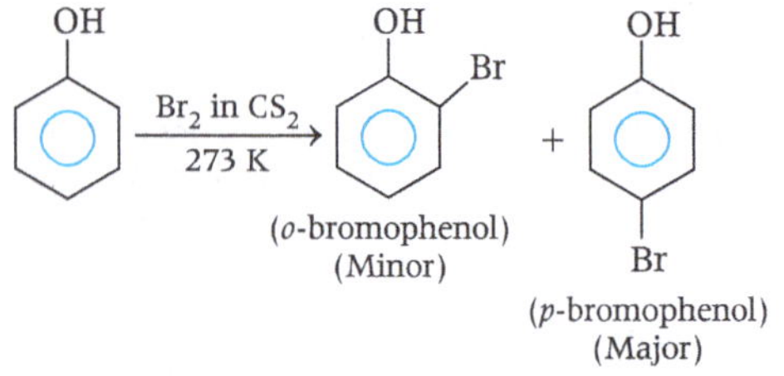

(iii) When phenol reacts with neutral $FeCl_3$ solution, then ferric phenoxide complex is formed.

Following reaction takes place

$$6C_6H_5OH + FeCl_3 \longrightarrow \underset{\text{Violet colour complex}}{[Fe(OC_6H_5)_6]^{3-}} + 3H^+ + 3HCl$$

(iv) Picric acid is prepared by first treating phenol with conc. H_2SO_4 at 373 K and then with HNO_3.

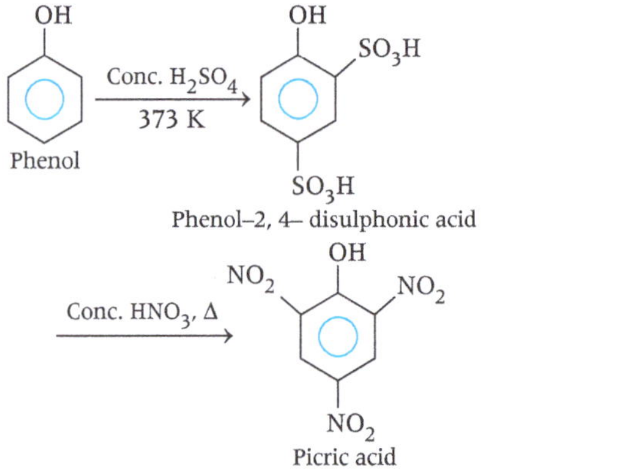

(v) On treating phenol with chloroform in the presence of sodium hydroxide, —CHO group is introduced at *ortho*-position of benzene ring.

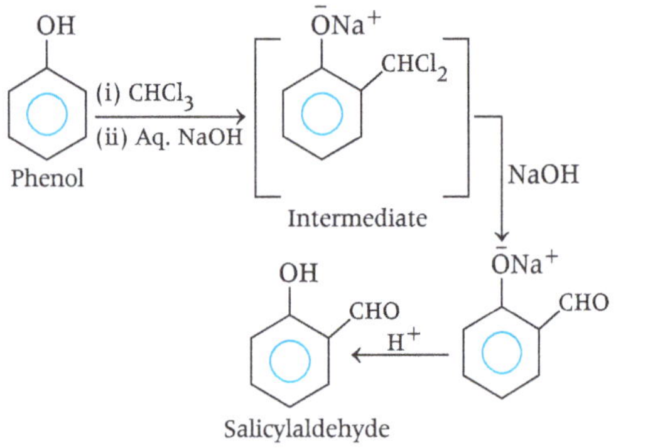

20. (i) (a) When oxalic acid is added to acidic solution of $KMnO_4$, its colour disappear due to the reduction of MnO_4^- ion to Mn^{2+}. Following chemical reaction takes place.

$$5C_2O_4^{2-} + 2MnO_4^- + 16H^+ \longrightarrow \underset{\text{(Colourless)}}{2Mn^{2+}} + 8H_2O + 10CO_2$$

(b) Some transition metals and their compounds are attracted towards magnetic field due to presence of unpaired electrons in *d*-orbitals.

(c) Mn^{2+} compounds (E.C, [Ar]$3d^5$) are more stable towards (+3) oxidation state due to half-filled *d*-orbitals.

On the other hand, Fe^{2+} compounds (E.C, [Ar]$3d^6$) are comparatively less stable as they have six electrons in their orbitals.

So, they tend to lose one electron from Fe^{3+} and get stable $3d^5$ configuration.

(ii) (a) $2KMnO_4 + 8H_2SO_4 + 10FeSO_4 \longrightarrow K_2SO_4 + 2MnSO_4 + 5Fe_2(SO_4)_3 + 8H_2O$

(b) $K_2Cr_2O_7 + 7H_2SO_4 + 6KI \longrightarrow 4K_2SO_4 + Cr_2(SO_4)_3 + 3I_2 + 7H_2O$

21. (i) Two solutions having same osmotic pressure at a given temperature are called isotonic solutions.

(ii) Given, $\pi = 8.21$ atm

$$T = 273 + 27 = 300\text{ K}$$
$$V = 100\text{ mL} = 0.1\text{ L}$$

As we know that, $\pi = \frac{n}{V}RT$

$$\therefore 8.21 = \frac{W_2 \times 0.0821 \times 300}{180 \times 0.1}$$

$$\Rightarrow W_2 = \frac{8.21 \times 180 \times 0.1}{0.0821 \times 300} = 6\text{ g}$$

(iii) Given, $\pi = 8.21$ atm

$$T = 273 + 37 = 310\text{ K}$$
$$V = 0.1\text{ L}$$

As we know that,

$$\pi = \frac{n}{V}RT$$

$$\therefore \quad \pi = \frac{6 \times 0.0821 \times 310}{180 \times 0.1}$$

$$\pi = 8.48\text{ atm}$$

(iv) The given statement is false. As solution having less osmotic pressure than the other solution is called hypotonic solution. Thus, a pure NaCl solution with salt concentration less than 0.91% (mass/volume) is hypotonic with human blood.

(v) Edema is caused by taking a lot of salt or salty food. This happens because people experience water retention in tissue, cells and intercellular spaces because of osmosis.

Or

(i) Mass of urea, $W_2 = 8.0$ g

Mass of water, $W_1 = 250$ g

$$T_b^\circ = 373\text{ K}$$
$$K_b = 0.52\text{ K kg mol}^{-1}$$

Molecular mass of urea, $M_2 = 60$ g/mol

As we know that,

$$\Delta T_b = \frac{K_b \times W_2 \times 1000}{M_2 \times W_1}$$

$$\therefore \quad \Delta T_b = \frac{0.52 \times 8 \times 1000}{250 \times 60}$$

$$\Delta T_b = 0.277\text{ K}$$

Now, $\Delta T_b = T_b - T_b^\circ$

$\because$ Freezing point of urea solution,

$$T_b = (0.277 + 373)\text{ K}$$
$$= 373.277\text{ K}$$

(ii) Mass of water, $W_1 = 4$ kg or 4000 g

$$T_f = -6°\text{C}$$
$$K_f = 1.86\text{ K kg mol}^{-1}$$

As we know that,

$$\Delta T_f = T_f^\circ - T_f$$
$$= 0 - (-6°\text{C})$$
$$= 6°\text{C or } 6\text{ K}$$

Now, $\Delta T_f = \frac{K_f \times W_2 \times 1000}{W_1 \times M_2}$

$$W_2 = \frac{6 \times 4000 \times 62.07}{1000 \times 1.86}$$

Amount of urea, $W_2 = 800.9$ g

(iii) Molality does not change with change in temperature. While, molarity of a solution decrease with rise in temperature due to increase in volume.

ISC

SAMPLE PAPER 1

Time : 3 hrs
Marks : 70

Chemistry

General Instructions

(See Latest ISC Specimen Paper)

SECTION A

(14 Marks)

1. (A) Fill in the blanks by choosing the appropriate word(s) from those given in brackets.

[oxidation, *p*-benzoquinone, reduction, benzoic acid, mol $L^{-1}s^{-1}$, $mol^{-1}L\ s^{-1}$, s^{-1}, red, black, white, paramagnetic, diamagnetic, octahedral, tetrahedral] **[4×1]**

(i) For a first order reaction, the unit of rate is ...... and that of rate constant is ....

(ii) When formic acid reacts with Tollen's reagent and Fehling solution it gives ...... and ...... ppt. respectively.

(iii) The complex $[Mn(H_2O)_6]^{2+}$ ion has ...... geometry and is ...... in nature.

(iv) Phenol on ...... with chromic acid gives ....

(B) Select and write the correct alternative from the choices given below. **[7×1]**

(i) Which of the following is resistant to nucleophilic attack by hydroxyl ions?

(a) Methyl acetate (b) Acetonitrile
(c) Acetamide (d) Diethyl ether

(ii) At pH = 4, glycine exists as

(a) $H_3N^+—CH_2—COO^-$ (b) $H_3N^+—CH_2—COOH$
(c) $H_2N—CH_2—COOH$ (d) $H_2N—CH_2COO^-$

(iii) For strong electrolytes, the plot of molar conductance *versus* $\sqrt{C}$ is

(a) parabolic (b) linear (c) sinusoidal (d) circular

(iv) During a chemical reaction with increase in temperature, rate of a reaction

(a) decreases (b) increases
(c) remains constant (d) show irregular trends

(v) Which of the following statements are correct, when a mixture of NaCl and $K_2Cr_2O_7$ is gently warmed with conc. H_2SO_4?

I. A deep red vapours is evolved.
II. The vapours when passed into NaOH solution gives a yellow solution of Na_2CrO_4.
III. Chlorine gas is evolved.
IV. Chromyl chloride is formed.

Choose the correct option.

(a) Both I and II (b) I, II and III
(c) I, II and IV (d) Both III and IV

(vi) **Assertion** (A) On increasing dilution, specific conductance increases.

Reason (R) Degree of ionisation of weak electrolyte increases and mobility of ions also increases.

(a) Both (A) and (R) are correct and (R) is the correct explanation of (A).
(b)Both (A) and (R) are correct but (R) is not the correct explanation of (A).
(c) (A) is correct and (R) is incorrect.
(d)(A) is incorrect and (R) is correct.

(vii) **Assertion** (A) Nitration of chlorobenzene leads to the formation of *ortho* and *para*-nitrochlorobenzene.

Reason (R) $—NO_2$ group is a *o*, *p*-directing group.

(a) Both (A) and (R) are correct and (R) is the correct explanation of (A).
(b) Both (A) and (R) are correct but (R) is not the correct explanation of (A).
(c) (A) is correct and (R) is incorrect.
(d) (A) is incorrect and (R) is correct.

(C) Read the passage given below and answer the questions that follows **[3×1]**

There are nuclear reactions constantly occuring in our body, but there are very few of them compared to the chemical reactions, and they do not affect our bodies much. Nuclear reactions occuring in our bodies is radioactive decay.

The most common natural radioactive isotopes in human are carbon-14 and potassium 40. The natural occurrence of carbon-14 decay in the body is the core principle behind carbon dating.

(i) Why is carbon-14 radioactive while carbon-12 not? (Atomic number of carbon=6)

(ii) Which are the two most common radioactive decays happening in human body?

(iii) Approximately how old is a fossil with 12 g of carbon-14, if it initially possessed 32 g of carbon-14? (Given : $t_{1/2}$ = 6000 s, log 2.667=0.4260)

SECTION B

(20 Marks)

2. The vapour pressure of water is 15.6 kPa at 300 K. Calculate the vapour pressure of a one molal solution of a non-volatile, non-ionic solute in water. **[2]**

3. Complete the following equations. **[2]**

(i) $2CrO_4^{2-} + 2H^+ \longrightarrow$ (ii) $KMnO_4 \xrightarrow{\text{Heat}}$

4. Calculate the mass of compound (molar mass = 256 g mol^{-1}) to be dissolved in 75 g of benzene to lower its freezing point by 0.48 K.

(K_f = 5.12 K kg mol^{-1}) **[2]**

5. Write equations involved in following reactions. **[2]**

(i) Williamson's ether synthesis (ii) Kolbe's reaction

6. Give reason for the following. **[2]**

(i) Zn^{2+} salts are white while Ni^{2+} salts are blue.

(ii) Why Mn^{3+} acts as strong oxidising agent?

7. Deficiency of which vitamin causes the following diseases. **[2]**

(i) Bleeding gums (ii) Weak eyesight

8. (i) During working of a mercury cell, write the reaction taking place at (a) anode (b) cathode

(ii) Given that the standard reduction potential for $Cr^{3+}/Cr = -0.72$ V and $Fe^{2+}/Fe = -0.42$ V. What will be the standard potential of the cell? **[2]**

9. Identify compounds [*A*] and [*B*] in the following reactions. **[2]**

(i)

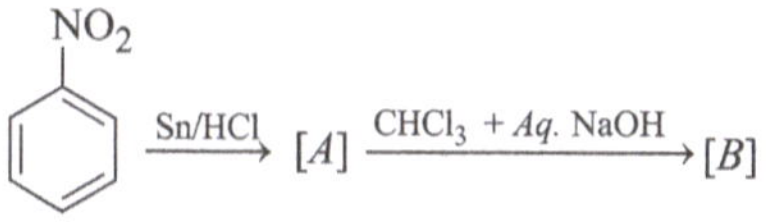

(ii)

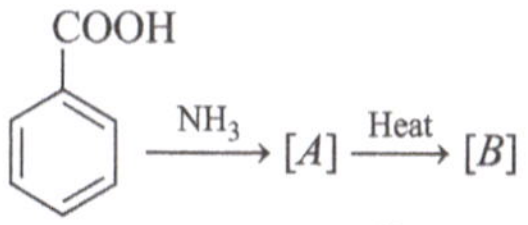

Or

An aromatic compound [*A*] on heating with Br_2 and KOH forms a compound [*B*] of molecular formula C_6H_7N which on reaction with $CHCl_3$ and alc. KOH produces a foul smelling compound *C*. Identify the compounds [*A*], [*B*], [*C*] and give the IUPAC name of [*C*]. **[2]**

10. A reactant has a half-life of 10 minutes.

(i) Calculate the rate constant for the first order reaction.

(ii) What fraction of the reactant will be left after an hour of the reaction has occurred? **[2]**

11. Write chemical equations when **[2]**

(i) ethyl chloride is treated with aqueous KOH.

(ii) CH_3Br is treated with KCN.

SECTION C

(21 Marks)

12. In a reaction between *A* and *B*, the initial rate of reaction (r_0) was measured for different initial concentrations of *A* and *B* as given below:

A / mol L^{-1}	0.20	0.20	0.40
B / mol L^{-1}	0.30	0.10	0.05
r_0 / mol L^{-1} s^{-1}	5.07×10^{-5}	5.07×10^{-5}	1.43×10^{-4}

What is the order of the reaction with respect to *A* and *B*? **[3]**

13. Give reasons for the following.

(i) Ethyl iodide undergoes S_N2 reaction faster than ethyl bromide.

(ii) (±) 2-butanol is optically inactive.

(iii) C—*X* bond length in halobenzene is smaller than C—*X* bond length in CH_3—*X*. **[3]**

14. Arrange the following compounds in the increasing order of their property as indicated.

$CH_3CH_2CH(Br)COOH, CH_3CH(Br)CH_2COOH, (CH_3)_2CHCOOH, CH_3CH_2CH_2COOH.$ **[3]**

(i) in the increasing order of their acidic strength.

(ii) in the increasing order of their pK_a values.

15. (i) Henry's law constant for the molality of methane in benzene at 298 K is 4.27×10^5 mm of Hg. Calculate the solubility of methane in benzene at 298 K under 760 mm of Hg.

(ii) The solubility of $Ba(OH)_2 \cdot 8H_2O$ in water is 5.6 g per 100 g of water at 288 K. Calculate the molality of hydroxide ion in saturated solution of $Ba(OH)_2 \cdot 8H_2O$ at that temperature. **[3]**

16. Give reason for the following.
   (i) *d*-block elements exhibit a large number of oxidation states than *f*-block elements.
   (ii) Sc^{3+} ion do not show paramagnetism.
   (iii) Transition metal exhibit high enthalpy of atomisation. **[3]**

17. Identify the structures of *A*, *B* and *C* in the following reactions. **[3]**

   (i) $C_6H_5N_2Cl \xrightarrow{CuCN} [A] \xrightarrow[\Delta]{H_2O/H^+} [B] \xrightarrow[\Delta]{NH_3} [C]$

   (ii) $CH_3CH_2I \xrightarrow{NaCN} [A] \xrightarrow[\text{Partial hydrolysis}]{OH^-} [B] \xrightarrow{NaOH+Br_2} [C]$

Or

How will the following be converted? (Give chemical equations)
   (i) Nitrobenzene to aniline
   (ii) Acetamide to ethylamine
   (iii) Benzene to acetanilide

18. Predict the major product of acid catalysed dehydration of **[3]**
   (i) 1-methyl cyclohexanol. (ii) butan-1-ol.

SECTION D **(15 Marks)**

19. (i) A steady current of 2 amperes was passed through two electrolytic cells *X* and *Y* connected in series containing electrolytes $FeSO_4$ and $ZnSO_4$ until 2.8 g of Fe deposited at the cathode of cell *X*. How long did the current flow? Calculate the mass of Zn deposited at the cathode of cell *Y*. (Molar mass : $Fe = 56\ g\ mol^{-1}$
$Zn = 653\ g\ mol^{-1}$, $1F = 96500\ C\ mol^{-1}$)

(ii) In the plot of molar conductivity (Λ_m) *vs* square root of concentration ($C^{1/2}$), following curves are obtained for two electrolytes *A* and *B*.

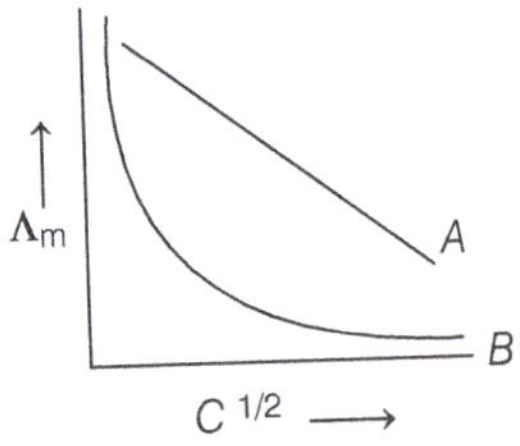

Predict the nature of electrolytes *A* and *B*. Justify your answer.

Or

(i) Calculate E°_{cell} for the following reaction at 298 K:

$$2Al(s)+3Cu^{2+}(0.01\,M) \longrightarrow 2Al^{3+}(0.01\,M)+3Cu(s)$$

Given, $E_{cell} = 1.98\ V$

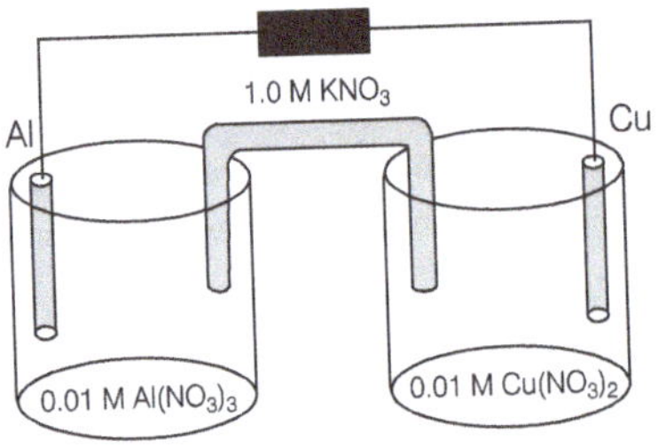

(ii) Calculate the potential of hydrogen electrode in contact with a solution whose pH is 10. **[5]**

20. (i) Write the chemical equation to illustrate the following name reactions.
   (a) Clemmensen reduction (b) Rosenmund reduction
   (c) HVZ reaction
   (ii) Give one chemical test to distinguish between the pair of compounds.
   (a) Formaldehyde and acetaldehyde
   (b) Acetone and acetic acid **[5]**

21. (i) Name the type of isomerism shown by the following pairs of coordination compounds.
   (a) $[Cu(NH_3)_4][PtCl_4]$ and $[Pt(NH_3)_4][CuCl_4]$
   (b) $[Cr(SCN)(H_2O)_5]^{2+}$ and $[Cr(NCS)(H_2O)_5]^{2+}$
   (c) $[Cr(H_2O)_6]Cl_3$ and $[CrCl(H_2O)_5]Cl_2 \cdot H_2O$
   (ii) Find the hybridisation and magnetic nature of the complex $[Fe(H_2O)_6]^{2+}$. **[5]**

Solutions

1. (A) (i) $mol\ L^{-1}s^{-1}$, s^{-1}
   (ii) black, red
   (iii) octahedral, paramagnetic
   (iv) oxidation, *p*-benzoquinone

(B) (i) (d) Diethyl ether is resistant to nucleophilic attack by hydroxyl ions because it is a Lewis base and is not easily attacked by nucleophile (OH^-).

(ii) (b) At pH = 4, glycine exist as
$H_3N^+—CH_2—COOH$.

In the acidic medium (pH = 4), COO^- group gets protonated.

(iii) (b) The plot of molar conductance (Λ_m) *versus* $\sqrt{C}$ is linear.

(iv) (b) Rate of a reaction increases with increase in temperature.

(v) (c) Statements I, II and IV are correct, while the statement III is incorrect. It's corrected form is as follows

On warming the mixture of NaCl and $K_2Cr_2O_7$ gently with conc. H_2SO_4, deep red vapours of chromyl chloride are evolved. When they are passed into NaOH solution, it gives a yellow solution of Na_2CrO_4.

(vi) (d) (A) is incorrect, but (R) is correct. On dilution, conductance (G) decreases, so specific conductance (κ) also decreases because according to relation, $\kappa = G\sigma$ and $\kappa \propto G$.

(vii) (c) (A) is correct, but (R) is incorrect. Presence of —Cl in chlorobenzene activates the ring at *ortho* and *para*-positions and therefore, nitration of chlorobenzene leads to formation of *o*, *p*-nitrochlorobenezne. While $—NO_2$ group is a *meta*-directing group.

(C) (i) C-14 and C-12 have same number of protons (i.e. 6) but different number of neutrons (i.e. 8 and 6 respectively). As C-14 atom has more neutrons than protons in its nucleus, therefore, its nucleus becomes unstable and shows radioactivity.

(ii) The two most common radioactive decays happening in human body are

(a) carbon-14 decay to stable nitrogen atom and

(b) potassium-40 atoms decay to stable calcium.

(iii) Given, initial amount of C-14 present in fossil

$C_0 = 32$ g

Final amount of C-14, i.e. $C_t = 12$ g.

Time $(t) = ?$

For 1st order reaction, $k = \dfrac{0.693}{6000}$

[half-life, i.e. 6000 s, is given in passage]

For 1st order reactions

$$t = \frac{2.303}{k}\log\left(\frac{C_0}{C_t}\right) \quad \ldots(i)$$

Substituting the given value in Eqn. (i), we get

$$t = \frac{2.303}{0.693}\times 6000 \times \log\frac{32}{12}$$

$$= 19939.4 \log 2.667$$

$$= 19939.4 \times 0.426 = 8494 \text{ years}$$

2. As solution is 1 molal, it means that 1 mole of solute is dissolved in 1000 g of solvent (water).

Moles of solute = 1 mol

Moles of water $= \dfrac{1000}{18} = 55.55$ mol

$\therefore$ Total moles = 56.55

Mole fraction of water $= \dfrac{55.55}{56.55}$

$$\left[\because \text{Mole fraction of solvent } (\chi) = \frac{\text{Moles of solvent}}{\text{Total moles}}\right]$$

Now, according to Raoult's law,

$$p_{\text{solution}} = p_{\text{solution}} \times \chi_{\text{solvent }(H_2O)}$$

$$p_{\text{solution}} = 15.6 \times \frac{55.55}{56.55}$$

$$= 15.32 \text{kPa}$$

3. (i) $2CrO_4^{2-} + 2H^+ \longrightarrow Cr_2O_7^{2-} + H_2O$

(ii) $2KMnO_4 \xrightarrow{\text{Heat}} K_2MnO_4 + MnO_2 + O_2$

4. Given that, $K_f = 5.12$ K kg mol^{-1}

Mass of benzene, $W_1 = 75$ g

Depression in freezing point,

$\Delta T_f = 0.48$ K, $M_2 = 256$ g mol^{-1}

If w_2 is the mass of compound.

Then, $\Delta T_f = \dfrac{K_f \times w_2 \times 1000}{W_1 \times M_2}$

(where, M_2 is molar mass of compound)

or $\quad 0.48 = \dfrac{5.12 \times w_2 \times 1000}{75 \times 256}$

$\therefore \quad w_2 = \dfrac{0.489 \times 75 \times 256}{5.12 \times 1000} = 1.8$ g

5. (i) When alkyl halide reacts with sodium alkoxide, ether is formed. This reaction is known as **Williamson's ether synthesis.**

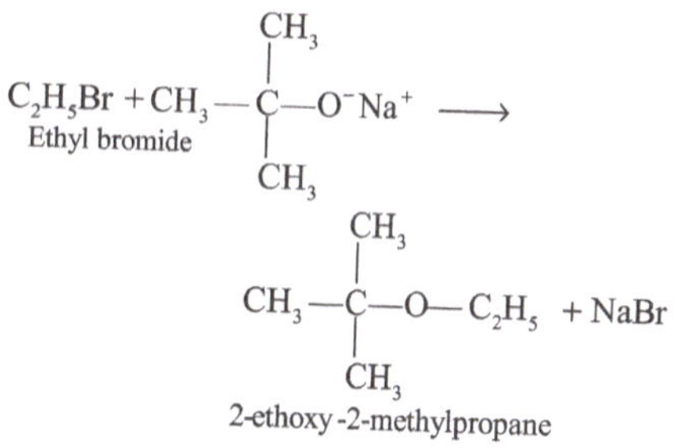

(ii) **Kolbe's reaction** When sodium phenoxide [generated by treating phenol with NaOH] is heated with CO_2 at about 400 K and under 4 to 7 atmospheric pressure, sodium salicylate is formed as major product, which on acidification gives salicylic acid.

e.g.

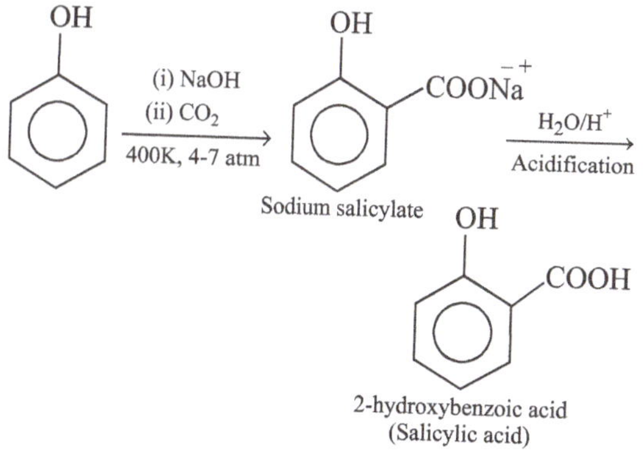

6. (i) Electronic configuration of $Zn^{2+} = 3d^{10}4s^0$

= [↑↓][↑↓][↑↓][↑↓][↑↓]

Electronic configuration of $Ni^{2+} = 3d^8 4s^0$

= [↑↓][↑↓][↑↓][↑][↑]

Salts that contains unpaired electrons are coloured thus, Zn^{2+} salts are white while Ni^{2+} salts are blue.

(ii) In the +3 oxidation state, Mn is a strong oxidising agent as its electronic configuration is $3d^4$, which is less stable and it can reduce to Mn^{2+} giving a more stable $3d^5$-configuration. Hence, it acts as a strong oxidising agent.

7. (i) Vitamin C (ii) Vitamin A

8. (i) In mercury cell, anode is made up of zinc mercury amalgam and cathode is of paste of HgO and carbon.

Electrode reactions are as follows.

(a) At anode

$$Zn(Hg) + 2\bar{O}H \longrightarrow ZnO(s) + H_2O + 2e^-$$

(b) At cathode

$$HgO + H_2O + 2e^- \longrightarrow Hg(l) + 2OH^-$$

(ii) $E^\circ_{cell} = E^\circ_{cathode} - E^\circ_{anode} = -0.42 - (-0.72) = 0.3\,V$

9. (i)

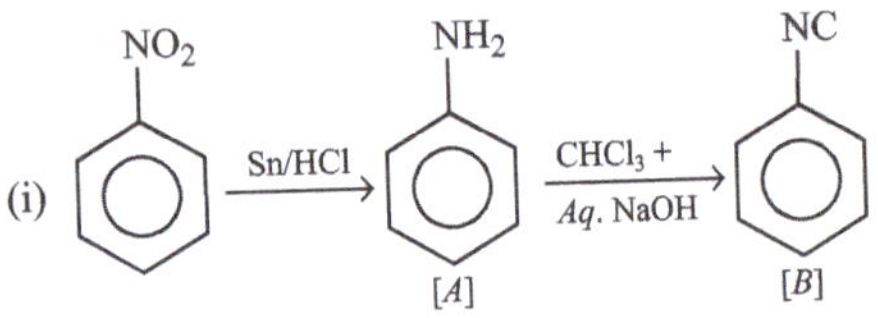

(ii)

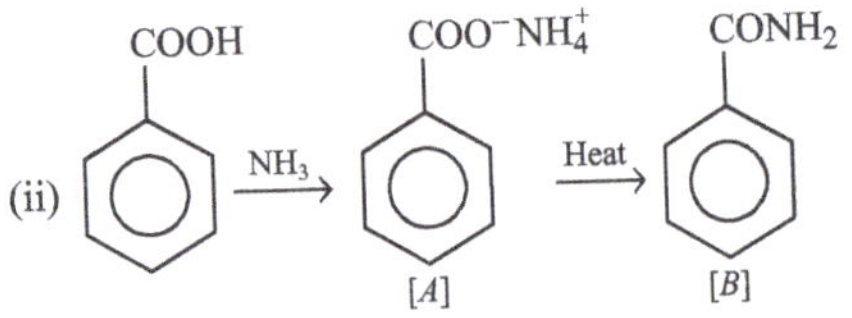

Or

Since, compound '*A*' on heating with Br_2 and KOH forms a compound '*B*' which further reacts with $CHCl_3$ and alc. KOH producing a foul smelling compound '*C*'.

Thus, compound '*C*' is an aromatic isocyanide and compound *B* is aniline with formula $C_6H_5NH_2$ and compound *A* must be benzamide. Reaction involved are as follows

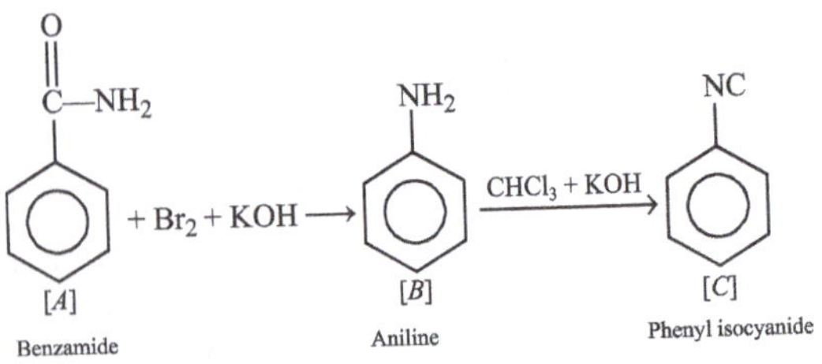

10. (i) $k = \frac{0.693}{t_{1/2}} = \frac{0.693}{10} = 0.0693\ \text{min}^{-1}$

(ii) $N = N_0\left(\frac{1}{2}\right)^n$

where, $n = \frac{\text{Total time}}{t_{1/2}} = \frac{60}{10} = 6$

$$\frac{N}{N_0} = \left(\frac{1}{2}\right)^6 = \frac{1}{64}$$

[where, N_0 = initial amount of reactant and N = amount of reactant left after time, t]

11. (i) Ethyl chloride undergoes hydrolysis when treated with aqueous KOH to form ethyl alcohol. (Through S_N2 nucleophilic substitution)

$$\underset{\text{Chloromethane}}{C_2H_5Cl} + KOH(aq) \longrightarrow \underset{\text{Ethanol}}{C_2H_5OH} + KCl$$

(ii) When CH_3Br is treated with KCN, methyl cyanide is obtained.

$$\underset{\text{Bromomethane}}{CH_3—Br} + K—CN \longrightarrow \underset{\text{Methyl cyanide}}{CH_3—CN} + KBr$$

12. Rate law states that rate $= k[A]^x[B]^y$

$(Rate)_1 = k[0.20]^x[0.30]^y = 5.07 \times 10^{-5}$ ...(i)

$(Rate)_2 = k[0.20]^x[0.10]^y = 5.07 \times 10^{-5}$ ...(ii)

$(Rate)_3 = k[0.40]^x[0.05]^y = 1.43 \times 10^{-4}$ ...(iii)

On dividing Eq. (i) by Eq. (ii), we get

$$\frac{(Rate)_1}{(Rate)_2} = \frac{k[0.20]^x[0.30]^y}{k[0.20]^x[0.10]^y} = \frac{5.07 \times 10^{-5}}{5.07 \times 10^{-5}} = 1$$

$$[3]^y = [3]^0$$

$$y = 0$$

Now, on dividing Eq. (iii) by Eq. (ii), we get

$$\frac{(Rate)_3}{(Rate)_2} = \frac{k(0.40)^x(0.05)^0}{k(0.20)^x(0.10)^0} = \frac{1.43 \times 10^{-4}}{5.07 \times 10^{-5}}$$

$$2.8205 = 2^x\left(\frac{1}{2}\right)^0 = 2^x$$

$$\log 2.8205 = x \log 2$$

$$x = \frac{0.4503}{0.3010} = 1.5$$

Thus, order of the reaction with respect to *A* and *B* are 1.5 and 0, respectively.

13. (i) Iodide is a better leaving group because of its larger size than bromide, therefore, ethyl iodide undergoes S_N2 reaction faster than ethyl bromide.

(ii) (±) 2-butanol is a racemic mixture. It is a mixture which contains two enantiomers in equal proportion and thus, have zero optical rotation due to internal compensation. Therefore, it is optically inactive.

(iii) In halobenzenes (like chlorobenzene), the lone pair of electrons on halogen atom is delocalised on the benzene ring. As a result, C—*X* bond (C—Cl bond in case of chlorobenzene) acquires some double bond character while in $CH_3—X$, C—*X* bond is a pure single bond. Therefore, C—*X* bond in halobenzene is shorter than in $CH_3—X$.

14. (i) As $+I$-effect of isopropyl group is more than that of n-propyl group, therefore, $(CH_3)_2CHCOOH$ is a weaker acid than $CH_3CH_2CH_2COOH$. Since, $-I$-effect decreases with distance, therefore, $CH_3CH_2CH(Br)COOH$ is a stronger acid than $CH_3CH_2CH(Br)CH_2COOH$.

Hence, increasing order of acidic strength is:

$$(CH_3)_2CHCOOH < CH_3CH_2CH_2COOH < CH_3CH(Br)CH_2COOH < CH_3CH_2CH(Br)COOH$$

(ii) The pK_a values indicates the strength of an acid. Lower pK_a value means stronger acid. So, the correct order of their pK_a values is

$$CH_3CH_2CH(Br)COOH < CH_3CH(Br)CH_2COOH < CH_3CH_2CH_2COOH < (CH_3)_2CHCOOH$$

15. (i) According to Henry's law, $p = K_H \cdot \chi$

So, $$\chi = \frac{p}{K_H} = \frac{760}{4.27 \times 10^5} = 1.78 \times 10^{-3}$$

Solubility or the mole fraction of methane in benzene is 1.78×10^{-3}.

(ii) Molar mass of $Ba(OH)_2 \cdot 8H_2O$

$$= 137 + 2 \times 17 + 8 \times 18$$
$$= 315 \text{ g mol}^{-1}$$

$\therefore$ 100 g water has 5.6 g of $Ba(OH)_2 \cdot 8H_2O$

$\therefore$ 1000 g water will have $Ba(OH)_2 \cdot 8H_2O = 56$ g

Number of moles of

$$Ba(OH)_2 \cdot 8H_2O = \frac{56}{315} = 0.178 \text{ mol}$$

Thus, molality of $Ba(OH)_2 = 0.178$ m

$$Ba(OH)_2 \longrightarrow Ba^{2+} + 2OH^-$$

Molality of OH^- ions $= 2 \times$ Molality of $Ba(OH)_2$

$$= 2 \times 0.178 = 0.356 \text{ m}$$

16. (i) This is because the difference of energy between $(n-1)d$ and ns-orbitals is very small. Hence, electrons from both the energy levels can be removed to exhibit variable oxidation states.

In f-block elements, there is large gap in energy of $4f$ and $5d$-subshells, thus the number of oxidatioin states of f-block is limited.

(ii) E.C. of $Sc = [Ar]4s^2 3d^1$ E.C. of $Sc^{3+} = [Ar]$

Sc^{3+} ion do not show paramagnetism because it achieves noble gas configuration of Ar (argon), so it's d-orbitals is empty, hence no unpaired electron is present.

(iii) The transition element exhibit higher enthalpies of atomisation because of strong interatomic interaction due to large number of unpaired electrons in d-orbitals, hence the bond becomes stronger.

17. (i) $$C_6H_5N_2Cl \xrightarrow{CuCN} \underset{\substack{\text{Benzonitrile} \\ (A)}}{C_6H_5CN} \xrightarrow[\Delta]{H_2O/H^+} \underset{\substack{\text{Benzoic acid} \\ (B)}}{C_6H_5COOH} \xrightarrow[\Delta]{NH_3} \underset{\substack{\text{Benzamide} \\ (C)}}{C_6H_5CONH_2}$$

(ii) $$CH_3CH_2I \xrightarrow{NaCN} \underset{\substack{\text{Ethyl cyanide} \\ (A)}}{CH_3CH_2CN} \xrightarrow{OH^-}$$

$$\underset{\substack{\text{Propanamide} \\ (B)}}{CH_3CH_2CONH_2} \xrightarrow{NaOH + Br_2} \underset{\substack{\text{Ethylamine} \\ (C)}}{CH_3CH_2NH_2}$$

Or

(i) $$\underset{\text{Nitrobenzene}}{C_6H_5NO_2} + 3H_2 \xrightarrow[\text{Fe + HCl}]{\text{Sn + HCl Or}} \underset{\text{Aniline}}{C_6H_5NH_2} + 2H_2O$$

(ii) $$\underset{\text{Acetamide}}{CH_3-\overset{\overset{\displaystyle O}{\|}}{C}-NH_2} \xrightarrow[P_2O_5]{\Delta} \underset{\text{Methyl cyanide}}{CH_3C \equiv N} + H_2O$$

$$\xrightarrow[LiAlH_4]{4[H]} \underset{\text{Ethylamine}}{CH_3CH_2NH_2}$$

(iii) $$\underset{\text{Benzene}}{C_6H_6} \xrightarrow{HNO_3/H_2SO_4} \underset{\text{Nitrobenzene}}{C_6H_5NO_2} \xrightarrow[(Sn + HCl)]{4[H]}$$

$$\underset{\text{Aniline}}{C_6H_5NH_2} \xrightarrow[-HCl]{CH_3COCl} \underset{\text{Acetanilide}}{C_6H_5NHCOCH_3}$$

18. (i)

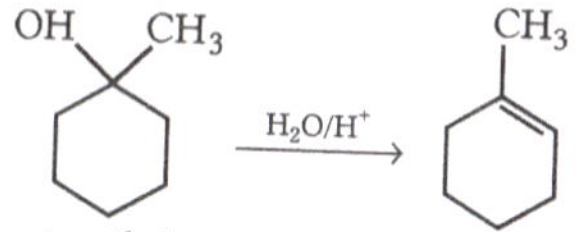

1-methyl cyclohexanol   1-methyl cyclohex-1-ene

(ii) $$\underset{\text{Butan-1-ol}}{CH_3CH_2CH_2CH_2-\ddot{O}H} \xrightarrow{+H^+}$$

$$\underset{\text{Protonated alcohol}}{CH_3CH_2CH_2CH_2-\overset{+}{O}H_2} \xrightarrow{-H_2O} \underset{1^\circ \text{ carbocation}}{CH_3CH_2-\underset{H}{\underset{|}{C}H}-\overset{+}{C}H_2}$$

$$\xrightarrow{\text{1, 2-hydride shift}} \underset{\substack{2^\circ \text{ carbocation (II)} \\ \text{(More stable)}}}{CH_3-CH_2-\overset{\oplus}{C}H-CH_3} \xrightarrow{-H^+}$$

$$\underset{\substack{\text{But-1-ene} \\ \text{(Minor)}}}{CH_3CH_2CH=CH_2} + \underset{\substack{\text{But-2-ene} \\ \text{(Major)}}}{CH_3-CH=CH-CH_3}$$

19. (i) $$Fe^{2+} + \underset{2F}{2e^-} \longrightarrow \underset{56g}{Fe}$$

$\because$ 56 g of Fe is deposited by 2F or 2×96500 C charge

$\therefore$ 2.8 g of Fe will be deposited by

$$\frac{96500 \times 2 \times 2.8}{56} \text{ C charge} = 9650 \text{ C}$$

Now, $$Q = It$$

$\therefore$ $$\text{Time, } t = \frac{9650}{2} = 4825 \text{ s}$$

$$Zn^{2+} + 2e^- \rightarrow Zn$$

$\because 2\times 96500$ C charge deposits Zn = 65.3 g

$\therefore$ 9650 C charge will deposit

$$Zn = \frac{65.3\times 9650}{96500\times 2} = 3.27\,g$$

(ii) '*A*' is a strong electrolyte since there is a small increase in Λ_m with dilution while '*B*' is a weak electrolyte since Λ_m increases sharply near high dilution.

Or

(i) $2Al(s) + 3Cu^{2+}\ (0.01\ M) \longrightarrow$

$$2Al^{3+}\ (0.01\ M) + 3\,Cu(s);\ E_{cell} = 1.98\ V$$

Applying Nernst equation for the given cell reaction,

$$E_{cell} = E^\circ_{cell} - \frac{0.0591}{n}\log\frac{[Al^{3+}]^2}{[Cu^{2+}]^3}$$

$$E^\circ_{cell} = E_{cell} + \frac{0.0591}{n}\log\frac{[Al^{3+}]^2}{[Cu^{2+}]^3}$$

Here, $n = 6$ (n = number of electrons transferred)

$$E^\circ_{cell} = 1.98 + \frac{0.0591}{6}\log\frac{(0.01)^2}{(0.01)^3}$$

$$= 1.98 + \frac{0.0591}{6}\log 100 = 1.98 + \frac{0.0591}{6}\times 2$$

$[\because \log 100 = \log 10^2 = 2\log 10 = 2 \text{ as } \log 10 = 1]$

$$= 1.9997\ V \approx 2.0\ V$$

(ii) For hydrogen electrode, $H^+ + e^- \longrightarrow \frac{1}{2}H_2$

Applying Nernst equation,

$$E_{(H^+/1/2H_2)} = E^\circ_{(H^+/1/2H_2)} - \frac{0.0591}{n}\log\frac{1}{[H^+]}$$

$$= 0 - \frac{0.0591}{1}\log\frac{1}{(10^{-10})}$$

$$(\because pH = 10, [H^+] = 10^{-10}M)$$

$$= 0 - \frac{0.0591}{1}\times(10\log 10) = -0.591\ V$$

Thus, $E_{(H^+/1/2H_2)} = -0.591\ V$

20. (i) (a) $\underset{\text{Acetone}}{CH_3-\overset{O}{\overset{\|}{C}}-CH_3} \xrightarrow[\text{(Clemmensen reduction)}]{\text{Zn-Hg, Conc. HCl}} \underset{\text{Propane}}{CH_3CH_2CH_3} + H_2O$

(b) $\underset{\text{Acetyl chloride}}{CH_3-\overset{O}{\overset{\|}{C}}-Cl} + H_2 \xrightarrow[\text{(Rosenmund reduction)}]{Pd-BaSO_4} \underset{\text{Acetaldehyde}}{CH_3-\overset{O}{\overset{\|}{C}}-H} + HCl$

(c) $\underset{\text{Carboxylic acid}}{CH_3-CH_2-COOH} \xrightarrow[\text{(II) } H_3O^+]{\text{(I) } Br_2,\ P} \underset{\alpha\text{-bromocarboxylic acid}}{CH_3(Br)C-COOH}$

(ii) (a) **Iodoform test** When formaldehyde and acetaldehyde are treated with iodine in the presence of alkali, acetaldehyde gives yellow precipitate of iodoform, but formaldehyde does not give such precipitate.

$$\underset{\text{Acetaldehyde}}{CH_3CHO} + 4NaOH + 3I_2 \longrightarrow \underset{\text{Yellow ppt.}}{CHI_3\downarrow} + HCOONa + 3NaI + 3H_2O$$

$$\underset{\text{Formaldehyde}}{HCHO} + 4NaOH + 3I_2 \longrightarrow \text{No iodoform test}$$

(b) Acetic acid when heated with ethyl alcohol in the presence of conc. H_2SO_4, gives a fruity smell of an ester, (ethyl ethanoate) while acetone does not give this test.

$$\underset{\text{Acetic acid}}{CH_3COOH} + \underset{\text{Ethyl alcohol}}{C_2H_5OH} \xrightarrow[\text{Conc. } H_2SO_4]{\Delta} \underset{\text{Ethyl ethanoate}}{CH_3COOC_2H_5} + H_2O$$

$$\underset{\text{Acetone}}{CH_3-\overset{O}{\overset{\|}{C}}-CH_3} + \underset{\text{Ethyl alcohol}}{C_2H_5OH} \xrightarrow[\text{Conc. } H_2SO_4]{\Delta} \text{No reaction}$$

21. (i) (a) In both the given compounds, interchange of ligands (NH_3 and Cl) between cationic and anionic entities of different metal ion (Cu and Pt) takes place. Hence, they show **coordination isomerism**.

(b) In both compounds ambidentate ligand SCN is present. In $[Cr(SCN)(H_2O)_5]^{2+}$complex,

SCN is attached through S with Cr while in $[Cr(NCS)(H_2O)_5]^{2+}$ complex, NCS is attached through N with Cr.

Hence, they show **linkage isomerism**.

(c) In both the compounds, number of solvent ligand molecules and counter ions differ in the crystal lattice. So, they show **hydrate isomerism**.

(ii) Let oxidation number of Fe in the complex ion $[Fe(H_2O)_6]^{2+}$ is x, then

$$x + 6\times 0 = +2$$

$$\Rightarrow \quad x = +2$$

Electronic configuration of Fe is $[Ar]\,3d^6 4s^2$.

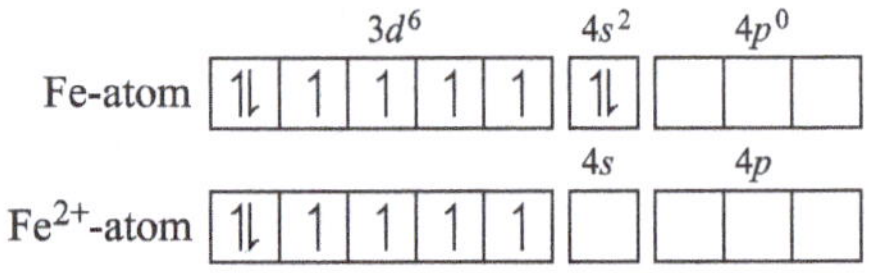

H_2O is a weak field ligand, so it will not pair up $3d^6$ electrons. Thus,

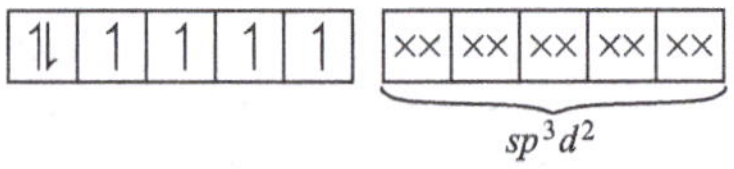

Coordination number of complex is 6. Hence, hybridisation is sp^3d^2.

It contains four unpaired electrons. So, it is paramagnetic.

ISC

SAMPLE PAPER 2

Time : 3 hrs
Marks : 70

Chemistry

General Instructions

1. This paper is divided into four Sections A, B , C and D. Answer all questions.
   Section A consists of one question having sub-parts of one mark each. **Section B** consists of ten questions of two marks each. **Section C** consists of seven questions of three marks each and **Section D** consists of three questions of five marks each.
2. Internal choices have been provided in one question each in Section B, Section C, Section D.
3. All working, including rough work, should be done on the same sheet as, and adjacent to the rest of the answer.
4. The intended marks for questions or parts of questions are given in brackets [].
5. Balanced equations must be given wherever possible and diagrams where they are helpful.
6. When solving numerical problems, all essential working must be shown.
   In working out problems, use the following data :
   Gas constant R = 1.987 cal deg^{-1} mol^{-1} = 8.314 JK^{-1} mol^{-1} = 0.0821 dm^3 atm K^{-1} mol^{-1}
   1 atm = 1 dm^3 atm = 101.3 J. 1 Faraday = 96500 coulombs. **Avogadro's number** = 6.023×10^{23}

SECTION A

(14 Marks)

1. (A) Fill in the blanks by choosing the appropriate word(s) from those given in the brackets.

[mol L^{-1}s^{-1}, Co, second order, mol L s^{-1}, nucleophilic, resonance stabilisation, CO_2, H_2O, first order, dihydric, explosive, trihydric] **[4×1]**

(i) The unit of the rate of a reaction is ...... and all radioactive disintegration reactions follow ...... kinetics.

(ii) The acidity of phenol is due to the .... of its anion and formation of phenol from chlorobenzene is an example of ...... aromatic substitution.

(iii) Formic acid when heated with conc. H_2SO_4 produces ...... and ....

(iv) Glycerol is a ...... alcohol and is used in making ....

(B) Select and write the correct alternative from the choices given below. **[7×1]**

(i) Which of the following is/are rechargeable batteries?

(a) Nickel-cadmium (b) Lead storage
(c) Both (a) and (b) (d) None of these

(ii) Expression for the half-life of zero order reaction is given as

(a) $t_{1/2} = \frac{[R]}{2k}$ (b) $t_{1/2} = \frac{[R]_0}{2k}$
(c) $t_{1/2} = \frac{0.693}{k}$ (d) $t_{1/2} = \frac{0.301}{k}$

(iii) The electrophile used in Reimer-Tiemann reaction is

(a) $CCl_3^{\oplus}$ (b) $:CCl_2$ (c) $Cl^{\oplus}$ (d) H_2O

(iv) The spatial arrangement of the two or more polypeptide chains with respect to each other is known as ...*A*... of protein. Here, '*A*' is

(a) primary structure (b) secondary structure
(c) tertiary structure (d) quaternary structure

(v) Which of the following statements are true about osmotic pressure?

I. Flow of solvent from solution across a semipermeable membrane can be stopped, if some extra pressure is applied on solution.

II. It is the pressure that stops the flow of solvent towards solution.

III. It is the pressure that allows flow of solvent across the semipermeable membrane.

Choose the correct option.

(a) Both I and II
(b) Both II and III
(c) Both I and III
(d) I, II and III

(vi) **Assertion** (A) H_2—O_2 fuel cell gives a constant voltage throughout its life.

Reason (R) In this fuel cell, H_2 reacts with OH^- ions yet the overall concentration of OH^- ions does not change. **[2×1]**

(a) Both (A) and (R) are correct and (R) is the correct explanation of (A).
(b) Both (A) and (R) are correct but (R) is not the correct explanation of (A).
(c) (A) is correct and (R) is incorrect.
(d) (A) is incorrect and (R) is correct.

(vii) **Assertion** (A) S_N1 mechanism is ruled out in case of haloarene.

Reason (R) Phenyl cation is formed as a result of self ionisation which is not stabilised by resonance.

(a) Both (A) and (R) are correct and (R) is the correct explanation of (A).
(b) Both (A) and (R) are correct but (R) is not the correct explanation of (A).
(c) (A) is correct and (R) is incorrect.
(d) (A) is incorrect and (R) is correct.

(C) Read the passage given below and answer the questions that follows. **[3×1]**

In phenol, OH-group directly attached to sp^2-hybridised carbon of benzene ring acts as a electron donating group and is responsible for the acidic nature of phenol. Due to this, the lone pair of electrons of O—H are involved in resonance with C-atoms of benzene ring. As a result of resonance, the oxygen atom acquires a partial positive charge. This weakens the O—H bond and, thus facilitates the release of a proton.

As a result, phenols behave as Bronsted acids. The reaction of phenol with aqueous NaOH indicates that phenols are stronger acids than alcohols. The reactions of phenol with metals such as Na, Al and NaOH indicate its acidic nature.

(i) Give the equation for the reaction of phenol with chloroform in presence of aqueous NaOH.
(ii) Which one is stronger acid, phenol or ethanol?
(iii) Give one reaction showing the acidic nature of phenol.

SECTION B

(20 Marks)

2. Calculate the molality of K_2CO_3 solution which is formed by dissolving 2.5 g of it in 1L of solution. Density of solution is 0.85 g mL^{-1}. [**Ans.** 0.02 m] **[2]**

3. (i) A first order reaction has rate constant of $k = 1.15 \times 10^{-3} s^{-1}$. How long will it take for 6 g of reactant to reduce to 3 g. [**Ans.** $t = 602.8$ s]

(ii) Express the rate of following reaction **[2]**

$$N_2(g) + 3H_2(g) \longrightarrow 2NH_3(g)$$

4. (i) Arrange the following solutions in order of increasing boiling point.

1 M glucose, 2 M glucose and 3 M glucose.

(ii) What happens when the external pressure applied becomes more than osmotic pressure of the solutions. **[2]**

5. Complete the following chemical equation.

(i) $Cr_2O_7^{2-} + 6Fe^{2+} + 14H^+ \longrightarrow$

(ii) $2MnO_4^- + 16H^+ + 5C_2O_4^{2-} \longrightarrow$ **[2]**

6. Complete then following equation. **[2]**

(i) $2MnO_4^- + 5S^{2-} + 16H^+ \longrightarrow$

(ii) $Cr_2O_7^{2-} + 2OH^- \longrightarrow$

7. (i) Give the reaction for the formation of phosgene gas.

(ii) What happens when phosgene gas reacts with ethanol? **[2]**

8. How will you convert **[2]**

(i) ethanoic acid into methanamine?

(ii) hexane nitrile into 1-aminopentane?

Or

An unknown aldehyde (A) reacts with an alkali to form β-hydroxy aldehyde which on heating produce but-2-en-1-al (B). Compound (B) on reaction with conc. alkali produces two compounds (C) and (D). D is an alcohol with molecular formula C_7H_8O. Identify the compounds (A), (B), (C) and (D).

9. Write IUPAC name of the following compound. **[2]**

(i) 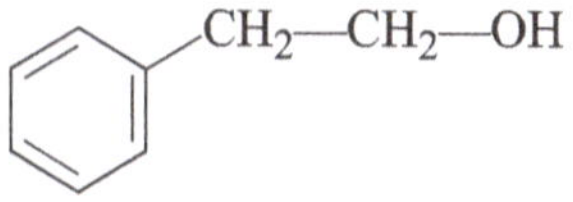

(ii) $H_3C—C{=}C—CH_2—OH$ (with CH_3 on the second carbon and Br on the third carbon)

10. Give a reason for each of the following. **[2]**

(i) Amino acids show amphoteric behaviour.

(ii) Vitamin-C cannot be stored in our body.

11. Predict the product of electrolysis in each of the following. **[2]**

(i) An aqueous solution of $AgNO_3$ with platinum electrodes.

(ii) An aqueous solution of H_2SO_4 with platinum electrode.

SECTION C

(21 Marks)

12. Give reasons.

(i) *n*-butyl bromide has higher boiling point than *t*-butyl bromide.

(ii) Racemic mixture is optically inactive.

(iii) The presence of nitro group ($—NO_2$) at *o*/*p*-positions, increases the reactivity of haloarenes towards nucleophilic substitution reactions. **[3]**

13. (i) What is lanthanoid contraction? What are the consequences of lanthanoid contraction?

(ii) Name the element which show only + 3 oxidation state. **[3]**

Or How would you account for following?

(i) Transition metal shows variable oxidation state.

(ii) Orange colour of $Cr_2O_7^{2-}$ ion changes to yellow when treated with alkali.

(iii) Mn^{3+} is paramagnetic. **[3]**

14. At some temperature, the vapour pressure of pure C_6H_6 is 0.256 bar and that of pure $C_6H_5CH_3$ (toluene) is 0.0925 bar. If the mole fraction of toluene in solution is 0.6. Then, **[3]**

(i) what will be the total pressure of the solution?

(ii) what will be the mole fraction of each component in vapour phase?

15. Identify the compounds [*A*], [*B*] and [*C*] **[3]**

(i) $C_6H_5Br \xrightarrow{\text{Mg/dry ether}} [A] \xrightarrow[\text{(b) } H_3O^+]{\text{(a) } CO_2(g)} [B] \xrightarrow{PCl_5} [C]$

(ii) $CH_3CN \xrightarrow[\text{(ii) } H_3O^+]{\text{(i) } SnCl_2/HCl} [A] \xrightarrow{\text{Dil. NaOH}} [B] \xrightarrow{\Delta} [C]$

16. The following results have been obtained during kinetic studies of the reaction: **[3]**

$$2A + B \longrightarrow C + D$$

Exp. No.	[*A*]	[*B*]	Initial rate of formation of *D*
1.	0.1 M	0.1 M	6.0×10^{-3} M min^{-1}
2.	0.3 M	0.2 M	7.2×10^{-3} M min^{-1}
3.	0.3 M	0.4 M	2.88×10^{-2} M min^{-1}
4.	0.4 M	0.1 M	2.40×10^{-2} M min^{-1}

Determine rate law and the rate constant for the reaction.

17. Synthesize the following. **[3]**

(i) Butene to butanol

(ii) 1-chloropropane to propan-1-ol

(iii) Benzoic acid to benzyl alcohol

18. Arrange the following compounds. **[3]**

$(CH_3)_3N, C_2H_5NH_2, C_2H_5OH$

(i) In the increasing order of their basic strength.

(ii) in the decreasing order of their boiling point.

SECTION D

(15 Marks)

19. (i) For the reaction,

$$2AgCl(s) + H_2(g)\,(1\text{ atm}) \longrightarrow 2Ag(s) + 2H^+(0.1\text{ M}) + 2Cl^-(0.1\text{ M}),$$

$\Delta G° = -43600$ J at 25° C.

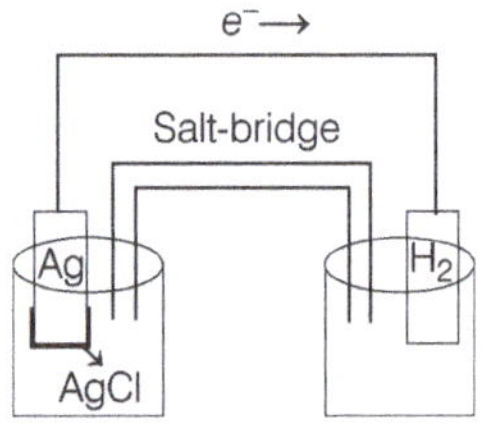

Calculate the emf of the cell. [log $10^{-n} = -n$]

(ii) Define fuel cell and write its two advantages. **[5]**

Or

(i) The molar conductivity (Λ_m) of KCl solutions, at different concentration at 298 K, is plotted as shown in the figure given below.

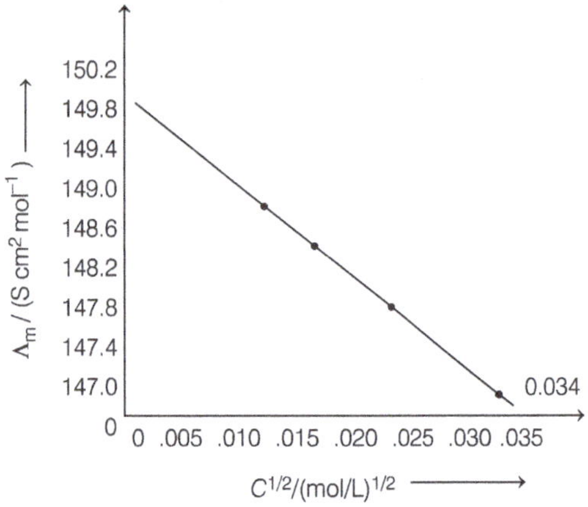

Determine the value of Λ_m° and A for KCl.

(ii) Calculate the emf of the following cell at 298 K.

$$Mg(s)|Mg^{2+}(0.1\text{ M})\,||\,Cu^{2+}(1.0\times10^{-3}\text{ M})|Cu(s)$$

[Given : $E^\circ_{cell} = 2.71$ V] [**Ans.** 2.6509 V] **[5]**

20. (i) Write the hybridisation and magnetic character of the following complexes.

(a) $[Fe(CN)_6]^{2+}$

(b) $[Ni(CN)_4]^{2-}$

(c) $[Cr(NH_3)_3Cl_3]$

(Atomic number : Fe = 26, Ni = 28, Cr = 24]

(ii) Discuss the nature of bonding in the following coordiantion entities on the basis of valence bond theory. **[5]**

(a) $[Fe(CN)_6]^{4-}$

(b) $[Co[C_2O_4)_3]^{3-}$

21. (i) Write the products formed when CH_3CHO reacts with the following reagents.

(a) HCN

(b) $H_2N—OH$

(c) CH_3CHO in the presence of dilute NaOH.

(ii) Complete the following reaction.

(a) $2H—\underset{\underset{O}{\|}}{C}—H \xrightarrow{\text{Conc. KOH}}$

(b) 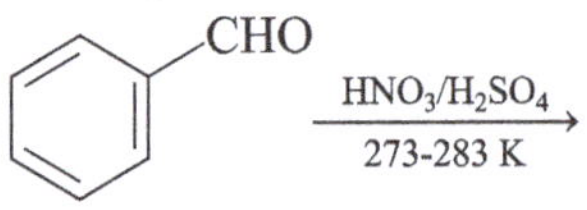

[5]

ISC

SAMPLE PAPER 3

Time : 3 hrs
Marks : 70

Chemistry

General Instructions

1. This paper is divided into four Sections A, B , C and D. Answer all questions.
   Section A consists of one question having sub-parts of one mark each. **Section B** consists of ten questions of two marks each. **Section C** consists of seven questions of three marks each and **Section D** consists of three questions of five marks each.
2. Internal choices have been provided in one question each in Section B, Section C, Section D.
3. All working, including rough work, should be done on the same sheet as, and adjacent to the rest of the answer.
4. The intended marks for questions or parts of questions are given in brackets [].
5. Balanced equations must be given wherever possible and diagrams where they are helpful.
6. When solving numerical problems, all essential working must be shown.
   In working out problems, use the following data :
   Gas constant $R = 1.987$ cal deg^{-1} mol^{-1} = 8.314 JK^{-1} mol^{-1} = 0.0821 dm^3 atm K^{-1} mol^{-1}
   1 atm = 1 dm^3 atm = 101.3 J. 1 Faraday = 96500 coulombs. **Avogadro's number** = 6.023×10^{23}

SECTION A

(14 Marks)

1. (A) Fill in the blanks by choosing the appropriate word(s) from those given in brackets.

[log R, $\frac{1}{T}$, ln k, T, deoxyribose, ribose, HCl, H_2SO_4, anhydrous $ZnCl_2$, anhydrous $AlCl_3$, 1°, 2°, 3°] **[4×1]**

(i) The plot of ...... *versus* ...... has slopes equal to E_a/R.

(ii) In RNA, the sugar is ... but in DNA, it is ....

(iii) Lucas reagent is a mixture of conc. ... and ... .

(iv) Aldehyde gives ...... alcohol whereas ketones gives ...... alcohol on reduction.

(B) Select and write the correct alternative from the choices given below. **[7 × 1]**

(i) Ionic mobility of Ag^+ is ($\lambda_{Ag^+} = 5 \times 10^{-4}$ ohm^{-1} cm^2 eq^{-1})

(a) 5.2×10^{-9} (b) 2.4×10^{-9}
(c) 8.25×10^{-9} (d) 152×10^{-9}

(ii) Which of the following is most acidic?

(a) Phenol (b) Benzyl alcohol
(c) *m*-chlorophenol (d) Cyclohexanol

(iii) 75% of first order reaction was completed in 32 min so, 50% of the reaction was completed in

(a) 24 min (b) 8 min
(c) 16 min (d) 4 min

(iv) The unit of rate constant for first order reaction is

(a) mol L^{-1} s^{-1} (b) s^{-1}
(c) L mol^{-1} s^{-1} (d) s^{-2}

(v) Some of the following gases are soluble in water due to formation of their ions.

I. CO_2 II. H_2 III. HCl IV. CH_4

Choose the water insoluble gases among them and mark the correct option.

(a) only I and II (b) only II and IV
(c) only II and III (d) only I and II

(vi) **Assertion** (A) Anhyd. HCl is a bad conductor of electricity while *aq*. HCl is a good conductor.

Reason (R) Aqueous HCl is not fully ionised but anhyd. HCl is ionised to produce H^+ and Cl^- ions.

(a) Both (A) and (R) are correct and (R) is the correct explanation of (A).

(b) Both (A) and (R) are correct but (R) is not the correct explanation of (A).

(c) (A) is correct and (R) is incorrect.

(d) (A) is incorrect and (R) is correct.

(vii) **Assertion** (A) CH_4 does not react with Cl_2 in dark.

Reason (R) Chlorination of CH_4 takes place in sunlight.

(a) Both (A) and (R) are correct and (R) is the correct explanation of (A).

(b) Both (A) and (R) are correct but (R) is not the correct explanation of (A).

(c) (A) is correct and (R) is incorrect.

(d) (A) is incorrect and (R) is correct.

(C) Read the passage given below and answer the questions that follows. **[3×1]**

Electrolysis is a process by which electric current passes through a substance to produce a chemical change. During electrolysis, the reactions occurring at the electrodes are the oxidation and reduction reactions.

Therefore, the products of electrolysis can be predicted on the basis of electrode potentials of different reactions.

The products of electrolysis depend on the nature of material being electrolysed and the types of electrodes being used. If the electrode is inert such as gold or platinum, it does not take part in the chemical reaction and acts only as a source or sink for electrons. On the other hand, if the electrode is reactive, it takes part in the electrode reaction. Thus, the products of electrolysis may be different for inert and reactive electrodes.

The products of electrolysis mainly depend upon different oxidising and reducing species present in the electrolytic cell and their standard electrode potentials. It may be noted that some electrochemical processes, though feasible, are so slow kinetically that at lower voltages, these do not seem to occur.

(i) Why sugar cannot conduct electricity in aqueous solution ?

(ii) At which electrode do oxidation and reduction takes place in electrolysis ?

(iii) A solution of $Ni(NO_3)_2$ is electrolysed between platinum electrodes using a current of 5.0 A for 20 min. What mass nickel will be deposited at the cathode?

(Given : Atomic mass of Ni = 58.7 g mol^{-1}, 1F = 96500 C mol^{-1})

SECTION B (20 Marks)

2. (i) Arrange the following equimolar solutions in order of decreasing order of osmotic pressure.

NaCl, $BaCl_2$, $AlCl_3$ and Glucose.

(ii) Elevation of boiling point of 1 M KCl solution is nearly double than that of 1 M sugar solution. Justify the statement. **[2]**

3. (i) On the basis of crystal field energy, write the electronic configuration of d^4 in terms of t_{2g} and e_g in an octahedral field when

(a) $\Delta_o > P$ (b) $\Delta_o < P$

(ii) Find the no. of unpaired electrons in complex $[Fe(H_2O)_6]^{3+}$ having magnetic moment value of 5.92 BM. **[2]**

4. On mixing liquid *X* and liquid *Y*, volume of the resulting solution decreases. What type of deviation from Raoult's law is shown by the resulting solution? What change in temperature would you observe after mixing liquids *X* and *Y*? **[2]**

5. Balance and complete the following equations. **[2]**

(i) $(CH_3)_3—C—O—CH_3 + HI \longrightarrow$

(ii) $CH_3—CH{=}CH_2 \xrightarrow[\text{(b) } 3H_2O_2/10OH^-]{\text{(a) } B_2H_6}$

6. Give reason for the following. **[2]**

(i) Lanthanoids do not form their carbonyl compounds.